Selected Economics Statistics for Various Years, 1929–1982

Statistics in rows 1–5 are in billions of dollars in the year specified. Numbers may not add to totals because of rounding.

GDP AND INCOME DATA	1929	1933	1939	1940	1942	1944	1946	1948	1950	1952	1954
1 Gross domestic product	103.6	56.4	92.2	101.4	161.9	219.8	222.2	269.1	293.7	358.3	380.4
1A Personal consumption expenditures	77.4	45.9	67.2	71.3	89.0	108.7	144.3	175.0	192.2	219.5	240.0
1B Gross private domestic investment	16.5	1.7	9.3	13.6	10.4	7.8	31.1	48.1	54.1	54.0	53.8
1C Government purchases	9.4	8.7	14.8	15.0	62.7	105.3	39.6	40.5	46.7	83.6	86.1
1D Net exports of goods and services	0.4	0.1	0.8	1.5	−0.3	−2.0	7.2	5.5	0.7	1.2	0.4
2 Net domestic product	93.9	49.0	82.9	91.8	148.2	200.2	199.1	240.7	263.8	322.0	339.8
3 National income	93.9	48.1	82.0	90.9	149.5	198.0	198.6	242.6	263.9	321.3	338.7
3A Wages and salaries	51.1	29.6	48.1	52.2	85.3	121.3	119.6	142.0	155.3	196.2	209.2
3B Rent	6.2	2.9	3.8	3.9	5.5	6.4	7.1	7.8	9.1	11.2	13.4
3C Interest	4.6	4.0	3.6	3.3	3.2	2.4	1.9	2.6	3.2	4.1	5.6
3D Profits	10.7	−0.3	6.4	9.6	20.4	24.8	17.9	30.9	35.6	38.8	38.3
3E Proprietor's income	14.1	5.3	11.1	12.3	23.4	29.4	35.7	39.2	37.5	43.1	42.3
3F Taxes on production and imports*	7.2	6.6	9.0	9.6	11.7	13.7	16.4	20.1	23.2	27.9	29.9
4 Personal income	84.9	65.2	72.9	78.4	123.4	166.0	178.6	209.7	228.9	275.2	294.3
5 Disposable income	83.2	46.0	71.4	76.8	118.5	148.3	161.4	190.5	209.9	243.2	264.1
6 Disposable income per capita	683	366	545	581	879	1072	1142	1299	1384	1550	1627
7 Personal saving as percent of DI	4.3	3.7	4.4	5.7	24.1	26.0	9.6	6.9	7.1	8.4	7.5

OTHER STATISTICS	1929	1933	1939	1940	1942	1944	1946	1948	1950	1952	1954
8 Real GDP (billions of 2005 dollars)	977.0	716.4	1072.8	1166.9	1618.2	2035.2	1792.2	1854.2	2006.0	2243.9	2332.4
9 Economic growth rate (change in real GDP)	—	−1.3	8.1	8.8	18.5	8.1	−10.9	4.4	8.7	3.8	−0.6
10 Consumer Price Index (1982–1984 = 100)	17.1	13.0	13.9	14.0	16.3	17.6	19.5	24.1	24.1	26.5	26.9
11 Rate of inflation (percent change in CPI)	0.0	−5.1	−1.4	0.7	10.9	1.7	8.3	8.1	1.3	1.9	0.7
12 Money supply, M1 (billions of $)	26.6	19.9	34.2	39.7	55.4	85.3	106.5	112.5	114.1	125.2	130.3
13 Federal funds interest rate (%)	—	—	—	—	—	—	—	1.75	2.07	3.00	3.05
14 Prime interest rate (%)	5.50	1.50	1.50	1.50	1.50	1.50	1.50	1.75	2.70	3.00	3.05
15 Population (millions)	121.8	125.6	131.0	132.1	134.9	138.4	141.4	146.6	152.3	157.6	163.0
16 Civilian labor force (millions)	49.2	51.6	55.2	55.6	56.4	54.6	57.5	60.6	62.2	62.1	63.6
16A Employment (millions)	47.6	38.8	45.7	47.5	53.8	54.0	55.3	58.3	58.9	60.3	60.1
16B Unemployment (millions)	1.6	12.8	9.5	8.1	2.7	0.7	2.3	2.3	3.3	1.9	3.5
17 Unemployment rate (%)	3.2	24.9	17.2	14.6	4.7	1.2	3.9	3.8	5.3	3.0	5.5
18 Productivity growth, business sector (%)	—	—	—	—	—	—	—	4.6	8.2	2.8	2.1
19 After-tax manufacturing profit per dollar of sales (cents)	—	—	—	—	—	—	—	7.0	7.1	4.3	4.5
20 Price of crude oil (U.S. average, dollars per barrel)	1.27	0.67	1.02	1.02	1.19	1.21	1.41	2.60	2.51	2.53	2.78
21 Federal budget surplus (+) or deficit (−) (billions of dollars)	—	—	—	−2.9	−20.5	−47.6	−15.2	11.8	−3.1	−1.5	−1.2
22 Public debt (billions of dollars)	16.9	22.5	48.2	50.7	79.2	204.1	271.0	252.0	256.9	259.1	270.8
23 Trade balance on current account (billions of dollars)	—	—	—	—	—	—	4.9	2.4	−1.8	0.6	0.2

*Combines items from other smaller accounts.

1956	1958	1960	1962	1964	1966	1968	1970	1972	1974	1976	1978	1980	1982
437.4	467.2	526.4	585.7	663.6	787.7	909.8	1038.3	1237.9	1499.5	1824.6	2293.8	2788.1	3253.2
271.7	296.2	331.8	363.3	411.5	480.9	558.0	648.3	770.2	932.9	1151.3	1427.6	1755.8	2075.5
72.0	64.5	78.9	88.1	102.1	131.3	141.2	152.4	207.6	249.4	292.0	438.0	479.3	517.2
91.4	106.0	111.5	130.1	143.2	171.6	209.3	233.7	263.4	317.9	383.0	453.6	566.1	680.4
2.4	0.5	4.2	4.1	6.9	3.9	1.4	4.0	−3.4	−0.8	−1.6	−25.4	−13.1	−20.0
390.3	413.9	469.9	525.1	597.3	711.2	819.4	930.0	1110.7	1335.8	1616.4	2032.3	2444.1	2819.7
394.9	415.6	473.9	528.9	601.4	710.1	821.2	929.5	1110.3	1341.5	1609.8	2027.9	2433.0	2851.4
244.5	259.5	296.4	327.1	370.7	442.7	524.3	617.2	725.1	890.2	1059.3	1335.5	1647.6	1919.6
14.1	15.2	17.0	18.6	19.4	20.5	20.6	21.1	23.1	24.0	22.1	20.9	28.5	38.1
6.9	9.5	10.6	14.2	17.4	22.4	27.1	39.1	47.9	70.8	85.5	115.0	181.8	271.1
48.0	42.5	53.1	62.3	75.5	92.5	97.3	82.5	111.4	115.1	161.6	218.4	201.4	205.7
45.9	50.2	50.7	55.3	59.4	68.2	74.2	78.5	96.0	113.5	132.2	167.5	173.5	174.8
35.5	38.7	46.1	51.4	59.0	63.8	77.7	91.1	106.8	127.9	169.1	244.1	200.2	242.1
339.5	368.9	411.3	456.4	514.3	603.8	711.7	838.6	992.6	1222.7	1474.7	1836.7	2301.5	2766.8
302.9	330.4	365.2	404.9	462.3	537.4	624.7	735.5	869.0	1071.7	1302.3	1607.3	2002.7	2412.7
1800	1897	2020	2170	2408	2733	3112	3586	4140	5010	5972	7220	8794	10,390
8.5	8.5	7.2	8.3	8.8	8.2	8.4	9.4	8.9	10.7	9.4	8.9	9.8	10.9

1956	1958	1960	1962	1964	1966	1968	1970	1972	1974	1976	1978	1980	1982
2549.7	2577.6	2830.9	3072.4	3392.3	3845.3	4133.4	4269.9	4647.7	4889.9	5141.3	5677.6	5839.0	5870.9
2.0	−0.9	2.5	6.1	5.8	6.5	4.8	0.2	5.3	−0.6	5.4	5.6	−0.3	−1.9
27.2	28.9	29.6	30.2	31.0	32.4	34.8	38.8	41.8	49.3	56.9	65.2	82.4	96.5
1.5	2.8	1.7	1.0	1.3	2.9	4.2	5.7	3.2	11.0	5.8	7.6	13.5	6.2
136.0	138.4	140.7	145.2	160.3	172.0	197.4	214.4	249.2	274.2	306.2	357.3	408.5	474.8
2.73	1.57	3.21	2.71	3.50	5.11	5.66	7.17	4.44	10.51	5.05	7.94	13.35	12.24
3.77	3.83	4.82	4.50	4.50	5.63	6.31	5.25	5.73	10.81	6.84	9.06	15.26	14.85
168.9	174.9	180.7	186.5	191.9	196.6	200.7	205.1	209.9	213.9	218.0	222.6	227.7	232.2
66.6	67.6	69.6	70.6	73.1	75.8	78.7	82.8	87.0	91.9	96.2	102.3	106.9	110.2
63.8	63.0	65.8	66.7	69.3	72.9	75.9	78.7	82.2	86.8	88.8	96.0	99.3	99.5
2.8	4.6	3.9	3.9	3.8	2.9	2.8	4.1	4.9	5.2	7.4	6.2	7.6	10.7
4.1	6.8	5.5	5.5	5.2	3.8	3.6	4.9	5.6	5.6	7.7	6.1	7.1	9.7
0.1	2.8	1.7	4.6	3.4	4.1	3.4	2.0	3.2	−1.7	3.2	1.1	−0.3	−0.8
5.3	4.2	4.4	4.5	5.2	5.6	5.1	4.0	4.3	5.5	5.4	5.4	4.8	3.5
2.79	3.01	2.88	2.90	2.88	2.88	2.94	3.18	3.39	6.87	8.19	9.00	21.59	28.52
3.9	−2.8	0.3	−7.1	−5.9	−3.7	−25.2	−2.8	−23.4	−6.1	−73.7	−59.2	−73.8	−128.0
272.7	279.7	290.5	302.9	316.1	328.5	368.7	380.9	435.9	483.9	629.0	776.6	909.1	1137.3
2.7	0.8	2.8	3.4	6.8	3.0	0.6	2.3	−5.8	2.0	4.3	−15.1	2.3	−5.5

(Continued in back of book)

Selected Economics Statistics for Various Years, 1984–2009

Statistics in rows 1–5 are in billions of dollars in the year specified. Numbers may not add to totals because of rounding.

GDP AND INCOME DATA	1984	1986	1987	1988	1989	1990	1991	1992	1993	1994	1995
1 Gross domestic product	3930.9	4460.1	4736.4	5100.4	5482.1	5800.5	5992.1	6342.3	6667.4	7085.2	7414.7
1A Personal consumption expenditures	2501.1	2896.7	3097.0	3350.1	3594.5	3835.5	3980.1	4236.9	4483.6	4750.8	4987.3
1B Gross private domestic investment	735.6	746.5	785.0	821.6	874.9	861.0	802.9	864.8	953.3	1097.3	1144.0
1C Government purchases	796.9	949.3	999.4	1038.9	1100.6	1181.7	1236.1	1273.5	1294.8	1329.8	1374.0
1D Net exports of goods and services	−102.7	−132.5	−145.0	−110.1	−87.9	−77.6	−27.0	−32.8	−64.4	−92.7	−90.7
2 Net domestic product	3456.5	3921.6	4165.3	4489.4	4830.7	5109.3	5267.7	5598.0	5889.3	6266.0	6545.2
3 National income	3461.3	3871.5	4150.0	4522.3	4800.5	5059.5	5217.9	5517.1	5784.7	6181.3	6522.3
3A Wages and salaries	2245.4	2557.7	2735.6	2954.2	3131.3	3326.3	3438.3	3631.4	3797.1	3998.5	4195.2
3B Rent	40.0	33.8	34.2	40.2	42.4	49.8	61.6	84.6	114.1	142.9	154.6
3C Interest	327.1	367.1	366.7	385.3	434.1	444.2	418.2	387.7	364.6	362.2	358.3
3D Profits	318.6	314.1	367.8	426.6	425.6	434.4	457.3	496.2	543.7	628.2	716.2
3E Proprietor's income	233.1	262.6	294.2	334.8	351.6	365.1	367.3	414.9	449.6	485.1	516.0
3F Taxes on production and imports*	297.1	336.2	351.5	381.2	415.5	439.7	475.2	502.5	515.6	564.4	582.0
4 Personal income	3268.9	3696.0	3924.4	4231.2	4557.5	4846.7	5031.5	5347.3	5568.1	5874.8	6200.9
5 Disposable income	2891.5	3258.8	3435.3	3726.3	3991.4	4254.0	4444.9	4736.7	4921.6	5184.3	5457.0
6 Disposable income per capita	12,232	13,540	14,146	15,206	16,134	17,004	17,532	18,436	18,909	19,678	20,470
7 Personal saving as percent of DI	10.2	7.6	6.5	6.9	6.6	6.5	7.0	7.3	5.8	5.2	5.2

OTHER STATISTICS	1984	1986	1987	1988	1989	1990	1991	1992	1993	1994	1995
8 Real GDP (billions of 2005 dollars)	6577.1	7086.5	7313.3	7613.9	7885.9	8033.9	8015.1	8287.1	8523.4	8870.7	9093.7
9 Economic growth rate (change in real GDP)	7.2	3.5	3.2	4.1	3.6	1.9	−0.2	3.4	2.9	4.1	2.5
10 Consumer Price Index (1982–1984 =100)	103.9	109.6	113.6	118.3	124.0	130.7	136.2	140.3	144.5	148.2	152.4
11 Rate of inflation (percent change in CPI)	4.3	1.9	3.6	4.1	4.8	5.4	4.2	3.0	3.0	2.6	2.8
12 Money supply, M1 (billions of $)	551.6	724.7	750.2	786.7	792.9	824.7	897.0	1024.9	1129.6	1150.6	1127.5
13 Federal funds interest rate (%)	10.23	6.80	6.66	7.57	9.21	8.10	5.69	3.52	3.02	4.21	5.83
14 Prime interest rate (%)	12.04	8.33	8.21	9.32	10.87	10.01	8.46	6.25	6.00	7.15	8.83
15 Population (millions)	236.3	240.7	242.8	245.0	247.3	250.1	253.5	256.9	260.3	263.4	266.6
16 Civilian labor force (millions)	113.5	117.8	119.9	121.7	123.9	125.8	126.3	128.1	129.2	131.1	132.3
16A Employment (millions)	105.0	109.6	112.4	115.0	117.3	118.8	117.7	118.5	120.3	123.1	124.9
16B Unemployment (millions)	8.5	8.2	7.4	6.7	6.5	7.0	8.6	9.6	8.9	8.0	7.4
17 Unemployment rate (%)	7.5	7.0	6.2	5.5	5.3	5.6	6.8	7.5	6.9	6.1	5.6
18 Productivity growth, business sector (%)	2.7	2.9	0.3	1.5	1.0	2.1	1.5	4.2	0.5	0.9	0.0
19 After-tax manufacturing profit per dollar of sales (cents)	4.6	3.7	4.9	5.9	4.9	3.9	2.4	0.8	2.8	5.4	5.6
20 Price of crude oil (U.S. average, dollars per barrel)	25.88	12.51	15.40	12.58	15.86	20.03	16.54	15.99	14.25	13.19	14.62
21 Federal budget surplus (+) or deficit (−) (billions of dollars)	−185.4	−221.2	−149.7	−155.2	−152.6	−221.0	−269.2	−290.3	−255.1	−203.2	−164.0
22 Public debt (billions of dollars)	1564.7	2120.6	2346.1	2601.3	2868.0	3206.6	3598.5	4002.1	4351.4	4643.7	4921.0
23 Trade balance on current account (billions of dollars)	−94.3	−147.2	−160.7	−121.1	−99.5	−79.0	2.9	−50.1	−84.8	−121.6	−113.6

*Combines items from other smaller accounts.

1996	1997	1998	1999	2000	2001	2002	2003	2004	2005	2006	2007	2008	2009**
7838.5	8332.4	8793.5	9353.5	9951.5	10,286.2	10,642.3	11,142.1	11,867.8	12,638.4	13,398.9	14,077.6	14,441.4	14,256.3
5273.6	5570.6	5918.5	6342.8	6830.4	7148.8	7439.2	7804.0	8285.1	8819.0	9322.7	9826.4	10,129.9	10,089.1
1240.2	1388.7	1510.8	1641.5	1772.2	1661.9	1647.0	1729.7	1968.6	2172.2	2327.2	2288.5	2136.1	1628.8
1421.0	1474.4	1526.1	1631.3	1731.0	1846.4	1983.3	2112.6	2232.8	2369.9	2518.4	2676.5	2883.2	2930.7
−96.3	−101.4	−161.8	−262.1	−382.1	−371.0	−427.2	−504.1	−618.7	−722.7	−769.3	−713.8	−707.8	−392.4
6925.9	7368.6	7772.9	8259.1	8767.2	9029.9	9337.3	9788.1	10,435.0	11,097.0	11,738.2	12,317.6	12,594.3	12,392.3
6931.7	7406.0	7875.6	8358.0	8938.9	9185.2	9408.5	9840.2	10,534.0	11,273.8	12,031.2	12,448.2	12,635.2	12,288.1
4391.4	4665.6	5023.2	5353.9	5788.8	5979.3	6110.8	6382.6	6693.4	7065.0	7477.0	7856.5	8037.4	7791.6
170.4	176.5	191.5	208.2	215.3	232.4	218.7	204.2	198.4	178.2	146.5	144.9	210.4	268.1
371.1	407.6	479.3	481.4	539.3	544.4	506.4	504.1	461.6	543.0	652.2	739.2	815.1	788.2
801.5	884.8	812.4	856.3	819.2	784.2	872.2	977.8	1246.9	1456.1	1608.3	1541.7	1360.4	1308.9
583.7	628.2	687.5	746.8	817.5	870.7	890.3	930.6	1033.8	1069.8	1133.0	1096.4	1106.3	1041.0
613.3	643.3	681.7	711.6	758.8	774.2	810.1	840.9	889.9	961.7	1014.2	1069.5	1105.6	1090.3
6591.6	7000.7	7525.4	7910.8	8559.4	8883.3	9060.1	9378.1	9937.2	10,485.9	11,268.1	11,894.1	12,238.8	12,026.1
5759.6	6074.6	6498.9	6803.3	7327.2	7648.5	8009.7	8377.8	8889.4	9277.3	9915.7	10,403.1	10,806.4	10,923.6
21,355	22,255	23,534	24,356	25,944	26,805	27,799	28,805	30,287	31,318	33,157	34,445	35,450	35,526
4.9	4.6	5.3	3.1	2.9	2.7	3.5	3.5	3.4	1.4	2.4	1.7	2.7	4.3

1996	1997	1998	1999	2000	2001	2002	2003	2004	2005	2006	2007	2008	2009**
9433.9	9854.3	10,283.5	10,779.8	11,226.0	11,347.2	11,553.0	11,840.7	12,263.8	12,638.4	12,976.2	13,254.1	13,312.2	12,987.4
3.7	4.5	4.4	4.8	4.1	1.1	1.8	2.5	3.6	3.1	2.7	2.1	0.4	−2.4
156.9	160.5	163.0	166.6	172.2	177.1	179.9	184.0	188.9	195.3	201.6	207.3	215.3	214.5
3.0	2.3	1.6	2.2	3.4	2.8	1.6	2.3	2.7	3.4	3.2	2.8	3.8	−0.4
1081.6	1072.8	1095.8	1122.7	1087.7	1182.2	1220.4	1306.9	1377.1	1375.3	1367.9	1375.8	1594.7	1693.3
5.30	5.46	5.35	4.97	6.24	3.88	1.67	1.13	1.35	3.22	4.97	5.02	1.92	0.16
8.27	8.44	8.35	8.00	9.23	6.91	4.67	4.12	4.34	6.19	7.96	8.05	5.09	3.25
269.7	272.9	276.1	279.3	282.4	285.3	288.0	290.7	293.3	296.0	298.8	301.7	304.5	307.2
133.9	136.3	137.7	139.4	142.6	143.7	144.9	146.5	147.4	149.3	151.4	153.1	154.3	154.1
126.7	129.6	131.5	133.5	136.9	136.9	136.5	137.8	139.3	141.7	144.4	146.0	145.4	139.9
7.2	6.7	6.2	5.9	5.7	6.8	8.4	8.8	8.1	7.6	7.0	7.1	8.9	14.3
5.4	4.9	4.5	4.2	4.0	4.7	5.8	6.0	5.5	5.1	4.6	4.6	5.8	9.3
2.9	1.8	3.0	3.5	3.5	3.0	4.5	3.8	2.9	1.7	1.0	1.8	2.1	3.8
6.0	6.2	5.9	6.2	6.1	0.8	3.2	5.4	7.1	7.4	8.1	7.3	4.2	5.4
18.46	17.23	10.87	15.56	26.72	21.84	22.51	27.56	36.77	50.28	59.63	66.52	94.04	56.39
−107.4	−21.9	69.3	125.6	236.2	128.2	−157.8	−377.6	−412.7	−318.3	−248.2	−160.7	−458.6	−1412.7
5181.9	5369.7	5478.7	5605.5	5628.7	5769.9	6198.4	6760.0	7354.7	7905.3	8451.4	8950.7	9986.1	11,875.9
−124.8	−140.7	−215.1	−301.6	−417.4	−398.3	−459.2	−521.5	−631.1	−748.7	−803.5	−726.6	−706.1	−419.9

**Data for 2009 and the years immediately prior are subject to change because of subsequent government data revisions.

Sources: Bureau of Economic Analysis; Bureau of Labor Statistics; Federal Reserve System; Economic Report of the President, 2010; and U.S. Energy Information Administration.

Dhaval

Macroeconomics

NINETEENTH EDITION

Campbell R. McConnell
University of Nebraska

Stanley L. Brue
Pacific Lutheran University

Sean M. Flynn
Scripps College

A Custom Value Edition for ECON 201

WILLIAM PATERSON UNIVERSITY

 **Learning Solutions**

Boston   Burr Ridge, IL   Dubuque, IA   New York   San Francisco   St. Louis
Bangkok   Bogotá   Caracas   Lisbon   London   Madrid
Mexico City   Milan   New Delhi   Seoul   Singapore   Sydney   Taipei   Toronto

A Custom Value Edition for ECON 201
William Paterson University

1 2 3 4 5 6 7 8 9 0 TFR TFR 13 12 11

ISBN-13: 978-0-07-764413-0
ISBN-10: 0-07-764413-1

Learning Solutions Consultant: Philip Rudder
Production Editor: Jeni McAtee
Printer/Binder: TFR Printing
Cover Images © 2012 JupiterImages Corporation

To **Mem** and to **Terri** and **Craig**, and to **past instructors**

About the Authors

CAMPBELL R. MCCONNELL earned his Ph.D. from the University of Iowa after receiving degrees from Cornell College and the University of Illinois. He taught at the University of Nebraska–Lincoln from 1953 until his retirement in 1990. He is also coauthor of *Contemporary Labor Economics*, ninth edition; *Essentials of Economics*, second edition; *Macroeconomics: Brief Edition*; and *Microeconomics: Brief Edition* (all The McGraw-Hill Companies), and has edited readers for the principles and labor economics courses. He is a recipient of both the University of Nebraska Distinguished Teaching Award and the James A. Lake Academic Freedom Award and is past president of the Midwest Economics Association. Professor McConnell was awarded an honorary Doctor of Laws degree from Cornell College in 1973 and received its Distinguished Achievement Award in 1994. His primary areas of interest are labor economics and economic education. He has an extensive collection of jazz recordings and enjoys reading jazz history.

STANLEY L. BRUE did his undergraduate work at Augustana College (South Dakota) and received its Distinguished Achievement Award in 1991. He received his Ph.D. from the University of Nebraska–Lincoln. He is retired from a long career at Pacific Lutheran University, where he was honored as a recipient of the Burlington Northern Faculty Achievement Award. Professor Brue has also received the national Leavey Award for excellence in economic education. He has served as national president and chair of the Board of Trustees of Omicron Delta Epsilon International Economics Honorary. He is coauthor of *Economic Scenes*, fifth edition (Prentice-Hall); *Contemporary Labor Economics*, ninth edition; *Essentials of Economics*, second edition; *Macroeconomics: Brief Edition*; *Microeconomics: Brief Edition* (all The McGraw-Hill Companies); and *The Evolution of Economic Thought*, seventh edition (South-Western). For relaxation, he enjoys international travel, attending sporting events, and skiing with family and friends.

SEAN M. FLYNN did his undergraduate work at the University of Southern California before completing his Ph.D. at U.C. Berkeley, where he served as the Head Graduate Student Instructor for the Department of Economics after receiving the Outstanding Graduate Student Instructor Award. He teaches at Scripps College (of the Claremont Colleges) and is the author of *Economics for Dummies* (Wiley) and coauthor of *Essentials of Economics*, second edition; *Macroeconomics: Brief Edition*; and *Microeconomics: Brief Edition* (all The McGraw-Hill Companies). His research interests include finance and behavioral economics. An accomplished martial artist, he has represented the United States in international aikido tournaments and is the author of *Understanding Shodokan Aikido* (Shodokan Press). Other hobbies include running, traveling, and enjoying ethnic food.

List of Key Graphs

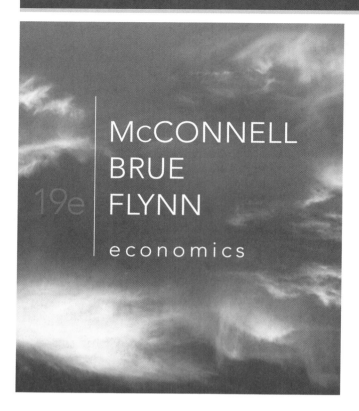

MᴄCONNELL
BRUE
FLYNN
19e

economics

Welcome to the 19th edition of *Economics*, the best-selling economics textbook in the world. An estimated 14 million students have used *Economics* or its companion editions, *Macroeconomics* and *Microeconomics*. *Economics* has been adapted into Australian and Canadian editions and translated into Italian, Russian, Chinese, French, Spanish, Portuguese, and other languages. We are pleased that *Economics* continues to meet the market test: nearly one out of four U.S. students in principles courses used the 18th edition.

Fundamental Objectives

We have three main goals for *Economics*:

- Help the beginning student master the principles essential for understanding the economizing problem, specific economic issues, and policy alternatives.
- Help the student understand and apply the economic perspective and reason accurately and objectively about economic matters.
- Promote a lasting student interest in economics and the economy.

What's New and Improved?

One of the benefits of writing a successful text is the opportunity to revise—to delete the outdated and install the new, to rewrite misleading or ambiguous statements, to introduce more relevant illustrations, to improve the organizational structure, and to enhance the learning aids.

We trust that you will agree that we have used this opportunity wisely and fully. Some of the more significant changes include the following.

Restructured Introductory Chapters

We have divided the five-chapter grouping of introductory chapters common to *Economics*, *Microeconomics*, and *Macroeconomics* into two parts. Part 1 contains Chapter 1 (Limits, Alternatives, and Choices) and Chapter 2 (The Market System and the Circular Flow). The content in Part 2 has changed and now consists of three chapters: Chapter 3 (Demand, Supply, and Market Equilibrium), Chapter 4 (Elasticity), and Chapter 5 (Market Failures: Public Goods and Externalities).

The chapters in Part 2 are much more concept-oriented and analytical and much less general and descriptive than in the previous edition. Our new approach responds to suggestions by reviewers made over the years to:

- Locate the elasticity chapter immediately after the supply and demand chapter.
- Put the elasticity chapter into *Macroeconomics* for those who cover elasticity in their macro course.
- Eliminate the mainly descriptive Chapter 4 on the private and public sectors and move the relevant content to where it fits more closely with related micro and macro materials.
- Provide a single chapter on international trade, rather than two separate chapters that have overlapping coverage (Chapters 5 and 37 in *Economics*, 18th edition).
- Boost the analysis of market failures (public goods and externalities) in the introductory sections to complement and balance the strong but highly stylized introduction to the market system discussed in Chapter 2.

Our new approach embraces these suggestions. For micro instructors, the new ordering provides a clear supply-and-demand path to the subsequent chapters on consumer and producer behavior. For macro instructors, the new ordering provides the option of assigning elasticity or market failures or both. And because this content is both optional and modular, macro instructors can also skip it and move directly to the macroeconomic analysis.

The content on the United States in the global economy that appeared in Chapter 5 of the 18th edition of *Macroeconomics* is now integrated into Chapter 20 (International Trade). Because Chapter 20 draws only on production possibilities analysis and supply and demand analysis, it can be assigned at any point after Chapter 3 (Demand, Supply, and Market Equilibrium). Therefore, instructors who want to introduce international economics early in their courses can assign Chapter 20 within the introductory chapters found in Parts 1 and 2.

For instructors who prefer Chapter 5 of the prior edition to Chapter 20 of the new edition, we have fully updated the previous Chapter 5 content and made it freely available for viewing and printing at both the instructor and student portions of our Web site, **www.mcconnell19e.com**. Look for it under the new category called Content Options for Instructors (COI). This substitute for Chapter 20 is fully supported by both the instructor supplement package and the student supplement package.

New "Consider This" and "Last Word" Pieces

Our "Consider This" boxes are used to provide analogies, examples, or stories that help drive home central economic ideas in a student-oriented, real-world manner. For instance, a "Consider This" box titled "McHits and McMisses" illustrates consumer sovereignty through a listing of successful and unsuccessful products. The difference between stocks and flows is illustrated through a "Consider This" box that contrasts the pool of water above a dam and the flow of water into and out of the reservoir. These brief vignettes, each accompanied by a photo, illustrate key points in a lively, colorful, and easy-to-remember way. We have added 16 new "Consider This" boxes in this edition of *Economics*.

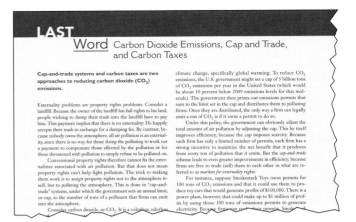

CONSIDER THIS . . .

The Fable of the Bees

Economist Ronald Coase received the Nobel Prize for his so-called **Coase theorem**, which pointed out that under the right conditions, private individuals could often negotiate their own mutually agreeable solutions to externality problems through *private bargaining* without the need for government interventions like pollution taxes.

This is a very important insight because it means that we shouldn't automatically call for government intervention every time we see a potential externality problem. Consider the positive externalities that bees provide by pollinating farmers' crops. Should we assume that beekeeping will be underprovided unless the government intervenes with, for instance, subsidies to encourage more hives and hence more pollination?

As it turns out, no. Research has shown that farmers and beekeepers long ago used private bargaining to develop customs and payment systems that avoid free riding by farmers and encourage beekeepers to keep the optimal number of hives. Free riding is avoided by the custom that all farmers in an area simultaneously hire beekeepers to provide bees to pollinate their crops. And farmers always pay the beekeepers for their pollination services because if they didn't, then no beekeeper would ever work with them in the future—a situation that would lead to massively reduced crop yields due to a lack of pollination.

The "Fable of the Bees" is a good reminder that it is a fallacy to assume that the government must always get involved to remedy externalities. In many cases, the private sector can solve both positive and negative externality problems on its own.

Our "Last Word" pieces are lengthier applications or case studies that are placed near the end of each chapter. For example, the "Last Word" section for Chapter 1 (Limits, Alternatives, and Choices) examines pitfalls to sound economic reasoning, while the "Last Word" section for

LAST

Word Carbon Dioxide Emissions, Cap and Trade, and Carbon Taxes

Cap-and-trade systems and carbon taxes are two approaches to reducing carbon dioxide (CO_2) emissions.

Externality problems are property rights problems. Consider a landfill. Because the owner of the landfill has full rights to his land, people wishing to dump their trash into the landfill have to pay him. This payment implies that there is no externality: He happily accepts their trash in exchange for a dumping fee. By contrast, because nobody owns the atmosphere, all air pollution is an externality, since there is no way for those doing the polluting to work out a payment to compensate those affected by the pollution or for those threatened with pollution to simply refuse to be polluted on.

Conventional property rights therefore cannot fix the externalities associated with air pollution. But that does not mean property rights can't help fight pollution. The trick to making them work is to assign property rights not to the atmosphere itself, but to *polluting* the atmosphere. This is done in "cap-and-trade" systems, under which the government sets an annual limit, or cap, to the number of tons of a pollutant that firms can emit into the atmosphere.

Consider carbon dioxide, or CO_2. It is a colorless, odorless

climate change, specifically global warming. To reduce CO_2 emissions, the U.S. government might set a cap of 5 billion tons of CO_2 emissions per year in the United States (which would be about 10 percent below 2009 emissions levels for that molecule). The government then prints out emissions permits that sum to the limit set in the cap and distributes them to polluting firms. Once they are distributed, the only way a firm can legally emit a ton of CO_2 is if it owns a permit to do so.

Under this policy, the government can obviously adjust the total amount of air pollution by adjusting the cap. This by itself improves efficiency, because the cap imposes scarcity. Because each firm has only a limited number of permits, each firm has a strong incentive to maximize the net benefit that it produces from every ton of pollution that it emits. But the *cap-and-trade* scheme leads to even greater improvements in efficiency, because firms are free to trade (sell) them to each other in what are referred to as *markets for externality rights*.

For instance, suppose Smokestack Toys owns permits for 100 tons of CO_2 emissions and that it could use them to produce toy cars that would generate profits of $100,000. There is a power plant, however, that could make up to $1 million of profits by using those 100 tons of emissions permits to generate electricity. Because firms can trade their permits, Smok

Chapter 5 (Market Failures: Public Goods and Externalities) examines cap-and-trade versus carbon taxes as policy responses to excessive carbon dioxide emissions. There are 10 new "Last Word" sections in this edition of *Economics*.

If you are unfamiliar with *Economics* or *Macroeconomics*, we encourage you to thumb through the chapters to take a quick look at these highly visible features.

New Discussions of the Financial Crisis and the Recession

Our modernization of the macroeconomics in the previous edition has met with great success, measured by reviews, instructor feedback, and market response. We recast the entire macro analysis in terms of the modern, dominant paradigm of macroeconomics, using economic growth as the central backdrop and viewing business fluctuations as significant and costly variations in the rate of growth. In this paradigm, business cycles result from demand shocks (or, less often, supply shocks) in conjunction with inflexible short-run product prices and wages. The degree of price and wage stickiness decreases with time. In our models, the *immediate short run* is a period in which both the price level and wages are not only sticky, but stuck; the *short run* is a period in which product prices are flexible but wages are not; and the *long run* is a period in which both product prices and wages are fully flexible. Each of these three periods—and thus each of the models based on them—is relevant to understanding the actual macro economy and its occasional difficulties.

In this edition, we have mainly focused on incorporating into our new macroeconomic schema an analysis of the financial crisis, the recession, and the hesitant recovery. We first introduce the recession in Chapter 6 (An Introduction to Macroeconomics) via a new "Consider This" box that ties to the chapter's discussion of Buzzer Auto, demand shocks, and short-run sticky prices. In Chapter 7 (Measuring Domestic Output and National Income) we point out that the main flows in the National Income and Product Accounts usually expand over time, but not always, as demonstrated by the recession. In Chapter 8 (Economic Growth) we discuss how the recession relates to the growth/production possibilities dynamics of Figure 8.2. In Chapter 9 (Business Cycles, Unemployment, and Inflation) we provide a telling comparison of unemployment rates for various demographic groups for the prerecession year 2007 and the recession year 2009.

In Chapter 10 (Basic Macroeconomic Relationships) we have added two "Consider This" boxes, one on how the paradox of thrift applied to consumer behavior during the recession and the other on the riddle of plunging investment spending at the same time the interest rate dropped to near zero during the recession. In Chapter 11 (The Aggregate Expenditures Model) we use the recession as a timely application of how a decline in aggregate expenditures can produce a recessionary expenditure gap and a highly negative GDP gap. In Chapter 12 (Aggregate Demand and Aggregate Supply) we use the recession as a good application of how negative demand shocks can produce large declines in real output with no or very little deflation. Chapter 13 (Fiscal Policy, Deficits, and Debt) provided a terrific opportunity to bring each of these timely and relevant subjects up-to-date, and we took full advantage of that opportunity.

In Chapter 14 (Money, Banking, and Financial Institutions) we added a major new section on the financial crisis, with emphasis on the mortgage debt crisis, mortgage-backed securities, failures and near-failures of financial firms, the Treasury's TARP rescue, the Fed's extraordinary use of lender-of-last-resort facilities, and the Wall Street Reform and Consumer Protection Act of 2010. In Chapter 15 (Money Creation), we stress that the Fed now pays interest on required reserves, and we also use the "Last Word" on the bank panics of 1930–1933 to explain how the Fed handled things very differently during the recent financial crisis.

Chapter 16 (Interest Rates and Monetary Policy) features several new discussions relating to Fed policies during the recession, including a new discussion on the liquidity trap. Along with giving the Fed high marks for dealing with the crisis, we also say that some economists think the Fed contributed to the financial crisis by keeping interest rates too low for too long during the recovery from the 2001 recession. We also replaced a dated "Consider This" piece with a new one on the ballooning Fed balance sheet and the problems it could pose for monetary policy during the eventual postrecession expansion. Chapter 17 (Financial Economics) presented a new opportunity for us to demonstrate how a sharp decline of the "appetite for risk" alters the slope of the Securities Market Line (SML) and changes investment patterns between stocks and bonds.

Other mentions of the recession are spread throughout the remainder of the macro chapters, including in the discussions of macro debates, trade protectionism, and trade deficits.

Although we found these various ways to work the recession into our macro chapters, we are confident that our basic macroeconomic models will serve equally well in explaining economic recovery and expansion back to the economy's historical growth path. The new inclusions relating to the recession simply help students see the relevance of the models to what they are seeing in the news and perhaps experiencing in their own lives. The overall tone of the book, including the macro, continues to be optimistic with respect to the long-term growth prospects of market economies.

Reworked End-of-Chapter Questions and Problems

We have extensively reworked the end-of-chapter Study Questions, splitting them into questions and problems and adding many new problems. The questions are analytic and often ask for free responses, whereas the problems are mainly quantitative. We have aligned the questions and problems with the learning objectives presented at the beginning of the chapters. All of the questions and problems are assignable through McGraw-Hill's *Connect Economics*; all of the problems also contain additional algorithmic variations and can be automatically graded within the system. The new lists of questions and problems were well-received by reviewers, many of them long-time users of the book.

Current Discussions and Examples

The 19th edition of *Macroeconomics* refers to and discusses many current topics. Examples include the cost of the war in Iraq; surpluses and shortages of tickets at the Olympics; the myriad impacts of ethanol subsidies; core inflation; China's continued rapid growth; the severe recession of 2007–2009; the paradox of thrift; the stimulus package of 2008; ballooning Federal budget deficits and public debt; the long-run funding shortfalls in Social Security and Medicare; securitization and the mortgage debt crisis; the Wall Street Reform and Consumer Protection Act of 2010; recent Fed monetary policy; the liquidity trap; the Fed's new term auction facility; the Fed's payment of interest on required reserves; the Taylor rule in relation to Fed policy; the jump in the size of the Fed's balance sheet; U.S. trade deficits; offshoring of American jobs; trade adjustment assistance; the European Union and the Euro Zone; changes in exchange rates; and many other current topics.

Chapter-by-Chapter Changes

Each chapter of *Macroeconomics*, 19th edition, contains updated data reflecting the current economy, streamlined Learning Objectives, and reorganized end-of-chapter content.

Chapter-specific updates include:

Chapter 1: Limits, Alternatives, and Choices features a new Learning Objective on consumption possibilities and a revised definition of "entrepreneur" that clarifies why risk taking is socially beneficial and, thus, why entrepreneurial ability is a valuable economic resource.

Chapter 2: The Market System and the Circular Flow includes a revised explanation of property rights, a clarified discussion of firms' motives for choosing the lowest-cost production methods, an updated "McHits and McMisses" "Consider This" box, and a revised discussion of the circular flow model.

Chapter 3: Demand, Supply, and Market Equilibrium contains wording improvements that clarify the main concepts.

Chapter 4: Elasticity is a new chapter that focuses solely on elasticity. This content has been moved forward from Chapter 6 of *Economics*, 18th edition, allowing this topic to be covered directly after supply and demand. This content will be available in both the Macro and Micro splits. The material on consumer and producer surplus from that chapter has been moved to Chapter 5 of *Macroeconomics*, 19th edition.

Chapter 5: Market Failures: Public Goods and Externalities is a new chapter that first examines consumer surplus, producer surplus, efficiency, and efficiency losses (all from Chapter 6, *Economics*, 18th edition). It then devotes the remainder of the chapter to market failures, specifically public goods and externalities (both from Chapter 16, *Economics*, 18th edition.) The chapter also features a new "Last Word" section that discusses the pros and cons of cap-and-trade emissions-control policies and a new "Consider This" box that concisely discusses the Coase Theorem.

Chapter 6: An Introduction to Macroeconomics includes two new "Consider This" boxes. The first contrasts economic investment with financial investment and the second discusses the recession of 2007–2009 in the context of the introductory analysis.

Chapter 7: Measuring Domestic Output and National Income adds new definitions and data for the terms *durable goods*, *nondurable goods*, and *services* in the discussion of personal consumption.

Chapter 8: Economic Growth has substantially revised Learning Objectives that provide a better preview of the chapter; tightened discussions in the "Consider This" boxes on patents in India and on women, the labor force, and economic growth; a new discussion relating the recession to the growth and production possibilities analysis in Figure 8.2; and updates on growth accounting from the *Economic Report of the President*.

Chapter 9: Business Cycles, Unemployment, and Inflation includes a revised discussion on business cycles, new data on unemployment rates during the recent recession, and a new discussion of core inflation.

Chapter 10: Basic Macroeconomic Relationships features new "Consider This" boxes discussing the Great Recession, the paradox of thrift, and the investment riddle, and an improved discussion of investment instability.

Chapter 11: The Aggregate Expenditures Model provides a revised introduction that links to the prior chapters, improved discussions in the "Assumptions and Simplifications" and "International Linkages" sections, and a new application that relates the Great Recession to the AE model.

Chapter 12: Aggregate Demand and Aggregate Supply has a new introduction that provides a current and relevant example for students, and a reorganized and updated "Last Word" on oil prices.

Chapter 13: Fiscal Policy, Deficits, and Debt provides explicit definitions of expansionary and contractionary fiscal policy and political business cycles, an updated discussion of current fiscal policy, detailed coverage of the 2008 and 2009 stimulus packages, and a new "Last Word" on Social Security and Medicare funding shortfalls.

Chapter 14: Money, Banking, and Financial Institutions features a new section on the financial crisis of 2007–2008, with emphasis on the mortgage default crisis, mortgage-backed securitization, failures and near failures of financial firms, the Treasury's TARP rescue, the Fed's extraordinary new lender-of-last resort facilities, and the Wall Street Reform and Consumer Protection Act of 2010. Also new is a "Last Word" on electronic banking.

Chapter 15: Money Creation contains a clarified discussion of a bank's balance sheet and an updated "Last Word" that contrasts the lack of action by the Fed during the early 1930s compared to the Fed's forceful actions during the financial crisis of 2007–2008.

Chapter 16: Interest Rates and Monetary Policy features a fully updated discussion of recent U.S. monetary policy, a new "Consider This" box on the ballooning balance sheet of the Fed during the recession of 2007–2009, and the conversion of the AD-AS summary figure from the previous edition to a new "Last Word" section.

Chapter 17: Financial Economics provides a revised introduction to the discussion of present value, a new section on applications of the security market line, and a new "Consider This" piece that discusses Ponzi schemes and Bernie Madoff.

Chapter 18: Extending the Analysis of Aggregate Supply features a crisper discussion of economic growth with ongoing inflation, along with a modified Figure 18.7, and an updated discussion of the Phillips Curve.

Chapter 19: Current Issues in Macro Theory and Policy has a new "Consider This" box on the Fed's actions prior to the financial crisis and an updated discussion of the Taylor Rule in the "Last Word."

Chapter 20: International Trade contains relevant content from Chapter 5 of the 18th edition. This chapter features additional explanation that clarifies how comparative advantage differs from absolute advantage, a new "Consider This" box on misunderstanding the gains from trade, and a streamlined discussion of multilateral trade agreements and free-trade zones.

Chapter 21: The Balance of Payments, Exchange Rates, and Trade Deficits features a streamlined explanation of why the balance-of-payments statement always balances, a revised discussion of official reserves and balance-of-payments deficits and surpluses, and updated discussions of exchange rates.

Chapter 22 Web: The Economics of Developing Countries includes a revised discussion of large populations and the standard of living and updated coverage of the role of government in improving the growth prospects of developing countries.

Distinguishing Features

Comprehensive Explanations at an Appropriate Level
Economics is comprehensive, analytical, and challenging yet fully accessible to a wide range of students. The thoroughness and accessibility enable instructors to select topics for special classroom emphasis with confidence that students can read and comprehend other independently assigned material in the book. Where needed, an extra sentence of explanation is provided. Brevity at the expense of clarity is false economy.

Fundamentals of the Market System
Many economies throughout the world are still making difficult transitions from planning to markets while a handful of other countries such as Venezuela seem to be trying to re-establish government-controlled, centrally planned economies. Our detailed description of the institutions and operation of the market system in Chapter 2 (The Market System and the Circular Flow) is therefore even more relevant than before. We pay particular attention to property rights, entrepreneurship, freedom of enterprise and choice, competition, and the role of profits because these concepts are often misunderstood by beginning students worldwide.

Extensive Treatment of International Economics
We give the principles and institutions of the global economy extensive treatment. The appendix to Chapter 3 (Demand, Supply, and Market Equilibrium) has an application on exchange rates. Chapter 20 (International Trade) examines key facts of international trade, specialization and comparative advantage, arguments for protectionism, impacts of tariffs and subsidies, and various trade agreements. Chapter 21 (Balance of Payments, Exchange Rates, and Trade Deficits) discusses the balance of payments, fixed and floating exchange rates, and U.S. trade deficits. Web Chapter 22 (The Economics of Developing Countries) takes a look at the special problems faced by developing countries and how the advanced industrial countries try to help them.

As noted previously in this preface, Chapter 20 (International Trade) is constructed such that instructors who want to cover international trade early in the course can assign it immediately after Chapter 3. Chapter 20 requires only a good understanding of production possibilities analysis and supply and demand analysis to comprehend. International competition, trade flows, and financial flows are integrated throughout *Macroeconomics*. "Global Perspective" boxes add to the international flavor of the text.

Early and Extensive Treatment of Government
The public sector is an integral component of modern capitalism. This book introduces the role of government early. Chapter 5 (Market Failures: Public Goods and Externalities) systematically discusses public goods and government policies toward externalities. Government's role (including the role of the Fed) in promoting price-stability, full employment, and economic growth is central to the macroeconomic policy chapters. Considerable attention is given to the issues related to budget deficits and the Federal debt.

Step-by-Step, Two-Path Macro
As in the previous edition, our macro continues to be distinguished by a

systematic step-by-step approach to developing ideas and building models. Explicit assumptions about price and wage stickiness are posited and then systematically peeled away, yielding new models and extensions, all in the broader context of growth, expectations, shocks, and degrees of price and wage stickiness over time.

In crafting this step-by-step macro approach, we took care to preserve the "two-path macro" that many instructors appreciated. Instructors who want to bypass the immediate short-run model (Chapter 11: The Aggregate Expenditures Model) can proceed without loss of continuity directly to the short-run AD-AS model (Chapter 12: Aggregate Demand and Aggregate Supply), fiscal policy, money and banking, monetary policy, and the long-run AD-AS analysis.

Focus on Economic Policy and Issues For many students, the macro chapters on fiscal policy and monetary policy are where the action is centered. We guide that action along logical lines through the application of appropriate analytical tools.

Integrated Text and Web Site *Macroeconomics* and its Web site are highly integrated through in-text Web buttons, Web-based end-of-chapter questions, bonus Web chapters, multiple-choice self-tests at the Web site, math notes, and other features. Our Web site is part and parcel of our student learning package, customized to the book.

The in-text Web buttons (or indicators) merit special mention. Three differing colors of rectangular indicators appear throughout the book, informing readers that complementary content on a subject can be found at our Web site, **www.mcconnell19e.com**. The indicator types are:

Worked Problems Written by Norris Peterson of Pacific Lutheran University (WA), these pieces consist of side-by-side computational questions and computational procedures used to derive the answers. In essence, they extend the textbook's explanations

WORKED PROBLEMS

W 1.1

Budget lines

of various computations—for example, of real GDP, real GDP per capita, the unemployment rate, the inflation rate, and more. From a student's perspective, they provide "cookbook" help for solving numerical problems.

Interactive Graphs These pieces (developed under the supervision of Norris Peterson) depict 30 major graphs in *Economics* and instruct students to shift the curves, observe

INTERACTIVE GRAPHS

G 1.1

Production possibilities curve

the outcomes, and derive relevant generalizations. This hands-on graph work will greatly reinforce the graphs and their meaning.

Origin of the Ideas These pieces, written by Randy Grant of Linfield College (OR), are brief histories of 70 major ideas identified in *Economics*. They identify the particular economists who developed ideas such as opportunity cost, equilibrium price, the multiplier, comparative advantage, and elasticity.

ORIGIN OF THE IDEA

O 1.1

Origin of the term "economics"

Organizational Alternatives

Although instructors generally agree on the content of principles of economics courses, they sometimes differ on how to arrange the material. *Macroeconomics* includes 7 parts, and thus provides considerable organizational flexibility. For example, the two-path macro enables covering the full aggregate expenditures model or advancing directly from the chapter on basic macro relationships to the AD-AS model. Also, the section of Chapter 18 on the intricacies of the relationship between short-run and long-run aggregate supply can easily be appended to Chapter 12 on AD and AS.

Finally, as noted before, Chapter 20 on international trade can easily be moved up to immediately after Chapter 3 on supply and demand for instructors who want an early discussion of international trade.

Pedagogical Aids

Macroeconomics is highly student-oriented. The "To the Student" statement at the beginning of Part 1 details the book's many pedagogical aids. The 19th edition is also accompanied by a variety of high-quality supplements that help students master the subject and help instructors implement customized courses.

Supplements for Students and Instructors

Study Guide One of the world's leading experts on economic education, William Walstad of the University of Nebraska–Lincoln, prepared the *Study Guide*. Many students find either the printed or digital version indispensable. Each chapter contains an introductory statement, a checklist of behavioral objectives, an outline, a list of important terms, fill-in questions, problems and projects, objective questions, and discussion questions.

The *Guide* comprises a superb "portable tutor" for the principles student. Separate *Study Guides* are available for the macro and micro paperback editions of the text.

Instructor's Manual

Laura Maghoney of Solano Community College revised and updated the *Instructor's Manual*, and Shawn Knabb of Western Washington University checked and brought the end-of-chapter questions, problems, and solutions to the *Manual*. The revised *Instructor's Manual* includes:

- Chapter summaries.
- Listings of "what's new" in each chapter.
- Teaching tips and suggestions.
- Learning objectives.
- Chapter outlines.
- Extra questions and problems.
- Answers to the end-of-chapter questions and problems, plus correlation guides mapping content to the learning objectives.

The *Instructor's Manual* is available on the instructor's side of the Online Learning Center.

Three Test Banks

Test Bank I contains about 6500 multiple-choice and true-false questions, most of which were written by the text authors. Randy Grant revised Test Bank I for the 19th edition. Test Bank II contains around 6000 multiple-choice and true-false questions, updated by Felix Kwan of Maryville University. All Test Bank I and II questions are organized by learning objective, topic, AACSB Assurance of Learning, and Bloom's Taxonomy guidelines. Test Bank III, written by William Walstad, contains more than 600 pages of short-answer questions and problems created in the style of the book's end-of-chapter questions. Test Bank III can be used to construct student assignments or design essay and problem exams. Suggested answers to the essay and problem questions are included. In all, more than 14,000 questions give instructors maximum testing flexibility while ensuring the fullest possible text correlation.

Test Banks I and II are available in *Connect Economics*, through EZ Test Online, and in MS Word. EZ Test Online allows professors to create customized tests that contain both questions that they select from the test banks as well as questions that they craft themselves. Test Bank III is available in MS Word on the password-protected instructor's side of the Online Learning Center, and on the Instructor Resource CD.

PowerPoint Presentations

With the assistance of Laura Maghoney, the Web site PowerPoint Presentations

for the 19th edition were updated by a dedicated team of instructors: Jill Beccaris-Pescatore of Montgomery County Community College, Stephanie Campbell of Mineral Area College, Amy Chataginer of Mississippi Gulf Coast Community College, and Dorothy Siden of Salem State College. Each chapter is accompanied by a concise yet thorough tour of the key concepts. Instructors can use these Web site presentations in the classroom, and students can use them on their computers.

Digital Image Library

Every graph and table in the text is available on the instructor's side of the Web site and on the Instructor's Resource CD-ROM.

McGraw-Hill Connect Economics

McGraw-Hill *Connect Economics* is an online assignment and assessment solution that connects students with the tools and resources  they'll need to achieve success. McGraw-Hill *Connect Economics* helps prepare students for their future by enabling faster learning, more efficient studying, and higher retention of knowledge.

All of the end-of-chapter questions and problems, the thousands of questions from Test Banks I and II, and additional resources are available in *Connect Economics*. For more information on *Connect Economics* and other technology, please see pages xiv–xxi.

Online Learning Center (www.mcconnell19e.com)

The Web site accompanying this book is a central resource for students and instructors alike. The optional Web Chapter (Chapter 22W: The Economics of Developing Countries) plus the two new Content Options for Instructors (The United States in the Global Economy and Previous International Exchange-Rate Systems), are posted as full-color PDF files. The in-text Web buttons alert the students to points in the book where they can springboard to the Web site to get more information. Students can also review PowerPoint presentations and test their knowledge of a chapter's concepts with a self-graded multiple-choice quiz. The password-protected Instructor Center houses the Instructor's Manual, all three Test Banks, and links to EZ Test Online, PowerPoint presentations, and the Digital Image Library.

Computerized Test Bank Online

A comprehensive bank of test questions is provided within McGraw-Hill's flexible electronic testing program EZ Test Online (**www.eztestonline.com**). EZ Test Online allows instructors to simply and quickly create tests or quizzes for their students. Instructors can select questions from multiple McGraw-Hill test banks or author their own, and then either print the finalized test or quiz for paper distribution or publish it online for access via the Internet.

This user-friendly program allows instructors to sort questions by format; select questions by learning objectives or Bloom's taxonomy tags; edit existing questions or add new ones; and scramble questions for multiple versions of the same test. Instructors can export their tests for use in WebCT, Blackboard, and PageOut, making it easy to share assessment materials with colleagues, adjuncts, and TAs. Instant scoring and feedback is provided, and EZ Test Online's record book is designed to easily export to instructor gradebooks.

Assurance-of-Learning Ready Many educational institutions are focused on the notion of assurance of learning, an important element of some accreditation standards. *Macroeconomics* is designed to support your assurance-of-learning initiatives with a simple yet powerful solution. Each chapter in the book begins with a list of numbered learning objectives to which each end-of-chapter question and problem is then mapped. In this way, student responses to those questions and problems can be used to assess how well students are mastering each particular learning objective. Each test bank question for *Macroeconomics* also maps to a specific learning objective.

You can use our test bank software, EZ Test Online, or *Connect Economics* to easily query for learning outcomes and objectives that directly relate to the learning objectives for your course. You can then use the reporting features to aggregate student results in a similar fashion, making the collection and presentation of assurance-of-learning data simple and easy.

AACSB Statement The McGraw-Hill Companies is a proud corporate member of AACSB International. Understanding the importance and value of AACSB accreditation, *Macroeconomics*, 19th edition, has sought to recognize the curricula guidelines detailed in the AACSB standards for business accreditation by connecting end-of-chapter questions in *Macroeconomics*, 19th edition, and the accompanying test banks to the general knowledge and skill guidelines found in the AACSB standards.

This AACSB Statement for *Macroeconomics*, 19th edition, is provided only as a guide for the users of this text. The AACSB leaves content coverage and assessment within the purview of individual schools, their respective missions, and their respective faculty. While *Macroeconomics*, 19th edition, and the teaching package make no claim of any specific AACSB qualification or evaluation, we have, within *Macroeconomics*, 19th edition, labeled selected questions according to the six general knowledge and skills areas.

Acknowledgments

We give special thanks to Norris Peterson and Randy Grant, who created the "button" content on our Web site. We again thank James Reese of the University of South Carolina at Spartanburg, who wrote the original Internet exercises. Although many of those questions were replaced or modified in the typical course of revision, several remain virtually unchanged. We also thank Laura Maghoney and the team of instructors who updated the PowerPoint slides for the 19th edition. Shawn Knabb deserves great thanks for accuracy-checking the end-of-chapter questions and problems and their solutions, as well as for creating the variations of all of the problems. Thanks to the dedicated instructors who created and revised our additional study tools, including Steve Price, Shannon Aucoin, Brian Motii, Amy Scott, Emilio Gomez, Amy Stapp, Richard Kramer, and Mark Wilson. Finally, we thank William Walstad and Tom Barbiero (the coauthor of our Canadian edition) for their helpful ideas and insights.

We are greatly indebted to an all-star group of professionals at McGraw-Hill—in particular Douglas Reiner, Noelle Fox Bathurst, Harvey Yep, Lori Koetters, Jen Saxton, Melissa Larmon, and Brent Gordon—for their publishing and marketing expertise.

We thank Keri Johnson for her selection of the "Consider This" and "Last Word" photos and Mary Kazak Sander and Maureen McCutcheon for the design.

The 19th edition has benefited from a number of perceptive formal reviews. The reviewers, listed at the end of the preface, were a rich source of suggestions for this revision. To each of you, and others we may have inadvertently overlooked, thank you for your considerable help in improving *Macroeconomics*.

Stanley L. Brue
Sean M. Flynn
Campbell R. McConnell

Reviewers

Virden Harrison, *Modesto Junior College*
Richard Hawkins, *University of West Florida*
Kim Hawtrey, *Hope College*
Glenn Haynes, *Western Illinois University*
Michael Heslop, *NOVA Community College Annandale*
Jesse Hill, *Tarrant County College SE*
Calvin Hoy, *County College of Morris*
James Hubert, *Seattle Central Community College*
Greg Hunter, *California State Polytechnic University, Pomona*
Christos Ioannou, *University of Minnesota–Minneapolis*
Faridul Islam, *Utah Valley University*
Mahshid Jalilvand, *University of Wisconsin–Stout*
Ricot Jean, *Valencia Community College–Osceola*
Jonatan Jelen, *City College of New York*
Brad Kamp, *University of South Florida–Sarasota*
Kevin Kelley, *Northwest Vista College*
Chris Klein, *Middle Tennessee State University*
Barry Kotlove, *Edmonds Community College*
Richard Kramer, *New England College*
Felix Kwan, *Maryville University*
Ted Labay, *Bishop State Community College*
Tina Lance, *Germanna Community College–Fredericksburg*
Yu-Feng Lee, *New Mexico State University–Las Cruces*
Adam Lei, *Midwestern State University*
Phillip Letting, *Harrisburg Area Community College*
Brian Lynch, *Lake Land College*
Zagros Madjd-Sadjadi, *Winston-Salem State University*
Laura Maghoney, *Solano Community College*
Vincent Mangum, *Grambling State University*
Benjamin Matta, *New Mexico State University–Las Cruces*
Pete Mavrokordatos, *Tarrant County College NE*
Michael McIntyre, *Copiah Lincoln Community College*
Bob McKizzie, *Tarrant County College SE*
Kevin McWoodson, *Moraine Valley Community College*
Edwin Mensah, *University of North Carolina at Pembroke*
Randy Methenitis, *Richland College*
Ida Mirzaie, *Ohio State University*
David Mitch, *University of Maryland–Baltimore City*
Ramesh Mohan, *Bryant University*
Daniel Morvey, *Piedmont Technical College*
Shahriar Mostashari, *Campbell University*
Richard Mount, *Monmouth University*
Ted Muzio, *St. John's University*

Cliff Nowell, *Weber State University*
Albert Okunade, *University of Memphis*
Mary Ellen Overbay, *Seton Hall University*
Tammy Parker, *University of Louisiana at Monroe*
David Peterson, *American River College*
Alberto Perez, *Harford Community College*
Mary Anne Pettit, *Southern Illinois University*
Jeff Phillips, *Morrisville State College*
William Piper, *Piedmont College*
Robert Poulton, *Graceland University*
Dezzie Prewitt, *Rio Hondo College*
Joe Prinzinger, *Lynchburg College*
Jaishankar Raman, *Valparaiso University*
Natalie Reaves, *Rowan University*
Virginia Reilly, *Ocean County College*
Tim Reynolds, *Alvin Community College*
John Romps, *Saint Anselm College*
Tom Scheiding, *Elizabethtown College*
Amy Schmidt, *Saint Anselm College*
Ron Schuelke, *Santa Rosa Junior College*
Alexandra Shiu, *Temple College*
Dorothy Siden, *Salem State College*
Timothy Simpson, *Central New Mexico Community College*
Jonathan Sleeper, *Indian River State College Central*
Camille Soltau-Nelson, *Texas A&M University*
Robert Sonora, *Fort Lewis College*
Nick Spangenberg, *Ozarks Tech Community College*
Dennis Spector, *Naugatuck Valley Community College*
Thomas Stevens, *University of Massachusetts, Amherst*
Tamika Steward, *Tarrant Count College SE*
Robin Sturik, *Cuyahoga Community College Western–Parma*
Travis Taylor, *Christopher Newport University*
Ross Thomas, *Central New Mexico Community College*
Mark Thompson, *Augusta State University*
Deborah Thorsen, *Palm Beach Community College–Lake Worth*
Mike Toma, *Armstrong Atlantic State University*
Dosse Toulaboe, *Fort Hays State University*
Jeff Vance, *Sinclair Community College*
Cheryl Wachenheim, *North Dakota State University–Fargo*
Christine Wathen, *Middlesex County College*
Scott Williams, *County College of Morris*
Wendy Wysocki, *Monroe County Community College*
Edward Zajicek, *Winston-Salem State University*

Brief Contents

Contents

PART TWO
Price, Quantity, and Efficiency   46

Chapter 3
Demand, Supply, and Market Equilibrium   47

PART ONE

INTRODUCTION TO ECONOMICS AND THE ECONOMY

To the Student

This book and its ancillaries contain several features designed to help you learn economics:

- **Web buttons (indicators)** A glance through the book reveals many pages with rectangular icons set into the text. These "buttons" alert you to helpful learning aids available with the book. The green button denotes "Interactive Graphs" found at the text's Web site, **www. mcconnell19e.com**. Brief exercises have you interact with the graphs, for example, by clicking on a specific curve and dragging it to a new location. These exercises will enhance your understanding of the underlying concepts. The blue button symbolizes "Worked Problems." Numeric problems are presented and then solved, side-by-side, step-by-step. Seeing how the problems are worked will help you solve similar problems on quizzes and exams. The purple button stands for "Origin of the Idea." Each of these pieces traces a particular idea to the person or persons who first developed it.

INTERACTIVE GRAPHS

G 3.1

Supply and demand

WORKED PROBLEMS

W 2.1

Least-cost production

ORIGIN OF THE IDEA

O 1.4

Ceteris paribus

After reading a chapter, thumb back through it to note the Web buttons and their associated numbers. On the home page of our Internet site select Student Edition and use the pull-down list under "Choose one" to find the Web button content for each chapter.

- **Other Internet aids** Our Web site contains many other aids. In the Student Edition you will find self-testing multiple-choice quizzes, PowerPoint presentations, and much more. For those of you with a very strong mathematics background, be sure to note the "See the Math" section on the Web site. There you will find nearly 50 notes that develop the algebra and, in a few cases, the calculus that underlie the economic concepts.

- **Appendix on graphs** Be assured, however, that you will need only basic math skills to do well in the principles course. In particular, you will need to be comfortable with basic graphical analysis and a few quantitative concepts. The appendix at the end of

Chapter 1 reviews graphs and slopes of curves. You may want to read it before starting Chapter 1.

- **Reviews** Each chapter contains two to four Quick Reviews and an end-of-chapter summary. These reviews will help you focus on essential ideas and study for exams.

- **Key terms and Key Graphs** Key terms are set in boldface type within the chapters, listed at the end of each chapter, and again defined in the glossary at the end of the book. Graphs with special importance are labeled Key Graphs, and each includes a multiple-choice Quick Quiz. Your instructor may or may not emphasize all of these figures, but you should pay special attention to those that are discussed in class; you can be certain there will be exam questions on them.

- **Consider This and Last Word boxes** Many chapters include a "Consider This" box. These brief pieces provide commonplace analogies, examples, and stories that help you understand and remember central economic ideas. Each chapter concludes with a "Last Word" box. Some of them are revealing applications of economic ideas; others are short case studies. While it is tempting to ignore in-text boxes, don't. Most are fun to read, and all will improve your grasp of economics.

- **Questions and Problems** The end of each chapter features separate sections of Questions and Problems. The Questions are analytic and often ask for free-responses, while the Problems are more computational. Each is keyed to a particular learning objective (LO) in the list of LOs at the beginning of the chapter. At the Web site is a multiple-choice quiz for each chapter.

- **Study Guide** We enthusiastically recommend the *Study Guide* accompanying this text. This "portable tutor" contains not only a broad sampling of various kinds of questions but a host of useful learning aids. Software-driven tutorials, including the Self Quiz and Study in *Connect Economics*, are also available with the text.

Our two main goals are to help you understand and apply economics and help you improve your analytical skills. An understanding of economics will enable you to comprehend a whole range of economic, social, and political problems that otherwise would seem puzzling and perplexing. Also, your study will enhance reasoning skills that are highly prized in the workplace.

Good luck with your study. We think it will be well worth your time and effort.

AFTER READING THIS CHAPTER, YOU SHOULD BE ABLE TO:

1 **Define economics and the features of the economic perspective.**

2 **Describe the role of economic theory in economics.**

3 **Distinguish microeconomics from macroeconomics and positive economics from normative economics.**

4 **List the categories of scarce resources and delineate the nature of the economizing problem.**

5 **Apply production possibilities analysis, increasing opportunity costs, and economic growth.**

6 **Explain how economic growth and international trade increase consumption possibilities.**

7 **(Appendix) Understand graphs, curves, and slopes as they relate to economics.**

Limits, Alternatives, and Choices

(An appendix on understanding graphs follows this chapter. If you need a quick review of this mathematical tool, you might benefit by reading the appendix first.) People's wants are numerous and varied. Biologically, people need only air, water, food, clothing, and shelter. But in modern societies people also desire goods and services that provide a more comfortable or affluent standard of living. We want bottled water, soft drinks, and fruit juices, not just water from the creek. We want salads, burgers, and pizzas, not just berries and nuts. We want jeans, suits, and coats, not just woven reeds. We want apartments, condominiums, or houses, not just mud huts. And, as the saying goes, "That is not the half of it." We also want flat-panel TVs, Internet service, education, homeland security, cell phones, health care, and much more.

Fortunately, society possesses productive resources, such as labor and managerial talent, tools and machinery, and land and mineral deposits. These resources, employed in the economic system (or simply the economy), help us produce goods and services that satisfy many of our economic

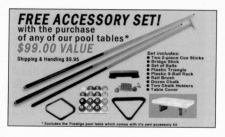

ORIGIN OF THE IDEA

O 1.1

Origin of the term "Economics"

wants. But the blunt reality is that our economic wants far exceed the productive capacity of our scarce (limited) resources. We are forced to make choices. This unyielding truth underlies the definition of **economics,** which is the social science concerned with how individuals, institutions, and society make optimal (best) choices under conditions of scarcity.

The Economic Perspective

Economists view things from a unique perspective. This **economic perspective,** or economic way of thinking, has several critical and closely interrelated features.

Scarcity and Choice

Scarce economic resources mean limited goods and services. Scarcity restricts options and demands choices. Because we "can't have it all," we must decide what we will have and what we must forgo.

At the core of economics is the idea that "there is no free lunch." You may be treated to lunch, making it "free" from your perspective, but someone bears a cost. Because all resources are either privately or collectively owned by members of society, ultimately society bears the cost. Scarce inputs of land, equipment, farm labor, the labor of cooks and waiters, and managerial talent are required. Because society could have used these resources to produce something else, it sacrifices those other goods and services in making the lunch available. Economists call such sacrifices **opportunity costs:** To obtain more of one thing, society forgoes the opportunity of getting the next best thing. That sacrifice is the opportunity cost of the choice.

Purposeful Behavior

Economics assumes that human behavior reflects "rational self-interest." Individuals look for and pursue opportunities to increase their **utility**—the pleasure, happiness, or satisfaction obtained from consuming a good or service. They allocate their time, energy, and money to maximize their satisfaction. Because they weigh costs and benefits, their economic decisions are "purposeful" or "rational," not "random" or "chaotic."

ORIGIN OF THE IDEA

O 1.2

Utility

Consumers are purposeful in deciding what goods and services to buy. Business firms are purposeful in deciding what products to produce and how to produce them. Government entities are purposeful in deciding what public services to provide and how to finance them.

"Purposeful behavior" does not assume that people and institutions are immune from faulty logic and therefore are perfect decision makers. They sometimes make mistakes. Nor does it mean that people's decisions are unaffected by emotion or the decisions of those around them. Indeed, economists acknowledge that people are sometimes impulsive or emulative. "Purposeful behavior" simply means that people make decisions with some desired outcome in mind.

Rational self-interest is not the same as selfishness. In the economy, increasing one's own wage, rent, interest, or

CONSIDER THIS . . .

Free for All?

Free products are seemingly everywhere. Sellers offer free software, free cell phones, and free checking accounts. Dentists give out free toothbrushes. At state visitor centers, there are free brochures and maps.

Does the presence of so many free products contradict the economist's assertion "There is no free lunch"? No! Resources are used to produce each of these products, and because those resources have alternative uses, society gives up something else to get the "free" good. Where resources are used to produce goods or services, there is no free lunch.

So why are these goods offered for free? In a word: marketing! Firms sometimes offer free products to entice people to try them, hoping they will then purchase those goods later. The free software may eventually entice you to buy the producer's upgraded software. In other instances, the free brochures contain advertising for shops and restaurants, and that free e-mail program is filled with ads. In still other cases, the product is free only in conjunction with a larger purchase. To get the free bottle of soda, you must buy the large pizza. To get the free cell phone, you need to sign up for a year's worth of cell phone service.

So while "free" products may come at no cost to the individuals receiving them, they are never free to society.

profit normally requires identifying and satisfying *somebody else's* wants! Also, people make personal sacrifices for others. They contribute time and money to charities because they derive pleasure from doing so. Parents help pay for their children's education for the same reason. These self-interested, but unselfish, acts help maximize the givers'

CONSIDER THIS . . .

Fast-Food Lines

The economic perspective is useful in analyzing all sorts of behaviors. Consider an everyday example: the behavior of fast-food customers. When customers enter the restaurant, they go to the shortest line, believing that line will minimize their time cost of obtaining food. They are acting purposefully; time is limited, and people prefer using it in some way other than standing in line.

If one fast-food line is temporarily shorter than other lines, some people will move to that line. These movers apparently view the time saving from the shorter line (marginal benefit) as exceeding the cost of moving from their present line (marginal cost). The line switching tends to equalize line lengths. No further movement of customers between lines occurs once all lines are about equal.

Fast-food customers face another cost-benefit decision when a clerk opens a new station at the counter. Should they move to the new station or stay put? Those who shift to the new line decide that the time saving from the move exceeds the extra cost of physically moving. In so deciding, customers must also consider just how quickly they can get to the new station compared with others who may be contemplating the same move. (Those who hesitate in this situation are lost!)

Customers at the fast-food establishment do not have perfect information when they select lines. Thus, not all decisions turn out as expected. For example, you might enter a short line and find someone in front of you is ordering hamburgers and fries for 40 people in the Greyhound bus parked out back (and the employee is a trainee!). Nevertheless, at the time you made your decision, you thought it was optimal.

Finally, customers must decide what food to order when they arrive at the counter. In making their choices, they again compare marginal costs and marginal benefits in attempting to obtain the greatest personal satisfaction for their expenditure.

Economists believe that what is true for the behavior of customers at fast-food restaurants is true for economic behavior in general. Faced with an array of choices, consumers, workers, and businesses rationally compare marginal costs and marginal benefits in making decisions.

satisfaction as much as any personal purchase of goods or services. Self-interested behavior is simply behavior designed to increase personal satisfaction, however it may be derived.

Marginal Analysis: Comparing Benefits and Costs

The economic perspective focuses largely on **marginal analysis**—comparisons of marginal benefits and marginal costs, usually for decision making. To economists, "marginal" means "extra," "additional," or "a change in." Most choices or decisions involve changes in the status quo, meaning the existing state of affairs.

Should you attend school for another year? Should you study an extra hour for an exam? Should you supersize your fries? Similarly, should a business expand or reduce its output? Should government increase or decrease its funding for a missile defense system?

Each option involves marginal benefits and, because of scarce resources, marginal costs. In making choices rationally, the decision maker must compare those two amounts. Example: You and your fiancée are shopping for an engagement ring. Should you buy a $\frac{1}{2}$-carat diamond, a $\frac{3}{4}$-carat diamond, a 1-carat diamond, or something even larger? The marginal cost of a larger-size diamond is the added expense beyond the cost of the smaller-size diamond. The marginal benefit is the perceived lifetime pleasure (utility) from the larger-size stone. If the marginal benefit of the larger diamond exceeds its marginal cost (and you can

ORIGIN OF THE IDEA
O 1.3
Marginal analysis

afford it), buy the larger stone. But if the marginal cost is more than the marginal benefit, you should buy the smaller diamond instead—even if you can afford the larger stone!

In a world of scarcity, the decision to obtain the marginal benefit associated with some specific option always includes the marginal cost of forgoing something else. The money spent on the larger-size diamond means forgoing some other product. An opportunity cost—the value of the next best thing forgone—is always present whenever a choice is made.

Theories, Principles, and Models

Like the physical and life sciences, as well as other social sciences, economics relies on the **scientific method.** That procedure consists of several elements:

- Observing real-world behavior and outcomes.
- Based on those observations, formulating a possible explanation of cause and effect (hypothesis).

- Testing this explanation by comparing the outcomes of specific events to the outcome predicted by the hypothesis.
- Accepting, rejecting, and modifying the hypothesis, based on these comparisons.
- Continuing to test the hypothesis against the facts. If favorable results accumulate, the hypothesis evolves into a theory. A very well-tested and widely accepted theory is referred to as an economic law or an **economic principle**—a statement about economic behavior or the economy that enables prediction of the probable effects of certain actions. Combinations of such laws or principles are incorporated into models, which are simplified representations of how something works, such as a market or segment of the economy.

Economists develop theories of the behavior of individuals (consumers, workers) and institutions (businesses, governments) engaged in the production, exchange, and consumption of goods and services. Theories, principles, and models are "purposeful simplifications." The full scope of economic reality itself is too complex and bewildering to be understood as a whole. In developing theories, principles, and models economists remove the clutter and simplify.

Economic principles and models are highly useful in analyzing economic behavior and understanding how the economy operates. They are the tools for ascertaining cause and effect (or action and outcome) within the economic system. Good theories do a good job of explaining and predicting. They are supported by facts concerning how individuals and institutions actually behave in producing, exchanging, and consuming goods and services.

There are some other things you should know about economic principles.

- *Generalizations* Economic principles are generalizations relating to economic behavior or to the economy itself. Economic principles are expressed as the tendencies of typical or average consumers, workers, or business firms. For example, economists say that consumers buy more of a particular product when its price falls. Economists recognize that some consumers may increase their purchases by a large amount, others by a small amount, and a few not at all. This "price-quantity" principle, however, holds for the typical consumer and for consumers as a group.
- *Other-things-equal assumption* In constructing their theories, economists use the *ceteris paribus* or **other-things-equal assumption**—the assumption that factors other than those being considered do not change. They assume that all variables except those under immediate consideration are held constant for a particular analysis. For example, consider the relationship between the price of Pepsi and the amount of it purchased. Assume that of all the factors that might influence the amount of Pepsi purchased (for example, the price of Pepsi, the price of Coca-Cola, and consumer incomes and preferences), only the price of Pepsi varies. This is helpful because the economist can then focus on the relationship between the price of Pepsi and purchases of Pepsi in isolation without being confused by changes in other variables.

ORIGIN OF THE IDEA

O 1.4

Ceteris paribus

- *Graphical expression* Many economic models are expressed graphically. Be sure to read the special appendix at the end of this chapter as a review of graphs.

Microeconomics and Macroeconomics

Economists develop economic principles and models at two levels.

Microeconomics

Microeconomics is the part of economics concerned with decision making by individual customers, workers, households, and business firms. At this level of analysis, we observe the details of their behavior under a figurative microscope. We measure the price of a specific product, the number of workers employed by a single firm, the revenue or income of a particular firm or household, or the expenditures of a specific firm, government entity, or family. In microeconomics, we examine the sand, rocks, and shells, not the beach.

Macroeconomics

Macroeconomics examines either the economy as a whole or its basic subdivisions or aggregates, such as the government, household, and business sectors. An **aggregate** is a collection of specific economic units treated as if they were one unit. Therefore, we might lump together the millions of consumers in the U.S. economy and treat them as if they were one huge unit called "consumers."

In using aggregates, macroeconomics seeks to obtain an overview, or general outline, of the structure of the economy and the relationships of its major aggregates. Macroeconomics speaks of such economic measures as total output, total employment, total income, aggregate expenditures, and the general level of prices in analyzing various economic problems. Very little attention is given to the specific units making up the various aggregates.

Figuratively, macroeconomics looks at the beach, not the pieces of sand, the rocks, and the shells.

The micro–macro distinction does not mean that economics is so highly compartmentalized that every topic can be readily labeled as either micro or macro; many topics and subdivisions of economics are rooted in both. Example: While the problem of unemployment is usually treated as a macroeconomic topic (because unemployment relates to aggregate production), economists recognize that the decisions made by *individual* workers on how long to search for jobs and the way *specific* labor markets encourage or impede hiring are also critical in determining the unemployment rate.

Positive and Normative Economics

Both microeconomics and macroeconomics contain elements of positive economics and normative economics. **Positive economics** focuses on facts and cause-and-effect relationships. It includes description, theory development, and theory testing. Positive economics avoids value judgments. It tries to establish scientific statements about economic behavior and deals with what the economy is actually like. Such scientific-based analysis is critical to good policy analysis.

Economic policy, on the other hand, involves **normative economics,** which incorporates value judgments about what the economy should be like or what particular policy actions should be recommended to achieve a desirable goal. Normative economics looks at the desirability of certain aspects of the economy. It underlies expressions of support for particular economic policies.

Positive economics concerns *what is,* whereas normative economics embodies subjective feelings about *what ought to be.* Examples: Positive statement: "The unemployment rate in France is higher than that in the United States." Normative statement: "France ought to undertake policies to make its labor market more flexible to reduce unemployment rates." Whenever words such as "ought" or "should" appear in a sentence, you are very likely encountering a normative statement.

Most of the disagreement among economists involves normative, value-based policy questions. Of course, economists sometime disagree about which theories or models best represent the economy and its parts, but they agree on a full range of economic principles. Most economic controversy thus reflects differing opinions or value judgments about what society should be like.

QUICK REVIEW 1.1

- Economics examines how individuals, institutions, and society make choices under conditions of scarcity.
- The economic perspective stresses (a) resource scarcity and the necessity of making choices, (b) the assumption of purposeful (or rational) behavior, and (c) comparisons of marginal benefit and marginal cost.
- In choosing the best option, people incur an opportunity cost—the value of the next-best option.
- Economists use the scientific method to establish economic theories—cause-effect generalizations about the economic behavior of individuals and institutions.
- Microeconomics focuses on specific decision-making units of the economy, macroeconomics examines the economy as a whole.
- Positive economics deals with factual statements ("what is"); normative economics involves value judgments ("what ought to be").

Individual's Economizing Problem

A close examination of the **economizing problem**—the need to make choices because economic wants exceed economic means—will enhance your understanding of economic models and the difference between microeconomic and macroeconomic analysis. Let's first build a microeconomic model of the economizing problem faced by an individual.

Limited Income

We all have a finite amount of income, even the wealthiest among us. Even Donald Trump must decide how to spend his money! And the majority of us have much more limited means. Our income comes to us in the form of wages, interest, rent, and profit, although we may also receive money from government programs or family members. As Global Perspective 1.1 shows, the average income of Americans in 2008 was $47,580. In the poorest nations, it was less than $500.

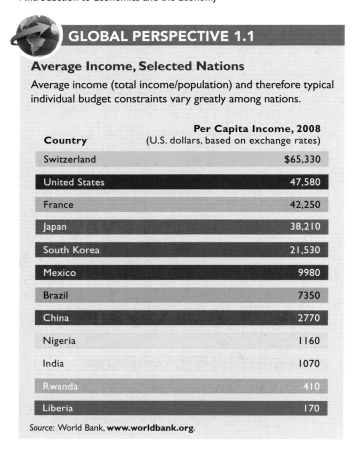

GLOBAL PERSPECTIVE 1.1

Average Income, Selected Nations

Average income (total income/population) and therefore typical individual budget constraints vary greatly among nations.

Country	Per Capita Income, 2008 (U.S. dollars, based on exchange rates)
Switzerland	$65,330
United States	47,580
France	42,250
Japan	38,210
South Korea	21,530
Mexico	9980
Brazil	7350
China	2770
Nigeria	1160
India	1070
Rwanda	410
Liberia	170

Source: World Bank, **www.worldbank.org**.

Unlimited Wants

For better or worse, most people have virtually unlimited wants. We desire various goods and services that provide utility. Our wants extend over a wide range of products, from *necessities* (for example, food, shelter, and clothing) to *luxuries* (for example, perfumes, yachts, and sports cars). Some wants such as basic food, clothing, and shelter have biological roots. Other wants, for example, specific kinds of food, clothing, and shelter, arise from the conventions and customs of society.

Over time, as new and improved products are introduced, economic wants tend to change and multiply. Only recently have people wanted iPods, Internet service, or camera phones because those products did not exist a few decades ago. Also, the satisfaction of certain wants may trigger others: the acquisition of a Ford Focus or a Honda Civic has been known to whet the appetite for a Lexus or a Mercedes.

Services, as well as goods, satisfy our wants. Car repair work, the removal of an inflamed appendix, legal and accounting advice, and haircuts all satisfy human wants.

Actually, we buy many goods, such as automobiles and washing machines, for the services they render. The differences between goods and services are often smaller than they appear to be.

For most people, the desires for goods and services cannot be fully satisfied. Bill Gates may have all that he wants for himself, but his massive charitable giving suggests that he keenly wants better health care for the world's poor. Our desires for a particular good or service can be satisfied; over a short period of time we can surely get enough toothpaste or pasta. And one appendectomy is plenty. But our broader desire for more goods and services and higher-quality goods and services seems to be another story.

Because we have only limited income (usually through our work) but seemingly insatiable wants, it is in our self-interest to economize: to pick and choose goods and services that maximize our satisfaction given the limitations we face.

A Budget Line

We can clarify the economizing problem facing consumers by visualizing a **budget line** (or, more technically, a *budget constraint*). It is a schedule or curve that shows various combinations of two products a consumer can purchase with a specific money income. Although we assume two products, the analysis generalizes to the full range of products available to consumers.

To understand the idea of a budget line, suppose that you received a Barnes & Noble (or Borders) gift card as a birthday present. The $120 card is soon to expire. You take the card to the store and confine your purchase decisions to two alternatives: DVDs and paperback books. DVDs are $20 each and paperback books are $10 each. Your purchase options are shown in the table in Figure 1.1.

At one extreme, you might spend all of your $120 "income" on 6 DVDs at $20 each and have nothing left to spend on books. Or, by giving up 2 DVDs and thereby gaining $40, you can have 4 DVDs at $20 each and 4 books at $10 each. And so on to the other extreme, at which you could buy 12 books at $10 each, spending your entire gift card on books with nothing left to spend on DVDs.

The graph in Figure 1.1 shows the budget line. Note that the graph is not restricted to whole units of DVDs and books as is the table. Every point on the graph represents a possible combination of DVDs and books, including fractional quantities. The slope of the graphed budget line measures the ratio of the price of books (P_b) to the price of DVDs (P_{dvd}); more precisely, the slope is $P_b/P_{dvd} = \$-10/\$+20 = -\frac{1}{2}$. So you must forgo 1 DVD

FIGURE 1.1 A consumer's budget line. The budget line (or budget constraint) shows all the combinations of any two products that can be purchased, given the prices of the products and the consumer's money income.

The Budget Line: Whole-Unit Combinations of DVDs and Paperback Books Attainable with an Income of $120		
Units of DVDs (Price = $20)	Units of Books (Price = $10)	Total Expenditure
6	0	$120 (= $120 + $0)
5	2	$120 (= $100 + $20)
4	4	$120 (= $80 + $40)
3	6	$120 (= $60 + $60)
2	8	$120 (= $40 + $80)
1	10	$120 (= $20 + $100)
0	12	$120 (= $0 + $120)

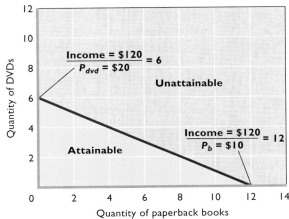

(measured on the vertical axis) to buy 2 books (measured on the horizontal axis). This yields a slope of $-\frac{1}{2}$ or $-.5$.

The budget line illustrates several ideas.

Attainable and Unattainable Combinations All the combinations of DVDs and books on or inside the budget line are *attainable* from the $120 of money income. You can afford to buy, for example, 3 DVDs at $20 each and 6 books at $10 each. You also can obviously afford to buy 2 DVDs and 5 books, thereby using up only $90 of the $120 available on your gift card. But to achieve maximum utility you will want to spend the full $120. The budget line shows all combinations that cost exactly the full $120.

In contrast, all combinations beyond the budget line are *unattainable*. The $120 limit simply does not allow you to purchase, for example, 5 DVDs at $20 each and 5 books at $10 each. That $150 expenditure would clearly exceed the $120 limit. In Figure 1.1 the attainable combinations are on and within the budget line; the unattainable combinations are beyond the budget line.

Trade-Offs and Opportunity Costs The budget line in Figure 1.1 illustrates the idea of trade-offs arising from limited income. To obtain more DVDs, you have to give up some books. For example, to obtain the first DVD, you trade off 2 books. So the opportunity cost of the first DVD

ORIGIN OF THE IDEA

O 1.5

Opportunity costs

is 2 books. To obtain the second DVD the opportunity cost is also 2 books. The straight-line budget constraint, with its constant slope, indicates constant opportunity cost. That is, the opportunity cost of 1 extra DVD remains the same (= 2 books) as more DVDs are purchased. And, in

CONSIDER THIS . . .

Did Gates, Winfrey, and Rodriguez Make Bad Choices?

Opportunity costs come into play in decisions well beyond simple buying decisions. Consider the different choices people make with respect to college. College graduates usually earn about 50 percent more during their lifetimes than persons with just high school diplomas. For most capable students, "Go to college, stay in college, and earn a degree" is very sound advice.

Yet Microsoft cofounder Bill Gates and talk show host Oprah Winfrey* both dropped out of college, and baseball star Alex Rodriguez ("A-Rod") never even bothered to start classes. What were they thinking? Unlike most students, Gates faced enormous opportunity costs for staying in college. He had a vision for his company, and his starting work young helped ensure Microsoft's success. Similarly, Winfrey landed a spot in local television news when she was a teenager, eventually producing and starring in the Oprah Winfrey Show when she was 32 years old. Getting a degree in her twenties might have interrupted the string of successes that made her famous talk show possible. And Rodriguez knew that professional athletes have short careers. Therefore, going to college directly after high school would have taken away four years of his peak earning potential.

So Gates, Winfrey, and Rodriguez understood opportunity costs and made their choices accordingly. The size of opportunity costs greatly matters in making individual decisions.

*Winfrey eventually went back to school and earned a degree from Tennessee State University when she was in her thirties.

reverse, the opportunity cost of 1 extra book does not change ($= \frac{1}{2}$ DVD) as more books are bought.

Choice Limited income forces people to choose what to buy and what to forgo to fulfill wants. You will select the combination of DVDs and paperback books that you think is "best." That is, you will evaluate your marginal benefits and marginal costs (here, product price) to make choices that maximize your satisfaction. Other people, with the same $120 gift card, would undoubtedly make different choices.

Income Changes The location of the budget line varies with money income. An increase in money income shifts the budget line to the right; a decrease in money income shifts it to the left. To verify this, recalculate the table in Figure 1.1, assuming the card value (income) is (a) $240 and (b) $60, and plot the new budget lines in the graph. No wonder people like to have more income: That shifts their budget lines outward and enables them to buy more goods and services. But even with more income, people will still face spending trade-offs, choices, and opportunity costs.

> **WORKED PROBLEMS**
>
> **W 1.1**
>
> Budget lines

QUICK REVIEW 1.2

- Because wants exceed incomes, individuals face an economizing problem; they must decide what to buy and what to forgo.
- A budget line (budget constraint) shows the various combinations of two goods that a consumer can purchase with a specific money income.
- Straight-line budget constraints imply constant opportunity costs for both goods.

Society's Economizing Problem

Society must also make choices under conditions of scarcity. It, too, faces an economizing problem. Should it devote more of its limited resources to the criminal justice system (police, courts, and prisons) or to education (teachers, books, and schools)? If it decides to devote more resources to both, what other goods and services does it forgo? Health care? Energy development?

Scarce Resources

Society has limited or scarce **economic resources,** meaning all natural, human, and manufactured resources that go into the production of goods and services. This includes the entire set of factory and farm buildings and all the equipment, tools, and machinery used to produce manufactured goods and agricultural products; all transportation and communication facilities; all types of labor; and land and mineral resources.

Resource Categories

Economists classify economic resources into four general categories.

Land Land means much more to the economist than it does to most people. To the economist **land** includes all natural resources ("gifts of nature") used in the production process. These include forests, mineral and oil deposits, water resources, wind power, sunlight, and arable land.

Labor The resource **labor** consists of the physical actions and mental activities that people contribute to the production of goods and services. The work-related activities of a logger, retail clerk, machinist, teacher, professional football player, and nuclear physicist all fall under the general heading "labor."

Capital For economists, **capital** (or capital goods) includes all manufactured aids used in producing consumer goods and services. Included are all factory, storage, transportation, and distribution facilities, as well as tools and machinery. Economists use the term **investment** to describe spending that pays for the production and accumulation of capital goods.

Capital goods differ from consumer goods because consumer goods satisfy wants directly, whereas capital goods do so indirectly by aiding the production of consumer goods. For example, large commercial baking ovens (capital goods) help make loaves of bread (consumer goods). Note that the term "capital" as used by economists refers not to money but to tools, machinery, and other productive equipment. Because money produces nothing, economists do not include it as an economic resource. Money (or money capital or financial capital) is simply a means for purchasing goods and services, including capital goods.

Entrepreneurial Ability Finally, there is the special human resource, distinct from labor, called **entrepreneurial ability.** The entrepreneur performs several socially useful functions:

- The entrepreneur takes the initiative in combining the resources of land, labor, and capital to produce a good or a service. Both a sparkplug and a catalyst, the entrepreneur is the driving force behind production and the agent who combines the other resources in what is hoped will be a successful business venture.

- The entrepreneur makes the strategic business decisions that set the course of an enterprise.
- The entrepreneur innovates. He or she commercializes new products, new production techniques, or even new forms of business organization.
- The entrepreneur bears risk. Innovation is risky, as nearly all new products and ideas are subject to the possibility of failure as well as success. Progress would cease without entrepreneurs who are willing to take on risk by devoting their time, effort, and ability—as well as their own money and the money of others—to commercializing new products and ideas that may enhance society's standard of living.

Because land, labor, capital, and entrepreneurial ability are combined to produce goods and services, they are called the **factors of production,** or simply "inputs."

Production Possibilities Model

Society uses its scarce resources to produce goods and services. The alternatives and choices it faces can best be understood through a macroeconomic model of production possibilities. To keep things simple, let's initially assume:

- *Full employment* The economy is employing all of its available resources.
- *Fixed resources* The quantity and quality of the factors of production are fixed.
- *Fixed technology* The state of technology (the methods used to produce output) is constant.
- *Two goods* The economy is producing only two goods: pizzas and industrial robots. Pizzas symbolize **consumer goods,** products that satisfy our wants directly; industrial robots (for example, the kind used to weld automobile frames) symbolize **capital goods,** products that satisfy our wants indirectly by making possible more efficient production of consumer goods.

Production Possibilities Table

A production possibilities table lists the different combinations of two products that can be produced with a specific set of resources, assuming full employment. Table 1.1 presents a simple, hypothetical economy that is producing pizzas and

industrial robots; the data are, of course, hypothetical. At alternative A, this economy would be devoting all its available resources to the production of industrial robots (capital goods); at alternative E, all resources would go to pizza production (consumer goods). Those alternatives are unrealistic extremes; an economy typically produces both capital goods and consumer goods, as in B, C, and D. As we move from alternative A to E, we increase the production of pizzas at the expense of the production of industrial robots.

Because consumer goods satisfy our wants directly, any movement toward E looks tempting. In producing more pizzas, society increases the satisfaction of its current wants. But there is a cost: More pizzas mean fewer industrial robots. This shift of resources to consumer goods catches up with society over time because the stock of capital goods expands more slowly, thereby reducing potential future production. By moving toward alternative E, society chooses "more now" at the expense of "much more later."

By moving toward A, society chooses to forgo current consumption, thereby freeing up resources that can be used to increase the production of capital goods. By building up its stock of capital this way, society will have greater future production and, therefore, greater future consumption. By moving toward A, society is choosing "more later" at the cost of "less now."

Generalization: At any point in time, a fully employed economy must sacrifice some of one good to obtain more of another good. Scarce resources prohibit such an economy from having more of both goods. Society must choose among alternatives. There is no such thing as a free pizza, or a free industrial robot. Having more of one thing means having less of something else.

Production Possibilities Curve

The data presented in a production possibilities table are shown graphically as a **production possibilities curve.** Such a curve displays the different combinations of goods

INTERACTIVE GRAPHS
G 1.1
Production possibilities curve

and services that society can produce in a fully employed economy, assuming a fixed availability of supplies of resources and fixed technology. We arbitrarily represent the economy's output of capital goods (here, industrial robots) on the vertical axis and the output of consumer goods (here, pizzas) on the horizontal axis, as shown in **Figure 1.2 (Key Graph).**

Each point on the production possibilities curve represents some maximum output of the two products. The

TABLE 1.1 Production Possibilities of Pizzas and Industrial Robots

		Production Alternatives			
Type of Product	A	B	C	D	E
Pizzas (in hundred thousands)	0	1	2	3	4
Robots (in thousands)	10	9	7	4	0

key graph

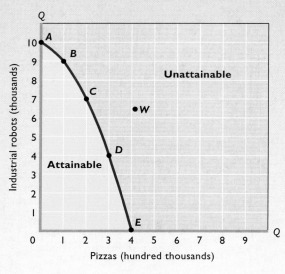

FIGURE 1.2 The production possibilities curve. Each point on the production possibilities curve represents some maximum combination of two products that can be produced if resources are fully employed. When an economy is operating on the curve, more industrial robots means fewer pizzas, and vice versa. Limited resources and a fixed technology make any combination of industrial robots and pizzas lying outside the curve (such as at *W*) unattainable. Points inside the curve are attainable, but they indicate that full employment is not being realized.

QUICK QUIZ FOR FIGURE 1.2

1. Production possibilities curve *ABCDE* is bowed out from the origin because:
   a. the marginal benefit of pizzas declines as more pizzas are consumed.
   b. the curve gets steeper as we move from *E* to *A*.
   c. it reflects the law of increasing opportunity costs.
   d. resources are scarce.
2. The marginal opportunity cost of the second unit of pizza is:
   a. 2 units of robots.
   b. 3 units of robots.
   c. 7 units of robots.
   d. 9 units of robots.
3. The total opportunity cost of 7 units of robots is:
   a. 1 unit of pizza.
   b. 2 units of pizza.
   c. 3 units of pizza.
   d. 4 units of pizza.
4. All points on this production possibilities curve necessarily represent:
   a. society's optimal choice.
   b. less than full use of resources.
   c. unattainable levels of output.
   d. full employment.

Answers: 1. c; 2. a; 3. b; 4. d

---

curve is a "constraint" because it shows the limit of attainable outputs. Points on the curve are attainable as long as the economy uses all its available resources. Points lying inside the curve are also attainable, but they reflect less total output and therefore are not as desirable as points on the curve. Points inside the curve imply that the economy could have more of both industrial robots and pizzas if it achieved full employment of its resources. Points lying beyond the production possibilities curve, like *W*, would represent a greater output than the output at any point on the curve. Such points, however, are unattainable with the current availability of resources and technology.

Law of Increasing Opportunity Costs

Figure 1.2 clearly shows that more pizzas means fewer industrial robots. The number of units of industrial robots that must be given up to obtain another unit of pizzas, of course, is the opportunity cost of that unit of pizzas.

In moving from alternative A to alternative B in Table 1.1, the cost of 1 additional unit of pizzas is 1 fewer unit of industrial robots. But when additional units are considered—B to C, C to D, and D to E—an important economic principle is revealed: For society, the opportunity cost of each additional unit of pizzas is greater than the opportunity cost of the preceding one. When we move from A to B, just 1 unit of industrial robots is sacrificed for 1 more unit of pizzas; but in going from B to C we sacrifice 2 additional units of industrial robots for 1 more unit of pizzas; then 3 more of industrial robots for 1 more of pizzas; and finally 4 for 1. Conversely, confirm that as we move from E to A, the cost of an additional unit of industrial robots (on average) is $\frac{1}{4}$, $\frac{1}{3}$, $\frac{1}{2}$, and 1 unit of pizzas, respectively, for the four successive moves.

Our example illustrates the **law of increasing opportunity costs.** As the production of a particular good increases, the opportunity cost of producing an additional unit rises.

Shape of the Curve The law of increasing opportunity costs is reflected in the shape of the production possibilities curve: The curve is bowed out from the origin of the graph. Figure 1.2 shows that when the economy moves from *A* to *E*, it must give up successively larger amounts of industrial robots (1, 2, 3, and 4) to acquire equal increments of pizzas (1, 1, 1, and 1). This is shown in the slope of the production possibilities curve, which becomes steeper as we move from *A* to *E*.

Economic Rationale The law of increasing opportunity costs is driven by the fact that economic resources are not completely adaptable to alternative uses. Many resources are better at producing one type of good than at producing others. Consider land. Some land is highly suited to growing the ingredients necessary for pizza production. But as pizza production expands, society has to start using land that is less bountiful for farming. Other land is rich in mineral deposits and therefore well-suited to producing the materials needed to make industrial robots. That land will be the first land devoted to the production of industrial robots. But as society steps up the production of robots, it must use land that is less and less suited to making their components.

If we start at *A* and move to *B* in Figure 1.2, we can shift resources whose productivity is relatively high in pizza production and low in industrial robots. But as we move from *B* to *C*, *C* to *D*, and so on, resources highly

WORKED PROBLEMS

W 1.2
Production possibilities

productive in pizzas become increasingly scarce. To get more pizzas, resources whose productivity in industrial robots is relatively great will be needed. Increasingly more of such resources, and hence greater sacrifices of industrial robots, will be needed to achieve each 1-unit increase in pizzas. This lack of perfect flexibility, or interchangeability, on the part of resources is the cause of increasing opportunity costs for society.

Optimal Allocation

Of all the attainable combinations of pizzas and industrial robots on the curve in Figure 1.2, which is optimal (best)? That is, what specific quantities of resources should be allocated to pizzas and what specific quantities should be allocated to industrial robots in order to maximize satisfaction?

Recall that economic decisions center on comparisons of marginal benefit (MB) and marginal cost (MC). Any economic activity should be expanded as long as marginal benefit exceeds marginal cost and should be reduced if marginal cost exceeds marginal benefit. The optimal amount of the activity occurs where MB = MC. Society needs to make a similar assessment about its production decision.

Consider pizzas. We already know from the law of increasing opportunity costs that the marginal cost of additional units of pizza will rise as more units are produced. At the same time, we need to recognize that the extra or marginal benefits that come from producing and consuming pizza decline with each successive unit of pizza. Consequently, each successive unit of pizza brings with it both increasing marginal costs and decreasing marginal benefits.

The optimal quantity of pizza production is indicated by point *e* at the intersection of the MB and MC curves: 200,000 units in Figure 1.3. Why is this amount the optimal quantity? If only 100,000 units of pizzas were

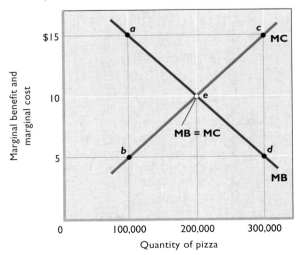

FIGURE 1.3 Optimal output: MB = MC. Achieving the optimal output requires the expansion of a good's output until its marginal benefit (MB) and marginal cost (MC) are equal. No resources beyond that point should be allocated to the product. Here, optimal output occurs at point e, where 200,000 units of pizzas are produced.

produced, the marginal benefit of an extra unit of pizza (point *a*) would exceed its marginal cost (point *b*). In money terms, MB is $15, while MC is only $5. When society gains something worth $15 at a marginal cost of only $5, it is better off. In Figure 1.3, net gains can continue to be realized until pizza-product production has been increased to 200,000.

The Economics of War

Production possibilities analysis is helpful in assessing the costs and benefits of waging the broad war on terrorism, including the wars in Afghanistan and Iraq. At the end of 2010, the estimated cost of these efforts exceeded $1.05 trillion.

If we categorize all U.S. production as either "defense goods" or "civilian goods," we can measure them on the axes of a production possibilities diagram such as that shown in Figure 1.2. The opportunity cost of using more resources for defense goods is the civilian goods sacrificed. In a fully employed economy, more defense goods are achieved at the opportunity cost of fewer civilian goods—health care, education, pollution control, personal computers, houses, and so on. The cost of war and defense is the other goods forgone. The benefits of these activities are numerous and diverse but clearly include the gains from protecting against future loss of American lives, assets, income, and well-being.

Society must assess the marginal benefit (MB) and marginal cost (MC) of additional defense goods to determine their optimal amounts—where to locate on the defense goods–civilian goods production possibilities curve. Although estimating marginal benefits and marginal costs is an imprecise art, the MB-MC framework is a useful way of approaching choices. An optimal allocation of resources requires that society expand production of defense goods until MB = MC.

The events of September 11, 2001, and the future threats they foreshadowed increased the marginal benefits of defense goods, as perceived by Americans. If we label the horizontal axis in Figure 1.3 "defense goods" and draw in a rightward shift of the MB curve, you will see that the optimal quantity of defense goods rises. In view of the concerns relating to September 11, the United States allocated more of its resources to defense. But the MB-MC analysis also reminds us we can spend too much on defense, as well as too little. The United States should not expand defense goods beyond the point where MB = MC. If it does, it will be sacrificing civilian goods of greater value than the defense goods obtained.

In contrast, the production of 300,000 units of pizzas is excessive. There the MC of an added unit is $15 (point *c*) and its MB is only $5 (point *d*). This means that 1 unit of pizza is worth only $5 to society but costs it $15 to obtain. This is a losing proposition for society!

So resources are being efficiently allocated to any product when the marginal benefit and marginal cost of its output are equal (MB = MC). Suppose that by applying the same analysis to industrial robots, we find that the optimal (MB = MC) quantity of robots is 7000. This would mean that alternative *C* (200,000 units of pizzas and 7000 units of industrial robots) on the production possibilities curve in Figure 1.2 would be optimal for this economy.

- Economists categorize economic resources as land, labor, capital, and entrepreneurial ability.
- The production possibilities curve illustrates several ideas: (a) scarcity of resources is implied by the area of unattainable combinations of output lying outside the production possibilities curve; (b) choice among outputs is reflected in the variety of attainable combinations of goods lying along the curve; (c) opportunity cost is illustrated by the downward slope of the curve; (d) the law of increasing opportunity costs is reflected in the bowed-outward shape of the curve.
- A comparison of marginal benefits and marginal costs is needed to determine the best or optimal output mix on a production possibilities curve.

Unemployment, Growth, and the Future

In the depths of the Great Depression of the 1930s, one-quarter of U.S. workers were unemployed and one-third of U.S. production capacity was idle. Subsequent downturns have been much less severe. During the deep 2007–2009 recession, for instance, production fell by a comparably smaller 3.7 percent and 1-in-10 workers was without a job.

Almost all nations have experienced widespread unemployment and unused production capacity from business downturns at one time or another. Since 2000, for example, several nations—including Argentina, Japan, Mexico, Germany, and South Korea—have had economic downturns and unemployment.

How do these realities relate to the production possibilities model? Our analysis and conclusions change if we relax the assumption that all available resources are fully employed. The five alternatives in Table 1.1 represent

FIGURE 1.4 Unemployment and the production possibilities curve. Any point inside the production possibilities curve, such as U, represents unemployment or a failure to achieve full employment. The arrows indicate that by realizing full employment, the economy could operate on the curve. This means it could produce more of one or both products than it is producing at point U.

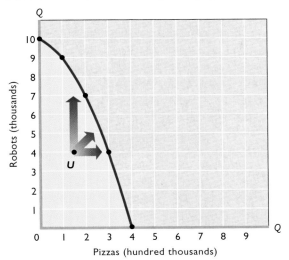

though unsteady, rate. And although some of our energy and mineral resources are being depleted, new sources are also being discovered. The development of irrigation systems, for example, adds to the supply of arable land.

The net result of these increased supplies of the factors of production is the ability to produce more of both consumer goods and capital goods. Thus, 20 years from now, the production possibilities may supersede those shown in Table 1.1. The new production possibilities might look like those in the table in Figure 1.5. The greater abundance of resources will result in a greater potential output of one or both products at each alternative. The economy will have achieved economic growth in the form of expanded potential output. Thus, when an increase in the quantity or quality of resources occurs, the production possibilities curve shifts outward and to the right, as illustrated by the move from the inner curve to curve $A'B'C'D'E'$ in Figure 1.5. This sort of shift represents growth of economic capacity, which, when used, means **economic growth:** a larger total output.

maximum outputs; they illustrate the combinations of pizzas and industrial robots that can be produced when the economy is operating at full employment. With unemployment, this economy would produce less than each alternative shown in the table.

Graphically, we represent situations of unemployment by points inside the original production possibilities curve (reproduced here in Figure 1.4). Point U is one such point. Here the economy is falling short of the various maximum combinations of pizzas and industrial robots represented by the points on the production possibilities curve. The arrows in Figure 1.4 indicate three possible paths back to full employment. A move toward full employment would yield a greater output of one or both products.

A Growing Economy

When we drop the assumptions that the quantity and quality of resources and technology are fixed, the production possibilities curve shifts positions and the potential maximum output of the economy changes.

Increases in Resource Supplies Although resource supplies are fixed at any specific moment, they change over time. For example, a nation's growing population brings about increases in the supplies of labor and entrepreneurial ability. Also, labor quality usually improves over time via more education and training. Historically, the economy's stock of capital has increased at a significant,

FIGURE 1.5 Economic growth and the production possibilities curve. The increase in supplies of resources, improvements in resource quality, and technological advances that occur in a dynamic economy move the production possibilities curve outward and to the right, allowing the economy to have larger quantities of both types of goods.

Type of Product	Production Alternatives				
	A'	B'	C'	D'	E'
Pizzas (in hundred thousands)	0	2	4	6	8
Robots (in thousands)	14	12	9	5	0

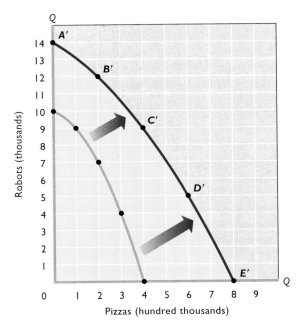

LAST Word Pitfalls to Sound Economic Reasoning

Because They Affect Us So Personally, We Often Have Difficulty Thinking Accurately and Objectively About Economic Issues.

Here are some common pitfalls to avoid in successfully applying the economic perspective.

Biases Most people bring a bundle of biases and preconceptions to the field of economics. For example, some might think that corporate profits are excessive or that lending money is always superior to borrowing money. Others might believe that government is necessarily less efficient than businesses or that more government regulation is always better than less. Biases cloud thinking and interfere with objective analysis. All of us must be willing to shed biases and preconceptions that are not supported by facts.

Loaded Terminology The economic terminology used in

newspapers and broadcast media is sometimes emotionally biased, or loaded. The writer or spokesperson may have a cause to promote or an ax to grind and may slant comments accordingly. High profits may be labeled "obscene," low wages may be called "exploitative" or self-interested behavior may be "greed." Government workers may be referred to as "mindless bureaucrats" and those favoring stronger government regulations may be called "socialists." To objectively analyze economic issues, you must be prepared to reject or discount such terminology.

Fallacy of Composition Another pitfall in economic thinking is the assumption that what is true for one individual or part of a whole is necessarily true for a group of individuals or the whole. This is a logical fallacy called the *fallacy of composition*; the assumption is not correct. A statement that is valid for an individual or part is not necessarily valid for the larger group or whole. You may see the action better if you leap to your feet to see an outstanding play at a

Advances in Technology An advancing technology brings both new and better goods and improved ways of producing them. For now, let's think of technological advance as being only improvements in the methods of production, for example, the introduction of computerized systems to manage inventories and schedule production. These advances alter our previous discussion of the economizing problem by allowing society to produce more goods with available resources. As with increases in resource supplies, technological advances make possible the production of more industrial robots *and* more pizzas.

A real-world example of improved technology is the recent surge of new technologies relating to computers, communications, and biotechnology. Technological advances have dropped the prices of computers and greatly increased their speed. Improved software has greatly increased the everyday usefulness of computers. Cellular phones and the Internet have increased communications capacity, enhancing production and improving the

efficiency of markets. Advances in biotechnology have resulted in important agricultural and medical discoveries. These and other new and improved technologies have contributed to U.S. economic growth (outward shifts of the nation's production possibilities curve).

Conclusion: Economic growth is the result of (1) increases in supplies of resources, (2) improvements in resource quality, and (3) technological advances. The consequence of growth is that a full-employment economy can enjoy a greater output of both consumption goods and capital goods. Whereas static, no-growth economies must sacrifice some of one good to obtain more of another, dynamic, growing economies can have larger quantities of both goods.

Present Choices and Future Possibilities

An economy's current choice of positions on its production possibilities curve helps determine the future location football game. But if all the spectators leap to their feet at the same time, nobody—including you—will have a better view than when all remained seated.

Here are two economic examples: An individual stockholder can sell shares of, say, Google stock without affecting the price of the stock. The individual's sale will not noticeably reduce the share price because the sale is a negligible fraction of the total shares of Google being bought and sold. But if all the Google shareholders decide to sell their shares the same day, the market will be flooded with shares and the stock price will fall precipitously. Similarly, a single cattle ranch can increase its revenue by expanding the size of its livestock herd. The extra cattle will not affect the price of cattle when they are brought to market. But if all ranchers as a group expand their herds, the total output of cattle will increase so much that the price of cattle will decline when the cattle are sold. If the price reduction is relatively large, ranchers as a group might find that their income has fallen despite their having sold a greater number of cattle because the fall in price overwhelms the increase in quantity.

Post Hoc Fallacy You must think very carefully before concluding that because event A precedes event B, A is the cause of B. This kind of faulty reasoning is known as the *post hoc, ergo propter hoc,* or "after this, therefore because of this," fallacy. Noneconomic example: A professional football team hires a new coach and the team's record improves. Is the new coach the cause? Maybe. Perhaps the presence of more experienced and talented players or an easier schedule is the true cause. The rooster crows before dawn but does not cause the sunrise.

Economic example: Many people blamed the Great Depression of the 1930s on the stock market crash of 1929. But the crash did not cause the Great Depression. The same severe weaknesses in the economy that caused the crash caused the Great Depression. The depression would have occurred even without the preceding stock market crash.

Correlation but Not Causation Do not confuse correlation, or connection, with causation. Correlation between two events or two sets of data indicates only that they are associated in some systematic and dependable way. For example, we may find that when variable X increases, Y also increases. But this correlation does not necessarily mean that there is causation—that increases in X cause increases in Y. The relationship could be purely coincidental or dependent on some other factor, Z, not included in the analysis.

Here is an example: Economists have found a positive correlation between education and income. In general, people with more education earn higher incomes than those with less education. Common sense suggests education is the cause and higher incomes are the effect; more education implies a more knowledgeable and productive worker, and such workers receive larger salaries.

But might the relationship be explainable in other ways? Are education and income correlated because the characteristics required for succeeding in education—ability and motivation—are the same ones required to be a productive and highly paid worker? If so, then people with those traits will probably both obtain more education and earn higher incomes. But greater education will not be the sole cause of the higher income.

of that curve. Let's designate the two axes of the production possibilities curve as "goods for the future" and "goods for the present," as in Figure 1.6. Goods for the future are such things as capital goods, research and education, and preventive medicine. They increase the quantity and quality of property resources, enlarge the stock of technological information, and improve the quality of human resources. As we have already seen, goods for the future such as capital goods are the ingredients of economic growth. Goods for the present are consumer goods such as food, clothing, and entertainment.

Now suppose there are two hypothetical economies, Presentville and Futureville, that are initially identical in every respect except one: Presentville's current choice of positions on its production possibilities curve strongly favors present goods over future goods. Point P in Figure 1.6a

INTERACTIVE GRAPHS

G 1.2

Present choices and future possibilities

indicates that choice. It is located quite far down the curve to the right, indicating a high priority for goods for the present, at the expense of less goods for the future. Futureville, in contrast, makes a current choice that stresses larger amounts of future goods and smaller amounts of present goods, as shown by point F in Figure 1.6b.

Now, other things equal, we can expect Futureville's future production possibilities curve to be farther to the right than Presentville's future production possibilities curve. By currently choosing an output more favorable to technological advances and to increases in the quantity and quality of resources, Futureville will achieve greater economic growth than Presentville. In terms of capital goods, Futureville is choosing to make larger current additions to its "national factory" by devoting more of its current output to capital than Presentville. The payoff from this choice for Futureville is greater future production capacity and economic growth. The opportunity cost is fewer consumer goods in the present for Futureville to enjoy.

FIGURE 1.6 Present choices and future locations of production possibilities curves. A nation's current choice favoring "present goods," as made by Presentville in (a), will cause a modest outward shift of the production possibilities curve in the future. A nation's current choice favoring "future goods," as made by Futureville in (b), will result in a greater outward shift of the curve in the future.

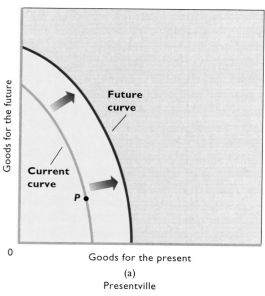

(a)
Presentville

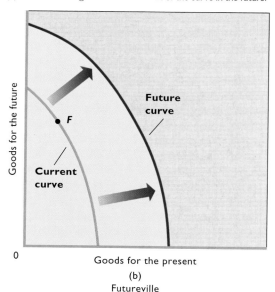

(b)
Futureville

Is Futureville's choice thus necessarily "better" than Presentville's? That, we cannot say. The different outcomes simply reflect different preferences and priorities in the two countries. But each country will have to live with the economic consequences of its choice.

A Qualification: International Trade

Production possibilities analysis implies that an individual nation is limited to the combinations of output indicated by its production possibilities curve. But we must modify this principle when international specialization and trade exist.

You will see in later chapters that an economy can circumvent, through international specialization and trade, the output limits imposed by its domestic production possibilities curve. Under international specialization and trade, each nation first specializes in the production of those items for which it has the lowest opportunity costs (due to an abundance of the necessary resources). Countries then engage in international trade, with each country exchanging the items that it can produce at the lowest opportunity costs for the items that other countries can produce at the lowest opportunity costs.

International specialization and trade allow a nation to get more of a desired good at less sacrifice of some other good. Rather than sacrifice three units of domestically-

produced robots to get a third unit of domestically-produced pizza, as in Table 1.1, a nation that engages in international specialization and trade might be able to do much better. If it specializes in robots while another country specializes in pizza, then it may be able to obtain the third unit of pizza by trading only two units of domestically-produced robots for one unit of foreign-produced pizza. Specialization and trade have the same effect as having more and better resources or discovering improved production techniques; both increase the quantities of capital and consumer goods available to society. Expansion of domestic production possibilities and international trade are two separate routes for obtaining greater output.

QUICK REVIEW 1.4

- Unemployment causes an economy to operate at a point inside its production possibilities curve.

- Increases in resource supplies, improvements in resource quality, and technological advance cause economic growth, which is depicted as an outward shift of the production possibilities curve.

- An economy's present choice of capital and consumer goods helps determine the future location of its production possibilities curve.

- International specialization and trade enable a nation to obtain more goods than its production possibilities curve indicates.

Summary

1. Economics is the social science that examines how individuals, institutions, and society make optimal choices under conditions of scarcity. Central to economics is the idea of opportunity cost: the value of the next-best good or service forgone to obtain something.

2. The economic perspective includes three elements: scarcity and choice, purposeful behavior, and marginal analysis. It sees individuals and institutions making rational decisions based on comparisons of marginal costs and marginal benefits.

3. Economists employ the scientific method, in which they form and test hypotheses of cause-and-effect relationships to generate theories, laws, and principles. Economists often combine theories into representations called models.

4. Microeconomics examines the decision making of specific economic units or institutions. Macroeconomics looks at the economy as a whole or its major aggregates.

5. Positive economic analysis deals with facts; normative economics reflects value judgments.

6. Individuals face an economizing problem. Because their wants exceed their incomes, they must decide what to purchase and what to forgo. Society also faces an economizing problem. Societal wants exceed the available resources necessary to fulfill them. Society therefore must decide what to produce and what to forgo.

7. Graphically, a budget line (or budget constraint) illustrates the economizing problem for individuals. The line shows the various combinations of two products that a consumer can purchase with a specific money income, given the prices of the two products.

8. Economic resources are inputs into the production process and can be classified as land, labor, capital, or entrepreneurial ability. Economic resources are also known as factors of production or inputs.

9. Economists illustrate society's economizing problem through production possibilities analysis. Production possibilities tables and curves show the different combinations of goods and services that can be produced in a fully employed economy, assuming that resource quantity, resource quality, and technology are fixed.

10. An economy that is fully employed and thus operating on its production possibilities curve must sacrifice the output of some types of goods and services to increase the production of others. The gain of one type of good or service is always accompanied by an opportunity cost in the form of the loss of some of the other type.

11. Because resources are not equally productive in all possible uses, shifting resources from one use to another creates increasing opportunity costs. The production of additional units of one product requires the sacrifice of increasing amounts of the other product.

12. The optimal (best) point on the production possibilities curve represents the most desirable mix of goods and is determined by expanding the production of each good until its marginal benefit (MB) equals its marginal cost (MC).

13. Over time, technological advances and increases in the quantity and quality of resources enable the economy to produce more of all goods and services, that is, to experience economic growth. Society's choice as to the mix of consumer goods and capital goods in current output is a major determinant of the future location of the production possibilities curve and thus of the extent of economic growth.

14. International trade enables a nation to obtain more goods from its limited resources than its production possibilities curve indicates.

Terms and Concepts

economics

economic perspective

opportunity cost

utility

marginal analysis

scientific method

economic principle

other-things-equal assumption

microeconomics

macroeconomics

aggregate

positive economics

normative economics

economizing problem

budget line

economic resources

land

labor

capital

investment

entrepreneurial ability

factors of production

consumer goods

capital goods

production possibilities curve

law of increasing opportunity costs

economic growth

Questions

1. What is an opportunity cost? How does the idea relate to the definition of economics? Which of the following decisions would entail the greater opportunity cost: Allocating a square block in the heart of New York City for a surface parking lot or allocating a square block at the edge of a typical suburb for such a lot? Explain. **LO1**

2. Cite three examples of recent decisions that you made in which you, at least implicitly, weighed marginal cost and marginal benefit. **LO1**

3. What is meant by the term "utility" and how does the idea relate to purposeful behavior? **LO1**

4. What are the key elements of the scientific method and how does this method relate to economic principles and laws? **LO2**

5. Indicate whether each of the following statements applies to microeconomics or macroeconomics: **LO3**
   a. The unemployment rate in the United States was 9.7 percent in March 2010.
   b. A U.S. software firm discharged 15 workers last month and transferred the work to India.
   c. An unexpected freeze in central Florida reduced the citrus crop and caused the price of oranges to rise.
   d. U.S. output, adjusted for inflation, decreased by 2.4 percent in 2009.
   e. Last week Wells Fargo Bank lowered its interest rate on business loans by one-half of 1 percentage point.
   f. The consumer price index rose by 2.7 percent from December 2008 to December 2009.

6. State (a) a positive economic statement of your choice, and then (b) a normative economic statement relating to your first statement. **LO3**

7. What are economic resources? What categories do economists use to classify them? Why are resources also called factors of production? Why are they called inputs? **LO4**

8. Why is money not considered to be a capital resource in economics? Why is entrepreneurial ability considered a category of economic resource, distinct from labor? What are the major functions of the entrepreneur? **LO4**

9. Specify and explain the typical shapes of marginal-benefit and marginal-cost curves. How are these curves used to determine the optimal allocation of resources to a particular product? If current output is such that marginal cost exceeds marginal benefit, should more or fewer resources be allocated to this product? Explain. **LO5**

10. Explain how (if at all) each of the following events affects the location of a country's production possibilities curve: **LO5**
    a. The quality of education increases.
    b. The number of unemployed workers increases.
    c. A new technique improves the efficiency of extracting copper from ore.
    d. A devastating earthquake destroys numerous production facilities.

11. Suppose that, on the basis of a nation's production possibilities curve, an economy must sacrifice 10,000 pizzas domestically to get the 1 additional industrial robot it desires but that it can get the robot from another country in exchange for 9000 pizzas. Relate this information to the following statement: "Through international specialization and trade, a nation can reduce its opportunity cost of obtaining goods and thus 'move outside its production possibilities curve.'" **LO6**

12. **LAST WORD** Studies indicate that married men on average earn more income than unmarried men of the same age and education level. Why must we be cautious in concluding that marriage is the cause and higher income is the effect?

Problems

1. Potatoes cost Janice $1 per pound, and she has $5.00 that she could possibly spend on potatoes or other items. If she feels that the first pound of potatoes is worth $1.50, the second pound is worth $1.14, the third pound is worth $1.05, and all subsequent pounds are worth $0.30, how many pounds of potatoes will she purchase? What if she only had $2 to spend? **LO1**

2. Pham can work as many or as few hours as she wants at the college bookstore for $9 per hour. But due to her hectic schedule, she has just 15 hours per week that she can spend working at either the bookstore or at other potential jobs. One potential job, at a café, will pay her $12 per hour for up to 6 hours per week. She has another job offer at a garage that will pay her $10 an hour for up to 5 hours per week. And she has a potential job at a daycare center that will pay her $8.50 per hour for as many hours as she can work. If her goal is to maximize the amount of money she can make each week, how many hours will she work at the bookstore? **LO1**

3. Suppose you won $15 on a lotto ticket at the local 7-Eleven and decided to spend all the winnings on candy bars and bags of peanuts. The price of candy bars is $0.75 and the price of peanuts is $1.50. **LO4**
   a. Construct a table showing the alternative combinations of the two products that are available.
   b. Plot the data in your table as a budget line in a graph. What is the slope of the budget line? What is the opportunity cost of one more candy bar? Of one more bag of peanuts? Do these opportunity costs rise, fall, or remain constant as each additional unit of the product is purchased?

c. Does the budget line tell you which of the available combinations of candy bars and bags of peanuts to buy?

d. Suppose that you had won $30 on your ticket, not $15. Show the $30 budget line in your diagram. Has the number of available combinations increased or decreased?

4. Suppose that you are on a desert island and possess exactly 20 coconuts. Your neighbor, Friday, is a fisherman, and he is willing to trade 2 fish for every 1 coconut that you are willing to give him. Another neighbor, Kwame, is also a fisherman, and he is willing to trade 3 fish for every 1 coconut. LO4

a. On a single figure, draw budget lines for trading with Friday and for trading with Kwame. (Put coconuts on the vertical axis.)

b. What is the slope of the budget line from trading with Friday?

c. What is the slope of the budget line from trading with Kwame?

d. Which budget line features a larger set of attainable combinations of coconuts and fish?

e. If you are going to trade coconuts for fish, would you rather trade with Friday or Kwame?

5. To the right is a production possibilities table for consumer goods (automobiles) and capital goods (forklifts): LO5

a. Show these data graphically. Upon what specific assumptions is this production possibilities curve based?

b. If the economy is at point C, what is the cost of one more automobile? Of one more forklift? Which characteristic of the production possibilities curve reflects the law of increasing opportunity costs: its shape or its length?

c. If the economy characterized by this production possibilities table and curve were producing 3 automobiles and 20 forklifts, what could you conclude about its use of its available resources?

d. Is production at a point outside the production possibilities curve currently possible? Could a future advance in technology allow production beyond the current production possibilities curve? Could international trade allow a country to consume beyond its current production possibilities curve?

Type of Production	Production Alternatives				
	A	B	C	D	E
Automobiles	0	2	4	6	8
Forklifts	30	27	21	12	0

6. Look at Figure 1.3. Suppose that the cost of cheese falls, so that the marginal cost of producing pizza decreases. Will the MC curve shift up or down? Will the optimal amount of pizza increase or decrease? LO5

7. Referring to the table in problem 5, suppose improvement occurs in the technology of producing forklifts but not in the technology of producing automobiles. Draw the new production possibilities curve. Now assume that a technological advance occurs in producing automobiles but not in producing forklifts. Draw the new production possibilities curve. Now draw a production possibilities curve that reflects technological improvement in the production of both goods. LO6

8. On average, households in China save 40 percent of their annual income each year, whereas households in the United States save less than 5 percent. Production possibilities are growing at roughly 9 percent annually in China and 3.5 percent in the United States. Use graphical analysis of "present goods" versus "future goods" to explain the differences in growth rates. LO6

FURTHER TEST YOUR KNOWLEDGE AT
www.mcconnell19e.com

At the text's Online Learning Center (OLC), **www.mcconnell19e.com**, you will find one or more Web-based questions that require information from the Internet to answer. We urge you to check them out; they will familiarize you with Web sites that may be helpful in other courses and perhaps even in your career. The OLC also features multiple-choice questions that give instant feedback and provides other helpful ways to further test your knowledge of the chapter.

Graphs and Their Meaning

If you glance quickly through this text, you will find many graphs. Some seem simple, while others seem more formidable. All are included to help you visualize and understand economic relationships. Physicists and chemists sometimes illustrate their theories by building arrangements of multicolored wooden balls, representing protons, neutrons, and electrons, that are held in proper relation to one another by wires or sticks. Economists most often use graphs to illustrate their models. By understanding these "pictures," you can more readily comprehend economic relationships. Most of our principles or models explain relationships between just two sets of economic facts, which can be conveniently represented with two-dimensional graphs.

Construction of a Graph

A *graph* is a visual representation of the relationship between two variables. The table in Figure 1 is a hypothetical illustration showing the relationship between income and consumption for the economy as a whole. Without even studying economics, we would logically expect that people would buy more goods and services when their incomes go up. Thus, it is not surprising to find in the table that total consumption in the economy increases as total income increases.

The information in the table is expressed graphically in Figure 1. Here is how it is done: We want to show visually how consumption changes as income changes. We therefore represent income on the **horizontal axis** of the graph and consumption on the **vertical axis.**

Now we arrange the vertical and horizontal scales of the graph to reflect the ranges of values of consumption and income and mark the scales in convenient increments. As you can see, the values marked on the scales cover all the values in the table. The increments on both scales are $100.

Because the graph has two dimensions, each point within it represents an income value and its associated consumption value. To find a point that represents one of the five income-consumption combinations in the table in Figure 1, we draw straight lines from the appropriate values on the vertical and horizontal axes. For example, to plot point *c* (the $200 income–$150 consumption point), we draw straight lines up from the horizontal (income) axis at $200 and across from the vertical (consumption) axis at $150. These lines intersect at point *c*, which represents this particular income-consumption combination. You should verify that the other income-consumption combinations shown in the table are properly located in the graph in Figure 1. Finally, by assuming that the same general relationship between income and consumption prevails for all other incomes, we draw a line or smooth curve to connect these points. That line or curve represents the income-consumption relationship.

If the curve is a straight line, as in Figure 1, we say the relationship is *linear*. (It is permissible, and even customary, to call straight lines in graphs "curves.")

FIGURE 1 **Graphing the direct relationship between consumption and income.** Two sets of data that are positively or directly related, such as consumption and income, graph as an upsloping line.

Income per Week	Consumption per Week	Point
$ 0	$ 50	a
100	100	b
200	150	c
300	200	d
400	250	e

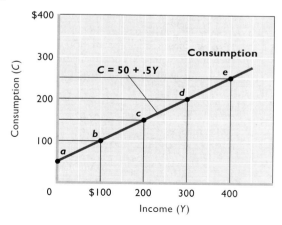

Direct and Inverse Relationships

The line in Figure 1 slopes upward to the right, so it depicts a direct relationship between income and consumption. By a **direct relationship** (or positive relationship) we mean that two variables—in this case, consumption and income—change in the *same* direction. An increase in consumption is associated with an increase in income; a decrease in consumption accompanies a decrease in income. When two sets of data are positively or directly related, they always graph as an *upsloping* line, as in Figure 1.

In contrast, two sets of data may be inversely related. Consider the table in Figure 2, which shows the relationship between the price of basketball tickets and game attendance at Gigantic State University (GSU). Here we have an **inverse relationship** (or negative relationship) because the two variables change in *opposite* directions. When ticket prices decrease, attendance increases. When ticket prices increase, attendance decreases. The six data points in the table in Figure 2 are plotted in the graph. Observe that an inverse relationship always graphs as a *downsloping* line.

Dependent and Independent Variables

Although it is not always easy, economists seek to determine which variable is the "cause" and which is the "effect." Or, more formally, they seek the independent variable and the dependent variable. The **independent** variable is the cause or source; it is the variable that changes first. The **dependent variable** is the effect or outcome; it is the variable that changes because of the change in the independent variable. As in our income-consumption example, income generally is the independent variable and consumption the dependent variable. Income causes consumption to be what it is rather than the other way around. Similarly, ticket prices (set in advance of the season and printed on the ticket) determine attendance at GSU basketball games; attendance at games does not determine the printed ticket prices for those games. Ticket price is the independent variable and the quantity of tickets purchased is the dependent variable.

You may recall from your high school courses that mathematicians put the independent variable (cause) on the horizontal axis and the dependent variable (effect) on the vertical axis. Economists are less tidy; their graphing of independent and dependent variables is more arbitrary. Their conventional graphing of the income-consumption relationship is consistent with mathematical convention, but economists put price and cost data on the vertical axis. Hence, economists' graphing of GSU's ticket price–attendance data differs from normal mathematical procedure. This does not present a problem, but we want you to be aware of this fact to avoid any possible confusion.

Other Things Equal

Our simple two-variable graphs purposely ignore many other factors that might affect the amount of consumption

FIGURE 2 Graphing the inverse relationship between ticket prices and game attendance. Two sets of data that are negatively or inversely related, such as ticket price and the attendance at basketball games, graph as a downsloping line.

Ticket Price	Attendance, Thousands	Point
$50	0	a
40	4	b
30	8	c
20	12	d
10	16	e
0	20	f

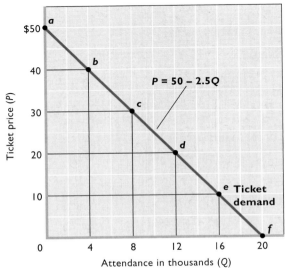

occurring at each income level or the number of people who attend GSU basketball games at each possible ticket price. When economists plot the relationship between any two variables, they employ the *ceteris paribus* (other-things-equal) assumption. Thus, in Figure 1 all factors other than income that might affect the amount of consumption are presumed to be constant or unchanged. Similarly, in Figure 2 all factors other than ticket price that might influence attendance at GSU basketball games are assumed constant. In reality, "other things" are not equal; they often change, and when they do, the relationship represented in our two tables and graphs will change. Specifically, the lines we have plotted would *shift* to new locations.

Consider a stock market "crash." The dramatic drop in the value of stocks might cause people to feel less wealthy and therefore less willing to consume at each level of income. The result might be a downward shift of the consumption line. To see this, you should plot a new consumption line in Figure 1, assuming that consumption is, say, $20 less at each income level. Note that the relationship remains direct; the line merely shifts downward to reflect less consumption spending at each income level.

Similarly, factors other than ticket prices might affect GSU game attendance. If GSU loses most of its games, attendance at GSU games might be less at each ticket price. To see this, redraw Figure 2 assuming that 2000 fewer fans attend GSU games at each ticket price.

Slope of a Line

Lines can be described in terms of their slopes. The **slope of a straight line** is the ratio of the vertical change (the rise or drop) to the horizontal change (the run) between any two points of the line.

Positive Slope
Between point *b* and point *c* in Figure 1, the rise or vertical change (the change in consumption) is +$50 and the run or horizontal change (the change in income) is +$100. Therefore:

$$\text{Slope} = \frac{\text{vertical change}}{\text{horizontal change}} = \frac{+50}{+100} = \frac{1}{2} = .5$$

Note that our slope of $\frac{1}{2}$ or .5 is positive because consumption and income change in the same direction; that is, consumption and income are directly or positively related.

The slope of .5 tells us there will be a $1 increase in consumption for every $2 increase in income. Similarly, it indicates that for every $2 decrease in income there will be a $1 decrease in consumption.

Negative Slope
Between any two of the identified points in Figure 2, say, point *c* and point *d*, the vertical change is −10 (the drop) and the horizontal change is +4 (the run). Therefore:

$$\text{Slope} = \frac{\text{vertical change}}{\text{horizontal change}} = \frac{-10}{+4}$$

$$= -2\frac{1}{2} = -2.5$$

This slope is negative because ticket price and attendance have an inverse relationship.

Note that on the horizontal axis attendance is stated in thousands of people. So the slope of −10/+4 or −2.5 means that lowering the price by $10 will increase attendance by 4000 people. This is the same as saying that a $2.50 price reduction will increase attendance by 1000 persons.

Slopes and Measurement Units
The slope of a line will be affected by the choice of units for either variable. If, in our ticket price illustration, we had chosen to measure attendance in individual people, our horizontal change would have been 4000 and the slope would have been

$$\text{Slope} = \frac{-10}{+4000} = \frac{-1}{+400} = -.0025$$

The slope depends on the way the relevant variables are measured.

Slopes and Marginal Analysis
Recall that economics is largely concerned with changes from the status quo. The concept of slope is important in economics because it reflects marginal changes—those involving 1 more (or 1 fewer) unit. For example, in Figure 1 the .5 slope shows that $.50 of extra or marginal consumption is associated with each $1 change in income. In this example, people collectively will consume $.50 of any $1 increase in their incomes and reduce their consumption by $.50 for each $1 decline in income.

Infinite and Zero Slopes
Many variables are unrelated or independent of one another. For example, the quantity of wristwatches purchased is not related to the price of bananas. In Figure 3a we represent the price of bananas on the vertical axis and the quantity of watches demanded on the horizontal axis. The graph of their relationship is the line parallel to the vertical axis,

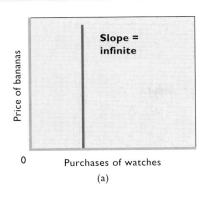

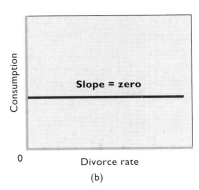

FIGURE 3 Infinite and zero slopes. (a) A line parallel to the vertical axis has an infinite slope. Here, purchases of watches remain the same no matter what happens to the price of bananas. (b) A line parallel to the horizontal axis has a slope of zero. In this case, consumption remains the same no matter what happens to the divorce rate. In both (a) and (b), the two variables are totally unrelated to one another.

indicating that the same quantity of watches is purchased no matter what the price of bananas. The slope of such a line is *infinite*.

Similarly, aggregate consumption is completely unrelated to the nation's divorce rate. In Figure 3b we put consumption on the vertical axis and the divorce rate on the horizontal axis. The line parallel to the horizontal axis represents this lack of relatedness. This line has a slope of *zero*.

Vertical Intercept

A line can be located on a graph (without plotting points) if we know just two things: its slope and its vertical intercept. We have already discussed slope. The **vertical intercept** of a line is the point where the line meets the vertical axis. In Figure 1 the intercept is $50. This intercept means that if current income were zero, consumers would still spend $50. They might do this through borrowing or by selling some of their assets. Similarly, the $50 vertical intercept in Figure 2 shows that at a $50 ticket price, GSU's basketball team would be playing in an empty arena.

Equation of a Linear Relationship

If we know the vertical intercept and slope, we can describe a line succinctly in equation form. In its general form, the equation of a straight line is

$$y = a + bx$$

where y = dependent variable
a = vertical intercept
b = slope of line
x = independent variable

For our income-consumption example, if C represents consumption (the dependent variable) and Y represents income (the independent variable), we can write $C = a + bY$.

By substituting the known values of the intercept and the slope, we get

$$C = 50 + .5Y$$

This equation also allows us to determine the amount of consumption C at any specific level of income. You should use it to confirm that at the $250 income level, consumption is $175.

When economists reverse mathematical convention by putting the independent variable on the vertical axis and the dependent variable on the horizontal axis, then y stands for the independent variable, rather than the dependent variable in the general form. We noted previously that this case is relevant for our GSU ticket price—attendance data. If P represents the ticket price (independent variable) and Q represents attendance (dependent variable), their relationship is given by

$$P = 50 - 2.5Q$$

where the vertical intercept is 50 and the negative slope is $-2\frac{1}{2}$, or -2.5. Knowing the value of P lets us solve for Q, our dependent variable. You should use this equation to predict GSU ticket sales when the ticket price is $15.

Slope of a Nonlinear Curve

We now move from the simple world of linear relationships (straight lines) to the more complex world of nonlinear relationships. The slope of a straight line is the same at all its points. The slope of a line representing a nonlinear relationship changes from one point to another. Such lines are always referred to as *curves*.

Consider the downsloping curve in Figure 4. Its slope is negative throughout, but the curve flattens as we move down along it. Thus, its slope constantly changes; the curve has a different slope at each point.

To measure the slope at a specific point, we draw a straight line tangent to the curve at that point. A straight line is *tangent* at a point if it touches, but does not intersect, the curve at that point. Thus line *aa* is tangent to the curve in Figure 4 at point *A*. The slope of the curve at that point is equal to the slope of the tangent line. Specifically,

> **INTERACTIVE GRAPHS**
> **G 1.3**
> Curves and slopes

the total vertical change (drop) in the tangent line *aa* is −20 and the total horizontal change (run) is +5. Because the slope of the tangent line *aa* is −20/+5, or −4, the slope of the curve at point *A* is also −4.

Line *bb* in Figure 4 is tangent to the curve at point *B*. Following the same procedure, we find the slope at *B* to be −5/+15, or −$\frac{1}{3}$. Thus, in this flatter part of the curve, the slope is less negative.

FIGURE 4 **Determining the slopes of curves.**
The slope of a nonlinear curve changes from point to point on the curve. The slope at any point (say, *B*) can be determined by drawing a straight line that is tangent to that point (line *bb*) and calculating the slope of that line.

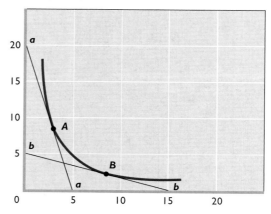

Appendix Summary

1. Graphs are a convenient and revealing way to represent economic relationships.

2. Two variables are positively or directly related when their values change in the same direction. The line (curve) representing two directly related variables slopes upward.

3. Two variables are negatively or inversely related when their values change in opposite directions. The line (curve) representing two inversely related variables slopes downward.

4. The value of the dependent variable (the "effect") is determined by the value of the independent variable (the "cause").

5. When the "other factors" that might affect a two-variable relationship are allowed to change, the graph of the relationship will likely shift to a new location.

6. The slope of a straight line is the ratio of the vertical change to the horizontal change between any two points. The slope of an upsloping line is positive; the slope of a downsloping line is negative.

7. The slope of a line or curve depends on the units used in measuring the variables. The slope is especially relevant for economics because it measures marginal changes.

8. The slope of a horizontal line is zero; the slope of a vertical line is infinite.

9. Together, the vertical intercept and slope of a line determine its location; they are used in expressing the line—and the relationship between the two variables—as an equation.

10. The slope of a curve at any point is determined by calculating the slope of a straight line tangent to the curve at that point.

Appendix Terms and Concepts

horizontal axis

vertical axis

direct relationship

inverse relationship

independent variable

dependent variable

slope of a straight line

vertical intercept

Appendix Questions connect ECONOMICS

1. Briefly explain the use of graphs as a way to represent economic relationships. What is an inverse relationship? How does it graph? What is a direct relationship? How does it graph? LO7

2. Describe the graphical relationship between ticket prices and the number of people choosing to visit amusement parks. Is that relationship consistent with the fact that, historically, park attendance and ticket prices have both risen? Explain. LO7

3. Look back at Figure 2, which shows the inverse relationship between ticket prices and game attendance at Gigantic State University. (a) Interpret the meaning of both the slope and the intercept. (b) If the slope of the line were steeper, what would that say about the amount by which ticket sales respond to increases in ticket prices? (c) If the slope of the line stayed the same but the intercept increased, what can you say about the amount by which ticket sales respond to increases in ticket prices? LO7

Appendix Problems

1. Graph and label as either direct or indirect the relationships you would expect to find between (a) the number of inches of rainfall per month and the sale of umbrellas, (b) the amount of tuition and the level of enrollment at a university, and (c) the popularity of an entertainer and the price of her concert tickets. LO7

2. Indicate how each of the following might affect the data shown in the table and graph in Figure 2 of this appendix: LO7
   a. GSU's athletic director schedules higher-quality opponents.
   b. An NBA team locates in the city where GSU plays.
   c. GSU contracts to have all its home games televised.

3. The following table contains data on the relationship between saving and income. Rearrange these data into a meaningful order and graph them on the accompanying grid. What is the slope of the line? The vertical intercept? Write the equation that represents this line. What would you predict saving to be at the $12,500 level of income? LO7

Income per Year	Saving per Year
$15,000	$1,000
0	−500
10,000	500
5,000	0
20,000	1,500

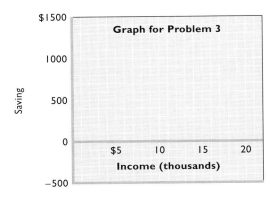

4. Construct a table from the data shown on the graph below. Which is the dependent variable and which the independent variable? Summarize the data in equation form. LO7

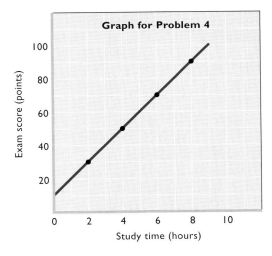

5. Suppose that when the interest rate on loans is 16 percent, businesses find it unprofitable to invest in machinery and equipment. However, when the interest rate is 14 percent, $5 billion worth of investment is profitable. At 12 percent interest, a total of $10 billion of investment is profitable. Similarly, total investment increases by $5 billion for each successive 2-percentage-point decline in the interest rate. Describe the relevant relationship between the interest rate and investment in a table, on a graph, and as an equation. Put the interest rate on the vertical axis and investment on the horizontal axis. In your equation use the form $i = a + bI$, where i is the interest rate, a is the vertical intercept, b is the slope of the line (which is negative), and I is the level of investment. LO7

6. Suppose that $C = a + bY$, where C = consumption, a = consumption at zero income, b = slope, and Y = income. LO7
   a. Are C and Y positively related or are they negatively related?

b. If graphed, would the curve for this equation slope upward or slope downward?

c. Are the variables C and Y inversely related or directly related?

d. What is the value of C if $a = 10$, $b = .50$, and $Y = 200$?

e. What is the value of Y if $C = 100$, $a = 10$, and $b = .25$?

7. The accompanying graph shows curve XX' and tangents at points A, B, and C. Calculate the slope of the curve at these three points. **LO7**

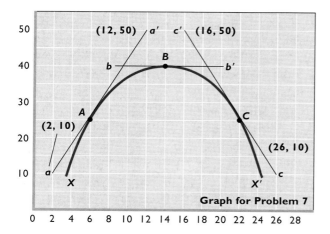

Graph for Problem 7

8. In the accompanying graph, is the slope of curve AA' positive or negative? Does the slope increase or decrease as we move along the curve from A to A'? Answer the same two questions for curve BB'. **LO7**

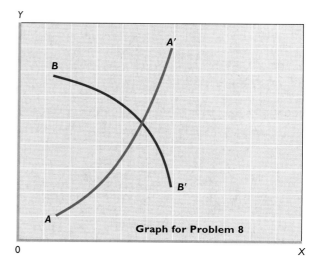

Graph for Problem 8

The Market System and the Circular Flow

You are at the mall. Suppose you were assigned to compile a list of all the individual goods and services there, including the different brands and variations of each type of product. That task would be daunting and the list would be long! And even though a single shopping mall contains a remarkable quantity and variety of goods, it is only a tiny part of the national economy.

Who decided that the particular goods and services available at the mall and in the broader economy should be produced? How did the producers determine which technology and types of resources to use in producing these particular goods? Who will obtain these products? What accounts for the new and improved products among these goods? This chapter will answer these and related questions.

Economic Systems

Every society needs to develop an **economic system**—a particular set of institutional arrangements and a coordinating mechanism—to respond to the economizing problem. The economic system has to determine what goods are produced, how they are produced, who gets them, how to accommodate change, and how to promote technological progress.

Economic systems differ as to (1) who owns the factors of production and (2) the method used to motivate, coordinate, and direct economic activity. Economic systems have two polar extremes: the command system and the market system.

The Command System

The **command system** is also known as *socialism* or *communism*. In a command system, government owns most property resources and economic decision making occurs through a central economic plan. A central planning board appointed by the government makes nearly all the major decisions concerning the use of resources, the composition and distribution of output, and the organization of production. The government owns most of the business firms, which produce according to government directives. The central planning board determines production goals for each enterprise and specifies the amount of resources to be allocated to each enterprise so that it can reach its production goals. The division of output between capital and consumer goods is centrally decided, and capital goods are allocated among industries on the basis of the central planning board's long-term priorities.

A pure command economy would rely exclusively on a central plan to allocate the government-owned property resources. But, in reality, even the preeminent command economy—the Soviet Union—tolerated some private ownership and incorporated some markets before its collapse in 1992. Recent reforms in Russia and most of the eastern European nations have to one degree or another transformed their command economies to capitalistic, market-oriented systems. China's reforms have not gone as far, but they have greatly reduced the reliance on central planning. Although government ownership of resources and capital in China is still extensive, the nation has increasingly relied on free markets to organize and coordinate its economy. North Korea and Cuba are the last prominent remaining examples of largely centrally planned economies. Other countries using mainly the command system include Turkmenistan, Laos, Belarus, Libya, Myanmar, and Iran. Later in this chapter, we will explore the main reasons for the general demise of the command systems.

The Market System

The polar alternative to the command system is the **market system**, or *capitalism*. The system is characterized by the private ownership of resources and the use of markets and prices to coordinate and direct economic activity. Participants act in their own self-interest. Individuals and businesses seek to achieve their economic goals through their own decisions regarding work, consumption, or production. The system allows for the private ownership of capital, communicates through prices, and coordinates economic activity through *markets*—places where buyers and sellers come together to buy and sell goods, services, and resources. Goods and services are produced and resources are supplied by whoever is willing and able to do so. The result is competition among independently acting buyers and sellers of each product and resource. Thus, economic decision making is widely dispersed. Also, the high potential monetary rewards create powerful incentives for existing firms to innovate and entrepreneurs to pioneer new products and processes.

In *pure* capitalism—or *laissez-faire* capitalism—government's role would be limited to protecting private property and establishing an environment appropriate

ORIGIN OF THE IDEA

O 2.1

Laissez-faire

to the operation of the market system. The term "laissez-faire" means "let it be," that is, keep government from interfering with the economy. The idea is that such interference will disturb the efficient working of the market system.

But in the capitalism practiced in the United States and most other countries, government plays a substantial role in the economy. It not only provides the rules for economic activity but also promotes economic stability and growth, provides certain goods and services that would otherwise be underproduced or not produced at all, and modifies the distribution of income. The government, however, is not the dominant economic force in deciding what to produce, how to produce it, and who will get it. That force is the market.

Characteristics of the Market System

An examination of some of the key features of the market system in detail will be very instructive.

Private Property

In a market system, private individuals and firms, not the government, own most of the property resources (land

and capital). It is this extensive private ownership of capital that gives capitalism its name. This right of **private property,** coupled with the freedom to negotiate binding legal contracts, enables individuals and businesses to obtain, use, and dispose of property resources as they see fit. The right of property owners to designate who will receive their property when they die helps sustain the institution of private property.

The most important consequence of property rights is that they encourage people to cooperate by helping to ensure that only *mutually agreeable* economic transactions take place. To consider why this is true, imagine a world without legally enforceable property rights. In such a world, the strong could simply take whatever they wanted from the weak without giving them any compensation. But in a world of legally enforceable property rights, any person wanting something from you has to get you to agree to give it to them. And you can say no. The result is that if they really want what you have, they must offer you something that you value more highly in return. That is, they must offer you a mutually agreeable economic transaction—one that benefits you as well as them.

Property rights also encourage investment, innovation, exchange, maintenance of property, and economic growth. Nobody would stock a store, build a factory, or clear land for farming if someone else, or the government itself, could take that property for his or her own benefit.

Property rights also extend to intellectual property through patents, copyrights, and trademarks. Such long-term protection encourages people to write books, music, and computer programs and to invent new products and production processes without fear that others will steal them and the rewards they may bring.

Moreover, property rights facilitate exchange. The title to an automobile or the deed to a cattle ranch assures the buyer that the seller is the legitimate owner. Also, property rights encourage owners to maintain or improve their property so as to preserve or increase its value. Finally, property rights enable people to use their time and resources to produce more goods and services, rather than using them to protect and retain the property they have already produced or acquired.

Freedom of Enterprise and Choice

Closely related to private ownership of property is freedom of enterprise and choice. The market system requires that various economic units make certain choices, which are expressed and implemented in the economy's markets:

- **Freedom of enterprise** ensures that entrepreneurs and private businesses are free to obtain and use economic resources to produce their choice of goods and services and to sell them in their chosen markets.
- **Freedom of choice** enables owners to employ or dispose of their property and money as they see fit. It also allows workers to try to enter any line of work for which they are qualified. Finally, it ensures that consumers are free to buy the goods and services that best satisfy their wants and that their budgets allow.

These choices are free only within broad legal limitations, of course. Illegal choices such as selling human organs or buying illicit drugs are punished through fines and imprisonment. (Global Perspective 2.1 reveals that the degree of economic freedom varies greatly from economy to economy.)

Self-Interest

In the market system, **self-interest** is the motivating force of the various economic units as they express their free choices. Self-interest simply means that each economic unit tries to achieve its own particular goal, which usually requires delivering something of value to others. Entrepreneurs try to maximize

ORIGIN OF THE IDEA
O 2.2
Self-interest

profit or minimize loss. Property owners try to get the highest price for the sale or rent of their resources. Workers try to maximize their utility (satisfaction) by finding jobs that offer the best combination of wages, hours, fringe benefits, and working conditions. Consumers try to obtain the products they want at the lowest possible price and apportion their expenditures to maximize their utility. The motive of self-interest gives direction and consistency to what might otherwise be a chaotic economy.

Competition

The market system depends on **competition** among economic units. The basis of this competition is freedom of choice exercised in pursuit of a monetary return. Very broadly defined, competition requires

- Two or more buyers and two or more sellers acting independently in a particular product or resource market. (Usually there are many more than two buyers or sellers.)
- Freedom of sellers and buyers to enter or leave markets, on the basis of their economic self-interest.

Competition among buyers and sellers diffuses economic power within the businesses and households that make up the economy. When there are many buyers and sellers acting independently in a market, no single buyer

GLOBAL PERSPECTIVE 2.1

Index of Economic Freedom, Selected Economies

The Index of Economic Freedom measures economic freedom using 10 broad categories such as trade policy, property rights, and government intervention, with each category containing more than 50 specific criteria. The index then ranks 179 economies according to their degree of economic freedom. A few selected rankings for 2010 are listed below.

FREE

1 Hong Kong
3 Australia
6 Switzerland

MOSTLY FREE

8 United States
19 Japan
28 Botswana

MOSTLY UNFREE

113 Brazil
140 China
143 Russia

REPRESSED

168 Iran
174 Venezuela
179 North Korea

Source: Used by permission of The Heritage Foundation, **www.heritage.org**.

or seller can dictate the price of the product or resource because others can undercut that price.

Competition also implies that producers can enter or leave an industry; no insurmountable barriers prevent an industry's expanding or contracting. This freedom of an industry to expand or contract provides the economy with the flexibility needed to remain efficient over time. Freedom of entry and exit enables the economy to adjust to changes in consumer tastes, technology, and resource availability.

The diffusion of economic power inherent in competition limits the potential abuse of that power. A producer that charges more than the competitive market price will lose sales to other producers. An employer who pays less than the competitive market wage rate will lose workers to other employers. A firm that fails to exploit new technology will lose profits to firms that do. A firm that produces shoddy products will be punished as customers switch to higher-quality items made by rival firms. Competition is the basic regulatory force in the market system.

Markets and Prices

We may wonder why an economy based on self-interest does not collapse in chaos. If consumers want breakfast cereal but businesses choose to produce running shoes and resource suppliers decide to make computer software, production would seem to be deadlocked by the apparent inconsistencies of free choices.

In reality, the millions of decisions made by households and businesses are highly coordinated with one another by markets and prices, which are key components of the market system. They give the system its ability to coordinate millions of daily economic decisions. A **market** is an institution or mechanism that brings buyers ("demanders") and sellers ("suppliers") into contact. A market system conveys the decisions made by buyers and sellers of products and resources. The decisions made on each side of the market determine a set of product and resource prices that guide resource owners, entrepreneurs, and consumers as they make and revise their choices and pursue their self-interest.

Just as competition is the regulatory mechanism of the market system, the market system itself is the organizing and coordinating mechanism. It is an elaborate communication network through which innumerable individual free choices are recorded, summarized, and balanced. Those who respond to market signals and heed market dictates are rewarded with greater profit and income; those who do not respond to those signals and choose to ignore market dictates are penalized. Through this mechanism society decides what the economy should produce, how production can be organized efficiently, and how the fruits of production are to be distributed among the various units that make up the economy.

QUICK REVIEW 2.1

- The market system rests on the private ownership of property and on freedom of enterprise and freedom of choice.
- Property rights encourage people to cooperate and make mutually agreeable economic transactions.
- The market system permits consumers, resource suppliers, and businesses to pursue and further their self-interest.
- Competition diffuses economic power and limits the actions of any single seller or buyer.
- The coordinating mechanism of capitalism is a system of markets and prices.

Technology and Capital Goods

In the market system, competition, freedom of choice, self-interest, and personal reward provide the opportunity and motivation for technological advance. The monetary rewards for new products or production techniques accrue directly to the innovator. The market system therefore encourages extensive use and rapid development of complex capital goods: tools, machinery, large-scale factories, and facilities for storage, communication, transportation, and marketing.

Advanced technology and capital goods are important because the most direct methods of production are often the least efficient. The only way to avoid that inefficiency is to rely on capital goods. It would be ridiculous for a farmer to go at production with bare hands. There are huge benefits to be derived from creating and using such capital equipment as plows, tractors, and storage bins. The more efficient production means much more abundant output.

Specialization

The extent to which market economies rely on **specialization** is extraordinary. Specialization means using the resources of an individual, firm, region, or nation to produce one or a few goods or services rather than the entire range of goods and services. Those goods and services are then exchanged for a full range of desired products. The majority of consumers produce virtually none of the goods and services they consume, and they consume little or nothing of the items they produce. The person working nine to five installing windows in commercial aircraft may rarely fly. Many farmers sell their milk to the local dairy and then buy margarine at the local grocery store. Society learned long ago that self-sufficiency breeds inefficiency. The jack-of-all-trades may be a very colorful individual but is certainly not an efficient producer.

Division of Labor Human specialization—called the **division of labor**—contributes to a society's output in several ways:

- ***Specialization makes use of differences in ability.*** Specialization enables individuals to take advantage of existing differences in their abilities and skills. If

ORIGIN OF THE IDEA

O 2.3

Specialization: division of labor

Peyton is strong, athletic, and good at throwing a football and Beyoncé is beautiful, agile, and can sing, their distribution of talents can be most efficiently used if Peyton plays professional football and Beyoncé records songs and gives concerts.

- ***Specialization fosters learning by doing.*** Even if the abilities of two people are identical, specialization may still be advantageous. By devoting time to a single task, a person is more likely to develop the skills required and to improve techniques than by working at a number of different tasks. You learn to be a good lawyer by studying and practicing law.
- ***Specialization saves time.*** By devoting time to a single task, a person avoids the loss of time incurred in shifting from one job to another. Also, time is saved by not "fumbling around" with tasks that one is not trained to do.

For all these reasons, specialization increases the total output society derives from limited resources.

Geographic Specialization Specialization also works on a regional and international basis. It is conceivable that oranges could be grown in Nebraska, but because of the unsuitability of the land, rainfall, and temperature, the costs would be very high. And it is conceivable that wheat could be grown in Florida, but such production would be costly for similar geographical reasons. So Nebraskans produce products—wheat in particular—for which their resources are best suited, and Floridians do the same, producing oranges and other citrus fruits. By specializing, both economies produce more than is needed locally. Then, very sensibly, Nebraskans and Floridians swap some of their surpluses—wheat for oranges, oranges for wheat.

Similarly, on an international scale, the United States specializes in producing such items as commercial aircraft and software, which it sells abroad in exchange for video cameras from Japan, bananas from Honduras, and woven baskets from Thailand. Both human specialization and geographic specialization are needed to achieve efficiency in the use of limited resources.

Use of Money

A rather obvious characteristic of any economic system is the extensive use of money. Money performs several functions, but first and foremost it is a **medium of exchange.** It makes trade easier.

Specialization requires exchange. Exchange can, and sometimes does, occur through **barter**—swapping goods for goods, say, wheat for oranges. But barter poses serious problems because it requires a *coincidence of wants* between the buyer and the seller. In our example, we assumed that Nebraskans had excess wheat to trade and wanted oranges. And we assumed that Floridians had excess oranges to trade and wanted wheat. So an exchange occurred. But if such a coincidence of wants is missing, trade is stymied.

FIGURE 2.1 **Money facilitates trade when wants do not coincide.** The use of money as a medium of exchange permits trade to be accomplished despite a noncoincidence of wants. (I) Nebraska trades the wheat that Florida wants for money from Floridians; (2) Nebraska trades the money it receives from Florida for the potatoes it wants from Idaho; (3) Idaho trades the money it receives from Nebraska for the oranges it wants from Florida.

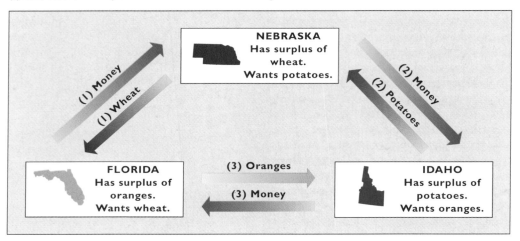

Suppose that Nebraska has no interest in Florida's oranges but wants potatoes from Idaho. And suppose that Idaho wants Florida's oranges but not Nebraska's wheat. And, to complicate matters, suppose that Florida wants some of Nebraska's wheat but none of Idaho's potatoes. We summarize the situation in Figure 2.1.

In none of the cases shown in the figure is there a coincidence of wants. Trade by barter clearly would be difficult. Instead, people in each state use **money,** which is simply a convenient social invention to facilitate exchanges of goods and services. Historically, people have used cattle, cigarettes, shells, stones, pieces of metal, and many other commodities, with varying degrees of success, as money. To serve as money, an item needs to pass only one test: It must be generally acceptable to sellers in exchange for their goods and services. Money is socially defined; whatever society accepts as a medium of exchange *is* money.

Today, most economies use pieces of paper as money. The use of paper dollars (currency) as a medium of exchange is what enables Nebraska, Florida, and Idaho to overcome their trade stalemate, as demonstrated in Figure 2.1.

On a global basis, specialization and exchange are complicated by the fact that different nations have different currencies. But markets in which currencies are bought and sold make it possible for people living in different countries to exchange goods and services without resorting to barter.

Active, but Limited, Government

An active, but limited, government is the final characteristic of market systems in modern advanced industrial economies. Although a market system promotes a high

degree of efficiency in the use of its resources, it has certain inherent shortcomings, called "market failures." We will discover in subsequent chapters that government can increase the overall effectiveness of a market system in several ways.

QUICK REVIEW 2.2

- The market systems of modern industrial economies are characterized by extensive use of technologically advanced capital goods. Such goods help these economies achieve greater efficiency in production.
- Specialization is extensive in market systems; it enhances efficiency and output by enabling individuals, regions, and nations to produce the goods and services for which their resources are best suited.
- The use of money in market systems facilitates the exchange of goods and services that specialization requires.

Five Fundamental Questions

The key features of the market system help explain how market economies respond to five fundamental questions:

- What goods and services will be produced?
- How will the goods and services be produced?
- Who will get the goods and services?
- How will the system accommodate change?
- How will the system promote progress?

These five questions highlight the economic choices underlying the production possibilities curve discussed in

Chapter 1. They reflect the reality of scarce resources in a world of unlimited wants. All economies, whether market or command, must address these five questions.

What Will Be Produced?

How will a market system decide on the specific types and quantities of goods to be produced? The simple answer is this: The goods and services that can be produced at a continuing profit will be produced, while those whose production generates a continuing loss will be discontinued. Profits and losses are the difference between the total revenue (TR) a firm receives from the sale of its products and the total cost (TC) of producing those products. (For economists, total costs include not only wage and salary payments to labor, and interest and rental payments for capital and land, but also payments to the entrepreneur for organizing and combining the other resources to produce a product.)

Continuing economic profit (TR > TC) in an industry results in expanded production and the movement of resources toward that industry. Existing firms grow and new firms enter. The industry expands. Continuing losses (TC > TR) in an industry leads to reduced production and the exit of resources from that industry. Some existing firms shrink in size; others go out of business. The industry contracts. In the market system, consumers are sovereign (in command). **Consumer sovereignty** is crucial in determining the types and quantities of goods produced. Consumers spend their income on the goods they are most willing and able to buy. Through these **"dollar votes"** they register their wants in the market. If the dollar votes for a certain product are great enough to create a profit, businesses will produce that product and offer it for sale. In contrast, if the dollar votes do not create sufficient revenues to cover costs, businesses will not produce the product. So the consumers are sovereign. They collectively direct resources to industries that are meeting consumer wants and away from industries that are not meeting consumer wants.

The dollar votes of consumers determine not only which industries will continue to exist but also which products will survive or fail. Only profitable industries, firms, and products survive. So firms are not as free to produce whatever products they wish as one might otherwise think. Consumers' buying decisions make the production of some products profitable and the production of other products unprofitable, thus restricting the choice of businesses in deciding what to produce. Businesses must match their production choices with consumer choices or else face losses and eventual bankruptcy.

The same holds true for resource suppliers. The employment of resources derives from the sale of the goods

and services that the resources help produce. Autoworkers are employed because automobiles are sold. There are few remaining professors of early Latin because there are few people desiring to learn the Latin language. Resource suppliers, desiring to earn income, are not truly free to allocate their resources to the production of goods that consumers do not value highly. Consumers register their preferences in the market; producers and resource suppliers, prompted by their own self-interest, respond appropriately.

How Will the Goods and Services Be Produced?

What combinations of resources and technologies will be used to produce goods and services? How will the production be organized? The answer: In combinations and ways that minimize the cost per unit of output. This is true

TABLE 2.1 Three Techniques for Producing $15 Worth of Bar Soap

Resource	Price per Unit of Resource	Units of Resource					
		Technique 1		Technique 2		Technique 3	
		Units	Cost	Units	Cost	Units	Cost
Labor	$2	4	$ 8	2	$ 4	1	$ 2
Land	1	1	1	3	3	4	4
Capital	3	1	3	1	3	2	6
Entrepreneurial ability	3	1	3	1	3	1	3
Total cost of $15 worth of bar soap			$15		$13		$15

because inefficiency drives up costs and lowers profits. As a result, any firm wishing to maximize its profits will make great efforts to minimize production costs. These efforts will include using the right mix of labor and capital, given the prices and productivity of those resources. They also mean locating production facilities optimally to hold down production and transportation expenses.

Those efforts will be intensified if the firm faces competition, as consumers strongly prefer low prices and will shift their purchases over to the firms that can produce a quality product at the lowest possible price. Any firm foolish enough to use higher-cost production methods will go bankrupt as it is undersold by its more efficient competitors who can still make a profit when selling at a lower price. Simply stated: Competition eliminates high-cost producers.

Least-cost production means that firms must employ the most economically efficient technique of production in producing their output. The most efficient production technique depends on

- The available technology, that is, the available body of knowledge and techniques that can be used to combine economic resources to produce the desired results.
- The prices of the needed resources.

A technique that requires just a few inputs of resources to produce a specific output may be highly inefficient economically if those resources are valued very highly in the market. Economic efficiency requires obtaining a particular output of product with the least input of scarce resources, when both output and resource inputs are measured in dollars and cents. The combination of resources that will produce, say, $15 worth of bathroom soap at the lowest possible cost is the most efficient.

Suppose there are three possible techniques for producing the desired $15 worth of bars of soap. Suppose also that the quantity of each resource required by each production technique and the prices of the required resources are as shown in Table 2.1. By multiplying the required

quantities of each resource by its price in each of the three techniques, we can determine the total cost of producing $15 worth of soap by means of each technique.

Technique 2 is economically the most efficient, because it is the least costly. It enables society to obtain $15 worth of output by using a smaller amount of resources—

WORKED PROBLEMS

W 2.1

Least-cost production

$13 worth—than the $15 worth required by the two other techniques. Competition will dictate that producers use technique 2. Thus, the question of how goods will be produced is answered. They will be produced in a least-cost way.

A change in either technology or resource prices, however, may cause a firm to shift from the technology it is using. If the price of labor falls to $.50, technique 1 becomes more desirable than technique 2. Firms will find they can lower their costs by shifting to a technology that uses more of the resource whose price has fallen. Exercise: Would a new technique involving 1 unit of labor, 4 of land, 1 of capital, and 1 of entrepreneurial ability be preferable to the techniques listed in Table 2.1, assuming the resource prices shown there?

Who Will Get the Output?

The market system enters the picture in two ways when determining the distribution of total output. Generally, any product will be distributed to consumers on the basis of their ability and willingness to pay its existing market price. If the price of some product, say, a small sailboat, is $3000, then buyers who are willing and able to pay that price will "sail, sail away." Consumers who are unwilling or unable to pay the price will be "sitting on the dock of the bay."

The ability to pay the prices for sailboats and other products depends on the amount of income that consumers have, along with the prices of, and preferences for, various goods. If consumers have sufficient income and want to spend their money on a particular good, they can have it.

The amount of income they have depends on (1) the quantities of the property and human resources they supply and (2) the prices those resources command in the resource market. Resource prices (wages, interest, rent, profit) are crucial in determining the size of each person's income and therefore each person's ability to buy part of the economy's output. If a lawyer earning $200 an hour and a janitor earning $10 an hour both work the same number of hours each year, then each year the lawyer will be able to purchase 20 times more of society's output than the janitor.

How Will the System Accommodate Change?

Market systems are dynamic: Consumer preferences, technology, and supplies of resources all change. This means that the particular allocation of resources that is now the most efficient for a specific pattern of consumer tastes, range of technological alternatives, and amount of available resources will become obsolete and inefficient as consumer preferences change, new techniques of production are discovered, and resource supplies change over time. Can the market economy adjust to such changes?

Suppose consumer tastes change. For instance, assume that consumers decide they want more fruit juice and less milk than the economy currently provides. Those changes in consumer tastes will be communicated to producers through an increase in spending on fruit and a decline in spending on milk. Other things equal, prices and profits in the fruit juice industry will rise and those in the milk industry will fall. Self-interest will induce existing competitors to expand output and entice new competitors to enter the prosperous fruit industry and will in time force firms to scale down—or even exit—the depressed milk industry.

The higher prices and greater economic profit in the fruit-juice industry will not only induce that industry to expand but will also give it the revenue needed to obtain the resources essential to its growth. Higher prices and profits will permit fruit producers to attract more resources from less urgent alternative uses. The reverse occurs in the milk industry, where fewer workers and other resources are employed. These adjustments in the economy are appropriate responses to the changes in consumer tastes. This is consumer sovereignty at work.

The market system is a gigantic communications system. Through changes in prices and profits, it communicates changes in such basic matters as consumer tastes and elicits appropriate responses from businesses and resource suppliers. By affecting price and profits, changes in consumer tastes direct the expansion of some industries and the contraction of others. Those adjustments are conveyed to the resource market. As expanding industries employ more resources and contracting industries employ fewer, the resulting changes in resource prices (wages and salaries, for example) and income flows guide resources from the contracting industries to the expanding industries.

This directing or guiding function of prices and profits is a core element of the market system. Without such a system, a government planning board or some other administrative agency would have to direct businesses and resources into the appropriate industries. A similar analysis shows that the system can and does adjust to other fundamental changes—for example, to changes in technology and in the prices of various resources.

How Will the System Promote Progress?

Society desires economic growth (greater output) and higher standards of living (greater output *per person*). How does the market system promote technological improvements and capital accumulation, both of which contribute to a higher standard of living for society?

Technological Advance The market system provides a strong incentive for technological advance and enables better products and processes to supplant inferior ones. An entrepreneur or firm that introduces a popular new product will gain revenue and economic profit at the expense of rivals. Firms that are highly profitable one year may find they are in financial trouble just a few years later. Technological advance also includes new and improved methods that reduce production or distribution costs. By passing part of its cost reduction on to the consumer through a lower product price, a firm can increase sales and obtain economic profit at the expense of rival firms.

Moreover, the market system promotes the *rapid spread* of technological advance throughout an industry. Rival firms must follow the lead of the most innovative firm or else suffer immediate losses and eventual failure. In some cases, the result is **creative destruction:** The creation of new products and production methods completely destroys the market positions of firms that are wedded to existing products and older ways of doing business. Example: The advent of compact discs largely demolished long-play vinyl records, and iPods and other digital technologies are now supplanting CDs.

Capital Accumulation Most technological advances require additional capital goods. The market system provides the resources necessary to produce additional capital goods through increased dollar votes for those goods. That is, the market system acknowledges dollar voting for capital goods as well as for consumer goods.

But who counts the dollar votes for capital goods? Answer: Entrepreneurs and business owners. As receivers of profit income, they often use part of that income to purchase capital goods. Doing so yields even greater profit income in the future if the technological innovation that required the additional capital goods is successful. Also, by paying interest or selling ownership shares, the entrepreneur and firm can attract some of the income of households as saving to increase their dollar votes for the production of more capital goods.

QUICK REVIEW 2.3

- The output mix of the market system is determined by profits, which in turn depend heavily on consumer preferences. Economic profits cause industries to expand; losses cause industries to contract.
- Competition forces industries to use the least costly production methods.
- Competitive markets reallocate resources in response to changes in consumer tastes, technological advances, and changes in availability of resources.
- In a market economy, consumer income and product prices determine how output will be distributed.
- Competitive markets create incentives for technological advance and capital accumulation, both of which contribute to increases in standards of living.

The "Invisible Hand"

In his 1776 book *The Wealth of Nations*, Adam Smith first noted that the operation of a market system creates a curious unity between private interests and social interests. Firms and resource suppliers, seeking to further their own self-interest and operating within the framework of a highly competitive market system, will simultaneously, as though guided by an **"invisible hand,"** promote the public or social interest. For example, we have seen that in a competitive environment, businesses seek to build new and improved products to increase profits. Those enhanced products increase society's well-being. Businesses also use the least costly combination of resources to produce a specific output because doing so is in their self-interest. To act otherwise would be to forgo profit or even to risk business failure. But, at the same time, to use scarce resources in the least costly way is clearly in the social interest as well. It "frees up" resources to produce something else that society desires.

Self-interest, awakened and guided by the competitive market system, is what induces responses appropriate to the changes in society's wants. Businesses seeking to make higher profits and to avoid losses, and resource suppliers pursuing greater monetary rewards, negotiate changes in the allocation of resources and end up with the output that society wants. Competition controls or guides self-interest such that self-interest automatically and quite unintentionally furthers the best interest of society. The invisible hand ensures that when firms maximize their profits and resource suppliers maximize their incomes, these groups also help maximize society's output and income.

Of the various virtues of the market system, three merit reemphasis:

- *Efficiency* The market system promotes the efficient use of resources by guiding them into the production of the goods and services most wanted by society. It forces the use of the most efficient techniques in organizing resources for production, and it encourages the development and adoption of new and more efficient production techniques.

- *Incentives* The market system encourages skill acquisition, hard work, and innovation. Greater work skills and effort mean greater production and higher incomes, which usually translate into a higher standard of living. Similarly, the assuming of risks by entrepreneurs can result in substantial profit incomes. Successful innovations generate economic rewards.

- *Freedom* The major noneconomic argument for the market system is its emphasis on personal freedom. In contrast to central planning, the market system coordinates economic activity without coercion. The market system permits—indeed, it thrives on—freedom of enterprise and choice. Entrepreneurs and workers are free to further their own self-interest, subject to the rewards and penalties imposed by the market system itself.

Of course, no economic system, including the market system, is flawless. In Chapter 5 we will explain two well-known shortcomings of the market system and examine the government policies that try to remedy them.

The Demise of the Command Systems

Our discussion of how a market system answers the five fundamental questions provides insights on why the command systems of the Soviet Union, eastern Europe, and China (prior to its market reforms) failed. Those systems encountered two insurmountable problems.

The Coordination Problem

The first difficulty was the coordination problem. The central planners had to coordinate the millions of individual decisions by consumers, resource suppliers, and businesses. Consider the setting up of a factory to produce tractors. The central planners had to establish a realistic annual production target, for example, 1000 tractors. They then had to make available all the necessary inputs—labor, machinery, electric power, steel, tires, glass, paint, transportation—for the production and delivery of those 1000 tractors.

Because the outputs of many industries serve as inputs to other industries, the failure of any single industry to achieve its output target caused a chain reaction of repercussions. For example, if iron mines, for want of machinery or labor or transportation, did not supply the steel industry with the required inputs of iron ore, the steel mills were unable to fulfill the input needs of the many industries that depended on steel. Those steel-using industries (such as tractor, automobile, and transportation) were unable to fulfill their planned production goals. Eventually the chain reaction spread to all firms that used steel as an input and from there to other input buyers or final consumers.

The coordination problem became more difficult as the economies expanded. Products and production processes grew more sophisticated and the number of industries requiring planning increased. Planning techniques that worked for the simpler economy proved highly inadequate and inefficient for the larger economy. Bottlenecks and production stoppages became the norm, not the exception. In trying to cope, planners further suppressed product variety, focusing on one or two products in each product category.

A lack of a reliable success indicator added to the coordination problem in the Soviet Union and China prior to its market reforms. We have seen that market economies rely on profit as a success indicator. Profit depends on consumer demand, production efficiency, and product quality. In contrast, the major success indicator for the command economies usually was a quantitative production target that the central planners assigned. Production costs, product quality, and product mix were secondary considerations. Managers and workers often sacrificed product quality and variety because they were being awarded bonuses for meeting quantitative, not qualitative, targets. If meeting production goals meant sloppy assembly work and little product variety, so be it.

It was difficult at best for planners to assign quantitative production targets without unintentionally producing distortions in output. If the plan specified a production target for producing nails in terms of *weight* (tons of nails), the enterprise made only large nails. But if it specified the target as a *quantity* (thousands of nails), the firm made all small nails, and lots of them! That is precisely what happened in the centrally planned economies.

The Incentive Problem

The command economies also faced an incentive problem. Central planners determined the output mix. When they misjudged how many automobiles, shoes, shirts, and chickens were wanted at the government-determined prices, persistent shortages and surpluses of those products arose. But as long as the managers who oversaw the production of those goods were rewarded for meeting their assigned production goals, they had no incentive to adjust production in response to the shortages and surpluses. And there were no fluctuations in prices and profitability to signal that more or less of certain products was desired. Thus, many products were unavailable or in short supply, while other products were overproduced and sat for months or years in warehouses.

The command systems of the former Soviet Union and China before its market reforms also lacked entrepreneurship. Central planning did not trigger the profit motive, nor did it reward innovation and enterprise.

CONSIDER THIS . . .

The Two Koreas

North Korea is one of the few command economies still standing. After the Second World War, the Korean peninsula was divided into North Korea and South Korea. North Korea, under the influence of the Soviet Union, established a command economy that emphasized government ownership and central government planning. South Korea, protected by the United States, established a market economy based upon private ownership and the profit motive. Today, the differences in the economic outcomes of the two systems are striking:

	North Korea	South Korea
GDP	$40 billion*	$1.3 trillion*
GDP per capita	$1800*	$27,700*
Exports	$2.0 billion	$355 billion
Imports	$3.5 billion	$313 billion
Agrculture as % of GDP	23 percent	3 percent

*Based on purchasing power equivalencies to the U.S. dollar.
Source: *CIA World Fact Book,* 2010, **www.cia.gov**.

key graph

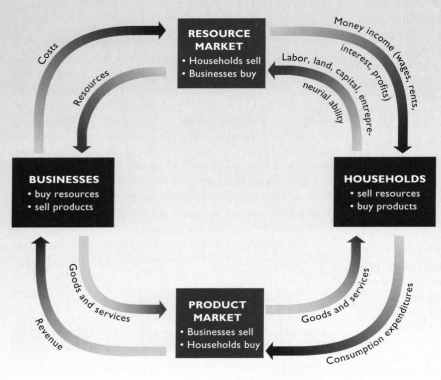

FIGURE 2.2 The circular flow diagram.
Resources flow from households to businesses through the resource market, and products flow from businesses to households through the product market. Opposite these real flows are monetary flows. Households receive income from businesses (their costs) through the resource market, and businesses receive revenue from households (their expenditures) through the product market.

QUICK QUIZ FOR FIGURE 2.2

1. The resource market is the place where:
   a. households sell products and businesses buy products.
   b. businesses sell resources and households sell products.
   c. households sell resources and businesses buy resources (or the services of resources).
   d. businesses sell resources and households buy resources (or the services of resources).

2. Which of the following would be determined in the product market?
   a. a manager's salary.
   b. the price of equipment used in a bottling plant.
   c. the price of 80 acres of farmland.
   d. the price of a new pair of athletic shoes.

3. In this circular flow diagram:
   a. money flows counterclockwise.
   b. resources flow counterclockwise.
   c. goods and services flow clockwise.
   d. households are on the selling side of the product market.

4. In this circular flow diagram:
   a. households spend income in the product market.
   b. firms sell resources to households.
   c. households receive income through the product market.
   d. households produce goods.

Answers: 1. c; 2. d; 3. b; 4. a

The route for getting ahead was through participation in the political hierarchy of the Communist Party. Moving up the hierarchy meant better housing, better access to health care, and the right to shop in special stores. Meeting production targets and maneuvering through the minefields of party politics were measures of success in "business." But a definition of business success based solely on political savvy was not conducive to technological advance, which is often disruptive to existing products, production methods, and organizational structures.

The Circular Flow Model

The dynamic market economy creates continuous, repetitive flows of goods and services, resources, and money. The **circular flow diagram,** shown in **Figure 2.2 (Key Graph),** illustrates those flows for a simplified economy in which there is no government. Observe that in the diagram we group this economy's decision makers into *businesses*

> **ORIGIN OF THE IDEA**
>
> **O 2.4**
>
> Circular flow diagram

and *households*. Additionally, we divide this economy's markets into the *resource market* and the *product market*.

Households

The blue rectangle on the right side of the circular flow diagram in Figure 2.2 represents **households,** which are defined as one or more persons occupying a housing unit. There are currently about 116 million households in the U.S. economy. Households buy the goods and services that businesses make available in the product market. Households obtain the income needed to buy those products by selling resources in the resource market.

All the resources in our no-government economy are ultimately owned or provided by households. For instance, the members of one household or another directly provide all of the labor and entrepreneurial ability in the economy. Households also own all of the land and all of the capital in the economy either directly, as personal property, or indirectly, as a consequence of owning all of the businesses in the economy (and thereby controlling all of the land and capital owned by businesses). Thus, all of the income in the economy—all wages, rents, interest, and profits—flows to households because they provide the economy's labor, land, capital, and entrepreneurial ability.

Businesses

The blue rectangle on the left side of the circular flow diagram represents **businesses,** which are commercial establishments that attempt to earn profits for their owners by offering goods and services for sale. Businesses fall into three main categories.

- A **sole proprietorship** is a business owned and managed by a single person. The proprietor (the owner) may work alone or have employees. Examples include a woman who runs her own tree-cutting business and an independent accountant who, with two assistants, helps his clients with their taxes.
- The **partnership** form of business organization is a natural outgrowth of the sole proprietorship. In a partnership, two or more individuals (the partners) agree to own and operate a business together. They pool their financial resources and business skills to operate the business, and they share any profits or losses that the business may generate. Many law firms and dental practices are organized as partnerships, as are a wide variety of firms in many other industries.
- A **corporation** is an independent legal entity that can—on its own behalf—acquire resources, own assets, produce and sell products, incur debts, extend

credit, sue and be sued, and otherwise engage in any legal business activity.

The fact that a corporation is an independent legal entity means that its owners bear no personal financial responsibility for the fulfillment of the corporation's debts and obligations. For instance, if a corporation has failed to repay a loan to a bank, the bank can sue the corporation but not its owners. Professional managers run most corporations. They are hired and supervised by a board of directors that is elected annually by the corporation's owners. Google, Ford, and American Airlines are examples of large corporations, but corporations come in all sizes and operate in every type of industry.

There currently are about 30 million businesses in the United States, ranging from enormous corporations like Walmart, with 2009 sales of $406 billion and 2.1 million employees, to single-person sole proprietorships with sales of less than $100 per day.

Businesses sell goods and services in the product market in order to obtain revenue, and they incur costs in the resource market when they purchase the labor, land, capital, and entrepreneurial ability that they need to produce their respective goods and services.

Product Market

The red rectangle at bottom of the diagram represents the **product market,** the place where the goods and services produced by businesses are bought and sold. Households use the income they receive from the sale of resources to buy goods and services. The money that they spend on goods and services flows to businesses as revenue.

Resource Market

Finally, the red rectangle at the top of the circular flow diagram represents the **resource market** in which households sell resources to businesses. The households sell resources to generate income, and the businesses buy resources to produce goods and services. Productive resources flow from households to businesses, while money flows from businesses to households in the form of wages, rents, interest, and profits.

To summarize, the circular flow model depicts a complex web of economic activity in which businesses and households are both buyers and sellers. Businesses buy resources and sell products. Households buy products and sell resources. The counterclockwise flow of economic resources and finished products that is illustrated by the red arrows in Figure 2.2 is paid for by the clockwise flow of money income and consumption expenditures illustrated by the blue arrows.

LAST

Word   Shuffling the Deck

Economist Donald Boudreaux Marvels at the Way the Market System Systematically and Purposefully Arranges the World's Tens of Billions of Individual Resources.

In *The Future and Its Enemies*, Virginia Postrel notes the astonishing fact that if you thoroughly shuffle an ordinary deck of 52 playing cards, chances are practically 100 percent that the resulting arrangement of cards has never before existed. *Never.* Every time you shuffle a deck, you produce an arrangement of cards that exists for the first time in history.

The arithmetic works out that way. For a very small number of items, the number of possible arrangements is small. Three items, for example, can be arranged only six different ways. But the number of possible arrangements grows very large very quickly. The number of different ways to arrange five items is 120 . . . for ten items it's 3,628,800 . . . for fifteen items it's 1,307,674,368,000.

The number of different ways to arrange 52 items is 8.066 $\times 10^{67}$. This is a *big* number. No human can comprehend its enormousness. By way of comparison, the number of possible ways to arrange a mere 20 items is 2,432,902,008,176,640,000— a number larger than the total number of seconds that have elapsed since the beginning of time ten billion years ago—and this number is Lilliputian compared to 8.066×10^{67}.

What's the significance of these facts about numbers? Consider the number of different resources available in the world— my labor, your labor, your land, oil, tungsten, cedar, coffee beans, chickens, rivers, the Empire State Building, [Microsoft] Windows, the wharves at Houston, the classrooms at Oxford, the airport at Miami, and on and on and on. No one can possibly count all of the different productive resources available for our use. But we can be sure that this number is at least in the tens of billions.

When you reflect on how incomprehensibly large is the number of ways to arrange a deck containing a mere 52 cards, the mind boggles at the number of different ways to arrange all the world's resources.

If our world were random—if resources combined together haphazardly, as if a giant took them all into his hands and tossed them down like so many [cards]—it's a virtual certainty that the resulting combination of resources would be useless. Unless this chance arrangement were quickly rearranged according to some productive logic, nothing worthwhile would be produced. We would all starve to death. Because only a tiny fraction of possible arrangements serves human ends, any arrangement will be useless if it is chosen randomly or with inadequate knowledge of how each and every resource might be productively combined with each other.

And yet, we witness all around us an arrangement of resources that's productive and serves human goals. Today's arrangement of resources might not be perfect, but it is vastly superior to most of the trillions upon trillions of other possible arrangements.

How have we managed to get one of the minuscule number of arrangements that works? The answer is private property—a social institution that encourages mutual accommodation.

Private property eliminates the possibility that resource arrangements will be random, for each resource owner chooses a course of action only if it promises rewards to the owner that exceed the rewards promised by all other available courses.

[The result] is a breathtakingly complex and productive arrangement of countless resources. This arrangement emerged over time (and is still emerging) as the result of billions upon billions of individual, daily, small decisions made by people seeking to better employ their resources and labor in ways that other people find helpful.

Source: Abridged from Donald J. Boudreaux, "Mutual Accommodation," *Ideas on Liberty*, May 2000, pp. 4–5. Used by permission of *The Freeman*.

Summary

1. The market system and the command system are the two broad types of economic systems used to address the economizing problem. In the market system (or capitalism), private individuals own most resources, and markets coordinate most economic activity. In the command system (or socialism or communism), government owns most resources and central planners coordinate most economic activity.

2. The market system is characterized by the private ownership of resources, including capital, and the freedom of individuals to engage in economic activities of their choice to advance their material well-being. Self-interest is the driving force of such an economy and competition functions as a regulatory or control mechanism.

3. In the market system, markets, prices, and profits organize and make effective the many millions of individual economic decisions that occur daily.

4. Specialization, use of advanced technology, and the extensive use of capital goods are common features of market systems. Functioning as a medium of exchange, money eliminates the problems of bartering and permits easy trade and greater specialization, both domestically and internationally.

5. Every economy faces five fundamental questions: (a) What goods and services will be produced? (b) How will the goods and services be produced? (c) Who will get the goods and services? (d) How will the system accommodate change? (e) How will the system promote progress?

6. The market system produces products whose production and sale yield total revenue sufficient to cover total cost. It does not produce products for which total revenue continuously falls short of total cost. Competition forces firms to use the lowest-cost production techniques.

7. Economic profit (total revenue minus total cost) indicates that an industry is prosperous and promotes its expansion. Losses signify that an industry is not prosperous and hasten its contraction.

8. Consumer sovereignty means that both businesses and resource suppliers are subject to the wants of consumers. Through their dollar votes, consumers decide on the composition of output.

9. The prices that a household receives for the resources it supplies to the economy determine that household's income. This income determines the household's claim on the economy's output. Those who have income to spend get the products produced in the market system.

10. By communicating changes in consumer tastes to entrepreneurs and resource suppliers, the market system prompts appropriate adjustments in the allocation of the economy's resources. The market system also encourages technological advance and capital accumulation, both of which raise a nation's standard of living.

11. Competition, the primary mechanism of control in the market economy, promotes a unity of self-interest and social interests. As if directed by an invisible hand, competition harnesses the self-interest motives of businesses and resource suppliers to further the social interest.

12. The command systems of the Soviet Union and pre-reform China met their demise because of coordination difficulties caused by central planning and the lack of a profit incentive. The coordination problem resulted in bottlenecks, inefficiencies, and a focus on a limited number of products. The incentive problem discouraged product improvement, new product development, and entrepreneurship.

13. The circular flow model illustrates the flows of resources and products from households to businesses and from businesses to households, along with the corresponding monetary flows. Businesses are on the buying side of the resource market and the selling side of the product market. Households are on the selling side of the resource market and the buying side of the product market.

Terms and Concepts

economic system	specialization	circular flow diagram
command system	division of labor	households
market system	medium of exchange	businesses
private property	barter	sole proprietorship
freedom of enterprise	money	partnership
freedom of choice	consumer sovereignty	corporation
self-interest	dollar votes	product market
competition	creative destruction	resource market
market	"invisible hand"	

Questions

1. Contrast how a market system and a command economy try to cope with economic scarcity. **LO1**

2. How does self-interest help achieve society's economic goals? Why is there such a wide variety of desired goods and services in a market system? In what way are entrepreneurs and businesses at the helm of the economy but commanded by consumers? **LO2**

3. Why is private property, and the protection of property rights, so critical to the success of the market system? How do property rights encourage cooperation? **LO2**

4. What are the advantages of using capital in the production process? What is meant by the term "division of labor"? What are the advantages of specialization in the use of human and material resources? Explain why exchange is the necessary consequence of specialization. **LO2**

5. What problem does barter entail? Indicate the economic significance of money as a medium of exchange. What is meant by the statement "We want money only to part with it"? **LO2**

6. Evaluate and explain the following statements: **LO2**
   a. The market system is a profit-and-loss system.
   b. Competition is the disciplinarian of the market economy.

7. Assume that a business firm finds that its profit is greatest when it produces $40 worth of product A. Suppose also that each of the three techniques shown in the table to the right will produce the desired output. **LO3**
   a. With the resource prices shown, which technique will the firm choose? Why? Will production using that technique entail profit or loss? What will be the amount of that profit or loss? Will the industry expand or contract? When will that expansion or contraction end?
   b. Assume now that a new technique, technique 4, is developed. It combines 2 units of labor, 2 of land, 6 of capital, and 3 of entrepreneurial ability. In view of the resource prices in the table, will the firm adopt the new technique? Explain your answer.
   c. Suppose that an increase in the labor supply causes the price of labor to fall to $1.50 per unit, all other resource prices remaining unchanged. Which technique will the producer now choose? Explain.
   d. "The market system causes the economy to conserve most in the use of resources that are particularly scarce

in supply. Resources that are scarcest relative to the demand for them have the highest prices. As a result, producers use these resources as sparingly as is possible." Evaluate this statement. Does your answer to part *c*, above, bear out this contention? Explain.

Resource	Price per Unit of Resource	Resource Units Required		
		Technique 1	Technique 2	Technique 3
Labor	$3	5	2	3
Land	4	2	4	2
Capital	2	2	4	5
Entrepreneurial ability	2	4	2	4

8. Some large hardware stores, such as Home Depot, boast of carrying as many as 20,000 different products in each store. What motivated the producers of those individual products to make them and offer them for sale? How did the producers decide on the best combinations of resources to use? Who made those resources available, and why? Who decides whether these particular hardware products should continue to be produced and offered for sale? **LO3**

9. What is meant by the term "creative destruction"? How does the emergence of MP3 (or iPod) technology relate to this idea? **LO3**

10. In a sentence, describe the meaning of the phrase "invisible hand." **LO4**

11. In market economies, firms rarely worry about the availability of inputs to produce their products, whereas in command economies input availability is a constant concern. Why the difference? **LO4**

12. Distinguish between the resource market and the product market in the circular flow model. In what way are businesses and households both sellers and buyers in this model? What are the flows in the circular flow model? **LO5**

13. **LAST WORD** What explains why millions of economic resources tend to get arranged logically and productively rather than haphazardly and unproductively?

Problems

1. Table 2.1 contains information on three techniques for producing $15 worth of bar soap. Assume that we said "$15 worth of bar soap" because soap cost $3 per bar and all three techniques produce 5 bars of soap ($15 = $3 per bar × 5 bars). So you know each technique produces 5 bars of soap. **LO3**
   a. What technique will you want to use if the price of a bar of soap falls to $2.75? What if the price of a bar of soap rises to $4? To $5?

   b. How many bars of soap will you want to produce if the price of a bar of soap falls to $2.00?
   c. Suppose that the price of soap is again $3 per bar but that the prices of all four resources are now $1 per unit. Which is now the least-profitable technique?
   d. If the resource prices return to their original levels (the ones shown in the table) but a new technique is invented that can produce 3 bars of soap (yes, 3 bars, not 5 bars!)

using 1 unit of each of the four resources, will firms prefer the new technique?

2. Suppose Natasha currently makes $50,000 per year working as a manager at a cable TV company. She then develops two possible entrepreneurial business opportunities. In one, she will quit her job to start an organic soap company. In the other, she will try to develop an Internet-based competitor to the local cable company. For the soap-making opportunity, she anticipates annual revenue of $465,000 and costs for the necessary land, labor, and capital of $395,000 per year. For the Internet opportunity, she anticipates costs for land, labor, and capital of $3,250,000 per year as compared to revenues of $3,275,000 per year. (a) Should she quit her current job to become an entrepreneur? (b) If she does quit her current job, which opportunity would she pursue? LO3

3. With current technology, suppose a firm is producing 400 loaves of banana bread daily. Also assume that the least-cost combination of resources in producing those loaves is 5 units of labor, 7 units of land, 2 units of capital, and 1 unit of entrepreneurial ability, selling at prices of $40, $60, $60, and $20, respectively. If the firm can sell these 400 loaves at $2 per unit, what is its total revenue? Its total cost? Its profit or loss? Will it continue to produce banana bread? If this firm's situation is typical for the other makers of banana bread, will resources flow toward or away from this bakery good? LO3

4. Let's put dollar amounts on the flows in the circular flow diagram of Figure 2.2. LO5

   a. Suppose that businesses buy a total of $100 billion of the four resources (labor, land, capital, and entrepreneurial ability) from households. If households receive $60 billion in wages, $10 billion in rent, and $20 billion in interest, how much are households paid for providing entrepreneurial ability?

   b. If households spend $55 billion on goods and $45 billion on services, how much in revenues do businesses receive in the product market?

FURTHER TEST YOUR KNOWLEDGE AT
www.mcconnell19e.com

At the text's Online Learning Center (OLC), **www.mcconnell19e.com**, you will find one or more Web-based questions that require information from the Internet to answer. We urge you to check them out; they will familiarize you with Web sites that may be helpful in other courses and perhaps even in your career. The OLC also features multiple-choice questions that give instant feedback and provides other helpful ways to further test your knowledge of the chapter.

PRICE, QUANTITY, AND EFFICIENCY

AFTER READING THIS CHAPTER, YOU SHOULD BE ABLE TO:

1 Describe *demand* and explain how it can change.

2 Describe *supply* and explain how it can change.

3 Relate how supply and demand interact to determine market equilibrium.

4 Explain how changes in supply and demand affect equilibrium prices and quantities.

5 Identify what government-set prices are and how they can cause product surpluses and shortages.

6 (Appendix) Illustrate how supply and demand analysis can provide insights on actual-economy situations.

Demand, Supply, and Market Equilibrium

ORIGIN OF THE IDEA

O 3.1

Demand and supply

The model of supply and demand is the economics profession's greatest contribution to human understanding because it explains the operation of the markets on which we depend for nearly everything that we eat, drink, or consume. The model is so powerful and so widely used that to many people it *is* economics.

This chapter explains how the model works and how it can explain both the *quantities* that are bought and sold in markets as well as the *prices* at which they trade.

Markets

Markets bring together buyers ("demanders") and sellers ("suppliers"). The corner gas station, an e-commerce site, the local music store, a farmer's roadside stand—all are familiar markets. The New York Stock Exchange and the Chicago Board of Trade are markets in which buyers and sellers from all over the world communicate with one another to buy and sell bonds, stocks, and commodities. Auctioneers bring together potential buyers and sellers of art, livestock, used farm equipment, and, sometimes, real estate. In labor markets, new college graduates "sell" and employers "buy" specific labor services.

Some markets are local; others are national or international. Some are highly personal, involving face-to-face contact between demander and supplier; others are faceless, with buyer and seller never seeing or knowing each other.

To keep things simple, we will focus in this chapter on markets in which large numbers of independently acting buyers and sellers come together to buy and sell standardized products. Markets with these characteristics are the economy's most highly competitive. They include the wheat market, the stock market, and the market for foreign currencies. All such markets involve demand, supply, price, and quantity. As you will soon see, the price is "discovered" through the interacting decisions of buyers and sellers.

Demand

Demand is a schedule or a curve that shows the various amounts of a product that consumers are willing and able to purchase at each of a series of possible prices during a specified period of time.[1] Demand shows the quantities of a product that will be purchased at various possible prices, *other things equal*. Demand can easily be shown in table form. The table in Figure 3.1 is a hypothetical **demand schedule** for a *single consumer* purchasing bushels of corn.

The table reveals the relationship between the various prices of corn and the quantity of corn a particular consumer would be willing and able to purchase at each of these prices. We say "willing and able" because willingness alone is not effective in the market. You may be willing to buy a plasma television set, but if that willingness is not backed by the necessary dollars, it will not be effective and, therefore, will not be reflected in the market. In the table in Figure 3.1, if the price of corn were $5 per bushel, our consumer would be willing and able to buy 10 bushels per week; if it were $4, the consumer would be willing and able to buy 20 bushels per week; and so forth.

The table does not tell us which of the five possible prices will actually exist in the corn market. That depends

---

[1]This definition obviously is worded to apply to product markets. To adjust it to apply to resource markets, substitute the word "resource" for "product" and the word "businesses" for "consumers."

FIGURE 3.1 An individual buyer's demand for corn. Because price and quantity demanded are inversely related, an individual's demand schedule graphs as a downsloping curve such as D. Other things equal, consumers will buy more of a product as its price declines and less of the product as its price rises. (Here and in later figures, P stands for price and Q stands for quantity demanded or supplied.)

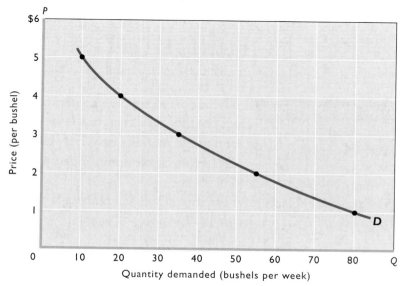

Demand for Corn	
Price per Bushel	Quantity Demanded per Week
$5	10
4	20
3	35
2	55
1	80

on the interaction between demand and supply. Demand is simply a statement of a buyer's plans, or intentions, with respect to the purchase of a product.

To be meaningful, the quantities demanded at each price must relate to a specific period—a day, a week, a month. Saying "A consumer will buy 10 bushels of corn at $5 per bushel" is meaningless. Saying "A consumer will buy 10 bushels of corn *per week* at $5 per bushel" is meaningful. Unless a specific time period is stated, we do not know whether the demand for a product is large or small.

Law of Demand

A fundamental characteristic of demand is this: Other things equal, as price falls, the quantity demanded rises, and as price rises, the quantity demanded falls. In short, there is a negative or *inverse* relationship between price and quantity demanded. Economists call this inverse relationship the **law of demand.**

ORIGIN OF THE IDEA
O 3.2
Law of demand

The other-things-equal assumption is critical here. Many factors other than the price of the product being considered affect the amount purchased. For example, the quantity of Nikes purchased will depend not only on the price of Nikes but also on the prices of such substitutes as Reeboks, Adidas, and New Balances. The law of demand in this case says that fewer Nikes will be purchased if the price of Nikes rises and if the prices of Reeboks, Adidas, and New Balances all remain constant. In short, if the *relative price* of Nikes rises, fewer Nikes will be bought. However, if the price of Nikes and the prices of all other competing shoes increase by some amount—say, $5—consumers might buy more, fewer, or the same number of Nikes.

Why the inverse relationship between price and quantity demanded? Let's look at three explanations, beginning with the simplest one:

- The law of demand is consistent with common sense. People ordinarily *do* buy more of a product at a low price than at a high price. Price is an obstacle that deters consumers from buying. The higher that obstacle, the less of a product they will buy; the lower the price obstacle, the more they will buy. The fact that businesses have "sales" to clear out unsold items is evidence of their belief in the law of demand.
- In any specific time period, each buyer of a product will derive less satisfaction (or benefit, or utility) from each successive unit of the product consumed. The second Big Mac will yield less satisfaction to the

ORIGIN OF THE IDEA
O 3.3
Diminishing marginal utility

consumer than the first, and the third still less than the second. That is, consumption is subject to **diminishing marginal utility.** And because successive units of a particular product yield less and less marginal utility, consumers will buy additional units only if the price of those units is progressively reduced.

- We can also explain the law of demand in terms of income and substitution effects. The **income effect** indicates that a lower price increases the purchasing power of a buyer's money income, enabling the buyer to purchase more of the product than before. A higher price has the opposite effect. The **substitution effect** suggests that at a lower price buyers have the incentive to substitute what is now a less expensive product for other products that are now *relatively* more expensive. The product whose price has fallen is now "a better deal" relative to the other products.

For example, a decline in the price of chicken will increase the purchasing power of consumer incomes, enabling people to buy more chicken (the income effect). At a lower price, chicken is relatively more attractive and consumers tend to substitute it for pork, lamb, beef, and fish (the substitution effect). The income and substitution effects combine to make consumers able and willing to buy more of a product at a low price than at a high price.

ORIGIN OF THE IDEA
O 3.4
Income and substitution effects

The Demand Curve

The inverse relationship between price and quantity demanded for any product can be represented on a simple graph, in which, by convention, we measure *quantity demanded* on the horizontal axis and *price* on the vertical axis. In the graph in Figure 3.1 we have plotted the five price-quantity data points listed in the accompanying table and connected the points with a smooth curve, labeled *D*. Such a curve is called a **demand curve.** Its downward slope reflects the law of demand—people buy more of a product, service, or resource as its price falls. The relationship between price and quantity demanded is inverse (or negative).

The table and graph in Figure 3.1 contain exactly the same data and reflect the same relationship between price and quantity demanded. But the graph shows that relationship much more simply and clearly than a table or a description in words.

Market Demand

So far, we have concentrated on just one consumer. But competition requires that more than one buyer be present in each market. By adding the quantities demanded by all consumers at each of the various possible prices, we can get from *individual* demand to *market* demand. If there are just three buyers in the market, as represented in the table in Figure 3.2, it is relatively easy to determine the total quantity demanded at each price. Figure 3.2 shows the graphical summing procedure: At each price we sum horizontally the quantities demanded by Joe, Jen, and Jay to obtain the total quantity demanded at that price; we then plot the price and the total quantity demanded as one point on the market demand curve.

Competition, of course, ordinarily entails many more than three buyers of a product. To avoid hundreds or thousands or millions of additions, we suppose that all the buyers in a market are willing and able to buy the same amounts at each of the possible prices. Then we just multiply those amounts by the number of buyers to obtain the market demand. That is how we arrived at the demand schedule and demand curve D_1 in Figure 3.3 for a market of 200 corn buyers, each with a demand as shown in the table in Figure 3.1.

In constructing a demand curve such as D_1 in Figure 3.3, economists assume that price is the most important influence on the amount of any product purchased. But economists know that other factors can and do affect purchases. These factors, called **determinants of demand,** are assumed to be constant when a demand curve like D_1 is drawn. They are the "other things equal" in the relationship between price and quantity demanded. When any of these determinants changes, the demand curve will shift to the right or left. For this reason, determinants of demand are sometimes referred to as *demand shifters*.

The basic determinants of demand are (1) consumers' tastes (preferences), (2) the number of buyers in the market, (3) consumers' incomes, (4) the prices of related goods, and (5) consumer expectations.

Changes in Demand

A change in one or more of the determinants of demand will change the demand data (the demand schedule) in the table accompanying Figure 3.3 and therefore the location of the demand curve there. A change in the demand schedule or, graphically, a shift in the demand curve is called a *change in demand*.

If consumers desire to buy more corn at each possible price than is reflected in column 2 in the table in Figure 3.3, that *increase in demand* is shown as a shift of the demand curve to the right, say, from D_1 to D_2. Conversely, a *decrease in demand* occurs when consumers buy less corn

FIGURE 3.2 Market demand for corn, three buyers. The market demand curve D is the horizontal summation of the individual demand curves (D_1, D_2, and D_3) of all the consumers in the market. At the price of $3, for example, the three individual curves yield a total quantity demanded of 100 bushels (= 35 + 39 + 26).

	Market Demand for Corn, Three Buyers					
Price per Bushel	Joe	Quantity Demanded Jen		Jay		Total Quantity Demanded per Week
$5	10	+	12	+	8	= 30
4	20	+	23	+	17	= 60
3	35	+	39	+	26	= 100
2	55	+	60	+	39	= 154
1	80	+	87	+	54	= 221

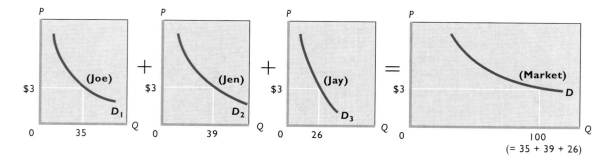

FIGURE 3.3 Changes in the demand for corn. A change in one or more of the determinants of demand causes a change in demand. An increase in demand is shown as a shift of the demand curve to the right, as from D_1 to D_2. A decrease in demand is shown as a shift of the demand curve to the left, as from D_1 to D_3. These changes in demand are to be distinguished from a change in quantity demanded, which is caused by a change in the price of the product, as shown by a movement from, say, point a to point b on fixed demand curve D_1.

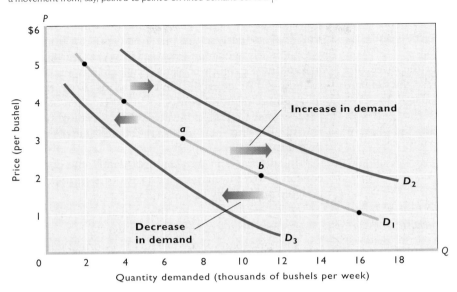

Market Demand for Corn, 200 Buyers, (D_1)	
(1) Price per Bushel	(2) Total Quantity Demanded per Week
$5	2000
4	4000
3	7000
2	11,000
1	16,000

at each possible price than is indicated in column 2. The leftward shift of the demand curve from D_1 to D_3 in Figure 3.3 shows that situation.

Now let's see how changes in each determinant affect demand.

Tastes A favorable change in consumer tastes (preferences) for a product—a change that makes the product more desirable—means that more of it will be demanded at each price. Demand will increase; the demand curve will shift rightward. An unfavorable change in consumer preferences will decrease demand, shifting the demand curve to the left.

New products may affect consumer tastes; for example, the introduction of digital cameras greatly decreased the demand for film cameras. Consumers' concern over the health hazards of cholesterol and obesity have increased the demand for broccoli, low-calorie beverages, and fresh fruit while decreasing the demand for beef, veal, eggs, and whole milk. Over the past several years, the demand for coffee drinks and table wine has greatly increased, driven by a change in tastes. So, too, has the demand for touch-screen mobile phones and fuel-efficient hybrid vehicles.

Number of Buyers An increase in the number of buyers in a market is likely to increase demand; a decrease in the number of buyers will probably decrease demand. For example, the rising number of older persons in the United

States in recent years has increased the demand for motor homes, medical care, and retirement communities. Large-scale immigration from Mexico has greatly increased the demand for a range of goods and services in the Southwest, including Mexican food products in local grocery stores. Improvements in communications have given financial markets international range and have thus increased the demand for stocks and bonds. International trade agreements have reduced foreign trade barriers to American farm commodities, increasing the number of buyers and therefore the demand for those products.

In contrast, emigration (out-migration) from many small rural communities has reduced the population and thus the demand for housing, home appliances, and auto repair in those towns.

Income How changes in income affect demand is a more complex matter. For most products, a rise in income causes an increase in demand. Consumers typically buy more steaks, furniture, and electronic equipment as their incomes increase. Conversely, the demand for such products declines as their incomes fall. Products whose demand varies *directly* with money income are called *superior goods*, or **normal goods.**

Although most products are normal goods, there are some exceptions. As incomes increase beyond some point, the demand for used clothing, retread tires, and third-hand automobiles may decrease, because the higher incomes enable consumers to buy new versions of those products. Rising incomes may also decrease the demand for soy-enhanced hamburger. Similarly, rising incomes may cause the demand for charcoal grills to decline as wealthier consumers switch to gas grills. Goods whose demand varies *inversely* with money income are called **inferior goods.**

Prices of Related Goods

A change in the price of a related good may either increase or decrease the demand for a product, depending on whether the related good is a substitute or a complement:

- A **substitute good** is one that can be used in place of another good.
- A **complementary good** is one that is used together with another good.

Substitutes Häagen-Dazs ice cream and Ben & Jerry's ice cream are substitute goods or, simply, *substitutes*. When two products are substitutes, an increase in the price of one will increase the demand for the other. Conversely, a decrease in the price of one will decrease the demand for the other. For example, when the price of Häagen-Dazs ice cream rises, consumers will buy less of it and increase their demand for Ben & Jerry's ice cream. When the price of Colgate toothpaste declines, the demand for Crest decreases. So it is with other product pairs such as Nikes and Reeboks, Budweiser and Miller beer, or Chevrolets and Fords. They are *substitutes in consumption*.

Complements Because complementary goods (or, simply, *complements*) are used together, they are typically demanded jointly. Examples include computers and software, cell phones and cellular service, and snowboards and lift tickets. If the price of a complement (for example, lettuce) goes up, the demand for the related good (salad dressing) will decline. Conversely, if the price of a complement (for example, tuition) falls, the demand for a related good (textbooks) will increase.

Unrelated Goods The vast majority of goods are not related to one another and are called *independent goods*. Examples are butter and golf balls, potatoes and automobiles, and bananas and wristwatches. A change in the price of one has little or no effect on the demand for the other.

Consumer Expectations

Changes in consumer expectations may shift demand. A newly formed expectation of higher future prices may cause consumers to buy now in order to "beat" the anticipated price rises, thus increasing current demand. That is often what happens in so-called hot real estate markets. Buyers rush in because they think the price of new homes will continue to escalate rapidly. Some buyers fear being "priced out of the market" and therefore not obtaining the home they desire. Other buyers—speculators—believe they will be able to sell the houses later at a higher price. Whichever their motivation, these buyers increase the current demand for houses.

Similarly, a change in expectations concerning future income may prompt consumers to change their current spending. For example, first-round NFL draft choices may splurge on new luxury cars in anticipation of lucrative professional football contracts. Or workers who become fearful of losing their jobs may reduce their demand for, say, vacation travel.

In summary, an *increase* in demand—the decision by consumers to buy larger quantities of a product at each possible price—may be caused by:

- A favorable change in consumer tastes.
- An increase in the number of buyers.
- Rising incomes if the product is a normal good.
- Falling incomes if the product is an inferior good.
- An increase in the price of a substitute good.
- A decrease in the price of a complementary good.
- A new consumer expectation that either prices or income will be higher in the future.

You should "reverse" these generalizations to explain a *decrease* in demand. Table 3.1 provides additional illustrations of the determinants of demand.

TABLE 3.1 Determinants of Demand: Factors That Shift the Demand Curve

Determinant	Examples
Change in buyer tastes	Physical fitness rises in popularity, increasing the demand for jogging shoes and bicycles; cell phone popularity rises, reducing the demand for landline phones.
Change in number of buyers	A decline in the birthrate reduces the demand for children's toys.
Change in income	A rise in incomes increases the demand for normal goods such as restaurant meals, sports tickets, and necklaces while reducing the demand for inferior goods such as cabbage, turnips, and inexpensive wine.
Change in the prices of related goods	A reduction in airfares reduces the demand for bus transportation (substitute goods); a decline in the price of DVD players increases the demand for DVD movies (complementary goods).
Change in consumer expectations	Inclement weather in South America creates an expectation of higher future coffee bean prices, thereby increasing today's demand for coffee beans.

Changes in Quantity Demanded

A *change in demand* must not be confused with a *change in quantity demanded*. A **change in demand** is a shift of the demand curve to the right (an increase in demand) or to the left (a decrease in demand). It occurs because the consumer's state of mind about purchasing the product has been altered in response to a change in one or more of the determinants of demand. Recall that "demand" is a schedule or a curve; therefore, a "change in demand" means a change in the schedule and a shift of the curve.

In contrast, a **change in quantity demanded** is a movement from one point to another point—from one price-quantity combination to another—on a fixed demand curve. The cause of such a change is an increase or decrease in the price of the product under consideration. In the table in Figure 3.3, for example, a decline in the price of corn from $5 to $4 will increase the quantity demanded of corn from 2000 to 4000 bushels.

In Figure 3.3 the shift of the demand curve D_1 to either D_2 or D_3 is a change in demand. But the movement from point *a* to point *b* on curve D_1 represents a change in quantity demanded: Demand has not changed; it is the entire curve, and it remains fixed in place.

QUICK REVIEW 3.1

- Demand is a schedule or a curve showing the amount of a product that buyers are willing and able to purchase, in a particular time period, at each possible price in a series of prices.
- The law of demand states that, other things equal, the quantity of a good purchased varies inversely with its price.
- The demand curve shifts because of changes in (a) consumer tastes, (b) the number of buyers in the market, (c) consumer income, (d) the prices of substitute or complementary goods, and (e) consumer expectations.
- A change in demand is a shift of the demand curve; a change in quantity demanded is a movement from one point to another on a fixed demand curve.

Supply

Supply is a schedule or curve showing the various amounts of a product that producers are willing and able to make available for sale at each of a series of possible prices during a specific period.[2] The table in Figure 3.4 is a hypothetical

---

[2]This definition is worded to apply to product markets. To adjust it to apply to resource markets, substitute "resource" for "product" and "owners" for "producers."

---

supply schedule for a single producer of corn. It shows the quantities of corn that will be supplied at various prices, other things equal.

Law of Supply

The table in Figure 3.4 shows that a positive or direct relationship prevails between price and quantity supplied. As price rises, the quantity supplied rises; as price falls, the quantity supplied falls. This relationship is called the **law of supply.** A supply schedule tells us that, other things equal, firms will produce and offer for sale more of their product at a high price than at a low price. This, again, is basically common sense.

Price is an obstacle from the standpoint of the consumer, who is on the paying end. The higher the price, the less the consumer will buy. But the supplier is on the receiving end of the product's price. To a supplier, price represents *revenue*, which serves as an incentive to produce and sell a product. The higher the price, the greater this incentive and the greater the quantity supplied.

Consider a farmer who is deciding on how much corn to plant. As corn prices rise, as shown in the table in Figure 3.4, the farmer finds it profitable to plant more corn. And the higher corn prices enable the farmer to cover the increased costs associated with more intensive cultivation and the use of more seed, fertilizer, and pesticides. The overall result is more corn.

Now consider a manufacturer. Beyond some quantity of production, manufacturers usually encounter increases in *marginal cost*—the added cost of producing one more unit of output. Certain productive resources—in particular, the firm's plant and machinery—cannot be expanded quickly, so the firm uses more of other resources such as labor to produce more output. But as labor becomes more abundant relative to the fixed plant and equipment, the additional workers have relatively less space and access to equipment. For example, the added workers may have to wait to gain access to machines. As a result, each added worker produces less added output, and the marginal cost of successive units of output rises accordingly. The firm will not produce the more costly units unless it receives a higher price for them. Again, price and quantity supplied are directly related.

The Supply Curve

As with demand, it is convenient to represent individual supply graphically. In Figure 3.4, curve *S* is the **supply curve** that corresponds with the price–quantity supplied data in the accompanying table. The upward slope of the curve reflects the law of supply—producers offer more of

FIGURE 3.4 An individual producer's supply of corn. Because price and quantity supplied are directly related, the supply curve for an individual producer graphs as an upsloping curve. Other things equal, producers will offer more of a product for sale as its price rises and less of the product for sale as its price falls.

Supply of Corn	
Price per Bushel	Quantity Supplied per Week
$5	60
4	50
3	35
2	20
1	5

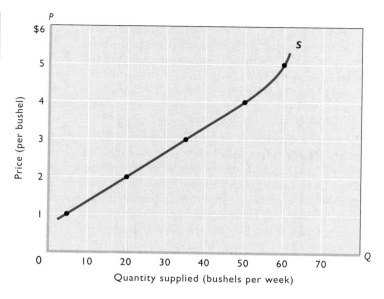

a good, service, or resource for sale as its price rises. The relationship between price and quantity supplied is positive, or direct.

Market Supply

Market supply is derived from individual supply in exactly the same way that market demand is derived from individual demand. We sum the quantities supplied by each producer at each price. That is, we obtain the market supply curve by "horizontally adding" the supply curves of the individual producers. The price–quantity supplied data in the table accompanying Figure 3.5 are for an assumed 200 identical producers in the market, each willing to supply corn according to the supply schedule shown in Figure 3.4. Curve S_1 in Figure 3.5 is a graph of the market supply data. Note that the values of the axes in Figure 3.5 are the same as those used in our graph of market demand (Figure 3.3). The only difference is that we change the label on the horizontal axis from "quantity demanded" to "quantity supplied."

Determinants of Supply

In constructing a supply curve, we assume that price is the most significant influence on the quantity supplied of any product. But other factors (the "other things equal") can and do affect supply. The supply curve is drawn on the assumption that these other things are fixed and do not change. If one of them does change, a *change in supply* will occur, meaning that the entire supply curve will shift.

The basic **determinants of supply** are (1) resource prices, (2) technology, (3) taxes and subsidies, (4) prices of other goods, (5) producer expectations, and (6) the number of sellers in the market. A change in any one or more of these determinants of supply, or *supply shifters*, will move the supply curve for a product either right or left. A shift to the *right*, as from S_1 to S_2 in Figure 3.5, signifies an *increase* in supply: Producers supply larger quantities of the product at each possible price. A shift to the *left*, as from S_1 to S_3, indicates a *decrease* in supply: Producers offer less output at each price.

Changes in Supply

Let's consider how changes in each of the determinants affect supply. The key idea is that costs are a major factor underlying supply curves; anything that affects costs (other than changes in output itself) usually shifts the supply curve.

Resource Prices The prices of the resources used in the production process help determine the costs of production incurred by firms. Higher *resource* prices raise production costs and, assuming a particular *product* price, squeeze profits. That reduction in profits reduces the incentive for firms to supply output at each product price. For example, an increase in the price of sand, crushed rock, or Portland cement will increase the cost of producing concrete and reduce its supply.

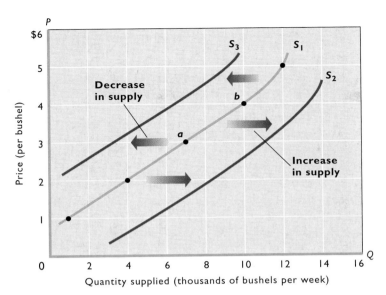

P

Price (per bushel)

$6

5

4

3

2

1

0   2   4   6   8   10   12   14   16   Q

Quantity supplied (thousands of bushels per week)

FIGURE 3.5 **Changes in the supply of corn.** A change in one or more of the determinants of supply causes a change in supply. An increase in supply is shown as a rightward shift of the supply curve, as from S_1 to S_2. A decrease in supply is depicted as a leftward shift of the curve, as from S_1 to S_3. In contrast, a change in the *quantity supplied* is caused by a change in the product's price and is shown by a movement from one point to another, as from b to a on fixed supply curve S_1.

Market Supply of Corn, 200 Producers, (S_1)	
(1) Price per Bushel	(2) Total Quantity Supplied per Week
$5	12,000
4	10,000
3	7000
2	4000
1	1000

In contrast, lower *resource* prices reduce production costs and increase profits. So when resource prices fall, firms supply greater output at each product price. For example, a decrease in the price of iron ore will decrease the price of steel.

Technology

Improvements in technology (techniques of production) enable firms to produce units of output with fewer resources. Because resources are costly, using fewer of them lowers production costs and increases supply. Example: Technological advances in producing flat-panel computer monitors have greatly reduced their cost. Thus, manufacturers will now offer more such monitors than previously at the various prices; the supply of flat-panel monitors has increased.

Taxes and Subsidies

Businesses treat most taxes as costs. An increase in sales or property taxes will increase production costs and reduce supply. In contrast, subsidies are "taxes in reverse." If the government subsidizes the production of a good, it in effect lowers the producers' costs and increases supply.

Prices of Other Goods

Firms that produce a particular product, say, soccer balls, can sometimes use their plant and equipment to produce alternative goods, say, basketballs and volleyballs. The higher prices of these "other goods" may entice soccer ball producers to switch production to those other goods in order to increase profits. This *substitution in production* results in a decline in the supply of soccer balls. Alternatively, when the prices of basketballs and volleyballs decline relative to the price of soccer balls, producers of those goods may decide to produce more soccer balls instead, increasing their supply.

Producer Expectations

Changes in expectations about the future price of a product may affect the producer's current willingness to supply that product. It is difficult, however, to generalize about how a new expectation of higher prices affects the present supply of a product. Farmers anticipating a higher wheat price in the future might withhold some of their current wheat harvest from the market, thereby causing a decrease in the current supply of wheat. In contrast, in many types of manufacturing industries, newly formed expectations that price will increase may induce firms to add another shift of workers or to expand their production facilities, causing current supply to increase.

Number of Sellers

Other things equal, the larger the number of suppliers, the greater the market supply. As more firms enter an industry, the supply curve shifts to the right. Conversely, the smaller the number of firms in the industry, the less the market supply. This means that as firms leave an industry, the supply curve shifts to the left. Example: The United States and Canada have imposed restrictions on haddock fishing to replenish dwindling stocks. As part of that policy, the Federal government has bought the boats of some of the haddock fishers as a way of putting

TABLE 3.2 Determinants of Supply: Factors That Shift the Supply Curve

Determinant	Examples
Change in resource prices	A decrease in the price of microchips increases the supply of computers; an increase in the price of crude oil reduces the supply of gasoline.
Change in technology	The development of more effective wireless technology increases the supply of cell phones.
Changes in taxes and subsidies	An increase in the excise tax on cigarettes reduces the supply of cigarettes; a decline in subsidies to state universities reduces the supply of higher education.
Change in prices of other goods	An increase in the price of cucumbers decreases the supply of watermelons.
Change in producer expectations	An expectation of a substantial rise in future log prices decreases the supply of logs today.
Change in number of suppliers	An increase in the number of tattoo parlors increases the supply of tattoos; the formation of women's professional basketball leagues increases the supply of women's professional basketball games.

them out of business and decreasing the catch. The result has been a decline in the market supply of haddock.

Table 3.2 is a checklist of the determinants of supply, along with further illustrations.

Changes in Quantity Supplied

The distinction between a *change in supply* and a *change in quantity supplied* parallels the distinction between a change in demand and a change in quantity demanded. Because supply is a schedule or curve, a **change in supply** means a change in the schedule and a shift of the curve. An increase in supply shifts the curve to the right; a decrease in supply shifts it to the left. The cause of a change in supply is a change in one or more of the determinants of supply.

In contrast, a **change in quantity supplied** is a movement from one point to another on a fixed supply curve. The cause of such a movement is a change in the price of the specific product being considered.

Consider supply curve S_1 in Figure 3.5. A decline in the price of corn from $4 to $3 decreases the quantity of corn supplied per week from 10,000 to 7000 bushels. This movement from point *b* to point *a* along S_1 is a change in quantity supplied, not a change in supply. Supply is the full schedule of prices and quantities shown, and this schedule does not change when the price of corn changes.

- A supply schedule or curve shows that, other things equal, the quantity of a good supplied varies directly with its price.
- The supply curve shifts because of changes in (a) resource prices, (b) technology, (c) taxes or subsidies, (d) prices of other goods, (e) expectations of future prices, and (f) the number of suppliers.
- A change in supply is a shift of the supply curve; a change in quantity supplied is a movement from one point to another on a fixed supply curve.

Market Equilibrium

With our understanding of demand and supply, we can now show how the decisions of buyers of corn and sellers of corn interact to determine the equilibrium price and quantity of corn. In the table in Figure 3.6, columns 1 and 2 repeat the market supply of corn (from the table in Figure 3.5), and columns 2 and 3 repeat the market demand for corn (from the table in Figure 3.3). We assume this is a competitive market so that neither buyers nor sellers can set the price.

Equilibrium Price and Quantity

We are looking for the equilibrium price and equilibrium quantity. The **equilibrium price** (or *market-clearing price*) is the price where the intentions of buyers and sellers match. It is the price where quantity demanded equals quantity supplied. The table in Figure 3.6 reveals that at $3, *and only at that price*, the number of bushels of corn that sellers wish to sell (7000) is identical to the number consumers want to buy (also 7000). At $3 and 7000 bushels of corn, there is neither a shortage nor a surplus of corn. So 7000 bushels of corn is the **equilibrium quantity**: the quantity at which the intentions of buyers and sellers match, so that the quantity demanded and the quantity supplied are equal.

INTERACTIVE GRAPHS
G 3.1
Supply and demand

Graphically, the equilibrium price is indicated by the intersection of the supply curve and the demand curve in **Figure 3.6 (Key Graph)**. (The horizontal axis now measures both quantity demanded and quantity supplied.) With neither a shortage nor a surplus at $3, the market is *in equilibrium*, meaning "in balance" or "at rest."

Competition among buyers and among sellers drives the price to the equilibrium price; once there, it will remain there unless it is subsequently disturbed by changes in

key graph

FIGURE 3.6 Equilibrium price and quantity. The intersection of the downsloping demand curve D and the upsloping supply curve S indicates the equilibrium price and quantity, here $3 and 7000 bushels of corn. The shortages of corn at below-equilibrium prices (for example, 7000 bushels at $2) drive up price. The higher prices increase the quantity supplied and reduce the quantity demanded until equilibrium is achieved. The surpluses caused by above-equilibrium prices (for example, 6000 bushels at $4) push price down. As price drops, the quantity demanded rises and the quantity supplied falls until equilibrium is established. At the equilibrium price and quantity, there are neither shortages nor surpluses of corn.

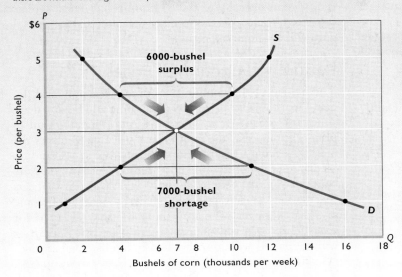

Market Supply of and Demand for Corn

(1) Total Quantity Supplied per Week	(2) Price per Bushel	(3) Total Quantity Demanded per Week	(4) Surplus (+) or Shortage (−)*
12,000	$5	2000	+10,000 ↓
10,000	4	4000	+6000 ↓
7000	**3**	**7000**	0
4000	2	11,000	−7000 ↑
1000	1	16,000	−15,000 ↑

*Arrows indicate the effect on price.

QUICK QUIZ FOR FIGURE 3.6

1. Demand curve D is downsloping because:
   a. producers offer less of a product for sale as the price of the product falls.
   b. lower prices of a product create income and substitution effects that lead consumers to purchase more of it.
   c. the larger the number of buyers in a market, the lower the product price.
   d. price and quantity demanded are directly (positively) related.

2. Supply curve S:
   a. reflects an inverse (negative) relationship between price and quantity supplied.
   b. reflects a direct (positive) relationship between price and quantity supplied.
   c. depicts the collective behavior of buyers in this market.

   d. shows that producers will offer more of a product for sale at a low product price than at a high product price.

3. At the $3 price:
   a. quantity supplied exceeds quantity demanded.
   b. quantity demanded exceeds quantity supplied.
   c. the product is abundant and a surplus exists.
   d. there is no pressure on price to rise or fall.

4. At price $5 in this market:
   a. there will be a shortage of 10,000 units.
   b. there will be a surplus of 10,000 units.
   c. quantity demanded will be 12,000 units.
   d. quantity demanded will equal quantity supplied.

Answers: 1. b; 2. b; 3. d; 4. b

demand or supply (shifts of the curves). To better understand the uniqueness of the equilibrium price, let's consider other prices. At any above-equilibrium price, quantity supplied exceeds quantity demanded. For example, at the $4 price, sellers will offer 10,000 bushels of corn, but buyers will purchase only 4000. The $4 price encourages sellers to offer lots of corn but discourages many consumers from buying it. The result is a **surplus** (or *excess supply*) of 6000 bushels. If corn sellers produced them all, they would find themselves with 6000 unsold bushels of corn.

Surpluses drive prices down. Even if the $4 price existed temporarily, it could not persist. The large surplus would prompt competing sellers to lower the price to encourage buyers to take the surplus off their hands. As the price fell, the incentive to produce corn would decline and the incentive for consumers to buy corn would increase. As shown in Figure 3.6, the market would move to its equilibrium at $3.

Any price below the $3 equilibrium price would create a shortage; quantity demanded would exceed quantity

57

supplied. Consider a $2 price, for example. We see both from column 2 of the table and from the demand curve in Figure 3.6 that quantity demanded exceeds quantity supplied at that price. The result is a **shortage** (or *excess demand*) of 7000 bushels of corn. The $2 price discourages sellers from devoting resources to corn and encourages

---

CONSIDER THIS . . .

Ticket Scalping: A Bum Rap!

Ticket prices for athletic events and musical concerts are usually set far in advance of the events. Sometimes the original ticket price is too low to be the equilibrium price. Lines form at the ticket window and a severe shortage of tickets occurs at the printed price. What happens next? Buyers who are willing to pay more than the original price bid up the ticket price in resale ticket markets.

Tickets sometimes get resold for much greater amounts than the original price—market transactions known as "scalping." For example, an original buyer may resell a $75 ticket to a concert for $200. Reporters sometimes denounce scalpers for "ripping off" buyers by charging "exorbitant" prices.

But is scalping really a rip-off? We must first recognize that such ticket resales are voluntary transactions. If both buyer and seller did not expect to gain from the exchange, it would not occur! The seller must value the $200 more than seeing the event, and the buyer must value seeing the event at $200 or more. So there are no losers or victims here: Both buyer and seller benefit from the transaction. The scalping market simply redistributes assets (game or concert tickets) from those who would rather have the money (and the other things that the money can buy) to those who would rather have the tickets.

Does scalping impose losses or injury on the sponsors of the event? If the sponsors are injured, it is because they initially priced tickets below the equilibrium level. Perhaps they did this to create a long waiting line and the attendant news media publicity. Alternatively, they may have had a genuine desire to keep tickets affordable for lower-income, ardent fans. In either case, the event sponsors suffer an opportunity cost in the form of less ticket revenue than they might have otherwise received. But such losses are self-inflicted and separate and distinct from the fact that some tickets are later resold at a higher price.

So is ticket scalping undesirable? Not on economic grounds! It is an entirely voluntary activity that benefits both sellers and buyers.

---

consumers to desire more bushels than are available. The $2 price cannot persist as the equilibrium price. Many consumers who want to buy corn at this price will not obtain it. They will express a willingness to pay more than $2 to get corn. Competition among these buyers will drive up the price, eventually to the $3 equilibrium level. Unless disrupted by changes of supply or demand, this $3 price of corn will continue to prevail.

Rationing Function of Prices

The ability of the competitive forces of supply and demand to establish a price at which selling and buying decisions are consistent is called the rationing function of prices. In our case, the equilibrium price of $3 clears the market, leaving no burdensome surplus for sellers and no inconvenient shortage for potential buyers. And it is the combination of freely made individual decisions that sets this market-clearing price. In effect, the market outcome says that all buyers who are willing and able to pay $3 for a bushel of corn will obtain it; all buyers who cannot or will not pay $3 will go without corn. Similarly, all producers who are willing and able to offer corn for sale at $3 a bushel will sell it; all producers who cannot or will not sell for $3 per bushel will not sell their product.

Efficient Allocation

A competitive market such as that we have described not only rations goods to consumers but also allocates society's resources efficiently to the particular product. Competition among corn producers forces them to use the best technology and right mix of productive resources. If they didn't, their costs would be too high relative to the market price, and they would be unprofitable. The result is **productive efficiency:** the production of any particular good in the least costly way. When society produces corn at the lowest achievable per-unit cost, it is expending the least-valued combination of resources to produce that product and therefore is making available more-valued resources to produce other desired goods. Suppose society has only $100 worth of resources available. If it can produce a bushel of corn using $3 of those resources, then it will have available $97 of resources remaining to produce other goods. This is clearly better than producing the corn for $5 and having only $95 of resources available for the alternative uses.

Competitive markets also produce **allocative efficiency:** the *particular mix* of goods and services most highly valued by society (minimum-cost production assumed). For example, society wants land suitable for growing corn used for that purpose, not to grow dandelions. It wants diamonds to be used for jewelry, not crushed up and used as an additive to give concrete more sparkle. It wants iPods and MP4 players, not cassette players and tapes. Moreover, society does not want to devote all its resources to corn, diamonds, and portable digital media players. It wants to assign some resources to wheat, gasoline, and cell phones. Competitive markets make those allocatively efficient assignments.

The equilibrium price and quantity in competitive markets usually produce an assignment of resources that is "right" from an economic perspective. Demand essentially reflects the marginal benefit (MB) of the good, based on the utility received. Supply reflects the marginal cost (MC) of producing the good. The market ensures that firms produce all units of goods for which MB exceeds MC and no units for which MC exceeds MB. At the intersection of the demand and supply curves, MB equals MC and allocative efficiency results. As economists say, there is neither an "underallocaton of resources" nor an "overallocation of resources" to the product.

Changes in Supply, Demand, and Equilibrium

We know that demand might change because of fluctuations in consumer tastes or incomes, changes in consumer expectations, or variations in the prices of related goods. Supply might change in response to changes in resource prices, technology, or taxes. What effects will such changes in supply and demand have on equilibrium price and quantity?

Changes in Demand Suppose that the supply of some good (for example, health care) is constant and demand increases, as shown in Figure 3.7a. As a result, the new intersection of the supply and demand curves is at higher values on both the price and the quantity axes. Clearly, an increase in demand raises both equilibrium price and equilibrium quantity. Conversely, a decrease in demand such as that shown in Figure 3.7b reduces both equilibrium price and equilibrium quantity. (The value of graphical analysis is now apparent: We need not fumble with columns of figures to determine the outcomes; we need only compare the new and the old points of intersection on the graph.)

Changes in Supply What happens if the demand for some good (for example, flash drives) is constant but supply increases, as in Figure 3.7c? The new intersection of supply and demand is located at a lower equilibrium price but at a higher equilibrium quantity. An increase in supply reduces equilibrium price but increases equilibrium quantity. In contrast, if supply decreases, as in Figure 3.7d, equilibrium price rises while equilibrium quantity declines.

Complex Cases When both supply and demand change, the effect is a combination of the individual effects.

Supply Increase; Demand Decrease What effect will a supply increase and a demand decrease for some good (for example, apples) have on equilibrium price? Both changes decrease price, so the net result is a price drop greater than that resulting from either change alone.

What about equilibrium quantity? Here the effects of the changes in supply and demand are opposed: the increase in supply increases equilibrium quantity, but the decrease in demand reduces it. The direction of the change in equilibrium quantity depends on the relative sizes of the changes in supply and demand. If the increase in supply is larger than the decrease in demand, the equilibrium quantity will increase. But if the decrease in demand is greater than the increase in supply, the equilibrium quantity will decrease.

Supply Decrease; Demand Increase A decrease in supply and an increase in demand for some good (for example, gasoline) both increase price. Their combined effect is an increase in equilibrium price greater than that caused by either change separately. But their effect on the equilibrium quantity is again indeterminate, depending on the relative sizes of the changes in supply and demand. If the decrease in supply is larger than the increase in demand, the equilibrium quantity will decrease. In contrast, if the increase in demand is greater than the decrease in supply, the equilibrium quantity will increase.

Supply Increase; Demand Increase What if supply and demand both increase for some good (for example, cell phones)? A supply increase drops equilibrium price, while a demand increase boosts it. If the increase in supply is greater than the increase in demand, the equilibrium price will fall. If the opposite holds, the equilibrium price will rise.

The effect on equilibrium quantity is certain: The increases in supply and demand both raise the equilibrium quantity. Therefore, the equilibrium quantity will increase by an amount greater than that caused by either change alone.

Supply Decrease; Demand Decrease What about decreases in both supply and demand for some good (for example, new homes)? If the decrease in supply is greater

FIGURE 3.7 Changes in demand and supply and the effects on price and quantity. The increase in demand from D_1 to D_2 in (a) increases both equilibrium price and equilibrium quantity. The decrease in demand from D_3 to D_4 in (b) decreases both equilibrium price and equilibrium quantity. The increase in supply from S_1 to S_2 in (c) decreases equilibrium price and increases equilibrium quantity. The decline in supply from S_3 to S_4 in (d) increases equilibrium price and decreases equilibrium quantity. The boxes in the top right corners summarize the respective changes and outcomes. The upward arrows in the boxes signify increases in equilibrium price (P) and equilibrium quantity (Q); the downward arrows signify decreases in these items.

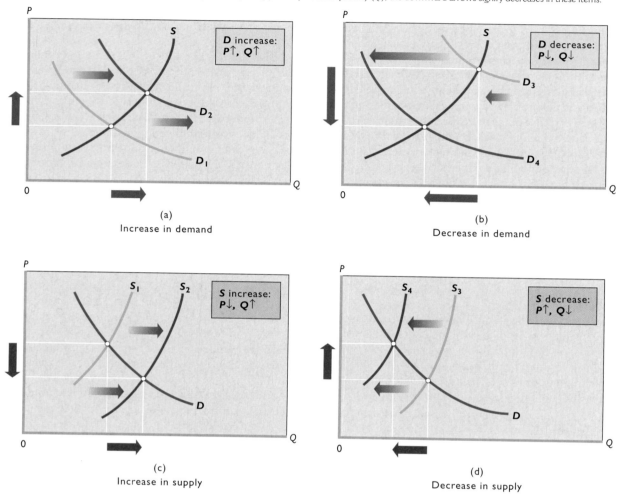

than the decrease in demand, equilibrium price will rise. If the reverse is true, equilibrium price will fall. Because the decreases in supply and demand each reduce equilibrium quantity, we can be sure that equilibrium quantity will fall.

Table 3.3 summarizes these four cases. To understand them fully, you should draw supply and demand diagrams for each case to confirm the effects listed in this table.

Special cases arise when a decrease in demand and a decrease in supply, or an increase in demand and an increase in supply, exactly cancel out. In both cases, the net effect on equilibrium price will be zero; price will not change.

The optional appendix accompanying this chapter provides additional examples of situations in which both supply and demand change at the same time.

TABLE 3.3 Effects of Changes in Both Supply and Demand

Change in Supply	Change in Demand	Effect on Equilibrium Price	Effect on Equilibrium Quantity
1. Increase	Decrease	Decrease	Indeterminate
2. Decrease	Increase	Increase	Indeterminate
3. Increase	Increase	Indeterminate	Increase
4. Decrease	Decrease	Indeterminate	Decrease

CONSIDER THIS . . .

Salsa and Coffee Beans

If you forget the other-things-equal assumption, you can encounter situations that *seem* to be in conflict with the laws of demand and supply. For example, suppose salsa manufacturers sell 1 million bottles of salsa at $4 a bottle in one year; 2 million bottles at $5 in the next year; and 3 million at $6 in the year thereafter. Price and quantity purchased vary directly, and these data seem to be at odds with the law of demand.

But there is no conflict here; the data do not refute the law of demand. The catch is that the law of demand's other-things-equal assumption has been violated over the three years in the example. Specifically, because of changing tastes and rising incomes, the demand for salsa has increased sharply, as in Figure 3.7a. The result is higher prices *and* larger quantities purchased.

Another example: The price of coffee beans occasionally shoots upward at the same time that the quantity of coffee beans harvested declines. These events seemingly contradict the direct relationship between price and quantity denoted by supply. The catch again is that the other-things-equal assumption underlying the upsloping supply curve is violated. Poor coffee harvests decrease supply, as in Figure 3.7d, increasing the equilibrium price of coffee and reducing the equilibrium quantity.

The laws of demand and supply are not refuted by observations of price and quantity made over periods of time in which either demand or supply curves shift.

Application: Government-Set Prices

Prices in most markets are free to rise or fall to their equilibrium levels, no matter how high or low those levels might be. However, government sometimes concludes that supply and demand will produce prices that are unfairly high for buyers or unfairly low for sellers. So government may place legal limits on how high or low a price or prices may go. Is that a good idea?

Price Ceilings on Gasoline

A **price ceiling** sets the maximum legal price a seller may charge for a product or service. A price at or below the ceiling is legal; a price above it is not. The rationale for establishing price ceilings (or ceiling prices) on specific products is that they purportedly enable consumers to obtain some "essential" good or service that they could not afford at the equilibrium price. Examples are rent controls and usury laws, which specify maximum "prices" in the forms of rent and interest that can be charged to borrowers.

Graphical Analysis We can easily show the effects of price ceilings graphically. Suppose that rapidly rising world income boosts the purchase of automobiles and shifts the demand for gasoline to the right so that the market equilibrium price reaches $3.50 per gallon, shown as P_0 in Figure 3.8. The rapidly rising price of gasoline greatly burdens low- and moderate-income households, which pressure government to "do something." To keep gasoline prices down, the government imposes a ceiling price P_c of $3 per gallon. To impact the market, a price ceiling must be below the equilibrium price. A ceiling price of $4, for example, would have had no effect on the price of gasoline in the current situation.

What are the effects of this $3 ceiling price? The rationing ability of the free market is rendered ineffective. Because the ceiling price P_c is below the market-clearing price P_0, there is a lasting shortage of gasoline. The quantity of gasoline demanded at P_c is Q_d and the quantity supplied is only Q_s; a persistent excess demand or shortage of amount $Q_d - Q_s$ occurs.

The price ceiling P_c prevents the usual market adjustment in which competition among buyers bids up price, inducing more production and rationing some buyers out of the market. That process would normally continue until the shortage disappeared at the equilibrium price and quantity, P_0 and Q_0.

By preventing these market adjustments from occurring, the price ceiling poses two related problems.

FIGURE 3.8 A price ceiling. A price ceiling is a maximum legal price such as P_c. When the ceiling price is below the equilibrium price, a persistent product shortage results. Here that shortage is shown by the horizontal distance between Q_d and Q_s.

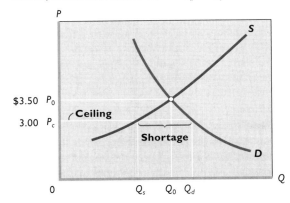

Word A Legal Market for Human Organs?

A Legal Market Might Eliminate the Present Shortage of Human Organs for Transplant. But There Are Many Serious Objections to "Turning Human Body Parts into Commodities" for Purchase and Sale.

It has become increasingly commonplace in medicine to transplant kidneys, lungs, livers, corneas, pancreases, and hearts from deceased individuals to those whose organs have failed or are failing. But surgeons and many of their patients face a growing problem: There are shortages of donated organs available for transplant. Not everyone who needs a transplant can get one. In 2010, there were 105,000 Americans on the waiting list for transplants. Indeed, an inadequate supply of donated organs causes an estimated 6900 deaths in the United States each year.

Why Shortages? Seldom do we hear of shortages of desired goods in market economies. What is different about organs for transplant? One difference is that no legal market exists for human organs. To understand this situation,

observe the demand curve D_1 and supply curve S_1 in the accompanying figure. The downward slope of the demand curve tells us that if there were a market for human organs, the quantity of organs demanded would be greater at lower prices than at higher prices. Vertical supply curve S_1 represents the fixed quantity of human organs now donated via consent before death. Because the price of these donated organs is in effect zero, quantity demanded Q_3 exceeds quantity supplied Q_1. The shortage of $Q_3 - Q_1$ is rationed through a waiting list of those in medical need of transplants. Many people die while still on the waiting list.

Use of a Market A market for human organs would increase the incentive to donate organs. Such a market might work like this: An individual might specify in a legal document that he or she is willing to sell one or more usable human organs upon death or near-death. The person could specify where the money from the sale would go, for example, to family, a church, an educational institution, or a charity. Firms would then emerge to purchase organs and resell them where needed for profit. Under such a

Rationing Problem How will the available supply Q_s be apportioned among buyers who want the greater amount Q_d? Should gasoline be distributed on a first-come, first-served basis, that is, to those willing and able to get in line the soonest or stay in line the longest? Or should gas stations distribute it on the basis of favoritism? Since an unregulated shortage does not lead to an equitable distribution of gasoline, the government must establish some formal system for rationing it to consumers. One option is to issue ration coupons, which authorize bearers to purchase a fixed amount of gasoline per month. The rationing system might entail first the printing of coupons for Q_s gallons of gasoline and then the equal distribution of the coupons among consumers so that the wealthy family of four and the poor family of four both receive the same number of coupons.

Black Markets But ration coupons would not prevent a second problem from arising. The demand curve in Figure 3.8 reveals that many buyers are willing to pay more than

the ceiling price P_c. And, of course, it is more profitable for gasoline stations to sell at prices above the ceiling. Thus, despite a sizable enforcement bureaucracy that would have to accompany the price controls, *black markets* in which gasoline is illegally bought and sold at prices above the legal limits will flourish. Counterfeiting of ration coupons will also be a problem. And since the price of gasoline is now "set by government," government might face political pressure to set the price even lower.

Rent Controls

About 200 cities in the United States, including New York City, Boston, and San Francisco, have at one time or another enacted rent controls: maximum rents established by law (or, more recently, maximum rent increases for existing tenants). Such laws are well intended. Their goals are to protect low-income families from escalating rents caused by perceived housing shortages and to make housing more affordable to the poor.

system, the supply curve of usable organs would take on the normal upward slope of typical supply curves. The higher the expected price of an organ, the greater the number of people who would be willing to have their organs sold at death. Suppose that the supply curve is S_2 in the figure. At the equilibrium price P_1, the number of organs made available for transplant (Q_2) would equal the number purchased for transplant (also Q_2). In this generalized case, the shortage of organs would be eliminated and, of particular importance, the number of organs available for transplanting would rise from Q_1 to Q_2. This means more lives would be saved and enhanced than under the present donor system.

Objections In view of this positive outcome, why is there no such market for human organs? Critics of market-based solutions have two main objections. The first is a moral objection: Critics feel that turning human organs into commodities commercializes human beings and diminishes the special nature of human life. They say there is something unseemly about selling and buying body organs as if they were bushels of wheat or ounces of gold. (There is, however, a market for blood!) Moreover, critics note that the market would ration the available organs (as represented by Q_2 in the figure) to people who either can afford them (at P_1) or have health insurance for transplants. The poor and uninsured would be left out.

Second, a health-cost objection suggests that a market for body organs would greatly increase the cost of health care. Rather than obtaining freely donated (although "too few") body organs, patients or their insurance companies would have to pay market prices for them, further increasing the cost of medical care.

Rebuttal Supporters of market-based solutions to organ shortages point out that the laws against selling organs are simply driving the market underground. Worldwide, an estimated $1 billion-per-year illegal market in human organs has emerged. As in other illegal markets, the unscrupulous tend to thrive. This fact is dramatized by the accompanying photo, in which four Pakistani villagers show off their scars after they each sold a kidney to pay off debts. Supporters say that legalization of the market for human organs would increase organ supply from legal sources, drive down the price of organs, and reduce the abuses such as those now taking place in illegal markets.

What have been the actual economic effects? On the demand side, the below-equilibrium rents attract a larger number of renters. Some are locals seeking to move into their own places after sharing housing with friends or family. Others are outsiders attracted into the area by the artificially lower rents. But a large problem occurs on the supply side. Price controls make it less attractive for landlords to offer housing on the rental market. In the short run, owners may sell their rental units or convert them to condominiums. In the long run, low rents make it unprofitable for owners to repair or renovate their rental units. (Rent controls are one cause of the many abandoned apartment buildings found in larger cities.) Also, insurance companies, pension funds, and other potential new investors in housing will find it more profitable to invest in office buildings, shopping malls, or motels, where rents are not controlled.

In brief, rent controls distort market signals and thus resources are misallocated: Too few resources are allocated to rental housing and too many to alternative uses.

Ironically, although rent controls are often legislated to lessen the effects of perceived housing shortages, controls in fact are a primary cause of such shortages. For that reason, most American cities either have abandoned or are in the process of dismantling rent controls.

Price Floors on Wheat

A **price floor** is a minimum price fixed by the government. A price at or above the price floor is legal; a price below it is not. Price floors above equilibrium prices are usually invoked when society feels that the free functioning of the market system has not provided a sufficient income for certain groups of resource suppliers or producers. Supported prices for agricultural products and current minimum wages are two examples of price (or wage) floors. Let's look at the former.

Suppose that many farmers have extremely low incomes when the price of wheat is at its equilibrium value of $2 per bushel. The government decides to help out by establishing a legal price floor or price support of $3 per bushel.

FIGURE 3.9 A price floor. A price floor is a minimum legal price such as P_f. When the price floor is above the equilibrium price, a persistent product surplus results. Here that surplus is shown by the horizontal distance between Q_s and Q_d.

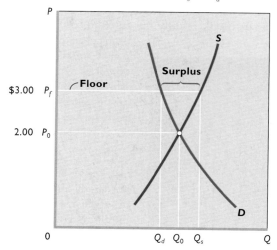

What will be the effects? At any price above the equilibrium price, quantity supplied will exceed quantity demanded—that is, there will be a persistent excess supply or surplus of the product. Farmers will be willing to produce and offer for sale more than private buyers are willing to purchase at the price floor. As we saw with a price ceiling, an imposed legal price disrupts the rationing ability of the free market.

Graphical Analysis Figure 3.9 illustrates the effect of a price floor graphically. Suppose that S and D are the supply and demand curves for wheat. Equilibrium price and quantity are P_0 and Q_0, respectively. If the government imposes a price floor of P_f, farmers will produce Q_s but private buyers will purchase only Q_d. The surplus is the excess of Q_s over Q_d.

The government may cope with the surplus resulting from a price floor in two ways:

- It can restrict supply (for example, by instituting acreage allotments by which farmers agree to take a certain amount of land out of production) or increase demand (for example, by researching new uses for the product involved). These actions may reduce the difference between the equilibrium price and the price floor and that way reduce the size of the resulting surplus.
- If these efforts are not wholly successful, then the government must purchase the surplus output at the $3 price (thereby subsidizing farmers) and store or otherwise dispose of it.

Additional Consequences Price floors such as P_f in Figure 3.9 not only disrupt the rationing ability of prices

but distort resource allocation. Without the price floor, the $2 equilibrium price of wheat would cause financial losses and force high-cost wheat producers to plant other crops or abandon farming altogether. But the $3 price floor allows them to continue to grow wheat and remain farmers. So society devotes too many of its scarce resources to wheat production and too few to producing other, more valuable, goods and services. It fails to achieve allocative efficiency.

That's not all. Consumers of wheat-based products pay higher prices because of the price floor. Taxpayers pay higher taxes to finance the government's purchase of the surplus. Also, the price floor causes potential environmental damage by encouraging wheat farmers to bring hilly, erosion-prone "marginal land" into production. The higher price also prompts imports of wheat. But, since such imports would increase the quantity of wheat supplied and thus undermine the price floor, the government needs to erect tariffs (taxes on imports) to keep the foreign wheat out. Such tariffs usually prompt other countries to retaliate with their own tariffs against U.S. agricultural or manufacturing exports.

INTERACTIVE GRAPHS
G 3.2
Price floors and ceilings

So it is easy to see why economists "sound the alarm" when politicians advocate imposing price ceilings or price floors such as price controls, rent controls, interest-rate lids, or agricultural price supports. In all these cases, good intentions lead to bad economic outcomes. Government-controlled prices cause shortages or surpluses, distort resource allocation, and produce negative side effects.

QUICK REVIEW 3.3

- In competitive markets, prices adjust to the equilibrium level at which quantity demanded equals quantity supplied.
- The equilibrium price and quantity are those indicated by the intersection of the supply and demand curves for any product or resource.
- An increase in demand increases equilibrium price and quantity; a decrease in demand decreases equilibrium price and quantity.
- An increase in supply reduces equilibrium price but increases equilibrium quantity; a decrease in supply increases equilibrium price but reduces equilibrium quantity.
- Over time, equilibrium price and quantity may change in directions that seem at odds with the laws of demand and supply because the other-things-equal assumption is violated.
- Government-controlled prices in the form of ceilings and floors stifle the rationing function of prices, distort resource allocations, and cause negative side effects.

Summary

1. Demand is a schedule or curve representing the willingness of buyers in a specific period to purchase a particular product at each of various prices. The law of demand implies that consumers will buy more of a product at a low price than at a high price. So, other things equal, the relationship between price and quantity demanded is negative or inverse and is graphed as a downsloping curve.

2. Market demand curves are found by adding horizontally the demand curves of the many individual consumers in the market.

3. Changes in one or more of the determinants of demand (consumer tastes, the number of buyers in the market, the money incomes of consumers, the prices of related goods, and consumer expectations) shift the market demand curve. A shift to the right is an increase in demand; a shift to the left is a decrease in demand. A change in demand is different from a change in the quantity demanded, the latter being a movement from one point to another point on a fixed demand curve because of a change in the product's price.

4. Supply is a schedule or curve showing the amounts of a product that producers are willing to offer in the market at each possible price during a specific period. The law of supply states that, other things equal, producers will offer more of a product at a high price than at a low price. Thus, the relationship between price and quantity supplied is positive or direct, and supply is graphed as an upsloping curve.

5. The market supply curve is the horizontal summation of the supply curves of the individual producers of the product.

6. Changes in one or more of the determinants of supply (resource prices, production techniques, taxes or subsidies, the prices of other goods, producer expectations, or the number of sellers in the market) shift the supply curve of a product. A shift to the right is an increase in supply; a shift to the left is a decrease in supply. In contrast, a change in the price of the product being considered causes a change in the quantity supplied, which is shown as a movement from one point to another point on a fixed supply curve.

7. The equilibrium price and quantity are established at the intersection of the supply and demand curves. The interaction of market demand and market supply adjusts the price to the point at which the quantities demanded and supplied are equal. This is the equilibrium price. The corresponding quantity is the equilibrium quantity.

8. The ability of market forces to synchronize selling and buying decisions to eliminate potential surpluses and shortages is known as the rationing function of prices. The equilibrium quantity in competitive markets reflects both productive efficiency (least-cost production) and allocative efficiency (producing the right amount of the product relative to other products).

9. A change in either demand or supply changes the equilibrium price and quantity. Increases in demand raise both equilibrium price and equilibrium quantity; decreases in demand lower both equilibrium price and equilibrium quantity. Increases in supply lower equilibrium price and raise equilibrium quantity; decreases in supply raise equilibrium price and lower equilibrium quantity.

10. Simultaneous changes in demand and supply affect equilibrium price and quantity in various ways, depending on their direction and relative magnitudes (see Table 3.3).

11. A price ceiling is a maximum price set by government and is designed to help consumers. Effective price ceilings produce persistent product shortages, and if an equitable distribution of the product is sought, government must ration the product to consumers.

12. A price floor is a minimum price set by government and is designed to aid producers. Effective price floors lead to persistent product surpluses; the government must either purchase the product or eliminate the surplus by imposing restrictions on production or increasing private demand.

13. Legally fixed prices stifle the rationing function of prices and distort the allocation of resources.

Terms and Concepts

demand

demand schedule

law of demand

diminishing marginal utility

income effect

substitution effect

demand curve

determinants of demand

normal goods

inferior goods

substitute good

complementary good

change in demand

change in quantity demanded

supply

supply schedule

law of supply

supply curve

determinants of supply

change in supply

change in quantity supplied

equilibrium price

equilibrium quantity

surplus

shortage

productive efficiency

allocative efficiency

price ceiling

price floor

Questions

1. Explain the law of demand. Why does a demand curve slope downward? How is a market demand curve derived from individual demand curves? **LO1**

2. What are the determinants of demand? What happens to the demand curve when any of these determinants change? Distinguish between a change in demand and a movement along a fixed demand curve, noting the cause(s) of each. **LO1**

3. What effect will each of the following have on the demand for small automobiles such as the Mini-Cooper and Smart car? **LO1**

   a. Small automobiles become more fashionable.

   b. The price of large automobiles rises (with the price of small autos remaining the same).

   c. Income declines and small autos are an inferior good.

   d. Consumers anticipate that the price of small autos will greatly come down in the near future.

   e. The price of gasoline substantially drops.

4. Explain the law of supply. Why does the supply curve slope upward? How is the market supply curve derived from the supply curves of individual producers? **LO2**

5. What are the determinants of supply? What happens to the supply curve when any of these determinants changes? Distinguish between a change in supply and a change in the quantity supplied, noting the cause(s) of each. **LO2**

6. What effect will each of the following have on the supply of *auto* tires? **LO2**

   a. A technological advance in the methods of producing tires.

   b. A decline in the number of firms in the tire industry.

   c. An increase in the prices of rubber used in the production of tires.

   d. The expectation that the equilibrium price of auto tires will be lower in the future than currently.

   e. A decline in the price of the large tires used for semi trucks and earth-hauling rigs (with no change in the price of auto tires).

   f. The levying of a per-unit tax on each auto tire sold.

   g. The granting of a 50-cent-per-unit subsidy for each auto tire produced.

7. "In the corn market, demand often exceeds supply and supply sometimes exceeds demand." "The price of corn rises and falls in response to changes in supply and demand." In which of these two statements are the terms "supply" and "demand" used correctly? Explain. **LO2**

8. In 2001 an outbreak of hoof-and-mouth disease in Europe led to the burning of millions of cattle carcasses. What impact do you think this had on the supply of cattle hides, hide prices, the supply of leather goods, and the price of leather goods? **LO4**

9. Critically evaluate: "In comparing the two equilibrium positions in Figure 3.7b, I note that a smaller amount is actually demanded at a lower price. This refutes the law of demand." **LO4**

10. For each stock in the stock market, the number of shares sold daily equals the number of shares purchased. That is, the quantity of each firm's shares demanded equals the quantity supplied. So, if this equality always occurs, why do the prices of stock shares ever change? **LO4**

11. Suppose the total demand for wheat and the total supply of wheat per month in the Kansas City grain market are as shown in the table below. Suppose that the government establishes a price ceiling of $3.70 for wheat. What might prompt the government to establish this price ceiling? Explain carefully the main effects. Demonstrate your answer graphically. Next, suppose that the government establishes a price floor of $4.60 for wheat. What will be the main effects of this price floor? Demonstrate your answer graphically. **LO5**

Thousands of Bushels Demanded	Price per Bushel	Thousands of Bushels Supplied
85	$3.40	72
80	3.70	73
75	4.00	75
70	4.30	77
65	4.60	79
60	4.90	81

12. What do economists mean when they say "price floors and ceilings stifle the rationing function of prices and distort resource allocation"? **LO5**

13. **LAST WORD** In some countries, such as France, every corpse is available for doctors to "harvest" for organs unless the deceased, while still alive, signed a form forbidding the organs to be harvested. In the USA, it is the opposite: No harvesting is allowed unless the deceased had signed, while still alive, an organ donor form authorizing doctors to harvest any needed organs. Use supply and demand figures to show in which country organ shortages are likely to be less severe.

Problems

1. Suppose there are three buyers of candy in a market: Tex, Dex, and Rex. The market demand and the individual demands of Tex, Dex, and Rex are shown on the next page. **LO1**

   a. Fill in the table for the missing values.

   b. Which buyer demands the least at a price of $5? The most at a price of $7?

   c. Which buyer's quantity demanded increases the most when the price is lowered from $7 to $6?

d. Which direction would the market demand curve shift if Tex withdrew from the market? What if Dex doubled his purchases at each possible price?

e. Suppose that at a price of $6, the total quantity demanded increases from 19 to 38. Is this a "change in the quantity demanded" or a "change in demand"?

Price per Candy	Individual Quantities Demanded			Total Quantity Demanded
	Tex	Dex	Rex	
$8	3 +	1 +	0 =	____
7	8 +	2 +	____ =	12
6	____ +	3 +	4 =	19
5	17 +	____ +	6 =	27
4	23 +	5 +	8 =	____

2. The figure below shows the supply curve for tennis balls, S_1, for Drop Volley Tennis, a producer of tennis equipment. Use the figure and the table below to give your answers to the following questions. LO2

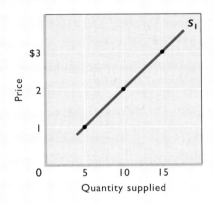

a. Use the figure to fill in the quantity supplied on supply curve S_1 for each price in the table below.

Price	S_1 Quantity Supplied	S_2 Quantity Supplied	Change in Quantity Supplied
$3	____	4	____
2	____	2	____
1	____	0	____

b. If production costs were to increase, the quantities supplied at each price would be as shown by the third column of the table ("S_2 Quantity Supplied"). Use that data to draw supply curve S_2 on the same graph as supply curve S_1.

c. In the fourth column of the table, enter the amount by which the quantity supplied at each price changes due to

the increase in product costs. (Use positive numbers for increases and negative numbers for decreases.)

d. Did the increase in production costs cause a "decrease in supply" or a "decrease in quantity supplied"?

3. Refer to the expanded table below from question 11. LO3

a. What is the equilibrium price? At what price is there neither a shortage nor a surplus? Fill in the surplus-shortage column and use it to confirm your answers.

b. Graph the demand for wheat and the supply of wheat. Be sure to label the axes of your graph correctly. Label equilibrium price P and equilibrium quantity Q.

c. How big is the surplus or shortage at $3.40? At $4.90? How big a surplus or shortage results if the price is 60 cents higher than the equilibrium price? 30 cents lower than the equilibrium price?

Thousands of Bushels Demanded	Price per Bushel	Thousands of Bushels Supplied	Surplus (+) or Shortage (−)
85	$3.40	72	_____
80	3.70	73	_____
75	4.00	75	_____
70	4.30	77	_____
65	4.60	79	_____
60	4.90	81	_____

4. How will each of the following changes in demand and/or supply affect equilibrium price and equilibrium quantity in a competitive market; that is, do price and quantity rise, fall, or remain unchanged, or are the answers indeterminate because they depend on the magnitudes of the shifts? Use supply and demand to verify your answers. LO4

a. Supply decreases and demand is constant.

b. Demand decreases and supply is constant.

c. Supply increases and demand is constant.

d. Demand increases and supply increases.

e. Demand increases and supply is constant.

f. Supply increases and demand decreases.

g. Demand increases and supply decreases.

h. Demand decreases and supply decreases.

5. Use two market diagrams to explain how an increase in state subsidies to public colleges might affect tuition and enrollments in both public and private colleges. LO4

6. ADVANCED ANALYSIS Assume that demand for a commodity is represented by the equation $P = 10 - .2Q_d$ and supply by the equation $P = 2 + .2Q_s$, where Q_d and Q_s are quantity demanded and quantity supplied, respectively, and P is price. Using the equilibrium condition $Q_s = Q_d$, solve the equations to determine equilibrium price. Now determine equilibrium quantity. LO4

7. Suppose that the demand and supply schedules for rental apartments in the city of Gotham are as given in the table below. **LO5**

Monthly Rent	Apartments Demanded	Apartments Supplied
$2500	10,000	15,000
2000	12,500	12,500
1500	15,000	10,000
1000	17,500	7500
500	20,000	5000

a. What is the market equilibrium rental price per month and the market equilibrium number of apartments demanded and supplied?

b. If the local government can enforce a rent-control law that sets the maximum monthly rent at $1500, will there be a surplus or a shortage? Of how many units? And how many units will actually be rented each month?

c. Suppose that a new government is elected that wants to keep out the poor. It declares that the minimum rent that can be charged is $2500 per month. If the government can enforce that price floor, will there be a surplus or a shortage? Of how many units? And how many units will actually be rented each month?

d. Suppose that the government wishes to decrease the market equilibrium monthly rent by increasing the supply of housing. Assuming that demand remains unchanged, by how many units of housing would the government have to increase the supply of housing in order to get the market equilibrium rental price to fall to $1500 per month? To $1000 per month? To $500 per month?

FURTHER TEST YOUR KNOWLEDGE AT
www.mcconnell19e.com

At the text's Online Learning Center (OLC), **www.mcconnell19e.com**, you will find one or more Web-based questions that require information from the Internet to answer. We urge you to check them out; they will familiarize you with Web sites that may be helpful in other courses and perhaps even in your career. The OLC also features multiple-choice questions that give instant feedback and provides other helpful ways to further test your knowledge of the chapter.

Additional Examples of Supply and Demand

Our discussion has clearly demonstrated that supply and demand analysis is a powerful tool for understanding equilibrium prices and quantities. The information provided in the main body of this chapter is fully sufficient for moving forward in the book, but you may find that additional examples of supply and demand are helpful. This optional appendix provides several concrete illustrations of changes in supply and demand.

Your instructor may assign all, some, or none of this appendix, depending on time availability and personal preference.

Changes in Supply and Demand

As Figure 3.7 of this chapter demonstrates, changes in supply and demand cause changes in price, quantity, or both. The following applications illustrate this fact in several real-world markets. The simplest situations are those in which either supply changes while demand remains constant or demand changes while supply remains constant. Let's consider two such simple cases first, before looking at more complex applications.

Lettuce

Every now and then we hear on the news that extreme weather has severely reduced the size of some crop. Suppose, for example, that a severe freeze destroys a sizable portion of the lettuce crop. This unfortunate situation implies a significant decline in supply, which we represent as a leftward shift of the supply curve from S_1 to S_2 in Figure 1. At each price, consumers desire as much lettuce as before, so the freeze does not affect the demand for lettuce. That is, demand curve D_1 does not shift.

What are the consequences of the reduced supply of lettuce for equilibrium price and quantity? As shown in Figure 1, the leftward shift of the supply curve disrupts the previous equilibrium in the market for lettuce and drives the equilibrium price upward upward from P_1 to P_2. Consumers respond to that price hike by reducing the quantity of lettuce demanded from Q_1 to Q_2. Equilibrium is restored at P_2 and Q_2.

Consumers who are willing and able to pay price P_2 obtain lettuce; consumers unwilling or unable to pay that

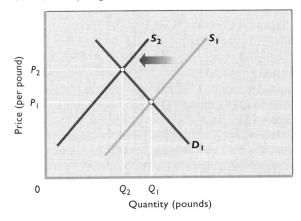

FIGURE 1 The market for lettuce. The decrease in the supply of lettuce, shown here by the shift from S_1 to S_2, increases the equilibrium price of lettuce from P_1 to P_2 and reduces the equilibrium quantity from Q_1 to Q_2.

price do not. Some consumers continue to buy as much lettuce as before, even at the higher price. Others buy some lettuce but not as much as before, and still others opt out of the market completely. The latter two groups use the money they would have spent on lettuce to obtain other products, say, carrots. (Because of our other-things-equal assumption, the prices of other products have not changed.)

Exchange Rates

Exchange rates are the prices at which one currency can be traded (exchanged) for another. Exchange rates are normally determined in foreign exchange markets. One of the largest foreign exchange markets is the euro-dollar market in which the currency used in most of Europe, the *euro*, is exchanged for U.S. dollars. In the United States, this market is set up so that euros are priced in dollars—that is, the "product" being traded is euros and the "price" to buy that product is quoted in dollars. Thus, the market equilibrium price one day might be $1.25 to buy 1 euro, while on another day it might be $1.50 to buy 1 euro.

Foreign exchange markets are used by individuals and companies that need to make purchases or payments in a different currency. U.S. companies exporting goods to Germany, for instance, wish to be paid in U.S. dollars.

FIGURE 2 The market for euros. The increase in the demand for euros, shown here by the shift from D_1 to D_2, increases the equilibrium price of one euro from $1.25 to $1.50 and increases the equilibrium quantity of euros that are exchanged from Q_1 to Q_2. The dollar has depreciated.

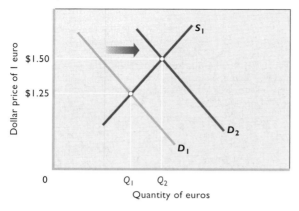

FIGURE 3 The market for pink salmon. In the last several decades, the supply of pink salmon has increased and the demand for pink salmon has decreased. As a result, the price of pink salmon has declined, as from P_1 to P_2. Because supply has increased by more than demand has decreased, the equilibrium quantity of pink salmon has increased, as from Q_1 to Q_2.

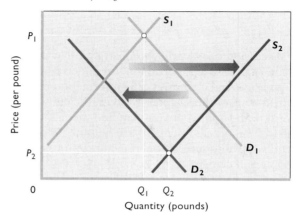

Thus, their German customers will need to convert euros into dollars. The euros that they bring to the euro-dollar market will become part of the overall market supply of euros. Conversely, an American mutual fund may wish to purchase some French real estate outside of Paris. But to purchase that real estate, it will need to pay in euros because the current French owners will only accept payment in euros. Thus, the American mutual fund has a demand to purchase euros that will form part of the overall market demand for euros. The fund will bring dollars to the euro-dollar foreign exchange market in order to purchase the euros it desires.

Sometimes, the demand for euros increases. This might be because a European product surges in popularity in foreign countries. For example, if a new German-made automobile is a big hit in the United States, American car dealers will demand more euros with which to pay for more units of that new model. This will shift the demand curve for euros to the right, as from D_1 to D_2 in Figure 2. Given the fixed euro supply curve S_1, the increase in demand raises the equilibrium exchange rate (the equilibrium number of dollars needed to purchase 1 euro) from $1.25 to $1.50. The equilibrium quantity of euros purchased increases from Q_1 to Q_2. Because a higher dollar amount is now needed to purchase one euro, economists say that the dollar has *depreciated*—gone down in value—relative to the euro. Alternatively, the euro has *appreciated*—gone up in value—relative to the dollar, because one euro now buys $1.50 rather than $1.25.

Pink Salmon

Now let's see what happens when both supply and demand change at the same time. Several decades ago, people who caught salmon earned as much as $1 for each pound of pink salmon—the type of salmon most commonly used for canning. In Figure 3 that price is represented as P_1, at the intersection of supply curve S_1 and demand curve D_1. The corresponding quantity of pink salmon is shown as Q_1 pounds.

As time passed, supply and demand changed in the market for pink salmon. On the supply side, improved technology in the form of larger, more efficient fishing boats greatly increased the catch and lowered the cost of obtaining it. Also, high profits at price P_1 encouraged many new fishers to enter the industry. As a result of these changes, the supply of pink salmon greatly increased and the supply curve shifted to the right, as from S_1 to S_2 in Figure 3.

Over the same years, the demand for pink salmon declined, as represented by the leftward shift from D_1 to D_2 in Figure 3. That decrease was caused by increases in consumer income and reductions of the price of substitute products. As buyers' incomes rose, consumers shifted demand away from canned fish and toward higher-quality fresh or frozen fish, including more-valued Atlantic, chinook, sockeye, and coho salmon. Moreover, the emergence of fish farming, in which salmon are raised in ocean net pens, lowered the prices of these substitute species. That, too, reduced the demand for pink salmon.

CHAPTER THREE APPENDIX 71

The altered supply and demand reduced the price of pink salmon to as low as \$.10 per pound, as represented by the drop in price from P_1 to P_2 in Figure 3. Both the supply increase and the demand decrease helped reduce the equilibrium price. However, in this particular case the equilibrium quantity of pink salmon increased, as represented by the move from Q_1 to Q_2. Both shifts reduced the equilibrium price, but equilibrium quantity increased because the increase in supply exceeded the decrease in demand.

Gasoline

The price of gasoline in the United States has increased rapidly several times during the past several years. For example, the average price of a gallon of gasoline rose from around \$2.25 in January 2007 to about \$4.10 in July 2008. What caused this 80 percent rise in the price of gasoline? How would we diagram this increase?

We begin in Figure 4 with the price of a gallon of gasoline at P_1, representing the \$2.25 price. Simultaneous supply and demand factors disturbed this equilibrium. Supply uncertainties relating to Middle East politics and warfare and expanded demand for oil by fast-growing countries such as China pushed up the price of a barrel of oil from \$50 per barrel in January 2007 to \$145 per barrel in July 2008. Oil is the main input for producing gasoline, so any sustained rise in its price boosts the per-unit cost of producing gasoline. Such cost rises decrease the supply of gasoline, as represented by the leftward shift of the supply curve from S_1 to S_2 in Figure 4. At times refinery breakdowns in the United States also contributed to this reduced supply.

While the supply of gasoline declined between January 2007 and July 2008, the demand for gasoline increased, as depicted by the rightward shift of the demand curve from D_1 to D_2. Incomes in general were rising over this period because the U.S. economy was rapidly expanding. Rising incomes raise demand for all normal goods, including gasoline. An increased number of low-gas-mileage SUVs and light trucks on the road also contributed to growing gas demand.

The combined decline in gasoline supply and increase in gasoline demand boosted the price of gasoline from \$2.25 to \$4.10, as represented by the rise from P_1 to P_2 in Figure 4. Because the demand increase outweighed the supply decrease, the equilibrium quantity expanded, here from Q_1 to Q_2.

In other periods the price of gasoline has *declined* as the demand for gasoline has increased. Test your understanding of the analysis by explaining how such a price decrease could occur.

Sushi

Sushi bars are springing up like Starbucks in American cities (well, maybe not that fast!). Consumption of sushi, the raw-fish delicacy from Japan, has soared in the United States in recent years. Nevertheless, the price of sushi has remained relatively constant.

Supply and demand analysis helps explain this circumstance of increased quantity and constant price. A change in tastes has increased the U.S. demand for sushi. Many consumers of sushi find it highly tasty when they try it. And, as implied by the growing number of sushi bars in the United States, the supply of sushi has also expanded.

We represent these supply and demand changes in Figure 5 as the rightward shift of the demand curve from D_1 to D_2 and the rightward shift of the supply curve from S_1 to S_2. Observe that the equilibrium quantity of sushi increases from Q_1 to Q_2 and equilibrium price remains constant at P_1. The increase in supply, which taken alone would reduce price, has perfectly offset the increase in demand, which taken alone would raise price. The price of sushi does not change, but the equilibrium quantity greatly increases because both the increase in demand and the increase in supply expand purchases and sales.

Simultaneous increases in demand and supply can cause price to either rise, fall, or remain constant, depending on the relative magnitudes of the supply and demand increases. In this case, price remained constant.

FIGURE 4 The market for gasoline. An increase in the demand for gasoline, as shown by the shift from D_1 to D_2, coupled with a decrease in supply, as shown by the shift from S_1 to S_2, boosts equilibrium price (here from P_1 to P_2). In this case, equilibrium quantity increases from Q_1 to Q_2 because the increase in demand outweighs the decrease in supply.

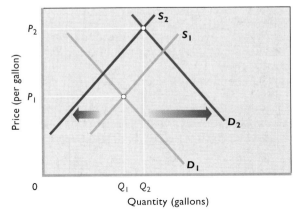

FIGURE 5 The market for sushi. Equal increases in the demand for sushi, as from D_1 to D_2, and in the supply of sushi, as from S_1 to S_2, expand the equilibrium quantity of sushi (here from Q_1 to Q_2) while leaving the price of sushi unchanged at P_1.

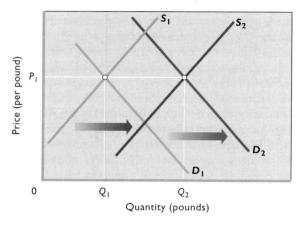

FIGURE 6 The market for tickets to the Olympic women's figure skating finals. The demand curve D and supply curve S for the Olympic women's figure skating finals produce an equilibrium price that is above the P_1 price printed on the ticket. At price P_1 the quantity of tickets demanded, Q_2, greatly exceeds the quantity of tickets available (Q_1). The resulting shortage of ab ($= Q_2Q_1$) gives rise to a legal or illegal secondary market.

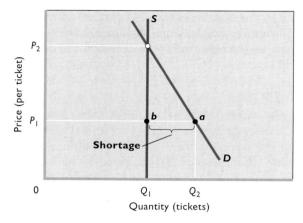

Preset Prices

In the body of this chapter, we saw that an effective government-imposed price ceiling (legal maximum price) causes quantity demanded to exceed quantity supplied—a shortage. An effective government-imposed price floor (legal minimum price) causes quantity supplied to exceed quantity demanded—a surplus. Put simply: Shortages result when prices are set below, and surpluses result when prices are set above, equilibrium prices.

We now want to establish that shortages and surpluses can occur in markets other than those in which government imposes price floors and ceilings. Such market imbalances happen when the seller or sellers set prices in advance of sales and the prices selected turn out to be below or above equilibrium prices. Consider the following two examples.

Olympic Figure Skating Finals

Tickets for the women's figure skating championship at the Olympics are among the world's "hottest tickets." The popularity of this event and the high incomes of buyers translate into tremendous ticket demand. The Olympic officials set the price for the tickets in advance. Invariably, the price, although high, is considerably below the equilibrium price that would equate quantity demanded and quantity supplied. A severe shortage of tickets therefore occurs in this *primary market*—the market involving the official ticket office.

The shortage, in turn, creates a *secondary market* in which buyers bid for tickets held by initial purchasers rather than the original seller. Scalping tickets—selling them above the original ticket price—may be legal or illegal, depending on local laws.

Figure 6 shows how the shortage in the primary ticket market looks in terms of supply and demand analysis. Demand curve D represents the strong demand for tickets and supply curve S represents the supply of tickets. The supply curve is vertical because a fixed number of tickets are printed to match the capacity of the arena. At the printed ticket price of P_1, the quantity of tickets demanded, Q_2, exceeds the quantity supplied, Q_1. The result is a shortage of ab—the horizontal distance between Q_2 and Q_1 in the primary market.

If the printed ticket price had been the higher equilibrium price P_2, no shortage of tickets would have occurred. But at the lower price P_1, a shortage and secondary ticket market will emerge among those buyers willing to pay more than the printed ticket price and those sellers willing to sell their purchased tickets for more than the original price. Wherever there are shortages and secondary markets, it is safe to assume the original price was set below the equilibrium price.

Olympic Curling Preliminaries

Contrast the shortage of tickets for the women's figure skating finals at the Olympics to the surplus of tickets for one of the preliminary curling matches. For the uninitiated, curling is a sport in which participants slide a heavy round object called a "stone" down the ice toward a target while teammates called "sweepers" use brooms to alter the course of the stone when desired.

Curling is a popular spectator sport in a few nations such as Canada, but it does not draw many fans in most countries. So the demand for tickets to most of the preliminary curling events is not very strong. We demonstrate this weak demand as D in Figure 7. As in our previous example, the supply of tickets is fixed by the size of the arena and is shown as vertical line S.

We represent the printed ticket price as P_1 in Figure 7. In this case the printed price is much higher than the equilibrium price of P_2. At the printed ticket price, quantity supplied is Q_1 and quantity demanded is Q_2. So a surplus of tickets of ba $(= Q_1 - Q_2)$ occurs. No ticket scalping occurs and there are numerous empty seats. Only if the Olympic officials had priced the tickets at the lower price P_2 would the event have been a sellout. (Actually, the Olympic officials try to adjust to demand realities for curling contests by holding them in smaller arenas and by charging less for tickets. Nevertheless, the stands are rarely full for the preliminary contests, which compete against final events in other winter Olympic sports.)

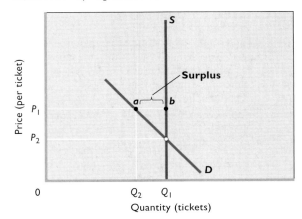

FIGURE 7 The market for tickets to the Olympic curling preliminaries. The demand curve D and supply curve S for the Olympic curling preliminaries produce an equilibrium price below the P_1 price printed on the ticket. At price P_1 the quantity of tickets demanded is less than the quantity of tickets available. The resulting surplus of ba $(= Q_1 - Q_2)$ means the event is not sold out.

Appendix Summary

1. A decrease in the supply of a product increases its equilibrium price and reduces its equilibrium quantity. In contrast, an increase in the demand for a product boosts both its equilibrium price and its equilibrium quantity.

2. Simultaneous changes in supply and demand affect equilibrium price and quantity in various ways, depending on the relative magnitudes of the changes in supply and demand. Equal increases in supply and demand, for example, leave equilibrium price unchanged.

3. Sellers set prices of some items such as tickets in advance of the event. These items are sold in the primary market that involves the original seller and buyers. If preset prices turn out to be below the equilibrium prices, shortages occur and scalping in legal or illegal secondary markets arises. The prices in the secondary market then rise above the preset prices. In contrast, surpluses occur when the preset prices happen to exceed the equilibrium prices.

Appendix Questions   [McGraw-Hill Connect] ECONOMICS

1. Why are shortages or surpluses more likely with preset prices, such as those on tickets, than flexible prices, such as those on gasoline? **LO6**

2. Most scalping laws make it illegal to sell—but not to buy—tickets at prices above those printed on the tickets. Assuming that is the case, use supply and demand analysis to explain why the equilibrium ticket price in an illegal secondary market tends to be higher than in a legal secondary market. **LO6**

3. Go to the Web site of the Energy Information Administration, **www.eia.doe.gov**, and follow the links to find the current retail price of gasoline. How does the current price of regular gasoline compare with the price a year ago? What must have happened to either supply, demand, or both to explain the observed price change? **LO6**

4. Suppose the supply of apples sharply increases because of perfect weather conditions throughout the growing season. Assuming no change in demand, explain the effect on the equilibrium price and quantity of apples. Explain why quantity demanded increases even though demand does not change. **LO6**

5. Assume the demand for lumber suddenly rises because of a rapid growth of demand for new housing. Assume no change in supply. Why does the equilibrium price of lumber rise? What would happen if the price did not rise under the demand and supply circumstances described? **LO6**

6. Suppose both the demand for olives and the supply of olives decline by equal amounts over some time period. Use graphical analysis to show the effect on equilibrium price and quantity. **LO6**

7. Assume that both the supply of bottled water and the demand for bottled water rise during the summer but that supply increases more rapidly than demand. What can you conclude about the directions of the impacts on equilibrium price and equilibrium quantity? LO6

Appendix Problems

1. Demand and supply often shift in the retail market for gasoline. Here are two demand curves and two supply curves for gallons of gasoline in the month of May in a small town in Maine. Some of the data are missing. LO6

	Quantities Demanded		Quantities Supplied	
Price	D_1	D_2	S_1	S_2
$4.00	5000	7500	9000	9500
___	6000	8000	8000	9000
2.00	___	8500	___	8500
___	___	9000	5000	___

a. Use the following facts to fill in the missing data in the table. If demand is D_1 and supply is S_1, the equilibrium quantity is 7000 gallons per month. When demand is D_2 and supply is S_1, the equilibrium price is $3.00 per gallon. When demand is D_2 and supply is S_1, there is an excess demand of 4000 gallons per month at a price of $1.00 per gallon. If demand is D_1 and supply is S_2, the equilibrium quantity is 8000 gallons per month.

b. Compare two equilibriums. In the first, demand is D_1 and supply is S_1. In the second, demand is D_1 and supply is S_2. By how much does the equilibrium quantity change? By how much does the equilibrium price change?

c. If supply falls from S_2 to S_1 while demand declines from D_2 to D_1, does the equilibrium price rise, fall, or stay the same? What if only supply falls? What if only demand falls?

d. Suppose that supply is fixed at S_1 and that demand starts at D_1. By how many gallons per month would demand have to increase at each price level such that the equilibrium price per gallon would be $3.00? $4.00?

2. The table below shows two demand schedules for a given style of men's shoe—that is, how many pairs per month will be demanded at various prices at a men's clothing store in Seattle called Stromnord.

Price	D_1 Quantity Demanded	D_2 Quantity Demanded
$75	53	13
70	60	15
65	68	18
60	77	22
55	87	27

Suppose that Stromnord has exactly 65 pairs of this style of shoe in inventory at the start of the month of July and will not receive any more pairs of this style until at least August 1. LO6

a. If demand is D_1, what is the lowest price that Stromnord can charge so that it will not run out of this model of shoe in the month of July? What if demand is D_2?

b. If the price of shoes is set at $75 for both July and August and demand will be D_2 in July and D_1 in August, how many pairs of shoes should Stromnord order if it wants to end the month of August with exactly zero pairs of shoes in its inventory? What if the price is set at $55 for both months?

3. Use the table below to answer the questions that follow: LO6

a. If this table reflects the supply of and demand for tickets to a particular World Cup soccer game, what is the stadium capacity?

b. If the preset ticket price is $45, would we expect to see a secondary market for tickets? Would the price of a ticket in the secondary market be higher than, the same as, or lower than the price in the primary (original) market?

c. Suppose for some other World Cup game the quantity of tickets demanded is 20,000 lower at each ticket price than shown in the table. If the ticket price remains $45, would the event be a sellout?

Quantity Demanded, Thousands	Price	Quantity Supplied, Thousands
80	$25	60
75	35	60
70	45	60
65	55	60
60	65	60
55	75	60
50	85	60

GDP, GROWTH, AND INSTABILITY

6

AFTER READING THIS CHAPTER, YOU SHOULD BE ABLE TO:

1 Interpret how macroeconomics studies both long-run economic growth and short-run fluctuations in output and unemployment.

2 Explain why economists focus on GDP, inflation, and unemployment when assessing the health of an entire economy.

3 Discuss why sustained increases in living standards are a historically recent phenomenon.

4 Identify why saving and investment are key factors in promoting rising living standards.

5 Describe why economists believe that "shocks" and "sticky prices" are responsible for short-run fluctuations in output and employment.

An Introduction to Macroeconomics

As you know from Chapter 1, macroeconomics studies the behavior of the economy as a whole. It is primarily concerned with two topics: long-run economic growth and the short-run fluctuations in output and employment that are often referred to as the **business cycle.** These phenomena are closely related because they happen simultaneously. Economies show a distinct growth trend that leads to higher output and higher standards of living in the long run, but in the short run there is considerable variability. Sometimes growth proceeds more rapidly and sometimes it proceeds more slowly. It may even turn negative for a while so that output and living standards actually decline, a situation referred to as a **recession.** That is precisely what happened in late 2007 and continued through 2008 and into 2009. The economy experienced what has come to be called the Great Recession.

This chapter provides an overview of the data that macroeconomists use to measure the status and growth of an entire economy as well as a preview of the models that they use to help explain both long-run growth and short-run fluctuations. Because it is an overview chapter, it raises many unanswered questions. Subsequent chapters will explain these topics in much greater detail.

Performance and Policy

To understand how economies operate and how their performance might be improved, economists collect and analyze economic data. An almost infinite number of data items can be looked at, including the amount of new construction taking place each month, how many ships laden with cargo are arriving at our ports each year, and how many new inventions have been patented in the last few weeks. That being said, macroeconomists tend to focus on just a few statistics when trying to assess the health and development of an economy. Chief among these are real GDP, unemployment, and inflation.

- **Real GDP,** or **real gross domestic product,** measures the value of final goods and services produced within the borders of a country during a specific period of time, typically a year. This statistic is very useful because it can tell us whether an economy's output is growing. For instance, if U.S. real GDP in one year is larger than in the previous year, we know that U.S. output increased from the first year to the next. To determine real GDP, government statisticians first calculate **nominal GDP,** which totals the dollar value of all goods and services produced within the borders of a country using *their current prices during the year that they were produced.* But because nominal GDP uses the prices in place in the year the output was produced, it suffers from a major problem: It can increase from one year to the next even if there is no increase in output. To see how, consider a commercial blacksmith who produced 10 iron spiral staircases last year and 10 identical staircases this year. Clearly, the blacksmith's output did not change. But if the price of each staircase rose from $10,000 last year to $20,000 this year, nominal GDP increased from $100,000 (= 10 × $10,000) to $200,000 (= 10 × $20,000). Without knowing about the price increase, we might unwisely conclude that the output of staircases increased from 10 to 20. Real GDP statistically eliminates these kinds of price changes. As a result, we can compare real GDP numbers from one year to the next and really know if there is a change in output (rather than prices). Because more output means greater consumption possibilities—including not only

the chance to consume more fun things such as movies, vacations, and video games, but also more serious things like better health care and safer roads—economists and policymakers are deeply committed to encouraging a large and growing real GDP.

- **Unemployment** is the state a person is in if he or she cannot get a job despite being willing to work and actively seeking work. High rates of unemployment are undesirable because they indicate that a nation is not using a large portion of its most important resource—the talents and skills of its people. Unemployment is a waste because we must count as a loss all the goods and services that unemployed workers could have produced if they had been working. Researchers have also drawn links between higher rates of unemployment and major social problems like higher crime rates and greater political unrest as well as higher rates of depression, heart disease, and other illnesses among unemployed individuals.

- **Inflation** is an increase in the overall level of prices. As an example, consider all the goods and services bought by a typical family over the course of one year. If the economy is experiencing inflation, it will cost the family more money to buy those goods and services this year than it cost to buy them last year. This can be troublesome for several reasons. First, if the family's income does not rise as fast as the prices of the goods and services that it consumes, it won't be able to purchase as much as it used to and its standard of living will fall. Along the same lines, a surprise jump in inflation reduces the purchasing power of people's savings. Savings that they believed would be able to buy them a specific amount of goods and services will turn out to buy them less than they expected due to the higher-than-expected prices.

Because these statistics are the standards by which economists keep track of long-run growth and short-run fluctuations, we will spend a substantial amount of time in the next few chapters examining how these statistics are computed, how well they are able to capture the well-being of actual people, and how they vary both across countries and over time. Once they are understood, we will build on them in subsequent chapters by developing macroeconomic models of both long-run growth and short-run fluctuations. These will help us understand how policymakers attempt to maximize growth while minimizing unemployment and inflation.

Macroeconomic models also clarify many important questions about the powers and limits of government economic policy. These include:

- Can governments promote long-run economic growth?
- Can they reduce the severity of recessions by smoothing out short-run fluctuations?
- Are certain government policy tools such as manipulating interest rates (monetary policy) more effective at mitigating short-run fluctuations than other government policy tools such as changes in tax rates or levels of government spending (fiscal policy)?
- Is there a trade-off between lower rates of unemployment and higher rates of inflation?
- Does government policy work best when it is announced in advance or when it is a surprise?

The answers to these questions are of crucial importance because of the vast differences in economic performance experienced by national economies at different times. For instance, the amount of output generated by the U.S. economy grew at an average rate of 2.7 percent per year between 1995 and the start of the recession of 2007–2009, while the amount of output generated by the Japanese economy grew at an average rate of only 1.0 percent per year over the same time period. Similarly, in 2007, unemployment in the United States was only 4.6 percent of the labor force, while it was 8.7 percent in Germany, 7.2 percent in India, 12.8 percent in Poland, and 80 percent in Zimbabwe. At the same time, the inflation rate in the United States was 2.7 percent, compared with 1.7 percent in Germany, 13.7 percent in Venezuela, and 26,470 percent in Zimbabwe. In 2008 and 2009, however, the U.S. economy lost 8 million jobs, and the unemployment rate rose from 4.6 percent to as high as 10.1 percent.

Our models will help us understand why such large differences in rates of growth, unemployment, and inflation exist among countries and why those rates can change so substantially from one period to another. These models also will provide significant insights on how government policies can influence rates of growth, unemployment, and inflation.

The Miracle of Modern Economic Growth

Rapid and sustained economic growth is a modern phenomenon. Before the Industrial Revolution began in the late 1700s in England, standards of living showed virtually no growth over hundreds or even thousands of years. For instance, the standard of living of the average Roman peasant was virtually the same at the start of the Roman Empire around the year 500 B.C. as it was at the end of the Roman Empire 1000 years later. Similarly, historians and archaeologists have estimated that the standard of living enjoyed by the average Chinese peasant was essentially the same in the year A.D. 1800 as it was in the year A.D. 100.

That is not to say that the Roman and Chinese economies did not expand over time. They did. In fact, their total outputs of goods and services increased many times over. The problem was that as they did, their populations went up by similar proportions so that the amount of output *per person* remained virtually unchanged.

This historical pattern continued until the start of the Industrial Revolution, which ushered in not only factory production and automation but also massive increases in research and development so that new and better technologies were constantly being invented. The result was that output began to grow faster than the population. This meant that living standards began to rise as the amount of output *per person* increased.

Not all countries experienced this phenomenon, but those that did were said to be experiencing **modern economic growth** (in which output per person rises) as compared with earlier times in which output (but not output per person) increased. Under modern economic growth, the annual increase in output per person is often not large, perhaps 2 percent per year in countries such as England that were the first to industrialize. But when compounded over time, an annual growth rate of 2 percent adds up very rapidly. Indeed, it implies that the standard of living will double every 35 years. So if the average citizen of a country enjoying 2 percent growth begins this year with an income of $10,000, in 35 years that person will have an income of $20,000. And 35 years after that there will be another doubling so that her income in 70 years will be $40,000. And 35 years after that, the average citizen's income will double again to $80,000. Such high rates of growth are amazing when compared to the period before modern economic growth when standards of living remained unchanged century after century.

The vast differences in living standards seen today between rich and poor countries are almost entirely the result of the fact that only some countries have experienced modern economic growth. Indeed, before the start of the Industrial Revolution in the late 1700s, living standards around the world were very similar, so much so that the average standard of living in the richest parts of the world was at most only two or three times higher than the standard of living in the poorest parts of the world. By contrast,

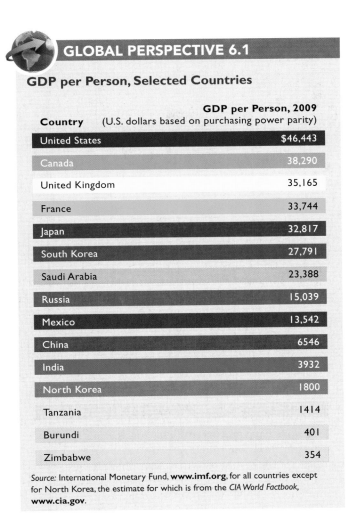

GLOBAL PERSPECTIVE 6.1

GDP per Person, Selected Countries

Country	GDP per Person, 2009 (U.S. dollars based on purchasing power parity)
United States	$46,443
Canada	38,290
United Kingdom	35,165
France	33,744
Japan	32,817
South Korea	27,791
Saudi Arabia	23,388
Russia	15,039
Mexico	13,542
China	6546
India	3932
North Korea	1800
Tanzania	1414
Burundi	401
Zimbabwe	354

Source: International Monetary Fund, **www.imf.org**, for all countries except for North Korea, the estimate for which is from the *CIA World Factbook*, **www.cia.gov**.

the citizens of the richest nations today have material standards of living that are on average more than 50 times higher than those experienced by citizens of the poorest nations, as can be seen by the GDP per person data for the year 2009 given in Global Perspective 6.1.

Global Perspective 6.1 facilitates international comparisons of living standards by making three adjustments to each country's GDP. First, it converts each country's GDP from its own currency into U.S. dollars so that there is no confusion about the values of different currencies. Second, it divides each country's GDP measured in dollars by the size of its population. The resulting number, *GDP per person*, is the average amount of output each person in each country could have if each country's total output were divided equally among its citizens. It is a measure of each country's average standard of living. Third, the table uses a method called *purchasing power*

parity to adjust for the fact that prices are much lower in some countries than others. By making this adjustment, we can trust that $1 of GDP per person in the United States represents about the same quantity of goods and services as $1 of GDP per person in any of the other countries. The resulting numbers—GDP per person adjusted for purchasing power parity—are presented in Global Perspective 6.1.

Saving, Investment, and Choosing between Present and Future Consumption

At the heart of economic growth is the principle that to raise living standards over time, an economy must devote at least some fraction of its current output to increasing future output. As implied in Chapter 1, this process requires flows of both saving and investment, which we will define and discuss before returning to why they are so important for economic growth.

- **Saving** occurs when current consumption is less than current output (or when current spending is less than current income).
- **Investment** happens when resources are devoted to increasing future output—for instance by building a new research facility in which scientists invent the next generation of fuel-efficient automobiles or by constructing a modern, super-efficient factory. (A caution: In economics, the term "investment" differs from common usage. To understand why, be sure to read the Consider This box located on the next page.)

When thinking about why saving and investment are so important for economic growth, the key point is that the amount of investment is ultimately limited by the amount of saving. The only way that more output can be directed at investment activities is if saving increases. But that, in turn, implies that individuals and society as a whole must make trade-offs between current and future consumption. This is true because the only way to pay for more investment—and the higher levels of future consumption that more investment can generate—is to increase present saving. But increased saving can only come at the price of reduced current consumption. Individuals and society as a whole must therefore wrestle with a choice between present consumption and future consumption. They must decide how to balance the reductions in current consumption required to fund current investment against the increases in future consumption that the added current investment will make possible.

CONSIDER THIS . . .

Economic versus Financial Investment

Economics students often are confused by how the word "investment" is used in economics. This is understandable, because economists draw a distinction between "financial investment" and "economic investment."

Financial investment captures what ordinary people mean when they say investment, namely, the purchase of assets like stocks, bonds, and real estate in the hope of reaping a financial gain. Anything of monetary value is an asset and, in everyday usage, people purchase—or "invest" in—assets hoping to receive a financial gain, either by eventually selling them at higher prices than they paid for them or by receiving a stream of payments from others who are allowed to use the asset. By contrast, when economists say "investment," they are referring to **economic investment,** which relates to the creation and expansion of business enterprises. Specifically, economic investment only includes spending on the production and accumulation of newly created capital goods such as machinery, tools, factories, and warehouses. For example, economic investment will occur when the airplane shown in the accompanying photo is purchased by a commercial airline.

For economists, purely financial transactions, such as swapping cash for a stock or a bond, are not "investment." Neither are the purchases of factories or apartment buildings built in previous years. These transactions simply transfer the ownership of financial assets or existing real assets from one party to another. They do not purchase newly created capital goods. As such, they are great examples of financial investment, but not of economic investment. So now that you know the difference, remember that purely financial transactions, like buying Google stock or a five-year-old factory, are indeed referred to as "investment"—except in economics!

Banks and Other Financial Institutions

Households are the principal source of savings. But businesses are the main economic investors. So how does the pool of savings generated by households when they spend less than they consume get transferred to businesses so that they can purchase newly created capital goods? The answer is through banks and other financial institutions such as mutual funds, pension plans, and insurance companies. These institutions collect the savings of households, rewarding savers with interest and dividends and sometimes capital gains (increases in asset values). The banks and other financial institutions then lend the funds to businesses, which invest in equipment, factories, and other capital goods.

Macroeconomics devotes considerable attention to money, banking, and financial institutions because a well-functioning financial system helps to promote economic growth and stability by encouraging saving and by properly directing that saving into the most productive possible investments. In contrast, a poorly functioning financial system can create serious problems for an economy.

Uncertainty, Expectations, and Shocks

Decisions about savings and investment are complicated by the fact that the future is uncertain. Investment projects sometimes produce disappointing results or even fail totally. As a result, firms spend considerable time trying to predict future trends so that they can, hopefully, invest only in projects that are likely to succeed. This implies that macroeconomics has to take into account **expectations** about the future.

Expectations are hugely important for two reasons. The more obvious reason involves the effect that changing expectations have on current behavior. If firms grow more pessimistic about the future returns that are likely to come from current investments, they are going to invest less today than they would if they were more optimistic. Expectations therefore have a large effect on economic growth since increased pessimism will lead to less current investment and, subsequently, less future consumption.

The less-obvious reason that expectations are so important has to do with what happens when expectations are unmet. Firms are often forced to cope with **shocks**—situations in which they were expecting one thing to happen but then something else happened. For instance, consider a situation in which a firm decides to build a high-speed railroad that will shuttle passengers between Los Angeles and Las Vegas. They do so expecting it to be very popular and make a handsome profit. But if it unexpectedly turns out to be unpopular and loses money, the railroad must figure out how to respond. Should the railroad go out of business completely? Should it attempt to see if it can turn a profit by hauling cargo instead of passengers? Is there a possibility that the venture might succeed if the firm borrows $30 million from a bank to pay for a massive advertising campaign? These sorts of decisions are necessitated by the shock and surprise of having to deal with an unexpected situation.

Economies are exposed to both demand shocks and supply shocks. **Demand shocks** are unexpected changes in the demand for goods and services. **Supply shocks** are unexpected changes in the supply of goods and services. Note that the word *shock* only reveals that something unexpected has happened. It does not tell us whether what has happened is unexpectedly good or unexpectedly bad. To clarify this, economists use more specific terms. For instance, a *positive demand shock* refers to a situation in which demand turns out to be higher than expected, while a *negative demand shock* refers to a situation in which demand turns out to be lower than expected.

Economists believe that most short-run fluctuations in GDP are the result of demand shocks. Supply shocks do happen in some cases and are very important when they do occur. But we will focus most of our attention in this chapter and subsequent chapters on demand shocks, how they affect the economy, and how government policy may be able to help the economy adjust to them.

But why are demand shocks such a big problem? Why would we have to consider calling in the government to help deal with them? And why can't firms deal with demand shocks on their own?

The answer to these questions is that the prices of many goods and services are inflexible (slow to change, or "sticky") in the short run. As we will explain, this implies that price changes do not quickly equalize the quantities demanded of such goods and services with their respective quantities supplied. Instead, because prices are inflexible, the economy is forced to respond in the short run to demand shocks primarily through changes in output and employment rather than through changes in prices.

Although an economy as a whole is vastly more complex than a single firm, an analogy that uses a single car factory will be helpful in explaining why demand shocks and inflexible prices are so important to understanding most of the short-run fluctuations that affect the entire economy. Consider a car manufacturing company named Buzzer Auto. Like most companies, Buzzer Auto is in business to try to make a profit. Part of turning a profit involves trying to develop accurate expectations about future market conditions. Consequently, Buzzer constantly does market research to estimate future demand conditions so that it will, hopefully, only build cars that people are going to want to buy.

After extensive market research, Buzzer concludes that it could earn a modest profit if it builds and staffs an appropriately sized factory to build an environmentally friendly SUV, which it decides to call the Prion. Buzzer's marketing economists collaborate with Buzzer's engineers and conclude that expected profits will be maximized if the firm builds a factory that has an optimal output rate of 900 cars

per week. If the factory operates at this rate, it can produce Prions for only $36,500 per vehicle. This is terrific because the firm's estimates for demand indicate that a supply of 900 vehicles per week can be sold at a price of $37,000 per vehicle—meaning that if everything goes according to plan, Buzzer Auto should make an accounting profit of $500 on each Prion that it produces and sells. Expecting these future conditions, Buzzer decides to build the factory, staff it with workers, and begin making the Prion.

Look at Figure 6.1a, which shows the market for Prions when the vertical supply curve for Prions is fixed at the factory's optimal output rate of 900 cars per week. Notice that we have drawn in three possible demand curves. D_L corresponds to low demand for the Prion; D_M corresponds to the medium level of demand that Buzzer's marketing economists are expecting to materialize; and D_H corresponds to high demand for the Prion. Figure 6.1a is consistent with the marketing economists' expectations: if all goes according to plan and the actual demand that materializes is D_M, the equilibrium price will in fact be $37,000 per Prion and the equilibrium quantity demanded will be 900 cars per week. Thus, if all goes according to expectations, the factory will have exactly the right capacity to meet the expected quantity demanded at the sales price of $37,000 per vehicle. In addition, the firm's books will show a profit of $500 per vehicle on each of the 900 vehicles that it builds and expects to sell each week at that price.

Here is the key point. If expectations are always fulfilled, Buzzer Auto will never contribute to any of the short-run fluctuations in output and unemployment that affect real-world economies. First, if everything always goes according to plan and Buzzer Auto's expectations always come true, then the factory will always produce and sell at its optimal output rate of 900 cars per week. This would mean that it would never experience any fluctuations in output—either in the short run or in the long run. At the same time, since producing a constant output of 900 cars each week will always require the same number of workers, the factory's labor demand and employment should never vary. So if everything always goes according to plan, Buzzer Auto will never have any effect on unemployment because it will always hire a constant number of workers.

These facts imply that the short-run fluctuations in output and unemployment that we do see in the real world must be the result of shocks and things *not* going according to plan. In particular, business cycle fluctuations typically arise because the actual demand that materializes ends up being either lower or higher than what people were expecting. When this occurs, some adjustments will be necessary to bring the quantity demanded and the quantity supplied back into alignment. As we are about to

FIGURE 6.1 **The effect of unexpected changes in demand under flexible and fixed prices.** (a) If prices are flexible, then no matter what demand turns out to be, Buzzer Auto can continue to sell its optimal output of 900 cars per week since the equilibrium price will adjust to equalize the quantity demanded with the quantity supplied. (b) By contrast, if Buzzer Auto sticks with a fixed-price policy, then the quantity demanded will vary with the level of demand. At the fixed price of $37,000 per vehicle, the quantity demanded will be 700 cars per week if demand is D_L, 900 cars per week if demand is D_M, and 1150 cars per week if demand is D_H.

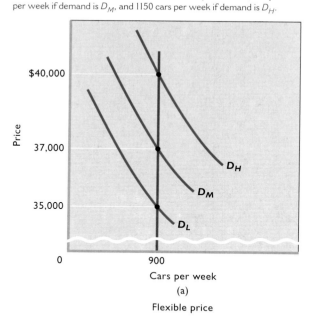

(a)

Flexible price

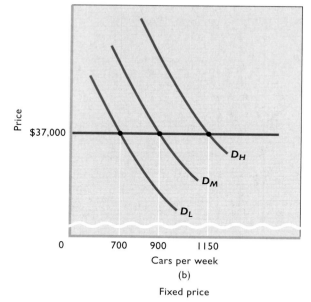

(b)

Fixed price

explain, the nature of these adjustments varies hugely depending on whether prices are flexible or inflexible.

Demand Shocks and Flexible Prices

Figure 6.1a illustrates the case of adjusting to unexpected changes in demand *when prices are flexible*. Here, if demand is unexpectedly low at D_L, the market price can adjust downward to $35,000 per vehicle so that the quantity demanded at that price will still be equal to the factory's optimal output rate of 900 cars per week. On the other hand, if demand is unexpectedly high at D_H, the market price can adjust upward to $40,000 per vehicle so that the quantity demanded will still be equal to the factory's optimal output rate of 900 cars per week. These adjustments imply that *if* the price of Prions is free to quickly adjust to new equilibrium levels in response to unexpected changes in demand, the factory could always operate at its optimal output rate of 900 cars per week. Only the amount of profit or loss will vary with demand.

Applying this logic to the economy as a whole, *if the prices of goods and services could always adjust quickly to unexpected changes in demand, then the economy could always produce at its optimal capacity* since prices would adjust to ensure that the quantity demanded of each good and service would always equal the quantity supplied. Simply put, if prices were fully flexible, there would be no

short-run fluctuations in output. Production levels would remain constant and unemployment levels would not change because firms would always need the same number of workers to produce the same amount of output.

Demand Shocks and Sticky Prices

In reality, many prices in the economy are inflexible and are not able to change rapidly when demand changes unexpectedly. Consider the extreme case shown in Figure 6.1b, in which the price of Prions is totally inflexible, fixed at $37,000 per Prion. Here, if demand unexpectedly falls from D_M to D_L, the quantity demanded at the fixed price of $37,000 will only be 700 cars per week, which is 200 cars fewer than the factory's optimal output of 900 cars per week. On the other hand, if demand is unexpectedly high at D_H, the quantity demanded at the fixed price of $37,000 will be 1150 cars per week, which is 250 cars more than the factory's optimal output of 900 cars per week.

One way for companies to deal with these unexpected shifts in quantity demanded would be to try to adjust the factory's output to match them. That is, during weeks of low demand, Buzzer Auto could attempt to produce only 700 Prions, while during weeks of high demand it could try to produce 1150 Prions. But this sort of flexible output strategy is very expensive because factories operate at their lowest costs when they are producing constantly at their optimal output levels; operating at either a higher or a lower production rate results in higher per-unit production costs.[1]

Knowing this, manufacturing firms typically attempt to deal with unexpected changes in demand by maintaining an inventory. An **inventory** is a store of output that has been produced but not yet sold. Inventories are useful because they can be allowed to grow or decline in periods when demand is unexpectedly low or high—thereby allowing production to proceed smoothly even when demand is variable. In our example, Buzzer Auto would maintain an inventory of unsold Prions. In weeks when demand is unexpectedly low, the inventory will increase by 200 Prions as the quantity demanded falls 200 vehicles short of the factory's optimal output. By contrast, during weeks when demand is unexpectedly high, the inventory will decrease as the quantity demanded exceeds the factory's optimal output by 250 cars. By allowing inventory levels to fluctuate with these unexpected shifts in demand, Buzzer Auto can respond by adjusting inventory levels rather than output levels. In addition, with any luck, the overall inventory level will stay roughly constant over time as unexpected increases and decreases in demand cancel each other out.

But consider what will happen if the firm experiences many successive weeks of unexpectedly low demand. For each such week, the firm's inventory of unsold Prions will increase by 200 cars. The firm's managers will not mind if this happens for a few weeks, but if it continues for many weeks, then the managers will be forced to cut production because, among other things, there will simply be no place to park so many unsold vehicles. More importantly, holding large numbers of unsold cars in inventory is unprofitable because while costs must be incurred to build an unsold car, an unsold car obviously brings in no revenue. Constantly rising inventories hurt firm profits and the management will want to reduce output if it sees inventories rising week after week due to unexpectedly low demand.

This simplified story about a single car company explains why economists believe that a combination of unexpected changes in demand and inflexible prices are the key to understanding the short-run fluctuations that affect real-world economies. If prices were flexible, then the firm could always operate at the factory's optimal output level because prices would always adjust to ensure that it could sell its optimal output of 900 cars per week no matter what happens to demand. But if prices are inflexible, then an unexpected decline in demand that persists for any length of

---

[1]If you have studied microeconomics, you will recognize that the firm's optimal output level of 900 cars per week is the level that minimizes the factory's average total cost (ATC) per vehicle of producing the Prion. Producing either more or fewer Prions will result in higher per-vehicle production costs.

CONSIDER THIS . . .

The Great Recession

In 2008 and 2009, the United States encountered its worst financial and economic crisis since the Great Depression of the 1930s.

The recession was so severe that it has been dubbed the Great Recession. The recession was triggered by a steep decline in housing prices and a crisis involving mortgage loans and the financial securities built on them. Several key U.S. financial institutions collapsed or nearly failed, and lending markets largely froze. Despite government bailout efforts, the financial crisis eventually spread to the broader economy. Employment fell by 8 million workers between 2007 and the end of 2009, and the unemployment rate rose from 4.7 percent to 10 percent over that same period. Economic growth slumped to 0.4 percent in 2008 and to a *negative* 2.4 percent in 2009, compared with the 2.7 percent annual increases occurring between 1995 and 2007.

And this is where Buzzer Auto comes into the picture. The situation in Figure 6.1b, where the price of Buzzer's autos is inflexible, is highly relevant to the Great Recession. Like Buzzer, actual auto producers such as GM, Ford, and Chrysler, as well as thousands of producers of other products across the economy, established their production capacity and set their expectations of product demand on the basis of normal times. But demand for their goods and services fell unexpectedly because of greater consumer difficulty in getting loans, declining consumer confidence, and eventually declining income. The economy's price level (essentially a weighted average of all prices) declined only slightly, and that was after the recession was well underway. Therefore, real output (not prices) took the major brunt of the decline of total demand in the economy. Output dropped, employment plummeted, and unemployment soared.

---

time will result in increasing inventories that will eventually force the firm's management to cut production to less than the optimal output level of 900 cars per week. When this happens, not only will output fall, but unemployment will also rise. The firm will lay off workers because fewer employees will be needed to produce fewer cars.

Generalizing this story to the economy as a whole, if demand falls off for many goods and services across the entire economy for an extended period of time, then the firms that make those goods and services will be forced to cut production. Manufacturing firms that maintain inventories will do so as they find inventories piling up due to sluggish sales. And services firms will do so as they encounter slow sales for their services. As both manufacturing and

Computerized Inventory Tracking Has Greatly Accelerated How Quickly Companies Can Respond to Unexpected Changes in Demand.

Before computers made it possible to track inventory changes in real time, firms could only react to unexpected shifts in demand very slowly. This was true because, before computers, tracking inventory was a painful, slow process that involved hiring people to physically count the items held in inventory—one at a time. Because this process was both costly and annoying, firms typically counted their inventories only a few times per year.

An unfortunate side effect of counting inventory so infrequently was that unexpected shifts in demand could cause large changes in inventory levels before anyone could find out about them. To see why, consider a firm that counts its inventory just twice per year, for example, once in January and once in July. If the demand for its product suddenly falls in February and then remains low, the decline in demand will not be discovered until the July inventory count. Only then will a high inventory level inform the firm's management that the demand for its product must have unexpectedly declined.

The long delay between when the shift in demand happens and when it is discovered means that the firm will very likely feel pressed to sharply reduce its production of new output, because the fastest way to reduce its high inventory level is to sharply reduce its output rate (so that new sales will exceed the reduced output rate). Following this policy, however, implies not only a large cut in output but also a substantial increase in unemployment, because fewer workers will be needed to produce less output. Infrequent inventory counting therefore leads to strong fluctuations in output and employment, because unexpected changes in demand have plenty of time to cause large changes in inventory levels.

By contrast, computerized inventory tracking systems enable companies to track their inventory levels in real time. These systems keep continuous track of inventory levels through technologies such as bar codes and laser scanners, and this tracking tells firms almost immediately when demand has changed unexpectedly. As a result, the firms with these systems can make much more subtle changes to output and employment, because they can discover the unexpected changes in demand before those unexpected changes have caused large increases or decreases in inventories.

Before the Great Recession of 2007–2009, the general thinking among economists was that real-time inventory systems had moderated business cycles. Between 1982 and 2007,

service output declines, the economy will recede, with GDP falling and unemployment rising.

On the other hand, if demand is unexpectedly high for a prolonged period of time, the economy will boom and unemployment will fall. In the case of our Prion example, for each week that demand is unexpectedly high, inventories will fall by 250 cars. If this keeps happening week after week, inventories will start to run out and the firm will have to react by increasing production to more than the optimal output rate of 900 cars per week so that orders do not go unfilled. When this happens, GDP will increase as more cars per week are produced and unemployment will fall because the factory will need to hire more workers to produce the larger number of cars.

How Sticky Are Prices?

We have just shown that **inflexible prices**—or **"sticky prices"** as economists are fond of saying—help to explain how unexpected changes in demand lead to the fluctuations in GDP and employment that occur over the course of the business cycle. Of course, not all prices are sticky. Indeed, the markets for many commodities and raw materials such as corn, oil, and natural gas feature extremely **flexible prices** that react within seconds to changes in supply and demand. By contrast, the prices of most of the final goods and services that people consume are quite sticky, with the average good or service going 4.3 months between price changes. To get a better appreciation for the fact that price stickiness varies greatly by product or service, look at Table 6.1, which gives the average number of months between price changes for various common goods and services. The prices of some products like gasoline and airline tickets change very rapidly—about once a month or even less than once a month. By contrast, haircuts and newspapers average more than two years between price changes. And coin-operated laundry machines average nearly four years between price changes!

An important recent study has found that product prices are particularly sticky in response to widespread

business cycles were less frequent and less deep than previously. Prior to 1982, recessions happened in the United States every five or so years and were often quite punishing, with high levels of unemployment and significant declines in output. But firms began to widely adopt computerized inventory management systems during the 1980s, and between 1982 and 2007 the U.S. economy experienced only two mild recessions: one in 1991–1992 and another in 2000–2001. Since these recessions were mild and about 10 years apart, some economists concluded that improvements in inventory management had helped dampen the business cycle.

Opinions vary, however, as to how much credit computerized inventory management should be given for the apparent reduction in the frequency and severity of the business cycle during this period. Indeed, several other explanations have been offered to explain why things seem to have improved. One explanation is that governments may have learned from past mistakes and shifted to better economic policies. But taking the various explanations into account, it is safe to say that most economists would give at least some of the credit to innovations in inventory management.

Ironically, the advantages of computerized inventory control that seemed to help moderate the business cycle for 25 years may have contributed to the suddenness and steepness of the severe recession of 2007–2009. As we have indicated, the immediate cause of the recession was a near-collapse of the financial system that nearly froze lending and produced a major, continuing demand shock in the form of significant reductions of spending by consumers and businesses. Firms immediately became aware of the severity and continuation of the demand shock through their computerized inventory systems and responded by reducing their current production and employment to keep their inventory levels from swelling in size. The computerized inventory management systems therefore transmitted the sudden and continuing demand shock to a rapid and lengthy decline in real GDP. The outcome was the worst recession in the United States since 1982.

TABLE 6.1 **Average Number of Months between Price Changes for Selected Goods and Services**

Item	Months
Coin-operated laundry machines	46.4
Newspapers	29.9
Haircuts	25.5
Taxi fare	19.7
Veterinary services	14.9
Magazines	11.2
Computer software	5.5
Beer	4.3
Microwave ovens	3.0
Milk	2.4
Electricity	1.8
Airline tickets	1.0
Gasoline	0.6

Source: Mark Bils and Peter J. Klenow, "Some Evidence on the Importance of Sticky Prices." *Journal of Political Economy,* October 2004, pp. 947–985. Used with permission of The University of Chicago Press.

macroeconomic and monetary disturbances.[2] In later chapters, we will identify and discuss several factors that cause short-run price stickiness. But to keep the current discussion brief, let's focus on just two factors here. One factor is that companies selling final goods and services know that consumers prefer stable, predictable prices that do not fluctuate rapidly with changes in demand. Consumers would be annoyed if the same bottle of soda or shampoo cost one price one day, a different price the next day, and yet another price a week later. Volatile prices make planning more difficult, and, in addition, consumers who come in to buy the product on a day when the price happens to be high will likely feel that they are being taken advantage of. To avoid this, most firms try to maintain stable prices that do not change very often. Firms do have

[2]Jean Boivin, Marc P. Giannoni, and Illian Mihov, "Sticky Prices and Monetary Policy: Evidence from Disaggregated US Data," *American Economic Review,* March 2009, pp. 350–384.

occasional sales where they lower prices, but on the whole they tend to try to keep prices stable and predictable—the result being price inflexibility.

Another factor that causes sticky prices has to do with the fact that in certain situations, a firm may be afraid that cutting its price may be counterproductive because its rivals might simply match the price cut—a situation often referred to as a "price war." This possibility is common among firms that only have one or two major rivals. Consider Coca-Cola and Pepsi. If Coca-Cola faces unexpectedly low demand for its product, it might be tempted to reduce its price in the hope that it can steal business away from Pepsi. But such a strategy would only work if Pepsi left its price alone when Coca-Cola cut its price. That, of course, is not likely. If Coca-Cola cuts its price, Pepsi will very likely cut its price in retaliation, doing its best to make sure that Coca-Cola doesn't steal away any of its customers. Thus, if Pepsi retaliates, Coca-Cola will only be made worse off by its decision to cut its price: It will not pick up much more business (because Pepsi also cut its price) and it will also be receiving less money for each bottle of Coke that it sells (because it lowered its own price.) Thus, firms that have to realistically consider the possibility of price wars often have sticky prices.

Categorizing Macroeconomic Models Using Price Stickiness

We have now demonstrated why price stickiness is believed to have such a large role in short-run economic fluctuations. It should be noted, however, that price stickiness moderates over time. This is true because firms that choose to use a fixed-price policy in the short run do not have to stick with that policy permanently. In particular, if unexpected changes in demand begin to look permanent, many firms will allow their prices to change so that price changes (in addition to quantity changes) can help to equalize quantities supplied with quantities demanded.

For this reason, economists speak of "sticky prices" rather than "stuck prices." Only in the very short run are prices totally inflexible. As time passes and prices are revised, the world looks much more like Figure 6.1a, in which prices are fully flexible, rather than Figure 6.1b, in which prices are totally inflexible. Indeed, the totally inflexible case shown in Figure 6.1b can be thought of as the extremely short-run response to an unexpected change in demand, while the fully flexible case shown in Figure 6.1a can be thought of as a longer-run response to an unexpected change in demand. In terms of time durations, the extreme short run can be thought of as the first few weeks and months after a demand shock, while the long run can be thought of as extending from many months to several years after a demand shock happens.

This realization is very useful in categorizing and understanding the differences between the various macroeconomic models that we will be presenting in subsequent chapters. For instance, the aggregate expenditures model presented in Chapter 11 assumes perfectly inflexible prices (and wages) and thus is a model in which prices are not just sticky but completely stuck. By contrast, the aggregate demand–aggregate supply model presented in Chapter 12 allows for flexible prices (with or without flexible wages) and is therefore useful for understanding how the economy behaves over longer periods of time.

As you study these various models, keep in mind that we need different models precisely because the economy behaves so differently depending on how much time has passed after a demand shock. The differences in behavior result from the fact that prices go from stuck in the extreme short run to fully flexible in the long run. Using different models for different stages in this process gives us much better insights into not only how economies actually behave but also how various government and central bank policies may have different effects in the short run when prices are fixed versus the long run when prices are flexible.

Where will we go from here? In the remainder of Part 3, we examine how economists measure GDP and why GDP has expanded over time. Then, we discuss the terminology of business cycles and explore the measurement and types of unemployment and inflation. At that point you will be well-prepared to examine the economic models, monetary considerations, and stabilization policies that lie at the heart of macroeconomics.

Summary

1. Macroeconomics studies long-run economic growth and short-run economic fluctuations.
2. Macroeconomists focus their attention on three key economic statistics: real GDP, unemployment, and inflation.

Real GDP measures the value of all final goods and services produced in a country during a specific period of time. The unemployment rate measures the percentage of all workers who are not able to find paid employment despite being willing and able to work at currently available wages. The inflation rate measures the extent to which the overall level of prices is rising in the economy.

3. Before the Industrial Revolution, living standards did not show any sustained increases over time. Economies grew, but any increase in output tended to be offset by an equally large increase in the population, so that the amount of output per person did not rise. By contrast, since the Industrial Revolution began in the late 1700s, many nations have experienced modern economic growth in which output grows faster than population—so that standards of living rise over time.

4. Macroeconomists believe that one of the keys to modern economic growth is the promotion of saving and investment (for economists, the purchase of capital goods). Investment activities increase the economy's future potential output level. But investment must be funded by saving, which is only possible if people are willing to reduce current consumption. Consequently, individuals and society face a trade-off between current consumption and future consumption since the only way to fund the investment necessary to increase future consumption is by reducing current consumption to gather the savings necessary to fund that investment. Banks and other financial institutions help to convert saving into investment by taking the savings generated by households and lending it to businesses that wish to make investments.

5. Expectations have an important effect on the economy for two reasons. First, if people and businesses are more positive about the future, they will save and invest more. Second, individuals and firms must make adjustments to shocks—situations in which expectations are unmet and the future does not turn out the way people were expecting. In

particular, shocks often imply situations where the quantity supplied of a given good or service does not equal the quantity demanded of that good or service.

6. If prices were always flexible and capable of rapid adjustment, then dealing with situations in which quantities demanded did not equal quantities supplied would always be easy since prices could simply adjust to the market equilibrium price at which quantities demanded equal quantities supplied. Unfortunately, real-world prices are often inflexible (or "sticky") in the short run so that the only way for the economy to adjust to such situations is through changes in output levels.

7. Sticky prices combine with shocks to drive short-run fluctuations in output and employment. Consider a negative demand shock in which demand is unexpectedly low. Because prices are fixed, the lower-than-expected demand will result in unexpectedly slow sales. This will cause inventories to increase. If demand remains low for an extended period of time, inventory levels will become too high and firms will have to cut output and lay off workers. Thus, when prices are inflexible, the economy adjusts to unexpectedly low demand through changes in output and employment rather than through changes in prices (which are not possible when prices are inflexible).

8. Prices are inflexible in the short run for various reasons, two of which are discussed in this chapter. First, firms often attempt to set and maintain stable prices to please customers who like predictable prices because they make for easy planning (and who might become upset if prices were volatile). Second, a firm with just a few competitors may be reluctant to cut its price due to the fear of starting a price war, a situation in which its competitors retaliate by cutting their prices as well—thereby leaving the firm worse off than it was to begin with.

Terms and Concepts

business cycle

recession

real GDP (Gross Domestic Product)

nominal GDP

unemployment

inflation

modern economic growth

saving

investment

financial investment

economic investment

expectations

shocks

demand shocks

supply shocks

inventory

inflexible prices ("sticky prices")

flexible prices

Questions

1. Draw a graph with "Level of real output" on the vertical axis and "Time" on the horizontal axis. If the long-run trend line of economic growth for the United States were to appear on your graph as a straight upsloping line, how would you pencil in economic fluctuations in relation to that straight line? Referring to your graph, briefly explain why economic fluctuations and economic growth are compatible concepts. Check your drawing against Figure 9.1, page 171. **LO1**

2. Why do you think macroeconomists focus on just a few key statistics when trying to understand the health and trajec-

tory of an economy? Would it be better to try to examine all possible data? **LO2**

3. Consider a nation in which the volume of goods and services is growing by 5 percent per year. What is the likely impact of this high rate of growth on the power and influence of its government relative to other countries experiencing slower rates of growth? What about the effect of this 5 percent growth on the nation's living standards? Will these also necessarily grow by 5 percent per year, given population growth? Why or why not? **LO2**

4. Did economic output start growing faster than population from the beginning of the human inhabitation of the earth? When did modern economic growth begin? Have all of the world's nations experienced the same extent of modern economic growth? LO3

5. Why is there a trade-off between the amount of consumption that people can enjoy today and the amount of consumption that they can enjoy in the future? Why can't people enjoy more of both? How does saving relate to investment and thus to economic growth? What role do banks and other financial institutions play in aiding the growth process? LO4

6. How does investment as defined by economists differ from investment as defined by the general public? What would happen to the amount of economic investment made today if firms expected the future returns to such investment to be very low? What if firms expected future returns to be very high? LO4

7. Why, in general, do shocks force people to make changes? Give at least two examples from your own experience. LO5

8. Catalog companies are committed to selling at the prices printed in their catalogs. If a catalog company finds its inventory of sweaters rising, what does that tell you about the demand for sweaters? Was it unexpectedly high, unexpectedly low, or as expected? If the company could change the price of sweaters, would it raise the price, lower the price, or keep the price the same? Given that the company cannot change the price of sweaters, consider the number of sweaters it orders each month from the company that makes its sweaters. If inventories become very high, will the catalog company increase, decrease, or keep orders the same? Given what the catalog company does with its orders, what is likely to happen to employment and output at the sweater manufacturer? LO5

9. **LAST WORD** Why do some economists believe that better inventory control software and systems may help to reduce the frequency and severity of recessions caused by mild demand shocks? How could those same inventory systems quickly transmit large demand shocks directly to sudden, deep recessions?

Problems

1. Suppose that the annual rates of growth of real GDP of Econoland over a five-year period were sequentially as follows: 3 percent, 1 percent, –2 percent, 4 percent, and 5 percent. What was the average of these growth rates in Econoland over these 5 years? What term would economists use to describe what happened in year 3? If the growth rate in year 3 had been a positive 2 percent rather than a negative 2 percent, what would have been the average growth rate? LO1

2. Suppose that Glitter Gulch, a gold mining firm, increased its sales revenues on newly mined gold from $100 million to $200 million between one year and the next. Assuming that the price of gold increased by 100 percent over the same period, by what numerical amount did Glitter Gulch's real output change? If the price of gold had not changed, what would have been the change in Glitter Gulch's real output? LO2

3. A mathematical approximation called the rule of 70 tells us that the number of years that it will take something that is growing to double in size is approximately equal to the number 70 divided by its percentage rate of growth. Thus, if Mexico's real GDP per person is growing at 7 percent per year, it will take about 10 years (= 70/7) to double. Apply the rule of 70 to solve the following problem. Real GDP per person in Mexico in 2005 was about $11,000 per person,

while it was about $44,000 per person in the United States. If real GDP per person in Mexico grows at the rate of 5 percent per year, about how long will it take Mexico's real GDP per person to reach the level that the United States was at in 2005? (Hint: How many times would Mexico's 2005 real GDP per person have to double to reach the United States' 2005 real GDP per person?) LO3

4. Assume that a national restaurant firm called BBQ builds 10 new restaurants at a cost of $1 million per restaurant. It outfits each restaurant with an additional $200,000 of equipment and furnishings. To help partially defray the cost of this expansion, BBQ issues and sells 200,000 shares of stock at $30 per share. What is the amount of economic investment that has resulted from BBQ's actions? How much purely financial investment took place? LO4

5. Refer to Figure 6.1b and assume that price is fixed at $37,000 and that Buzzer Auto needs 5 workers for every 1 automobile produced. If demand is D_M and Buzzer wants to perfectly match its output and sales, how many cars will Buzzer produce and how many workers will it hire? If instead, demand unexpectedly falls from D_M to D_L, how many fewer cars will Buzzer sell? How many fewer workers will it need if it decides to match production to these lower sales? LO5

FURTHER TEST YOUR KNOWLEDGE AT
www.mcconnell19e.com

At the text's Online Learning Center (OLC), **www.mcconnell19e.com**, you will find one or more Web-based questions that require information from the Internet to answer. We urge you to check them out; they will familiarize you with Web sites that may be helpful in other courses and perhaps even in your career. The OLC also features multiple-choice questions that give instant feedback and provides other helpful ways to further test your knowledge of the chapter.

7

8

AFTER READING THIS CHAPTER, YOU SHOULD BE ABLE TO:

1 Explain how gross domestic product (GDP) is defined and measured.

2 Describe the relationships among GDP, net domestic product, national income, personal income, and disposable income.

3 Discuss the nature and function of a GDP price index, and describe the difference between nominal GDP and real GDP.

4 List and explain some limitations of the GDP measure.

Measuring Domestic Output and National Income

"Disposable Income Flat." "Personal Consumption Surges." "Investment Spending Stagnates." "GDP Up 4 Percent." These headlines, typical of those found on Yahoo! Finance or in *The Wall Street Journal*, give knowledgeable readers valuable information on the state of the economy. This chapter will help you interpret such headlines and understand the stories reported under them. Specifically, it will help you become familiar with the vocabulary and methods of national income accounting. Such accounting enables economists to measure the long-run rate of economic growth and identify the recessions and expansions associated with the economic ups and downs known as the business cycle. In addition, the terms and ideas that you encounter in this chapter will provide a needed foundation for the macroeconomic models found in subsequent chapters.

Assessing the Economy's Performance

National income accounting measures the economy's overall performance. It does for the economy as a whole what private accounting does for the individual firm or for the individual household.

A business firm measures its flows of income and expenditures regularly—usually every 3 months or once a year. With that information in hand, the firm can gauge its economic health. If things are going well and profits are good, the accounting data can be used to explain that success. Were costs down? Was output up? Have market prices risen? If things are going badly and profits are poor, the firm may be able to identify the reason by studying the record over several accounting periods. All this information helps the firm's managers plot their future strategy.

National income accounting operates in much the same way for the economy as a whole. The Bureau of Economic Analysis (BEA), an agency of the Commerce Department, compiles the National Income and Product Accounts (NIPA) for the U.S. economy. This accounting enables economists and policymakers to:

- Assess the health of the economy by comparing levels of production at regular intervals.
- Track the long-run course of the economy to see whether it has grown, been constant, or declined.
- Formulate policies that will safeguard and improve the economy's health.

Gross Domestic Product

The primary measure of the economy's performance is its annual total output of goods and services or, as it is called, its *aggregate output*. There are several ways to measure aggregate output depending upon how one wishes to define "an economy." For instance, should the value of the cars produced at a Toyota plant in Ohio count as part of the output of the U.S. economy because they are made within the United States or as part of the Japanese economy because Toyota is a Japanese company? As mentioned in Chapter 6, **gross domestic product (GDP)** defines aggregate output as the dollar value of all final goods and services produced within the borders of a country during a specific period of time, typically a year. Under this definition, the value of the cars produced at the Toyota factory in Ohio clearly count as part of U.S. aggregate output rather than Japanese

TABLE 7.1 Comparing Heterogeneous Output by Using Money Prices

Year	Annual Output	Market Value
1	3 sofas and 2 computers	3 at $500 + 2 at $2000 = $5500
2	2 sofas and 3 computers	2 at $500 + 3 at $2000 = $7000

aggregate output because the cars are made within the borders of the United States.[1]

A Monetary Measure

By necessity, GDP is a *monetary measure*. To see why, suppose that the economy produces three sofas and two computers in year 1 and two sofas and three computers in year 2. In which year is output greater? We can't answer that question until we attach a price tag to each of the two products to indicate how society evaluates their relative worth.

That's what GDP does. It measures the value of output in monetary terms. Without such a measure we would have no way of comparing the relative values of the vast number of goods and services produced in different years. In Table 7.1 the price of sofas is $500 and the price of computers is $2000. GDP would gauge the output of year 2 ($7000) as greater than the output of year 1 ($5500) because society places a higher monetary value on the output of year 2. Society is willing to pay $1500 more for the combination of goods produced in year 2 than for the combination of goods produced in year 1.

Avoiding Multiple Counting

To measure aggregate output accurately, all goods and services produced in a particular year must be counted once and only once. Because most products go through a series of production stages before they reach the market, some of their components are bought and sold many times. To avoid counting those components each time, GDP includes only the market value of *final goods* and ignores *intermediate goods* altogether.

Intermediate goods are products that are purchased for resale or further processing or manufacturing. **Final goods** are products that are purchased by their end users. Crude oil is an intermediate good; gasoline used for

---

[1] In contrast to GDP, U.S. gross *national* product (GNP) consists of the total value of all the final goods and services produced by American-supplied resources, whether those goods and services are produced within the borders of the United States or abroad. The U.S. switched from GNP to GDP accounting in 1992 to match the type of accounting used by other countries worldwide.

TABLE 7.2 **Value Added in a Five-Stage Production Process**

(1) Stage of Production	(2) Sales Value of Materials or Product	(3) Value Added
	$ 0	⌉——— $120 (= $120 − $ 0)
Firm A, sheep ranch	120	⌉——— 60 (= 180 − 120)
Firm B, wool processor	180	⌉——— 40 (= 220 − 180)
Firm C, coat manufacturer	220	⌉——— 50 (= 270 − 220)
Firm D, clothing wholesaler	270	⌉——— 80 (= 350 − 270)
Firm E, retail clothier	**350**	
Total sales values	$1140	
Value added (total income)		**$350**

personal transportation is a final good. Steel beams are intermediate goods; completed high-rise apartments are final goods. Lettuce, carrots, and vinegar in restaurant salads are intermediate goods; restaurant salads are final goods. Other examples of final goods are sunglasses bought by consumers, assembly machinery purchased by businesses, surveillance satellites bought by government, and smart phones purchased by foreign buyers.

Why is the value of final goods included in GDP but the value of intermediate goods excluded? Because the value of final goods already includes the value of all the intermediate goods that were used in producing them. Including the value of intermediate goods would amount to **multiple counting,** and that would distort the value of GDP.

To see why, suppose that five stages are needed to manufacture a wool coat and get it to the consumer—the final user. Table 7.2 shows that firm A, a sheep ranch, sells $120 worth of wool to firm B, a wool processor. Firm A pays out the $120 in wages, rent, interest, and profit. Firm B processes the wool and sells it to firm C, a coat manufacturer, for $180. What does firm B do with the $180 it receives? It pays $120 to firm A for the wool and uses the remaining $60 to pay wages, rent, interest, and profit for the resources used in processing the wool. Firm C, the manufacturer, sells the coat to firm D, a wholesaler, which sells it to firm E, a retailer. Then at last a consumer, the final user, comes in and buys the coat for $350.

How much of these amounts should we include in GDP to account for the production of the coat? Just $350, the value of the final product. The $350 includes all the intermediate transactions leading up to the product's final sale. Including the sum of all the intermediate sales, $1140, in GDP would amount to multiple counting. The production and sale of the final coat generated just $350 of output, not $1140.

Alternatively, we could avoid multiple counting by measuring and cumulating only the *value added* at each stage. **Value added** is the market value of a firm's output *less* the value of the inputs the firm has bought from others. At each stage, the difference between what a firm pays for inputs and what it receives from selling the product made from those inputs is paid out as wages, rent, interest, and profit. Column 3 of Table 7.2 shows that the value added by firm B is $60, the difference between the $180 value of its output and the $120 it paid for the input from firm A. We find the total value of the coat by adding together all the values added by the five firms. Similarly, by calculating and summing the values added to all the goods and services produced by all firms in the economy, we can find the market value of the economy's total output—its GDP.

GDP Excludes Nonproduction Transactions

Although many monetary transactions in the economy involve final goods and services, many others do not. These nonproduction transactions must be excluded from GDP because they have nothing to do with the generation of final goods. *Nonproduction transactions* are of two types: purely financial transactions and secondhand sales.

Financial Transactions Purely financial transactions include the following:

- *Public transfer payments* These are the social security payments, welfare payments, and veterans' payments that the government makes directly to households. Since the recipients contribute nothing to *current production* in return, to include such payments in GDP would be to overstate the year's output.

FIGURE 7.1 The expenditures and income approaches to GDP. There are two general approaches to measuring gross domestic product. We can determine GDP as the value of output by summing all expenditures on that output. Alternatively, with some modifications, we can determine GDP by adding up all the components of income arising from the production of that output.

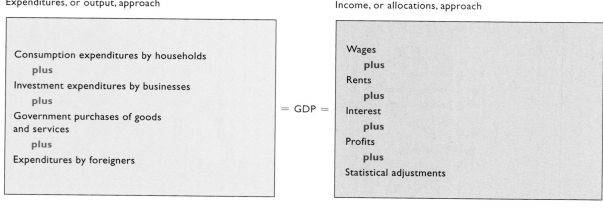

Expenditures, or output, approach

Income, or allocations, approach

Consumption expenditures by households
plus
Investment expenditures by businesses
plus
Government purchases of goods
and services
plus
Expenditures by foreigners

= GDP =

Wages
plus
Rents
plus
Interest
plus
Profits
plus
Statistical adjustments

- *Private transfer payments* Such payments include, for example, the money that parents give children or the cash gifts given during the holidays. They produce no output. They simply transfer funds from one private individual to another and consequently do not enter into GDP.
- *Stock market transactions* The buying and selling of stocks (and bonds) is just a matter of swapping bits of paper. Stock market transactions create nothing in the way of current production and are not included in GDP. Payments for the services provided by a stockbroker *are* included, however, because their services are currently provided and are thus a part of the economy's current output of goods and services.

Secondhand Sales Secondhand sales contribute nothing to current production and for that reason are excluded from GDP. Suppose you sell your 1995 Ford Mustang to a friend; that transaction would be ignored in reckoning this year's GDP because it generates no current production. The same would be true if you sold a brand-new Mustang to a neighbor a week after you purchased it.

Two Ways of Looking at GDP: Spending and Income

Let's look again at how the market value of total output—or of any single unit of total output—is measured. Given the data listed in Table 7.2, how can we measure the market value of a coat?

One way is to see how much the final user paid for it. That will tell us the market value of the final product. Or we can add up the entire wage, rental, interest, and profit

incomes that were created in producing the coat. The second approach is the value-added technique used in Table 7.2.

The final-product approach and the value-added approach are two ways of looking at the same thing. What is spent on making a product is income to those who helped make it. If $350 is spent on manufacturing a coat, then $350 is the total income derived from its production.

We can look at GDP in the same two ways. We can view GDP as the sum of all the money spent in buying it. That is the *output approach*, or **expenditures approach.** Or we can view GDP in terms of the income derived or created from producing it. That is the *earnings* or *allocations approach*, or the **income approach**.

As illustrated in Figure 7.1, we can determine GDP for a particular year either by adding up all that was spent to buy total output or by adding up all the money that was derived as income from its production. Buying (spending money) and selling (receiving income) are two aspects of the same transaction. On the expenditures side of GDP, all final goods produced by the economy are bought either by three domestic sectors (households, businesses, and government) or by foreign buyers. On the income side (once certain statistical adjustments are made), the total receipts acquired from the sale of that total output are allocated to the suppliers of resources as wage, rent, interest, and profit.

The Expenditures Approach

To determine GDP using the expenditures approach, we add up all the spending on final goods and services that has taken place throughout the year. National income accountants use precise terms for the types of spending listed on the left side of Figure 7.1.

Personal Consumption Expenditures (C)

What we have called "consumption expenditures by households," the national-income accountants call **personal consumption expenditures**. This term covers all expenditures by households on goods and services.

In a typical year, roughly 10 percent of these personal consumption expenditures are on **durable goods**—products that have expected lives of three years or more. Such goods include new automobiles, furniture, and refrigerators. Another 30 percent are on **nondurable goods**—products with less than three years of expected life. Included are goods like food, clothing, and gasoline. About 60 percent of personal consumption expenditures are on **services**—the work done by lawyers, hair stylists, doctors, mechanics, and other service providers. Because of this high percentage, economists sometimes refer to the U.S. economy as a *service economy*. National-income accountants combine the household spending on durable goods, nondurable goods, and services and use the symbol C to designate the personal consumption expenditures component of GDP.

Gross Private Domestic Investment (I_g)

Under the heading **gross private domestic investment**, the accountants include the following items:

- All final purchases of machinery, equipment, and tools by business enterprises.
- All construction.
- Changes in inventories.

Notice that this list, except for the first item, includes more than we have meant by "investment" so far. The second item includes residential construction as well as the construction of new factories, warehouses, and stores. Why do the accountants regard residential construction as investment rather than consumption? Because apartment buildings and houses, like factories and stores, earn income when they are rented or leased. Owner-occupied houses are treated as investment goods because they *could be* rented to bring in an income return. So the national income accountants treat all residential construction as investment. Finally, increases in inventories (unsold goods) are considered to be investment because they represent, in effect, "unconsumed output." For economists, all new output that is not consumed is, by definition, capital. An increase in inventories is an addition (although perhaps temporary) to the stock of capital goods, and such additions are precisely how we define investment.

Positive and Negative Changes in Inventories

We need to look at changes in inventories more closely. Inventories can either increase or decrease over some period. Suppose they increased by $10 billion between December 31, 2008, and December 31, 2009. Therefore, in 2009 the economy produced $10 billion more output than people purchased. We need to count all output produced in 2009 as part of that year's GDP, even though some of it remained unsold at the end of the year. This is accomplished by including the $10 billion increase in inventories as investment in 2009. That way the expenditures in 2009 will correctly measure the output produced that year.

Alternatively, suppose that inventories decreased by $10 billion in 2009. This "drawing down of inventories" means that the economy sold $10 billion more of output in 2009 than it produced that year. It did this by selling goods produced in prior years—goods already counted as GDP in those years. Unless corrected, expenditures in 2009 will overstate GDP for 2009. So in 2009 we consider the $10 billion decline in inventories as "negative investment" and subtract it from total investment that year. Thus, expenditures in 2009 will correctly measure the output produced in 2009.

Noninvestment Transactions So much for what investment *is*. You also need to know what it *isn't*. For economists and NIPA accountants, investment does *not* include noninvestment transactions such as the transfer of paper assets (stocks, bonds) or the resale of tangible assets (houses, jewelry, boats). Such financial transactions merely transfer the ownership of existing assets. The investment in the GDP accounts is economic investment—the creation of *new* capital assets. The mere transfer (sale) of claims to existing capital goods does not produce new capital goods. Therefore such transactions (so-called financial investments) are not included as investment in the GDP accounts.

Gross Investment versus Net Investment As we have seen, the category gross private domestic investment includes (1) all final purchases of machinery, equipment, and tools; (2) all construction; and (3) changes in inventories. The words "private" and "domestic" mean that we are speaking of spending by private businesses, not by government (public) agencies, and that the investment is taking place inside the country, not abroad.

The word "gross" means that we are referring to *all* investment goods—both those that replace machinery, equipment, and buildings that were used up (worn out or made obsolete) in producing the current year's output and any net additions to the economy's stock of capital. Gross investment includes investment in replacement capital *and* in added capital.

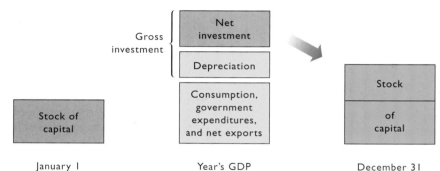

FIGURE 7.2 Gross investment, depreciation, net investment, and the stock of capital. When gross investment exceeds depreciation during a year, net investment occurs. This net investment expands the stock of private capital from the beginning of the year to the end of the year by the amount of the net investment. Other things equal, the economy's production capacity expands.

In contrast, **net private domestic investment** includes *only* investment in the form of added capital. The amount of capital that is used up over the course of a year is called *depreciation*. So

Net investment = gross investment − depreciation

In typical years, gross investment exceeds depreciation. Thus net investment is positive and the nation's stock of capital rises by the amount of net investment. As illustrated in Figure 7.2, the stock of capital at the end of the year exceeds the stock of capital at the beginning of the year by the amount of net investment.

Gross investment need not always exceed depreciation, however. When gross investment and depreciation *are equal*, net investment is zero and there is no change in the size of the capital stock. When gross investment *is less than* depreciation, net investment is negative. The economy then is *disinvesting*—using up more capital than it is producing—and the nation's stock of capital shrinks. That happened in the Great Depression of the 1930s.

National income accountants use the symbol *I* for private domestic investment spending. To differentiate between gross investment and net investment, they add either the subscript *g* or the subscript *n*. But it is gross investment, I_g, that they use when tallying up GDP.

Government Purchases (*G*)

The third category of expenditures in the national income accounts is **government purchases**, officially labeled "government consumption expenditures and gross investment." These expenditures have two components: (1) expenditures for goods and services that government consumes in providing public services and (2) expenditures for *publicly owned capital* such as schools and highways, which have long lifetimes. Government purchases (Federal, state, and local) include all government expenditures on final goods and all direct purchases of resources, including labor. It does *not* include government transfer

payments because, as we have seen, they merely transfer government receipts to certain households and generate

CONSIDER THIS . . .

Stocks versus Flows

An analogy of a reservoir is helpful in thinking about a nation's capital stock, investment, and depreciation. Picture a reservoir that has water flowing in from a river and flowing out from an outlet after it passes through turbines. The volume of water in the reservoir *at any particular point in time* is a "stock." In contrast, the inflow from the river and outflow from the outlet are "flows."

The volume or stock of water in the reservoir will rise if the weekly inflow exceeds the weekly outflow. It will fall if the inflow is less than the outflow. And it will remain constant if the two flows are equal.

Now let's apply this analogy to the stock of capital, gross investment, and depreciation. The stock of capital is the total capital in place at any point in time and is analogous to the level of water in the reservoir. Changes in this capital stock over some period, for example, 1 year, depend on *gross investment* and *depreciation*. Gross investment (analogous to the reservoir inflow) is an addition of capital goods and therefore adds to the stock of capital, while depreciation (analogous to the reservoir outflow) is the using up of capital and thus subtracts from the capital stock. The capital stock increases when gross investment exceeds depreciation, declines when gross investment is less than depreciation, and remains the same when gross investment and depreciation are equal.

Alternatively, the stock of capital increases when *net investment* (gross investment *minus* depreciation) is positive. When net investment is negative, the stock of capital declines, and when net investment is zero, the stock of capital remains constant.

TABLE 7.3 Accounting Statement for the U.S. Economy, 2009 (in Billions)*

Receipts: Expenditures Approach		Allocations: Income Approach	
Sum of:		Sum of:	
Personal consumption expenditures (C)	$10,089	Compensation of employees	$7792
Gross private domestic investment (I_g)	1628	Rents	268
Government purchases (G)	2931	Interest	788
Net exports (X_n)	−392	Proprietors' income	1041
		Corporate profits	1309
		Taxes on production and imports	1090
		Equals:	
		National income	**$12,288**
		National income	$12,288
		Less: Net foreign factor income	105
		Plus: Statistical discrepancy	209
		Plus: Consumption of fixed capital	1864
Equals:		*Equals:*	
Gross domestic product	**$14,256**	**Gross domestic product**	**$14,256**

*Some of the items in the Allocations column combine related categories that appear in the more detailed accounts. All data are subject to government revision.

Source: Bureau of Economic Analysis, **www.bea.gov**.

no production of any sort. National income accountants use the symbol *G* to signify government purchases.

Net Exports (X_n)

International trade transactions are a significant item in national income accounting. But when calculating U.S. GDP, we must keep in mind that we want to total up only those expenditures that are used to purchase goods and services produced *within the borders of the United States.* Thus, we must add in the value of exports, *X*, since exports are by definition goods and services produced within the borders of the United States. Don't be confused by the fact that the expenditures made to buy our exports are made by foreigners. The definition of GDP does not care about *who* is making expenditures on U.S.-made goods and services—only that the goods and services that they buy are made within the borders of the United States. Thus, foreign spending on our exports *must* be included in GDP.

At this point, you might incorrectly think that GDP should be equal to the sum of $C + I_g + G + X$. But this sum overstates GDP. The problem is that, once again, we must consider only expenditures made on *domestically produced* goods and services. As it stands, *C*, I_g, and *G* count expenditures on consumption, investment, and government purchases *regardless* of where those goods and services are made. Crucially, not all of the *C*, I_g, or *G* expenditures are for domestically produced goods and services. Some of the expenditures are for imports—

goods and services produced outside of the United States. Because we wish to count *only* the part of *C*, I_g, and *G* that goes to purchasing domestically produced goods and services, we must subtract the spending that goes to imports, *M*. That subtraction yields the correct formula for calculating gross domestic product: GDP = $C + I_g + G + X − M$.

Accountants simplify this formula for GDP by defining **net exports,** X_n, to be equal to exports minus imports:

$$\text{Net exports } (X_n) = \text{exports } (X) - \text{imports } (M)$$

Using this definition of net exports, the formula for gross domestic product simplifies to,

$$\text{GDP} = C + I_g + G + X_n$$

Table 7.3 shows that in 2009 Americans spent $392 billion more on imports than foreigners spent on U.S. exports. That is, net exports in 2009 were a *minus* $392 billion.

Putting It All Together: GDP = $C + I_g + G + X_n$

Taken together, the four categories of expenditures provide a measure of the market value of a specific year's total output—its GDP. For the United States in 2009 (Table 7.3),

$$\text{GDP} = \$10,089 + 1628 + 2931 - 392 = \$14,256 \text{ billion}$$

Global Perspective 7.1 lists the GDPs of several countries. The values of GDP are converted to dollars using international exchange rates.

GLOBAL PERSPECTIVE 7.1

Comparative GDPs in Trillions of U.S. Dollars, Selected Nations, 2009

The United States, Japan, and Germany have the world's highest GDPs. The GDP data charted below have been converted to U.S. dollars via international exchange rates.

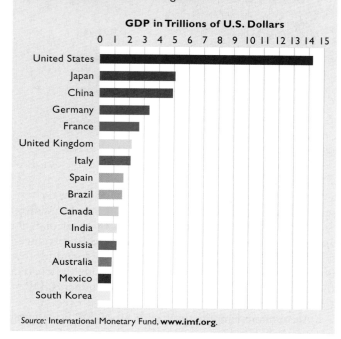

GDP in Trillions of U.S. Dollars

United States, Japan, China, Germany, France, United Kingdom, Italy, Spain, Brazil, Canada, India, Russia, Australia, Mexico, South Korea

Source: International Monetary Fund, **www.imf.org.**

The Income Approach

Table 7.3 shows how 2009's expenditures of $14,256 billion were allocated as income to those responsible for producing the output. It would be simple if we could say that the entire amount of expenditures flowed back to them in the form of wages, rent, interest, and profit. But some expenditures flow to other recipients (such as the government) or to other uses (such as paying to replace the capital goods that have worn out while producing this year's GDP). These must be accounted for to balance the expenditures and income sides of the overall account. We will begin by looking at the items that make up *national income.*

Compensation of Employees

By far the largest share of national income—$7792 billion in 2009—was paid as wages and salaries by business and government to their employees. That figure also includes wage and salary supplements, in particular, payments by employers into social insurance and into a variety of private pension, health, and welfare funds for workers.

Rents

Rents consist of the income received by the households and businesses that supply property resources. They include the monthly payments tenants make to landlords and the lease payments corporations pay for the use of office space. The figure used in the national accounts is *net* rent—gross rental income minus depreciation of the rental property.

Interest

Interest consists of the money paid by private businesses to the suppliers of loans used to purchase capital. It also includes such items as the interest households receive on savings deposits, certificates of deposit (CDs), and corporate bonds.

Proprietors' Income

What we have loosely termed "profits" is broken down by the national income accountants into two accounts: proprietors' income, which consists of the net income of sole proprietorships, partnerships, and other unincorporated businesses; and corporate profits. Proprietors' income flows to the proprietors.

Corporate Profits

Corporate profits are the earnings of corporations. National income accountants subdivide corporate profits into three categories:

- *Corporate income taxes* These taxes are levied on corporations' profits. They flow to the government.
- *Dividends* These are the part of after-tax profits that corporations choose to pay out, or distribute, to their stockholders. They thus flow to households—the ultimate owners of all corporations.
- *Undistributed corporate profits* Any after-tax profits that are not distributed to shareholders are saved, or retained, by corporations to be invested later in new plants and equipment. Undistributed corporate profits are also called *retained earnings.*

Taxes on Production and Imports

The account called **taxes on production and imports** includes general sales taxes, excise taxes, business property taxes, license fees, and customs duties. Why do national income accountants add these indirect business taxes to wages, rent, interest, and profits in determining national income? The answer is, "to account for expenditures that are diverted to the government." Consider an item that would otherwise sell for $1 but costs $1.05 because the government has imposed a 5 percent sales tax. When this item is purchased, consumers will expend $1.05 to buy it. But only $1 will go to the seller (who will then distribute it as income in the form of wages, rent, interest, and profit in order to compensate resource providers). The remaining 5 cents will flow as revenue to the government. The GDP accountants handle the extra 5 cents by placing it into the category called "Taxes on Production and Imports" and loosely consider it to be "income" to government.

From National Income to GDP

We have just shown that expenditures on final goods and services flow either as income to private citizens or as "income" to government. As a result, **national income** is the total of all sources of private income (employee compensation, rents, interest, proprietors' income, and corporate profits) plus government revenue from taxes on production and imports. National income is all the income that flows to American-supplied resources, whether here or abroad, plus taxes on production and imports. But notice that the figure for national income shown in Table 7.3— $12,288 billion—is less than GDP as reckoned by the expenditures approach shown on the left side of the table. The two sides of the accounting statement are brought into balance by subtracting one item from national income and adding two others.

Net Foreign Factor Income First, we need to make a slight adjustment in "national" income versus "domestic" income. National income includes the total income of Americans, whether it was earned in the United States or abroad. But GDP is a measure of *domestic* output—total output produced within the United States regardless of the nationality of those who provide the resources. So in moving from national income to GDP, we must take out the income Americans gain from supplying resources abroad and add in the income that foreigners gain by supplying resources in the United States. That process provides *net foreign factor income*. In 2009, net foreign factor income was $105 billion, meaning that American-owned resources earned $105 billion more in other countries than foreign-owned resources earned in the United States. Because this $105 billion is earnings of Americans, it is

included in U.S. national income. But this income is not part of U.S. domestic income because it reflects earnings from output produced in other nations. It is part of those nations' domestic income, derived from production of their domestic output. Thus, we subtract net foreign factor income from U.S. national income to stay on the correct path to use the income approach to determine the value of *U.S. domestic output* (output produced within the U.S. borders).

Statistical Discrepancy NIPA accountants add a statistical discrepancy to national income to make the income approach match the outcome of the expenditures approach. In 2009 that discrepancy was $209 billion.

Consumption of Fixed Capital Finally, we must recognize that the useful lives of private capital equipment (such as bakery ovens or automobile assembly lines) extend far beyond the year in which they were produced. To avoid understating profit and income in the year of purchase and to avoid overstating profit and income in succeeding years, the cost of such capital must be allocated over its lifetime. The amount allocated is an estimate of how much of the capital is being used up each year. It is called *depreciation*. Accounting for depreciation results in a more accurate statement of profit and income for the economy each year. Publicly owned capital, such as courthouses and bridges, also requires a depreciation allowance in the national income accounts.

The huge depreciation charge made against private and publicly owned capital each year is called **consumption of fixed capital** because it is the allowance for capital that has been "consumed" in producing the year's GDP. It is the portion of GDP that is set aside to pay for the ultimate replacement of those capital goods.

The money allocated to consumption of fixed capital (the depreciation allowance) is a cost of production and thus included in the gross value of output. But this money is not available for other purposes, and, unlike other costs of production, it does not add to anyone's income. So it is not included in national income. We must therefore add it to national income to achieve balance with the economy's expenditures, as in Table 7.3.

Table 7.3 summarizes the expenditures approach and income approach to GDP. The left side shows what the U.S. economy produced in 2009 and what was spent to purchase it. The right side shows how those expenditures were allocated either as income to individuals, as revenue to the government, or to other uses such as paying for the replacement of depreciated capital.

Other National Accounts

Several other national accounts provide additional useful information about the economy's performance. We can derive these accounts by making various adjustments to GDP.

Net Domestic Product

As a measure of total output, GDP does not make allowances for replacing the capital goods used up in each year's production. As a result, it does not tell us how much new output was available for consumption and for additions to the stock of capital. To determine that, we must subtract from GDP the capital that was consumed in producing the GDP and that had to be replaced. That is, we need to subtract consumption of fixed capital (depreciation) from GDP. The result is a measure of **net domestic product (NDP)**:

$$\text{NDP} = \text{GDP} - \text{consumption of fixed capital (depreciation)}$$

For the United States in 2009:

	Billions
Gross domestic product	$14,256
Less: Consumption of fixed capital	1864
Equals: Net domestic product	$12,392

NDP is simply GDP adjusted for depreciation. It measures the total annual output that the entire economy—households, businesses, government, and foreigners—can consume without impairing its capacity to produce in ensuing years.

National Income

Sometimes it is useful to know how much Americans earned for their contributions of land, labor, capital, and entrepreneurial talent. Recall that U.S. national income (NI) includes all income earned through the use of American-owned resources, whether they are located at home or abroad. It also includes taxes on production and imports. To derive NI from NDP, we must subtract the aforementioned statistical discrepancy from NDP and add net foreign factor income, since the latter is income earned by Americans overseas minus income earned by foreigners in the United States.

For the United States in 2009:

	Billions
Net domestic product	$12,392
Less: Statistical discrepancy	209
Plus: Net foreign factor income	105
Equals: National income	$12,288

We know, too, that we can calculate national income through the income approach by simply adding up employee compensation, rent, interest, proprietors' income, corporate profit, and taxes on production and imports.

Personal Income

Personal income (PI) includes all income received, whether earned or unearned. It is likely to differ from national income (income earned) because some income earned—taxes on production and imports, Social Security taxes (payroll taxes), corporate income taxes, and undistributed corporate profits—is not received by households. Conversely, some income received—such as Social Security payments, unemployment compensation payments, welfare payments, disability and education payments to veterans, and private pension payments—is not earned. These transfer payments must be added to obtain PI.

In moving from national income to personal income, we must subtract the income that is earned but not received and add the income that is received but not earned. For the United States in 2009:

	Billions
National income	$12,288
Less: Taxes on production and imports	1090
Less: Social Security contributions	967
Less: Corporate income taxes	315
Less: Undistributed corporate profits	418
Plus: Transfer payments	2528*
Equals: Personal income	$12,026

*Includes statistical discrepancy

Disposable Income

Disposable income (DI) is personal income less personal taxes. Personal taxes include personal income taxes, personal property taxes, and inheritance taxes. Disposable income is the amount of income that households have left over after paying their personal taxes. They are free to divide that income between consumption (C) and saving (S):

$$DI = C + S$$

For the United States in 2009:

	Billions
Personal income	$12,026
Less: Personal taxes	1102
Equals: Disposable income	$10,924

Table 7.4 summarizes the relationships among GDP, NDP, NI, PI, and DI.

The Circular Flow Revisited

Figure 7.3 is an elaborate flow diagram that shows the economy's four main sectors along with the flows of

TABLE 7.4 The Relationship between GDP, NDP, NI, PI, and DI in the United States, 2009*

	Billions
Gross domestic product (GDP)	$14,256
Less: Consumption of fixed capital	1864
Equals: Net domestic product	$12,392
Net domestic product (NDP)	$12,392
Less: Statistical discrepancy	209
Plus: Net foreign factor income	105
Equals: National income (NI)	$12,288
National income (NI)	$12,288
Less: Taxes on production and imports	1090
Less: Social Security contributions	967
Less: Corporate income taxes	315
Less: Undistributed corporate profits	418
Plus: Transfer payments	2528
Equals: Personal income (PI)	$12,026
Personal income (PI)	$12,026
Less: Personal taxes	1102
Equals: Disposable income (DI)	$10,924

*Some of the items combine categories that appear in the more detailed accounts.
Source: Bureau of Economic Analysis, **www.bea.gov**.

expenditures and allocations that determine GDP, NDP, NI, and PI. The orange arrows represent the spending flows—$C + I_g + G + X_n$—that together measure gross domestic product. To the right of the GDP rectangle are green arrows that show first the allocations of GDP and then the adjustments needed to derive NDP, NI, PI, and DI.

The diagram illustrates the adjustments necessary to determine each of the national income accounts. For example, net domestic product is smaller than GDP because consumption of fixed capital flows away from GDP in determining NDP. Also, disposable income is smaller than personal income because personal taxes flow away from PI (to government) in deriving DI.

Note the three domestic sectors of the economy: households, government, and businesses. The household sector has an inflow of disposable income and outflows of consumption spending and saving. The government sector has an inflow of revenue in the form of types of taxes and an outflow of government disbursements in the form of purchases and transfers. The business sector has inflows of three major sources of funds for business investment and an outflow of investment expenditures.

Also, take a look at the foreign sector (all other countries) in the flow diagram. Spending by foreigners on U.S. exports adds to U.S. GDP, but some of U.S. consumption, government, and investment expenditures buy imported products. The flow from foreign markets shows that we handle this complication by calculating net exports (U.S. exports minus U.S. imports). The net export flow may be a positive or negative amount, adding to or subtracting from U.S. GDP.

Finally, you need to be aware that the flows shown in Figure 7.3 are dynamic entities and generally expand in size over time as the economy grows. But not always! Case in point: The Great Recession of 2007–2009—first discussed in the Consider This box on page 123—produced a pronounced slowing of the main spending and income flows. Specifically, U.S. businesses greatly reduced investment expenditures and households initially reduced personal consumption expenditures. Consequently, GDP, NDP, NI, and PI all significantly declined.

QUICK REVIEW 7.2

- Net domestic product (NDP) is the market value of GDP minus consumption of fixed capital (depreciation).
- National income (NI) is all income earned through the use of American-owned resources, whether located at home or abroad. NI also includes taxes on production and imports.
- Personal income (PI) is all income received by households, whether earned or not.
- Disposable income (DI) is all income received by households minus personal taxes.

FIGURE 7.3 U.S. domestic output and the flows of expenditure and income. This figure is an elaborate circular flow diagram that fits the expenditures and allocations sides of GDP to one another. The expenditures flows are shown in orange; the allocations or income flows are shown in green. You should trace through the income and expenditures flows, relating them to the five basic national income accounting measures.

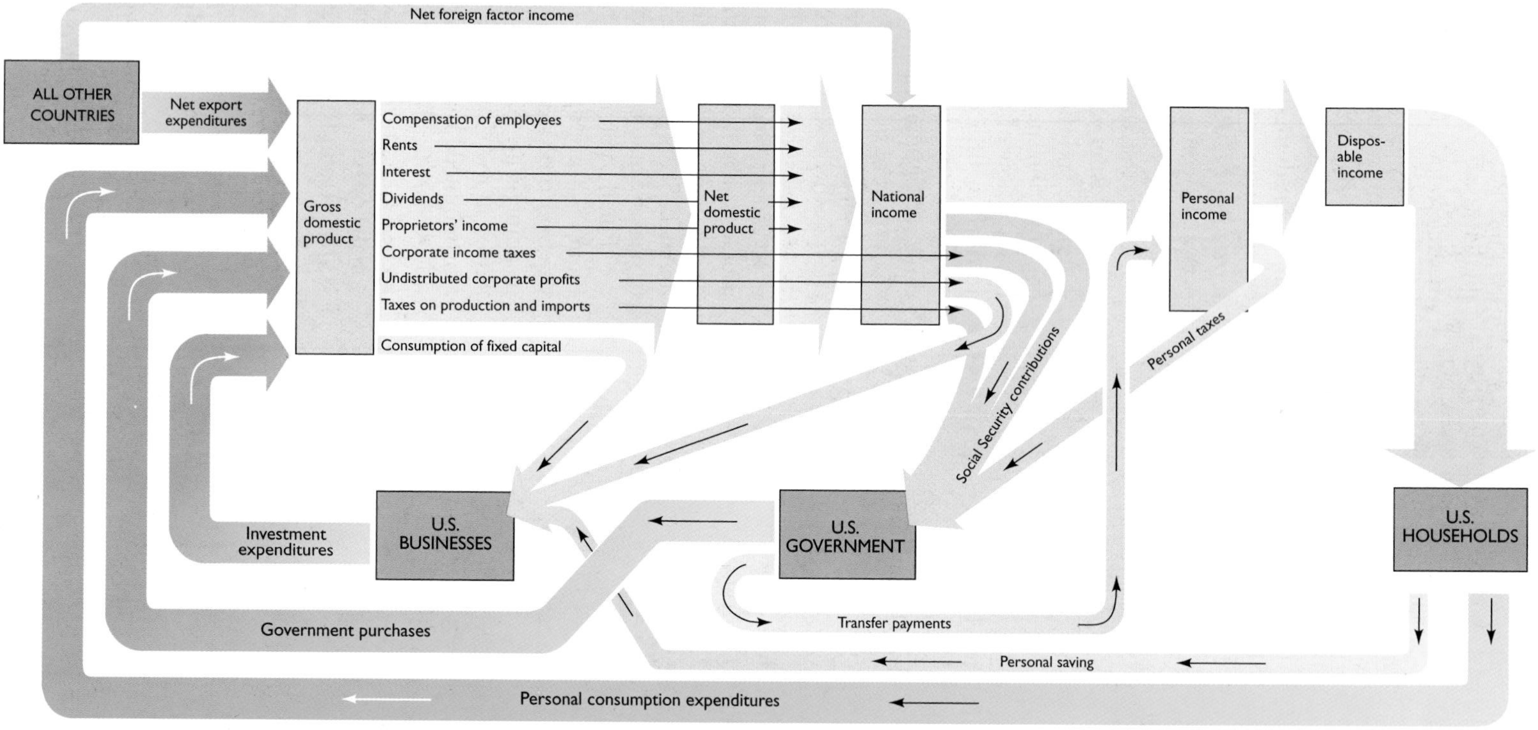

ALL OTHER COUNTRIES

U.S. BUSINESSES

U.S. GOVERNMENT

U.S. HOUSEHOLDS

Net foreign factor income

Net export expenditures

Gross domestic product

Compensation of employees
Rents
Interest
Dividends
Proprietors' income
Corporate income taxes
Undistributed corporate profits
Taxes on production and imports
Consumption of fixed capital

Net domestic product

National income

Personal income

Disposable income

Personal taxes

Social Security contributions

Transfer payments

Personal saving

Investment expenditures

Government purchases

Personal consumption expenditures

Nominal GDP versus Real GDP

Recall that GDP is a measure of the market or money value of all final goods and services produced by the economy in a given year. We use money or nominal values as a common denominator to sum that heterogeneous output into a meaningful total. But, as alluded to in Chapter 6, that creates a problem: How can we compare the market values of GDP from year to year if the value of money itself changes in response to inflation (rising prices) or deflation (falling prices)? After all, we determine the value of GDP by multiplying total output by market prices.

Whether there is a 5 percent increase in output with no change in prices or a 5 percent increase in prices with no change in output, the change in the value of GDP will be the same. And yet it is the *quantity* of goods and services that get produced and distributed to households that affects our standard of living, not the price of those goods and services. For instance, the McDonald's hamburger that sold for 99 cents in 2009 yields the same satisfaction as a nearly identical McDonald's hamburger that sold for 18 cents in 1967.

The way around this problem is to *deflate* GDP when prices rise and to *inflate* GDP when prices fall. These adjustments give us a measure of GDP for various years as if the value of the dollar had always been the same as it was in some reference year. A GDP based on the prices that prevailed when the output was produced is called unadjusted GDP, or **nominal GDP.** A GDP that has been deflated or inflated to reflect changes in the price level is called adjusted GDP, or **real GDP.**

Adjustment Process in a One-Product Economy

There are two ways we can adjust nominal GDP to reflect price changes. For simplicity, let's assume that the economy produces only one good, pizza, in the amounts indicated in Table 7.5 for years 1, 2, and 3. Suppose that we gather revenue data directly from the financial reports of the economy's pizza businesses to measure nominal GDP in various years. After completing our effort, we will have determined nominal GDP for each year, as shown in column 4 of Table 7.5. We will have no way of knowing to what extent changes in price and/or changes in quantity of output have accounted for the increases or decreases in nominal GDP that we observe.

GDP Price Index How can we determine real GDP in our pizza economy? One way is to assemble data on the price changes that occurred over various years (column 2) and use them to establish an overall price index for the entire period. Then we can use the index in each year to adjust nominal GDP to real GDP for that year.

A **price index** is a measure of the price of a specified collection of goods and services, called a "market basket," in a given year as compared to the price of an identical (or highly similar) collection of goods and services in a reference year. That point of reference, or benchmark, is known as the base period, base year, or simply, the reference year. More formally,

$$\frac{\text{Price}}{\text{index}} \underset{\text{in given}}{\text{in given}} = \frac{\text{price of market basket}}{\text{price of same market}} \times 100 \qquad (1)$$

By convention, the price ratio between a given year and the base year is multiplied by 100 to facilitate computation. For example, a price ratio of 2/1 (= 2) is expressed as a price index of 200. A price ratio of 1/3 (= .33) is expressed as a price index of 33.

In our pizza-only example, of course, our market basket consists of only one product. Column 2 of Table 7.5 reveals that the price of pizza was $10 in year 1, $20 in year 2, $25 in year 3, and so on. Let's select year 1 as our

TABLE 7.5 Calculating Real GDP (Base Year = Year 1)

Year	(1) Units of Output	(2) Price of Pizza per Unit	(3) Price Index (Year 1 = 100)	(4) Unadjusted, or Nominal, GDP, (1) × (2)	(5) Adjusted, or Real, GDP
1	5	$10	100	$ 50	$50
2	7	20	200	140	70
3	8	25	250	200	80
4	10	30	—	—	—
5	11	28	—	—	—

base year. Now we can express the successive prices of the contents of our market basket in, say, years 2 and 3 as compared to the price of the market basket in year 1:

$$\text{Price index, year 2} = \frac{\$20}{\$10} \times 100 = 200$$

$$\text{Price index, year 3} = \frac{\$25}{\$10} \times 100 = 250$$

For year 1 the index has to be 100, since that year and the base year are identical.

The index numbers tell us that the price of pizza rose from year 1 to year 2 by 100 percent {= [(200 − 100)/100] × 100} and from year 1 to year 3 by 150 percent {= [(250 − 100)/100] × 100}.

Dividing Nominal GDP by the Price Index

We can now use the index numbers shown in column 3 to deflate the nominal GDP figures in column 4. The simplest and most direct method of deflating is to express the index numbers as hundredths—in decimal form—and then to divide them into corresponding nominal GDP. That gives us real GDP:

$$\text{Real GDP} = \frac{\text{nominal GDP}}{\text{price index (in hundredths)}} \qquad (2)$$

Column 5 shows the results. These figures for real GDP measure the market value of the output of pizza in years 1,

> **WORKED PROBLEMS**
> **W 7.2**
> Real GDP and price indexes

2, and 3 as if the price of pizza had been a constant $10 throughout the 3-year period. In short, real GDP reveals the market value of each year's output measured in terms of dollars that have the same purchasing power as dollars had in the base year.

To test your understanding, extend Table 7.5 to years 4 and 5, using equations 1 and 2. Then run through

> **ORIGIN OF THE IDEA**
> **O 7.1**
> GDP price index

the entire deflating procedure, using year 3 as the base period. This time you will have to inflate some of the nominal GDP data, using the same procedure as we used in the examples.

An Alternative Method

Another way to calculate real GDP is to gather separate data on physical outputs (as in column 1) and their prices (as in column 2) of Table 7.5. We could then determine the market value of outputs in successive years *if the base-year*

TABLE 7.6 Steps for Deriving Real GDP from Nominal GDP

Method 1

1. Find nominal GDP for each year.
2. Compute a GDP price index.
3. Divide each year's nominal GDP by that year's price index (in hundredths) to determine real GDP.

Method 2

1. Break down nominal GDP into physical quantities of output and prices for each year.
2. Find real GDP for each year by determining the dollar amount that each year's physical output would have sold for if base-year prices had prevailed. (The GDP price index can then be found by dividing nominal GDP by real GDP.)

price ($10) had prevailed. In year 2, the 7 units of pizza would have a value of $70 (= 7 units × $10). As column 5 confirms, that $70 worth of output is year 2's real GDP. Similarly, we could determine the real GDP for year 3 by multiplying the 8 units of output that year by the $10 price in the base year.

Once we have determined real GDP through this method, we can identify the price index for a given year simply by dividing the nominal GDP by the real GDP for that year:

$$\frac{\text{Price index}}{\text{(in hundredths)}} = \frac{\text{nominal GDP}}{\text{real GDP}} \qquad (3)$$

Example: In year 2 we get a price index of 200—or, in hundredths, 2.00—which equals the nominal GDP of $140 divided by the real GDP of $70. Note that equation 3 is simply a rearrangement of equation 2. Table 7.6 summarizes the two methods of determining real GDP in our single-good economy.

Real-World Considerations and Data

In the real world of many goods and services, of course, determining GDP and constructing a reliable price index are far more complex matters than in our pizza-only economy. The government accountants must assign a "weight" to each of several categories of goods and services based on the relative proportion of each category in total output. They update the weights annually as expenditure patterns change and roll the base year forward year by year using a moving average of expenditure patterns. The GDP price index used in the United States is called the *chain-type annual-weights price index*—which hints at its complexity. We spare you the details.

Table 7.7 shows some of the relationships between nominal GDP, real GDP, and the GDP price index for the U.S. economy. Here the reference year is 2005, where the

TABLE 7.7 Nominal GDP, Real GDP, and GDP Price Index for the United States, Selected Years

(1) Year	(2) Nominal GDP, Billions	(3) Real GDP, Billions	(4) GDP Price Index (2005 = 100)
1980	$ 2788.1	$ 5839.0	——
1985	4717.5	6849.3	68.9
1990	5800.5	——	72.2
2000	9951.5	11,226.0	88.6
2005	12,638.4	——	100.0
2009	14,256.3	12,987.4	109.8

Source: Bureau of Economic Analysis, **www.bea.gov**.

value of the index is set at 100. Because the U.S. price level has been rising over the long run, the pre-2005 values of real GDP (column 3) are higher than the nominal values of GDP for those years (column 2). This upward adjustment acknowledges that prices were lower in the years before 2005, and thus nominal GDP understated the real output of those years in 2005 prices and must be inflated to show the correct relationship to other years.

Conversely, the rising price level of the post-2005 years caused nominal GDP figures for those years to overstate real output. So the statisticians deflate those figures to determine what real GDP would have been in other years if 2005 prices had prevailed. Doing so reveals that real GDP has been less than nominal GDP since 2005.

By inflating the nominal pre-2005 GDP data and deflating the post-2005 data, government accountants determine annual real GDP, which can then be compared with the real GDP of any other year in the series of years. So the real GDP values in column 3 are directly comparable with one another.

Once we have determined nominal GDP and real GDP, we can compute the price index. And once we have determined nominal GDP and the price index, we can calculate real GDP. Example: Nominal GDP in 2009 was $14,256.3 billion and real GDP was $12,987.4 billion. So the price level in 2009 was 109.8 (= $14,256.3/$12,987.4 × 100), or 9.8 percent higher than in 2005. If we knew the nominal GDP and the price level only, we could find the real GDP for 2009 by dividing the nominal GDP of $14,256.3 by the 2009 price index, expressed in hundredths (1.098).

To test your understanding of the relationships between nominal GDP, real GDP, and the price level, determine the values of the price index for 1980 in Table 7.7 and determine real GDP for 1990 and 2005. We have left those figures out on purpose.

QUICK REVIEW 7.3

- Nominal GDP is output valued at current prices. Real GDP is output valued at constant base-year prices.
- The GDP price index compares the price (market value) of all the goods and services included in GDP in a given year to the price of the same market basket in a reference year.
- Nominal GDP can be transformed into real GDP by dividing the nominal GDP by the GDP price index expressed in hundredths.

Shortcomings of GDP

GDP is a reasonably accurate and highly useful measure of how well or how poorly the economy is performing. But it has several shortcomings as a measure of both total output and well-being (total utility).

Nonmarket Activities

Certain productive activities do not take place in any market—the services of stay-at-home parents, for example, and the labor of carpenters who repair their own homes. Such activities never show up in GDP because the accountants who tally up GDP only get data on economic transactions involving *market activities*—that is, transactions in which output or resources are traded for money. Consequently, GDP understates a nation's total output because it does not count *unpaid work*. There is one exception: The portion of farmers' output that farmers consume themselves *is* estimated and included in GDP.

Leisure

The average workweek (excluding overtime) in the United States has declined since the beginning of the 1900s—from about 53 hours to about 35 hours. Moreover, the greater frequency of paid vacations, holidays, and leave time has shortened the work year itself. This increase in leisure time has clearly had a positive effect on overall well-being. But our system of national income accounting understates well-being by ignoring leisure's value. Nor does the system accommodate the satisfaction—the "psychic income"—that many people derive from their work.

Improved Product Quality

Because GDP is a quantitative measure rather than a qualitative measure, it fails to capture the full value of improvements in product quality. A $200 cell phone purchased today is of very different quality than a cell phone that cost $200 just a decade ago. Today's cell phone is digital and has greater memory capacity, a viewing screen, and quite likely a camera and a music player.

Obviously quality improvement has a great effect on economic well-being, as does the quantity of goods produced. Although the BEA adjusts GDP for quality improvement for selected items, the vast majority of such improvement for the entire range of goods and services does not get reflected in GDP.

The Underground Economy

Embedded in our economy is a flourishing, productive underground sector. Some of the people who conduct business there are gamblers, smugglers, prostitutes, "fences" of stolen goods, drug growers, and drug dealers. They have good reason to conceal their incomes.

Most participants in the underground economy, however, engage in perfectly legal activities but choose illegally not to report their full incomes to the Internal Revenue Service (IRS). A barista at a coffee shop may report just a portion of the tips received from customers. Storekeepers may report only a portion of their sales receipts. Workers who want to hold on to their unemployment compensation benefits may take an "off-the-books" or "cash-only" job. A brick mason may agree to rebuild a neighbor's fireplace in exchange for the neighbor's repairing his boat engine. The value of none of these transactions shows up in GDP.

The value of underground transactions is estimated to be about 8 percent of the recorded GDP in the United States. That would mean that GDP in 2009 was understated by about $1.14 trillion. Global Perspective 7.2 shows estimates of the relative sizes of underground economies in selected nations.

GDP and the Environment

The growth of GDP is inevitably accompanied by "gross domestic by-products," including dirty air and polluted water, toxic waste, congestion, and noise. The social costs of the negative by-products reduce our economic well-being. And since those costs are not deducted from total output, GDP overstates our national well-being. Ironically, when money is spent to clean up pollution and reduce congestion, those expenses are added to the GDP!

Composition and Distribution of Output

The composition of output is undoubtedly important for well-being. But GDP does not tell us whether the currently produced mix of goods and services is enriching or potentially detrimental to society. GDP assigns equal

GLOBAL PERSPECTIVE 7.2

The Underground Economy as a Percentage of GDP, Selected Nations

Underground economies vary in size worldwide. Three factors that help explain the variation are (1) the extent and complexity of regulation, (2) the type and degree of taxation, and (3) the effectiveness of law enforcement.

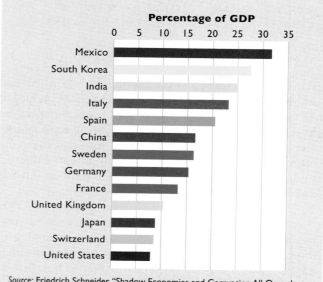

Percentage of GDP

Mexico, South Korea, India, Italy, Spain, China, Sweden, Germany, France, United Kingdom, Japan, Switzerland, United States

Source: Friedrich Schneider, "Shadow Economies and Corruption All Over the World: New Estimates for 145 Countries," *Economics: The Open-Access, Open-Assessment E-Journal*, vol. 1, 2007-9. Used with permission of Friedrich Schneider.

weight to an assault rifle and a set of encyclopedias, as long as both sell for the same price. Moreover, GDP reveals nothing about the way output is distributed. Does 90 percent of the output go to 10 percent of the households, for example, or is the output more evenly distributed? The distribution of output may make a big difference for society's overall well-being.

Noneconomic Sources of Well-Being

Finally, the connection between GDP and well-being is problematic for another reason. Just as a household's income does not measure its total happiness, a nation's GDP does not measure its total well-being. Many things could make a society better off without necessarily raising GDP: a reduction of crime and violence, peaceful relations with other countries, people's greater civility toward one another, better understanding between parents and children, and a reduction of drug and alcohol abuse.

The Bureau of Economic Analysis (BEA), an Agency of the Department of Commerce, Compiles the NIPA Tables. Where Does It Get the Actual Data?

Discussions of national income accounting often leave the impression that the data for the National Income and Product Accounts magically appear from some mysterious place. Let's take a tour to see where economists get their data.

Consumption The BEA derives the data for the consumption component of the GDP accounts from four main sources:

- The Census Bureau's *Retail Trade Survey*, which gains sales information from a sample of 22,000 firms.
- The Census Bureau's *Survey of Manufacturers*, which gathers information on shipments of consumer goods from 50,000 establishments.
- The Census Bureau's *Service Survey*, which collects sales data from 30,000 service businesses.
- Industry trade sources. For example, data on auto sales and aircraft are collected directly from auto and aircraft manufacturers.

Investment The sources of the data for the investment component of GDP include:

- All the sources above used to determine consumption. Purchases of capital goods are separated from purchases of consumer goods. For example, estimates of investment in equipment and software are based on manufacturers' shipments reported in the *Survey of Manufacturers*, the *Service Survey*, and industry sources.
- Census construction surveys. The Census Bureau's *Housing Starts Survey* and *Housing Sales Survey* produce the data

used to measure the amount of housing construction, and the *Construction Progress Reporting Survey* is the source of data on nonresidential construction. The BEA determines changes in business inventories through the *Retail Trade Survey*, the *Wholesale Trade Survey* (of 7100 wholesale firms), and the *Survey of Manufacturing.*

Government Purchases The data for government purchases (officially "government consumption and investment expenditures") are obtained through the following sources:

- The U.S. Office of Personnel Management, which collects data on wages and benefits, broken out by the private and public sector. Wages and benefits of government employees are the single largest "purchase" by Federal, state, and local government.
- The previously mentioned Census Bureau's construction surveys, which break out private and public sector construction expenditures.
- The Census Bureau's *Survey of Government Finance*, which provides data on government consumption and investment expenditures.

Net Exports The BEA determines net exports through two main sources:

- The U.S. Customs Service, which collects data on exports and imports of goods.
- BEA surveys of potential domestic exporters and importers of services, which collect data on exports and imports of services.

So there you have it. Not so magical after all!

Source: Based on Joseph A. Ritter, "Feeding the National Accounts," Federal Reserve Bank of St. Louis *Review*, March–April 2000, pp. 11–20. For those interested, this article also provides information on the sources of data for the income side of the national accounts.

Summary

1. Gross domestic product (GDP), a basic measure of an economy's economic performance, is the market value of all final goods and services produced within the borders of a nation in a year.

2. Final goods are those purchased by end users, whereas intermediate goods are those purchased for resale or for further processing or manufacturing. Intermediate goods, nonproduction transactions, and secondhand sales are purposely excluded in calculating GDP.

3. GDP may be calculated by summing total expenditures on all final output or by summing the income derived from the production of that output.

4. By the expenditures approach, GDP is determined by adding consumer purchases of goods and services, gross investment spending by businesses, government purchases, and net exports: $GDP = C + I_g + G + X_n$.

5. Personal consumption expenditures consist of expenditures on goods (durable goods and nondurable goods) and services. About 60 percent of consumer expenditures in the United States are on services, leading economists to refer to the U.S. economy as a *service economy*.

6. Gross investment is divided into (a) replacement investment (required to maintain the nation's stock of capital at its existing level) and (b) net investment (the net increase in the stock of capital). In most years, net investment is positive and therefore the economy's stock of capital and production capacity increase.

7. By the income or allocations approach, GDP is calculated as the sum of compensation to employees, rents, interest, proprietors' income, corporate profits, taxes on production and imports *minus* net foreign factor income, *plus* a statistical discrepancy and consumption of fixed capital.

8. Other national accounts are derived from GDP. Net domestic product (NDP) is GDP less the consumption of fixed capital. National income (NI) is total income earned by a nation's resource suppliers plus taxes on production and imports; it is found by subtracting a statistical discrepancy from NDP and adding net foreign factor income to NDP. Personal income (PI) is the total income paid to households prior to any allowance for personal taxes. Disposable income (DI) is personal income after personal taxes have been paid. DI measures the amount of income available to households to consume or save.

9. Price indexes are computed by dividing the price of a specific collection or market basket of output in a particular period by the price of the same market basket in a base period and multiplying the result (the quotient) by 100. The GDP price index is used to adjust nominal GDP for inflation or deflation and thereby obtain real GDP.

10. Nominal (current-dollar) GDP measures each year's output valued in terms of the prices prevailing in that year. Real (constant-dollar) GDP measures each year's output in terms of the prices that prevailed in a selected base year. Because real GDP is adjusted for price-level changes, differences in real GDP are due only to differences in production activity.

11. GDP is a reasonably accurate and very useful indicator of a nation's economic performance, but it has its limitations. It fails to account for nonmarket and illegal transactions, changes in leisure and in product quality, the composition and distribution of output, and the environmental effects of production. GDP should not be interpreted as a complete measure of well-being.

Terms and Concepts

national income accounting

gross domestic product (GDP)

intermediate goods

final goods

multiple counting

value added

expenditures approach

income approach

personal consumption expenditures (C)

durable goods

nondurable goods

services

gross private domestic investment (I_g)

net private domestic investment

government purchases (G)

net exports (X_n)

taxes on production and imports

national income

consumption of fixed capital

net domestic product (NDP)

personal income (PI)

disposable income (DI)

nominal GDP

real GDP

price index

Questions

1. In what ways are national-income statistics useful? **LO1**
2. Why do national-income accountants compare the market value of the total outputs in various years rather than actual physical volumes of production? What problem is posed by any comparison over time of the market values of various total outputs? How is this problem resolved? **LO1**

3. Which of the following goods are usually intermediate goods and which are usually final goods: running shoes, cotton fibers, watches, textbooks, coal, sunscreen lotion, lumber? **LO1**

4. Why do economists include only final goods and services in measuring GDP for a particular year? Why don't they include the value of the stocks and bonds bought and sold? Why don't they include the value of the used furniture bought and sold? **LO1**

5. Explain why an economy's output, in essence, is also its income. **LO1**

6. Provide three examples of each: consumer durable goods, consumer nondurable goods, and services. **LO1**

7. Why are changes in inventories included as part of investment spending? Suppose inventories declined by $1 billion during 2010. How would this affect the size of gross private domestic investment and gross domestic product in 2010? Explain. **LO1**

8. What is the difference between gross private domestic investment and net private domestic investment? If you were to determine net domestic product (NDP) through the expenditures approach, which of these two measures of investment spending would be appropriate? Explain. **LO2**

9. Use the concepts of gross investment and net investment to distinguish between an economy that has a rising stock of capital and one that has a falling stock of capital. Explain: "Though net investment can be positive, negative, or zero, it is impossible for gross investment to be less than zero." **LO2**

10. Define net exports. Explain how U.S. exports and imports each affect domestic production. How are net exports determined? Explain how net exports might be a negative amount. **LO2**

11. Contrast the ideas of nominal GDP and real GDP. Why is one more reliable than the other for comparing changes in the standard of living over a series of years? What is the GDP price index and what is its role in differentiating nominal GDP and real GDP? **LO3**

12. Which of the following are included or excluded in this year's GDP? Explain your answer in each case. **LO4**
   a. Interest received on an AT&T corporate bond.
   b. Social Security payments received by a retired factory worker.
   c. Unpaid services of a family member in painting the family home.
   d. Income of a dentist from the dental services provided.
   e. A monthly allowance a college student receives from home.
   f. Money received by Josh when he resells his nearly brand-new Honda automobile to Kim.
   g. The publication and sale of a new college textbook.
   h. An increase in leisure resulting from a 2-hour decrease in the length of the workweek, with no reduction in pay.
   i. A $2 billion increase in business inventories.
   j. The purchase of 100 shares of Google common stock.

13. **LAST WORD** What government agency compiles the U.S. NIPA tables? In what U.S. department is it located? Of the several specific sources of information, name one source for each of the four components of GDP: consumption, investment, government purchases, and net exports.

Problems

1. Suppose that annual output in year 1 in a 3-good economy is 3 quarts of ice cream, 1 bottle of shampoo, and 3 jars of peanut butter. In year 2, the output mix changes to 5 quarts of ice cream, 2 bottles of shampoo, and 2 jars of peanut butter. If the prices in both years are $4 per quart for ice cream, $3 per bottle of shampoo, and $2 per jar of peanut butter, what was the economy's GDP in year 1? What was its GDP in year 2? **LO1**

2. If in some country personal consumption expenditures in a specific year are $50 billion, purchases of stocks and bonds are $30 billion, net exports are –$10 billion, government purchases are $20 billion, sales of secondhand items are $8 billion, and gross investment is $25 billion, what is the country's GDP for the year? **LO1**

3. Assume that a grower of flower bulbs sells its annual output of bulbs to an Internet retailer for $70,000. The retailer, in turn, brings in $160,000 from selling the bulbs directly to final customers. What amount would these two transactions add to personal consumption expenditures and thus to GDP during the year? **LO1**

4. To the right is a list of domestic output and national income figures for a certain year. All figures are in billions. The questions that follow ask you to determine the major national

Personal consumption expenditures	$245
Net foreign factor income	4
Transfer payments	12
Rents	14
Statistical discrepancy	8
Consumption of fixed capital (depreciation)	27
Social Security contributions	20
Interest	13
Proprietors' income	33
Net exports	11
Dividends	16
Compensation of employees	223
Taxes on production and imports	18
Undistributed corporate profits	21
Personal taxes	26
Corporate income taxes	19
Corporate profits	56
Government purchases	72
Net private domestic investment	33
Personal saving	20

income measures by both the expenditures and the income approaches. The results you obtain with the different methods should be the same. LO2

   a. Using the above data, determine GDP by both the expenditures and the income approaches. Then determine NDP.
   b. Now determine NI in two ways: first, by making the required additions or subtractions from NDP; and second, by adding up the types of income and taxes that make up NI.
   c. Adjust NI (from part *b*) as required to obtain PI.
   d. Adjust PI (from part *c*) as required to obtain DI.

5. Using the following national income accounting data, compute (*a*) GDP, (*b*) NDP, and (*c*) NI. All figures are in billions. LO2

Compensation of employees	$194.2
U.S. exports of goods and services	17.8
Consumption of fixed capital	11.8
Government purchases	59.4
Taxes on production and imports	14.4
Net private domestic investment	52.1
Transfer payments	13.9
U.S. imports of goods and services	16.5
Personal taxes	40.5
Net foreign factor income	2.2
Personal consumption expenditures	219.1
Statistical discrepancy	0

6. Suppose that in 1984 the total output in a single-good economy was 7000 buckets of chicken. Also suppose that in 1984 each bucket of chicken was priced at $10. Finally, assume that in 2005 the price per bucket of chicken was $16 and that 22,000 buckets were produced. Determine the GDP price index for 1984, using 2005 as the base year. By what percentage did the price level, as measured by this index, rise between 1984 and 2005? What were the amounts of real GDP in 1984 and 2005? LO3

7. The following table shows nominal GDP and an appropriate price index for a group of selected years. Compute real GDP. Indicate in each calculation whether you are inflating or deflating the nominal GDP data. LO3

Year	Nominal GDP, Billions	Price Index (2005 = 100)	Real GDP, Billions
1968	$ 909.8	22.01	$_____
1978	2293.8	40.40	$_____
1988	5100.4	66.98	$_____
1998	8793.5	85.51	$_____
2008	14,441.4	108.48	$_____

8. Assume that the total value of the following items is $600 billion in a specific year for Upper Mongoose: net exports = $50 billion; value of new goods and services produced in the underground economy = $75 billion; personal consumption expenditures = $300 billion; value of the services of stay-at-home parents = $25 billion; gross domestic investment = $100 billion; government purchases = $50 billion. What is Upper Mongoose's GDP for the year? What is the size of the underground economy as a percentage of GDP? By what percentage would GDP be boosted if the value of the services of stay-at-home spouses were included in GDP? LO4

FURTHER TEST YOUR KNOWLEDGE AT
www.mcconnell19e.com

At the text's Online Learning Center (OLC), **www.mcconnell19e.com**, you will find one or more Web-based questions that require information from the Internet to answer. We urge you to check them out; they will familiarize you with Web sites that may be helpful in other courses and perhaps even in your career. The OLC also features multiple-choice questions that give instant feedback and provides other helpful ways to further test your knowledge of the chapter.

Economic Growth

People living in rich countries tend to take economic growth and rising standards of living for granted. Recessions—periods during which output declines—are normally infrequent and temporary, usually lasting less than a year. Once they pass, modern capitalistic economies return to growing, and living standards continue their seemingly inexorable rise.

But a look back at history or a look around the world today quickly dispels any confidence that economic growth and rising standards of living are automatic or routine. Historically, continually rising living standards are a recent phenomenon, seen only during the last century or two. Before that time, living standards barely rose—if at all—from one generation to the next. And a look around the world today reveals huge differences in standards of living resulting from the disturbing fact that, although some countries have enjoyed decades or even centuries of steadily rising per capita income levels, other countries have experienced hardly any economic growth at all.

This chapter investigates the causes of economic growth, what institutional structures appear to promote economic growth, and the controversies surrounding the benefits and costs of economic growth. As you will see, economic growth has been perhaps the most revolutionary and powerful force in history. Consequently, no study of economics is complete without a thorough understanding of the causes and consequences of economic growth.

Economic Growth

Economists define and measure **economic growth** as either:

- An increase in real GDP occurring over some time period.
- An increase in real GDP per capita occurring over some time period.

With either definition, economic growth is calculated as a percentage rate of growth per quarter (3-month period) or per year. For the first definition, for example, real GDP in the United States was $12,976.2 billion in 2006 and $13,254.1 billion in 2007. So the U.S. economic growth rate for 2007 was 2.1 percent $\{= [(\$13,254.1 \text{ billion} - \$12,976.2 \text{ billion})/\$12,976.2 \text{ billion}] \times 100\}$. Growth rates normally are positive, but not always. In recession year 2009, for instance, the U.S. rate of economic growth was a *minus* 2.4 percent.

The second definition of economic growth in the bulleted list takes into consideration the size of the population. **Real GDP per capita** (or per capita output) is the amount of real output per person in a country. It is calculated, as follows:

$$\text{Real GDP per capita} = \frac{\text{Real GDP}}{\text{Population}}$$

For example, in 2006 the real GDP in the United States was $12,976.2 billion and population was 298.8 million. Therefore, real GDP per capita in that year was $43,432. In 2007 real GDP per capita increased to $43,929. So the growth rate of real GDP per capita in 2007 was 1.1 percent $\{= [(\$43,929 - \$43,432)/\$43,432] \times 100\}$. In contrast, real GDP per capita fell by 3.3 percent in recession year 2009.

For measuring expansion of military potential or political preeminence, the growth of real GDP is more useful. Unless specified otherwise, growth rates reported in the news and by international agencies use this definition of economic growth. For comparing living standards, however, the second definition is superior. While China's GDP in 2008 was $4326 billion compared with Denmark's $343 billion, Denmark's real GDP per capita was $62,118 compared with China's hugely lower $3267. And in some cases growth of real GDP can be misleading. The African nation

of Eritrea had real GDP growth of 1.3 percent per year from 2000–2008. But over the same period its annual growth of population was 3.8 percent, resulting in a decline in real GDP per capita of roughly 2.5 percent per year.

Growth as a Goal

Growth is a widely held economic goal. The expansion of total output relative to population results in rising real wages and incomes and thus higher standards of living. An economy that is experiencing economic growth is better able to meet people's wants and resolve socioeconomic problems. Rising real wages and income provide richer opportunities to individuals and families—a vacation trip, a personal computer, a higher education—without sacrificing other opportunities and pleasures. A growing economy can undertake new programs to alleviate poverty, embrace diversity, cultivate the arts, and protect the environment without impairing existing levels of consumption, investment, and public goods production.

In short, *growth lessens the burden of scarcity*. A growing economy, unlike a static economy, can consume more today while increasing its capacity to produce more in the future. By easing the burden of scarcity—by relaxing society's constraints on production—economic growth enables a nation to attain its economic goals more readily and to undertake new endeavors that require the use of goods and services to be accomplished.

Arithmetic of Growth

Why do economists pay so much attention to small changes in the rate of economic growth? Because those changes really matter! For the United States, with a current nominal GDP of about $14.3 trillion, the difference between a 3 percent and a 4 percent rate of growth is about $143 billion of output each year. For a poor country, a difference of one-half of a percentage point in the rate of growth may mean the difference between starvation and mere hunger.

The mathematical approximation called the **rule of 70** provides a quantitative grasp of the effect of economic growth. The rule of 70 tells us that we can find the number of years it will take for some measure to double, given its annual percentage increase, by dividing that percentage increase into the number 70. So

$$\begin{matrix} \text{Approximate} \\ \text{number of years} \\ \text{required to double} \\ \text{real GDP} \end{matrix} = \frac{70}{\begin{matrix} \text{annual percentage rate} \\ \text{of growth} \end{matrix}}$$

Examples: A 3 percent annual rate of growth will double real GDP in about 23 (= 70 ÷ 3) years. Growth of 8 percent per year will double real GDP in about 9 (= 70 ÷ 8) years. The rule of 70 is applicable generally. For example, it works for estimating how long it will take the price level or a savings account to double at various percentage rates of inflation or interest. When compounded over many years, an apparently small difference in the rate of growth thus becomes highly significant. Suppose China and Italy start with identical GDPs, but then China grows at an 8 percent yearly rate, while Italy grows at 2 percent. China's GDP would double in about 9 years, while Italy's GDP would double in 35 years.

WORKED PROBLEMS

W 8.1

GDP growth

Growth in the United States

Table 8.1 gives an overview of economic growth in the United States since 1950. Column 2 reveals strong growth as measured by increases in real GDP. Note that between 1950 and 2009 real GDP increased about sixfold. But the U.S. population also increased. Nevertheless, in column 4 we find that real GDP per capita rose more than threefold over these years.

What has been the *rate* of U.S. growth? Real GDP grew at an annual rate of about 3.2 percent between 1950 and 2009. Real GDP per capita increased 2 percent per year over that time. But we must qualify these raw numbers in several ways:

- *Improved products and services* Since the numbers in Table 8.1 do not fully account for improvements in products and services, they understate the growth of economic well-being. Such purely quantitative data do not fully compare an era of vacuum tube computers and low-efficiency V8 hot rods with an era of digital cell phone networks and fuel-sipping, hybrid-drive vehicles.

- *Added leisure* The increases in real GDP and per capita GDP identified in Table 8.1 were accomplished despite increases in leisure. The average workweek, once 50 hours, is now about 35 hours (excluding overtime hours). Again the raw growth numbers understate the gain in economic well-being.

- *Other impacts* These measures of growth do not account for any effects growth may have had on the environment and the quality of life. If growth debases the physical environment, excessively warms the planet, and creates a stressful work environment, the bare growth numbers will overstate the gains in well-being that result from growth. On the other hand, if growth leads to stronger environmental protections or a more secure and stress-free lifestyle, these numbers will understate the gains in well-being.

In Chapter 6, we made two other key points about U.S. growth rates. First, they are not constant or smooth over time. Like those of other countries, U.S. growth rates vary quarterly and annually depending on a variety of factors such as the introduction of major new inventions and the economy's current position in the business cycle. Second, many countries share the U.S. experience of positive and ongoing economic growth. But sustained growth is both a historically new occurrence and also one that is not shared equally by all countries.

TABLE 8.1 Real GDP and Real GDP per Capita, Selected Years, 1950–2009

(1) Year	(2) Real GDP, Billions of 2005 $	(3) Population, Millions	(4) Real GDP Per Capita, 2005 $ (2) ÷ (3)
1950	$ 2006	152	$13,197
1960	2831	181	15,640
1970	4270	205	20,829
1980	5839	228	25,610
1990	8034	250	32,136
2000	11,226	282	39,809
2009	12,987	307	42,303

Source: Data are from the Bureau of Economic Analysis, **www.bea.gov**, and the U.S. Census Bureau, **www.census.gov**.

QUICK REVIEW 8.1

- Economists measure economic growth as either (a) an increase in real GDP over time or (b) an increase in real GDP per capita over time.

- Real GDP in the United States has grown at an average annual rate of about 3.2 percent since 1950; real GDP per capita has grown at roughly a 2 percent annual rate over that same period.

Modern Economic Growth

We now live in an era of wireless high-speed Internet connections, genetic engineering, and space exploration. New inventions and new technologies drive continual economic growth and ongoing increases in living standards. But it wasn't always like this. Economic growth and sustained increases in living standards are a historically recent phenomenon that started with the Industrial Revolution of the late 1700s. Before the Industrial Revolution, living standards were basically flat over long periods of time so that, for instance, Greek peasants living in the year 300 B.C. had about the same material standard of living as Greek peasants living in the year A.D. 1500. By contrast, our current era of **modern economic growth** is characterized by sustained and ongoing increases in living standards that can cause dramatic increases in the standard of living within less than a single human lifetime.

Economic historians informally date the start of the Industrial Revolution to the year 1776, when the Scottish inventor James Watt perfected a powerful and efficient steam engine. This steam engine inaugurated the modern era since the device could be used to drive industrial factory equipment, steamships, and steam locomotives.

The new industrial factories mass-produced goods for the first time. This meant that nearly all manufacturing shifted from items produced by hand by local craftsmen to items mass-produced in distant factories. The new steamships and steam locomotives meant that resources could easily flow to factories and that the products of factories could be shipped to distant consumers at low cost. The result was a huge increase in long-distance trade and a major population shift as people left farms to go work in the towns and cities where the new industrial factories were concentrated.

Steam power would later be largely replaced by electric power, and many more inventions would follow the steam engine that started the Industrial Revolution. These included railroads, motorized vehicles, telephones, airplanes, container ships, computers, the Internet, and many more. But the key point is that the last 200 or so years of history have been fundamentally different from anything that went before.

The biggest change has been change itself. Whereas in earlier times material standards of living and the goods and services that people produced and consumed changed very little even over the course of an entire human lifespan, today people living in countries experiencing modern economic growth are constantly exposed to new technologies, new products, and new services.

What is more, modern economic growth has vastly affected cultural, social, and political arrangements.

- Culturally, the vast increases in wealth and living standards have allowed ordinary people for the first time in history to have significant time for leisure activities and the arts.
- Socially, countries experiencing modern economic growth have abolished feudalism, instituted universal public education, and largely eliminated ancient social norms and legal restrictions against women and minorities doing certain jobs or holding certain positions.
- Politically, countries experiencing modern economic growth have tended to move toward democracy, a form of government that was extremely rare before the start of the Industrial Revolution.

In addition, the average human lifespan has more than doubled, from an average of less than 30 years before modern economic growth began in the late 1700s to a worldwide average of over 67 years today. Thus, for the first time in world history, the average person can expect to live into old age. These and other changes speak to the truly revolutionary power of economic growth and naturally lead economists to consider the causes of economic growth and what policies could be pursued to sustain and promote it. Their desire is intensified by the reality that economic growth is distributed so unevenly around the world.

The Uneven Distribution of Growth

Modern economic growth has spread only slowly from its British birthplace. It first advanced to France, Germany, and other parts of western Europe in the early 1800s before spreading to the United States, Canada, and Australia by the mid 1800s. Japan began to industrialize in the 1870s, but the rest of Asia did not follow until the early to mid 1900s, at which time large parts of Central and South America as well as the Middle East also began to experience modern economic growth. Most recent has been Africa, which for the most part did not experience modern economic growth until the last few decades. Notably, some parts of the world have yet to experience modern economic growth at all.

The different starting dates for modern economic growth in various parts of the world are the main cause of the vast differences in per capita GDP levels seen today. The current huge gaps between rich countries like the United States and Japan and poor countries like North Korea and Burundi were shown previously in Global Perspective 6.1. But the huge divergence in living standards caused by the fact that different countries started modern economic growth at different times is best seen in Figure 8.1, which shows how GDP per capita has evolved since 1820 in the United States, western Europe, Latin America, Asia, and Africa.

FIGURE 8.1 The great divergence in standards of living. Income levels around the world were very similar in 1820. But they are now very different because certain areas, including the United States and western Europe, began experiencing modern economic growth much earlier than other areas.

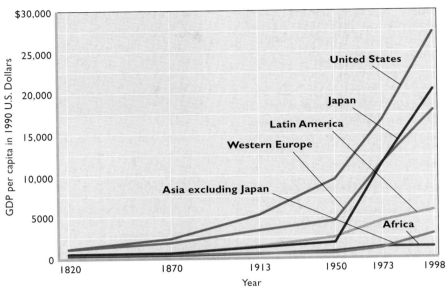

Source: Angus Maddison, *The World Economy: A Millennial Perspective*, (Paris: OECD, 2001), p. 264.

To make the comparison of living standards easier, income levels in all places and at all times have been converted into 1990 U.S. dollars. Using this convention, it is clear that in 1820 per capita incomes in all areas were quite similar, with the richest area in the world in 1820, western Europe, having an average per capita income of $1232, while the poorest area of the world at that time, Africa, had an average per capita income of $418. Thus, in 1820, average incomes in the richest area were only about three times larger than those in the poorest area.

But because western Europe and the United States started experiencing modern economic growth earlier than other areas, they have now ended up vastly richer than other areas, despite the fact that per capita incomes in nearly all places have increased at least a bit. For instance, per capita GDP in the United States in 1998 was $27,331 while it was only $1368 in Africa. Thus, because modern economic growth has occurred for nearly two centuries in the United States compared to a few decades in Africa, average living standards in the United States in 1998 were nearly 20 times higher than those in Africa.

Catching Up Is Possible

Do not get the wrong impression looking at Figure 8.1. Countries that began modern economic growth more recently are *not* doomed to be permanently poorer than the countries that began modern economic growth at an earlier date. This is true because people can adopt technology more quickly than they can invent it. Broadly speaking, the richest countries today have achieved that status because they have the most advanced technology. But because they already have the most advanced technology, they must invent new technology to get even richer. Because inventing and implementing new technology is slow and costly, real GDP per capita in the richest **leader countries** typically grows by an average annual rate of just 2 or 3 percent per year.

By contrast, poorer **follower countries** can grow much faster because they can simply adopt existing technologies from rich leader countries. For instance, in many places in Africa today, the first telephones most people have ever been able to use are cell phones. That is, these countries have not even bothered to install the copper wires necessary for land-line telephones, which are basically a nineteenth-century technology. Instead, they have gone directly for Internet-capable mobile phone networks, a twenty-first-century technology. By doing so, they skip past many stages of technology and development that the United States and other currently rich countries had to pass through. In effect, they jump directly to the most modern, most highly productive technology. The result is that, under the right circumstances, it is possible for poorer countries to experience extremely rapid increases

TABLE 8.2 Real GDP per Capita in 1960 and 2007 Plus Average Annual Growth Rates of Real GDP per Capita from 1960–2007 for Selected Countries. (Figures are in 2005 dollars.)

Country	Real GDP per Capita, 1960	Real GDP per Capita, 2007	Average Annual Growth Rate, 1960–2007
United States	$14,766	$42,887	2.3
United Kingdom	11,257	32,181	2.3
France	9347	29,663	2.5
Ireland	6666	41,625	4.0
Japan	5472	30,585	3.7
Singapore	4149	44,619	5.2
Hong Kong	3849	43,121	5.3
South Korea	1765	23,850	5.7

Note: GDP figures for all countries are measured in "international dollars" of equal value to U.S. dollars in 2005.

Source: Penn World Table version 6.3, **pwt.econ.upenn.edu**. Used by permission of the Center for International Comparisons at the University of Pennsylvania.

in living standards. This can continue until they have caught up with the leader countries and become leader countries themselves. Once that happens, their growth rates fall down to the 2 or 3 percent rate typical of leader countries. This happens because once they are also rich and using the latest technology, their growth rates are limited by the rate at which new technology can be invented and applied.

Table 8.2 shows both how the growth rates of leader countries are constrained by the rate of technological progress as well as how certain follower countries have been able to catch up by adopting more advanced technologies and growing rapidly. Table 8.2 shows real GDP per capita in 1960 and 2007 as well as the average annual growth rate of real GDP per capita between 1960 and 2007 for three countries—the United States, the United Kingdom, and France—that were already rich leader countries in 1960 as well as for five other nations that were relatively poor follower countries at that time. To make comparisons easy, the GDPs and GDPs per capita for all countries are expressed in terms of 2005 U.S. dollars. The countries are ordered by their respective GDPs per capita in 1960, so that the richest country in the world at the time, the United States, is listed first while the poorest of the eight selected countries at the time, South Korea, is listed last.

First, notice that the average annual growth rates of the three leader countries—the United States, the United Kingdom, and France—have all been between 2.2 and 2.5 percent per year because their growth rates are limited by the rate at which new technologies can be invented and applied. By contrast, the five countries that were follower countries in 1960 have been able to grow much faster, between 3.7 percent per year and 5.7 percent per year. This

Economic Growth Rates Matter!

When compounded over many decades, small absolute differences in rates of economic growth add up to substantial differences in real GDP and standards of living. Consider three hypothetical countries—Slogo, Sumgo, and Speedo. Suppose that in 2008 these countries have identical levels of real GDP ($6 trillion), population (200 million), and real GDP per capita ($30,000). Also, assume that annual real GDP growth is 2 percent in Slogo, 3 percent in Sumgo, and 4 percent in Speedo.

How will these alternative growth rates affect real GDP and real GDP per capita over a long period, say, a 70-year life span? By 2078 the 2, 3, and 4 percent growth rates would boost real GDP from $6 trillion to:
- $24 trillion in Slogo.
- $47 trillion in Sumgo.
- $93 trillion in Speedo.

For illustration, let's assume that each country experienced an average annual population growth of 1 percent over the 70 years. Then, in 2078 real GDP per capita would be about:
- $60,000 in Slogo.
- $118,000 in Sumgo.
- $233,000 in Speedo.

Even small differences in growth rates matter!

has had remarkable effects on their standards of living relative to the leader countries. For instance, Ireland's GDP per capita was only 60 percent that of its neighbor, the United Kingdom, in 1960. But because Ireland grew at a 4 percent rate for the next 47 years while the United Kingdom grew at only a 2.3 percent rate over that time period, by 2007 Ireland's GDP per capita was actually higher than the United Kingdom's GDP per capita. Ireland had become a leader country, too.

The growth experiences of the other four nations that were poor in 1960 have been even more dramatic. Hong Kong, for instance, moved from a GDP per capita that was less than one-third of that enjoyed by the United Kingdom in 1960 to a GDP per capita 25 percent higher than that of the United Kingdom in 2007. The Consider This box above emphasizes how quickly small differences in growth rates can change both the level of real GDP per capita and how countries stand in relation to each other in terms of real GDP per capita. This chapter's Last Word on rapid economic growth in China also reinforces our point.

Finally, you may be puzzled as to why the GDP per capita of the United States in 2007 in Table 8.2 is so much higher than that of other rich leader countries. Why, for instance, is U.S. GDP per capita 44 percent higher than French GDP per capita? One important reason is that U.S. citizens put in substantially more labor time than do the citizens of most other leader countries. First, a much larger fraction of the U.S. population is employed than in other rich leader countries. Second, U.S. employees work many more hours per year than do employees in other rich leader countries. For example, 62.1 percent of the working-age population of the United States was employed in 2005 compared to 51.0 percent in France. That's a difference of about 20 percent. And American employees worked an average of 1804 total hours during 2005, compared to an average of 1505 total hours for French workers. That's also a difference of about 20 percent. Added together, these two differences between U.S. and French labor supply imply about a 40 percent difference in the total number of hours worked in the French and American economies. Thus, differences in labor supply help explain differences between rich leader countries in terms of their differing levels of GDP per person.

Buy why do Americans supply so much more labor than workers in France and some of the other rich leader countries? Explanations put forth by economists include cultural differences regarding the proper balance between work and leisure, stronger unions in France and other rich leader countries, and more generous unemployment and welfare programs in France and other rich leader countries. France and other rich leader countries also tend to have higher tax rates than the United States—something that may significantly discourage employment. And, finally, the legal work-week is shorter in some countries than it is in the United States.

QUICK REVIEW 8.2

- Before the advent of modern economic growth starting in England in the late 1700s, living standards showed no sustained increases over time.
- Large differences in standards of living exist today because certain areas like the United States have experienced nearly 200 years of modern economic growth while other areas have had only a few decades of economic growth.
- Poor follower countries can catch up with and even surpass the living standards of rich leader countries by adopting the cutting-edge technologies and institutions already developed by rich leader countries.
- Substantial differences in GDP per capita among technologically advanced leader countries are often caused by differences in the amount of labor supplied.

Institutional Structures That Promote Growth

Table 8.2 demonstrates that poor follower countries can catch up and become rich leader countries by growing rapidly. But how does a country start that process and enter into modern economic growth? And once it has started modern economic growth, how does it keep the process going?

Economic historians have identified several institutional structures that promote and sustain modern economic growth. Some structures increase the savings and investment that are needed to fund the construction and maintenance of the huge amounts of infrastructure required to run modern economies. Other institutional structures promote the development of new technologies. And still others act to ensure that resources flow efficiently to their most productive uses. These growth-promoting institutional structures include:

- **Strong property rights** These appear to be absolutely necessary for rapid and sustained economic growth. People will not invest if they believe that thieves, bandits, or a rapacious and tyrannical government will steal their investments or their expected returns.
- **Patents and copyrights** These are necessary if a society wants a constant flow of innovative new technologies and sophisticated new ideas. Before patents and copyrights were first issued and enforced, inventors and authors usually saw their ideas stolen before they could profit from them. By giving inventors and authors the exclusive right to market and sell their creations, patents and copyrights give a strong financial incentive to invent and create.
- **Efficient financial institutions** These are needed to channel the savings generated by households toward the businesses, entrepreneurs, and inventors that do most of society's investing and inventing. Banks as well as stock and bond markets appear to be institutions crucial to modern economic growth.
- **Literacy and widespread education** Without highly educated inventors, new technologies do not get developed. And without a highly educated work-force, it is impossible to implement those technologies and put them to productive use.
- **Free trade** Free trade promotes economic growth by allowing countries to specialize so that different types of output can be produced in the countries where they can be made most efficiently. In addition, free trade promotes the rapid spread of new ideas so that innovations made in one country quickly spread to other countries.

Patents and Innovation

It costs U.S. and European drug companies about $1 billion to research, patent, and safety-test a new drug because literally thousands of candidate drugs fail for each drug that succeeds. The only way to cover these costs is by relying on patent protections that give a drug's developer the exclusive monopoly right to market and sell the new drug for 20 year following the patent application. The revenues over that time period will hopefully be enough to cover the drug's development costs and—if the drug is popular—generate a profit for the drug company.

Leader and follower countries have gotten into heated disputes over patented drugs, however, because the follower countries have often refused to recognize the patents granted to pharmaceutical companies in rich countries. India, for instance, has allowed local drug companies to copy and sell drugs that were developed by U.S. companies and are still under patent protection in the United States.

This benefits Indian consumers because competition among the local drug companies drives down the price to below the monopoly price that would be charged by the patent owner. But the weak patent protections in India have a side effect. They make it completely unprofitable for local drug producers to try to develop innovative new drugs. Local rivals would simply copy the new drugs and sell them at very low prices. So India has recently moved to strengthen its patent protections to try to provide financial incentives to transform its local drug companies from copycats into innovators. But note that the innovative new drugs that may result from the increased patent protections are not without a cost. As patent protections in India are improved, inexpensive local drugs copied from the leader countries will no longer be available to Indian consumers.

- *A competitive market system* Under a market system, prices and profits serve as the signals that tell firms what to make and how much of it to make. Rich leader countries vary substantially in terms of how much government regulation they impose on markets, but in all cases, firms have substantial autonomy to follow market signals in deciding on current production and in making investments to produce what they believe consumers will demand in the future.

Several other difficult-to-measure factors also influence a nation's capacity for economic growth. The overall social-cultural-political environment of the United States, for example, has encouraged economic growth. Beyond the market system that has prevailed in the United States, the United States also has had a stable political system characterized by democratic principles, internal order, the right of property ownership, the legal status of enterprise, and the enforcement of contracts. Economic freedom and political freedom have been "growth-friendly."

In addition, and unlike some nations, there are virtually no social or moral taboos on production and material progress in the United States. The nation's social philosophy has embraced wealth creation as an attainable and desirable goal and the inventor, the innovator, and the business-person are accorded high degrees of prestige and respect in American society. Finally, Americans have a positive attitude toward work and risk taking, resulting in an ample supply of willing workers and innovative entrepreneurs. A flow of energetic immigrants has greatly augmented that supply.

The nearby Consider This box deals with how fast-growing follower countries such as India sometimes alter their growth-related institutional structures as they grow richer. Web Chapter 22 looks at the special problems of economic growth in developing nations.

Determinants of Growth

Our discussion of modern economic growth and the institutional structures that promote it has purposely been general. We now want to focus our discussion on six factors that directly affect the *rate* of economic growth. These determinants of economic growth can be grouped into four supply factors, one demand factor, and one efficiency factor.

Supply Factors

Four of the determinants of economic growth relate to the physical ability of the economy to expand. They are:
- Increases in the quantity and quality of natural resources.
- Increases in the quantity and quality of human resources.
- Increases in the supply (or stock) of capital goods.
- Improvements in technology.

These **supply factors**—changes in the physical and technical agents of production—enable an economy to expand its potential GDP.

Demand Factor

The fifth determinant of economic growth is the **demand factor:**

- To achieve the higher production potential created by the supply factors, households, businesses, and government must *purchase* the economy's expanding output of goods and services.

When that occurs, there will be no unplanned increases in inventories and resources will remain fully employed. Economic growth requires increases in total spending to realize the output gains made available by increased production capacity.

Efficiency Factor

The sixth determinant of economic growth is the **efficiency factor:**

- To reach its full production potential, an economy must achieve economic efficiency as well as full employment.

The economy must use its resources in the least costly way (productive efficiency) to produce the specific mix of goods and services that maximizes people's well-being (allocative efficiency). The ability to expand production, together with the full use of available resources, is not sufficient for achieving maximum possible growth. Also required is the efficient use of those resources.

The supply, demand, and efficiency factors in economic growth are related. Unemployment caused by insufficient total spending (the demand factor) may lower the rate of new capital accumulation (a supply factor) and delay expenditures on research (also a supply factor). Conversely, low spending on investment (a supply factor) may cause insufficient spending (the demand factor) and unemployment. Widespread inefficiency in the use of resources (the efficiency factor) may translate into higher costs of goods and services and thus lower profits, which in turn may slow innovation and reduce the accumulation of capital (supply factors). Economic growth is a dynamic process in which the supply, demand, and efficiency factors all interact.

ORIGIN OF THE IDEA
O 8.1
Growth theory

Production Possibilities Analysis

To put the six factors affecting the rate of economic growth into better perspective, let's use the production possibilities analysis introduced in Chapter 1.

FIGURE 8.2 Economic growth and the production possibilities curve. Economic growth is made possible by the four supply factors that shift the production possibilities curve outward, as from *AB* to *CD*. Economic growth is realized when the demand factor and the efficiency factor move the economy from point *a* to point *b*.

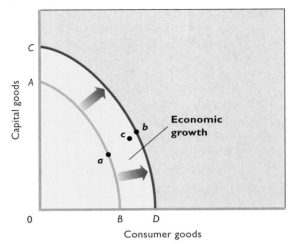

Growth and Production Possibilities

Recall that a curve like *AB* in Figure 8.2 is a production possibilities curve. It indicates the various *maximum* combinations of products an economy can produce with its fixed quantity and quality of natural, human, and capital resources and its stock of technological knowledge. An improvement in any of the supply factors will push the production possibilities curve outward, as from *AB* to *CD*.

But the demand factor reminds us that an increase in total spending is needed to move the economy from a point like *a* on curve *AB* to any of the points on the higher curve *CD*. And the efficiency factor reminds us that we need least-cost production and an optimal location on *CD* for the resources to make their maximum possible dollar contribution to total output. You will recall from Chapter 1 that this "best allocation" is determined by expanding production of each good until its marginal benefit equals its marginal cost. Here, we assume that this optimal combination of capital and consumer goods occurs at point *b*.

Example: The net increase in the size of the labor force in the United States in recent years has been 1.5 to 2 million workers per year. That increment raises the economy's production capacity. But obtaining the extra output that these added workers could produce depends on their success in finding jobs. It also depends on whether or not the jobs are in firms and industries where the workers' talents are fully and optimally used. Society does not want new labor-force entrants to be unemployed. Nor does it want pediatricians working as plumbers or pediatricians producing services for which marginal costs exceed marginal benefits.

Normally, increases in total spending match increases in production capacity, and the economy moves from a point on the previous production possibilities curve to a point on the expanded curve. Moreover, the competitive market system tends to drive the economy toward productive and allocative efficiency. Occasionally, however, the economy may end up at some point such as *c* in Figure 8.2. That kind of outcome occurred in the United States during the severe recession of 2007–2009. Real output fell far below the real output that the economy would have produced if it had achieved full employment and operated on its production possibilities curve.

Labor and Productivity

Although the demand and efficiency factors are important, discussions of economic growth focus primarily on supply factors. Society can increase its real output and income in two fundamental ways: (1) by increasing its inputs of resources and (2) by raising the productivity of those inputs. Figure 8.3 concentrates on the input of *labor* and provides a useful framework for discussing the role of supply factors in growth. A nation's real GDP in any year depends on the input of labor (measured in hours of work) multiplied by **labor productivity** (measured as real output per hour of work):

Real GDP = hours of work × labor productivity

Thought of this way, a nation's economic growth from one year to the next depends on its *increase* in labor inputs (if any) and its *increase* in labor productivity (if any).

Illustration: Assume that the hypothetical economy of Ziam has 10 workers in year 1, each working 2000 hours per year (50 weeks at 40 hours per week). The total input

> **WORKED PROBLEMS**
>
> **W 8.2**
>
> Productivity and economic growth

of labor therefore is 20,000 hours. If productivity (average real output per hour of work) is $10, then real GDP in Ziam will be $200,000 (= 20,000 × $10). If work hours rise to 20,200 and labor productivity rises to $10.40, Ziam's real GDP will increase to $210,080 in year 2. Ziam's rate of economic growth will be about 5% [= ($210,080 − $200,000)/$200,000] for the year.

Hours of Work What determines the number of hours worked each year? As shown in Figure 8.3, the hours of labor input depend on the size of the employed labor force and the length of the average workweek. Labor-force size

FIGURE 8.3 The supply determinants of real output.

Real GDP is usefully viewed as the product of the quantity of labor inputs (hours of work) multiplied by labor productivity.

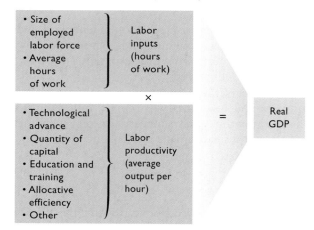

depends on the size of the working-age population and the **labor-force participation rate**—the percentage of the working-age population actually in the labor force. The length of the average workweek is governed by legal and institutional considerations and by collective bargaining agreements negotiated between unions and employers.

Labor Productivity Figure 8.3 tells us that labor productivity is determined by technological progress, the quantity of capital goods available to workers, the quality of the labor itself, and the efficiency with which inputs are allocated, combined, and managed. Productivity rises when the health, training, education, and motivation of workers improve; when workers have more and better machinery and natural resources with which to work; when production is better organized and managed; and when labor is reallocated from less-efficient industries to more-efficient industries.

Accounting for Growth

The president's Council of Economic Advisers uses a system called **growth accounting** to assess the relative importance of the supply-side elements that contribute to changes in real GDP. This system groups these elements into two main categories:

- Increases in hours of work.
- Increases in labor productivity.

Labor Inputs versus Labor Productivity

Table 8.3 provides the relevant data for the United States for five periods. The symbol "Q" in the table stands for "quarter" of the year. The beginning points for the first four

TABLE 8.3 Accounting for the Growth of U.S. Real GDP, 1953–2007 Plus Projection from 2009 to 2020 (Average Annual Percentage Changes)

Item	Actual				Projected
	1953 Q2 to 1973 Q4	1973 Q4 to 1995 Q2	1995 Q2 to 2001 Q1	2001 Q1 to 2007 Q3	2009 Q1 to 2020 Q4
Increase in real GDP	3.6	2.8	3.8	2.6	2.5
Increase in quantity of labor	1.1	1.3	1.4	−0.1	0.2
Increase in labor productivity	2.5	1.5	2.4	2.7	2.3

Source: Derived from *Economic Report of the President, 2008,* p. 45; and *Economic Report of the President, 2010,* p. 76.

periods are business-cycle peaks, and the last period includes future projections by the Council of Economic Advisers. It is clear from the table that both increases in the quantity of labor and increases in labor productivity are important sources of economic growth. Between 1953 and 2009, the labor force increased from 63 million to 154 million workers. Over that period the average length of the workweek remained relatively stable. Falling birthrates slowed the growth of the native population, but increased immigration partly offset that slowdown. As indicated in the Consider This box on the next page, of particular significance was a surge of women's participation in the labor force. Partly as a result, U.S. labor-force growth averaged 1.6 million workers per year over those 56 years.

The growth of labor productivity also has been important to economic growth. In fact, productivity growth has usually been the more significant factor, with the exception of 1973–1995 when productivity growth greatly slowed. For example, between 2001 and 2007, productivity growth was responsible for all of the 2.6 percent average annual economic growth. As shown in the far right column of Table 8.3, productivity growth is projected to account for 92 percent of the growth of real GDP between 2009 and 2020.

Because increases in labor productivity are so important to economic growth, economists go to the trouble of investigating and assessing the relative importance of the factors that contribute to productivity growth. There are five factors that, together, appear to explain changes in productivity growth rates: technological advance, the amount of capital each worker has to work with, education and training, economies of scale, and resource allocation. We will examine each factor in turn, noting how much each factor contributes to productivity growth.

Technological Advance

The largest contributor to productivity growth is technological advance, which is thought to account for about 40 percent of productivity growth. As economist Paul Romer stated, "Human history teaches us that economic growth springs from better recipes, not just from more cooking."

Technological advance includes not only innovative production techniques but new managerial methods and new forms of business organization that improve the process of production. Generally, technological advance is generated by the discovery of new knowledge, which allows resources to be combined in improved ways that increase output. Once discovered and implemented, new knowledge soon becomes available to entrepreneurs and firms at relatively low cost. Technological advance therefore eventually spreads through the entire economy, boosting productivity and economic growth.

Technological advance and capital formation (investment) are closely related, since technological advance usually promotes investment in new machinery and equipment. In fact, technological advance is often *embodied* within new capital. For example, the purchase of new computers brings into industry speedier, more powerful computers that incorporate new technology.

Technological advance has been both rapid and profound. Gas and diesel engines, conveyor belts, and assembly lines are significant developments of the past. So, too, are fuel-efficient commercial aircraft, integrated microcircuits, personal computers, digital photography, and containerized shipping. More recently, technological advance has exploded, particularly in the areas of computers, photography, wireless communications, and the Internet. Other fertile areas of recent innovation are medicine and biotechnology.

Quantity of Capital

A second major contributor to productivity growth is increased capital, which explains roughly 30 percent of productivity growth. More and better plant and equipment make workers more productive. And a nation acquires more capital by saving some of its income and using that savings to invest in plant and equipment.

Although some capital substitutes for labor, most capital is complementary to labor—it makes labor more productive. A key determinant of labor productivity is the amount of capital goods available *per worker.* If both the aggregate stock of capital goods and the size of the labor

CONSIDER THIS . . .

Women, the Labor Force, and Economic Growth

The substantial rise in the number of women working in the paid workforce in the United States has been one of the major labor market trends of the last 50 years. In 1960, about 40 percent of women worked full-time or part-time in paid jobs. Today, that number is about 60 percent.

Women have greatly increased their productivity in the workplace, mostly by becoming better educated and professionally trained. Rising productivity has increased women's wage rates. Those higher wages have raised the opportunity costs—the forgone wage earnings—of staying at home. Women have therefore substituted employment in the labor market for traditional home activities. This substitution has been particularly pronounced among married women. (Single women have always had high labor-force participation rates.)

Furthermore, changing lifestyles and the widespread availability of birth control have freed up time for greater labor-force participation by women. Women not only have fewer children, but those children are spaced closer together in age. Thus women who leave their jobs during their children's early years return to the labor force sooner.

Greater access to jobs by women also has raised the labor-force participation of women. Service industries—teaching, nursing, and office work, for instance—that traditionally have employed many women have expanded rapidly in the past several decades. Also, the population in general has shifted from farms and rural regions to urban areas, where jobs for women are more abundant and more geographically accessible. Additionally, occupational barriers to professions have greatly eroded, resulting in many more women becoming business managers, lawyers, professors, and physicians.

In summary, women in the United States are better educated, more productive, and more efficiently employed than ever before. Their greater presence in the labor force has contributed greatly to U.S. economic growth.

force increase over a given period, the individual worker is not necessarily better equipped and productivity will not necessarily rise. But the quantity of capital equipment available per U.S. worker has increased greatly over time. (In 2008 it was about $118,200 per worker.)

Public investment in the U.S. **infrastructure** (highways and bridges, public transit systems, wastewater treatment facilities, water systems, airports, educational facilities, and so on) has also grown over the years. This publicly owned capital complements private capital. Investments in new highways promote private investment in new factories and retail stores along their routes. Industrial parks developed by local governments attract manufacturing and distribution firms.

Private investment in infrastructure also plays a large role in economic growth. One example is the tremendous growth of private capital relating to communications systems over the years.

Education and Training

Ben Franklin once said, "He that hath a trade hath an estate," meaning that education and training contribute to a worker's stock of **human capital**—the knowledge and skills that make a worker productive. Investment in human capital includes not only formal education but also on-the-job training. Like investment in physical capital, investment in human capital is an important means of increasing labor productivity and earnings. An estimated 15 percent of productivity growth derives from investments in people's education and skills.

One measure of a nation's quality of labor is its level of educational attainment. Figure 8.4 shows large gains in education attainment over the past several decades. In 1960 only 41 percent of the U.S. population age 25 or older had at least a high school education; and only 8 percent had a college or postcollege education. By 2009, those numbers had increased to 87 and 29 percent, respectively. Clearly, more people are receiving more education than ever before.

But all is not upbeat with education in the United States. Many observers think that the quality of education in the United States has declined. For example, U.S.

FIGURE 8.4 Changes in the educational attainment of the U.S. adult population. The percentage of the U.S. adult population, age 25 or older, completing high school and college has been rising over recent decades.

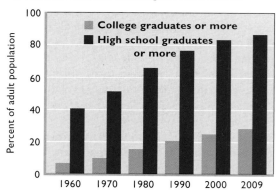

Source: U.S. Census Bureau, **www.census.gov**.

GLOBAL PERSPECTIVE 8.1

Average Test Scores of Eighth-Grade Students in Math and Science, Top 10 Test-Taking Countries and the United States

The test performance of U.S. eighth-grade students did not compare favorably with that of eighth-graders in several other nations in the Fourth International Math and Science Study (2007).

Mathematics

Rank		Score
1	Taiwan	598
2	South Korea	597
3	Singapore	593
4	Hong Kong	572
5	Japan	570
6	Hungary	517
7	Great Britain	513
8	Russia	512
9	United States	508
10	Lithuania	506

Science

Rank		Score
1	Singapore	567
2	Taiwan	561
3	Japan	554
4	South Korea	553
5	Great Britain	542
6	Hungary	539
7	Czech Republic	539
8	Slovenia	538
9	Hong Kong	530
10	Russia	530
11	United States	520

students perform poorly on science and math tests relative to students in many other nations (see Global Perspective 8.1). And the United States has been producing fewer engineers and scientists, a problem that may trace back to inadequate training in math and science in elementary and high schools. For these reasons, much recent public policy discussion and legislation has been directed toward improving the quality of the U.S. education and training system.

Economies of Scale and Resource Allocation

Economies of scale and improved resource allocation are a fourth and fifth source of productivity growth, and together they explain about 15 percent of productivity growth.

Economies of Scale Reductions in per-unit production costs that result from increases in output levels are called **economies of scale.** Markets have increased in size over time, allowing firms to increase output levels and thereby achieve production advantages associated with greater size. As firms expand their size and output, they are able to use larger, more productive equipment and employ methods of manufacturing and delivery that increase productivity. They also are better able to recoup substantial investments in developing new products and production methods. Examples: A large manufacturer of autos can use elaborate assembly lines with computerization and robotics, while smaller producers must settle for less-advanced technologies using more labor inputs. Large pharmaceutical firms greatly reduce the average amount of labor (researchers, production workers) needed to produce each pill as they increase the number of pills produced. Accordingly, economies of scale result in greater real GDP and thus contribute to economic growth.

Improved Resource Allocation Improved resource allocation means that workers over time have moved from low-productivity employment to high-productivity employment. Historically, many workers have shifted from agriculture, where labor productivity is low, to manufacturing, where it is quite high. More recently, labor has shifted away from some manufacturing industries to even higher-productivity industries such as computer software, business consulting, and pharmaceuticals. As a result of such shifts, the average productivity of U.S. workers has increased.

Also, discrimination in education and the labor market has historically deterred some women and minorities from entering high-productivity jobs. With the decline of such discrimination over time, many members of those groups have shifted from lower-productivity jobs to higher-productivity jobs. The result has been higher overall labor productivity and real GDP.

Finally, things such as tariffs, import quotas, and other barriers to international trade tend to relegate resources to relatively unproductive pursuits. The long-run movement toward liberalized international trade through international agreements has improved the allocation of resources, increased labor productivity, and expanded real output, both here and abroad.

The Rise in the Average Rate of Productivity Growth

Figure 8.5 shows the growth of labor productivity (as measured by changes in the index of labor productivity) in the United States from 1973 to 2009, along with separate trend lines for 1973–1995 and 1995–2009. Labor productivity in the business sector grew by an average of only 1.5 percent yearly over the 1973–1995 period. But productivity growth averaged 2.8 percent between 1995 and 2009. Many economists believe that this higher productivity growth resulted from a significant new wave of technological advance, coupled with global competition. Some economists think there is a good chance that the higher trend rates of productivity growth could continue for many years to come.

This increase in productivity growth is important because real output, real income, and real wages are linked to labor productivity. To see why, suppose you are alone on an uninhabited island. The number of fish you can catch or coconuts you can pick per hour—your productivity—is your real wage (or real income) per hour. By *increasing* your productivity, you can improve your standard of living because you can gather more fish and more coconuts (goods) for each hour of work.

So it is for the economy as a whole: Over long periods, the economy's labor productivity determines its average real hourly wage, which includes fringe benefits such as health care insurance and contributions to pensions. The economy's income per hour is equal to its output per hour. So productivity growth is the economy's main route for improving the living standards for its workers. It allows firms to pay higher wages without lowering their business profits.

Reasons for the Rise in the Average Rate of Productivity Growth

Why has productivity growth increased relative to earlier periods?

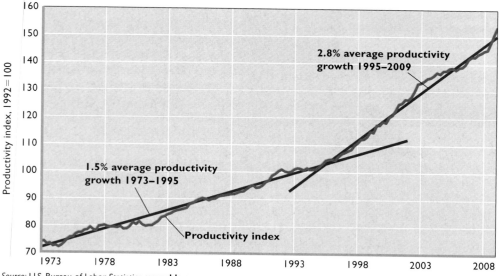

FIGURE 8.5 Growth of labor productivity in the United States, 1973–2009. U.S. labor productivity (here, for the business sector) increased at an average annual rate of only 1.5 percent from 1973 to 1995. But between 1995 and 2009, it rose to an annual rate of 2.8 percent.

Source: U.S. Bureau of Labor Statistics, **www.bls.gov**.

The Microchip and Information Technology

The core element of the productivity speedup is an explosion of entrepreneurship and innovation based on the microprocessor, or *microchip*, which bundles transistors on a piece of silicon. Some observers liken the invention of the microchip to that of electricity, the automobile, air travel, the telephone, and television in importance and scope.

The microchip has found its way into thousands of applications. It has helped create a wide array of new products and services and new ways of doing business. Its immediate results were the pocket calculator, the bar-code scanner, the personal computer, the laptop computer, and more powerful business computers. But the miniaturization of electronic circuits also advanced the development of many other products such as cell phones and pagers, computer-guided lasers, global positioning equipment, energy conservation systems, Doppler radar, digital cameras, and machines to decipher the human genome.

Perhaps of greatest significance, the widespread availability of personal and laptop computers stimulated the desire to tie them together. That desire promoted rapid development of the Internet and all its many manifestations, such as business-to-household and business-to-business electronic commerce (e-commerce). The combination of the computer, fiber-optic cable, wireless technology, and the Internet constitutes a spectacular advance in **information technology,** which has been used to connect all parts of the world.

New Firms and Increasing Returns

Hundreds of new **start-up firms** advanced various aspects of the new information technology. Many of these firms created more "hype" than goods and services and quickly fell by the wayside. But a number of firms flourished, eventually to take their places among the nation's largest firms. Examples of those firms include Intel (microchips); Apple and Dell (personal computers); Microsoft and Oracle (computer software); Cisco Systems (Internet switching systems); America Online (Internet service provision); Yahoo and Google (Internet search engines); and eBay and Amazon.com (electronic commerce). There are scores more! Most of these firms were either "not on the radar" or "a small blip on the radar" 30 years ago. Today each of them has large annual revenue and employs thousands of workers.

Successful new firms often experience **increasing returns,** a situation in which a given percentage increase in the amount of inputs a firm uses leads to an even larger percentage increase in the amount of output the firm produces. For example, suppose that a company called Techco decides to double the size of its operations to meet the growing demand for its services. After doubling its plant and equipment and doubling its workforce, say, from 100 workers to 200

workers, it finds that its total output has tripled from 8000 units to 24,000 units. Techco has experienced increasing returns; its output has increased by 200 percent, while its inputs have increased by only 100 percent. That is, its labor productivity has gone up from 80 units per worker (= 8000 units/100 workers) to 120 units per worker (= 24,000 units/200 workers). Increasing returns boost labor productivity and reduce per-unit production costs. Since these cost reductions result from increases in output levels, they are examples of *economies of scale.*

Both emerging firms as well as established firms can exploit several different sources of increasing returns and economies of scale:

- *More specialized inputs* Firms can use more specialized and thus more productive capital and workers as they expand their operations. A growing new e-commerce business, for example, can purchase highly specialized inventory management systems and hire specialized personnel such as accountants, marketing managers, and system maintenance experts.

- *Spreading of development costs* Firms can spread high product development costs over greater output. For example, suppose that a new software product costs $100,000 to develop and only $2 per unit to manufacture and sell. If the firm sells 1000 units of the software, its per-unit cost will be $102 [= ($100,000 + $2000)/1000], but if it sells 500,000 units, that cost will drop to only $2.20 [= ($100,000 + $1 million)/500,000].

- *Simultaneous consumption* Many recently developed products and services can satisfy large numbers of customers at the same time. Unlike a gallon of gas that needs to be produced for each buyer, a software program needs to be produced only once. It then becomes available at very low expense to thousands or even millions of buyers. The same is true of books delivered to electronic reading devices, movies distributed on DVDs, and information disseminated through the Internet.

- *Network effects* Software and Internet service become more beneficial to a buyer the greater the number of households and businesses that also buy them. When others have Internet service, you can send e-mail messages to them. And when they also have software that allows display of documents and photos, you can attach those items to your e-mail messages. These interconnectivity advantages are called **network effects,** which are increases in the value of a product to each user, including existing users, as the total number of users rises. The domestic and global expansion of the Internet in particular has produced network effects, as have cell phones, pagers, palm computers, and other aspects of wireless communication. Network effects magnify the value of output well beyond the costs of inputs.

- *Learning by doing* Finally, firms that produce new products or pioneer new ways of doing business experience increasing returns through **learning by doing**. Tasks that initially may have taken firms hours may take them only minutes once the methods are perfected.

Whatever the particular source of increasing returns, the result is higher productivity, which tends to reduce the per-unit cost of producing and delivering products.

Global Competition The recent economy is characterized not only by information technology and increasing returns but also by heightened global competition. The collapse of the socialist economies in the late 1980s and early 1990s, together with the success of market systems, has led to a reawakening of capitalism throughout the world. The new information technologies have "shrunk the globe" and made it imperative for all firms to lower their costs and prices and to innovate in order to remain competitive. Free-trade zones such as NAFTA and the European Union (EU), along with trade liberalization through the World Trade Organization (WTO), have also heightened competition internationally by removing trade protection from domestic firms. The larger geographic markets, in turn, have enabled firms to expand beyond their national borders.

Implications for Economic Growth

Other things equal, stronger productivity growth and heightened global competition allow the economy to achieve a higher rate of economic growth. A glance back at Figure 8.2 will help make this point. Suppose that the shift of the production possibilities curve from *AB* to *CD* reflects annual changes in potential output levels before the recent increase in growth rates. Then the higher growth rates of the more recent period of accelerated productivity growth would be depicted by a *larger* outward shift of the economy's production possibilities from *AB* to a curve beyond *CD*. When coupled with economic efficiency and increased total spending, the economy's real GDP would rise by even more than what is shown.

Two cautions: Although the trend line of productivity growth seems to be steeper than in the past and bodes well for long-term economic growth, fluctuations of the rate of economic growth will still occur. Because of demand factors, real output periodically deviates below and above the growth trend—as it certainly did during the recession of 2007–2009. Also, you need to know that the growth of the U.S. labor force may be declining. That slowing may offset some or all of the extra potential for economic growth that would arise from greater productivity growth.

Skepticism about Longevity

Although most macroeconomists have revised their forecasts for long-term productivity growth upward, at least slightly, others are still skeptical and urge a "wait-and-see" approach. These macroeconomists acknowledge that the economy has experienced a rapid advance of new technology, some new firms have experienced increasing returns, and global competition has increased. But they wonder if these factors are sufficiently profound to produce a long-lasting new era of substantially higher rates of productivity growth and real GDP growth.

They also point out that productivity surged between 1975 and 1978 and between 1983 and 1986 but in each case soon reverted to its lower long-run trend. The higher trend line of productivity inferred from the short-run spurt of productivity could prove to be transient. Only by looking backward over long periods can economists distinguish the start of a new long-run trend from a shorter-term boost in productivity related to the business cycle and temporary factors.

What Can We Conclude?

Given the different views on the recent productivity acceleration, what should we conclude? Perhaps the safest conclusions are these:

- The prospects for a lasting increase in productivity growth are good (see Global Perspective 8.2). Studies indicate that productivity increases related to information technology have spread to a wide range of industries, including services. Even in the recession year 2001 and then in 2002, when the economy was sluggish, productivity growth remained strong. Specifically, it averaged about 3.3 percent in the business sector over those two years. Productivity rose by 3.8 percent in 2003, 2.9 percent in 2004, and 2.0 percent in 2005, as the economy vigorously expanded.

- Time will tell. Productivity growth was 1.0 percent in 2006, 1.8 percent in 2007, 2.7 percent in 2008, and 2.1 percent is 2009. The average growth rate over those four years is lower than the 2.8 percent rate shown by the trend line in Figure 8.5, but it is higher than the 1.5 percent rate for the 1973–1995 period. Clearly, many more years must elapse before economists will be ready to declare the post-1995 productivity acceleration a long-run, sustainable trend.

Global Competitiveness Index

The Global Competitiveness Index published annually by the World Economic Forum measures each country's potential for economic growth. The index uses various factors—such as innovativeness, the capability to transfer technology among sectors, the efficiency of the financial system, rates of investment, and the degree of integration with the rest of the world—to measure a country's ability to achieve economic growth over time. Here is the top 10 list for 2009–2010.

Country	Global Competitiveness Ranking, 2009–2010
Switzerland	1
United States	2
Singapore	3
Sweden	4
Denmark	5
Finland	6
Germany	7
Japan	8
Canada	9
Netherlands	10

Source: Copyright World Economic Forum, **www.weforum.org**.

QUICK REVIEW 8.4

- Over long time periods, labor productivity growth determines an economy's growth of real wages and its standard of living.

- Many economists believe that the United States has entered a period of faster productivity growth and possibly higher rates of economic growth.

- The rise in the average rate of productivity growth is based on rapid technological change in the form of the microchip and information technology, increasing returns and lower per-unit costs, and heightened global competition that helps hold down prices.

- More-rapid U.S. productivity growth means that, other things equal, the U.S. economy can grow at higher annual rates than it could with less-rapid productivity growth. Nonetheless, many economists caution that it is still too early to determine whether the recent higher rates of productivity growth are a lasting long-run trend or a fortunate short-lived occurrence.

Is Growth Desirable and Sustainable?

Economists usually take for granted that economic growth is desirable and sustainable. But not everyone agrees.

The Antigrowth View

Critics of growth say industrialization and growth result in pollution, climate change, ozone depletion, and other environmental problems. These adverse negative externalities occur because inputs in the production process reenter the environment as some form of waste. The more rapid our growth and the higher our standard of living, the more waste the environment must absorb—or attempt to absorb. In an already wealthy society, further growth usually means satisfying increasingly trivial wants at the cost of mounting threats to the ecological system.

Critics of growth also argue that there is little compelling evidence that economic growth has solved sociological problems such as poverty, homelessness, and discrimination. Consider poverty: In the antigrowth view, American poverty is a problem of distribution, not production. The requisite for solving the problem is a firm commitment to redistribute wealth and income, not further increases in output.

Antigrowth sentiment also says that while growth may permit us to "make a better living," it does not give us "the good life." We may be producing more and enjoying it less. Growth means frantic paces on jobs, worker burnout, and alienated employees who have little or no control over decisions affecting their lives. The changing technology at the core of growth poses new anxieties and new sources of insecurity for workers. Both high-level and low-level workers face the prospect of having their hard-earned skills and experience rendered obsolete by onrushing technology. High-growth economies are high-stress economies, which may impair our physical and mental health.

Finally, critics of high rates of growth doubt that they are sustainable. The planet Earth has finite amounts of natural resources available, and they are being consumed at alarming rates. Higher rates of economic growth simply speed up the degradation and exhaustion of the earth's resources. In this view, slower economic growth that is environmentally sustainable is preferable to faster growth.

In Defense of Economic Growth

The primary defense of growth is that it is the path to the greater material abundance and higher living standards

LAST Word Economic Growth in China

China's Economic Growth Rate in the Past 25 Years Is Among the Highest Recorded for Any Country During Any Period of World History.

Propelled by capitalistic reforms, China has experienced nearly 9 percent annual growth rates over the past 25 years. Real output has more than quadrupled over that period. China's growth rate was 13 percent in 2007, 9 percent in 2008, and 8.7 percent in 2009. Expanded output and income have boosted domestic saving and investment, and the growth of capital goods has further increased productivity, output, and income. The rising income, together with inexpensive labor, has attracted more foreign direct investment (a total of over $170 billion between 2005 and 2007).

China's real GDP and real income have grown much more rapidly than China's population. Per capita income has increased at a high annual rate of 8 percent since 1980. This is particularly noteworthy because China's population has expanded by 14 million a year (despite a policy that encourages one child per family). Based on exchange rates, China's per capita income was $3678 in 2009. But because the prices of many basic items in China are still low and are not totally reflected in exchange rates, Chinese per capita purchasing power for 2009 was estimated to be equivalent to $6000 of income in the United States.

The growth of per capita income in China has resulted from increased use of capital, improved technology, and shifts of labor away from lower-productivity toward higher-productivity uses. One such shift of employment has been from agriculture toward rural and urban manufacturing. Another shift has been from state-owned enterprises toward private firms. Both shifts have raised the productivity of Chinese workers.

Chinese economic growth had been accompanied by a huge expansion of China's international trade. Chinese exports rose from $5 billion in 1978 to $1.2 trillion in 2009. These exports have provided the foreign currency needed to import consumer goods and capital goods. Imports of capital goods from industrially advanced countries have brought with them highly advanced technology that is embodied in, for example, factory design, industrial machinery, office equipment, and telecommunications systems.

China still faces some significant problems in its transition to the market system, however. At times, investment booms in China have resulted in too much spending relative to production capacity.

The result has been some periods of 15 to 25 percent annual rates of inflation. China confronted the inflation problem by giving its central bank more power so that, when appropriate, the bank can raise interest rates to damp down investment spending. This greater monetary control has reduced inflation significantly. China's inflation rate was a mild 1.2 percent in 2003, 4.1 percent in 2004, and 1.9 percent in 2005. After rising to 4.8 percent in 2007 and 5.9 percent in 2008, it fell to zero in 2009 because of the worldwide recession.

In addition, the overall financial system in China remains weak and inadequate. Many unprofitable state-owned enterprises owe colossal sums of money on loans made by the Chinese state-owned banks (an estimate is nearly $100 billion). Because most of these loans are not collectible, the government may need to bail out the banks to keep them in operation.

Unemployment is also a problem. Even though the transition from an agriculture-dominated economy to a more urban, industrial economy has been gradual, considerable displacement of labor has occurred. Although the official rate for the nation hovers around 4 percent, there is substantial unemployment and underemployment in the interior regions of China.

China still has much work to do to integrate its economy fully into the world's system of international finance and trade. As a condition of joining the World Trade Organization in 2001, China agreed to reduce its high tariffs on imports and remove restrictions on foreign ownership. In addition, it agreed to change its poor record of protecting intellectual property rights such as copyrights, trademarks, and patents. Unauthorized copying of products is a major source of trade friction between China and the United States. So, too, is the artificially low international value of China's currency, which has contributed to a $227 billion annual trade surplus with the United States.

China's economic development has been very uneven geographically. Hong Kong is a wealthy capitalist city with a per capita income of about $32,000 in 2009. The standard of living is also relatively high in China's southern provinces and coastal cities, although not nearly as high as it is in Hong Kong. In fact, people living in these special economic zones have been the major beneficiaries of China's rapid growth. In contrast, the majority of people living elsewhere in China have very low incomes. Despite its remarkable recent economic successes, China remains a relatively low-income nation. But that status is quickly changing.

desired by the vast majority of people. Rising output and incomes allow people to buy

> more education, recreation, and travel, more medical care, closer communications, more skilled personal and professional services, and better-designed as well as more numerous products. It also means more art, music, and poetry, theater, and drama. It can even mean more time and resources devoted to spiritual growth and human development.[1]

Growth also enables society to improve the nation's infrastructure, enhance the care of the sick and elderly, provide greater access for the disabled, and provide more police and fire protection. Economic growth may be the only realistic way to reduce poverty, since there is only limited political support for greater redistribution of income. The way to improve the economic position of the poor is to increase household incomes through higher productivity and economic growth. Also, a no-growth policy among industrial nations might severely limit growth in poor nations. Foreign investment and development assistance in those nations would fall, keeping the world's poor in poverty longer.

Economic growth has not made labor more unpleasant or hazardous, as critics suggest. New machinery is usually less taxing and less dangerous than the machinery it replaces. Air-conditioned workplaces are more pleasant than steamy workshops. Furthermore, why would an end to economic growth reduce materialism or alienation? The loudest protests against materialism are heard in those nations and groups that now enjoy the highest levels of material abundance! The high standard of living that growth provides has increased our leisure and given us more time for reflection and self-fulfillment.

[1]Alice M. Rivlin, *Reviving the American Dream* (Washington, D.C.: Brookings Institution, 1992), p. 36.

Does growth threaten the environment? The connection between growth and environment is tenuous, say growth proponents. Increases in economic growth need not mean increases in pollution. Pollution is not so much a by-product of growth as it is a "problem of the commons." Much of the environment—streams, lakes, oceans, and the air—is treated as common property, with insufficient or no restrictions on its use. The commons have become our dumping grounds; we have overused and debased them. Environmental pollution is a case of negative externalities, and correcting this problem involves regulatory legislation, specific taxes ("effluent charges"), or market-based incentives to remedy misuse of the environment.

Those who support growth admit there are serious environmental problems. But they say that limiting growth is the wrong solution. Growth has allowed economies to reduce pollution, be more sensitive to environmental considerations, set aside wilderness, create national parks and monuments, and clean up hazardous waste, while still enabling rising household incomes.

Is growth sustainable? Yes, say the proponents of growth. If we were depleting natural resources faster than their discovery, we would see the prices of those resources rise. That has not been the case for most natural resources; in fact, the prices of most of them have declined. And if one natural resource becomes too expensive, another resource will be substituted for it. Moreover, say economists, economic growth has to do with the expansion and application of human knowledge and information, not of extractable natural resources. In this view, economic growth is limited only by human imagination.

Summary

1. A nation's economic growth can be measured either as an increase in real GDP over time or as an increase in real GDP per capita over time. Real GDP in the United States has grown at an average annual rate of about 3.2 percent since 1950; real GDP per capita has grown at roughly a 2 percent annual rate over that same period.

2. Sustained increases in real GDP per capita did not happen until the past two centuries, when England and then other countries began to experience modern economic growth, which is characterized by institutional structures that encourage savings, investment, and the development of new technologies. Institutional structures that promote growth include strong property rights, patents, efficient financial institutions, education, and a competitive market system.

3. Because some nations have experienced nearly two centuries of modern economic growth while others have only recently begun to experience modern economic growth, some countries today are much richer than other countries.

4. It is possible, however, for countries that are currently poor to grow faster than countries that are currently rich because the growth of real GDP per capita for rich countries is limited to about 2 percent per year. To continue growing, rich countries must invent and apply new technologies. By contrast, poor countries can grow much

faster because they can simply adopt the institutions and cutting-edge technologies already developed by the rich countries.

5. The determinants of economic growth to which we can attribute changes in growth rates include four supply factors (changes in the quantity and quality of natural resources, changes in the quantity and quality of human resources, changes in the stock of capital goods, and improvements in technology); one demand factor (changes in total spending); and one efficiency factor (changes in how well an economy achieves allocative and productive efficiency).

6. The growth of a nation's capacity to produce output can be illustrated graphically by an outward shift of its production possibilities curve.

7. Growth accounting attributes increases in real GDP either to increases in the amount of labor being employed or to increases in the productivity of the labor being employed. Increases in U.S. real GDP are mostly the result of increases in labor productivity. The increases in labor productivity can be attributed to technological progress, increases in the quantity of capital per worker, improvements in the education and training of workers, the exploitation of economies of scale, and improvements in the allocation of labor across different industries.

8. Over long time periods, the growth of labor productivity underlies an economy's growth of real wages and its standard of living. U.S. productivity rose by 2.8 percent annually between 1995 and 2009, compared to 1.5 percent annually between 1973 and 1995.

9. This post-1995 increase in the average rate of productivity growth is based on (*a*) rapid technological change in the form of the microchip and information technology, (*b*) increasing returns and lower per-unit costs, and (*c*) heightened global competition that holds down prices.

10. The main sources of increasing returns in recent years are (*a*) the use of more specialized inputs as firms grow, (*b*) the spreading of development costs, (*c*) simultaneous consumption by consumers, (*d*) network effects, and (*e*) learning by doing. Increasing returns mean higher productivity and lower per-unit production costs.

11. Skeptics wonder if the recent rise in the average rate of productivity growth is permanent, and suggest a wait-and-see approach. They point out that surges in productivity and real GDP growth have previously occurred but do not necessarily represent long-lived trends.

12. Critics of rapid growth say that it adds to environmental degradation, increases human stress, and exhausts the earth's finite supply of natural resources. Defenders of rapid growth say that it is the primary path to the rising living standards nearly universally desired by people, that it need not debase the environment, and that there are no indications that we are running out of resources. Growth is based on the expansion and application of human knowledge, which is limited only by human imagination.

Terms and Concepts

economic growth

real GDP per capita

rule of 70

modern economic growth

leader countries

follower countries

supply factors

demand factor

efficiency factor

labor productivity

labor-force participation rate

growth accounting

infrastructure

human capital

economies of scale

information technology

start-up firms

increasing returns

network effects

learning by doing

Questions

1. How is economic growth measured? Why is economic growth important? Why could the difference between a 2.5 percent and a 3 percent annual growth rate be of great significance over several decades? **LO1**

2. When and where did modern economic growth first happen? What are the major institutional factors that form the foundation for modern economic growth? What do they have in common? **LO2**

3. Why are some countries today much poorer than other countries? Are today's poor countries destined to always be poorer than today's rich countries? If so, explain why. If not, explain how today's poor countries can catch or even pass today's rich countries. **LO2**

4. What are the four supply factors of economic growth? What is the demand factor? What is the efficiency factor? Illustrate these factors in terms of the production possibilities curve. **LO3**

5. Suppose that Alpha and Omega have identically sized working-age populations but that total annual hours of work are much greater in Alpha than in Omega. Provide two possible reasons for this difference. **LO3**

6. What is growth accounting? To what extent have increases in U.S. real GDP resulted from more labor inputs? From greater labor productivity? Rearrange the following contributors to the growth of productivity in order of their quantitative importance: economies of scale, quantity of

capital, improved resource allocation, education and training, and technological advance. **LO4**

7. True or false? If false, explain why. **LO4**
    a. Technological advance, which to date has played a relatively small role in U.S. economic growth, is destined to play a more important role in the future.
    b. Many public capital goods are complementary to private capital goods.
    c. Immigration has slowed economic growth in the United States.

8. Explain why there is such a close relationship between changes in a nation's rate of productivity growth and changes in its average real hourly wage. **LO5**

9. Relate each of the following to the recent increase in the trend rate of productivity growth: **LO5**

    a. Information technology.
    b. Increasing returns.
    c. Network effects.
    d. Global competition.

10. What, if any, are the benefits and costs of economic growth, particularly as measured by real GDP per capita? **LO6**

11. **LAST WORD** Based on the information in this chapter, contrast the economic growth rates of the United States and China over the last 25 years. How does the real GDP per capita of China compare with that of the United States? Why is there such a huge disparity of per capita income between China's coastal cities and its interior regions?

Problems

1. Suppose an economy's real GDP is $30,000 in year 1 and $31,200 in year 2. What is the growth rate of its real GDP? Assume that population is 100 in year 1 and 102 in year 2. What is the growth rate of real GDP per capita? **LO1**

2. What annual growth rate is needed for a country to double its output in 7 years? In 35 years? In 70 years? In 140 years? **LO1**

3. Assume that a "leader country" has real GDP per capita of $40,000, whereas a "follower country" has real GDP per capita of $20,000. Next suppose that the growth of real GDP per capita falls to zero percent in the leader country and rises to 7 percent in the follower country. If these rates continue for long periods of time, how many years will it take for the follower country to catch up to the living standard of the leader country? **LO2**

4. Refer to Figure 8.2 and assume that the values for points *a*, *b*, and *c* are $10 billion, $20 billion, and $18 billion respec-

tively. If the economy moves from point *a* to point *b* over a 10-year period, what must have been its annual rate of economic growth? If, instead, the economy was at point *c* at the end of the 10-year period, by what percentage did it fall short of its production capacity? **LO3**

5. Suppose that work hours in New Zombie are 200 in year 1 and productivity is $8 per hour worked. What is New Zombie's real GDP? If work hours increase to 210 in year 2 and productivity rises to $10 per hour, what is New Zombie's rate of economic growth? **LO4**

6. The per-unit cost of an item is its average total cost (= total cost/quantity). Suppose that a new cell phone application costs $100,000 to develop and only $.50 per unit to deliver to each cell phone customer. What will be the per-unit cost of the application if it sells 100 units? 1000 units? 1 million units? **LO5**

FURTHER TEST YOUR KNOWLEDGE AT
www.mcconnell19e.com

At the text's Online Learning Center (OLC), **www.mcconnell19e.com**, you will find one or more Web-based questions that require information from the Internet to answer. We urge you to check them out; they will familiarize you with Web sites that may be helpful in other courses and perhaps even in your career. The OLC also features multiple-choice questions that give instant feedback and provides other helpful ways to further test your knowledge of the chapter.

Business Cycles, Unemployment, and Inflation

As indicated in Chapter 8, the United States has experienced remarkable economic growth over time. But this growth has not been smooth, steady, and predictable from year to year. At various times the United States has experienced recessions, high unemployment rates, or high inflation rates. For example, U.S. unemployment rose by 8 million workers and the unemployment rate increased from 4.7 percent to 10.1 percent during the recent recession. Other nations have also suffered high unemployment rates at times. As just one example, Spain's unemployment rate was nearly 20 percent in 2009. Also, inflation has occasionally plagued the United States and other nations. For instance, the U.S. inflation rate in 1980 was 13.5 percent. Zimbabwe's inflation soared to 26,000 percent in 2007!

Our goal in this chapter is to examine the concepts, terminology, and facts relating to macroeconomic instability. Specifically, we want to discuss the business cycle, unemployment, and inflation. The concepts discussed are extremely important for understanding subsequent chapters on economic theory and economic policy.

The Business Cycle

The long-run trend of the U.S. economy is one of economic growth, as stylized by the upsloping line labeled "Growth Trend" in Figure 9.1. But growth has been interrupted by periods of economic instability usually associated with **business cycles.** Business cycles are alternating rises and declines in the level of economic activity, sometime over several years. Individual cycles (one "up" followed by one "down") vary substantially in duration and intensity.

ORIGIN OF THE IDEA

O 9.1

Business cycles

Phases of the Business Cycle

Figure 9.1 shows the four phases of a generalized business cycle:

- At a **peak,** such as the middle peak shown in Figure 9.1, business activity has reached a temporary maximum. Here the economy is near or at full employment and the level of real output is at or very close to the economy's capacity. The price level is likely to rise during this phase.
- A **recession** is a period of decline in total output, income, and employment. This downturn, which lasts 6 months or more, is marked by the widespread contraction of business activity in many sectors of the

economy. Along with declines in real GDP, significant increases in unemployment occur. Table 9.1 documents the 10 recessions in the United States since 1950.

- In the **trough** of the recession or depression, output and employment "bottom out" at their lowest levels. The trough phase may be either short-lived or quite long.
- A recession is usually followed by a recovery and **expansion,** a period in which real GDP, income, and employment rise. At some point, the economy again approaches full employment. If spending then expands more rapidly than does production capacity, prices of nearly all goods and services will rise. In other words, inflation will occur.

Although business cycles all pass through the same phases, they vary greatly in duration and intensity. Many economists prefer to talk of business "fluctuations" rather than cycles because cycles imply regularity while fluctuations do not. The Great Depression of the 1930s resulted in a 27 percent decline in real GDP over a 3-year period in the United States and seriously impaired business activity for a decade. By comparison, the U.S. recessions detailed in Table 9.1 were less severe in both intensity and duration.

The Business Cycle Dating Committee of the National Bureau of Economic Research (NBER), a nonprofit economic research organization, declares the start and end

FIGURE 9.1 The business cycle. Economists distinguish four phases of the business cycle; the duration and strength of each phase may vary.

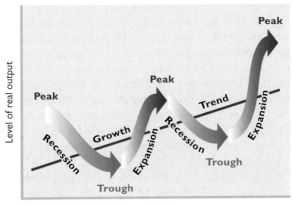

TABLE 9.1 U.S. Recessions since 1950

Period	Duration, Months	Depth (Decline in Real Output)
1953–54	10	−2.6%
1957–58	8	−3.7
1960–61	10	−1.1
1969–70	11	−0.2
1973–75	16	−3.2
1980	6	−2.2
1981–82	16	−2.9
1990–91	8	−1.4
2001	8	−0.4
2007–09	18	−3.7

Source: National Bureau of Economic Research, **www.nber.org**, and Minneapolis Federal Reserve Bank, "The Recession and Recovery in Perspective," **www.minneapolisfed.gov**. Output data are in 2000 dollars.

of recessions in the United States. Citing evidence of declining real output and falling employment, the NBER officially declared that the latest recession began in December 2007. The NBER subsequently declared that the Great Recession ended in June 2009, 18 months after it began. In making this announcement, the NBER pointed out that its declaration was not a forecast for the future path of the economy.

Recessions, of course, occur in other countries, too. For example, nearly all industrial nations and many developing nations have suffered recessions in the past several years.

Causation: A First Glance

The long-run trend of the U.S. economy is expansion and growth. That is why the business cycles in Figure 9.1 are drawn against a trend of economic growth. A key issue in macroeconomics is why the economy sees business cycle fluctuations rather than slow, smooth growth. In terms of Figure 9.1, why does output move up and down rather than just staying on the smooth growth trend line?

Economists have developed several possible explanations. But before turning to them, recall that in Chapter 6 we explained that these theories are founded on the idea that fluctuations are driven by shocks—unexpected events that individuals and firms may have trouble adjusting to. Also recall that short-run price stickiness is widely believed to be a major factor preventing the economy from rapidly adjusting to shocks. With prices sticky in the short run, price changes cannot quickly equalize the quantities demanded of goods and services with their respective quantities supplied after a shock has happened. Instead, the economy is forced to respond to shocks in the short run primarily through changes in output and employment rather than through changes in prices.

Economists cite several possible general sources of shocks that can cause business cycles.

- *Irregular innovation* Significant new products or production methods, such as those associated with the railroad, automobile, computer, and the Internet, can rapidly spread through the economy, sparking sizable increases in investment, consumption, output, and employment. After the economy has largely absorbed the new innovation, the economy may for a time slow down or possibly decline. Because such innovations occur irregularly and unexpectedly, they may contribute to the variability of economic activity.

- *Productivity changes* When productivity—output per unit of input—unexpectedly increases, the economy booms; when productivity unexpectedly decreases, the economy recedes. Such changes in

productivity can result from unexpected changes in resource availability (of, say, oil or agricultural commodities) or from unexpected changes in the general rate of technological advance.

- *Monetary factors* Some economists see business cycles as purely monetary phenomena. When a nation's central bank shocks the economy by creating more money than people were expecting, an inflationary boom in output occurs. By contrast, printing less money than people were expecting triggers an output decline and, eventually, a price-level fall.

- *Political events* Unexpected political events, such as peace treaties, new wars, or the 9/11 terrorist attacks, can create economic opportunities or strains. In adjusting to these shocks, the economy may experience upswings or downswings.

- *Financial instability* Unexpected financial bubbles (rapid asset price increases) or bursts (abrupt asset price decreases) can spill over to the general economy by expanding or contracting lending, and boosting or eroding the confidence of consumers and businesses. Booms and busts in the rest of the economy may follow.

The severe recession of 2007–2009 was precipitated by a combination of excessive money and a financial frenzy that led to overvalued real estate and unsustainable mortgage debt. Institutions bundled this debt into new securities ("derivatives") that were sold to financial investors. Some of the investors, in turn, bought insurance against losses that might arise from the securities. As real estate prices plummeted and mortgage defaults unexpectedly rocketed, the securitization and insurance structure buckled and nearly collapsed. Credit markets froze, pessimism prevailed, and spending by businesses and households declined.

Whatever the source of economic shocks, most economists agree that the *immediate* cause of the large majority of cyclical changes in the levels of real output and employment is unexpected changes in the level of total spending. If total spending unexpectedly sinks and firms cannot lower prices, firms will find themselves selling fewer units of output (since with prices fixed, a decreased amount of spending implies fewer items purchased). Slower sales will cause firms to cut back on production. As they do, GDP will fall. And because fewer workers will be needed to produce less output, employment also will fall. The economy will contract and enter a recession.

By contrast, if the level of spending unexpectedly rises, output, employment, and incomes will rise. This is true because, with prices sticky, the increased spending will mean that consumers will be buying a larger volume of goods and services (since, with prices fixed, more spending means more items purchased). Firms will respond by increasing output. This will increase GDP. And because they will need to hire more workers to produce the larger volume of output, employment also will increase. The economy will boom and enjoy an expansion. Eventually, as time passes and prices become more flexible, prices are also likely to rise as a result of the increased spending.

Cyclical Impact: Durables and Nondurables

Although the business cycle is felt everywhere in the economy, it affects different segments in different ways and to different degrees.

Firms and industries producing *capital goods* (for example, housing, commercial buildings, heavy equipment, and farm implements) and *consumer durables* (for example, automobiles, personal computers, and refrigerators) are affected most by the business cycle. Within limits, firms can postpone the purchase of capital goods. For instance, when the economy goes into recession, producers frequently delay the purchase of new equipment and the construction of new plants. The business outlook simply does not warrant increases in the stock of capital goods. In good times, capital goods are usually replaced before they depreciate completely. But when recession strikes, firms patch up their old equipment and make do. As a result, investment in capital goods declines sharply. Firms that have excess plant capacity may not even bother to replace all the capital that is depreciating. For them, net investment may be negative. The pattern is much the same for consumer durables such as automobiles and major appliances. When recession occurs and households must trim their budgets, purchases of these goods are often deferred. Families repair their old cars and appliances rather than buy new ones, and the firms producing these products suffer. (Of course, producers of capital goods and consumer durables also benefit most from expansions.)

In contrast, *service* industries and industries that produce *nondurable consumer goods* are somewhat insulated from the most severe effects of recession. People find it difficult to cut back on needed medical and legal services, for example. And a recession actually helps some service firms, such as pawnbrokers and law firms that specialize in bankruptcies. Nor are the purchases of many nondurable goods such as food and clothing easy to postpone. The quantity and quality of purchases of nondurables will decline, but not so much as will purchases of capital goods and consumer durables.

QUICK REVIEW 9.1

- The typical business cycle goes through four phases: peak, recession, trough, and expansion.
- Fluctuations in output and employment are caused by economic shocks combining with sticky prices.
- Sources of shocks that cause recessions include irregular innovation, productivity changes, monetary factors, political events, and financial instability.
- During a recession, industries that produce capital goods and consumer durables normally suffer greater output and employment declines than do service and nondurable consumer goods industries.

Unemployment

Two problems that arise over the course of the business cycle are unemployment and inflation. Let's look at unemployment first.

Measurement of Unemployment

The U.S. Bureau of Labor Statistics (BLS) conducts a nationwide random survey of some 60,000 households each month to determine who is employed and who is not employed. In a series of questions, it asks which members of the household are working, unemployed and looking for work, not looking for work, and so on. From the answers, it determines an unemployment rate for the entire nation.

Figure 9.2 helps explain the mathematics. The BLS divides the total U.S. population into three groups. One group is made up of people under 16 years of age and people who are institutionalized, for example, in mental hospitals or correctional institutions. Such people are not considered potential members of the labor force.

A second group, labeled "Not in labor force," is composed of adults who are potential workers but are not employed and are not seeking work. For example, they are stay-at-home parents, full-time students, or retirees.

The third group is the **labor force,** which constituted slightly more than 50 percent of the total population in 2009. The labor force consists of people who are able and willing to work. Both those who are employed and those who are unemployed but actively seeking work are counted as being in the labor force. The **unemployment rate** is the percentage of the labor force unemployed:

$$\text{Unemployment rate} = \frac{\text{unemployed}}{\text{labor force}} \times 100$$

FIGURE 9.2 The U.S. labor force, employment, and unemployment, 2009.* The labor force consists of persons 16 years of age or older who are not in institutions and who are (1) employed or (2) unemployed but seeking employment.

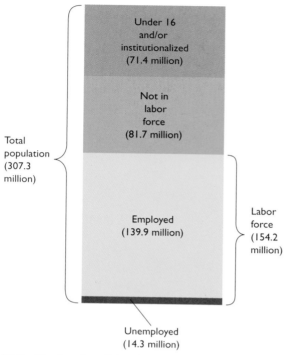

*Civilian labor-force data, which excludes military employment.
Source: Bureau of Labor Statistics, **www.bls.gov**.

The statistics underlying the rounded numbers in Figure 9.2 show that in 2009 the unemployment rate averaged

$$\frac{14{,}265{,}000}{154{,}142{,}000} \times 100 = 9.3\%$$

WORKED PROBLEMS

W 9.1

Unemployment rate

Unemployment rates for selected years appear on the inside covers of this book.

Despite the use of scientific sampling and interviewing techniques, the data collected in this survey are subject to criticism:

- **Part-time employment** The BLS lists all part-time workers as fully employed. In 2009 about 29 million people worked part-time as a result of personal choice. But another 9 million part-time workers either wanted to work full-time and could not find suitable full-time work or worked fewer hours because of a temporary slack in consumer demand. These last two groups were, in effect, partially employed and partially unemployed. By counting them as fully employed, say critics, the official BLS data understate the unemployment rate.

- **Discouraged workers** You must be actively seeking work in order to be counted as unemployed. An unemployed individual who is not actively seeking employment is classified as "not in the labor force." The problem is that many workers, after unsuccessfully seeking employment for a time, become discouraged and drop out of the labor force. The number of such **discouraged workers** was roughly 778,000 in 2009, up from 396,000 in 2007. By not counting discouraged workers as unemployed, say critics, the official BLS data understate the unemployment problem.

Types of Unemployment

There are three *types* of unemployment: frictional, structural, and cyclical.

Frictional Unemployment At any given time some workers are "between jobs." Some of them will be moving voluntarily from one job to another. Others will have been fired and will be seeking reemployment. Still others will have been laid off temporarily because of seasonal demand. In addition to those between jobs, many young workers will be searching for their first jobs.

As these unemployed people find jobs or are called back from temporary layoffs, other job seekers and laid-off workers will replace them in the "unemployment pool." It is important to keep in mind that while the pool itself persists because there are always newly unemployed workers flowing into it, most workers do *not* stay in the unemployment pool for very long. Indeed, when the economy is strong, the majority of unemployed workers find new jobs within a couple of months. One should be careful not to make the mistake of confusing the permanence of the pool itself with the false idea that the pool's membership is permanent, too. On the other hand, there are workers who do remain unemployed and in the pool for very long periods of time—sometimes for many years. As we discuss the different types of unemployment below, notice that certain types tend to be transitory while others are associated with much longer spells of unemployment.

Economists use the term **frictional unemployment**—consisting of *search unemployment* and *wait unemployment*—for workers who are either searching for jobs or waiting to take jobs in the near future. The word "frictional" implies that the labor market does not operate perfectly and instantaneously (without friction) in matching workers and jobs.

Frictional unemployment is inevitable and, at least in part, desirable. Many workers who are voluntarily between jobs are moving from low-paying, low-productivity jobs to higher-paying, higher-productivity positions. That means greater income for the workers, a better allocation of labor resources, and a larger real GDP for the economy.

Structural Unemployment Frictional unemployment blurs into a category called **structural unemployment.** Here, economists use "structural" in the sense of "compositional." Changes over time in consumer demand and in technology alter the "structure" of the total demand for labor, both occupationally and geographically.

Occupationally, the demand for certain skills (for example, sewing clothes or working on farms) may decline or even vanish. The demand for other skills (for example, designing software or maintaining computer systems) will intensify. Unemployment results because the composition of the labor force does not respond immediately or completely to the new structure of job opportunities. Workers who find that their skills and experience have become obsolete or unneeded thus find that they have no marketable talents. They are structurally unemployed until they adapt or develop skills that employers want.

Geographically, the demand for labor also changes over time. An example: the migration of industry and thus of employment opportunities from the Snowbelt to the Sunbelt over the past few decades. Another example is the movement of jobs from inner-city factories to suburban industrial parks. And a final example is the so-called *offshoring* of jobs that occurs when the demand for a particular type of labor shifts from domestic firms to foreign firms. As job opportunities shift from one place to another, some workers become structurally unemployed.

The distinction between frictional and structural unemployment is hazy at best. The key difference is that *frictionally* unemployed workers have marketable skills and either live in areas where jobs exist or are able to move to areas where they do. *Structurally* unemployed workers find it hard to obtain new jobs without retraining, gaining additional education, or relocating. Frictional unemployment is short-term; structural unemployment is more likely to be long-term and consequently more serious.

Cyclical Unemployment Unemployment that is caused by a decline in total spending is called **cyclical unemployment** and typically begins in the recession phase of the business cycle. As the demand for goods and services decreases, employment falls and unemployment rises. Cyclical unemployment results from insufficient demand for goods and services. The 25 percent unemployment rate in the depth of the Great Depression in 1933 reflected mainly cyclical unemployment, as did significant parts of the 9.7 percent unemployment rate in 1982, the 7.5 percent rate in 1992, the 5.8 percent rate in 2002, and the 9.3 percent rate in 2009.

Cyclical unemployment is a very serious problem when it occurs. We will say more about its high costs later, but first we need to define "full employment."

Definition of Full Employment

Because frictional and structural unemployment is largely unavoidable in a dynamic economy, *full employment* is something less than 100 percent employment of the labor force. Economists say that the economy is "fully employed" when it is experiencing only frictional and structural unemployment. That is, full employment occurs when there is no cyclical unemployment.

Economists describe the unemployment rate that is consistent with full employment as the **full-employment rate of unemployment,** or the **natural rate of unemployment (NRU).** At the NRU, the economy is said to be producing its **potential output.** This is the real GDP that occurs when the economy is "fully employed."

Note that a fully employed economy does not mean zero unemployment. Even when the economy is fully employed, the NRU is some positive percentage because it takes time for frictionally unemployed job seekers to find open jobs they can fill. Also, it takes time for the structurally unemployed to achieve the skills and geographic relocation needed for reemployment.

"Natural" does not mean, however, that the economy will always operate at this rate and thus realize its potential output. When cyclical unemployment occurs, the economy has much more unemployment than that which would occur at the NRU. Moreover, the economy can operate for a while at an unemployment rate *below* the NRU. At times, the demand for labor may be so great that firms take a stronger initiative to hire and train the structurally unemployed. Also, some parents, teenagers, college students, and retirees who were casually looking for just the right part-time or full-time jobs may quickly find them. Thus the unemployment rate temporarily falls below the natural rate.

Also, the NRU can vary over time as demographic factors, job-search methods, and public policies change. In the 1980s, the NRU was about 6 percent. Today, it is 4 to 5 percent.

Economic Cost of Unemployment

Unemployment that is excessive involves great economic and social costs.

GDP Gap and Okun's Law The basic economic cost of unemployment is forgone output. When the economy fails to create enough jobs for all who are able and willing to work, potential production of goods and services is irretrievably lost. In terms of Chapter 1's analysis, unemployment above the natural rate means that society is operating at some point inside its production possibilities curve. Economists call this sacrifice of output a **GDP gap**—the difference between actual and potential GDP. That is:

$$\text{GDP gap} = \text{actual GDP} - \text{potential GDP}$$

The GDP gap can be either negative (actual GDP < potential GDP) or positive (actual GDP > potential GDP). In the case of unemployment above the natural rate, it is negative because actual GDP falls short of potential GDP.

Potential GDP is determined by assuming that the natural rate of unemployment prevails. The growth of potential GDP is simply projected forward on the basis of the economy's "normal" growth rate of real GDP. Figure 9.3 shows the GDP gap for recent years in the United States. It also indicates the close correlation between the actual unemployment rate (Figure 9.3b) and the GDP gap (Figure 9.3a). The higher the unemployment rate, the larger is the GDP gap.

Macroeconomist Arthur Okun was the first to quantify the relationship between the unemployment rate and the GDP gap. **Okun's law** indicates that for every 1 percentage point by which the actual unemployment rate exceeds the natural rate, a negative GDP gap of about 2 percent occurs. With

WORKED PROBLEMS

W 9.2

Okun's law

this information, we can calculate the absolute loss of output associated with any above-natural unemployment rate. For example, in 2009 the unemployment rate was 9.3 percent, or 4.3 percentage points above that period's 5.0 percent natural rate of unemployment. Multiplying this 4.3 percent by Okun's 2 indicates that 2009's GDP gap was 8.6 percent of potential GDP (in real terms). By applying this 8.6 percent loss to 2009's potential GDP of $13,894 billion, we find that the economy sacrificed $1,195 billion of real output because the natural rate of unemployment was not achieved.

As you can see in Figure 9.3, sometimes the economy's actual output will exceed its potential or full-employment output. Figure 9.3 reveals that an economic expansion in 1999 and 2000, for example, caused actual GDP to exceed potential GDP in those years. There was a positive GDP gap in 1999 and 2000. Actual GDP for a time can exceed potential GDP, but positive GDP gaps create inflationary pressures and cannot be sustained indefinitely.

Unequal Burdens An increase in the unemployment rate from 5 to, say, 9 or 10 percent might be more tolerable to society if every worker's hours of work and wage income were reduced proportionally. But this is not the case. Part of the burden of unemployment is that its cost is unequally distributed.

Table 9.2 examines unemployment rates for various labor market groups for 2 periods. In 2007, the economy achieved full employment, with a 4.6 percent unemployment rate. The economy receded in December 2007 and two years later was feeling the full unemployment impact of the Great Recession. By observing the large variance in unemployment rates for the different groups within each period and comparing the rates between the 2 periods, we can generalize as follows:

- **Occupation** Workers in lower-skilled occupations (for example, laborers) have higher unemployment rates than workers in higher-skilled occupations (for

TABLE 9.2 Unemployment Rates by Demographic Group: Full Employment Year (2007) and Recession Year (2009)*

Demographic Group	Unemployment Rate	
	2007	2009
Overall	4.6%	9.3%
Occupation:		
Managerial and professional	2.1	4.6
Construction and extraction	7.6	19.7
Age:		
16–19	15.7	24.3
African American, 16–19	29.4	39.5
White, 16–19	13.9	21.8
Male, 20+	4.1	9.6
Female, 20+	4.0	7.5
Race and ethnicity:		
African American	8.3	14.8
Hispanic	5.6	12.1
White	4.1	8.5
Gender:		
Women	4.5	8.1
Men	4.7	10.3
Education:†		
Less than high school diploma	7.1	14.6
High school diploma only	4.4	9.7
College degree or more	2.0	4.6
Duration:		
15 or more weeks	1.5	4.7

*Civilian labor-force data.
†People age 25 or over.
Source: Economic Report of the President; Bureau of Labor Statistics, **www.bls.gov**; Census Bureau, **www.census.gov**.

FIGURE 9.3 Actual and potential real GDP and the unemployment rate. (a) The difference between actual and potential GDP is the GDP gap. A negative GDP gap measures the output the economy sacrifices when actual GDP falls short of potential GDP. A positive GDP gap indicates that actual GDP is above potential GDP. (b) A high unemployment rate means a large GDP gap (negative), and a low unemployment rate means a small or even positive GDP gap.

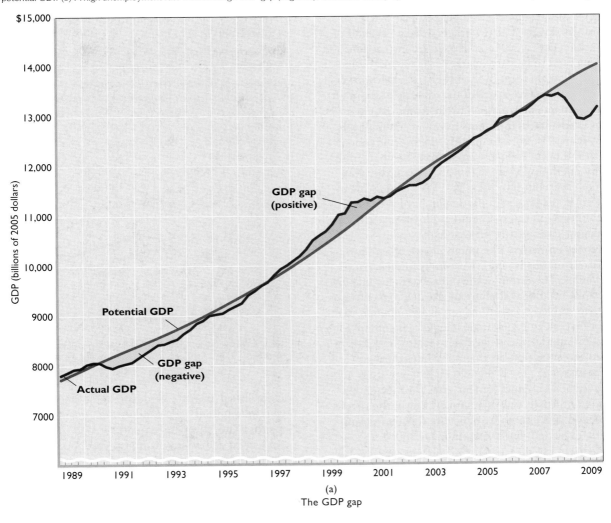

(a)
The GDP gap

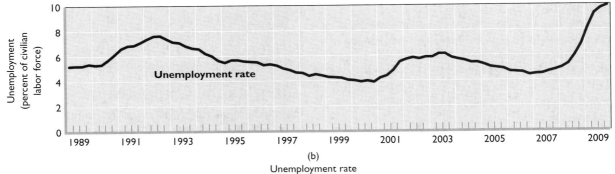

(b)
Unemployment rate

Source: Congressional Budget Office, **www.cbo.gov**, Bureau of Economic Analysis, **www.bea.gov**, and the Bureau of Labor Statistics, **www.bls.gov**.

example, professionals). Lower-skilled workers have more and longer spells of structural unemployment than higher-skilled workers. They also are less likely to be self-employed than are higher-skilled workers. Moreover, lower-skilled workers usually bear the brunt of recessions. Manufacturing, construction, and mining tend to be particularly hard-hit, and businesses generally retain most of their higher-skilled workers, in whom they have invested the expense of training.

- *Age* Teenagers have much higher unemployment rates than adults. Teenagers have lower skill levels, quit their jobs more frequently, are more frequently fired, and have less geographic mobility than adults. Many unemployed teenagers are new in the labor market, searching for their first jobs. Male African-American teenagers, in particular, have very high unemployment rates. The unemployment rate for all teenagers rises during recessions.

- *Race and ethnicity* The unemployment rate for African Americans and Hispanics is higher than that for whites. The causes of the higher rates include lower rates of educational attainment, greater concentration in lower-skilled occupations, and discrimination in the labor market. In general, the unemployment rate for African Americans is twice that of whites and rises by more percentage points than for whites during recessions.

- *Gender* The unemployment rates for men and women normally are very similar. But in the recent recession, the unemployment rate for men significantly exceeded that for women.

- *Education* Less-educated workers, on average, have higher unemployment rates than workers with more education. Less education is usually associated with lower-skilled, less-permanent jobs; more time between jobs; and jobs that are more vulnerable to cyclical layoff.

- *Duration* The number of persons unemployed for long periods—15 weeks or more—as a percentage of the labor force is much lower than the overall unemployment rate. But that percentage rises significantly during recessions. Notice from Table 9.2 that it rose from 1.5 percent of the labor force in 2007 to 4.7 percent in 2009.

Noneconomic Costs

Severe cyclical unemployment is more than an economic malady; it is a social catastrophe. Unemployment means idleness. And idleness means loss of skills, loss of self-respect, plummeting morale, family disintegration, and

GLOBAL PERSPECTIVE 9.1

Unemployment Rates in Five Industrial Nations, 1999–2009

Compared with Italy, France, and Germany, the United States had a relatively low unemployment rate in recent years.

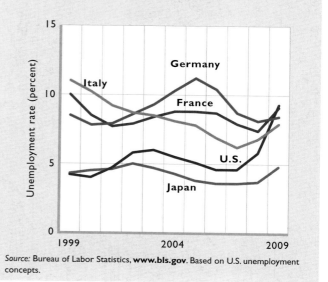

Source: Bureau of Labor Statistics, **www.bls.gov**. Based on U.S. unemployment concepts.

sociopolitical unrest. Widespread joblessness increases poverty, heightens racial and ethnic tensions, and reduces hope for material advancement.

History demonstrates that severe unemployment can lead to rapid and sometimes violent social and political change. Witness Hitler's ascent to power against a background of unemployment in Germany. Furthermore, relatively high unemployment among some racial and ethnic minorities has contributed to the unrest and violence that has periodically plagued some cities in the United States and abroad. At the individual level, research links increases in suicide, homicide, fatal heart attacks and strokes, and mental illness to high unemployment.

International Comparisons

Unemployment rates differ greatly among nations at any given time. One reason is that nations have different natural rates of unemployment. Another is that nations may be in different phases of their business cycles. Global Perspective 9.1 shows unemployment rates for five industrialized nations for the years 1999 through 2009. During most of this period, the U.S. unemployment rate was considerably lower than the rates in Italy, France, and Germany.

Inflation

We now turn to inflation, another aspect of macroeconomic instability. The problems inflation poses are subtler than those posed by unemployment.

Meaning of Inflation

Inflation is a rise in the general level of prices. When inflation occurs, each dollar of income will buy fewer goods and services than before. Inflation reduces the "purchasing power" of money. But inflation does not mean that *all* prices are rising. Even during periods of rapid inflation, some prices may be relatively constant and others may even fall. For example, although the United States experienced high rates of inflation in the 1970s and early 1980s, the prices of video recorders, digital watches, and personal computers declined.

Measurement of Inflation

The main measure of inflation in the United States is the **Consumer Price Index (CPI)**, compiled by the Bureau of Labor Statistics (BLS). The government uses this index to report inflation rates each month and each year. It also uses the CPI to adjust Social Security benefits and income tax brackets for inflation. The CPI reports the price of a "market basket" of some 300 consumer goods and services that are purchased by a typical urban consumer. (The GDP price index of Chapter 7 is a much broader measure of inflation since it includes not only consumer goods and services but also capital goods, goods and services purchased by government, and goods and services that enter world trade.)

The composition of the market basket for the CPI is based on spending patterns of urban consumers in a specific period, presently 2005–2006. The BLS updates the composition of the market basket every 2 years so that it reflects the most recent patterns of consumer purchases and captures the inflation that consumers are currently experiencing. The BLS arbitrarily sets the CPI equal to 100 for 1982–1984. So the CPI for any particular year is found as follows:

$$\text{CPI} = \frac{\text{price of the most recent market basket in the particular year}}{\text{price estimate of the market basket in 1982–1984}} \times 100$$

The rate of inflation is equal to the percentage growth of CPI from one year to the next. For example, the CPI was 207.3 in 2007, up from 201.6 in 2006. So the rate of inflation for 2007 is calculated as follows:

$$\text{Rate of inflation} = \frac{207.3 - 201.6}{201.6} \times 100 = 2.8\%$$

In rare cases, the CPI declines from one year to the next. For example, the CPI fell from 215.3 in 2008 to 214.5 in 2009. The rate of inflation for 2009 therefore was −0.4 percent. Such price level declines are called **deflation.**

In Chapter 8, we discussed the mathematical approximation called *the rule of 70*, which tells us that we can find the number of years it will take for some measure to double, given its annual percentage increase, by dividing that percentage increase into the number 70. So a 3 percent annual rate of inflation will double the price level in about 23 (= 70 ÷ 3) years. Inflation of 8 percent per year will double the price level in about 9 (= 70 ÷ 8) years.

Facts of Inflation

Figure 9.4 shows December-to-December rates of annual inflation in the United States between 1960 and 2009. Observe that inflation reached double-digit rates in the 1970s and early 1980s but has since declined and has been relatively mild recently.

In recent years U.S. inflation has been neither unusually high nor low relative to inflation in several other industrial countries (see Global Perspective 9.2). Some nations (not shown) have had double-digit or even higher annual rates of inflation in recent years. In 2009, for example, the annual inflation rate in the Democratic Republic of Congo was 46 percent; Eritrea, 35 percent; Afghanistan, 31 percent; and Venezuela, 27 percent. Zimbabwe's inflation rate was 14.9 billion percent in 2008 before Zimbabwe did away with its existing currency.

Types of Inflation

Nearly all prices in the economy are set by supply and demand. Consequently, if the economy is experiencing

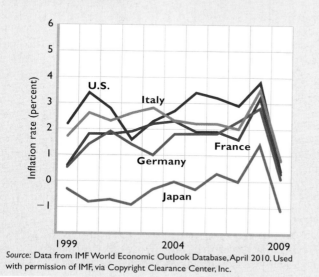

GLOBAL PERSPECTIVE 9.2

Inflation Rates in Five Industrial Nations, 1999–2009

Inflation rates in the United States in recent years were neither extraordinarily high nor extraordinarily low relative to rates in other industrial nations.

Source: Data from IMF World Economic Outlook Database, April 2010. Used with permission of IMF, via Copyright Clearance Center, Inc.

economy's capacity to produce. Where inflation is rapid and sustained, the cause invariably is an overissuance of money by the central bank (the Federal Reserve in the United States). When resources are already fully employed, the business sector cannot respond to excess demand by expanding output. So the excess demand bids up the prices of the limited output, producing **demand-pull inflation.** The essence of this type of inflation is "too much spending chasing too few goods."

Cost-Push Inflation Inflation also may arise on the supply, or cost, side of the economy. During some periods in U.S. economic history, including the mid-1970s, the price level increased even though total spending was not excessive. These were periods when output and employment were both *declining* (evidence that total spending was not excessive) while the general price level was *rising*.

The theory of **cost-push inflation** explains rising prices in terms of factors that raise **per-unit production costs** at each level of spending. A per-unit production cost is the average cost of a particular level of output. This average cost is found by dividing the total cost of all resource inputs by the amount of output produced. That is,

$$\text{Per-unit production cost} = \frac{\text{total input cost}}{\text{units of output}}$$

inflation and the overall level of prices is rising, we need to look for an explanation in terms of supply and demand.

Demand-Pull Inflation Usually, increases in the price level are caused by an excess of total spending beyond the

Rising per-unit production costs squeeze profits and reduce the amount of output firms are willing to supply at the existing price level. As a result, the economy's supply of goods and services declines and the price level rises. In this scenario, costs are *pushing* the price level upward,

---

FIGURE 9.4 Annual inflation rates in the United States, 1960–2009 (December-to-December changes in the CPI). The major periods of inflation in the United States in the past 49 years were in the 1970s and 1980s.

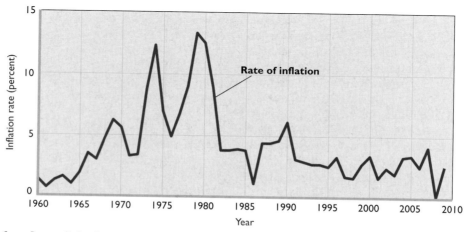

Source: Bureau of Labor Statistics, **www.bls.gov**.

whereas in demand-pull inflation demand is *pulling* it upward.

The major source of cost-push inflation has been so-called *supply shocks*. Specifically, abrupt increases in the costs of raw materials or energy inputs have on occasion driven up per-unit production costs and thus product prices. The rocketing prices of imported oil in 1973–1974 and again in 1979–1980 are good illustrations. As energy prices surged upward during these periods, the costs of producing and transporting virtually every product in the economy rose. Cost-push inflation ensued.

Complexities

The real world is more complex than the distinction between demand-pull and cost-push inflation suggests. It is difficult to distinguish between demand-pull inflation and cost-push inflation unless the original source of inflation is known. For example, suppose a significant increase in total spending occurs in a fully employed economy, causing demand-pull inflation. But as the demand-pull stimulus works its way through various product and resource markets, individual firms find their wage costs, material costs, and fuel prices rising. From their perspective they must raise their prices because production costs (someone else's prices) have risen. Although this inflation is clearly demand-pull in origin, it may mistakenly appear to be cost-push inflation to business firms and to government. Without proper identification of the source of the inflation, government and the Federal Reserve may be slow to undertake policies to reduce excessive total spending.

Another complexity is that cost-push inflation and demand-pull inflation differ in their sustainability. Demand-pull inflation will continue as long as there is excess total spending. Cost-push inflation is automatically self-limiting; it will die out by itself. Increased per-unit costs will reduce supply, and this means lower real output and employment. Those decreases will constrain further per-unit cost increases. In other words, cost-push inflation generates a recession. And in a recession, households and businesses concentrate on keeping their resources employed, not on pushing up the prices of those resources.

Core Inflation

Another complication relating to inflation (regardless of type) is noteworthy. Some price-flexible items within the consumer price index—particularly, food and energy—experience rapid changes in supply and demand and therefore considerable price volatility from month to month and year to year. For example, the prices of grain, fruit, vegetables, and livestock sometimes move rapidly in one

CONSIDER THIS . . .

Clipping Coins

Some interesting early episodes of demand-pull inflation occurred in Europe from the ninth century to the fifteenth century under feudalism. In that economic system, *lords* (or *princes*) ruled individual fiefdoms and their *vassals* (or *peasants*) worked the fields. The peasants initially paid parts of their harvest as taxes to the princes. Later, when the princes began issuing "coins of the realm," peasants began paying their taxes with gold coins.

Some princes soon discovered a way to transfer purchasing power from their vassals to themselves without explicitly increasing taxes. As coins came into the treasury, princes clipped off parts of the gold coins, making them slightly smaller. From the clippings they minted new coins and used them to buy more goods for themselves.

This practice of clipping coins was a subtle form of taxation. The quantity of goods being produced in the fiefdom remained the same, but the number of gold coins increased. With "too much money chasing too few goods," inflation occurred. Each gold coin earned by the peasants therefore had less purchasing power than previously because prices were higher. The increase of the money supply shifted purchasing power away from the peasants and toward the princes just as surely as if the princes had increased taxation of the peasants.

In more recent eras some dictators have simply printed money to buy more goods for themselves, their relatives, and their key loyalists. These dictators, too, have levied hidden taxes on their population by creating inflation.

The moral of the story is quite simple: A society that values price-level stability should not entrust the control of its money supply to people who benefit from inflation.

direction or the other, leading to sizable changes in the prices of food items such as bread, oranges, lettuce, and beef. Also, energy items such as gasoline and natural gas can rise or fall rapidly from period to period. These ups and downs of food and energy prices usually are temporary and often cancel each other out over longer periods.

In tracking inflation, policymakers want to avoid being misled by rapid but temporary price changes that may distort the inflation picture. They mainly are interested in how rapidly the prices of the typically more stable components of the CPI are rising. By stripping volatile food and energy prices from the CPI, policymakers isolate so-called

core inflation, the underlying increases in the CPI after volatile food and energy prices are removed.

If core inflation is low and stable, policymakers may be satisfied with current policy even though changes in the overall CPI index may be suggesting a rising rate of inflation. But policymakers become greatly concerned when core inflation is high and rising and take deliberate measures to try to halt it. We discuss these policies in later chapters.

QUICK REVIEW 9.3

- Inflation is a rising general level of prices and is measured as a percentage change in a price index such as the CPI; deflation is a decline in the general level of prices.

- For the past several years, the U.S. inflation rate has been within the general range of the rates of other advanced industrial nations and far below the rates experienced by some nations.

- Demand-pull inflation occurs when total spending exceeds the economy's ability to provide goods and services at the existing price level; total spending *pulls* the price level upward.

- Cost-push inflation occurs when factors such as rapid increases in the prices of imported raw materials drive up per-unit production costs at each level of output; higher costs *push* the price level upward.

- Core inflation is the underlying inflation rate after volatile food and energy prices have been removed.

Redistribution Effects of Inflation

Inflation redistributes real income. This redistribution helps some people and hurts some others while leaving many people largely unaffected. Who gets hurt? Who benefits? Before we can answer, we need some terminology.

Nominal and Real Income There is a difference between money (or nominal) income and real income. **Nominal income** is the number of dollars received as wages, rent, interest, or profit. **Real income** is a measure of the amount of goods and services nominal income can buy; it is the purchasing power of nominal income, or income adjusted for inflation. That is,

$$\text{Real income} = \frac{\text{nominal income}}{\text{price index (in hundredths)}}$$

Inflation need not alter an economy's overall real income—its total purchasing power. It is evident from the above equation that real income will remain the same when nominal income rises at the same percentage rate as does the price index.

But when inflation occurs, not everyone's nominal income rises at the same pace as the price level. Therein lies the potential for redistribution of real income from some to others. If the change in the price level differs from the change in a person's nominal income, his or her real income will be affected. The following approximation (shown by the $\cong$ sign) tells us roughly how much real income will change:

$$
\begin{array}{ccc}
\text{Percentage} & & \text{percentage} & & \text{percentage} \\
\text{change in} & \cong & \text{change in} & - & \text{change in} \\
\text{real income} & & \text{nominal income} & & \text{price level}
\end{array}
$$

WORKED PROBLEMS

W 9.3

Nominal and real income

For example, suppose that the price level rises by 6 percent in some period. If Bob's nominal income rises by 6 percent, his real income will *remain unchanged.* But if his nominal income instead rises by 10 percent, his real income will *increase* by about 4 percent. And if Bob's nominal income rises by only 2 percent, his real income will *decline* by about 4 percent.[1]

Anticipations The redistribution effects of inflation depend upon whether or not it is expected. We will first discuss situations involving **unanticipated inflation.** As you will see, these cause real income and wealth to be redistributed, harming some and benefiting others. We will then discuss situations involving **anticipated inflation.** These are situations in which people see an inflation coming in advance. With the ability to plan ahead, people are able to avoid or lessen the redistribution effects associated with inflation.

Who Is Hurt by Inflation?

Unanticipated inflation hurts fixed-income recipients, savers, and creditors. It redistributes real income away from them and toward others.

Fixed-Income Receivers People whose incomes are fixed see their real incomes fall when inflation occurs. The

---

[1]A more precise calculation uses our equation for real income. In our first illustration above, if nominal income rises by 10 percent from $100 to $110 and the price level (index) rises by 6 percent from 100 to 106, then real income has increased as follows:

$$\frac{\$110}{1.06} = \$103.77$$

The 4 percent increase in real income shown by the simple formula in the text is a reasonable approximation of the 3.77 percent yielded by our more precise formula.

classic case is the elderly couple living on a private pension or annuity that provides a fixed amount of nominal income each month. They may have retired in, say, 1993 on what appeared to be an adequate pension. However, by 2009 they would have discovered that inflation had cut the annual purchasing power of that pension—their real income—by one-third.

Similarly, landlords who receive lease payments of fixed dollar amounts will be hurt by inflation as they receive dollars of declining value over time. Likewise, public sector workers whose incomes are dictated by fixed pay schedules may suffer from inflation. The fixed "steps" (the upward yearly increases) in their pay schedules may not keep up with inflation. Minimum-wage workers and families living on fixed welfare incomes also will be hurt by inflation.

Savers Unanticipated inflation hurts savers. As prices rise, the real value, or purchasing power, of an accumulation of savings deteriorates. Paper assets such as savings accounts, insurance policies, and annuities that were once adequate to meet rainy-day contingencies or provide for a comfortable retirement decline in real value during inflation. The simplest case is the person who hoards money as a cash balance. A $1000 cash balance would have lost one-half its real value between 1985 and 2009. Of course, most forms of savings earn interest. But the value of savings will still decline if the rate of inflation exceeds the rate of interest.

Example: A household may save $1000 in a certificate of deposit (CD) in a commercial bank or savings and loan association at 6 percent annual interest. But if inflation is 13 percent (as it was in 1980), the real value or purchasing power of that $1000 will be cut to about $938 by the end of the year. Although the saver will receive $1060 (equal to $1000 plus $60 of interest), deflating that $1060 for 13 percent inflation means that its real value is only about $938 (= $1060 ÷ 1.13).

Creditors Unanticipated inflation harms creditors (lenders). Suppose Chase Bank lends Bob $1000, to be repaid in 2 years. If in that time the price level doubles, the $1000 that Bob repays will have only half the purchasing power of the $1000 he borrowed. True, if we ignore interest charges, the same number of dollars will be repaid as was borrowed. But because of inflation, each of those dollars will buy only half as much as it did when the loan was negotiated. As prices go up, the purchasing power of the dollar goes down. So the borrower pays back less valuable dollars than those received from the lender. The owners of Chase Bank suffer a loss of real income.

Who Is Unaffected or Helped by Inflation?

Some people are unaffected by inflation and others are actually helped by it. For the second group, inflation redistributes real income toward them and away from others.

Flexible-Income Receivers People who have flexible incomes may escape inflation's harm or even benefit from it. For example, individuals who derive their incomes solely from Social Security are largely unaffected by inflation because Social Security payments are *indexed* to the CPI. Benefits automatically increase when the CPI increases, preventing erosion of benefits from inflation. Some union workers also get automatic **cost-of-living adjustments (COLAs)** in their pay when the CPI rises, although such increases rarely equal the full percentage rise in inflation.

Some flexible-income receivers and all borrowers are helped by unanticipated inflation. The strong product demand and labor shortages implied by rapid demand-pull inflation may cause some nominal incomes to spurt ahead of the price level, thereby enhancing real incomes. For some, the 3 percent increase in nominal income that occurs when inflation is 2 percent may become a 7 percent increase when inflation is 5 percent. As an example, property owners faced with an inflation-induced real estate boom may be able to boost rents more rapidly than the rate of inflation. Also, some business owners may benefit from inflation. If product prices rise faster than resource prices, business revenues will increase more rapidly than costs. In those cases, the growth rate of profit incomes will outpace the rate of inflation.

Debtors Unanticipated inflation benefits debtors (borrowers). In our earlier example, Chase Bank's loss of real income from inflation is Bob's gain of real income. Debtor Bob borrows "dear" dollars but, because of inflation, pays back the principal and interest with "cheap" dollars whose purchasing power has been eroded by inflation. Real income is redistributed away from the owners of Chase Bank toward borrowers such as Bob.

The Federal government, which had amassed $11.9 trillion of public debt through 2009, has also benefited from inflation. Historically, the Federal government regularly paid off its loans by taking out new ones. Inflation permitted the Treasury to pay off its loans with dollars of less purchasing power than the dollars originally borrowed. Nominal national income and therefore tax collections rise with inflation; the amount of public debt owed does not. Thus, inflation reduces the real burden of the public debt to the Federal government.

Anticipated Inflation

The redistribution effects of inflation are less severe or are eliminated altogether if people anticipate inflation and can adjust their nominal incomes to reflect the expected price-level rises. The prolonged inflation that began in the late 1960s prompted many labor unions in the 1970s to insist on labor contracts with cost-of-living adjustment clauses.

Similarly, if inflation is anticipated, the redistribution of income from lender to borrower may be altered. Suppose a lender (perhaps a commercial bank or a savings and loan institution) and a borrower (a household) both agree that 5 percent is a fair rate of interest on a 1-year loan provided the price level is stable. But assume that inflation has been occurring and is expected to be 6 percent over the next year. If the bank lends the household $100 at 5 percent interest, the bank will be paid back $105 at the end of the year. But if 6 percent inflation does occur during that year, the purchasing power of the $105 will have been reduced to about $99. The lender will, in effect, have paid the borrower $1 for the use of the lender's money for a year.

The lender can avoid this subsidy by charging an *inflation premium*—that is, by raising the interest rate by 6 percent, the amount of the anticipated inflation. By charging 11 percent, the lender will receive back $111 at the end of the year. Adjusted for the 6 percent inflation, that amount will have roughly the purchasing power of $105 worth of today's money. The result then will be a mutually agreeable transfer of purchasing power from borrower to lender of $5, or 5 percent, for the use of $100 for 1 year. Financial institutions have also developed variable-interest-rate mortgages to protect themselves from the adverse effects of inflation. (Incidentally, this example points out that, rather than being a *cause* of inflation, high nominal interest rates are a *consequence* of inflation.)

Our example reveals the difference between the real rate of interest and the nominal rate of interest. The **real interest rate** is the percentage increase in *purchasing power* that the borrower pays the lender. In our example the real interest rate is 5 percent. The **nominal interest rate** is the percentage increase in *money* that the borrower pays the lender, including that resulting from the built-in expectation of inflation, if any. In equation form:

ORIGIN OF THE IDEA
O 9.2
Real interest rates

$$\text{Nominal interest rate} = \text{real interest rate} + \text{inflation premium (the expected rate of inflation)}$$

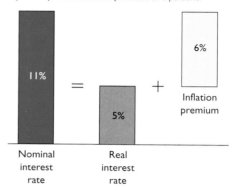

FIGURE 9.5 The inflation premium and nominal and real interest rates. The inflation premium—the expected rate of inflation—gets built into the nominal interest rate. Here, the nominal interest rate of 11 percent comprises the real interest rate of 5 percent plus the inflation premium of 6 percent.

As illustrated in Figure 9.5, the nominal interest rate in our example is 11 percent.

Other Redistribution Issues

We end our discussion of the redistribution effects of inflation by making three final points:

- *Deflation* The effects of unanticipated deflation—declines in the price level—are the reverse of those of inflation. People with fixed nominal incomes will find their real incomes enhanced. Creditors will benefit at the expense of debtors. And savers will discover that the purchasing power of their savings has grown because of the falling prices.

- *Mixed effects* A person who is simultaneously an income earner, a holder of financial assets, and a debtor will probably find that the redistribution impact of unanticipated inflation is cushioned. If the person owns fixed-value monetary assets (savings accounts, bonds, and insurance policies), inflation will lessen their real value. But that same inflation may produce an increase in the person's nominal wage. Also, if the person holds a fixed-interest-rate mortgage, the real burden of that debt will decline. In short, many individuals are simultaneously hurt and helped by inflation. All these effects must be considered before we can conclude that any particular person's net position is better or worse because of inflation.

- *Arbitrariness* The redistribution effects of inflation occur regardless of society's goals and values. Inflation lacks a social conscience and takes from some and gives to others, whether they are rich, poor, young, old, healthy, or infirm.

Does Inflation Affect Output?

Thus far, our discussion has focused on how inflation redistributes a specific level of total real income. But inflation also may affect an economy's level of real output (and thus its level of real income). The direction and significance of this effect on output depend on the type of inflation and its severity.

Cost-Push Inflation and Real Output

Recall that abrupt and unexpected rises in key resource prices such as oil can sufficiently drive up overall production costs to cause cost-push inflation. As prices rise, the quantity demanded of goods and services falls. So firms respond by producing less output, and unemployment goes up.

Economic events of the 1970s provide an example of how inflation can reduce real output. In late 1973 the Organization of Petroleum Exporting Countries (OPEC), by exerting its market power, managed to quadruple the price of oil. The cost-push inflationary effects generated rapid price-level increases in the 1973–1975 period. At the same time, the U.S. unemployment rate rose from slightly less than 5 percent in 1973 to 8.5 percent in 1975. Similar outcomes occurred in 1979–1980 in response to a second OPEC oil supply shock.

In short, cost-push inflation reduces real output. It redistributes a decreased level of real income.

Demand-Pull Inflation and Real Output

Economists do not fully agree on the effects of mild inflation (less than 3 percent) on real output. One perspective is that even low levels of inflation reduce real output because inflation diverts time and effort toward activities designed to hedge against inflation. Examples:

- Businesses must incur the cost of changing thousands of prices on their shelves and in their computers simply to reflect inflation.
- Households and businesses must spend considerable time and effort obtaining the information they need

to distinguish between real and nominal values such as prices, wages, and interest rates.

- To limit the loss of purchasing power from inflation, people try to limit the amount of money they hold in their billfolds and checking accounts at any one time and instead put more money into interest-bearing accounts and stock and bond funds. But cash and checks are needed in even greater amounts to buy the higher-priced goods and services. So more frequent trips, phone calls, or Internet visits to financial institutions are required to transfer funds to checking accounts and billfolds, when needed.

Without inflation, these uses of resources, time, and effort would not be needed, and they could be diverted toward producing more valuable goods and services. Proponents of "zero inflation" bolster their case by pointing to cross-country studies that indicate that lower rates of inflation are associated with higher rates of economic growth. Even mild inflation, say these economists, is detrimental to economic growth.

In contrast, other economists point out that full employment and economic growth depend on strong levels of total spending. Such spending creates high profits, strong demand for labor, and a powerful incentive for firms to expand their plants and equipment. In this view, the mild inflation that is a by-product of strong spending is a small price to pay for full employment and continued economic growth. Moreover, a little inflation may have positive effects because it makes it easier for firms to adjust real wages downward when the demands for their products fall. With mild inflation, firms can reduce real wages by holding nominal wages steady. With zero inflation firms would need to cut nominal wages to reduce real wages. Such cuts in nominal wages are highly visible and may cause considerable worker resistance and labor strife.

Finally, defenders of mild inflation say that it is much better for an economy to err on the side of strong spending, full employment, economic growth, and mild inflation than on the side of weak spending, unemployment, recession, and deflation.

Hyperinflation

All economists agree that **hyperinflation,** which is extraordinarily rapid inflation, can have a devastating impact on real output and employment.

As prices shoot up sharply and unevenly during hyperinflation, people begin to anticipate even more rapid inflation and normal economic relationships are disrupted. Business owners do not know what to charge for their products. Consumers do not know what to pay. Resource

LAST

Word The Stock Market and the Economy

How, If at All, Do Changes in Stock Prices Relate to Macroeconomic Instability?

Every day, the individual stocks (ownership shares) of thousands of corporations are bought and sold in the stock market. The owners of the individual stocks receive dividends—a portion of the firm's profit. Supply and demand in the stock market determine the price of each firm's stock, with individual stock prices generally rising and falling in concert with the collective expectations for each firm's profits. Greater profits normally result in higher dividends to the stock owners, and, in anticipation of higher dividends, people are willing to pay a higher price for the stock.

The media closely monitor and report stock market averages such as the Dow Jones Industrial Average (DJIA)—the weighted-average price of the stocks of 30 major U.S. industrial firms. It is common for these price averages to change over time or even to rise or fall sharply during a single day. On "Black Monday," October 19, 1987, the DJIA fell by 20 percent. A sharp drop in stock prices also occurred in October 1997, mainly in response to rapid declines in stock prices in Hong Kong and other southeast Asia stock markets. In contrast, the stock market averages rose spectacularly in 1998 and 1999, with the DJIA rising 16 and 25 percent in those two years. In 2002, the DJIA fell 17 percent. In 2003, it rose by 25 percent. In 2008, it plummeted by 34 percent, the steepest decline since the 1930s.

The volatility of the stock market raises this question: Do changes in stock price averages and thus stock market wealth cause macroeconomic instability? Linkages between the stock market and the economy might lead us to answer "yes." Consider a sharp increase in stock prices. Feeling wealthier, stock owners respond by increasing their spending (the *wealth effect*). Firms react by increasing their purchases of new capital goods because they can finance such purchases through issuing new shares of high-valued stock (the *investment effect*). Of course, sharp declines in stock prices would produce the opposite results.

Studies find that changes in stock prices do affect consumption and investment but that these consumption and investment impacts are relatively weak. For example, a 10 percent sustained increase in stock market values in 1 year is associated with a 4 percent increase in consumption spending over the next 3 years. The investment response is even weaker. So typical day-to-day and year-to-year changes in stock market values have little impact on the macroeconomy.

In contrast, *stock market bubbles* can be detrimental to an economy. Such bubbles are huge run-ups of overall stock prices, caused by excessive optimism and frenzied buying. The rising stock values are unsupported by realistic prospects of the future strength of the economy and the firms operating in it. Rather than slowly decompress, such bubbles may burst and cause harm to the economy. The free fall of stock values, if long-lasting, causes reverse wealth effects. The stock market crash also may create an overall pessimism about the economy that undermines consumption and investment spending even further. Indeed, the plunge of the stock market in 2007 and 2008 contributed to the severe recession of 2007–2009 by stressing financial institutions and creating a tremendous amount of pessimism about the direction of the economy.

A related question: Even though typical changes in stock prices do not cause recession or inflation, might they predict such maladies? That is, since stock market values are based on expected profits, wouldn't we expect rapid changes in stock price averages to forecast changes in future business conditions? Indeed, stock prices often do fall prior to recessions and rise prior to expansions. For this reason stock prices are among a group of 10 variables that constitute an index of leading indicators. Such an index may provide a useful clue to the future direction of the economy. But taken alone, stock market prices are not a reliable predictor of changes in GDP. Stock prices have fallen rapidly in some instances with no recession following. Black Monday itself did not produce a recession during the following 2 years. In other instances, recessions have occurred with no prior decline in stock market prices.

suppliers want to be paid with actual output, rather than with rapidly depreciating money. Money eventually becomes almost worthless and ceases to do its job as a medium of exchange. Businesses, anticipating further price increases, may find that hoarding both materials and finished products is profitable. Individual savers may decide to buy nonproductive wealth—jewels, gold, and other precious metals, real estate, and so forth—rather than providing funds that can be borrowed to purchase capital equipment. The economy may be thrown into a state of barter, and production and exchange drop further. The net result is economic collapse and, often, political chaos.

Examples of hyperinflation are Germany after the First World War and Japan after the Second World War. In Germany, "prices increased so rapidly that waiters changed the prices on the menu several times during the course of a lunch. Sometimes customers had to pay double the price listed on the menu when they ordered."[2]

In postwar Japan in 1947, "fisherman and farmers . . . used scales to weigh currency and change, rather than bothering to count it."[3]

There are also more recent examples: Between June 1986 and March 1991 the cumulative inflation in Nicaragua was 11,895,866,143 percent. From November 1993 to December 1994 the cumulative inflation rate in the Democratic Republic of Congo was 69,502 percent. From February 1993 to January 1994 the cumulative inflation rate in Serbia was 156,312,790 percent.[4]

Such dramatic hyperinflations are always the consequence of highly imprudent expansions of the money supply by government. The rocketing money supply produces frenzied total spending and severe demand-pull inflation. Zimbabwe's 14.9 billion percent inflation in 2008 is just the latest example.

---

[2]Theodore Morgan, *Income and Employment*, 2nd ed. (Englewood Cliffs, N.J.: Prentice Hall, 1952), p. 361.

[3]Raburn M. Williams, *Inflation! Money, Jobs, and Politicians* (Arlington Heights, Ill.: AHM Publishing, 1980), p. 2.

[4]Stanley Fischer, Ratna Sahay, and Carlos Végh, "Modern Hyper- and High Inflations," *Journal of Economic Literature*, September 2002, p. 840.

Summary

1. The United States and other industrial economies have gone through periods of fluctuations in real GDP, employment, and the price level. Although they have certain phases in common—peak, recession, trough, expansion—business cycles vary greatly in duration and intensity.

2. Although economists explain the business cycle in terms of underlying causal factors such as major innovations, productivity shocks, money creation, and financial crises, they generally agree that changes in the level of total spending are the immediate causes of fluctuating real output and employment.

3. The business cycle affects all sectors of the economy, though in varying ways and degrees. The cycle has greater effects on output and employment in the capital goods and durable consumer goods industries than in the services and nondurable goods industries.

4. Economists distinguish between frictional, structural, and cyclical unemployment. The full-employment or natural rate of unemployment, which is made up of frictional and structural unemployment, is currently between 4 and 5 percent. The presence of part-time and discouraged workers makes it difficult to measure unemployment accurately.

5. The GDP gap, which can be either a positive or a negative value, is found by subtracting potential GDP from actual GDP. The economic cost of unemployment, as measured by the GDP gap, consists of the goods and services forgone by

society when its resources are involuntarily idle. Okun's law suggests that every 1-percentage-point increase in unemployment above the natural rate causes an additional 2 percent negative GDP gap.

6. Inflation is a rise in the general price level and is measured in the United States by the Consumer Price Index (CPI). When inflation occurs, each dollar of income will buy fewer goods and services than before. That is, inflation reduces the purchasing power of money. Deflation is a decline in the general price level.

7. Unemployment rates and inflation rates vary widely globally. Unemployment rates differ because nations have different natural rates of unemployment and often are in different phases of their business cycles. Inflation and unemployment rates in the United States recently have been in the middle to low range compared with rates in other industrial nations.

8. Economists discern both demand-pull and cost-push (supply-side) inflation. Demand-pull inflation results from an excess of total spending relative to the economy's capacity to produce. The main source of cost-push inflation is abrupt and rapid increases in the prices of key resources. These supply shocks push up per-unit production costs and ultimately raise the prices of consumer goods.

9. Unanticipated inflation arbitrarily redistributes real income at the expense of fixed-income receivers, creditors, and

savers. If inflation is anticipated, individuals and businesses may be able to take steps to lessen or eliminate adverse redistribution effects.

10. When inflation is anticipated, lenders add an inflation premium to the interest rate charged on loans. The nominal interest rate thus reflects the real interest rate plus the inflation premium (the expected rate of inflation).

11. Cost-push inflation reduces real output and employment. Proponents of zero inflation argue that even mild demand-pull inflation (1 to 3 percent) reduces the economy's real output. Other economists say that mild inflation may be a necessary by-product of the high and growing spending that produces high levels of output, full employment, and economic growth.

12. Hyperinflation, caused by highly imprudent expansions of the money supply, may undermine the monetary system and cause severe declines in real output.

Terms and Concepts

business cycles

peak

recession

trough

expansion

labor force

unemployment rate

discouraged workers

frictional unemployment

structural unemployment

cyclical unemployment

full-employment rate of unemployment

natural rate of unemployment (NRU)

potential output

GDP gap

Okun's law

inflation

deflation

Consumer Price Index (CPI)

demand-pull inflation

cost-push inflation

per-unit production costs

core inflation

nominal income

real income

unanticipated inflation

anticipated inflation

cost-of-living adjustments (COLAs)

real interest rate

nominal interest rate

hyperinflation

Questions

1. What are the four phases of the business cycle? How long do business cycles last? Why does the business cycle affect output and employment in capital goods industries and consumer durable goods industries more severely than in industries producing consumer nondurables? **LO1**

2. How, in general, can a financial crisis lead to a recession? How, in general, can a major new invention lead to an expansion? **LO1**

3. How is the labor force defined and who measures it? How is the unemployment rate calculated? Does an increase in the unemployment rate necessarily mean a decline in the size of the labor force? Why is a positive unemployment rate—one more than zero percent—fully compatible with full employment? **LO2**

4. How, in general, do unemployment rates vary by race and ethnicity, gender, occupation, and education? Why does the average length of time people are unemployed rise during a recession? **LO2**

5. Why is it difficult to distinguish between frictional, structural, and cyclical unemployment? Why is unemployment an economic problem? What are the consequences of a negative GDP gap? What are the noneconomic effects of unemployment? **LO2**

6. Because the United States has an unemployment compensation program that provides income for those out of work, why should we worry about unemployment? **LO2**

7. What is the Consumer Price Index (CPI) and how is it determined each month? How does the Bureau of Labor Statistics calculate the rate of inflation from one year to the next? What effect does inflation have on the purchasing power of a dollar? How does it explain differences between nominal and real interest rates? How does deflation differ from inflation? **LO3**

8. Distinguish between demand-pull inflation and cost-push inflation. Which of the two types is most likely to be associated with a negative GDP gap? Which with a positive GDP gap, in which actual GDP exceeds potential GDP? What is core inflation? Why is it calculated? **LO3**

9. Explain how an increase in your nominal income and a decrease in your real income might occur simultaneously. Who loses from inflation? Who gains? **LO3**

10. Explain how hyperinflation might lead to a severe decline in total output. **LO3**

11. **LAST WORD** Suppose that stock prices were to fall by 10 percent in the stock market. All else equal, would the lower stock prices be likely to cause a recession? How might lower stock prices help predict a recession?

Problems

1. Suppose that a country's annual growth rates were 5, 3, 4, −1, −2, 2, 3, 4, 6, and 3 in yearly sequence over a 10-year period. What was the country's trend rate of growth over this period? Which set of years most clearly demonstrates an expansionary phase of the business cycle? Which set of years best illustrates a recessionary phase of the business cycle? LO1

2. Assume the following data for a country: total population, 500; population under 16 years of age or institutionalized, 120; not in labor force, 150; unemployed, 23; part-time workers looking for full-time jobs, 10. What is the size of the labor force? What is the official unemployment rate? LO2

3. Suppose that the natural rate of unemployment in a particular year is 5 percent and the actual rate of unemployment is 9 percent. Use Okun's law to determine the size of the GDP gap in percentage-point terms. If the potential GDP is $500 billion in that year, how much output is being forgone because of cyclical unemployment? LO2

4. If the CPI was 110 last year and is 121 this year, what is this year's rate of inflation? In contrast, suppose that the CPI was 110 last year and is 108 this year. What is this year's rate of inflation? What term do economists use to describe this second outcome? LO3

5. How long would it take for the price level to double if inflation persisted at (a) 2 percent per year, (b) 5 percent per year, and (c) 10 percent per year? LO3

6. If your nominal income rose by 5.3 percent and the price level rose by 3.8 percent in some year, by what percentage would your real income (approximately) increase? If your nominal income rose by 2.8 percent and your real income rose by 1.1 percent in some year, what must have been the (approximate) rate of inflation? LO3

7. Suppose that the nominal rate of inflation is 4 percent and the inflation premium is 2 percent. What is the real interest rate? Alternatively, assume that the real interest rate is 1 percent and the nominal interest rate is 6 percent. What is the inflation premium? LO3

FURTHER TEST YOUR KNOWLEDGE AT
www.mcconnell19e.com

At the text's Online Learning Center (OLC), **www.mcconnell19e.com**, you will find one or more Web-based questions that require information from the Internet to answer. We urge you to check them out; they will familiarize you with Web sites that may be helpful in other courses and perhaps even in your career. The OLC also features multiple-choice questions that give instant feedback and provides other helpful ways to further test your knowledge of the chapter.

MACROECONOMIC MODELS AND FISCAL POLICY

AFTER READING THIS CHAPTER, YOU SHOULD BE ABLE TO:

1 Describe how changes in income affect consumption (and saving).

2 List and explain factors other than income that can affect consumption.

3 Explain how changes in real interest rates affect investment.

4 Identify and explain factors other than the real interest rate that can affect investment.

5 Illustrate how changes in investment increase or decrease real GDP by a multiple amount.

Basic Macroeconomic Relationships*

In Chapter 9 we discussed the business cycle, unemployment, and inflation. Our eventual goal is to build economic models that can explain these phenomena. This chapter begins that process by examining the basic relationships that exist between three different pairs of economic aggregates. (Recall that to economists "aggregate" means "total" or "combined.") Specifically, this chapter looks at the relationships between:

• income and consumption (and income and saving).

• the interest rate and investment.

• changes in spending and changes in output.

*Note to the Instructor: If you wish to bypass the aggregate expenditures model (Keynesian cross model) covered in full in Chapter 11, assigning the present chapter will provide a seamless transition to the AD-AS model of Chapter 12 and the chapters beyond. If you want to cover the aggregate expenditure model, this present chapter provides the necessary building blocks.

What explains the trends in consumption (consumer spending) and saving reported in the news? How do changes in interest rates affect investment? How can initial changes in spending ultimately produce multiplied changes in GDP? The basic macroeconomic relationships discussed in this chapter answer these questions.

The Income-Consumption and Income-Saving Relationships

The other-things-equal relationship between income and consumption is one of the best-established relationships in macroeconomics. In examining that relationship, we are also exploring the relationship between income and saving. Recall that economists define *personal saving* as "not spending" or as "that part of disposable (after-tax) income not consumed." Saving (*S*) equals disposable income (DI) *minus* consumption (*C*).

Many factors determine a nation's levels of consumption and saving, but the most significant is disposable income. Consider some recent historical data for the United

States. In Figure 10.1 each dot represents consumption and disposable income for 1 year since 1987. The line *C* that is loosely fitted to these points shows that consumption is directly (positively) related to disposable income; moreover, households spend most of their income.

But we can say more. The **45°(degree) line** is a reference line. Because it bisects the 90° angle formed by the two axes of the graph, each point on it is equidistant from the two axes. At each point on the 45° line, consumption would equal disposable income, or *C* = DI. Therefore, the vertical distance between the 45° line and any point on the horizontal axis measures either consumption *or* disposable income. If we let it measure disposable income, the vertical distance between it and the consumption line labeled *C*

FIGURE 10.1 Consumption and disposable income, 1987–2009. Each dot in this figure shows consumption and disposable income in a specific year. The line *C*, which generalizes the relationship between consumption and disposable income, indicates a direct relationship and shows that households consume most of their after-tax incomes.

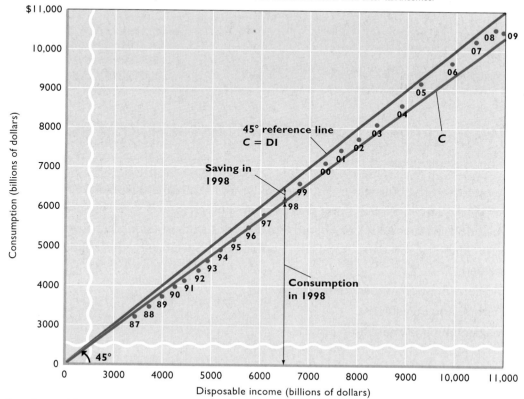

Source: Bureau of Economic Analysis, **www.bea.gov**.

represents the amount of saving (*S*) in that year. Saving is the amount by which actual consumption in any year falls short of the 45° line—(*S* = DI − *C*). For example, in 1998 disposable income was $6498.9 billion and consumption was $6157.5 billion, so saving was $341.4 billion. Observe that the vertical distance between the 45° line and line *C* increases as we move rightward along the horizontal axis and decreases as we move leftward. Like consumption, saving typically varies directly with the level of disposable income. However, that historical pattern broke down somewhat in several years preceding the recession of 2007–2009.

The Consumption Schedule

The dots in Figure 10.1 represent historical data—the actual amounts of DI, *C*, and *S* in the United States over a period of years. But, because we want to understand how the economy would behave under different possible scenarios, we need a schedule showing the various amounts that households would *plan* to consume at each of the various levels of disposable income that might prevail at some specific time. Columns 1 and 2 of Table 10.1, represented in **Figure 10.2a (Key Graph)**, show the hypothetical consumption schedule that we require. This **consumption schedule** (or "consumption function") reflects the direct consumption–disposable income relationship suggested by the data in Figure 10.1, and it is consistent with many household budget studies. In the aggregate, households increase their spending as their disposable income rises

ORIGIN OF THE IDEA

O 10.1

Income-consumption relationship

and spend a larger proportion of a small disposable income than of a large disposable income.

The Saving Schedule

It is relatively easy to derive a **saving schedule** (or "saving function"). Because saving equals disposable income less consumption (*S* = DI − *C*), we need only subtract consumption (Table 10.1, column 2) from disposable income (column 1) to find the amount saved (column 3) at each DI. Thus, columns 1 and 3 in Table 10.1 are the saving schedule, represented in Figure 10.2b. The graph shows that there is a direct relationship between saving and DI but that saving is a smaller proportion of a small DI than of a large DI. If households consume a smaller and smaller proportion of DI as DI increases, then they must be saving a larger and larger proportion.

Remembering that at each point on the 45° line consumption equals DI, we see that *dissaving* (consuming in excess of after-tax income) will occur at relatively low DIs. For example, at $370 billion (row 1, Table 10.1), consumption is $375 billion. Households can consume more than their current incomes by liquidating (selling for cash) accumulated wealth or by borrowing. Graphically, dissaving is shown as the vertical distance of the consumption schedule above the 45° line or as the vertical distance of the saving schedule below the horizontal axis. We have marked the dissaving at the $370 billion level of income in Figure 10.2a and 10.2b. Both vertical distances measure the $5 billion of dissaving that occurs at $370 billion of income.

In our example, the **break-even income** is $390 billion (row 2, Table 10.1). This is the income level at which

TABLE 10.1 Consumption and Saving Schedules (in Billions) and Propensities to Consume and Save

(1) Level of Output and Income (GDP = DI)	(2) Consumption (C)	(3) Saving (S), (1) − (2)	(4) Average Propensity to Consume (APC), (2)/(1)	(5) Average Propensity to Save (APS), (3)/(1)	(6) Marginal Propensity to Consume (MPC), Δ(2)/Δ(1)*	(7) Marginal Propensity to Save (MPS), Δ(3)/Δ(1)*
(1) $370	$375	$−5	1.01	−.01		
					.75	.25
(2) 390	390	0	1.00	.00		
					.75	.25
(3) 410	405	5	.99	.01		
					.75	.25
(4) 430	420	10	.98	.02		
					.75	.25
(5) 450	435	15	.97	.03		
					.75	.25
(6) 470	450	20	.96	.04		
					.75	.25
(7) 490	465	25	.95	.05		
					.75	.25
(8) 510	480	30	.94	.06		
					.75	.25
(9) 530	495	35	.93	.07		
					.75	.25
(10) 550	510	40	.93	.07		

*The Greek letter Δ, delta, means "the change in."

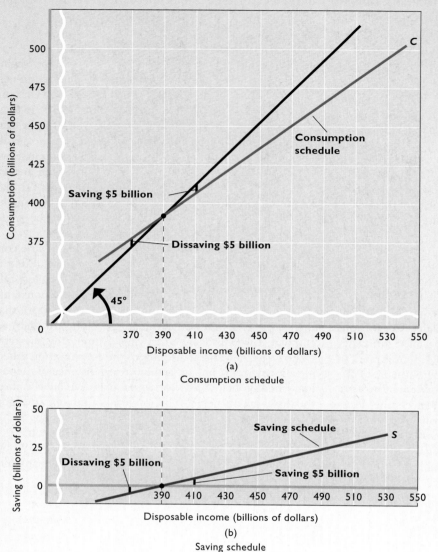

FIGURE 10.2 (a) Consumption and (b) saving schedules. The two parts of this figure show the income-consumption and income-saving relationships in Table 10.1 graphically. The saving schedule in (b) is found by subtracting the consumption schedule in (a) vertically from the 45° line. Consumption equals disposable income (and saving thus equals zero) at $390 billion for these hypothetical data.

QUICK QUIZ FOR FIGURE 10.2

1. The slope of the consumption schedule in this figure is .75. Thus, the:
   a. slope of the saving schedule is 1.33.
   b. marginal propensity to consume is .75.
   c. average propensity to consume is .25.
   d. slope of the saving schedule is also .75.

2. In this figure, when consumption is a positive amount, saving:
   a. must be a negative amount.
   b. must also be a positive amount.
   c. can be either a positive or a negative amount.
   d. is zero.

3. In this figure:
   a. the marginal propensity to consume is constant at all levels of income.
   b. the marginal propensity to save rises as disposable income rises.
   c. consumption is inversely (negatively) related to disposable income.
   d. saving is inversely (negatively) related to disposable income.

4. When consumption equals disposable income:
   a. the marginal propensity to consume is zero.
   b. the average propensity to consume is zero.
   c. consumption and saving must be equal.
   d. saving must be zero.

Answers: 1. b; 2. c; 3. a; 4. d

households plan to consume their entire incomes ($C = DI$). Graphically, the consumption schedule cuts the 45° line, and the saving schedule cuts the horizontal axis (saving is zero) at the break-even income level.

At all higher incomes, households plan to save part of their incomes. Graphically, the vertical distance between the consumption schedule and the 45° line measures this saving (see Figure 10.2a), as does the vertical distance between the saving schedule and the horizontal axis (see Figure 10.2b). For example, at the $410 billion level of income (row 3, Table 10.1), both these distances indicate $5 billion of saving.

Average and Marginal Propensities

Columns 4 to 7 in Table 10.1 show additional characteristics of the consumption and saving schedules.

APC and APS The fraction, or percentage, of total income that is consumed is the **average propensity to consume (APC).** The fraction of total income that is saved is the **average propensity to save (APS).** That is,

$$APC = \frac{consumption}{income}$$

and

$$APS = \frac{saving}{income}$$

For example, at $470 billion of income (row 6, Table 10.1), the APC is $\frac{450}{470} = \frac{45}{47}$, or about .96 (= 96 percent), while the APS is $\frac{20}{470} = \frac{2}{47}$, or about .04 (= 4 percent). Columns 4 and 5 in Table 10.1 show the APC and APS at each of the 10 levels of DI. As implied by our previous discussion, the APC falls as DI increases, while the APS rises as DI goes up.

Because disposable income is either consumed or saved, the fraction of any DI consumed plus the fraction saved (not consumed) must exhaust that income. Mathematically, APC + APS = 1 at any level of disposable income, as columns 4 and 5 in Table 10.1 illustrate. So if .96 of the $470 billion of income in row 6 in consumed, .04 must be saved. That is why APC + APS = 1.

Global Perspective 10.1 shows APCs for several countries.

MPC and MPS The fact that households consume a certain proportion of a particular total income, for example, $\frac{45}{47}$ of a $470 billion disposable income, does not guarantee they will consume the same proportion of any *change* in income they might receive. The proportion, or fraction, of any change in income consumed is called the **marginal propensity to consume (MPC),** "marginal" meaning "extra" or "a change in." Equivalently, the MPC is the

Average Propensities to Consume, Selected Nations

There are surprisingly large differences in average propensities to consume (APCs) among nations. In 2009, Australia, the United States, and Canada in particular had substantially higher APCs, and thus lower APSs, than several other advanced economies.

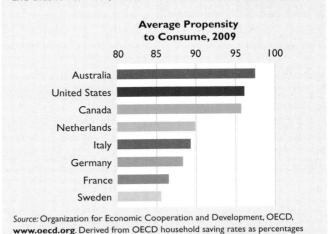

Average Propensity to Consume, 2009

Source: Organization for Economic Cooperation and Development, OECD, **www.oecd.org**. Derived from OECD household saving rates as percentages of disposable income. Econ Outlook 86, Annex Table 23, extracted March 2010.

ratio of a change in consumption to a change in the income that caused the consumption change:

$$MPC = \frac{change\ in\ consumption}{change\ in\ income}$$

Similarly, the fraction of any change in income saved is the **marginal propensity to save (MPS).** The MPS is the ratio of a change in saving to the change in income that brought it about:

$$MPS = \frac{change\ in\ saving}{change\ in\ income}$$

If disposable income is $470 billion (row 6 horizontally in Table 10.1) and household income rises by $20 billion to $490 billion (row 7), households will consume $\frac{15}{20}$, or $\frac{3}{4}$, and save $\frac{5}{20}$, or $\frac{1}{4}$, of that increase in income. In other words, the MPC is or .75, and the MPS is $\frac{1}{4}$ or .25, as shown in columns 6 and 7.

The sum of the MPC and the MPS for any change in disposable income must always be 1. Consuming or saving out of extra income is an either-or proposition; the fraction of any change in income not consumed is, by definition, saved. If .75 of extra disposable income is consumed, .25 must be saved. The fraction consumed (MPC) plus the fraction saved (MPS) must exhaust the whole change in income:

$$MPC + MPS = 1$$

In our example, .75 plus .25 equals 1.

MPC and MPS as Slopes

The MPC is the numerical value of the slope of the consumption schedule, and the MPS is the numerical value of the slope of the saving schedule. We know from the appendix to Chapter 1 that the slope of any line is the ratio of the vertical change to the horizontal change occasioned in moving from one point to another on that line.

Figure 10.3 measures the slopes of the consumption and saving lines, using enlarged portions of Figure 10.2a and 10.2b. Observe that consumption changes by $15 billion (the vertical change) for each $20 billion change in dispos-

able income (the horizontal change). The slope of the consumption line is thus .75 (= $15/$20), which is the value of the MPC. Saving changes by $5 billion (shown as the vertical change) for every $20 billion change in disposable income (shown as the horizontal change). The slope of the saving line therefore is .25 (= $5/$20), which is the value of the MPS.

Nonincome Determinants of Consumption and Saving

The amount of disposable income is the basic determinant of the amounts households will consume and save. But certain determinants other than income might prompt households to consume more or less at each possible level of income and thereby change the locations of the consumption and saving schedules. Those other determinants are wealth, borrowing, expectations, and interest rates.

Wealth

A household's wealth is the dollar amount of all the assets that it owns minus the dollar amount of its liabilities (all the debt that it owes). Households build wealth by saving money out of current income. The point of building wealth is to increase consumption possibilities. The larger the stock of wealth that a household can build up, the larger will be its present and future consumption possibilities.

Events sometimes suddenly boost the value of existing wealth. When this happens, households tend to increase their spending and reduce their saving. This so-called **wealth effect** shifts the consumption schedule upward and the saving schedule downward. They move in response to households taking advantage of the increased consumption possibilities afforded by the sudden increase in wealth. Examples: In the late 1990s, skyrocketing U.S. stock values expanded the value of household wealth by increasing the value of household assets. Predictably, households spent more and saved less. In contrast, a strong "reverse wealth effect" occurred in 2008. Plunging real estate and stock market prices joined together to erase $11.2 trillion (yes, trillion) of household wealth. Consumers quickly reacted by reducing their consumption spending. The consumption schedule shifted downward.

Borrowing

Household borrowing also affects consumption. When a household borrows, it can increase current consumption beyond what would be possible if its spending were limited to its disposable income. By allowing households to spend more, borrowing shifts the current consumption schedule upward.

But note that there is no "free lunch." While borrowing in the present allows for higher consumption in the present, it necessitates lower consumption in the future

FIGURE 10.3 The marginal propensity to consume and the marginal propensity to save. The MPC is the slope ($\Delta C/\Delta DI$) of the consumption schedule, and the MPS is the slope ($\Delta S/\Delta DI$) of the saving schedule. The Greek letter delta (Δ) means "the change in."

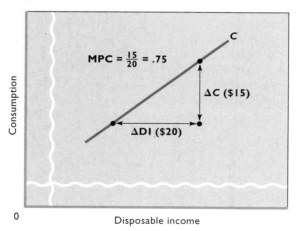

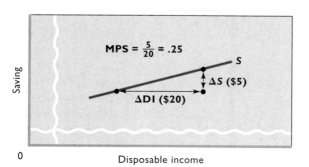

when the debts that are incurred due to the borrowing must be repaid. Stated a bit differently, increased borrowing increases debt (liabilities), which in turn reduces household wealth (since *wealth = assets − liabilities*). This reduction in wealth reduces future consumption possibilities in much the same way that a decline in asset values would. But note that the term "reverse wealth effect" is reserved for situations in which wealth unexpectedly changes because asset values unexpectedly change. It is not used to refer to situations such as the one being discussed here where wealth is intentionally reduced by households through borrowing and piling up debt to increase current consumption.

Expectations Household expectations about future prices and income may affect current spending and saving. For example, the expectation of higher prices tomorrow may cause households to buy more today while prices are still low. Thus, the current consumption schedule shifts up and the current saving schedule shifts down. Or expectations of a recession and thus lower income in the future may lead households to reduce consumption and save more today. Their greater present saving will help build wealth that will help them ride out the expected bad times. The consumption schedule therefore will shift down and the saving schedule will shift up.

Real Interest Rates When real interest rates (those adjusted for inflation) fall, households tend to borrow more, consume more, and save less. A lower interest rate, for example, decreases monthly loan payments and induces consumers to purchase automobiles and other goods bought on credit. A lower interest rate also diminishes the incentive to save because of the reduced interest "payment" to the saver. These effects on consumption and saving, however, are very modest. They mainly shift consumption toward some products (those bought on credit) and away from others. At best, lower interest rates shift the consumption schedule slightly upward and the saving schedule slightly downward. Higher interest rates do the opposite.

Other Important Considerations

There are several additional important points regarding the consumption and saving schedules:

- *Switching to real GDP* When developing macroeconomic models, economists change their focus from the relationship between consumption (and saving) and *disposable income* to the relationship between consumption (and saving) and *real domestic output (real GDP)*. This modification is reflected in Figure 10.4a and 10.4b, where the horizontal axes measure real GDP.

- *Changes along schedules* The movement from one point to another on a consumption schedule (for example, from *a* to *b* on C_0 in Figure 10.4a) is a *change in the amount consumed* and is solely caused by a change in real GDP. On the other hand, an upward or downward shift of the entire schedule, for example, a shift from C_0 to C_1 or C_2 in Figure 10.4a, is a *shift of the consumption schedule* and is caused by changes in any one or more of the *nonincome* determinants of consumption just discussed.

  A similar distinction in terminology applies to the saving schedule in Figure 10.4b.

- *Simultaneous shifts* Changes in wealth, expectations, interest rates, and household debt will shift the consumption schedule in one direction and the saving schedule in the opposite direction. If households

FIGURE 10.4 Shifts of the (a) consumption and (b) saving schedules. Normally, if households consume more at each level of real GDP, they are necessarily saving less. Graphically this means that an upward shift of the consumption schedule (C_0 to C_1) entails a downward shift of the saving schedule (S_0 to S_1). If households consume less at each level of real GDP, they are saving more. A downward shift of the consumption schedule (C_0 to C_2) is reflected in an upward shift of the saving schedule (S_0 to S_2). This pattern breaks down, however, when taxes change; then the consumption and saving schedules move in the *same* direction—opposite to the direction of the tax change.

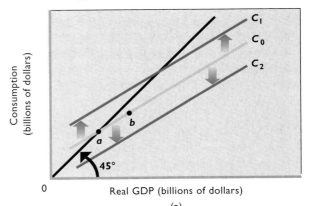

(a)
Consumption schedule

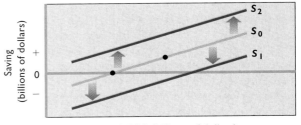

(b)
Saving schedule

CONSIDER THIS . . .

The Great Recession and the Paradox of Thrift

The Great Recession of 2007–2009 altered the prior consumption and saving behavior in the economy. Concerned about reduced wealth, high debt, and potential job losses, households increased their saving and reduced their consumption at each level of after-tax income (or each level of GDP). In Figure 10.4, this outcome is illustrated as the downward *shift* of the consumption schedule in the top graph and the upward *shift* of the saving schedule in the lower graph.

This change of behavior illustrates the so-called **paradox of thrift,** which refers to the possibility that a recession can be made worse when households become more thrifty and save in response to the downturn. The paradox of thrift rests on two major ironies. One irony is that saving more is *good* for the economy in the long run, as noted in Chapter 1 and Chapter 6. It finances investment and therefore fuels subsequent economic growth. But saving more can be *bad* for the economy during a recession. Because firms are pessimistic about future sales, the increased saving is not likely to be matched by an equal amount of added investment. The extra saving simply reduces spending on currently produced goods and services. That means that even more businesses suffer, more layoffs occur, and people's incomes decline even more.

The paradox of thrift has a second irony related to the *fallacy of composition* (Chapter 1, Last Word): Households as a group may inadvertently end up saving less when each individual household tries to save more during a recession. This is because each household's attempt to save more implies that it is also attempting to spend less. Across all households, that collective reduction in total spending in the economy creates additional job losses and further drives down total income. The decline in total income reduces the ability of households as a group to save as much as they did before their spending reduction and subsequent income decline.

decide to consume more at each possible level of real GDP, they must save less, and vice versa. (Even when they spend more by borrowing, they are, in effect, reducing their current saving by the amount borrowed since borrowing is, effectively, "negative saving.") Graphically, if the consumption schedule shifts upward

from C_0 to C_1 in Figure 10.4a, the saving schedule shifts downward, from S_0 to S_1 in Figure 10.4b. Similarly, a downward shift of the consumption schedule from C_0 to C_2 means an upward shift of the saving schedule from S_0 to S_2.

- *Taxation* In contrast, a change in taxes shifts the consumption and saving schedules in the same direction. Taxes are paid partly at the expense of consumption and partly at the expense of saving. So an increase in taxes will reduce both consumption and saving, shifting the consumption schedule in Figure 10.4a and the saving schedule in Figure 10.4b downward. Conversely, households will partly consume and partly save any decrease in taxes. Both the consumption schedule and saving schedule will shift upward.

- *Stability* The consumption and saving schedules usually are relatively stable unless altered by major tax increases or decreases. Their stability may be because consumption-saving decisions are strongly influenced by long-term considerations such as saving to meet emergencies or saving for retirement. It may also be because changes in the nonincome determinants frequently work in opposite directions and therefore may be self-canceling.

> **INTERACTIVE GRAPHS**
>
> **G 10.1**
>
> Consumption and saving schedules

QUICK REVIEW 10.1

- Both consumption spending and saving rise when disposable income increases; both fall when disposable income decreases.

- The average propensity to consume (APC) is the fraction of any specific level of disposable income that is spent on consumer goods; the average propensity to save (APS) is the fraction of any specific level of disposable income that is saved. The APC falls and the APS rises as disposable income increases.

- The marginal propensity to consume (MPC) is the fraction of a change in disposable income that is consumed and it is the slope of the consumption schedule; the marginal propensity to save (MPS) is the fraction of a change in disposable income that is saved and it is the slope of the saving schedule.

- Changes in consumer wealth, consumer expectations, interest rates, household debt, and taxes can shift the consumption and saving schedules (as they relate to real GDP).

The Interest-Rate–Investment Relationship

In our consideration of major macro relationships, we next turn to the relationship between the real interest rate and investment. Recall that investment consists of expenditures on new plants, capital equipment, machinery, inventories, and so on. The investment decision is a marginal-benefit–marginal-cost decision: The marginal benefit from investment is the expected rate of return businesses hope to realize. The marginal cost is the interest rate that must be paid for borrowed funds. Businesses will invest in all projects for which the expected rate of return exceeds the interest rate. Expected returns (profits) and the interest rate therefore are the two basic determinants of investment spending.

Expected Rate of Return

Investment spending is guided by the profit motive; businesses buy capital goods only when they think such purchases will be profitable. Suppose the owner of a small cabinetmaking shop is considering whether to invest in a new sanding machine that costs $1000 and has a useful life of only 1 year. (Extending the life of the machine beyond 1 year complicates the economic decision but does not change the fundamental analysis. We discuss the valuation of returns beyond 1 year in Chapter 17.) The new machine will increase the firm's output and sales revenue. Suppose the net expected revenue from the machine (that is, after such operating costs as power, lumber, labor, and certain taxes have been subtracted) is $1100. Then, after the $1000 cost of the machine is subtracted from the net expected revenue of $1100, the firm will have an expected profit of $100. Dividing this $100 profit by the $1000 cost of the machine, we find that the **expected rate of return**, r, on the machine is 10 percent ($= \$100/\$1000$). It is important to note that this is an *expected* rate of return, not a *guaranteed* rate of return. The investment may or may not generate as much revenue or as much profit as anticipated. Investment involves risk.

The Real Interest Rate

One important cost associated with investing that our example has ignored is interest, which is the financial cost of borrowing the $1000 of *money* "capital" to purchase the $1000 of *real* capital (the sanding machine).

The interest cost of the investment is computed by multiplying the interest rate, i, by the $1000 borrowed to buy the machine. If the interest rate is, say, 7 percent, the total interest cost will be $70. This compares favorably with the net expected return of $100, which produced the 10 percent expected rate of return. If the investment works out as expected, it will add $30 to the firm's profit.

We can generalize as follows: If the expected rate of return (10 percent) exceeds the interest rate (here, 7 percent), the investment should be undertaken. The firm expects the investment to be profitable. But if the interest rate (say, 12 percent) exceeds the expected rate of return (10 percent), the investment should not be undertaken. The firm expects the investment to be unprofitable. The firm should undertake all investment projects it thinks will be profitable. This means that the firm should array its prospective investment projects from the highest expected rate of return, r, downward and then invest in all projects for which r exceeds i. The firm therefore should invest to the point where $r = i$ because then it will have undertaken all investments for which r is greater than i.

This guideline applies even if a firm finances the investment internally out of funds saved from past profit rather than borrowing the funds. The role of the interest rate in the investment decision does not change. When the firm uses money from savings to invest in the sander, it incurs an opportunity cost because it forgoes the interest income it could have earned by lending the funds to someone else. That interest cost, converted to percentage terms, needs to be weighed against the expected rate of return.

The *real* rate of interest, rather than the *nominal* rate, is crucial in making investment decisions. Recall from Chapter 9 that the nominal interest rate is expressed in dollars of current value, while the real interest rate is stated in dollars of constant or inflation-adjusted value. Recall that the real interest rate is the nominal rate less the rate of inflation. In our sanding machine illustration, our implicit assumption of a constant price level ensures that all our data, including the interest rate, are in real terms.

But what if inflation *is* occurring? Suppose a $1000 investment is expected to yield a real (inflation-adjusted) rate of return of 10 percent and the nominal interest rate is 15 percent. At first, we would say the investment would be unprofitable. But assume there is ongoing inflation of 10 percent per year. This means the investing firm will pay back dollars with approximately 10 percent less in purchasing power. While the nominal interest rate is 15 percent, the real rate is only 5 percent ($= 15$ percent $- 10$ percent). By comparing this 5 percent real interest rate with the 10 percent expected real rate of return, we find that the investment is potentially profitable and should be undertaken.

Investment Demand Curve

We now move from a single firm's investment decision to total demand for investment goods by the entire business

key graph

FIGURE 10.5 The investment demand curve.
The investment demand curve is constructed by arraying all potential investment projects in descending order of their expected rates of return. The curve slopes downward, reflecting an inverse relationship between the real interest rate (the financial "price" of each dollar of investing) and the quantity of investment demanded.

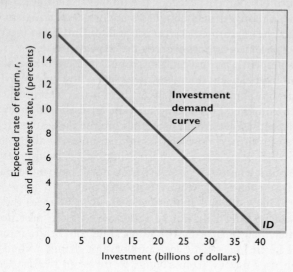

Real Interest Rate (*i*) and Expected Rate of Return (*r*)	Cumulative Amount of Investment Having This Rate of Return or Higher, Billions per Year
16%	$ 0
14	5
12	10
10	15
8	20
6	25
4	30
2	35
0	40

QUICK QUIZ FOR FIGURE 10.5

1. The investment demand curve:
   a. reflects a direct (positive) relationship between the real interest rate and investment.
   b. reflects an inverse (negative) relationship between the real interest rate and investment.
   c. shifts to the right when the real interest rate rises.
   d. shifts to the left when the real interest rate rises.

2. In this figure:
   a. greater cumulative amounts of investment are associated with lower real interest rates.
   b. lesser cumulative amounts of investment are associated with lower expected rates of return on investment.
   c. higher interest rates are associated with higher expected rates of return on investment, and therefore greater amounts of investment.
   d. interest rates and investment move in the same direction.

3. In this figure, if the real interest rate falls from 6 to 4 percent:
   a. investment will increase from 0 to $30 billion.
   b. investment will decrease by $5 billion.
   c. the expected rate of return will rise by $5 billion.
   d. investment will increase from $25 billion to $30 billion.

4. In this figure, investment will be:
   a. zero if the real interest rate is zero.
   b. $40 billion if the real interest rate is 16 percent.
   c. $30 billion if the real interest rate is 4 percent.
   d. $20 billion if the real interest rate is 12 percent.

Answers: 1. b; 2. a; 3. d; 4. c

---

sector. Assume that every firm has estimated the expected rates of return from all investment projects and has recorded those data. We can cumulate (successively sum) these data by asking: How many dollars' worth of investment projects have an expected rate of return of, say, 16 percent or more? How many have 14 percent or more? How many have 12 percent or more? And so on.

Suppose no prospective investments yield an expected return of 16 percent or more. But suppose there are $5 billion of investment opportunities with expected rates of re-

turn between 14 and 16 percent; an additional $5 billion yielding between 12 and 14 percent; still an additional $5 billion yielding between 10 and 12 percent; and an additional $5 billion in each successive 2 percent range of yield down to and including the 0 to 2 percent range.

To cumulate these figures for each rate of return, *r*, we add the amounts of investment that will yield each particular rate of return *r* or higher. This provides the data in the table in Figure 10.5. The data are shown graphically in **Figure 10.5 (Key Graph).** In the table, the number opposite 12 percent, for example, means there are $10 billion of investment opportunities that will yield an expected rate of return of 12 percent or more. The $10 billion includes the $5 billion of investment expected to yield a return of 14 percent or more plus the $5 billion expected to yield between 12 and 14 percent.

We know from our example of the sanding machine that an investment project will be undertaken if its expected rate of return, *r*, exceeds the real interest rate, *i*. Let's first suppose *i* is 12 percent. Businesses will undertake all investments for which *r* exceeds 12 percent. That is, they will invest until the 12 percent rate of return equals the 12 percent interest rate. Figure 10.5 reveals that $10 billion of investment spending will be undertaken at a 12 percent interest rate; that means $10 billion of investment projects have an expected rate of return of 12 percent or more.

Put another way: At a financial "price" of 12 percent, $10 billion of investment goods will be demanded. If the interest rate is lower, say, 8 percent, the amount of investment for which *r* equals or exceeds *i* is $20 billion. Thus, firms will demand $20 billion of investment goods at an 8 percent real interest rate. At 6 percent, they will demand $25 billion of investment goods.

By applying the marginal-benefit–marginal-cost rule that investment projects should be undertaken up to the point where *r* = *i*, we see

ORIGIN OF THE IDEA

O 10.2

Interest-rate–investment relationship

that we can add the real interest rate to the vertical axis in Figure 10.5. The curve in Figure 10.5 not only shows rates of return; it shows the quantity of investment demanded at each "price" *i* (interest rate) of investment. The vertical axis in Figure 10.5 shows the various possible real interest rates, and the horizontal axis shows the corresponding quantities of investment demanded. The inverse (downsloping) relationship between the interest rate (price) and dollar quantity of investment demanded conforms to the law of demand discussed in Chapter 3. The

INTERACTIVE GRAPHS

G 10.2

Investment demand curve

curve *ID* in Figure 10.5 is the economy's **investment demand curve.** It shows the amount of investment forthcoming at each real interest rate. The level of investment depends on the expected rate of return and the real interest rate.

Shifts of the Investment Demand Curve

Figure 10.5 shows the relationship between the interest rate and the amount of investment demanded, other things

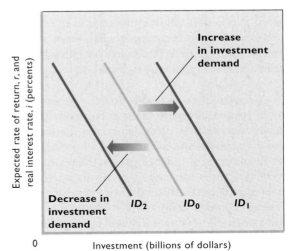

FIGURE 10.6 Shifts of the investment demand curve. Increases in investment demand are shown as rightward shifts of the investment demand curve; decreases in investment demand are shown as leftward shifts of the investment demand curve.

equal. When other things change, the investment demand curve shifts. In general, any factor that leads businesses collectively to expect greater rates of return on their investments increases investment demand. That factor shifts the investment demand curve to the right, as from ID_0 to ID_1 in Figure 10.6. Any factor that leads businesses collectively to expect lower rates of return on their investments shifts the curve to the left, as from ID_0 to ID_2. What are those non-interest-rate determinants of investment demand?

Acquisition, Maintenance, and Operating Costs
The initial costs of capital goods, and the estimated costs of operating and maintaining those goods, affect the expected rate of return on investment. When these costs rise, the expected rate of return from prospective investment projects falls and the investment demand curve shifts to the left. Example: Higher electricity costs associated with operating tools and machinery shifts the investment demand curve to the left. Lower costs, in contrast, shift it to the right.

Business Taxes When government is considered, firms look to expected returns *after taxes* in making their investment decisions. An increase in business taxes lowers the expected profitability of investments and shifts the investment demand curve to the left; a reduction of business taxes shifts it to the right.

Technological Change Technological progress—the development of new products, improvements in existing products, and the creation of new machinery and production processes—stimulates investment. The development of a more efficient machine, for example, lowers production costs or improves product quality and increases the expected rate of return from investing in the machine. Profitable new products (cholesterol medications, Internet services, high-definition televisions, cellular phones, and so on) induce a flurry of investment as businesses tool up for expanded production. A rapid rate of technological progress shifts the investment demand curve to the right.

Stock of Capital Goods on Hand The stock of capital goods on hand, relative to output and sales, influences investment decisions by firms. When the economy is overstocked with production facilities and when firms have excessive inventories of finished goods, the expected rate of return on new investment declines. Firms with excess production capacity have little incentive to invest in new capital. Therefore, less investment is forthcoming at each real interest rate; the investment demand curve shifts leftward.

When the economy is understocked with production facilities and when firms are selling their output as fast as they can produce it, the expected rate of return on new investment increases and the investment demand curve shifts rightward.

Planned Inventory Changes Recall from Chapter 7 that the definition of investment includes changes in inventories of unsold goods. An increase in inventories is counted as positive investment while a decrease in inventories is counted as negative investment. It is important to remember that some inventory changes are planned, while others are unplanned. Since the investment demand curve deals only with *planned* investment, it is only affected by *planned* changes that firms desire to make to their inventory levels. If firms are planning to increase their inventories, the investment demand curve shifts to the right. If firms are planning on decreasing their inventories, the investment demand curve shifts to the left.

Firms make planned changes to their inventory levels mostly because they are expecting either faster or slower sales. A firm that expects its sales to double in the next year will want to keep more inventory in stock, thereby increasing its investment demand. By contrast, a firm that is expecting slower sales will plan on reducing its inventory, thereby reducing its overall investment demand. But because life often does not turn out as expected, firms often find that the actual amount of inventory investment that they end up making is either greater or less than what they had planned. The size of the gap is, naturally, the dollar amount of their *unplanned* inventory changes. These unplanned inventory adjustments will play a large role in the aggregate expenditures model studied in Chapter 11.

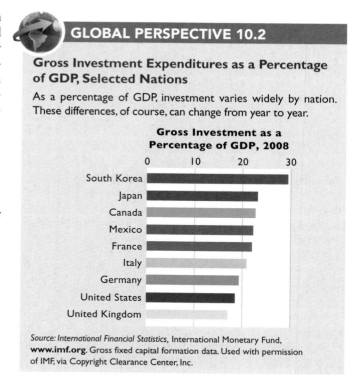

GLOBAL PERSPECTIVE 10.2

Gross Investment Expenditures as a Percentage of GDP, Selected Nations

As a percentage of GDP, investment varies widely by nation. These differences, of course, can change from year to year.

Gross Investment as a Percentage of GDP, 2008

South Korea
Japan
Canada
Mexico
France
Italy
Germany
United States
United Kingdom

Source: International Financial Statistics, International Monetary Fund, **www.imf.org**. Gross fixed capital formation data. Used with permission of IMF, via Copyright Clearance Center, Inc.

Expectations We noted that business investment is based on expected returns (expected additions to profit). Most capital goods are durable, with a life expectancy of 10 or 20 years. Thus, the expected rate of return on capital investment depends on the firm's expectations of future sales, future operating costs, and future profitability of the product that the capital helps produce. These expectations are based on forecasts of future business conditions as well as on such elusive and difficult-to-predict factors as changes in the domestic political climate, international relations, population growth, and consumer tastes. If executives become more optimistic about future sales, costs, and profits, the investment demand curve will shift to the right; a pessimistic outlook will shift the curve to the left.

Global Perspective 10.2 compares investment spending relative to GDP for several nations in a recent year. Domestic real interest rates and investment demand determine the levels of investment relative to GDP.

Instability of Investment

In contrast to consumption, investment is unstable; it rises and falls quite often. Investment, in fact, is the most volatile component of total spending—so much so that most of the fluctuations in output and employment that happen over the course of the business cycle can be attributed to demand shocks relating to unexpected increases

FIGURE 10.7 The volatility of investment, 1973–2009. Annual percentage changes in investment spending are often several times greater than the percentage changes in GDP. (Data are in real terms. Investment is gross private domestic investment).

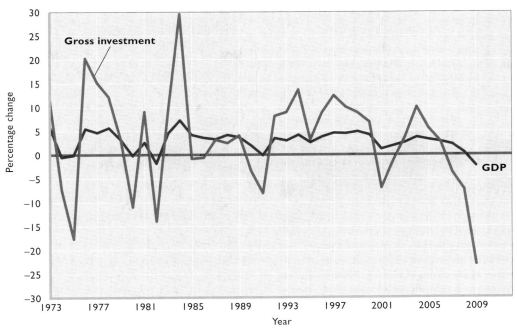

Source: Bureau of Economic Analysis, **www.bea.gov**.

and decreases in investment. Figure 10.8 shows just how volatile investment in the United States has been. Notice that the percentage swings in investment in real terms are greater than the percentage swings in real GDP. Several interrelated factors drawn from our previous discussion explain the variability of investment.

- *Variability of expectations* Business expectations can change quickly when some event suggests a significant possible change in future business conditions. Changes in exchange rates, trade barriers, legislative actions, stock market prices, government economic policies, the outlook for war or peace, court decisions in key labor or antitrust cases, and a host of similar considerations may cause substantial shifts in business expectations.

- *Durability* Because of their durability, capital goods have indefinite useful lifespans. Within limits, purchases of capital goods are discretionary and therefore can be postponed. Firms can scrap or replace older equipment and buildings, or they can patch them up and use them for a few more years. Optimism about the future may prompt firms to replace their older facilities and such modernizing will call for a high level of investment. A less optimistic view, however, may lead to smaller amounts of investment as firms repair older facilities and keep them in use.

- *Irregularity of innovation* New products and processes stimulate investment. Major innovations such as railroads, electricity, airplanes, automobiles, computers, the Internet, and cell phones induce vast upsurges or "waves" of investment spending that in time recede. But such innovations occur quite irregularly, adding to the volatility of investment.

- *Variability of profits* High current profits often generate optimism about the future profitability of new investments, whereas low current profits or losses spawn considerable doubt about the wisdom of new investments. Additionally, firms often save a portion of current profits as retained earnings and use these funds (as well as borrowed funds) to finance new investments. So current profits affect both the incentive and ability to invest. But profits themselves are highly variable from year to year, contributing to the volatility of investment.

In terms of our previous analysis, we would represent volatility of investment as occasional and substantial unexpected shifts of the investment demand curve (as in Figure 10.6), which cause significant changes in investment spending (as in Figure 10.7). These demand shocks can contribute to cyclical instability.

CONSIDER THIS . . .

The Great Recession and the Investment Riddle

During the severe recession of 2007–2009, real interest rates essentially declined to zero. Figure 10.5 suggests that this drop in interest rates should have boosted investment spending. But investment declined substantially during this period. On an annual basis, it declined by 7 percent in 2008 and 23 percent in 2009. Does this combination of lower real interest rates and reduced investment make Figure 10.5 irrelevant?

Definitely not! The key to the investment riddle is that during the recession, the investment demand curve shifted inward, as from ID_0 to ID_2 in Figure 10.6. This inward shift overwhelmed any investment-increasing effects of the decline of real interest rates. The net result turned out to be less investment, not more.

The leftward shift of the investment demand reflected a decline in the expected returns from investment. Firms envisioned zero or negative returns on investment in new capital because they were facing an overstock of existing capital relative to their current sales. Understandably, they therefore were not inclined to invest. Also, firms were extremely pessimistic about when the economy would regain its strength. This pessimism also contributed to low expected rates of return on investment and thus to exceptionally weak investment demand. Further, even though the interest rate was so low, firms that wanted to borrow and invest found that lenders were reluctant to lend them money for fear that they would not be able to pay back the loans.

QUICK REVIEW 10.2

- A specific investment will be undertaken if the expected rate of return, r, equals or exceeds the real interest rate, i.
- The investment demand curve shows the total monetary amounts that will be invested by an economy at various possible real interest rates.
- The investment demand curve shifts when changes occur in (a) the costs of acquiring, operating, and maintaining capital goods, (b) business taxes, (c) technology, (d) the stock of capital goods on hand, and (e) business expectations.

The Multiplier Effect*

A final basic relationship that requires discussion is the relationship between changes in spending and changes in real GDP. Assuming that the economy has room to expand—so

---

*Instructors who cover the full aggregate expenditures (AE) model (Chapter 11) rather than moving directly to aggregate demand and aggregate supply (Chapter 12) may choose to defer this discussion until after the analysis of equilibrium real GDP.

that increases in spending do not lead to increases in prices—there is a direct relationship between these two aggregates. More spending results in a higher GDP; less spending results in a lower GDP. But there is much more to this relationship. A change in spending, say, investment, ultimately changes output and income by more than the initial change in investment spending. That surprising result is called the *multiplier effect*: a change in a component of total spending leads to a larger change in GDP. The **multiplier** determines how much larger that change will be; it is the ratio of a change in GDP to the initial change in spending (in this case, investment). Stated generally,

$$\text{Multiplier} = \frac{\text{change in real GDP}}{\text{initial change in spending}}$$

By rearranging this equation, we can also say that

Change in GDP = multiplier × initial change in spending

So if investment in an economy rises by $30 billion and GDP increases by $90 billion as a result, we then know from our first equation that the multiplier is 3 (= $90/$30).

Note these three points about the multiplier:

- The "initial change in spending" is usually associated with investment spending because of investment's volatility. But changes in consumption (unrelated to changes in income), net exports, and government purchases also lead to the multiplier effect.
- The "initial change in spending" associated with investment spending results from a change in the real interest rate and/or a shift of the investment demand curve.
- Implicit in the preceding point is that the multiplier works in both directions. An increase in initial spending will create a multiple increase in GDP, while a decrease in spending will create a multiple decrease in GDP.

Rationale

The multiplier effect follows from two facts. First, the economy supports repetitive, continuous flows of expenditures and income through which dollars spent by Smith are received as income by Chin and then spent by Chin and received as income by Gonzales, and so on. (This chapter's Last Word presents this idea in a humorous way.) Second, any change in income will change both consumption and saving in the same direction as, and by a fraction of, the change in income.

It follows that an initial change in spending will set off a spending chain throughout the economy. That chain of spending, although of diminishing importance at each successive step, will cumulate to a multiple change in

GDP. Initial changes in spending produce magnified changes in output and income.

The table in Figure 10.8 illustrates the rationale underlying the multiplier effect. Suppose that a $5 billion increase in investment spending occurs. We assume that the MPC is .75, the MPS is .25, and prices remain constant. That is, neither the initial increase in spending nor any of the subsequent increases in spending will cause prices to rise.

The initial $5 billion increase in investment generates an equal amount of wage, rent, interest, and profit income because spending and receiving income are two sides of the same transaction. How much consumption will be induced by this $5 billion increase in the incomes of households? We find the answer by applying the marginal propensity to consume of .75 to this change in income. Thus, the $5 billion increase in income initially raises consumption by $3.75 (=

.75 × $5) billion and saving by $1.25 (= .25 × $5) billion, as shown in columns 2 and 3 in the table.

Other households receive as income (second round) the $3.75 billion of consumption spending. Those households consume .75 of this $3.75 billion, or $2.81 billion, and save .25 of it, or $.94 billion. The $2.81 billion that is consumed flows to still other households as income to be spent or saved (third round). And the process continues, with the added consumption and income becoming less in each round. The process ends when there is no more additional income to spend.

The bar chart in Figure 10.8 shows several rounds of the multiplier process of the table graphically. As shown by rounds 1 to 5, each round adds a smaller and smaller blue block to national income and GDP. The process, of course, continues beyond the five rounds shown (for

FIGURE 10.8 The multiplier process (MPC = .75). An initial change in investment spending of $5 billion creates an equal $5 billion of new income in round 1. Households spend $3.75 (= .75 × $5) billion of this new income, creating $3.75 of added income in round 2. Of this $3.75 of new income, households spend $2.81 (= .75 × $3.75) billion, and income rises by that amount in round 3. Such income increments over the entire process get successively smaller but eventually produce a total change of income and GDP of $20 billion. The multiplier therefore is 4 (= $20 billion/$5 billion).

	(1) Change in Income	(2) Change in Consumption (MPC = .75)	(3) Change in Saving (MPS = .25)
Increase in investment of **$5.00**	$5.00	$ 3.75	$1.25
Second round	3.75	2.81	.94
Third round	2.81	2.11	.70
Fourth round	2.11	1.58	.53
Fifth round	1.58	1.19	.39
All other rounds	4.75	3.56	1.19
Total	**$20.00**	$15.00	$5.00

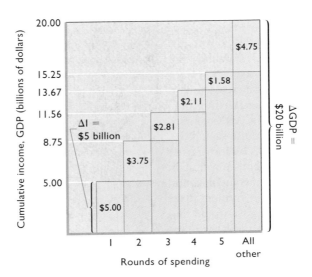

convenience we have simply cumulated the subsequent declining blocks into a single block labeled "All other"). The accumulation of the additional income in each round—the sum of the blue blocks—is the total change in income or GDP resulting from the initial $5 billion change in spending. Because the spending and respending effects of the increase in investment diminish with each successive round of spending, the cumulative increase in output and income eventually ends. In this case, the ending occurs when $20 billion of additional income accumulates. Thus, the multiplier is 4 (= $20 billion/$5 billion).

The Multiplier and the Marginal Propensities

You may have sensed from the table In Figure 10.8 that the fractions of an increase in income consumed (MPC) and saved (MPS) determine the cumulative respending effects of any initial change in spending and therefore determine the size of the multiplier. The MPC and the multiplier are directly related and the MPS and the multiplier are inversely related. The precise formulas are as shown in the next two equations:

$$\text{Multiplier} = \frac{1}{1 - \text{MPC}}$$

Recall, too, that MPC + MPS = 1. Therefore MPS = 1 − MPC, which means we can also write the multiplier formula as

$$\text{Multiplier} = \frac{1}{\text{MPS}}$$

This latter formula is a quick way to determine the multiplier. All you need to know is the MPS.

The smaller the fraction of any change in income saved, the greater the respending at each round and, therefore, the greater the multiplier. When the MPS is .25, as in our example, the multiplier is 4. If the MPS were .2, the multiplier would be 5. If the MPS were .33, the multiplier would be 3. Let's see why.

Suppose the MPS is .2 and businesses increase investment by $5 billion. In the first round of the table in Figure 10.8, consumption will rise by $4 billion (= MPC of .8 × $5 billion) rather than by $3.75 billion because saving will increase by $1 billion (= MPS of .2 × $5 billion) rather than $1.25 billion. The greater rise in consumption in round 1 will produce a greater increase in income in round 2. The same will be true for all successive rounds. If we worked through all rounds of the multiplier, we would find that the process ends when income has cumulatively increased by $25 billion, not the $20 billion shown in the ta-

FIGURE 10.9 The MPC and the multiplier. The larger the MPC (the smaller the MPS), the greater the size of the multiplier.

ble. When the MPS is .2 rather than .25, the multiplier is 5 (= $25 billion/$5 billion) as opposed to 4 (= $20 billion/$5 billion.)

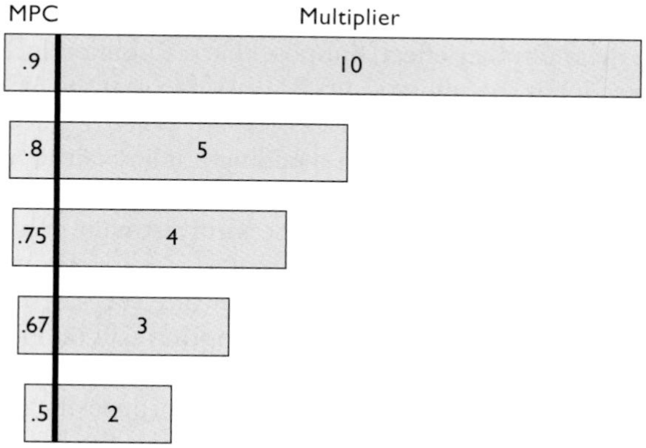

If the MPS were .33 rather than .25, the successive increases in consumption and income would be less than those in the table in Figure 10.8. We would discover that the process ended with a $15 billion increase in income rather than the $20 billion shown. When the MPS is .33, the multiplier is 3 (= $15 billion/$5 billion). The mathematics works such that the multiplier is equal to the reciprocal of the MPS. The reciprocal of any number is the quotient you obtain by dividing 1 by that number.

A large MPC (small MPS) means the succeeding rounds of consumption spending shown in Figure 10.8 diminish slowly and thereby cumulate to a large change in income. Conversely, a small MPC (a large MPS) causes the increases in consumption to decline quickly, so the cumulative change in income is small. The relationship between the MPC (and thus the MPS) and the multiplier is summarized in Figure 10.9.

WORKED PROBLEMS

W 10.2

Multiplier effect

QUICK REVIEW 10.3

- The multiplier effect reveals that an initial change in spending can cause a larger change in domestic income and output. The multiplier is the factor by which the initial change is magnified: multiplier = change in real GDP/initial change in spending.

- The higher the marginal propensity to consume (the lower the marginal propensity to save), the larger the multiplier: multiplier = 1/(1 − MPC) or 1/MPS.

LAST
Word Squaring the Economic Circle

Humorist Art Buchwald Examines the Multiplier

WASHINGTON—The recession hit so fast that nobody knows exactly how it happened. One day we were the land of milk and honey and the next day we were the land of sour cream and food stamps.

This is one explanation.

Hofberger, the Ford salesman in Tomcat, Va., a suburb of Washington, called up Littleton, of Littleton Menswear & Haberdashery, and said, "Good news, the new Fords have just come in and I've put one aside for you and your wife."

Littleton said, "I can't, Hofberger, my wife and I are getting a divorce."

"I'm sorry," Littleton said, "but I can't afford a new car this year. After I settle with my wife, I'll be lucky to buy a bicycle."

Hofberger hung up. His phone rang a few minutes later.

"This is Bedcheck the painter," the voice on the other end said. "When do you want us to start painting your house?"

"I changed my mind," said Hofberger, "I'm not going to paint the house."

"But I ordered the paint," Bedcheck said. "Why did you change your mind?"

"Because Littleton is getting a divorce and he can't afford a new car."

That evening when Bedcheck came home his wife said, "The new color television set arrived from Gladstone's TV Shop."

"Take it back," Bedcheck told his wife.

"Why?" she demanded.

"Because Hofberger isn't going to have his house painted now that the Littletons are getting a divorce."

The next day Mrs. Bedcheck dragged the TV set in its carton back to Gladstone. "We don't want it."

Gladstone's face dropped. He immediately called his travel agent, Sandstorm. "You know that trip you had scheduled for me to the Virgin Islands?"

"Right, the tickets are all written up."

"Cancel it. I can't go. Bedcheck just sent back the color TV set because Hofberger didn't sell a car to Littleton because they're going to get a divorce and she wants all his money."

Sandstorm tore up the airline tickets and went over to see his banker, Gripsholm. "I can't pay back the loan this month because Gladstone isn't going to the Virgin Islands."

Gripsholm was furious. When Rudemaker came in to borrow money for a new kitchen he needed for his restaurant, Gripsholm turned him down cold. "How can I loan you money when Sandstorm hasn't repaid the money he borrowed?"

Rudemaker called up the contractor, Eagleton, and said he couldn't put in a new kitchen. Eagleton laid off eight men.

Meanwhile, Ford announced it was giving a rebate on its new models. Hofberger called up Littleton immediately. "Good news," he said, "even if you are getting a divorce, you can afford a new car."

"I'm not getting a divorce," Littleton said. "It was all a misunderstanding and we've made up."

"That's great," Hofberger said. "Now you can buy the Ford."

"No way," said Littleton. "My business has been so lousy I don't know why I keep the doors open."

"I didn't realize that," Hofberger said.

"Do you realize I haven't seen Bedcheck, Gladstone, Sandstorm, Gripsholm, Rudemaker or Eagleton for more than a month? How can I stay in business if they don't patronize my store?"

Source: Art Buchwald, "Squaring the Economic Circle," *Cleveland Plain Dealer*, Feb. 22, 1975. Reprinted by permission.

How Large Is the Actual Multiplier Effect?

The multiplier we have just described is based on simplifying assumptions. Consumption of domestic output rises by the increases in income minus the increases in saving. But in reality, consumption of domestic output increases in each round by a lesser amount than implied by the MPS alone. In addition to saving, households use some of the extra income in each round to purchase additional goods from abroad (imports) and pay additional taxes. Buying imports and paying taxes drains off some of the additional consumption spending (on domestic output) created by the increases in income. So the multiplier effect is reduced and the 1/MPS formula for the multiplier overstates the actual outcome. To correct that problem, we would need to change the multiplier equation to read "1 divided by the fraction of the change in income that is not spent on domestic output." Also, we will find in later chapters that an increase in spending may be partly dissipated as inflation rather than realized fully as an increase in real GDP. This happens when increases in spending drive up prices. The multiplier process still happens, but it induces a much smaller change in real output because, at higher prices, any given amount of spending buys less real output. Economists disagree on the size of the actual multiplier in the United States. Estimates range from as high as 2.5 to as low as zero. So keep in mind throughout later discussions that the actual multiplier is much lower than the multipliers in our simple explanatory examples.

Summary

1. Other things equal, a direct (positive) relationship exists between income and consumption and income and saving. The consumption and saving schedules show the various amounts that households intend to consume and save at the various income and output levels, assuming a fixed price level.

2. The *average* propensities to consume and save show the fractions of any total income that are consumed and saved; APC + APS = 1. The *marginal* propensities to consume and save show the fractions of any change in total income that are consumed and saved; MPC + MPS = 1.

3. The locations of the consumption and saving schedules (as they relate to real GDP) are determined by (a) the amount of wealth owned by households, (b) expectations of future prices and incomes, (c) real interest rates, (d) household debt, and (e) tax levels. The consumption and saving schedules are relatively stable.

4. The immediate determinants of investment are (a) the expected rate of return and (b) the real rate of interest. The economy's investment demand curve is found by cumulating investment projects, arraying them in descending order according to their expected rates of return, graphing the result, and applying the rule that investment should be undertaken up to the point at which the real interest rate, i, equals the expected rate of return, r. The investment demand curve reveals an inverse (negative) relationship between the interest rate and the level of aggregate investment.

5. Shifts of the investment demand curve can occur as the result of changes in (a) the acquisition, maintenance, and operating costs of capital goods; (b) business taxes; (c) technology; (d) the stocks of capital goods on hand; and (e) expectations.

6. Either changes in interest rates or shifts of the investment demand curve can change the level of investment.

7. The durability of capital goods, the irregular occurrence of major innovations, profit volatility, and the variability of expectations all contribute to the instability of investment spending.

8. Through the multiplier effect, an increase in investment spending (or consumption spending, government purchases, or net export spending) ripples through the economy, ultimately creating a magnified increase in real GDP. The multiplier is the ultimate change in GDP divided by the initiating change in investment or some other component of spending.

9. The multiplier is equal to the reciprocal of the marginal propensity to save: The greater is the marginal propensity to save, the smaller is the multiplier. Also, the greater is the marginal propensity to consume, the larger is the multiplier.

10. Economists disagree on the size of the actual multiplier in the United States, with estimates ranging all the way from 2.5 to 0. But all estimates of actual-economy multipliers are less than the multiplier in our purposefully simple text illustrations.

Terms and Concepts

45° (degree) line

consumption schedule

saving schedule

break-even income

average propensity to consume (APC)

average propensity to save (APS)

marginal propensity to consume (MPC)

marginal propensity to save (MPS)

wealth effect

expected rate of return

investment demand curve

multiplier

paradox of thrift

Questions

1. What are the variables (the items measured on the axes) in a graph of the (*a*) consumption schedule and (*b*) saving schedule? Are the variables inversely (negatively) related or are they directly (positively) related? What is the fundamental reason that the levels of consumption and saving in the United States are each higher today than they were a decade ago? LO1

2. Precisely how do the MPC and the APC differ? How does the MPC differ from the MPS? Why must the sum of the MPC and the MPS equal 1? LO1

3. In what direction will each of the following occurrences shift the consumption and saving schedules, other things equal? LO2
   a. A large decrease in real estate values, including private homes.
   b. A sharp, sustained increase in stock prices.
   c. A 5-year increase in the minimum age for collecting Social Security benefits.
   d. An economy-wide expectation that a recession is over and that a robust expansion will occur.
   e. A substantial increase in household borrowing to finance auto purchases.

4. Why does a downshift of the consumption schedule typically involve an equal upshift of the saving schedule? What is the exception to this relationship? LO2

5. Why will a reduction in the real interest rate increase investment spending, other things equal? LO3

6. In what direction will each of the following occurrences shift the investment demand curve, other things equal? LO4
   a. An increase in unused production capacity occurs.
   b. Business taxes decline.
   c. The costs of acquiring equipment fall.
   d. Widespread pessimism arises about future business conditions and sales revenues.
   e. A major new technological breakthrough creates prospects for a wide range of profitable new products.

7. How is it possible for investment spending to increase even in a period in which the real interest rate rises? LO4

8. Why is investment spending unstable? LO4

9. Is the relationship between changes in spending and changes in real GDP in the multiplier effect a direct (positive) relationship or is it an inverse (negative) relationship? How does the size of the multiplier relate to the size of the MPC? The MPS? What is the logic of the multiplier-MPC relationship? LO5

10. Why is the actual multiplier in the U.S. economy less than the multiplier in this chapter's example? LO5

11. **LAST WORD** What is the central economic idea humorously illustrated in Art Buchwald's piece, "Squaring the Economic Circle"? How does the central idea relate to economic recessions, on the one hand, and vigorous economic expansions, on the other?

Problems

1. Refer to the table below. LO1
   a. Fill in the missing numbers in the table.
   b. What is the break-even level of income in the table? What is the term that economists use for the saving situation shown at the $240 level of income?
   c. For each of the following items, indicate whether the value in the table is either constant or variable as income changes: the MPS, the APC, the MPC, the APS.

2. Suppose that disposable income, consumption, and saving in some country are $200 billion, $150 billion, and $50 billion,

Level of Output and Income (GDP = DI)	Consumption	Saving	APC	APS	MPC	MPS
$240	$_____	$−4	—	—		
260	_____	0	—	—		
280	_____	4	—	—		
300	_____	8	—	—		
320	_____	12	—	—		
340	_____	16	—	—		
360	_____	20	—	—		
380	_____	24	—	—		
400	_____	28	—	—		

respectively. Next, assume that disposable income increases by $20 billion, consumption rises by $18 billion, and saving goes up by $2 billion. What is the economy's MPC? Its MPS? What was the APC before the increase in disposable income? After the increase? **LO1**

3. **ADVANCED ANALYSIS** Suppose that the linear equation for consumption in a hypothetical economy is $C = 40 + .8Y$. Also suppose that income (Y) is $400. Determine (*a*) the marginal propensity to consume, (*b*) the marginal propensity to save, (*c*) the level of consumption, (*d*) the average propensity to consume, (*e*) the level of saving, and (*f*) the average propensity to save. **LO1**

4. **ADVANCED ANALYSIS** Linear equations for the consumption and saving schedules take the general form $C = a + bY$ and $S = -a + (1 - b)Y$, where C, S, and Y are consumption, saving, and national income, respectively. The constant a represents the vertical intercept, and b represents the slope of the consumption schedule. **LO1, LO2**

a. Use the following data to substitute numerical values for a and b in the consumption and saving equations.

National Income (Y)	Consumption (C)
$ 0	$ 80
100	140
200	200
300	260
400	320

b. What is the economic meaning of b? Of $(1 - b)$?
c. Suppose that the amount of saving that occurs at each level of national income falls by $20 but that the values of b and $(1 - b)$ remain unchanged. Restate the saving and consumption equations inserting the new numerical values, and cite a factor that might have caused the change.

5. Use your completed table for problem 1 to solve this problem. Suppose the wealth effect is such that $10 changes in wealth produce $1 changes in consumption at each level of income. If real estate prices tumble such that wealth declines by $80, what will be the new level of consumption and saving at the $340 billion level of disposable income? The new level of saving? **LO2**

6. Suppose a handbill publisher can buy a new duplicating machine for $500 and the duplicator has a 1-year life. The machine is expected to contribute $550 to the year's net revenue. What is the expected rate of return? If the real interest rate at which funds can be borrowed to purchase the machine is 8 percent, will the publisher choose to invest in the machine? Will it invest in the machine if the real interest rate is 9 percent? If it is 11 percent? **LO3**

7. Assume there are no investment projects in the economy that yield an expected rate of return of 25 percent or more. But suppose there are $10 billion of investment projects yielding expected returns of between 20 and 25 percent; another $10 billion yielding between 15 and 20 percent; another $10 billion between 10 and 15 percent; and so forth. Cumulate these data and present them graphically, putting the expected rate of return (and the real interest rate) on the vertical axis and the amount of investment on the horizontal axis. What will be the equilibrium level of aggregate investment if the real interest rate is (*a*) 15 percent, (*b*) 10 percent, and (*c*) 5 percent? **LO3**

8. Refer to the table in Figure 10.5 and suppose that the real interest rate is 6 percent. Next, assume that some factor changes such that the expected rate of return declines by 2 percentage points at each prospective level of investment. Assuming no change in the real interest rate, by how much and in what direction will investment change? Which of the following might cause this change: (*a*) a decision to increase inventories; (*b*) an increase in excess production capacity? **LO4**

9. What will the multiplier be when the MPS is 0, .4, .6, and 1? What will it be when the MPC is 1, .90, .67, .50, and 0? How much of a change in GDP will result if firms increase their level of investment by $8 billion and the MPC is .80? If the MPC instead is .67? **LO5**

10. Suppose that an initial $10 billion increase in investment spending expands GDP by $10 billion in the first round of the multiplier process. If GDP and consumption both rise by $6 billion in the second round of the process, what is the MPC in this economy? What is the size of the multiplier? If, instead, GDP and consumption both rose by $8 billion in the second round, what would have been the size of the multiplier? **LO5**

FURTHER TEST YOUR KNOWLEDGE AT
www.mcconnell19e.com

At the text's Online Learning Center (OLC), **www.mcconnell19e.com**, you will find one or more Web-based questions that require information from the Internet to answer. We urge you to check them out; they will familiarize you with Web sites that may be helpful in other courses and perhaps even in your career. The OLC also features multiple-choice questions that give instant feedback and provides other helpful ways to further test your knowledge of the chapter.

AFTER READING THIS CHAPTER, YOU SHOULD BE ABLE TO:

1 **Illustrate how economists combine consumption and investment to depict an aggregate expenditures schedule for a private closed economy.**

2 **Discuss the three characteristics of the equilibrium level of real GDP in a private closed economy: aggregate expenditures = output; saving = investment; and no unplanned changes in inventories.**

3 **Analyze how changes in equilibrium real GDP can occur in the aggregate expenditures model and describe how those changes relate to the multiplier.**

4 **Explain how economists integrate the international sector (exports and imports) and the public sector (government expenditures and taxes) into the aggregate expenditures model.**

5 **Identify and describe the nature and causes of "recessionary expenditure gaps" and "inflationary expenditure gaps."**

The Aggregate Expenditures Model

In previous chapters we answered in detail two of the most critical questions in macroeconomics: How is an economy's output measured? Why does an economy grow? But we have been relatively general in addressing two other important questions: What determines the level of GDP, given a nation's production capacity? What causes real GDP to rise in one period and to fall in another? To provide more thorough answers to these two questions, we construct the aggregate expenditures

ORIGIN OF THE IDEA

O 11.1

Aggregate expenditures model

model, which has its origins in 1936 in the writings of British economist John Maynard Keynes (pronounced "Caines"). The basic premise of the aggregate expenditures model—also known as the "Keynesian cross" model—is that the amount of goods and services produced and therefore the level of employment depend directly on the level of aggregate expenditures (total spending). Businesses will produce only a level of output that they think they can profitably sell. They will idle their workers and machinery when there are no markets for their goods and services.

Assumptions and Simplifications

The simplifying assumptions underpinning the aggregate expenditures model reflect the economic conditions that were prevalent during the Great Depression. As discussed in this chapter's Last Word, Keynes created the model during the middle of the Great Depression in the hopes of understanding both why the Great Depression had happened as well as how it might be ended.

The most fundamental assumption behind the aggregate expenditures model is that prices in the economy are fixed. In the terminology of Chapter 6, the aggregate expenditures model is an extreme version of a sticky price model. In fact, it is a stuck-price model because the price-level cannot change at all.

Keynes made this simplifying assumption because he had observed that prices had not declined sufficiently during the Great Depression to boost spending and maintain output and employment at their pre-Depression levels. Such price declines had been predicted by macroeconomic theories that were popular before the Great Depression. But actual prices did not fall sufficiently during the Great Depression, and the economy sank far below its potential output. Real GDP in the United States declined by 27 percent from 1929 to 1933, and the unemployment rate rose to 25 percent. Thousands of factories sat idle, gathering dust and producing nothing, because nobody wanted to buy their output.

To Keynes, this massive unemployment of labor and capital resulted from firms reacting to information about how much they should produce. As households and businesses greatly reduced their spending, inventories of unsold goods rocketed. Unable or unwilling to slash their prices, firms could not sell all the goods they had already produced. So they greatly reduced their current production. This meant discharging workers, idling production lines, and even closing entire factories. Keynes thought that a new economic model was needed to show how all this could happen and how it might be reversed.

The Keynesian aggregate expenditures model is not just of historical interest. It is still insightful even today because many prices in the modern economy are inflexible downward over relatively short periods of time. The aggregate expenditures model therefore can help us understand how the modern economy is likely to initially adjust to various economic shocks. For example, it clarifies aspects of the recent severe recession, such as why unexpected initial declines in spending caused even larger declines in real GDP. It also illuminates the thinking underlying the stimulus programs (tax cuts, government spending increases) enacted by the government during the recession.

We will build up the aggregate expenditures model in simple stages. Let's first look at aggregate expenditures and equilibrium GDP in a *private closed economy*—one without international trade or government. Then we will "open" the "closed" economy to exports and imports and also convert our "private" economy to a more realistic "mixed" economy that includes government purchases (or, more loosely, "government spending") and taxes.

In addition, until we introduce taxes into the model, we will assume that real GDP equals disposable income (DI). For instance, if $500 billion of output is produced as GDP, households will receive exactly $500 billion of disposable income that they can then consume or save. And finally, unless specified otherwise, we will assume (as Keynes did) that the presence of excess production capacity and unemployed labor implies that an increase in aggregate expenditures will increase real output and employment but not raise the price level.

Consumption and Investment Schedules

In the private closed economy, the two components of aggregate expenditures are consumption, C, and gross investment, I_g. Because we examined the *consumption schedule* (Figure 10.2a) in the previous chapter, there is no need to repeat that analysis here. But to add the investment decisions of businesses to the consumption plans of households, we need to construct an investment schedule showing the amounts business firms collectively intend to invest—their **planned investment**—at each possible level of GDP. Such a schedule represents the investment plans of businesses in the same way the consumption schedule represents the consumption plans of households. In developing the investment schedule, we will assume that this planned investment is independent of the level of current disposable income or real output.

Suppose the investment demand curve is as shown in Figure 11.1a and the current real interest rate is 8 percent. This means that firms will spend $20 billion on investment goods. Our assumption tells us that this $20 billion of investment will occur at both low and high levels of GDP. The line I_g in Figure 11.1b shows this graphically; it is the economy's **investment schedule.** You should not confuse this investment schedule I_g with the investment demand curve ID in Figure 11.1a. The investment schedule shows the amount of investment forthcoming at each level of GDP. As indicated in Figure 11.1b, the interest rate and investment demand curve together determine this amount ($20 billion). Table 11.1 shows the investment schedule in tabular form. Note that investment (I_g) in column 2 is $20 billion at all levels of real GDP.

FIGURE 11.1 (a) The investment demand curve and (b) the investment schedule. (a) The level of investment spending (here, $20 billion) is determined by the real interest rate (here, 8 percent) together with the investment demand curve *ID*. (b) The investment schedule *I$_g$* relates the amount of investment ($20 billion) determined in (a) to the various levels of GDP.

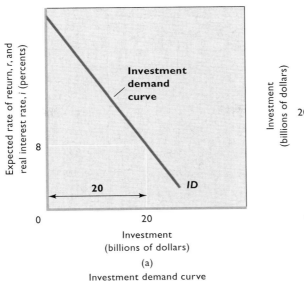

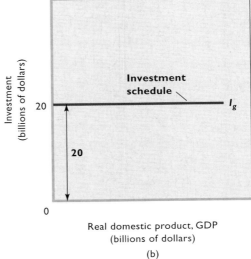

(a)
Investment demand curve

(b)
Investment schedule

TABLE 11.1 The Investment Schedule (in Billions)

(1) Level of Real Output and Income	(2) Investment (I$_g$)
$370	$20
390	20
410	20
430	20
450	20
470	20
490	20
510	20
530	20
550	20

Equilibrium GDP: $C + I_g$ = GDP

Now let's combine the consumption schedule of Chapter 10 and the investment schedule here to explain the equilibrium levels of output, income, and employment in the private closed economy.

Tabular Analysis

Columns 2 through 5 in Table 11.2 repeat the consumption and saving schedules of Table 10.1 and the investment schedule of Table 11.1.

Real Domestic Output Column 2 in Table 11.2 lists the various possible levels of total output—of real GDP— that the private sector might produce. Firms would be willing to produce any one of these 10 levels of output just as long as the revenue that they receive from selling any particular level equals or exceeds the costs they would incur to produce it. Those costs are the factor payments needed to obtain the required amounts of land, labor, capital, and entrepreneurship. For example, firms would be willing to produce $370 billion of output if the costs of production (wages, rents, interest, and the normal profit needed to attract entrepreneurship) are less than or equal to the $370 billion in revenue that they would get from selling the output.

Aggregate Expenditures In the private closed economy of Table 11.2, aggregate expenditures consist of consumption (column 3) plus investment (column 5). Their sum is shown in column 6, which along with column 2 makes up the **aggregate expenditures schedule** for the private closed economy. This schedule shows the amount ($C + I_g$) that will be spent at each possible output or income level.

At this point we are working with *planned investment*— the data in column 5, Table 11.2. These data show the amounts firms plan or intend to invest, not the amounts they actually will invest if there are unplanned changes in inventories. More about that shortly.

TABLE 11.2 Determination of the Equilibrium Levels of Employment, Output, and Income: A Private Closed Economy

(1) Possible Levels of Employment, Millions	(2) Real Domestic Output (and Income) (GDP = DI),* Billions	(3) Consumption (C), Billions	(4) Saving (S), Billions	(5) Investment (I_g), Billions	(6) Aggregate Expenditures (C + I_g), Billions	(7) Unplanned Changes in Inventories, (+ or −)	(8) Tendency of Employment, Output, and Income
(1) 40	$370	$375	$−5	$20	$395	$−25	Increase
(2) 45	390	390	0	20	410	−20	Increase
(3) 50	410	405	5	20	425	−15	Increase
(4) 55	430	420	10	20	440	−10	Increase
(5) 60	450	435	15	20	455	−5	Increase
(6) 65	470	450	20	20	470	0	Equilibrium
(7) 70	490	465	25	20	485	+5	Decrease
(8) 75	510	480	30	20	500	+10	Decrease
(9) 80	530	495	35	20	515	+15	Decrease
(10) 85	550	510	40	20	530	+20	Decrease

*If depreciation and net foreign factor income are zero, government is ignored and it is assumed that all saving occurs in the household sector of the economy, then GDP as a measure of domestic output is equal to NI, PI, and DI. This means that households receive a DI equal to the value of total output.

Equilibrium GDP Of the 10 possible levels of GDP in Table 11.2, which is the equilibrium level? Which total output is the economy capable of sustaining?

The equilibrium output is that output whose production creates total spending just sufficient to purchase that output. So the equilibrium level of GDP is the level at which the total quantity of goods produced (GDP) equals the total quantity of goods purchased (C + I_g). In the private closed economy, the **equilibrium GDP** is where

$$C + I_g = GDP$$

If you look at the domestic output levels in column 2 and the aggregate expenditures levels in column 6, you will see that this equality exists only at $470 billion of GDP (row 6). That is the only output at which economy-wide spending is precisely equal to the amount needed to move that output off the shelves. At $470 billion of GDP, the annual rates of production and spending are in balance. There is no overproduction, which would result in a piling up of unsold goods and consequently cutbacks in the production rate. Nor is there an excess of total spending, which would draw down inventories of goods and prompt increases in the rate of production. In short, there is no reason for businesses to alter this rate of production; $470 billion is the equilibrium GDP.

Disequilibrium No level of GDP other than the equilibrium level of GDP can be sustained. At levels of GDP *less than* equilibrium, spending always exceeds GDP. If, for example, firms produced $410 billion of GDP (row 3 in Table 11.2), they would find it would yield $405 billion in consumer spending. Supplemented by $20 billion of planned investment, aggregate expenditures (C + I_g) would be $425 billion, as shown in column 6. The economy would provide an annual rate of spending more than sufficient to purchase the $410 billion of annual production. Because buyers would be taking goods off the shelves faster than firms could produce them, an unplanned decline in business inventories of $15 billion would occur (column 7) if this situation continued. But businesses can adjust to such an imbalance between aggregate expenditures and real output by stepping up production. Greater output will increase employment and total income. This process will continue until the equilibrium level of GDP is reached ($470 billion).

The reverse is true at all levels of GDP *greater than* the $470 billion equilibrium level. Businesses will find that these total outputs fail to generate the spending needed to clear the shelves of goods. Being unable to recover their costs, businesses will cut back on production. To illustrate: At the $510 billion output (row 8), business managers would find spending is insufficient to permit the sale of all that output. Of the $510 billion of income that this output creates, $480 billion would be received back by businesses as consumption spending. Though supplemented by $20 billion of planned investment spending, total expenditures ($500 billion) would still be $10 billion below the $510 billion quantity produced. If this imbalance persisted, $10 billion of inventories would pile up (column 7). But businesses can adjust to this

WORKED PROBLEMS

W 11.1

Equilibrium GDP

key graph

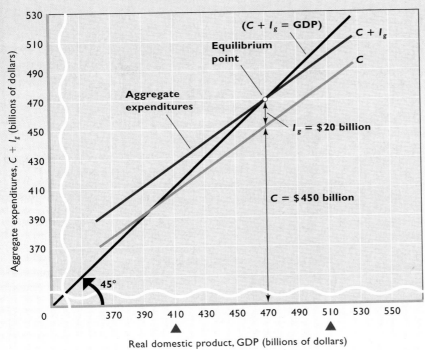

FIGURE 11.2 Equilibrium GDP in a private closed economy. The aggregate expenditures schedule, $C + I_g$, is determined by adding the investment schedule I_g to the upsloping consumption schedule C. Since investment is assumed to be the same at each level of GDP, the vertical distances between C and $C + I_g$ do not change. Equilibrium GDP is determined where the aggregate expenditures schedule intersects the 45° line, in this case at $470 billion.

QUICK QUIZ FOR FIGURE 11.2

1. In this figure, the slope of the aggregate expenditures schedule $C + I_g$:
   a. increases as real GDP increases.
   b. falls as real GDP increases.
   c. is constant and equals the MPC.
   d. is constant and equals the MPS.

2. At all points on the 45° line:
   a. equilibrium GDP is possible.
   b. aggregate expenditures exceed real GDP.
   c. consumption exceeds investment.
   d. aggregate expenditures are less than real GDP.

3. The $490 billion level of real GDP is not at equilibrium because:
   a. investment exceeds consumption.
   b. consumption exceeds investment.
   c. planned $C + I_g$ exceeds real GDP.
   d. planned $C + I_g$ is less than real GDP.

4. The $430 billion level of real GDP is not at equilibrium because:
   a. investment exceeds consumption.
   b. consumption exceeds investment.
   c. planned $C + I_g$ exceeds real GDP.
   d. planned $C + I_g$ is less than real GDP.

Answers: 1. c; 2. a; 3. d; 4. c

---

unintended accumulation of unsold goods by cutting back on the rate of production. The resulting decline in output would mean fewer jobs and a decline in total income.

Graphical Analysis

We can demonstrate the same analysis graphically. In **Figure 11.2 (Key Graph)** the 45° line developed in Chapter 10 now takes on increased significance. Recall that at any point on this line, the value of what is being measured on the horizontal axis (here, GDP) is equal to the value of what is being measured on the vertical axis

(here, aggregate expenditures, or $C + I_g$). Having discovered in our tabular analysis that the equilibrium level of domestic output is determined where $C + I_g$ equals GDP, we can say that the 45° line in Figure 11.2 is a graphical statement of that equilibrium condition.

Now we must graph the aggregate expenditures schedule onto Figure 11.2. To do this, we duplicate the consumption schedule C in Figure 10.2a and add to it vertically the constant $20 billion amount of investment I_g from Figure 11.1b. This $20 billion is the amount we assumed firms plan to invest at all levels of GDP. Or, more directly, we can plot the $C + I_g$ data in column 6, Table 11.2.

215

Observe in Figure 11.2 that the aggregate expenditures line $C + I_g$ shows that total spending rises with income and output (GDP), but not as much as income rises. That is true because the marginal propensity to consume—the slope of line C—is less than 1. A part of any increase in income will be saved rather than spent. And because the aggregate expenditures line $C + I_g$ is parallel to the consumption line C, the slope of the aggregate expenditures line also equals the MPC for the economy and is less than 1. For our particular data, aggregate expenditures rise by $15 billion for every $20 billion increase in real output and income because $5 billion of each $20 billion increment is saved. Therefore, the slope of the aggregate expenditures line is .75 (= $\Delta\$15/\Delta\$20$).

The equilibrium level of GDP is determined by the intersection of the aggregate expenditures schedule and the 45° line. This intersection locates the only point at which aggregate expenditures (on the vertical axis) are equal to GDP (on the horizontal axis). Because Figure 11.2 is based on the data in Table 11.2, we once again find that equilibrium output is $470 billion. Observe that consumption at this output is $450 billion and investment is $20 billion.

It is evident from Figure 11.2 that no levels of GDP *above* the equilibrium level are sustainable because at those levels $C + I_g$ falls short of GDP. Graphically, the aggregate expenditures schedule lies below the 45° line in those situations. At the $510 billion GDP level, for example, $C + I_g$ is only $500 billion. This underspending causes inventories to rise, prompting firms to readjust production downward, in the direction of the $470 billion output level.

Conversely, at levels of GDP *below* $470 billion, the economy wants to spend in excess of what businesses are producing. Then $C + I_g$ exceeds total output. Graphically, the aggregate expenditures schedule lies above the 45°

INTERACTIVE GRAPHS

G 11.1

Equilibrium GDP

line. At the $410 billion GDP level, for example, $C + I_g$ totals $425 billion. This excess spending causes inventories to fall below their planned level, prompting firms to adjust production upward, in the direction of the $470 billion output level. Once production reaches that level, it will be sustained there indefinitely unless there is some change in the location of the aggregate expenditures line.

Other Features of Equilibrium GDP

We have seen that $C + I_g$ = GDP at equilibrium in the private closed economy. A closer look at Table 11.2 reveals two more characteristics of equilibrium GDP:

- Saving and *planned* investment are equal ($S = I_g$).
- There are no *unplanned* changes in inventories.

Saving Equals Planned Investment

As shown by row 6 in Table 11.2, saving and planned investment are both $20 billion at the $470 billion equilibrium level of GDP.

Saving is a **leakage** or withdrawal of spending from the economy's circular flow of income and expenditures. Saving is what causes consumption to be less than total output or GDP. Because of saving, consumption by itself is insufficient to remove domestic output from the shelves, apparently setting the stage for a decline in total output.

However, firms do not intend to sell their entire output to consumers. Some of that output will be capital goods sold to other businesses. Investment—the purchases of capital goods—is therefore an **injection** of spending into the income-expenditures stream. As an adjunct to consumption, investment is thus a potential replacement for the leakage of saving.

If the leakage of saving at a certain level of GDP exceeds the injection of investment, then $C + I_g$ will be less than GDP and that level of GDP cannot be sustained. Any GDP for which saving exceeds investment is an above-equilibrium GDP. Consider GDP of $510 billion (row 8 in Table 11.2). Households will save $30 billion, but firms will plan to invest only $20 billion. This $10 billion excess of saving over planned investment will reduce total spending to $10 billion below the value of total output. Specifically, aggregate expenditures will be $500 billion while real GDP is $510 billion. This spending deficiency will reduce real GDP.

Conversely, if the injection of investment exceeds the leakage of saving, then $C + I_g$ will be greater than GDP and drive GDP upward. Any GDP for which investment exceeds saving is a below-equilibrium GDP. For example, at a GDP of $410 billion (row 3 in Table 11.2), households will save only $5 billion, but firms will invest $20 billion. So investment exceeds saving by $15 billion. The small leakage of saving at this relatively low GDP level is more than compensated for by the larger injection of investment spending. That causes $C + I_g$ to exceed GDP and drives GDP higher.

Only where $S = I_g$—where the leakage of saving of $20 billion is exactly offset by the injection of planned investment of $20 billion—will aggregate expenditures ($C + I_g$) equal real output (GDP). That $C + I_g$ = GDP equality is what defines the equilibrium GDP.

No Unplanned Changes in Inventories

As part of their investment plans, firms may decide to increase or decrease their inventories. But, as confirmed in line 6 of Table 11.2, there are no **unplanned changes in inventories** at equilibrium GDP. This fact, along with $C + I_g = $ GDP, and $S = I_g$ is a characteristic of equilibrium GDP in the private closed economy.

Unplanned changes in inventories play a major role in achieving equilibrium GDP. Consider, as an example, the $490 billion *above-equilibrium* GDP shown in row 7 of Table 11.2. What happens if firms produce that output, thinking they can sell it? Households save $25 billion of their $490 billion DI, so consumption is only $465 billion. Planned investment—which includes *planned* changes in inventories—is $20 billion (column 5). So aggregate expenditures $(C + I_g)$ are $485 billion and sales fall short of production by $5 billion. Firms retain that extra $5 billion of goods as an *unplanned* increase in inventories (column 7). It results from the failure of total spending to remove total output from the shelves.

Because changes in inventories are a part of investment, we note that *actual investment* is $25 billion. It consists of $20 billion of planned investment *plus* the $5 billion unplanned increase in inventories. Actual investment equals the saving of $25 billion, even though saving exceeds planned investment by $5 billion. Because firms cannot earn profits by accumulating unwanted inventories, the $5 billion unplanned increase in inventories will prompt them to cut back employment and production. GDP will fall to its equilibrium level of $470 billion, at which unplanned changes in inventories are zero.

Now look at the *below-equilibrium* $450 billion output (row 5, Table 11.2). Because households save only $15 billion of their $450 billion DI, consumption is $435 billion. Planned investment by firms is $20 billion, so aggregate expenditures are $455 billion. Sales exceed production by $5 billion. This is so only because a $5 billion unplanned decrease in business inventories has occurred. Firms must *disinvest* $5 billion in inventories (column 7). Note again that actual investment is $15 billion ($20 billion planned *minus* the $5 billion decline in inventory investment) and is equal to saving of $15 billion, even though planned investment exceeds saving by $5 billion. The unplanned decline in inventories, resulting from the excess of sales over production, will encourage firms to expand production. GDP will rise to $470 billion, at which unplanned changes in inventories are zero.

When economists say differences between investment and saving can occur and bring about changes in equilibrium GDP, they are referring to planned investment and saving. Equilibrium occurs only when planned investment and saving are equal. But when unplanned changes in inventories are considered, investment and saving are always equal, regardless of the level of GDP. That is true because actual investment consists of planned investment and unplanned investment (unplanned changes in inventories). Unplanned changes in inventories act as a balancing item that equates the actual amounts saved and invested in any period.

Changes in Equilibrium GDP and the Multiplier

In the previous chapter, we established that an initial change in spending can cause a greater change in real output through the multiplier effect. In equation form,

$$\text{Multiplier} = \frac{\text{change in real GDP}}{\text{initial change in spending}}$$

Further, we discovered that the size of the multiplier depends on the size of the MPS in the economy:

$$\text{Multiplier} = \frac{1}{\text{MPS}}$$

(Because the multiplier is such an important element of the aggregate expenditures model, we highly recommend that you quickly review Figure 10.8 at this time.)

In a private closed economy, the equilibrium GDP will change in response to changes in either the investment schedule or the consumption schedule. Because changes in the investment schedule are the main sources of instability, we will direct our attention toward them.

Figure 11.3 shows the effect of changes in investment spending on the equilibrium real GDP. Suppose that the expected rate of return on investment rises or that the real interest rate falls such that investment spending increases by $5 billion. That would be shown as an upward shift of the investment schedule in Figure 11.1b. In Figure 11.3, the $5 billion increase of investment spending will increase aggregate expenditures from $(C + I_g)_0$ to $(C + I_g)_1$ and raise equilibrium real GDP from $470 billion to $490 billion.

If the expected rate of return on investment decreases or if the real interest rate rises, investment spending will decline by, say, $5 billion. That would be shown as a downward shift of the investment schedule in Figure 11.1b and a downward shift of the aggregate expenditures schedule from $(C + I_g)_0$ to $(C + I_g)_2$ in Figure 11.3. Equilibrium GDP will fall from $470 billion to $450 billion.

In our examples, a $5 billion change in investment spending leads to a $20 billion change in output and income. So the *multiplier* is 4 (= $20/$5). The MPS is .25, meaning that for every $1 billion of new income, $.25 billion of new saving occurs. Therefore, $20 billion of new income is needed to generate $5 billion of new saving. Once that increase in income and saving occurs, the economy is back in equilibrium—$C + I_g = $ GDP; saving and investment are

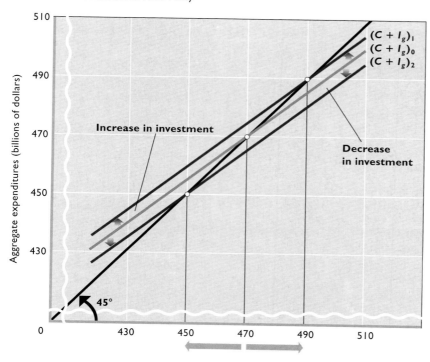

FIGURE 11.3 Changes in the aggregate expenditures schedule and the multiplier effect. An upward shift of the aggregate expenditures schedule from $(C + I_g)_0$ to $(C + I_g)_1$ will increase the equilibrium GDP. Conversely, a downward shift from $(C + I_g)_0$ to $(C + I_g)_2$ will lower the equilibrium GDP. The extent of the changes in equilibrium GDP will depend on the size of the multiplier, which in this case is 4 (=20/5). The multiplier is equal to 1/MPS (here, 4 = 1/.25).

equal; and there are no unplanned changes in inventories. You can see, then, why the multiplier is equal to 1/MPS and that the multiplier process is an integral part of the aggregate expenditures model.

QUICK REVIEW 11.1

- In a private closed economy, equilibrium GDP occurs where aggregate expenditures equal real domestic output ($C + I_g$ = GDP).
- At equilibrium GDP, saving equals planned investment ($S = I_g$) and unplanned changes in inventories are zero.
- Actual investment consists of planned investment plus unplanned changes in inventories (+ or −) and is always equal to saving in a private closed economy.
- Through the multiplier effect, an initial change in investment spending can cause a magnified change in domestic output and income.

Adding International Trade

We next move from a private closed economy to a private open economy that incorporates exports (X) and imports (M). Our focus will be on **net exports** (exports minus imports), which may be either positive or negative.

Net Exports and Aggregate Expenditures

Like consumption and investment, exports create domestic production, income, and employment for a nation. Although U.S. goods and services produced for export are sent abroad, foreign spending on those goods and services increases production and creates jobs and incomes in the United States. We must therefore include exports as a component of U.S. aggregate expenditures.

Conversely, when an economy is open to international trade, it will spend part of its income on imports—goods and services produced abroad. To avoid overstating the value of domestic production, we must subtract the amount spent on imported goods because such spending generates production and income abroad rather than at home. So, to correctly measure aggregate expenditures for domestic goods and services, we must subtract expenditures on imports from total spending.

In short, for a private closed economy, aggregate expenditures are $C + I_g$. But for an open economy, aggregate expenditures are $C + I_g + (X - M)$. Or, recalling that net exports (X_n) equal ($X - M$), we can say that aggregate expenditures for a private open economy are $C + I_g + X_n$.

TABLE 11.3 **Two Net Export Schedules (in Billions)**

(1) Level of GDP	(2) Net Exports, X_{n1} (X > M)	(3) Net Exports, X_{n2} (X < M)
$370	$+5	$−5
390	+5	−5
410	+5	−5
430	+5	−5
450	+5	−5
470	+5	−5
490	+5	−5
510	+5	−5
530	+5	−5
550	+5	−5

The Net Export Schedule

A net export schedule lists the amount of net exports that will occur at each level of GDP. Table 11.3 shows two possible net export schedules for the hypothetical economy represented in Table 11.2. In net export schedule X_{n1} (columns 1 and 2), exports exceed imports by $5 billion at each level of GDP. Perhaps exports are $15 billion while imports are $10 billion. In schedule X_{n2} (columns 1 and 3), imports are $5 billion higher than exports. Perhaps imports are $20 billion while exports are $15 billion. To simplify our discussion, we assume in both schedules that net exports are independent of GDP.[1]

Figure 11.4b represents the two net export schedules in Table 11.3. Schedule X_{n1} is above the horizontal axis and depicts positive net exports of $5 billion at all levels of GDP. Schedule X_{n2}, which is below the horizontal axis, shows negative net exports of $5 billion at all levels of GDP.

Net Exports and Equilibrium GDP

The aggregate expenditures schedule labeled $C + I_g$ in Figure 11.4a reflects the private closed economy. It shows the combined consumption and gross investment expenditures occurring at each level of GDP. With no foreign sector, the equilibrium GDP is $470 billion.

But in the private open economy, net exports can be either positive or negative. Let's see how each of the net export schedules in Figure 11.4b affects equilibrium GDP.

---

[1]In reality, although our exports depend on foreign incomes and are thus independent of U.S. GDP, our imports do vary directly with our own domestic national income. Just as our domestic consumption varies directly with our GDP, so do our purchases of foreign goods. As our GDP rises, U.S. households buy not only more Cadillacs and Harleys, but also more Mercedes and Kawasakis. However, for now we will ignore the complications of the positive relationship between imports and U.S. GDP.

Positive Net Exports Suppose the net export schedule is X_{n1}. The $5 billion of additional net export expenditures by the rest of the world is accounted for by adding that $5 billion to the $C + I_g$ schedule in Figure 11.4a. Aggregate expenditures at each level of GDP are then $5 billion higher than $C + I_g$ alone. The aggregate expenditures schedule for the open economy thus becomes $C + I_g + X_{n1}$. In this case, international trade increases equilibrium GDP from $470 billion in the private closed economy to $490 billion in the private open economy. Adding net exports of $5 billion has increased GDP by $20 billion, in this case implying a multiplier of 4.

Generalization: Other things equal, positive net exports increase aggregate expenditures and GDP beyond what they would be in a closed economy. Be careful to notice that this increase is the result of exports being larger than imports. This is true because exports and imports have opposite effects on the measurement of domestically produced output. Exports increase real GDP by increasing expenditures on domestically produced output. Imports, by contrast, must be subtracted when calculating real GDP because they are expenditures directed toward output produced abroad. It is only because net exports are positive in this example—so that the expansionary effect of exports outweighs the reductions caused by imports—that we get the overall increase in real GDP. As the next section shows, if net exports are negative, then the reductions caused by imports will outweigh the expansionary effect of exports so that domestic real GDP will decrease.

Negative Net Exports Suppose that net exports are a negative $5 billion as shown by X_{n2} in Figure 11.4b. This means that our hypothetical economy is importing $5 billion more of goods than it is exporting. The aggregate expenditures schedule shown as $C + I_g$ in Figure 11.4a therefore overstates the expenditures on domestic output at each level of GDP. We must reduce the sum of expenditures by the $5 billion net amount spent on imported goods. We do that by subtracting the $5 billion of net imports from $C + I_g$.

The relevant aggregate expenditures schedule in Figure 11.4a becomes $C + I_g + X_{n2}$ and equilibrium GDP falls from $470 billion to $450 billion. Again, a change in net exports of $5 billion has produced a fourfold change in GDP, reminding us that the multiplier in this example is 4.

This gives us a corollary to our first generalization: Other things equal, negative net exports reduce aggregate expenditures and GDP below what they would be in a closed economy. When imports exceed exports, the

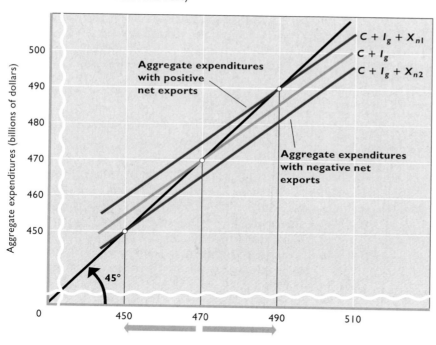

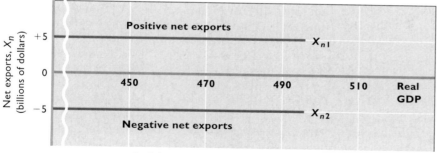

FIGURE 11.4 Net exports and equilibrium GDP. Positive net exports such as shown by the net export schedule X_{n1} in (b) elevate the aggregate expenditures schedule in (a) from the closed-economy level of $C + I_g$ to the open-economy level of $C + I_g + X_{n1}$. Negative net exports such as depicted by the net export schedule X_{n2} in (b) lower the aggregate expenditures schedule in (a) from the closed-economy level of $C + I_g$ to the open-economy level of $C + I_g + X_{n2}$.

contractionary effect of the larger amount of imports outweighs the expansionary effect of the smaller amount of exports, and equilibrium real GDP decreases.

Our generalizations of the effects of net exports on GDP mean that a decline in X_n—a decrease in exports or an increase in imports—reduces aggregate expenditures and contracts a nation's GDP. Conversely, an increase in X_n—the result of either an increase in exports or a decrease in imports—increases aggregate expenditures and expands GDP.

As is shown in Global Perspective 11.1, net exports vary greatly among the major industrial nations.

International Economic Linkages

Our analysis of net exports and real GDP suggests how circumstances or policies abroad can affect U.S. GDP.

Prosperity Abroad A rising level of real output and income among U.S. foreign trading partners enables the United States to sell more goods abroad, thus raising U.S. net exports and increasing U.S. real GDP (assuming initially there is excess capacity). There is good reason for Americans to be interested in the prosperity of our trading partners. Their good fortune enables them to buy more of our

GLOBAL PERSPECTIVE 11.1

Net Exports of Goods, Selected Nations, 2008

Some nations, such as China and Germany, have positive net exports; other countries, such as the United States and the United Kingdom, have negative net exports.

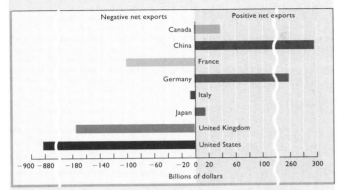

Negative net exports — Positive net exports

Canada
China
France
Germany
Italy
Japan
United Kingdom
United States

−900 −880 −180 −140 −100 −60 −20 0 20 60 100 260 300
Billions of dollars

Source: WTO Statistics Database, **www.wto.org**. Used with the permission of the World Trade Organization (WTO).

exports, increasing our income and enabling us in turn to buy more foreign imports. These imported goods are the ultimate benefit of international trade. Prosperity abroad transfers some of that prosperity to Americans.

Exchange Rates Depreciation of the dollar relative to other currencies enables people abroad to obtain more dollars with each unit of their own currencies. The price of U.S. goods in terms of those currencies will fall, stimulating purchases of U.S. exports. Also, U.S. customers will find they need more dollars to buy foreign goods and, consequently, will reduce their spending on imports. If the economy has available capacity, the increased exports and decreased imports will increase U.S. net exports and expand the nation's GDP.

This last example has been cast only in terms of depreciation of the dollar. You should think through the impact that appreciation of the dollar would have on net exports and equilibrium GDP.

A Caution on Tariffs and Devaluations Because higher net exports increase real GDP, countries often look for ways to reduce imports and increase exports during recessions or depressions. Thus, a recession might tempt the U.S. Federal government to increase tariffs and devalue the international value of the dollar (say, by supplying massive amounts of dollars in the foreign exchange mar-

ket) to try to increase net exports. Such an increase of net exports would expand domestic production, reduce domestic unemployment, and help the economy recover.

But this interventionist thinking is too simplistic. Suppose that the United States imposes high tariffs on foreign goods to reduce our imports and thus increase our domestic production and employment. Our imports, however, are our trading partners' exports. So when we restrict our imports to stimulate our economy, we depress the economies of our trading partners. They are likely to retaliate against us by imposing tariffs on our products. If so, our exports to them will decline and our net exports may in fact fall. With retaliation in the picture, it is possible that tariffs may decrease, not increase, our net exports.

That unfortunate possibility became a sad reality during the Great Depression of the 1930s, when various nations, including the United States, imposed trade barriers as a way of reducing domestic unemployment. The result was many rounds of retaliation that simply throttled world trade, worsened the depression, and increased unemployment. Abetting the problem were attempts by some nations to increase their net exports by devaluing their currencies. Other nations simply retaliated by devaluing their own currencies. The international exchange rate system collapsed, and world trade spiraled downward. Economic historians agree that tariffs and devaluations during the 1930s were huge policy mistakes!

Nations are tempted to use tariffs and currency devaluations because, *other things equal*, these policies *do* increase net exports and real GDP. But keep in mind that other things aren't likely to stay equal. In particular, other nations will almost certainly retaliate with their own tariffs and devaluations—the final result being lower net exports and lower GDP for those countries and for our own.

QUICK REVIEW 11.2

- Positive net exports increase aggregate expenditures relative to the closed economy and, other things equal, increase equilibrium GDP.
- Negative net exports decrease aggregate expenditures relative to the closed economy and, other things equal, reduce equilibrium GDP.
- In the open economy changes in (a) prosperity abroad, (b) tariffs, and (c) exchange rates can affect U.S. net exports and therefore U.S. aggregate expenditures and equilibrium GDP.
- Tariffs and deliberate currency depreciations are unlikely to increase net exports, because other nations will retaliate.

Adding the Public Sector

Our final step in constructing the full aggregate expenditures model is to move the analysis from a private (no-government) open economy to an economy with a public sector (sometimes called a "mixed economy"). This means adding government purchases and taxes to the model.

For simplicity, we will assume that government purchases are independent of the level of GDP and do not alter the consumption and investment schedules. Also, government's net tax revenues—total tax revenues less "negative taxes" in the form of transfer payments—are derived entirely from personal taxes. Finally, a fixed amount of taxes is collected regardless of the level of GDP.

Government Purchases and Equilibrium GDP

Suppose the government decides to purchase $20 billion of goods and services regardless of the level of GDP and tax collections.

Tabular Example Table 11.4 shows the impact of this purchase on the equilibrium GDP. Columns 1 through 4 are carried over from Table 11.2 for the private closed economy, in which the equilibrium GDP was $470 billion. The only new items are exports and imports in column 5 and government purchases in column 6. (Observe in column 5 that net exports are zero.) As shown in column 7, the addition of government purchases to private spending ($C + I_g + X_n$) yields a new, higher level of aggregate expenditures ($C + I_g + X_n + G$). Comparing columns 1 and 7, we find that aggregate expenditures and real output are equal at a higher

level of GDP. Without government purchases, equilibrium GDP was $470 billion (row 6); *with* government purchases, aggregate expenditures and real output are equal at $550 billion (row 10). Increases in public spending, like increases in private spending, shift the aggregate expenditures schedule upward and produce a higher equilibrium GDP.

Note, too, that government spending is subject to the multiplier. A $20 billion increase in government purchases has increased equilibrium GDP by $80 billion (from $470 billion to $550 billion). The multiplier in this example is 4.

This $20 billion increase in government spending is *not* financed by increased taxes. Shortly, we will demonstrate that increased taxes *reduce* equilibrium GDP.

Graphical Analysis In Figure 11.5, we vertically add $20 billion of government purchases, G, to the level of private spending, $C + I_g + X_n$. That added $20 billion raises the aggregate expenditures schedule (private plus public) to $C + I_g + X_n + G$, resulting in an $80 billion increase in equilibrium GDP, from $470 to $550 billion.

A decline in government purchases G will lower the aggregate expenditures schedule in Figure 11.5 and result in a multiplied decline in the equilibrium GDP. Verify in Table 11.4 that if government purchases were to decline from $20 billion to $10 billion, the equilibrium GDP would fall by $40 billion.

Taxation and Equilibrium GDP

The government not only spends but also collects taxes. Suppose it imposes a **lump-sum tax,** which is a tax of a constant amount or, more precisely, a tax yielding the same amount of tax revenue at each level of GDP. Let's

TABLE 11.4 The Impact of Government Purchases on Equilibrium GDP

(1) Real Domestic Output and Income (GDP = DI), Billions	(2) Consumption (C), Billions	(3) Savings (S), Billions	(4) Investment (I_g), Billions	(5) Net Exports (X_n), Billions — Exports (X)	Imports (M)	(6) Government Purchases (G), Billions	(7) Aggregate Expenditures ($C + I_g + X_n + G$), Billions (2) + (4) + (5) + (6)
(1) $370	$375	$−5	$20	$10	$10	$20	$415
(2) 390	390	0	20	10	10	20	430
(3) 410	405	5	20	10	10	20	445
(4) 430	420	10	20	10	10	20	460
(5) 450	435	15	20	10	10	20	475
(6) 470	450	20	20	10	10	20	490
(7) 490	465	25	20	10	10	20	505
(8) 510	480	30	20	10	10	20	520
(9) 530	495	35	20	10	10	20	535
(10) **550**	**510**	**40**	**20**	**10**	**10**	**20**	**550**

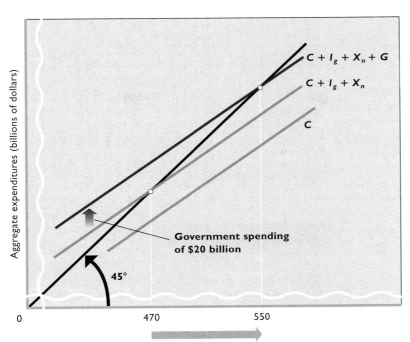

FIGURE 11.5 Government spending and equilibrium GDP. The addition of government expenditures of G to our analysis raises the aggregate expenditures ($C + I_g + X_n + G$) schedule and increases the equilibrium level of GDP, as would an increase in C, I_g, or X_n.

assume this tax is $20 billion, so that the government obtains $20 billion of tax revenue at each level of GDP regardless of the level of government purchases.

Tabular Example In Table 11.5, which continues our example, we find taxes in column 2, and we see in column 3 that disposable (after-tax) income is lower than GDP (column 1) by the $20 billion amount of the tax. Because

households use disposable income both to consume and to save, the tax lowers both consumption and saving. The MPC and MPS tell us how much consumption and saving will decline as a result of the $20 billion in taxes. Because the MPC is .75, the government tax collection of $20 billion will reduce consumption by $15 billion (= .75 × $20 billion). Since the MPS is .25, saving will drop by $5 billion (= .25 × $20 billion).

TABLE 11.5 Determination of the Equilibrium Levels of Employment, Output, and Income: Private and Public Sectors

(1) Real Domestic Output and Income (GDP = NI = PI), Billions	(2) Taxes (T), Billions	(3) Disposable Income (DI), Billions, (1) − (2)	(4) Consumption (C_a), Billions	(5) Saving (S_a), Billions (3)−(4)	(6) Investment (I_g), Billions	(7) Net Exports (X_n), Billions Exports (X)	Imports (M)	(8) Government Purchases (G), Billions	(9) Aggregate Expenditures ($C_a + I_g + X_n + G$), Billions, (4) + (6) + (7) + (8)
(1) $370	$20	$350	$360	$−10	$20	$10	$10	$20	$400
(2) 390	20	370	375	−5	20	10	10	20	415
(3) 410	20	390	390	0	20	10	10	20	430
(4) 430	20	410	405	5	20	10	10	20	445
(5) 450	20	430	420	10	20	10	10	20	460
(6) 470	20	450	435	15	20	10	10	20	475
(7) **490**	**20**	**470**	**450**	**20**	**20**	**10**	**10**	**20**	**490**
(8) 510	20	490	465	25	20	10	10	20	505
(9) 530	20	510	480	30	20	10	10	20	520
(10) 550	20	530	495	35	20	10	10	20	535

Columns 4 and 5 in Table 11.5 list the amounts of consumption and saving *at each level of GDP*. Note they are $15 billion and $5 billion smaller than those in Table 11.4. Taxes reduce disposable income relative to GDP by the amount of the taxes. This decline in DI reduces both consumption and saving at each level of GDP. The extent of the *C* and *S* reductions depend on the MPC and the MPS.

To find the effect of taxes on equilibrium GDP, we calculate aggregate expenditures again, as shown in column 9, Table 11.5. Aggregate spending is $15 billion less at each level of GDP than it was in Table 11.4. The reason is that after-tax consumption, designated by C_a, is $15 billion less at each level of GDP. A comparison of real output and aggregate expenditures in columns 1 and 9 shows that the aggregate amounts produced and purchased are equal only at $490 billion of GDP (row 7). The $20 billion lump-sum tax has reduced equilibrium GDP by $60 billion, from $550 billion (row 10, Table 11.3) to $490 billion (row 7, Table 11.4).

Graphical Analysis
In Figure 11.6 the $20 billion increase in taxes shows up as a $15 (not $20) billion decline in the aggregate expenditures ($C_a + I_g + X_n + G$) schedule. This decline in the schedule results solely from a decline in the consumption *C* component of aggregate expenditures. The equilibrium GDP falls from $550 billion to $490 billion because of this tax-caused drop in consumption. With no change in government expenditures,

tax increases lower the aggregate expenditures schedule relative to the 45° line and reduce the equilibrium GDP.

In contrast to our previous case, a *decrease* in existing taxes will raise the aggregate expenditures schedule in Figure 11.6 as a result of an increase in consumption at all GDP levels. You should confirm that a tax reduction of $10 billion (from the present $20 billion to $10 billion) would increase the equilibrium GDP from $490 billion to $520 billion.

Differential Impacts
You may have noted that equal changes in *G* and *T* do not have equivalent impacts on GDP. The $20 billion increase in *G* in our illustration, subject to the multiplier of 4, produced an $80 billion increase in real GDP. But the $20 billion increase in taxes reduced GDP by only $60 billion. Given an MPC of .75, the tax increase of $20 billion reduced consumption by only $15 billion (not $20 billion) because saving also fell by $5 billion. Subjecting the $15 billion decline in consumption to the multiplier of 4, we find the tax increase of $20 billion reduced GDP by $60 billion (not $80 billion).

> **WORKED PROBLEMS**
>
> **W 11.2**
>
> Complete aggregate expenditures model

Table 11.5 and Figure 11.6 constitute the complete aggregate expenditures model for an open economy with government. When total spending equals total produc-

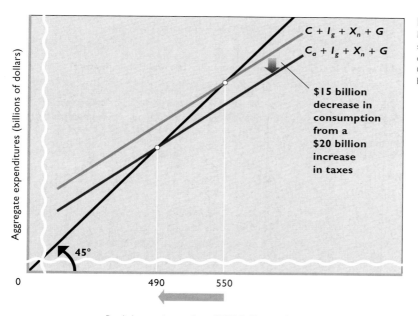

$C + I_g + X_n + G$

$C_a + I_g + X_n + G$

$15 billion decrease in consumption from a $20 billion increase in taxes

45°

0   490   550

Real domestic product, GDP (billions of dollars)

Aggregate expenditures (billions of dollars)

FIGURE 11.6 Taxes and equilibrium GDP. If the MPC is .75, the $20 billion of taxes will lower the consumption schedule by $15 billion and cause a $60 billion decline in the equilibrium GDP. In the open economy with government, equilibrium GDP occurs where C_a (after-tax income) $+ I_g + X_n + G =$ GDP. Here that equilibrium is $490 billion.

tion, the economy's output is in equilibrium. In the open mixed economy, equilibrium GDP occurs where

$$C_a + I_g + X_n + G = \text{GDP}$$

Injections, Leakages, and Unplanned Changes in Inventories The related characteristics of equilibrium noted for the private closed economy also apply to the full model. In particular, it is still the case that injections into the income-expenditures stream equal leakages from the income stream. For the private closed economy, $S = I_g$. For the expanded economy, imports and taxes are added leakages. Saving, importing, and paying taxes are all uses of income that subtract from potential consumption. Consumption will now be less than GDP—creating a potential spending gap—in the amount of after-tax saving (S_a), imports (M), and taxes (T). But exports (X) and government purchases (G), along with investment (I_g), are injections into the income-expenditures stream. At the equilibrium GDP, the sum of the leakages equals the sum of injections. In symbols:

$$S_a + M + T = I_g + X + G$$

You should use the data in Table 11.5 to confirm this equality between leakages and injections at the equilibrium GDP of $490 billion. Also, substantiate that a lack of such equality exists at all other possible levels of GDP.

Although not directly shown in Table 11.5, the equilibrium characteristic of "no unplanned changes in inventories" will also be fulfilled at the $490 billion GDP. Because aggregate expenditures equal GDP, all the goods and services produced will be purchased. There will be no unplanned increase in inventories, so firms will have no incentive to reduce their employment and production. Nor will they experience an unplanned decline in their inventories, which would prompt them to expand their employment and output to replenish their inventories.

INTERACTIVE GRAPHS

G 11.2

Changes in GDP

Equilibrium versus Full-Employment GDP

A key point about the equilibrium GDP of the aggregate expenditures model is that it need not equal the economy's full-employment GDP. In fact, Keynes specifically designed the model so that it could explain situations like the Great Depression, during which the economy was seemingly stuck at a bad equilibrium in which real GDP was far below potential output. As we will show you in a moment,

Keynes also used the model to suggest policy recommendations for moving the economy back toward potential output and full employment.

The fact that equilibrium and potential GDP in the aggregate expenditure model need not match also reveals critical insights about the causes of demand-pull inflation. We will first examine the "expenditure gaps" that give rise to differences between equilibrium and potential GDP and then see how the model helps to explain the recession of 2007–2009 and preview the policies used by the Federal government to try to halt and reverse it.

Recessionary Expenditure Gap

Suppose in **Figure 11.7 (Key Graph)**, panel (a), that the full-employment level of GDP is $510 billion and the aggregate expenditures schedule is AE_1. (For simplicity, we will now dispense with the $C_a + I_g + X_n + G$ labeling.) This schedule intersects the 45° line to the left of the economy's full-employment output, so the economy's equilibrium GDP of $490 billion is $20 billion short of its full-employment output of $510 billion. According to column 1 in Table 11.2, total employment at the full-employment GDP is 75 million workers. But the economy depicted in Figure 11.7a is employing only 70 million workers; 5 million available workers are not employed. For that reason, the economy is sacrificing $20 billion of output.

A **recessionary expenditure gap** is the amount by which aggregate expenditures *at the full-employment GDP* fall short of those required to achieve the full-employment GDP. Insufficient total spending contracts or depresses the economy. Table 11.5 shows that at the full-employment level of $510 billion (column 1), the corresponding level of aggregate expenditures is only $505 billion (column 9). The recessionary expenditure gap is thus $5 billion, the amount by which the aggregate expenditures curve would have to shift upward to realize equilibrium at the full-employment GDP. Graphically, the recessionary expenditure gap is the *vertical* distance (measured at the full-employment GDP) by which the actual aggregate expenditures schedule AE_1 lies below the hypothetical full-employment aggregate expenditures schedule AE_0. In Figure 11.7a, this recessionary expenditure gap is $5 billion. Because the multiplier is 4, there is a $20 billion differential (the recessionary expenditure gap of $5 billion times the multiplier of 4) between the equilibrium GDP and the full-employment GDP. This $20 billion difference is a negative *GDP gap*—an idea we first developed when discussing cyclical unemployment in Chapter 9.

FIGURE 11.7 Recessionary and inflationary expenditure gaps. The equilibrium and full-employment GDPs may not coincide. (a) A recessionary expenditure gap is the amount by which aggregate expenditures at the full-employment GDP fall short of those needed to achieve the full-employment GDP. Here, the $5 billion recessionary expenditure gap causes a $20 billion negative GDP gap. (b) An inflationary expenditure gap is the amount by which aggregate expenditures at the full-employment GDP exceed those just sufficient to achieve the full-employment GDP. Here, the inflationary expenditure gap is $5 billion; this overspending produces demand-pull inflation.

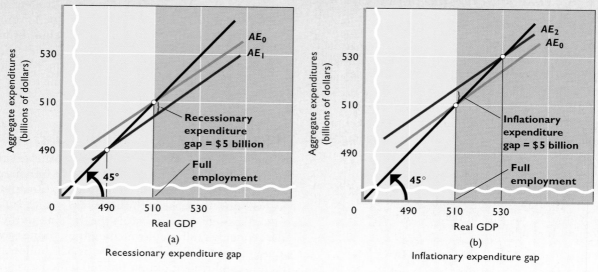

(a)
Recessionary expenditure gap

(b)
Inflationary expenditure gap

QUICK QUIZ FOR FIGURE 11.7

1. In the economy depicted:
   a. the MPS is .50.
   b. the MPC is .75.
   c. the full-employment level of real GDP is $530 billion.
   d. nominal GDP always equals real GDP.

2. The inflationary expenditure gap depicted will cause:
   a. demand-pull inflation.
   b. cost-push inflation.
   c. cyclical unemployment.
   d. frictional unemployment.

3. The recessionary expenditure gap depicted will cause:
   a. demand-pull inflation.
   b. cost-push inflation.

   c. cyclical unemployment.
   d. frictional unemployment.

4. In the economy depicted, the $5 billion inflationary expenditure gap:
   a. expands real GDP to $530 billion.
   b. leaves real GDP at $510 billion but causes inflation.
   c. could be remedied by equal $5 billion increases in taxes and government spending.
   d. implies that real GDP exceeds nominal GDP.

Answers: 1. b; 2. a; 3. c; 4. b

Keynes's Solution to a Recessionary Expenditure Gap

Keynes pointed to two different policies that a government might pursue to close a recessionary expenditure gap and achieve full employment. The first is to increase government spending. The second is to lower taxes. Both work by increasing aggregate expenditures.

Look back at Figure 11.5. There we showed how an increase in government expenditures G will increase overall aggregate expenditures and, consequently, the equilibrium real GDP. Applying this strategy to the situation in Figure 11.7a, government could completely close the

$20 billion negative GDP gap between the initial equilibrium of $490 billion and the economy's potential output of $510 billion if it increased spending by the $5 billion amount of the recessionary expenditure gap. Given the economy's multiplier of 4, the $5 billion increase in G would create a $20 billion increase in equilibrium real GDP, thereby bringing the economy to full employment.

Government also could lower taxes to close the recessionary expenditure gap and thus eliminate the negative GDP gap. Look back at Figure 11.6 in which an increase in taxes resulted in lower after-tax consumption spending and a smaller equilibrium real GDP. Keynes simply suggested a reversal of this process: Since an increase in taxes lowers equilibrium real GDP, a decrease in taxes will raise equilibrium GDP. The decrease in taxes will leave consumers with higher after-tax income. That will lead to higher consumption expenditures and an increase in equilibrium real GDP.

But by how much should the government cut taxes? By exactly $6.67 billion. That is because the MPC is .75. The tax cut of $6.67 billion will increase consumers' after-tax income by $6.67 billion. They will then increase consumption spending by .75 of that amount, or $5 billion. This will increase aggregate expenditures by the $5 billion needed to close the recessionary expenditure gap. The economy's equilibrium real GDP will rise to its potential output of $510 billion.

But a big warning is needed here: As the economy moves closer to its potential output, it becomes harder to justify Keynes's assumption that prices are stuck. As the economy closes its negative GDP gap, nearly all workers are employed and nearly all factories are operating at or near full capacity. In such a situation, there is no massive oversupply of productive resources to keep prices from rising. In fact, economists know from real-world experience that in such situations prices are not fully stuck. Instead, they become increasingly flexible as the economy moves nearer to potential output.

This fact is one of the major limitations of the aggregate expenditures model and is the reason why we will develop a different model that can handle inflation in the next chapter. That being said, it is nevertheless true that the aggregate expenditures model is still very useful despite its inability to handle flexible prices. For instance, as we explained in Chapter 6, even an economy operating near full employment will show sticky or even stuck prices in the short run. In such situations, the intuitions of the aggregate expenditures model will still hold true. The benefit of the aggregate demand–aggregate supply model that we develop in the next chapter is that it also can show us what happens over longer periods, as prices (and wages) become more flexible and are increasingly able to adjust.

> **WORKED PROBLEMS**
>
> **W 11.3**
>
> Expenditure gaps

Inflationary Expenditure Gap

Economists use the term **inflationary expenditure gap** to describe the amount by which an economy's aggregate expenditures *at the full-employment GDP* exceed those just necessary to achieve the full-employment level of GDP. In Figure 11.7b, there is a $5 billion inflationary expenditure gap at the $510 billion full-employment GDP. This is shown by the vertical distance between the actual aggregate expenditures schedule AE_2 and the hypothetical schedule AE_0 that would be just sufficient to achieve the $510 billion full-employment GDP. Thus, the inflationary expenditure gap is the amount by which the aggregate expenditures schedule would have to shift downward to realize equilibrium at the full-employment GDP.

But why does the name "inflationary expenditure gap" contain the word *inflationary*? In particular, what does the situation depicted in Figure 11.7b have to do with inflation? The answer lies in the answer to a different question: *Could the economy actually achieve and maintain an equilibrium real GDP that is substantially above the full-employment output level?*

The unfortunate answer is no. It is unfortunate because if such a thing were possible, then the government could make real GDP as high as it wanted by simply increasing G to an arbitrarily high number. Graphically, it could raise the AE_2 curve in Figure 11.7b as far up as it wanted, thereby increasing equilibrium real GDP as high as it wanted. Living standards would skyrocket! But this is not possible because, by definition, all the available workers in the economy are fully employed at the full-employment output level. Producing slightly more than the full-employment output level for a few months might be possible if you could convince all the workers to work overtime day after day. But there simply is not enough labor to have the economy produce at much more than potential output for any extended period of time.

So what *does* happen in situations in which aggregate expenditures are so high that the model predicts an equilibrium level of GDP beyond potential output? The answer is twofold. First, the economy ends up producing either at potential output or just above potential output due to the limited supply of labor. Second, the economy experiences demand-pull inflation. With the supply of output limited by the supply of labor, high levels of aggregate expenditures simply drive up prices. Nominal GDP will increase because of the higher price level, but real GDP will not.

Application: The Recession of 2007–2009

In December 2007 the U.S. economy entered the longest and one of the deepest recessions since the Great Depression of the 1930s. We will defer discussion of the underlying financial crisis until later chapters, but the ultimate effect of the crisis is easily portrayed through the aggregate expenditures model. We know that the AE_0 line in Figure 11.7a consists of the combined amount of after-tax

The Aggregate Expenditure Theory Emerged as a Critique of Classical Economics and as a Response to the Great Depression.

Until the Great Depression of the 1930s, many prominent economists, including David Ricardo (1772–1823) and John Stuart Mill (1806–1873), believed that the market system would ensure full employment of an economy's resources. These so-called *classical economists* acknowledged that now and then abnormal circumstances such as wars, political upheavals, droughts, speculative crises, and gold rushes would occur, deflecting the economy from full-employment status. But when such deviations occurred, the economy would automatically adjust and soon return to full-employment output. For example, a slump in output and employment would result in lower prices, wages, and interest rates, which in turn would increase consumer spending, employment, and investment spending. Any excess supply of goods and workers would soon be eliminated.

Classical macroeconomists denied that the level of spending in an economy could be too low to bring about the purchase of the entire full-employment output. They based their denial of inadequate spending in part on *Say's law*, attributed to the nineteenth-century French economist J. B. Say (1767–1832). This law is the disarmingly simple idea that the very act of producing goods generates income equal to the value of the goods produced. The production of any output automatically provides the income needed to buy that output. More succinctly stated, *supply creates its own demand*.

Say's law can best be understood in terms of a barter economy. A woodworker, for example, produces or supplies furniture as a means of buying or demanding the food and clothing produced by other workers. The woodworker's supply of furniture is the income that he will "spend" to satisfy his demand for other goods. The goods he buys (demands) will have a total value exactly equal to the goods he produces (supplies). And so it is for other producers and for the entire economy. Demand must be the same as supply!

THE GENERAL THEORY OF EMPLOYMENT, INTEREST, AND MONEY

JOHN MAYNARD KEYNES

GREAT MINDS SERIES

Assuming that the composition of output is in accord with consumer preferences, all markets would be cleared of their outputs. It would seem that all firms need to do to sell a full-employment output is to produce that level of output. Say's law guarantees there will be sufficient spending to purchase it all.

ORIGIN OF THE IDEA

O 11.2

Say's law

The Great Depression of the 1930s called into question the theory that supply creates its own demand (Say's law). In the United States, real GDP declined by 27 percent and the unemployment rate rocketed to nearly 25 percent. Other nations experienced similar impacts. And cyclical unemployment lingered for a decade. An obvious inconsistency exists between a theory that says that unemployment is virtually impossible and the actual occurrence of a 10 year siege of substantial unemployment.

In 1936 British economist John Maynard Keynes (1883–1946) explained why cyclical unemployment could occur in a market economy. In his *General Theory of Employment, Interest, and Money*, Keynes attacked the foundations of classical theory and developed the ideas underlying the aggregate expenditures model. Keynes disputed Say's law, pointing out that not all income need be spent in the same period that it is produced. In fact, some income is always saved. In normal times, that saving is borrowed by businesses to buy capital goods—thereby boosting total spending in the economy. But if expectations about the future grow pessimistic, businesses will slash investment spending and a lot of that saving will not be put to use. The result will be insufficient total spending. Unsold goods will accumulate in producers' warehouses, and producers will respond by reducing their output and discharging workers. A recession or depression will result, and widespread cyclical unemployment will occur. Moreover, said Keynes, recessions or depressions are not likely to correct themselves. In contrast to the more laissez-faire view of the classical economists, Keynes argued that government should play an active role in stabilizing the economy.

consumption expenditures (C_a), gross investment expenditures (I_g), net export expenditures (X_n), and government purchases (G) planned at each level of real GDP. During the recession, both after-tax consumption and investment expenditures declined, with planned investment expenditures suffering the largest drop by far.

Aggregate expenditures thus declined, as from AE_0 to AE_1 in Figure 11.7a. This set off a multiple decline in real GDP, illustrated in the figure by the decline from $510 billion to $490 billion. In the language of the aggregate expenditures model, a recessionary expenditure gap produced one of the largest negative GDP gaps since the Great Depression. Employment sank by more than 8 million people, and the unemployment rate jumped above 10 percent. As recessions go, this was a big one!

The Federal government undertook various Keynesian policies in 2008 and 2009 to try to eliminate the recessionary expenditure gap facing the economy. In 2008, the government provided $100 billion of tax rebate checks to taxpayers, hoping that recipients would use most of their checks to buy goods and services. (They didn't! Instead, they used substantial portions of their checks to pay off credit cards and reduce other debt.) In 2009, the Federal government enacted a $787 billion stimulus package

designed to boost aggregate expenditures, reduce the recessionary expenditure gap, and, through the multiplier effect, increase real GDP and employment.

We will defer discussion and further assessment of these stimulus attempts until Chapter 13, but Figure 11.7a clearly illuminates their purpose. If the government could drive up aggregate expenditures, such as from AE_1 to AE_0, the recession would come to an end and the recovery phase of the business cycle would begin.

QUICK REVIEW 11.3

- Government purchases shift the aggregate expenditures schedule upward and raise equilibrium GDP.
- Taxes reduce disposable income, lower consumption spending and saving, shift the aggregate expenditures schedule downward, and reduce equilibrium GDP.
- A recessionary expenditure gap is the amount by which an economy's aggregate expenditures schedule must shift upward to achieve the full-employment GDP; an inflationary expenditure gap is the amount by which the economy's aggregate expenditures schedule must shift downward to achieve full-employment GDP and eliminate demand-pull inflation.

Summary

1. The aggregate expenditures model views the total amount of spending in the economy as the primary factor determining the level of real GDP that the economy will produce. The model assumes that the price level is fixed. Keynes made this assumption to reflect the general circumstances of the Great Depression, in which declines in output and employment, rather than declines in prices, were the dominant adjustments made by firms when they faced huge declines in their sales.

2. For a private closed economy the equilibrium level of GDP occurs when aggregate expenditures and real output are equal or, graphically, where the $C + I_g$ line intersects the 45° line. At any GDP greater than equilibrium GDP, real output will exceed aggregate spending, resulting in unplanned investment in inventories and eventual declines in output and income (GDP). At any below-equilibrium GDP, aggregate expenditures will exceed real output, resulting in unplanned disinvestment in inventories and eventual increases in GDP.

3. At equilibrium GDP, the amount households save (leakages) and the amount businesses plan to invest (injections) are equal. Any excess of saving over planned investment will cause a shortage of total spending, forcing GDP to fall. Any excess of planned investment over saving will cause an excess of total spending, inducing GDP to rise. The change in

GDP will in both cases correct the discrepancy between saving and planned investment.

4. At equilibrium GDP, there are no unplanned changes in inventories. When aggregate expenditures diverge from real GDP, an unplanned change in inventories occurs. Unplanned increases in inventories are followed by a cutback in production and a decline of real GDP. Unplanned decreases in inventories result in an increase in production and a rise of GDP.

5. Actual investment consists of planned investment plus unplanned changes in inventories and is always equal to saving.

6. A shift in the investment schedule (caused by changes in expected rates of return or changes in interest rates) shifts the aggregate expenditures curve and causes a new equilibrium level of real GDP. Real GDP changes by more than the amount of the initial change in investment. This multiplier effect ($\Delta GDP/\Delta I_g$) accompanies both increases and decreases in aggregate expenditures and also applies to changes in net exports (X_n) and government purchases (G).

7. The net export schedule in the model of the open economy relates net exports (exports minus imports) to levels of real GDP. For simplicity, we assume that the level of net exports is the same at all levels of real GDP.

8. Positive net exports increase aggregate expenditures to a higher level than they would if the economy were "closed" to international trade. Negative net exports decrease aggregate expenditures relative to those in a closed economy, decreasing equilibrium real GDP by a multiple of their amount. Increases in exports or decreases in imports have an expansionary effect on real GDP, while decreases in exports or increases in imports have a contractionary effect.

9. Government purchases in the model of the mixed economy shift the aggregate expenditures schedule upward and raise GDP.

10. Taxation reduces disposable income, lowers consumption and saving, shifts the aggregate expenditures curve downward, and reduces equilibrium GDP.

11. In the complete aggregate expenditures model, equilibrium GDP occurs where $C_a + I_g + X_n + G = $ GDP. At the equilibrium GDP, *leakages* of after-tax saving (S_a), imports (M), and taxes (T) equal *injections* of investment (I_g), exports (X), and government purchases (G): $S_a + M + T = I_g + X_n + G$. Also, there are no unplanned changes in inventories.

12. The equilibrium GDP and the full-employment GDP may differ. A recessionary expenditure gap is the amount by which aggregate expenditures at the full-employment GDP fall short of those needed to achieve the full-employment GDP. This gap produces a negative GDP gap (actual GDP minus potential GDP). An inflationary expenditure gap is the amount by which aggregate expenditures at the full-employment GDP exceed those just sufficient to achieve the full-employment GDP. This gap causes demand-pull inflation.

13. Keynes suggested that the solution to the large negative GDP gap that occurred during the Great Depression was for government to increase aggregate expenditures. It could do this by increasing its own expenditures (G) or by lowering taxes (T) to increase after-tax consumption expenditures (C_a) by households. Because the economy had millions of unemployed workers and massive amounts of unused production capacity, government could boost aggregate expenditures without worrying about creating inflation.

14. The stuck-price assumption of the aggregate expenditures model is not credible when the economy approaches or attains its full-employment output. With unemployment low and excess production capacity small or nonexistent, an increase in aggregate expenditures will cause inflation along with any increase in real GDP.

Terms and Concepts

planned investment	leakage	lump-sum tax
investment schedule	injection	recessionary expenditure gap
aggregate expenditures schedule	unplanned changes in inventories	inflationary expenditure gap
equilibrium GDP	net exports	

Questions

1. What is an investment schedule and how does it differ from an investment demand curve? **LO1**

2. Why does equilibrium real GDP occur where $C + I_g = $ GDP in a private closed economy? What happens to real GDP when $C = I_g$ exceeds GDP? When $C = I_g$ is less than GDP? What two expenditure components of real GDP are purposely excluded in a private closed economy? **LO1**

3. Why is saving called a *leakage*? Why is planned investment called an *injection*? Why must saving equal planned investment at equilibrium GDP in the private closed economy? Are unplanned changes in inventories rising, falling, or constant at equilibrium GDP? Explain. **LO2**

4. Other things equal, what effect will each of the following changes independently have on the equilibrium level of real GDP in the private closed economy? **LO3**
   a. A decline in the real interest rate.
   b. An overall decrease in the expected rate of return on investment.
   c. A sizable, sustained increase in stock prices.

5. Depict graphically the aggregate expenditures model for a private closed economy. Now show a decrease in the aggregate expenditures schedule and explain why the decline in real GDP in your diagram is greater than the decline in the aggregate expenditures schedule. What is the term used for the ratio of a decline in real GDP to the initial drop in aggregate expenditures? **LO3**

6. Assuming the economy is operating below its potential output, what is the impact of an increase in net exports on real GDP? Why is it difficult, if not impossible, for a country to boost its net exports by increasing its tariffs during a global recession? **LO4**

7. Explain graphically the determination of equilibrium GDP for a private economy through the aggregate expenditures model. Now add government purchases (any amount you choose) to your graph, showing its impact on equilibrium GDP. Finally, add taxation (any amount of lump-sum tax that you choose) to your graph and show its effect on equilibrium GDP. Looking at your graph, determine whether

equilibrium GDP has increased, decreased, or stayed the same given the sizes of the government purchases and taxes that you selected. **LO4**

8. What is a recessionary expenditure gap? An inflationary expenditure gap? Which is associated with a positive GDP gap? A negative GDP gap? **LO5**

9. **LAST WORD** What is Say's law? How does it relate to the view held by classical economists that the economy generally will operate at a position on its production possibilities curve (Chapter 1)? Use production possibilities analysis to demonstrate Keynes's view on this matter.

Problems

1. Assuming the level of investment is $16 billion and independent of the level of total output, complete the table immediately below and determine the equilibrium levels of output and employment in this private closed economy. What are the sizes of the MPC and MPS? **LO1**

Possible Levels of Employment, Millions	Real Domestic Output (GDP = DI), Billions	Consumption, Billions	Saving, Billions
40	$240	$244	$ _____
45	260	260	_____
50	280	276	_____
55	300	292	_____
60	320	308	_____
65	340	324	_____
70	360	340	_____
75	380	356	_____
80	400	372	_____

2. Using the consumption and saving data in problem 1 and assuming investment is $16 billion, what are saving and planned investment at the $380 billion level of domestic output? What are saving and actual investment at that level?

What are saving and planned investment at the $300 billion level of domestic output? What are the levels of saving and actual investment? In which direction and by what amount will unplanned investment change as the economy moves from the $380 billion level of GDP to the equilibrium level of real GDP? From the $300 billion level of real GDP to the equilibrium level of GDP? **LO2**

3. By how much will GDP change if firms increase their investment by $8 billion and the MPC is .80? If the MPC is .67? **LO3**

4. Suppose that a certain country has an MPC of .9 and a real GDP of $400 billion. If its investment spending decreases by $4 billion, what will be its new level of real GDP? **LO3**

5. The data in columns 1 and 2 in the table below are for a private closed economy. **LO4**
   a. Use columns 1 and 2 to determine the equilibrium GDP for this hypothetical economy.
   b. Now open up this economy to international trade by including the export and import figures of columns 3 and 4. Fill in columns 5 and 6 and determine the equilibrium GDP for the open economy. What is the change in equilibrium GDP caused by the addition of net exports?
   c. Given the original $20 billion level of exports, what would be net exports and the equilibrium GDP if imports were $10 billion greater at each level of GDP?
   d. What is the multiplier in this example?

(1) Real Domestic Output (GDP = DI), Billions	(2) Aggregate Expenditures, Private Closed Economy, Billions	(3) Exports, Billions	(4) Imports, Billions	(5) Net Exports, Billions	(6) Aggregate Expenditures, Private Open Economy, Billions
$200	$240	$20	$30	$ _____	$ _____
250	280	20	30	_____	_____
300	320	20	30	_____	_____
350	360	20	30	_____	_____
400	400	20	30	_____	_____
450	440	20	30	_____	_____
500	480	20	30	_____	_____
550	520	20	30	_____	_____

6. Assume that, without taxes, the consumption schedule of an economy is as follows. **LO4**

GDP, Billions	Consumption, Billions
$100	$120
200	200
300	280
400	360
500	440
600	520
700	600

a. Graph this consumption schedule and determine the MPC.

b. Assume now that a lump-sum tax is imposed such that the government collects $10 billion in taxes at all levels of GDP. Graph the resulting consumption schedule and compare the MPC and the multiplier with those of the pretax consumption schedule.

7. Refer to columns 1 and 6 in the table for problem 5. Incorporate government into the table by assuming that it plans to tax and spend $20 billion at each possible level of GDP. Also assume that the tax is a personal tax and that government spending does not induce a shift in the private aggregate expenditures schedule. What is the change in equilibrium GDP caused by the addition of government? **LO4**

8. **ADVANCED ANALYSIS** Assume that the consumption schedule for a private open economy is such that consumption $C = 50 + 0.8Y$. Assume further that planned investment I_g and net exports X_n are independent of the level of real GDP and constant at $I_g = 30$ and $X_n = 10$. Recall also that, in equilibrium, the real output produced (Y) is equal to aggregate expenditures: $Y = C + I_g + X_n$. **LO4**

a. Calculate the equilibrium level of income or real GDP for this economy.

b. What happens to equilibrium Y if I_g changes to 10? What does this outcome reveal about the size of the multiplier?

9. Refer to the accompanying table in answering the questions that follow: **LO5**

(1) Possible Levels of Employment, Millions	(2) Real Domestic Output, Billions	(3) Aggregate Expenditures $(C_a + I_g + X_n + G)$, Billions
90	$500	$520
100	550	560
110	600	600
120	650	640
130	700	680

a. If full employment in this economy is 130 million, will there be an inflationary expenditure gap or a recessionary expenditure gap? What will be the consequence of this gap? By how much would aggregate expenditures in column 3 have to change at each level of GDP to eliminate the inflationary expenditure gap or the recessionary expenditure gap? What is the multiplier in this example?

b. Will there be an inflationary expenditure gap or a recessionary expenditure gap if the full-employment level of output is $500 billion? By how much would aggregate expenditures in column 3 have to change at each level of GDP to eliminate the gap? What is the multiplier in this example?

c. Assuming that investment, net exports, and government expenditures do not change with changes in real GDP, what are the sizes of the MPC, the MPS, and the multiplier?

10. Answer the following questions, which relate to the aggregate expenditures model: **LO5**

a. If C_a is $100, I_g is $50, X_n is −$10, and G is $30, what is the economy's equilibrium GDP?

b. If real GDP in an economy is currently $200, C_a is $100, I_g is $50, X_n is −$10, and G is $30, will the economy's real GDP rise, fall, or stay the same?

c. Suppose that full-employment (and full-capacity) output in an economy is $200. If C_a is $150, I_g is $50, X_n is −$10, and G is $30, what will be the macroeconomic result?

FURTHER TEST YOUR KNOWLEDGE AT
www.mcconnell19e.com

At the text's Online Learning Center (OLC), **www.mcconnell19e.com**, you will find one or more Web-based questions that require information from the Internet to answer. We urge you to check them out; they will familiarize you with Web sites that may be helpful in other courses and perhaps even in your career. The OLC also features multiple-choice questions that give instant feedback and provides other helpful ways to further test your knowledge of the chapter.

AFTER READING THIS CHAPTER, YOU SHOULD BE ABLE TO:

1 Define aggregate demand (AD) and explain the factors that cause it to change.

2 Define aggregate supply (AS) and explain the factors that cause it to change.

3 Discuss how AD and AS determine an economy's equilibrium price level and level of real GDP.

4 Describe how the AD-AS model explains periods of demand-pull inflation, cost-push inflation, and recession.

5 (Appendix) Identify how the aggregate demand curve relates to the aggregate expenditures model.

Aggregate Demand and Aggregate Supply

During the recession of 2007–2009, the economic terms *aggregate demand* and *aggregate supply* moved from the obscurity of economic journals and textbooks to the spotlight of national newspapers, Web sites, radio, and television.

The media and public asked: Why had *aggregate demand* declined, producing the deepest recession and highest rate of unemployment since 1982? Why hadn't the reductions in interest rates by the Federal Reserve boosted *aggregate demand*? Would the Federal government's $787 billion stimulus package increase *aggregate demand* and reduce unemployment, as intended? Would a resurgence of oil prices and other energy prices reduce *aggregate supply*, choking off an economic expansion?

Aggregate demand and aggregate supply are the featured elements of the **aggregate demand–aggregate supply model (AD-AS model),** the focus of this chapter. The aggregate expenditures model of the previous chapter is an immediate-short-run model, in which prices are assumed to be fixed. In contrast, the AD-AS model in this chapter is a "variable price–variable output" model that allows both the price level and level of real GDP to change. It can also show longer time horizons, distinguishing between the immediate short run, the short run, and the long run. Further, in subsequent chapters, we will see that the AD-AS model easily depicts fiscal and monetary policies such as those used in 2008 and 2009 to try to halt the downward slide of the economy and promote its recovery.

Aggregate Demand

Aggregate demand is a schedule or curve that shows the amount of a nation's output (real GDP) that buyers collectively desire to purchase at each possible price level. These buyers include the nation's households, businesses, and government along with consumers located abroad (households, businesses, and governments in other nations). The relationship between the price level (as measured by the GDP price index) and the amount of real GDP demanded is inverse or negative: When the price level rises, the quantity of real GDP demanded decreases; when the price level falls, the quantity of real GDP demanded increases.

Aggregate Demand Curve

The inverse relationship between the price level and real GDP is shown in Figure 12.1, where the aggregate demand curve AD slopes downward, as does the demand curve for an individual product.

Why the downward slope? The explanation is *not* the same as that for why the demand for a single product slopes downward. That explanation centered on the income effect and the substitution effect. When the price of an *individual* product falls, the consumer's (constant) nominal income allows a larger purchase of the product (the income effect). And, as price falls, the consumer wants to buy more of the product because it becomes relatively less expensive than other goods (the substitution effect).

But these explanations do not work for aggregates. In Figure 12.1, when the economy moves down its aggregate demand curve, it moves to a lower general price level. But our circular flow model tells us that when consumers pay lower prices for goods and services, less nominal income flows to resource suppliers in the form of wages, rents, interest, and profits. As a result, a decline in the price level does not necessarily mean an increase in the nominal income of the economy as a whole. Thus, a decline in the price level need not produce an income effect, where more output is purchased because lower nominal prices leave buyers with greater real income.

Similarly, in Figure 12.1, prices in general are falling as we move down the aggregate demand curve, so the rationale for the substitution effect (where more of a specific product is purchased because it becomes cheaper relative to all other products) is not applicable. There is no *overall* substitution effect among domestically produced goods when the price level falls.

If the conventional substitution and income effects do not explain the downward slope of the aggregate demand curve, what does? The explanation rests on three effects of a price-level change.

Real-Balances Effect A change in the price level produces a **real-balances effect**. Here is how it works: A higher price level reduces the real value or purchasing power of the public's accumulated savings balances. In particular, the real value of assets with fixed money values, such as savings accounts or bonds, diminishes. Because a higher price level erodes the purchasing power of such assets, the public is poorer in real terms and will reduce its spending. A household might buy a new car or a plasma TV if the purchasing power of its financial asset balances is, say, $50,000.

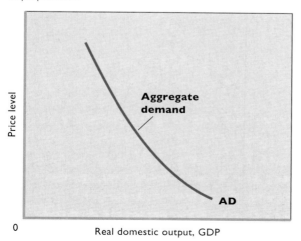

FIGURE 12.1 The aggregate demand curve. The downsloping aggregate demand curve AD indicates an inverse (or negative) relationship between the price level and the amount of real output purchased.

But if inflation erodes the purchasing power of its asset balances to $30,000, the household may defer its purchase. So a higher price level means less consumption spending.

Interest-Rate Effect The aggregate demand curve also slopes downward because of the **interest-rate effect.** When we draw an aggregate demand curve, we assume that the supply of money in the economy is fixed. But when the price level rises, consumers need more money for purchases and businesses need more money to meet their payrolls and to buy other resources. A $10 bill will do when the price of an item is $10, but a $10 bill plus a $1 bill is needed when the item costs $11. In short, a higher price level increases the demand for money. So, given a fixed supply of money, an increase in money demand will drive up the price paid for its use. That price is the interest rate.

Higher interest rates curtail investment spending and interest-sensitive consumption spending. Firms that expect a 6 percent rate of return on a potential purchase of capital will find that investment potentially profitable when the interest rate is, say, 5 percent. But the investment will be unprofitable and will not be made when the interest rate has risen to 7 percent. Similarly, consumers may decide not to purchase a new house or new automobile when the interest rate on loans goes up. So, by increasing the demand for money and consequently the interest rate, a higher price level reduces the amount of real output demanded.

Foreign Purchases Effect The final reason why the aggregate demand curve slopes downward is the **foreign purchases effect.** When the U.S. price level rises relative to foreign price levels (and exchange rates do not respond quickly or completely), foreigners buy fewer U.S. goods and Americans buy more foreign goods. Therefore, U.S. exports fall and U.S. imports rise. In short, the rise in the price level reduces the quantity of U.S. goods demanded as net exports.

These three effects, of course, work in the opposite direction for a decline in the price level. A decline in the price level increases consumption through the real-balances effect and interest-rate effect; increases investment through the interest-rate effect; and raises net exports by increasing exports and decreasing imports through the foreign purchases effect.

Changes in Aggregate Demand

Other things equal, a change in the price level will change the amount of aggregate spending and therefore change the amount of real GDP demanded by the economy. Movements along a fixed aggregate demand curve represent these changes in real GDP. However, if one or more of those "other things" change, the entire aggregate demand curve will shift. We call these other things **determinants of aggregate demand** or, less formally, *aggregate demand shifters.* They are listed in Figure 12.2.

Changes in aggregate demand involve two components:
- A change in one of the determinants of aggregate demand that directly changes the amount of real GDP demanded.
- A multiplier effect that produces a greater ultimate change in aggregate demand than the initiating change in spending.

In Figure 12.2, the full rightward shift of the curve from AD_1 to AD_2 shows an increase in aggregate demand, separated into these two components. The horizontal distance between AD_1 and the broken curve to its right illustrates an initial increase in spending, say, $5 billion of added investment. If the economy's MPC is .75, for example, then the simple multiplier is 4. So the aggregate demand curve shifts rightward from AD_1 to AD_2—four times the distance between AD_1 and the broken line. The multiplier process magnifies the initial change in spending into successive rounds of new consumption spending. After the shift, $20 billion (= $5 × 4) of additional real goods and services are demanded at each price level.

Similarly, the leftward shift of the curve from AD_1 to AD_3 shows a decrease in aggregate demand, the lesser amount of real GDP demanded at each price level. It also involves the initial decline in spending (shown as the horizontal distance between AD_1 and the dashed line to its left), followed by multiplied declines in consumption spending and the ultimate leftward shift to AD_3.

Let's examine each of the determinants of aggregate demand listed in Figure 12.2.

Consumer Spending

Even when the U.S. price level is constant, domestic consumers may alter their purchases of U.S.-produced real output. If those consumers decide to buy more output at each price level, the aggregate demand curve will shift to the right, as from AD_1 to AD_2 in Figure 12.2. If they decide to buy less output, the aggregate demand curve will shift to the left, as from AD_1 to AD_3.

Several factors other than a change in the price level may change consumer spending and therefore shift the aggregate demand curve. As Figure 12.2 shows, those factors are real consumer wealth, consumer expectations,

FIGURE 12.2 Changes in aggregate demand. A change in one or more of the listed determinants of aggregate demand will shift the aggregate demand curve. The rightward shift from AD$_1$ to AD$_2$ represents an increase in aggregate demand; the leftward shift from AD$_1$ to AD$_3$ shows a decrease in aggregate demand. The vertical distances between AD$_1$ and the dashed lines represent the initial changes in spending. Through the multiplier effect, that spending produces the full shifts of the curves.

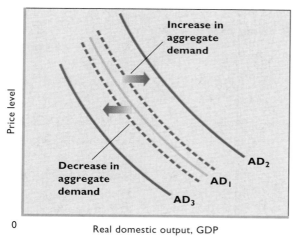

Determinants of Aggregate Demand: Factors That Shift the Aggregate Demand Curve

1. Change in consumer spending
   a. Consumer wealth
   b. Consumer expectations
   c. Household borrowing
   d. Taxes
2. Change in investment spending
   a. Interest rates
   b. Expected returns
      • Expected future business conditions
      • Technology
      • Degree of excess capacity
      • Business taxes
3. Change in government spending
4. Change in net export spending
   a. National income abroad
   b. Exchange rates

household debt, and taxes. Because our discussion here parallels that of Chapter 10, we will be brief.

Consumer Wealth

Consumer wealth is the total dollar value of all assets owned by consumers in the economy less the dollar value of their liabilities (debts). Assets include stocks, bonds, and real estate. Liabilities include mortgages, car loans, and credit card balances.

Consumer wealth sometimes changes suddenly and unexpectedly due to surprising changes in asset values. An unforeseen increase in the stock market is a good example. The increase in wealth prompts pleasantly surprised consumers to save less and buy more out of their current incomes than they had previously been planning. The resulting increase in consumer spending—the so-called *wealth effect*—shifts the aggregate demand curve to the right. In contrast, an unexpected decline in asset values will cause an unanticipated reduction in consumer wealth at each price level. As consumers tighten their belts in response to the bad news, a "reverse wealth effect" sets in. Unpleasantly surprised consumers increase savings and reduce consumption, thereby shifting the aggregate demand curve to the left.

Household Borrowing

Consumers can increase their consumption spending by borrowing. Doing so shifts the aggregate demand curve to the right. By contrast, a decrease in borrowing for consumption purposes shifts the aggregate demand curve to the left. The aggregate demand curve will also shift to the left if consumers increase their savings rates to pay off their debts. With more money flowing to debt repayment, consumption expenditures decline and the AD curve shifts left.

Consumer Expectations

Changes in expectations about the future may alter consumer spending. When people expect their future real incomes to rise, they tend to spend more of their current incomes. Thus, current consumption spending increases (current saving falls) and the aggregate demand curve shifts to the right. Similarly, a widely held expectation of surging inflation in the near future may increase aggregate demand today because consumers will want to buy products before their prices escalate. Conversely, expectations of lower future income or lower future prices may reduce current consumption and shift the aggregate demand curve to the left.

Personal Taxes

A reduction in personal income tax rates raises take-home income and increases consumer purchases at each possible price level. Tax cuts shift the aggregate demand curve to the right. Tax increases reduce consumption spending and shift the curve to the left.

Investment Spending

Investment spending (the purchase of capital goods) is a second major determinant of aggregate demand. A decline in investment spending at each price level will shift the aggregate demand curve to the left. An increase in investment spending will shift it to the right. In Chapter 10 we saw that investment spending depends on the real interest rate and the expected return from investment.

Real Interest Rates Other things equal, an increase in real interest rates will raise borrowing costs, lower investment spending, and reduce aggregate demand. We are not referring here to the "interest-rate effect" that results from a change in the price level. Instead, we are identifying a change in the real interest rate resulting from, say, a change in a nation's money supply. An increase in the money supply lowers the interest rate, thereby increasing investment and aggregate demand. A decrease in the money supply raises the interest rate, reducing investment and decreasing aggregate demand.

Expected Returns Higher expected returns on investment projects will increase the demand for capital goods and shift the aggregate demand curve to the right. Alternatively, declines in expected returns will decrease investment and shift the curve to the left. Expected returns, in turn, are influenced by several factors:

- *Expectations about future business conditions* If firms are optimistic about future business conditions, they are more likely to forecast high rates of return on current investment and therefore may invest more today. On the other hand, if they think the economy will deteriorate in the future, they will forecast low rates of return and perhaps will invest less today.
- *Technology* New and improved technologies enhance expected returns on investment and thus increase aggregate demand. For example, recent advances in microbiology have motivated pharmaceutical companies to establish new labs and production facilities.
- *Degree of excess capacity* A rise in excess capacity—unused capital—will reduce the expected return on new investment and hence decrease aggregate demand. Other things equal, firms operating factories at well below capacity have little incentive to build new factories. But when firms discover that their excess capacity is dwindling or has completely disappeared, their expected returns on new investment in factories and capital equipment rise. Thus, they increase their investment spending, and the aggregate demand curve shifts to the right.

- *Business taxes* An increase in business taxes will reduce after-tax profits from capital investment and lower expected returns. So investment and aggregate demand will decline. A decrease in business taxes will have the opposite effects.

The variability of interest rates and expected returns makes investment highly volatile. In contrast to consumption, investment spending rises and falls often, independent of changes in total income. Investment, in fact, is the least stable component of aggregate demand.

Government Spending

Government purchases are the third determinant of aggregate demand. An increase in government purchases (for example, more transportation projects) will shift the aggregate demand curve to the right, as long as tax collections and interest rates do not change as a result. In contrast, a reduction in government spending (for example, less military equipment) will shift the curve to the left.

Net Export Spending

The final determinant of aggregate demand is net export spending. Other things equal, higher U.S. *exports* mean an increased foreign demand for U.S. goods. So a rise in net exports (higher exports relative to imports) shifts the aggregate demand curve to the right. In contrast, a decrease in U.S. net exports shifts the aggregate demand curve leftward. (These changes in net exports are *not* those prompted by a change in the U.S. price level—those associated with the foreign purchases effect. The changes here are shifts of the AD curve, not movements along the AD curve.)

What might cause net exports to change, other than the price level? Two possibilities are changes in national income abroad and changes in exchange rates.

National Income Abroad Rising national income abroad encourages foreigners to buy more products, some of which are made in the United States. U.S. net exports thus rise, and the U.S. aggregate demand curve shifts to the right. Declines in national income abroad do the opposite: They reduce U.S. net exports and shift the U.S. aggregate demand curve to the left.

Exchange Rates Changes in the dollar's exchange rate—the price of foreign currencies in terms of the U.S. dollar—may affect U.S. exports and therefore aggregate demand. Suppose the dollar depreciates in terms of the euro (meaning the euro appreciates in terms of the dollar). The new, relatively lower value of dollars and higher value of euros enables European consumers to obtain more dollars with each euro. From their perspective, U.S. goods are now less expensive; it takes fewer euros to obtain them. So European consumers buy more U.S. goods, and U.S. exports rise. But American consumers can now obtain fewer euros for each dollar. Because they must pay more dollars to buy European goods, Americans reduce their imports. U.S. exports rise and U.S. imports fall. Conclusion: Dollar depreciation increases net exports (imports go down; exports go up) and therefore increases aggregate demand.

Dollar appreciation has the opposite effects: Net exports fall (imports go up; exports go down) and aggregate demand declines.

QUICK REVIEW 12.1

- Aggregate demand reflects an inverse relationship between the price level and the amount of real output demanded.
- Changes in the price level create real-balances, interest-rate, and foreign purchases effects that explain the downward slope of the aggregate demand curve.
- Changes in one or more of the determinants of aggregate demand (Figure 12.2) alter the amounts of real GDP demanded at each price level; they shift the aggregate demand curve. The multiplier effect magnifies initial changes in spending into larger changes in aggregate demand.
- An increase in aggregate demand is shown as a rightward shift of the aggregate demand curve; a decrease, as a leftward shift of the curve.

Aggregate Supply

Aggregate supply is a schedule or curve showing the relationship between a nation's price level and the amount of real domestic output that firms in the economy produce. This relationship varies depending on the time horizon and how quickly output prices and input prices can change. We will define three time horizons:

- In the *immediate short run*, both input prices as well as output prices are fixed.
- In the *short run*, input prices are fixed, but output prices can vary.
- In the *long run*, input prices as well as output prices can vary.

In Chapter 6, we discussed both the immediate short run and the long run in terms of how an automobile maker named Buzzer Auto responds to changes in the demand for its new car, the Prion. Here we extend the logic of that chapter to the economy as a whole to discuss how total output varies with the price level in the immediate short run, the short run, and the long run. As you will see, the relationship between the price level and total output is different in each of the three time horizons because input prices are stickier than output prices. Although both sets of prices become more flexible as time passes, output prices usually adjust more rapidly.

Aggregate Supply in the Immediate Short Run

Depending on the type of firm, the immediate short run can last anywhere from a few days to a few months. It lasts as long as *both* input prices and output prices stay fixed. Input prices are fixed in both the immediate short run and the short run by contractual agreements. In particular, 75 percent of the average firm's costs are wages and salaries—and these are almost always fixed by labor contracts for months or years at a time. As a result, they are usually fixed for a much longer duration than output prices, which can begin to change within a few days or a few months depending on the type of firm.

That being said, output prices are also typically fixed in the immediate short run. This is most often caused by firms setting fixed prices for their customers and then agreeing to supply whatever quantity demanded results at those fixed prices. For instance, once an appliance manufacturer sets its annual list prices for refrigerators, stoves, ovens, and microwaves, it is obligated to supply however many or few appliances customers want to buy at those prices. Similarly, a catalogue company is obliged to sell however much customers want to buy of its products at the prices listed in its current catalogue. And it is obligated to supply those quantities demanded until it sends out its next catalogue.

With output prices fixed and firms selling however much customers want to purchase at those fixed prices, the **immediate-short-run aggregate supply curve** AS_{ISR} is a horizontal line, as shown in Figure 12.3. The AS_{ISR} curve is horizontal at the overall price level P_1, which is calculated from all of the individual prices set by the various firms in the economy. Its horizontal shape implies that the total amount of output supplied in the economy depends directly on the volume of spending that results at price level P_1. If total spending is low at price level P_1, firms will supply a small amount of output to match the low level of spending. If total spending is high at price level P_1, they will supply a high level of output to match the high level of spending. The amount of output that results may be higher than or lower than the economy's full-employment output level Q_f.

Notice, however, that firms will respond in this manner to changes in total spending only as long as output

FIGURE 12.3 Aggregate supply in the immediate short

run. In the immediate short run, the aggregate supply curve AS_{ISR} is horizontal at the economy's current price level, P_1. With output prices fixed, firms collectively supply the level of output that is demanded at those prices.

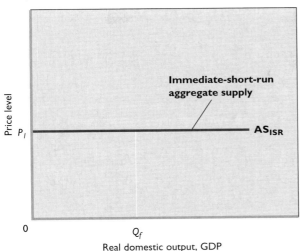

prices remain fixed. As soon as firms are able to change their product prices, they can respond to changes in aggregate spending not only by increasing or decreasing output but also by raising or lowering prices. This is the situation that leads to the upsloping short-run aggregate supply curve that we discuss next.

Aggregate Supply in the Short Run

The short run begins after the immediate short run ends. As it relates to macroeconomics, the short run is a period of time during which output prices are flexible, but input prices are either totally fixed or highly inflexible.

These assumptions about output prices and input prices are general—they relate to the economy in the aggregate. Naturally, some input prices are more flexible than others. Since gasoline prices are quite flexible, a package delivery firm like UPS that uses gasoline as an input will have at least one very flexible input price. On the other hand, wages at UPS are set by five-year labor contracts negotiated with its drivers' union, the Teamsters. Because wages are the firm's largest and most important input cost, UPS faces overall input prices that are inflexible for several years at a time. Thus, its "short run"—the period when it can change its shipping prices but not its substantially fixed input prices—is actually quite long. Keep this example in mind as we derive the short-run aggregate supply for the entire economy. Its applicability does not depend on some arbitrary definition of how long the "short run" should be.

Instead, the short-run for which the model is relevant is any period of time during which output prices are flexible, but input prices are fixed or nearly fixed.

As illustrated in Figure 12.4, the **short-run aggregate supply curve** AS slopes upward because, with input prices fixed, changes in the price level will raise or lower real firm profits. To see how this works, consider an economy that has only a single multiproduct firm called Mega Buzzer and in which the firm's owners must receive a real profit of $20 to produce the full-employment output of 100 units. Assume the owner's only input (aside from entrepreneurial talent) is 10 units of hired labor at $8 per worker, for a total wage cost of $80. Also, assume that the 100 units of output sell for $1 per unit, so total revenue is $100. Mega Buzzer's nominal profit is $20 (= $100 − $80), and using the $1 price to designate the base-price index of 100, its real profit is also $20 (= $20/1.00). Well and good; the full-employment output is produced.

Next consider what will happen if the price of Mega Buzzer's output doubles. The doubling of the price level will boost total revenue from $100 to $200, but since we are discussing the short run during which input prices are fixed, the $8 nominal wage for each of the 10 workers will remain unchanged so that total costs stay at $80. Nominal profit will rise from $20 (= $100 − $80) to $120 (= $200 − $80). Dividing that $120 profit by the

FIGURE 12.4 The aggregate supply curve (short

run). The upsloping aggregate supply curve AS indicates a direct (or positive) relationship between the price level and the amount of real output that firms will offer for sale. The AS curve is relatively flat below the full-employment output because unemployed resources and unused capacity allow firms to respond to price-level rises with large increases in real output. It is relatively steep beyond the full-employment output because resource shortages and capacity limitations make it difficult to expand real output as the price level rises.

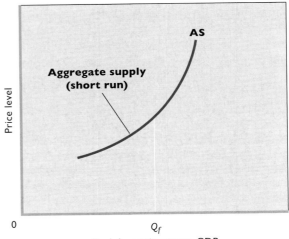

new price index of 200 (= 2.0 in hundredths), we find that Mega Buzzer's real profit is now $60. The rise in the real reward from $20 to $60 prompts the firm (economy) to produce more output. Conversely, price-level declines reduce real profits and cause the firm (economy) to reduce its output. So, in the short run, there is a direct, or positive, relationship between the price level and real output. When the price level rises, real output rises and when the price level falls, real output falls. The result is an upsloping short-run aggregate supply curve.

Notice, however, that the upslope of the short-run aggregate supply curve is not constant. It is flatter at outputs below the full-employment output level Q_f and steeper at outputs above it. This has to do with the fact that per-unit production costs underlie the short-run aggregate supply curve. Recall from Chapter 9 that

$$\text{Per-unit production cost} = \frac{\text{total input cost}}{\text{units of output}}$$

The per-unit production cost of any specific level of output establishes that output's price level because the associated price level must cover all the costs of production, including profit "costs."

As the economy expands in the short run, per-unit production costs generally rise because of reduced efficiency. But the extent of that rise depends on where the economy is operating relative to its capacity. When the economy is operating below its full-employment output, it has large amounts of unused machinery and equipment and large numbers of unemployed workers. Firms can put these idle human and property resources back to work with little upward pressure on per-unit production costs. And as output expands, few if any shortages of inputs or production bottlenecks will arise to raise per-unit production costs. That is why the slope of the short-run aggregate supply curve increases only slowly at output levels below the full-employment output level Q_f.

On the other hand, when the economy is operating beyond Q_f, the vast majority of its available resources are already employed. Adding more workers to a relatively fixed number of highly used capital resources such as plant and equipment creates congestion in the workplace and reduces the efficiency (on average) of workers. Adding more capital, given the limited number of available workers, leaves equipment idle and reduces the efficiency of capital. Adding more land resources when capital and labor are highly constrained reduces the efficiency of land resources. Under these circumstances, total input costs rise more rapidly than total output. The result is rapidly rising per-unit production costs that give the short-run

aggregate supply curve its rapidly increasing slope at output levels beyond Q_f.

Aggregate Supply in the Long Run

In macroeconomics, the long run is the time horizon over which both input prices as well as output prices are flexible. It begins after the short run ends. Depending on the type of firm and industry, this may be from a couple of weeks to several years in the future. But for the economy as a whole, it is the time horizon over which all output and input prices—including wage rates—are fully flexible.

The **long-run aggregate supply curve** AS_{LR} is vertical at the economy's full-employment output Q_f, as shown in Figure 12.5. The vertical curve means that in the long run the economy will produce the full-employment output level no matter what the price level is. How can this be? Shouldn't higher prices cause firms to increase output? The explanation lies in the fact that in the long run when both input prices as well as output prices are flexible, profit levels will always adjust to give firms exactly the right profit incentive to produce exactly the full-employment output level, Q_f.

To see why this is true, look back at the short-run aggregate supply curve AS shown in Figure 12.4. Suppose that the economy starts out producing at the full-employment output level Q_f and that the price level at that moment has an index value of $P = 100$. Now suppose that output prices double, so that the price index goes to $P = 200$. We

FIGURE 12.5 Aggregate supply in the long run. The long-run aggregate supply curve AS_{LR} is vertical at the full-employment level of real GDP (Q_f) because in the long run wages and other input prices rise and fall to match changes in the price level. So price-level changes do not affect firms' profits and thus they create no incentive for firms to alter their output.

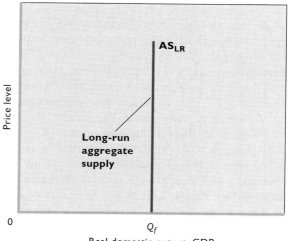

previously demonstrated for our single-firm economy that this doubling of the price level would cause profits to rise in the short run and that the higher profits would motivate the firm to increase output.

This outcome, however, is totally dependent on the fact that input prices are fixed in the short run. Consider what will happen in the long run when they are free to change. Firms can only produce beyond the full-employment output level by running factories and businesses at extremely high rates. This creates a great deal of demand for the economy's limited supply of productive resources. In particular, labor is in great demand because the only way to produce beyond full employment is if workers are working overtime.

As time passes and input prices are free to change, the high demand will start to raise input prices. In particular, overworked employees will demand and receive raises as employers scramble to deal with the labor shortages that arise when the economy is producing at above its full-employment output level. As input prices increase, firm profits will begin to fall. And as they decline, so does the motive firms have to produce more than the full-employment output level. This process of rising input prices and falling profits continues until the rise in input prices exactly matches the initial change in output prices (in our example, they both double). When that happens, firm profits in real terms return to their original level so that firms are once again motivated to produce at exactly the full-employment output level. This adjustment process means that in the long run the economy will produce at full employment regardless of the price level (in our example, at either $P = 100$ or $P = 200$). That is why the long-run aggregate supply curve AS_{LR} is vertical above the full-employment output level. Every possible price level on the vertical axis is associated with the economy producing at the full-employment output level in the long run once input prices adjust to exactly match changes in output prices.

Focusing on the Short Run

The immediate-short-run aggregate supply curve, the short-run aggregate supply curve, and the long-run aggregate supply curve are all important. Each curve is appropriate to situations that match their respective assumptions about the flexibility of input and output prices. In the remainder of the book, we will have several different opportunities to refer to each curve. But our focus in the rest of this chapter and the several chapters that immediately follow will be on short-run aggregate supply curves, such as the AS curve shown in Figure 12.4. Indeed, unless explicitly stated otherwise, all references to "aggregate supply" are to the AS curve and to aggregate supply in the short run.

Our emphasis on the short-run aggregate supply curve AS stems from out interest in understanding the business cycle in the simplest possible way. It is a fact that real-world economies typically manifest simultaneous changes in both their price levels and their levels of real output. The upsloping short-run AS curve is the only version of aggregate supply that can handle simultaneous movements in both of these variables. By contrast, the price level is assumed fixed in the immediate-short-run version of aggregate supply illustrated in Figure 12.3 and the economy's output is always equal to the full-employment output level in the long-run version of aggregate supply shown in Figure 12.5. This renders these versions of the aggregate supply curve less useful as part of a core model for analyzing business cycles and demonstrating the short-run government policies designed to deal with them. In our current discussion, we will reserve use of the immediate short run and long run for specific, clearly identified situations. Later in the book we will explore how the short-run and long-run AS curves are linked, and how that linkage adds several additional insights about business cycles and policy.

Changes in Aggregate Supply

An existing aggregate supply curve identifies the relationship between the price level and real output, other things equal. But when one or more of these other things change, the curve itself shifts. The rightward shift of the curve from AS_1 to AS_2 in Figure 12.6 represents an increase in aggregate supply, indicating that firms are willing to produce and sell more real output at each price level. The leftward shift of the curve from AS_1 to AS_3 represents a decrease in aggregate supply. At each price level, firms produce less output than before.

Figure 12.6 lists the other things that cause a shift of the aggregate supply curve. Called the **determinants of aggregate supply** or *aggregate supply shifters*, they collectively position the aggregate supply curve and shift the curve when they change. Changes in these determinants raise or lower per-unit production costs *at each price level (or each level of output)*. These changes in per-unit production cost affect profits, thereby leading firms to alter the amount of output they are willing to produce *at each price level*. For example, firms may collectively offer $9 trillion of real output at a price level of 1.0 (100 in index value), rather than $8.8 trillion. Or they may offer $7.5 trillion rather than $8 trillion. The point is that when one of the determinants listed in Figure 12.6 changes, the aggregate supply curve shifts to the right or left. Changes that reduce per-unit production costs shift the aggregate supply curve to the right, as from AS_1 to AS_2; changes that increase per-unit production costs shift it

FIGURE 12.6 Changes in aggregate supply. A change in one or more of the listed determinants of aggregate supply will shift the aggregate supply curve. The rightward shift of the aggregate supply curve from AS₁ to AS₂ represents an increase in aggregate supply; the leftward shift of the curve from AS₁ to AS₃ shows a decrease in aggregate supply.

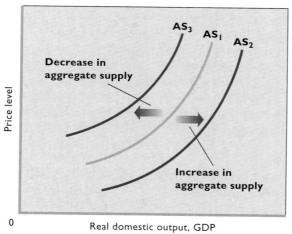

Determinants of Aggregate Supply: Factors That Shift the Aggregate Supply Curve

1. Change in input prices
   a. Domestic resource prices
   b. Prices of imported resources
2. Change in productivity
3. Change in legal-institutional environment
   a. Business taxes and subsidies
   b. Government regulations

to the left, as from AS₁ to AS₃. When per-unit production costs change for reasons other than changes in real output, the aggregate supply curve shifts.

The three aggregate supply determinants listed in Figure 12.6 require more discussion.

Input Prices

Input or resource prices—to be distinguished from the output prices that make up the price level—are a major ingredient of per-unit production costs and therefore a key determinant of aggregate supply. These resources can either be domestic or imported.

Domestic Resource Prices As stated earlier, wages and salaries make up about 75 percent of all business costs. Other things equal, decreases in wages reduce per-unit production costs. So when wages fall, the aggregate supply curve shifts to the right. Increases in wages shift the curve to the left. Examples:

- Labor supply increases because of substantial immigration. Wages and per-unit production costs fall, shifting the AS curve to the right.
- Labor supply decreases because a rapid increase in pension income causes many older workers to opt for early retirement. Wage rates and per-unit production costs rise, shifting the AS curve to the left.

Similarly, the aggregate supply curve shifts when the prices of land and capital inputs change. Examples:

- The price of machinery and equipment falls because of declines in the prices of steel and electronic

components. Per-unit production costs decline, and the AS curve shifts to the right.
- The supply of available land resources expands through discoveries of mineral deposits, irrigation of land, or technical innovations that transform "nonresources" (say, vast desert lands) into valuable resources (productive lands). The price of land declines, per-unit production costs fall, and the AS curve shifts to the right.

Prices of Imported Resources Just as foreign demand for U.S. goods contributes to U.S. aggregate demand, resources imported from abroad (such as oil, tin, and copper) add to U.S. aggregate supply. Added supplies of resources—whether domestic or imported—typically reduce per-unit production costs. A decrease in the price of imported resources increases U.S. aggregate supply, while an increase in their price reduces U.S. aggregate supply.

A good example of the major effect that changing resource prices can have on aggregate supply is the oil price hikes of the 1970s. At that time, a group of oil-producing nations called the Organization of Petroleum Exporting Countries (OPEC) worked in concert to decrease oil production in order to raise the price of oil. The 10-fold increase in the price of oil that OPEC achieved during the 1970s drove per-unit production costs up and jolted the U.S. aggregate supply curve leftward. By contrast, a sharp decline in oil prices in the mid-1980s resulted in a rightward shift of the U.S. aggregate supply curve. In 1999 OPEC again reasserted itself, raising oil prices and therefore per-unit production costs for some U.S. producers including airlines and shipping companies like FedEx and UPS. In 2007 the price of oil shot upward, but this increase was attributed to greater demand rather than to decreases in supply caused by OPEC. But keep in mind that no matter what their cause, increases in the price of oil and other resources raise production costs and decrease aggregate supply.

Exchange-rate fluctuations are another factor that may alter the price of imported resources. Suppose that the dollar appreciates, enabling U.S. firms to obtain more foreign currency with each dollar. This means that domestic producers face a lower *dollar* price of imported resources. U.S. firms will respond by increasing their imports of foreign resources, thereby lowering their per-unit production costs at each level of output. Falling per-unit production costs will shift the U.S. aggregate supply curve to the right.

A depreciation of the dollar will have the opposite set of effects and will shift the aggregate supply curve to the left.

Productivity

The second major determinant of aggregate supply is **productivity,** which is a measure of the relationship between a nation's level of real output and the amount of resources used to produce that output. Productivity is a measure of average real output, or of real output per unit of input:

$$\text{Productivity} = \frac{\text{total output}}{\text{total inputs}}$$

An increase in productivity enables the economy to obtain more real output from its limited resources. An increase in productivity affects aggregate supply by reducing the per-unit cost of output (per-unit production cost). Suppose, for example, that real output is 10 units, that 5 units of input are needed to produce that quantity, and that the price of each input unit is $2. Then

$$\text{Productivity} = \frac{\text{total output}}{\text{total inputs}} = \frac{10}{5} = 2$$

and

$$\text{Per-unit production cost} = \frac{\text{total input cost}}{\text{total output}}$$
$$= \frac{\$2 \times 5}{10} = \$1$$

Note that we obtain the total input cost by multiplying the unit input cost by the number of inputs used.

Now suppose productivity increases so that real output doubles to 20 units, while the price and quantity of the input remain constant at $2 and 5 units. Using the above equations, we see that productivity rises from 2 to 4 and

WORKED PROBLEMS

W 12.1

Productivity and costs

that the per-unit production cost of the output falls from $1 to $.50. The doubled productivity has reduced the per-unit production cost by half.

By reducing the per-unit production cost, an increase in productivity shifts the aggregate supply curve to the right. The main source of productivity advance is improved production technology, often embodied within new plant and equipment that replaces old plant and equipment. Other sources of productivity increases are a better-educated and better-trained workforce, improved forms of business enterprises, and the reallocation of labor resources from lower-productivity to higher-productivity uses.

Much rarer, decreases in productivity increase per-unit production costs and therefore reduce aggregate supply (shift the curve to the left).

Legal-Institutional Environment

Changes in the legal-institutional setting in which businesses operate are the final determinant of aggregate supply. Such changes may alter the per-unit costs of output and, if so, shift the aggregate supply curve. Two changes of this type are (1) changes in taxes and subsidies and (2) changes in the extent of regulation.

Business Taxes and Subsidies Higher business taxes, such as sales, excise, and payroll taxes, increase per-unit costs and reduce short-run aggregate supply in much the same way as a wage increase does. An increase in such taxes paid by businesses will increase per-unit production costs and shift aggregate supply to the left.

Similarly, a business subsidy—a payment or tax break by government to producers—lowers production costs and increases short-run aggregate supply. For example, the Federal government subsidizes firms that blend ethanol (derived from corn) with gasoline to increase the U.S. gasoline supply. This reduces the per-unit production cost of making blended gasoline. To the extent that this and other subsidies are successful, the aggregate supply curve shifts rightward.

Government Regulation It is usually costly for businesses to comply with government regulations. More regulation therefore tends to increase per-unit production costs and shift the aggregate supply curve to the left. "Supply-side" proponents of deregulation of the economy have argued forcefully that, by increasing efficiency and reducing the paperwork associated with complex regulations, deregulation will reduce per-unit costs and shift the aggregate supply curve to the right. Other economists are less certain. Deregulation that results in accounting manipulations, monopolization, and business failures is likely to shift the AS curve to the left rather than to the right.

QUICK REVIEW 12.2

- The immediate-short-run aggregate supply curve is horizontal; given fixed input and output prices, producers will supply whatever quantity of real output is demanded at the current price level.
- The short-run aggregate supply curve (or simply the "aggregate supply curve") is upsloping; given fixed resource prices, higher output prices raise firm profits and encourage them to increase their output levels.
- The long-run aggregate supply curve is vertical; given sufficient time, wages and other input prices rise or fall to match any change in the price level (that is, any change in the level of *output* prices).
- By altering per-unit production costs independent of changes in the level of output, changes in one or more of the determinants of aggregate supply (Figure 12.6) shift the aggregate supply curve.
- An increase in short-run aggregate supply is shown as a rightward shift of the aggregate supply curve; a decrease is shown as a leftward shift of the curve.

Equilibrium and Changes in Equilibrium

Of all the possible combinations of price levels and levels of real GDP, which combination will the economy gravitate toward, at least in the short run? **Figure 12.7 (Key Graph)** and its accompanying table provide the answer. Equilibrium occurs at the price level that equalizes the amounts of real output demanded and supplied. The intersection of the aggregate demand curve AD and the aggregate supply curve AS establishes the economy's **equilibrium price level** and **equilibrium real output**. So aggregate demand and aggregate supply *jointly* establish the price level and level of real GDP.

In Figure 12.7 the equilibrium price level and level of real output are 100 and $510 billion, respectively. To illustrate why, suppose the price level is 92 rather than 100. We see from the table that the lower price level will encourage businesses to produce real output of $502 billion. This is shown by point *a* on the AS curve in the graph. But, as revealed by the table and point *b* on the aggregate demand curve, buyers will want to purchase $514 billion of real output at price level 92. Competition among buyers

to purchase the lesser available real output of $502 billion will eliminate the $12 billion (= $514 billion − $502 billion) shortage and pull up the price level to 100.

As the table and graph show, the rise in the price level from 92 to 100 encourages producers to increase their real output from $502 billion to $510 billion and causes buyers to scale back their purchases from $514 billion to $510 billion. When equality occurs between the amounts of real output produced and purchased, as it does at price level 100, the economy has achieved equilibrium (here, at $510 billion of real GDP).

INTERACTIVE GRAPHS
G 12.1
Aggregate demand–aggregate supply

A final note: Although the equilibrium price level happens to be 100 in our example, nothing special is implied by that. Any price level can be an equilibrium price level.

Increases in AD: Demand-Pull Inflation

Now let's apply the AD-AS model to various situations that can confront the economy. For simplicity we will use P and Q symbols, rather than actual numbers. Remember that these symbols represent, respectively, price index values and amounts of real GDP.

Suppose the economy is operating at its full-employment output and businesses and government decide to increase their spending—actions that shift the aggregate demand curve to the right. Our list of determinants of aggregate demand (Figure 12.2) provides several reasons why this shift might occur. Perhaps firms boost their investment spending because they anticipate higher future profits from investments in new capital. Those profits are predicated on having new equipment and facilities that incorporate a number of new technologies. And perhaps government increases spending to expand national defense.

As shown by the rise in the price level from P_1 to P_2 in Figure 12.8, the increase in aggregate demand beyond the full-employment level of output causes inflation. This is *demand-pull inflation* because the price level is being pulled up by the increase in aggregate demand. Also, observe that the increase in demand expands real output from the full-employment level Q_f to Q_1. The distance between Q_1 and Q_f is a positive, or "inflationary," GDP gap. Actual GDP exceeds potential GDP.

The classic American example of demand-pull inflation occurred in the late 1960s. The escalation of the war in Vietnam resulted in a 40 percent increase in defense spending between 1965 and 1967 and another 15 percent increase in 1968. The rise in government spending, imposed on an already growing economy, shifted the

key graph

FIGURE 12.7 The equilibrium price level and equilibrium real GDP. The intersection of the aggregate demand curve and the aggregate supply curve determines the economy's equilibrium price level. At the equilibrium price level of 100 (in index-value terms), the $510 billion of real output demanded matches the $510 billion of real output supplied. So the equilibrium GDP is $510 billion.

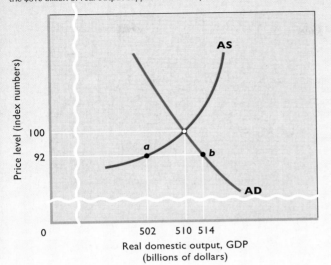

Real Output Demanded (Billions)	Price Level (Index Number)	Real Output Supplied (Billions)
$506	108	$513
508	104	512
510	**100**	**510**
512	96	507
514	92	502

QUICK QUIZ FOR FIGURE 12.7

1. The AD curve slopes downward because:
   a. per-unit production costs fall as real GDP increases.
   b. the income and substitution effects are at work.
   c. changes in the determinants of AD alter the amounts of real GDP demanded at each price level.
   d. decreases in the price level give rise to real-balances effects, interest-rate effects, and foreign purchases effects that increase the amount of real GDP demanded.

2. The AS curve slopes upward because:
   a. per-unit production costs rise as real GDP expands toward and beyond its full-employment level.
   b. the income and substitution effects are at work.
   c. changes in the determinants of AS alter the amounts of real GDP supplied at each price level.
   d. increases in the price level give rise to real-balances effects, interest-rate effects, and foreign purchases effects that increase the amounts of real GDP supplied.

3. At price level 92:
   a. a GDP surplus of $12 billion occurs that drives the price level up to 100.
   b. a GDP shortage of $12 billion occurs that drives the price level up to 100.
   c. the aggregate amount of real GDP demanded is less than the aggregate amount of GDP supplied.
   d. the economy is operating beyond its capacity to produce.

4. Suppose real output demanded rises by $4 billion at each price level. The new equilibrium price level will be:
   a. 108.
   b. 104.
   c. 96.
   d. 92.

Answers: 1. d; 2. a; 3. b; 4. b

economy's aggregate demand curve to the right, producing the worst inflation in two decades. Actual GDP exceeded potential GDP, thereby creating an inflationary GDP gap. Inflation jumped from 1.6 percent in 1965 to 5.7 percent by 1970.

A careful examination of Figure 12.8 reveals an interesting point concerning the multiplier effect. The increase in aggregate demand from AD₁ to AD₂ increases real output only to Q_1, not to Q_2, because part of the increase in aggregate demand is absorbed as inflation as the price level rises from P_1 to P_2. Had the price level remained at P_1, the shift of aggregate demand from AD₁ to AD₂ would have increased real output to Q_2. The full-strength multiplier effect of Chapters 10 and 11 would have occurred. But in Figure 12.8 inflation reduced the increase in real output—and thus the multiplier effect—by about one-half. For any initial increase in aggregate demand, the resulting increase in real output will be smaller the greater

245

FIGURE 12.8 An increase in aggregate demand that causes demand-pull inflation. The increase of aggregate demand from AD_1 to AD_2 causes demand-pull inflation, shown as the rise in the price level from P_1 to P_2. It also causes an inflationary GDP gap of Q_1 minus Q_f. The rise of the price level reduces the size of the multiplier effect. If the price level had remained at P_1, the increase in aggregate demand from AD_1 to AD_2 would increase output from Q_f to Q_2 and the multiplier would have been at full strength. But because of the increase in the price level, real output increases only from Q_f to Q_1 and the multiplier effect is reduced.

FIGURE 12.9 A decrease in aggregate demand that causes a recession. If the price level is downwardly inflexible at P_1, a decline of aggregate demand from AD_1 to AD_2 will move the economy leftward from a to b along the horizontal broken-line segment and reduce real GDP from Q_f to Q_1. Idle production capacity, cyclical unemployment, and a recessionary GDP gap (of Q_1 minus Q_f) will result. If the price level were flexible downward, the decline in aggregate demand would move the economy depicted from a to c instead of from a to b.

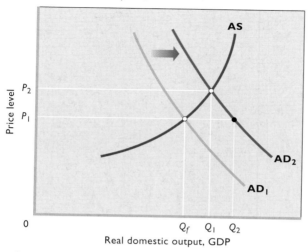

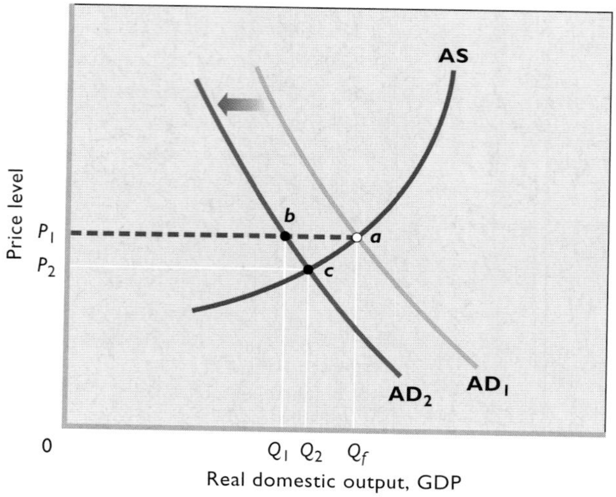

is the increase in the price level. Price-level flexibility weakens the realized multiplier effect.

Decreases in AD: Recession and Cyclical Unemployment

Decreases in aggregate demand describe the opposite end of the business cycle: recession and cyclical unemployment (rather than above-full employment and demand-pull inflation). For example, in 2008 investment spending in the United States greatly declined because of sharply lower expected returns on investment. These lower expectations resulted from the prospects of poor future business conditions and high degrees of current unused production capacity. In Figure 12.9 we show the resulting decline in aggregate demand as a leftward shift from AD_1 to AD_2.

But we now add an important twist to the analysis: *Deflation*—a decline in the price level—is not the norm in the American economy. We discussed "sticky prices" in Chapter 6 and previously explained how fixed prices lead to horizontal immediate-short-run aggregate supply curves. For reasons we will examine soon, many important prices in the U.S. economy are downwardly inflexible such that the price level is sticky downward even when aggregate demand substantially declines. Consider Figure 12.9, where the aggregate demand declines from AD_1 to AD_2. If

the price level is stuck at P_1, the economy moves from a to b along the broken horizontal line rather than from a to c along the short-run aggregate supply curve AS. The outcome is a decline of real output from Q_f to Q_1, with *no* change in the price level. In this case, it is as if the aggregate supply curve in Figure 12.9 is horizontal at P_1, to the left of Q_f, as indicated by the dashed line. This decline of real output from Q_f to Q_1 constitutes a *recession*, and since fewer workers are needed to produce the lower output, *cyclical unemployment* arises. The distance between Q_1 and Q_f is a negative, or "recessionary," GDP gap—the amount by which actual output falls short of potential output.

Close inspection of Figure 12.9 also reveals that without a fall in the price level, the multiplier is at full strength. With the price level stuck at P_1, real GDP decreases by $Q_f - Q_1$, which matches the full leftward shift of the AD curve. The multiplier of Chapters 10 and 11 is at full strength when changes in aggregate demand occur along what, in effect, is a horizontal segment of the AS curve. This full-strength multiplier would also exist for an increase in aggregate demand from AD_2 to AD_1 along this broken line, since none of the increase in output would be dissipated as inflation. We will say more about that in Chapter 13.

All recent recessions in the United States have generally mimicked the "GDP gap but no deflation" scenario

CONSIDER THIS . . .

Ratchet Effect

A *ratchet analogy* is a good way to think about the effects of changes in aggregate demand on the price level. A ratchet is a tool or mechanism such as a winch, car jack, or socket wrench that cranks a wheel forward but does not allow it to go backward. Properly set, each allows the operator to move an object (boat, car, or nut) in one direction while preventing it from moving in the opposite direction.

Product prices, wage rates, and per-unit production costs are highly flexible upward when aggregate demand increases along the aggregate supply curve. In the United States, the price level has increased in 57 of the 59 years since 1950.

But when aggregate demand decreases, product prices, wage rates, and per-unit production costs are inflexible downward. The U.S. price level has declined in only two years (1955 and 2009) since 1950, even though aggregate demand and real output have declined in a number of years.

In terms of our analogy, increases in aggregate demand ratchet the U.S. price level upward. Once in place, the higher price level remains until it is ratcheted up again. The higher price level tends to remain even with declines in aggregate demand.

shown in Figure 12.9. Consider the recession of 2007–2009, which resulted from chaos in the financial markets that quickly led to significant declines in spending by businesses and households. Because of the resulting decline in aggregate demand, real GDP fell short of potential real GDP by roughly $300 billion in 2008 and $1 trillion in 2009. The nation's unemployment rate rose from 4.7 percent in December 2007 to 10.1 percent in October 2009. The price level fell in some months and the rate of inflation declined—meaning that *disinflation* occurred. Considering the full period, however, *deflation* did not occur.

Real output takes the brunt of declines in aggregate demand in the U.S. economy because the price level tends to be downwardly rigid in the immediate short run. There are several reasons for this downward price stickiness.

- ***Fear of price wars*** Some large firms may be concerned that if they reduce their prices, rivals not only will match their price cuts but may retaliate by

making even deeper cuts. An initial price cut may touch off an unwanted *price war:* successively deeper and deeper rounds of price cuts. In such a situation, each firm eventually ends up with far less profit or higher losses than would be the case if each had simply maintained its prices. For this reason, each firm may resist making the initial price cut, choosing instead to reduce production and lay off workers.

- ***Menu costs*** Firms that think a recession will be relatively short-lived may be reluctant to cut their prices. One reason is what economists metaphorically call **menu costs,** named after their most obvious example: the cost of printing new menus when a restaurant decides to reduce its prices. But lowering prices also creates other costs. Additional costs derive from (1) estimating the magnitude and duration of the shift in demand to determine whether prices should be lowered, (2) repricing items held in inventory, (3) printing and mailing new catalogs, and (4) communicating new prices to customers, perhaps through advertising. When menu costs are present, firms may choose to avoid them by retaining current prices. That is, they may wait to see if the decline in aggregate demand is permanent.

- ***Wage contracts*** Firms rarely profit from cutting their product prices if they cannot also cut their wage rates. Wages are usually inflexible downward because large parts of the labor force work under contracts prohibiting wage cuts for the duration of the contract. (Collective bargaining agreements in major industries frequently run for 3 years.) Similarly, the wages and salaries of nonunion workers are usually adjusted once a year, rather than quarterly or monthly.

- ***Morale, effort, and productivity*** Wage inflexibility downward is reinforced by the reluctance of many employers to reduce wage rates. Some current wages may be so-called **efficiency wages**—wages that elicit maximum work effort and thus minimize labor costs per unit of output. If worker productivity (output per hour of work) remains constant, lower wages *do* reduce labor costs per unit of output. But lower wages might impair worker morale and work effort, thereby reducing productivity. Considered alone, lower productivity raises labor costs per unit of output because less output is produced. If the higher labor costs resulting from reduced productivity exceed the cost savings from the lower wage, then wage cuts will increase rather than reduce labor costs per unit of

ORIGIN OF THE IDEA

O 12.2

Efficiency wage

output. In such situations, firms will resist lowering wages when they are faced with a decline in aggregate demand.

- *Minimum wage* The minimum wage imposes a legal floor under the wages of the least-skilled workers. Firms paying those wages cannot reduce that wage rate when aggregate demand declines.

Decreases in AS: Cost-Push Inflation

Suppose that a major terrorist attack on oil facilities severely disrupts world oil supplies and drives up oil prices by, say, 300 percent. Higher energy prices would spread through the economy, driving up production and distribution costs on a wide variety of goods. The U.S. aggregate supply curve would shift to the left, say, from AS_1 to AS_2 in Figure 12.10. The resulting increase in the price level would be *cost-push inflation*.

The effects of a leftward shift in aggregate supply are doubly bad. When aggregate supply shifts from AS_1 to AS_2, the economy moves from a to b. The price level rises from P_1 to P_2 and real output declines from Q_f to Q_1. Along with the cost-push inflation, a recession (and negative GDP gap) occurs. That is exactly what happened in the United States in the mid-1970s when the price of oil rocketed upward. Then, oil expenditures were about 10 percent of U.S. GDP, compared to only 3 percent today. So, as indicated in this chapter's Last Word, the U.S. economy is now less vulnerable to cost-push inflation arising from such "aggregate supply shocks." That said, it is not *immune* from such shocks.

Increases in AS: Full Employment with Price-Level Stability

Between 1996 and 2000, the United States experienced a combination of full employment, strong economic growth, and very low inflation. Specifically, the unemployment rate fell to 4 percent and real GDP grew nearly 4 percent annually, *without igniting inflation*. At first thought, this "macroeconomic bliss" seems to be incompatible with the AD-AS model. The aggregate supply curve suggests that increases in aggregate demand that are sufficient for over-full employment will raise the price level (see Figure 12.8). Higher inflation, so it would seem, is the inevitable price paid for expanding output beyond the full-employment level.

But inflation remained very mild in the late 1990s. Figure 12.11 helps explain why. Let's first suppose that aggregate demand increased from AD_1 to AD_2 along aggregate supply curve AS_1. Taken alone, that increase in aggregate demand would move the economy from a to b. Real output would rise from full-employment output Q_1 to beyond-full-employment output Q_2. The economy would experience inflation, as shown by the increase in the price level from P_1 to P_3. Such inflation had occurred at the end of previous vigorous expansions of aggregate demand, including the expansion of the late 1980s.

FIGURE 12.10 A decrease in aggregate supply that causes cost-push inflation. A leftward shift of aggregate supply from AS_1 to AS_2 raises the price level from P_1 to P_2 and produces cost-push inflation. Real output declines and a recessionary GDP gap (of Q_1 minus Q_f) occurs.

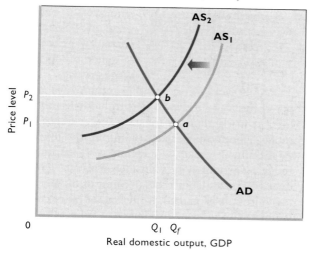

FIGURE 12.11 Growth, full employment, and relative price stability. Normally, an increase in aggregate demand from AD_1 to AD_2 would move the economy from a to b along AS_1. Real output would expand to Q_2, and inflation would result (P_1 to P_3). But in the late 1990s, significant increases in productivity shifted the aggregate supply curve, as from AS_1 to AS_2. The economy moved from a to c rather than from a to b. It experienced strong economic growth (Q_1 to Q_3), full employment, and only very mild inflation (P_1 to P_2) before receding in March 2001.

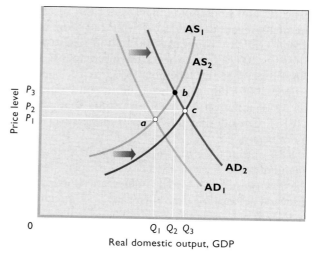

LAST

Word Has the Impact of Oil Prices Diminished?

Significant Changes in Oil Prices Historically Have Greatly Affected the U.S. Economy. Have the Effects of Such Changes Weakened?

The United States has experienced several aggregate supply shocks—abrupt changes in aggregate supply—caused by significant changes in oil prices. In the mid-1970s the nominal price of oil rose from $4 to $12 per barrel, and then again in the late 1970s it increased to $24 per barrel and eventually to $35. These oil prices reduced aggregate supply, causing rapid cost-push inflation. Accompanying the inflation was rising unemployment and a large, negative GDP gap.

In the late 1980s and through most of the 1990s, oil prices fell, sinking to a low of $11 per barrel in late 1998. This decline created a positive aggregate supply shock beneficial to the U.S. economy. In 2001 and 2002 the price of oil settled in at about $25 to $28 per barrel.

Then came a "perfect storm"—continuing conflict in Iraq, the rising demand for oil in India and China, an increase in economic growth in several industrial nations, disruption of oil production by hurricanes, and concern about political developments in Venezuela. The price of oil jumped upward to over $60 a barrel in 2005.

Many economists feared that energy prices would increase so much that the U.S. aggregate supply curve would shift to the left, causing severe cost-push inflation. But inflation in the United States remained modest. The U.S. inflation rate rose in 2005, but core inflation (the inflation rate after subtracting changes in the prices of food and energy) remained steady.

The price of oil surged upward again in 2007 and during the first half of 2008. In January 2007 it was slightly over $50 a barrel; in July 2008 it had reached $140 a barrel. Surely, such a huge increase of oil prices would be inflationary. But inflation did not occur. When world economies slowed in 2007 and receded in 2008, the price of oil sank rapidly. In March 2009, it was back to $40 a barrel.

Have rising oil prices completely lost their inflationary punch? There are two reasons to think so. First, oil prices clearly are a less significant factor in the U.S. economy than they were in the 1970s. Prior to 1980, changes in oil prices greatly affected core inflation in the United States. But since 1980 they have had very little effect on core inflation.* The main reason has been a significant decline in the amount of oil and gas used in producing each dollar of U.S. output. In 2005 producing a dollar of real GDP required about 7000 BTUs of oil and gas, compared to 14,000 BTUs in 1970. (A BTU, or British thermal unit, is the amount of energy required to heat one pound of water by one degree Fahrenheit.)

Part of this decline resulted from new production techniques spawned by the higher oil and energy prices. But equally important has been the changing relative composition of GDP, away from larger, heavier items (such as earth-moving equipment) that are energy intensive to make and transport and toward smaller, lighter items (such as microchips and software). Experts on energy economics estimate that the U.S. economy is about 33 percent less sensitive to oil price fluctuations than it was in the early 1980s and 50 percent less sensitive than in the mid-1970s.†

A second reason why increases in oil prices seem to have lost their inflationary impact is that the Federal Reserve has become more vigilant and adept at maintaining overall price stability through monetary policy. (We will discuss monetary policy in depth in Chapter 16.) The Fed simply has not let increases in oil prices become generalized as core inflation.

(You can find the current daily price of oil at OPEC's Web site, **www.opec.org**.)

---

*Mark A. Hooker, "Are Oil Shocks Inflationary? Asymmetric and Nonlinear Specifications versus Changes in Regimes," *Journal of Money, Credit and Banking*, May 2002, pp. 540–561.

†Stephen P. A. Brown and Mine K. Yücel, "Oil Prices and the Economy," Federal Reserve Bank of Dallas *Southwest Economy*, July–August 2000, pp. 1–6.

Between 1990 and 2000, however, larger-than-usual increases in productivity occurred because of a burst of new technology relating to computers, the Internet, inventory management systems, electronic commerce, and so on. We represent this higher-than-usual productivity growth as the rightward shift from AS_1 to AS_2 in Figure 12.11. The relevant aggregate demand and aggregate supply curves thus became AD_2 and AS_2, not AD_2 and AS_1. Instead of moving from a to b, the economy moved from a to c. Real output increased from Q_1 to Q_3, and the price level rose only modestly (from P_1 to P_2). The shift of the aggregate supply curve from AS_1 to AS_2 accommodated the rapid increase in aggregate demand and kept inflation mild. This remarkable combination of rapid productivity growth, rapid real GDP growth, full employment, and relative price-level stability led some observers to proclaim that the United States was experiencing a "new era" or a New Economy.

But in 2001 the New Economy came face-to-face with the old economic principles. Aggregate demand declined because of a substantial fall in investment spending, and in March 2001 the economy experienced a recession. The terrorist attacks of September 11, 2001, further dampened private spending and prolonged the recession throughout 2001. The unemployment rate rose from 4.2 percent in January 2001 to 6 percent in December 2002.

The economy rebounded between 2002 and 2007, eventually reachieving its earlier strong economic growth, low inflation, and low unemployment. Some economists began to refer to the period after 1982 as "The Great Moderation" because recessions were father apart and relatively mild. They drew the implication that businesses and government had smoothed out the business cycle. Wrong! The severity of the recession of 2007–2009 was a huge surprise.

QUICK REVIEW 12.3

- The equilibrium price level and amount of real output are determined at the intersection of the aggregate demand curve and the aggregate supply curve.
- Increases in aggregate demand beyond the full-employment level of real GDP cause demand-pull inflation.
- Decreases in aggregate demand cause recessions and cyclical unemployment, partly because the price level and wages tend to be inflexible in a downward direction.
- Decreases in aggregate supply cause cost-push inflation.
- Full employment, high economic growth, and price stability are compatible with one another if productivity-driven increases in aggregate supply are sufficient to balance growing aggregate demand.

Summary

1. The aggregate demand–aggregate supply model (AD-AS model) is a flexible-price model that enables analysis of simultaneous changes of real GDP and the price level.

2. The aggregate demand curve shows the level of real output that the economy demands at each price level.

3. The aggregate demand curve is downsloping because of the real-balances effect, the interest-rate effect, and the foreign purchases effect. The real-balances effect indicates that inflation reduces the real value or purchasing power of fixed-value financial assets held by households, causing cutbacks in consumer spending. The interest-rate effect means that, with a specific supply of money, a higher price level increases the demand for money, thereby raising the interest rate and reducing investment purchases. The foreign purchases effect suggests that an increase in one country's price level relative to the price levels in other countries reduces the net export component of that nation's aggregate demand.

4. The determinants of aggregate demand consist of spending by domestic consumers, by businesses, by government, and by foreign buyers. Changes in the factors listed in Figure 12.2 alter the spending by these groups and shift the aggregate demand curve. The extent of the shift is determined by the size of the initial change in spending and the strength of the economy's multiplier.

5. The aggregate supply curve shows the levels of real output that businesses will produce at various possible price levels. The slope of the aggregate supply curve depends upon the flexibility of input and output prices. Since these vary over time, aggregate supply curves are categorized into three time horizons, each having different underlying assumptions about the flexibility of input and output prices.

6. The *immediate-short-run aggregate supply curve* assumes that both input prices and output prices are fixed. With output prices fixed, the aggregate supply curve is a horizontal line at the current price level. The *short-run aggregate supply curve* assumes nominal wages and other input prices remain fixed while output prices vary. The aggregate supply curve is generally upsloping because per-unit production costs, and hence the prices that firms must receive, rise as real output expands. The aggregate supply curve is relatively steep to

the right of the full-employment output level and relatively flat to the left of it. The *long-run aggregate supply curve* assumes that nominal wages and other input prices fully match any change in the price level. The curve is vertical at the full-employment output level.

7. Because the short-run aggregate supply curve is the only version of aggregate supply that can handle simultaneous changes in the price level and real output, it serves well as the core aggregate supply curve for analyzing the business cycle and economic policy. Unless stated otherwise, all references to "aggregate supply" refer to short-run aggregate supply and the short-run aggregate supply curve.

8. Figure 12.6 lists the determinants of aggregate supply: input prices, productivity, and the legal-institutional environment. A change in any one of these factors will change per-unit production costs at each level of output and therefore will shift the aggregate supply curve.

9. The intersection of the aggregate demand and aggregate supply curves determines an economy's equilibrium price level and real GDP. At the intersection, the quantity of real GDP demanded equals the quantity of real GDP supplied.

10. Increases in aggregate demand to the right of the full-employment output cause inflation and positive GDP gaps (actual GDP exceeds potential GDP). An upsloping aggregate supply curve weakens the multiplier effect of an increase in aggregate demand because a portion of the increase in aggregate demand is dissipated in inflation.

11. Shifts of the aggregate demand curve to the left of the full-employment output cause recession, negative GDP gaps, and cyclical unemployment. The price level may not fall during recessions because of downwardly inflexible prices and wages. This inflexibility results from fear of price wars, menu costs, wage contracts, efficiency wages, and minimum wages. When the price level is fixed, changes in aggregate demand produce full-strength multiplier effects.

12. Leftward shifts of the aggregate supply curve reflect increases in per-unit production costs and cause cost-push inflation, with accompanying negative GDP gaps.

13. Rightward shifts of the aggregate supply curve, caused by large improvements in productivity, help explain the simultaneous achievement of full employment, economic growth, and price stability that occurred in the United States between 1996 and 2000. The recession of 2001, however, ended the expansionary phase of the business cycle. Expansion resumed in the 2002–2007 period, before giving way to the severe recession of 2007–2009.

Terms and Concepts

aggregate demand–aggregate supply (AD-AS) model

aggregate demand

real-balances effect

interest-rate effect

foreign purchases effect

determinants of aggregate demand

aggregate supply

immediate-short-run aggregate supply curve

short-run aggregate supply curve

long-run aggregate supply curve

determinants of aggregate supply

productivity

equilibrium price level

equilibrium real output

menu costs

efficiency wages

Questions

1. Why is the aggregate demand curve downsloping? Specify how your explanation differs from the explanation for the downsloping demand curve for a single product. What role does the multiplier play in shifts of the aggregate demand curve? **LO1**

2. Distinguish between "real-balances effect" and "wealth effect," as the terms are used in this chapter. How does each relate to the aggregate demand curve? **LO1**

3. What assumptions cause the immediate-short-run aggregate supply curve to be horizontal? Why is the long-run aggregate supply curve vertical? Explain the shape of the short-run aggregate supply curve. Why is the short-run curve relatively flat to the left of the full-employment output and relatively steep to the right? **LO2**

4. What effects would each of the following have on aggregate demand or aggregate supply, other things equal? In each case, use a diagram to show the expected effects on the equilibrium price level and the level of real output, assuming that the price level is flexible both upward and downward. **LO3**
   a. A widespread fear by consumers of an impending economic depression.
   b. A new national tax on producers based on the value added between the costs of the inputs and the revenue received from their output.
   c. A reduction in interest rates at each price level.
   d. A major increase in spending for health care by the Federal government.
   e. The general expectation of coming rapid inflation.

f. The complete disintegration of OPEC, causing oil prices to fall by one-half.

g. A 10 percent across-the-board reduction in personal income tax rates.

h. A sizable increase in labor productivity (with no change in nominal wages).

i. A 12 percent increase in nominal wages (with no change in productivity).

j. An increase in exports that exceeds an increase in imports (not due to tariffs).

5. Assume that (*a*) the price level is flexible upward but not downward and (*b*) the economy is currently operating at its full-employment output. Other things equal, how will each of the following affect the equilibrium price level and equilibrium level of real output in the short run? **LO3**

a. An increase in aggregate demand.

b. A decrease in aggregate supply, with no change in aggregate demand.

c. Equal increases in aggregate demand and aggregate supply.

d. A decrease in aggregate demand.

e. An increase in aggregate demand that exceeds an increase in aggregate supply.

6. Explain how an upsloping aggregate supply curve weakens the realized multiplier effect from an initial change in investment spending. **LO3**

7. Why does a reduction in aggregate demand in the actual economy reduce real output, rather than the price level?

Why might a full-strength multiplier apply to a decrease in aggregate demand? **LO3**

8. Explain: "Unemployment can be caused by a decrease of aggregate demand or a decrease of aggregate supply." In each case, specify the price-level outcomes. **LO4**

9. Use shifts of the AD and AS curves to explain (*a*) the U.S. experience of strong economic growth, full employment, and price stability in the late 1990s and early 2000s and (*b*) how a strong negative wealth effect from, say, a precipitous drop in house prices could cause a recession even though productivity is surging. **LO4**

10. In early 2001 investment spending sharply declined in the United States. In the two months following the September 11, 2001, attacks on the United States, consumption also declined. Use AD-AS analysis to show the two impacts on real GDP. **LO4**

11. **LAST WORD** Go to the OPEC Web site, **www.opec.org**, and find the current "OPEC basket price" of oil. By clicking on that amount, you will find the annual prices of oil for the past five years. By what percentage is the current price higher or lower than five years ago? Next, go to the Bureau of Economic Analysis Web site, **www.bea.gov**, and use the interactive feature to find U.S. real GDP for the past five years. By what percentage is real GDP higher or lower than it was five years ago? What, if anything, can you conclude about the relationship between the price of oil and the level of real GDP in the United States?

Problems

1. Suppose that consumer spending initially rises by $5 billion for every 1 percent rise in household wealth and that investment spending initially rises by $20 billion for every 1 percentage point fall in the real interest rate. Also assume that the economy's multiplier is 4. If household wealth falls by 5 percent because of declining house values, and the real interest rate falls by 2 percentage points, in what direction and by how much will the aggregate demand curve initially shift at each price level? In what direction and by how much will it eventually shift? **LO1**

2. Answer the following questions on the basis of the three sets of data for the country of North Vaudeville: **LO2**

a. Which set of data illustrates aggregate supply in the immediate short-run in North Vaudeville? The short run? The long run?

b. Assuming no change in hours of work, if real output per hour of work increases by 10 percent, what will be the new levels of real GDP in the right column of A? Does the new data reflect an increase in aggregate supply or does it indicate a decrease in aggregate supply?

3. Suppose that the aggregate demand and aggregate supply schedules for a hypothetical economy are as shown at the top left of the next page. **LO3**

(A)		(B)		(C)	
Price Level	**Real GDP**	**Price Level**	**Real GDP**	**Price Level**	**Real GDP**
110	275	100	200	110	225
100	250	100	225	100	225
95	225	100	250	95	225
90	200	100	275	90	225

Amount of Real GDP Demanded, Billions	Price Level (Price Index)	Amount of Real GDP Supplied, Billions
$100	300	$450
200	250	400
300	200	300
400	150	200
500	100	100

Input Quantity	Real GDP
150.0	$400
112.5	300
75.0	200

a. Use the data above to graph the aggregate demand and aggregate supply curves. What is the equilibrium price level and the equilibrium level of real output in this hypothetical economy? Is the equilibrium real output also necessarily the full-employment real output?

b. If the price level in this economy is 150, will quantity demanded equal, exceed, or fall short of quantity supplied? By what amount? If the price level is 250, will quantity demanded equal, exceed, or fall short of quantity supplied? By what amount?

c. Suppose that buyers desire to purchase $200 billion of extra real output at each price level. Sketch in the new aggregate demand curve as AD_1. What is the new equilibrium price level and level of real output?

4. Suppose that the table at the top right shows an economy's relationship between real output and the inputs needed to produce that output: LO3

a. What is productivity in this economy?

b. What is the per-unit cost of production if the price of each input unit is $2?

c. Assume that the input price increases from $2 to $3 with no accompanying change in productivity. What is the new per-unit cost of production? In what direction would the $1 increase in input price push the economy's aggregate supply curve? What effect would this shift of aggregate supply have on the price level and the level of real output?

d. Suppose that the increase in input price does not occur but, instead, that productivity increases by 100 percent. What would be the new per-unit cost of production? What effect would this change in per-unit production cost have on the economy's aggregate supply curve? What effect would this shift of aggregate supply have on the price level and the level of real output?

5. Refer to the data in the table that accompanies problem 2. Suppose that the present equilibrium price level and level of real GDP are 100 and $225, and that data set B represents the relevant aggregate supply schedule for the economy. LO4

a. What must be the current amount of real output demanded at the 100 price level?

b. If the amount of output demanded declined by $25 at the 100 price levels shown in B, what would be the new equilibrium real GDP? In business cycle terminology, what would economists call this change in real GDP?

FURTHER TEST YOUR KNOWLEDGE AT
www.mcconnell19e.com

At the text's Online Learning Center (OLC), **www.mcconnell19e.com**, you will find one or more Web-based questions that require information from the Internet to answer. We urge you to check them out; they will familiarize you with Web sites that may be helpful in other courses and perhaps even in your career. The OLC also features multiple-choice questions that give instant feedback and provides other helpful ways to further test your knowledge of the chapter.

The Relationship of the Aggregate Demand Curve to the Aggregate Expenditures Model*

The aggregate demand curve of this chapter and the aggregate expenditures model of Chapter 11 are intricately related.

Derivation of the Aggregate Demand Curve from the Aggregate Expenditures Model

We can directly connect the downsloping aggregate demand curve to the aggregate expenditures model by relating various possible price levels to corresponding equilibrium GDPs. In Figure 1 we have stacked the aggregate expenditures model (Figure 1a) and the aggregate demand curve (Figure 1b) vertically. This is possible because the horizontal axes of both models measure real GDP. Now let's derive the AD curve in three distinct steps. (Throughout this discussion, keep in mind that price level P_1 is lower than price level P_2, which is lower than price level P_3.)

- First suppose that the economy's price level is P_1 and its aggregate expenditures schedule is AE_1, the top schedule in Figure 1a. The equilibrium GDP is then Q_1 at point 1. So in Figure 1b we can plot the equilibrium real output Q_1 and the corresponding price level P_1. This gives us point 1′ in Figure 1b.
- Now assume the price level rises from P_1 to P_2. Other things equal, this higher price level will (1) decrease the value of real balances (wealth), decreasing consumption expenditures; (2) increase the interest rate, reducing investment and interest-sensitive consumption expenditures; and (3) increase imports and decrease exports, reducing net export expenditures. The aggregate expenditures schedule will fall from AE_1 to, say, AE_2 in Figure 1a, giving us

equilibrium Q_2 at point 2. In Figure 1b we plot this new price-level–real-output combination, P_2 and Q_2, as point 2′.

FIGURE 1 Deriving the aggregate demand curve from the aggregate expenditures model. (a) Rising price levels from P_1 to P_2 to P_3 shift the aggregate expenditures curve downward from AE_1 to AE_2 to AE_3 and reduce real GDP from Q_1 to Q_2 to Q_3. (b) The aggregate demand curve AD is derived by plotting the successively lower real GDPs from the upper graph against the P_1, P_2, and P_3 price levels.

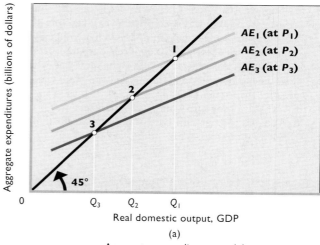

(a)
Aggregate expenditures model

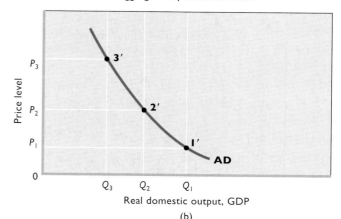

(b)
Aggregate demand–aggregate supply model

*This appendix presumes knowledge of the aggregate expenditures model discussed in Chapter 11 and should be skipped if Chapter 11 was not assigned.

- Finally, suppose the price level rises from P_2 to P_3. The value of real balances falls, the interest rate rises, exports fall, and imports rise. Consequently, the consumption, investment, and net export schedules fall, shifting the aggregate expenditures schedule downward from AE_2 to AE_3, which gives us equilibrium Q_3 at point 3. In Figure 1b, this enables us to locate point 3′, where the price level is P_3 and real output is Q_3.

In summary, increases in the economy's price level will successively shift its aggregate expenditures schedule downward and will reduce real GDP. The resulting price-level–real-GDP combinations will yield various points such as 1′, 2′, and 3′ in Figure 1b. Together, such points locate the downsloping aggregate demand curve for the economy.

Aggregate Demand Shifts and the Aggregate Expenditures Model

The determinants of aggregate demand listed in Figure 12.2 are the components of the aggregate expenditures model discussed in Chapter 11. When one of the determinants of aggregate demand changes, the aggregate expenditures schedule shifts upward or downward. We can easily link such shifts of the aggregate expenditures schedule to shifts of the aggregate demand curve.

Let's suppose that the price level is constant. In Figure 2 we begin with the aggregate expenditures schedule at AE_1 in the top diagram, yielding equilibrium real output Q_1. Assume now that investment increases in response to more optimistic business expectations, so the aggregate expenditures schedule rises from AE_1 to AE_2. (The notation "at P_1" reminds us that the price level is assumed constant.) The result will be a multiplied increase in equilibrium real output from Q_1 to Q_2.

In Figure 2b the increase in investment spending is reflected in the horizontal distance between AD_1 and the broken curve to its right. The immediate effect of the increase in investment is an increase in aggregate demand by the exact amount of the new spending. But then the multiplier process magnifies the initial increase in investment into successive rounds of consumption spending and an ultimate multiplied increase in aggregate demand from AD_1 to AD_2. Equilibrium real output rises from Q_1 to Q_2, the same multiplied increase in real GDP as that in the top graph. The initial increase in investment in the top graph has shifted the AD curve in

FIGURE 2 Shifts of the aggregate expenditures schedule and of the aggregate demand curve. (a) A change in some determinant of consumption, investment, or net exports (other than the price level) shifts the aggregate expenditures schedule upward from AE_1 to AE_2. The multiplier increases real output from Q_1 to Q_2. (b) The counterpart of this change is an initial rightward shift of the aggregate demand curve by the amount of initial new spending (from AD_1 to the broken curve). This leads to a multiplied rightward shift of the curve to AD_2, which is just sufficient to show the same increase in real output as that in the aggregate expenditures model.

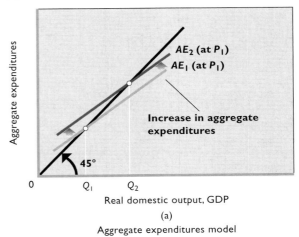

(a)
Aggregate expenditures model

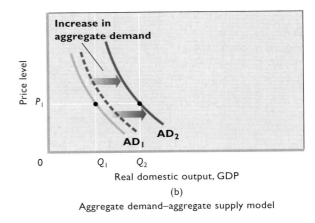

(b)
Aggregate demand–aggregate supply model

the lower graph by a horizontal distance equal to the change in investment times the multiplier. This particular change in real GDP is still associated with the constant price level P_1. To generalize,

$$\text{Shift of AD curve} = \text{initial change in spending} \times \text{multiplier}$$

Appendix Summary

1. A change in the price level alters the location of the aggregate expenditures schedule through the real-balances, interest-rate, and foreign purchases effects. The aggregate demand curve is derived from the aggregate expenditures model by allowing the price level to change and observing the effect on the aggregate expenditures schedule and thus on equilibrium GDP.

2. With the price level held constant, increases in consumption, investment, government, and net export expenditures shift the aggregate expenditures schedule upward and the aggregate demand curve to the right. Decreases in these spending components produce the opposite effects.

Appendix Questions

1. Explain carefully: "A change in the price level shifts the aggregate expenditures curve but not the aggregate demand curve." **LO5**

2. Suppose that the price level is constant and that investment decreases sharply. How would you show this decrease in the aggregate expenditures model? What would be the outcome for real GDP? How would you show this fall in investment in the aggregate demand–aggregate supply model, assuming the economy is operating in what, in effect, is a horizontal section of the aggregate supply curve? **LO5**

Appendix Problems

1. Refer to Figures 1a and 1b in the Appendix. Assume that Q_1 is 300, Q_2 is 200, Q_3 is 100, P_3 is 120, P_2 is 100, and P_1 is 80. If the price level increases from P_1 to P_3 in graph 1b, in what direction and by how much will real GDP change? If the slopes of the AE lines in Figure 1a are .8 and equal to the MPC, in what direction will the aggregate expenditures schedule in Figure 1a need to shift to produce the previously determined change in real GDP? What is the size of the multiplier in this example? **LO5**

2. Refer to Figure 2 in the Appendix and assume that Q_1 is $400 and Q_2 is $500, the price level is stuck at P_1, and the slopes of the AE lines in Figure 2a are .75 and equal to the MPC. In what direction and by how much does the aggregate expenditures schedule in Figure 2a need to shift to move the aggregate demand curve in Figure 2b from AD_1 to AD_2? What is the multiplier in this example? Given the multiplier, what must be the distance between AD_1 and the broken line to its right at P_1? **LO5**

AFTER READING THIS CHAPTER, YOU SHOULD BE ABLE TO:

1 Identify and explain the purposes, tools, and limitations of fiscal policy.

2 Explain the role of built-in stabilizers in moderating business cycles.

3 Describe how the cyclically adjusted budget reveals the status of U.S. fiscal policy.

4 Discuss the size, composition, and consequences of the U.S. public debt.

Fiscal Policy, Deficits, and Debt

In the previous chapter we saw that an excessive increase in aggregate demand can cause demand-pull inflation and that a significant decline in aggregate demand can cause recession and cyclical unemploy-

ORIGIN OF THE IDEA

O 13.1
Fiscal policy

ment. For these reasons, the Federal government sometimes uses budgetary actions to try to "stimulate the economy" or "rein in inflation." Such countercyclical **fiscal policy** consists of deliberate changes in government spending and tax collections designed to achieve full employ-

ment, control inflation, and encourage economic growth. (The adjective "fiscal" simply means "financial.")

We begin this chapter by examining the logic behind fiscal policy, its current status, and its limitations. Then we examine a closely related topic: the U.S. public debt.

Our discussion of fiscal policy and public debt is very timely. In 2009, Congress and the Obama administration began a $787 billion stimulus program designed to help lift the U.S. economy out of deep recession. This fiscal policy contributed to a $1.4 trillion Federal budget deficit in 2009, which increased the size of the U.S. public debt to $11.9 trillion.

Fiscal Policy and the AD-AS Model

The fiscal policy just defined is *discretionary* (or "active"). It is often initiated on the advice of the president's **Council of Economic Advisers (CEA),** a group of three economists appointed by the president to provide expertise and assistance on economic matters. Discretionary changes in government spending and taxes are *at the option* of the Federal government. They do not occur automatically. Changes that occur without congressional action are *nondiscretionary* (or "passive" or "automatic"), and we will examine them later in this chapter.

Expansionary Fiscal Policy

When recession occurs, an **expansionary fiscal policy** may be in order. This policy consists of government spending increases, tax reductions, or both, designed to increase aggregate demand and therefore raise real GDP. Consider Figure 13.1, where we suppose that a sharp decline in investment spending has shifted the economy's aggregate demand curve to the left from AD_1 to AD_2. (Disregard the arrows and dashed downsloping line for now.) The cause of the recession may be that profit expectations on investment projects have dimmed, curtailing investment spending and reducing aggregate demand.

Suppose the economy's potential or full-employment output is $510 billion in Figure 13.1. If the price level is inflexible downward at P_1, the broken horizontal line becomes relevant to the analysis. The aggregate demand curve moves leftward and reduces real GDP from $510 billion to $490 billion. A negative GDP gap of $20 billion (= $490 billion − $510 billion) arises. An increase in un-employment accompanies this negative GDP gap because fewer workers are needed to produce the reduced output. In short, the economy depicted is suffering both recession and cyclical unemployment.

What fiscal policy should the Federal government adopt to try to stimulate the economy? It has three main options: (1) increase government spending, (2) reduce taxes, or (3) use some combination of the two. If the Federal budget is balanced at the outset, expansionary fiscal policy will create a government **budget deficit**—government spending in excess of tax revenues.

Increased Government Spending Other things equal, a sufficient increase in government spending will shift an economy's aggregate demand curve to the right, from AD_2 to AD_1 in Figure 13.1. To see why, suppose that the recession prompts the government to initiate $5 billion of new spending on highways, education, and health care. We represent this new $5 billion of government spending as the horizontal distance between AD_2 and the dashed downsloping line immediately to its right. At each price level, the amount of real output that is demanded is now $5 billion greater than that demanded before the expansion of government spending.

But the initial increase in aggregate demand is not the end of the story. Through the multiplier effect, the aggregate demand curve shifts to AD_1, a distance that exceeds that represented by the originating $5 billion increase in government purchases. This greater shift occurs because the multiplier process magnifies the initial change in spending into successive rounds of new consumption spending. If the economy's MPC is .75, then the simple multiplier is 4. So the aggregate demand curve shifts rightward by four times the distance between AD_2 and the broken downslop-

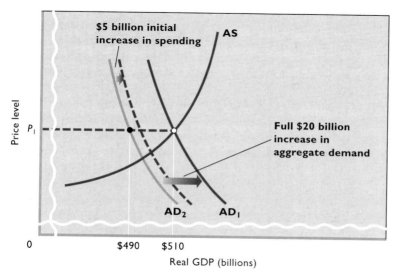

FIGURE 13.1 Expansionary fiscal policy. Expansionary fiscal policy uses increases in government spending or tax cuts to push the economy out of recession. In an economy with an MPC of .75, a $5 billion increase in government spending or a $6.67 billion decrease in personal taxes (producing a $5 billion initial increase in consumption) expands aggregate demand from AD_2 to the downsloping dashed curve. The multiplier then magnifies this initial increase in spending to AD_1. So real GDP rises along the broken horizontal line by $20 billion.

ing line. Because this *particular* increase in aggregate demand occurs along the horizontal broken-line segment, real output rises by the full extent of the multiplier. Observe that real output rises to $510 billion, up $20 billion from its recessionary level of $490 billion. Concurrently, unemployment falls as firms increase their employment to the full-employment level that existed before the recession.

Tax Reductions Alternatively, the government could reduce taxes to shift the aggregate demand curve rightward, as from AD_2 to AD_1. Suppose the government cuts personal income taxes by $6.67 billion, which increases disposable income by the same amount. Consumption will rise by $5 billion (= MPC of .75 × $6.67 billion) and saving will go up by $1.67 billion (= MPS of .25 × $6.67 billion). In this case the horizontal distance between AD_2 and the dashed downsloping line in Figure 13.1 represents only the $5 billion initial increase in consumption spending. Again, we call it "initial" consumption spending because the multiplier process yields successive rounds of increased consumption spending. The aggregate demand curve eventually shifts rightward by four times the $5 billion initial increase in consumption produced by the tax cut. Real GDP rises by $20 billion, from $490 billion to $510 billion, implying a multiplier of 4. Employment increases accordingly.

You may have noted that a tax cut must be somewhat larger than the proposed increase in government spending if it is to achieve the same amount of rightward shift in the aggregate demand curve. This is because part of a tax reduction increases saving, rather than consumption. To increase initial consumption by a specific amount, the government must reduce taxes by more than that amount. With an MPC of .75, taxes must fall by $6.67 billion for $5 billion of new consumption to be forthcoming because $1.67 billion is saved (not consumed). If the MPC had instead been, say, .6, an $8.33 billion reduction in tax collections would have been necessary to increase initial consumption by $5 billion. The smaller the MPC, the greater the tax cut needed to accomplish a specific initial increase in consumption and a specific shift in the aggregate demand curve.

Combined Government Spending Increases and Tax Reductions The government may combine spending increases and tax cuts to produce the desired initial increase in spending and the eventual increase in aggregate demand and real GDP. In the economy depicted in Figure 13.1, the government might increase its spending by $1.25 billion while reducing taxes by $5 billion. As an exercise, you should explain why this combination will produce the targeted $5 billion initial increase in new spending.

If you were assigned Chapter 11, think through these three fiscal policy options in terms of the recessionary-expenditure-gap analysis associated with the aggregate expenditures model (Figure 11.7). And recall from the appendix to Chapter 12 that rightward shifts of the aggregate demand curve relate directly to upward shifts of the aggregate expenditures schedule.

Contractionary Fiscal Policy

When demand-pull inflation occurs, a restrictive or **contractionary fiscal policy** may help control it. This policy consists of government spending reductions, tax increases, or both, designed to decrease aggregate demand and therefore lower or eliminate inflation. Look at Figure 13.2, where the full-employment level of real GDP is $510 billion. The economy starts at equilibrium at point *a*, where the initial aggregate demand curve AD_3 intersects aggregate supply

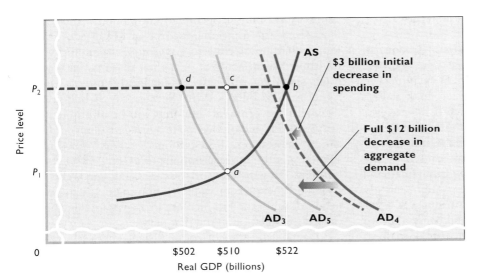

FIGURE 13.2 Contractionary fiscal policy. Contractionary fiscal policy uses decreases in government spending, increases in taxes, or both, to reduce demand-pull inflation. Here, an increase in aggregate demand from AD_3 to AD_4 has driven the economy to point *b* and ratcheted the price level up to P_2, where it becomes inflexible downward. If the economy's MPC is .75 and the multiplier therefore is 4, the government can either reduce its spending by $3 billion or increase its taxes by $4 billion (which will decrease consumption by $3 billion) to eliminate the inflationary GDP gap of $12 billion (= $522 billion − $510 billion). Aggregate demand will shift leftward, first from AD_4 to the dashed downsloping curve to its left, and then to AD_5. With the price level remaining at P_2, the economy will move from point *b* to point *c* and the inflationary GDP gap will disappear.

curve AS. Suppose that after going through the multiplier process, a $5 billion initial increase in investment and net export spending shifts the aggregate demand curve to the right by $20 billion, from AD_3 to AD_4. (Ignore the downsloping dashed line for now.) Given the upsloping AS curve, however, the equilibrium GDP does not rise by the full $20 billion. It only rises by $12 billion, to $522 billion, thereby creating an inflationary GDP gap of $12 billion ($522 billion − $510 billion). The upslope of the AS curve means that some of the rightward movement of the AD curve ends up causing demand-pull inflation rather than increased output. As a result, the price level rises from P_1 to P_2 and the equilibrium moves to point b.

Without a government response, the inflationary GDP gap will cause further inflation (as input prices rise in the long run to meet the increase in output prices). If the government looks to fiscal policy to eliminate the inflationary GDP gap, its options are the opposite of those used to combat recession. It can (1) decrease government spending, (2) raise taxes, or (3) use some combination of those two policies. When the economy faces demand-pull inflation, fiscal policy should move toward a government **budget surplus**—tax revenues in excess of government spending.

But before discussing how the government can either decrease government spending or increase taxes to move toward a government budget surplus and control inflation, we have to keep in mind that the price level is like a ratchet. While increases in aggregate demand that expand real output beyond the full-employment level tend to ratchet the price level upward, declines in aggregate demand do not seem to push the price level downward. This means that stopping inflation is a matter of halting the rise of the price level, not trying to lower it to the previous level. It also means that the government must take the ratchet effect into account when deciding how big a cut in spending or an increase in taxes it should undertake.

Decreased Government Spending

To control demand-pull inflation, the government can decrease aggregate demand by reducing government spending. To see why the ratchet effect matters so much, look at Figure 13.2 and consider what would happen if the government ignored the ratchet effect and attempted to design a spending-reduction policy to eliminate the inflationary GDP gap. Since the $12 billion gap was caused by the $20 billion rightward movement of the aggregate demand curve from AD_3 to AD_4, the government might naively think that it could solve the problem by causing a $20 billion leftward shift of the aggregate demand curve to move it back to where it originally was. It could attempt to do so by reducing government spending by $5 billion and then

allowing the multiplier effect to expand that initial decrease into a $20 billion decline in aggregate demand. That would shift the aggregate demand curve leftward by $20 billion, putting it back at AD_3.

This policy would work fine if there were no ratchet effect and if prices were flexible. The economy's equilibrium would move back from point b to point a, with equilibrium GDP returning to the full-employment level of $510 billion and the price level falling from P_2 back to P_1.

But because there *is* a ratchet effect, this scenario is not what will actually happen. Instead, the ratchet effect implies that the price level is stuck at P_2, so that the broken horizontal line at price level P_2 becomes important to the analysis. The fixed price level means that when the government reduces spending by $5 billion to shift the aggregate demand curve back to AD_3, it will actually cause a recession! The new equilibrium will not be at point a. It will be at point d, where aggregate demand curve AD_3 crosses the broken horizontal line. At point d, real GDP is only $502 billion, $8 billion below the full-employment level of $510 billion.

The problem is that, with the price level downwardly inflexible at P_2, the $20 billion leftward shift of the aggregate demand curve causes a full $20 billion decline in real GDP. None of the change in aggregate demand can be dissipated as a decline in the price level. As a result, equilibrium GDP declines by the full $20 billion, falling from $522 billion to $502 billion and putting it $8 billion below potential output. By not taking the ratchet effect into account, the government has overdone the decrease in government spending, replacing a $12 billion inflationary GDP gap with an $8 billion recessionary GDP gap. This is clearly not what it had in mind.

Here's how it can avoid this scenario. First, the government takes account of the size of the inflationary GDP gap. It is $12 billion. Second, it knows that with the price level fixed, the multiplier will be in full effect. Thus, it knows that any decline in government spending will be multiplied by a factor of 4. It then reasons that government spending will have to decline by only $3 billion rather than $5 billion. Why? Because the $3 billion initial decline in government spending will be multiplied by 4, creating a $12 billion decline in aggregate demand. Under the circumstances, a $3 billion decline in government spending is the correct amount to exactly offset the $12 billion GDP gap. This inflationary GDP gap is the problem that government wants to eliminate. To succeed, it need not undo the full increase in aggregate demand that caused the inflation in the first place.

Graphically, the horizontal distance between AD_4 and the dashed downsloping line to its left represents the

$3 billion decrease in government spending. Once the multiplier process is complete, this spending cut will shift the aggregate demand curve leftward from AD_4 to AD_5. With the price level fixed at P_2, the economy will come to equilibrium at point c. The economy will operate at its potential output of $510 billion, and the inflationary GDP gap will be eliminated. Furthermore, because the government took the ratchet effect correctly into account, the government will not accidentally push the economy into a recession by making an overly large initial decrease in government spending.

Increased Taxes Just as government can use tax cuts to increase consumption spending, it can use tax *increases* to *reduce* consumption spending. If the economy in Figure 13.2 has an MPC of .75, the government must raise taxes by $4 billion to achieve its fiscal policy objective. The $4 billion tax increase reduces saving by $1 billion (= the MPS of .25 × $4 billion). This $1 billion reduction in saving, by definition, is not a reduction in spending. But the $4 billion tax increase also reduces consumption spending by $3 billion (= the MPC of .75 × $4 billion), as shown by the distance between AD_4 and the dashed downsloping line to its left in Figure 13.2. After the multiplier process is complete, this initial $3 billion decline in consumption will cause aggregate demand to shift leftward by $12 billion at each price level (multiplier of 4 × $3 billion). With the economy moving to point c, the inflationary GDP gap will be closed and the inflation will be halted.

Combined Government Spending Decreases and Tax Increases The government may choose to combine spending decreases and tax increases in order to reduce aggregate demand and check inflation. To check your understanding, determine why a $1.5 billion decline in government spending combined with a $2 billion increase in taxes would shift the aggregate demand curve from AD_4 to AD_5. Also, if you were assigned Chapter 11, explain the three fiscal policy options for fighting inflation by referring to the inflationary-expenditure-gap concept developed with the aggregate expenditures model (Figure 11.7). And recall from the appendix to Chapter 12 that leftward shifts of the aggregate demand curve are associated with downshifts of the aggregate expenditures schedule.

INTERACTIVE GRAPHS

G 13.1

Fiscal policy

Policy Options: *G* or *T*?

Which is preferable as a means of eliminating recession and inflation? The use of government spending or the use of taxes? The answer depends largely on one's view as to whether the government is too large or too small.

Economists who believe there are many unmet social and infrastructure needs usually recommend that government spending be increased during recessions. In times of demand-pull inflation, they usually recommend tax increases. Both actions either expand or preserve the size of government.

Economists who think that the government is too large and inefficient usually advocate tax cuts during recessions and cuts in government spending during times of demand-pull inflation. Both actions either restrain the growth of government or reduce its size.

The point is that discretionary fiscal policy designed to stabilize the economy can be associated with either an expanding government or a contracting government.

QUICK REVIEW 13.1

- Discretionary fiscal policy is the purposeful change of government expenditures and tax collections by government to promote full employment, price stability, and economic growth.

- Expansionary fiscal policy consists of increases in government spending, reductions in taxes, or both, and is designed to expand real GDP by increasing aggregate demand.

- Contractionary fiscal policy entails decreases in government spending, increases in taxes, or both, and is designed to reduce aggregate demand and slow or halt demand-pull inflation.

- To be implemented correctly, contractionary fiscal policy must properly account for the ratchet effect and the fact that the price level will not fall as the government shifts the aggregate demand curve leftward.

Built-In Stability

To some degree, government tax revenues change automatically over the course of the business cycle and in ways that stabilize the economy. This automatic response, or built-in stability, constitutes nondiscretionary (or "passive" or "automatic") budgetary policy and results from the makeup of most tax systems. We did not include this built-in stability in our discussion of fiscal policy over the last few pages because we implicitly assumed that the same amount of tax revenue was being collected at each level of GDP. But the actual U.S. tax system is such that *net tax revenues* vary directly with GDP. (Net taxes are tax revenues less transfers and subsidies. From here on, we will use the simpler "taxes" to mean "net taxes.")

Virtually any tax will yield more tax revenue as GDP rises. In particular, personal income taxes have progressive rates and thus generate more-than-proportionate increases in tax revenues as GDP expands. Furthermore, as GDP rises and more goods and services are purchased, revenues from corporate income taxes and from sales taxes and excise taxes also increase. And, similarly, revenues from payroll taxes rise as economic expansion creates more jobs. Conversely, when GDP declines, tax receipts from all these sources also decline.

Transfer payments (or "negative taxes") behave in the opposite way from tax revenues. Unemployment compensation payments and welfare payments decrease during economic expansion and increase during economic contraction.

Automatic or Built-In Stabilizers

A **built-in stabilizer** is anything that increases the government's budget deficit (or reduces its budget surplus) during a recession and increases its budget surplus (or reduces its budget deficit) during an expansion without requiring explicit action by policymakers. As Figure 13.3 reveals, this is precisely what the U.S. tax system does. Government expenditures G are fixed and assumed to be independent of the level of GDP. Congress decides on a particular level of spending, but it does not determine the magnitude of tax revenues. Instead, it establishes tax rates, and the tax revenues then vary directly with the level of

GDP that the economy achieves. Line T represents that direct relationship between tax revenues and GDP.

Economic Importance The economic importance of the direct relationship between tax receipts and GDP becomes apparent when we consider that:

- Taxes reduce spending and aggregate demand.
- Reductions in spending are desirable when the economy is moving toward inflation, whereas increases in spending are desirable when the economy is slumping.

As shown in Figure 13.3, tax revenues automatically increase as GDP rises during prosperity, and since taxes reduce household and business spending, they restrain the economic expansion. That is, as the economy moves toward a higher GDP, tax revenues automatically rise and move the budget from deficit toward surplus. In Figure 13.3, observe that the high and perhaps inflationary income level GDP_3 automatically generates a contractionary budget surplus.

Conversely, as GDP falls during recession, tax revenues automatically decline, increasing spending by households and businesses and thus cushioning the economic contraction. With a falling GDP, tax receipts decline and move the government's budget from surplus toward deficit. In Figure 13.3, the low level of income GDP_1 will automatically yield an expansionary budget deficit.

Tax Progressivity Figure 13.3 reveals that the size of the automatic budget deficits or surpluses—and therefore built-in stability—depends on the responsiveness of tax revenues to changes in GDP. If tax revenues change sharply as GDP changes, the slope of line T in the figure will be steep and the vertical distances between T and G (the deficits or surpluses) will be large. If tax revenues change very little when GDP changes, the slope will be gentle and built-in stability will be low.

The steepness of T in Figure 13.3 depends on the tax system itself. In a **progressive tax system,** the average tax rate (= tax revenue/GDP) rises with GDP. In a **proportional tax system,** the average tax rate remains constant as GDP rises. In a **regressive tax system,** the average tax rate falls as GDP rises. The progressive tax system has the steepest tax line T of the three. However, tax revenues will rise with GDP under both the progressive and the proportional tax systems, and they may rise, fall, or stay the same under a regressive tax system. The main point is this: The more progressive the tax system, the greater the economy's built-in stability.

The built-in stability provided by the U.S. tax system has reduced the severity of business fluctuations, perhaps

FIGURE 13.3 Built-in stability. Tax revenues, T, vary directly with GDP, and government spending, G, is assumed to be independent of GDP. As GDP falls in a recession, deficits occur automatically and help alleviate the recession. As GDP rises during expansion, surpluses occur automatically and help offset possible inflation.

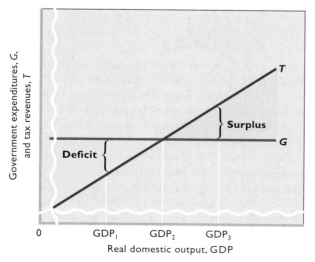

by as much as 8 to 10 percent of the change in GDP that otherwise would have occurred.[1] In recession-year 2009, for example, revenues from the individual income tax fell by a staggering 22 percent. This decline helped keep household spending and real GDP from falling even more than they did. But built-in stabilizers can only dampen, not counteract, swings in real GDP. Discretionary fiscal policy (changes in tax rates and expenditures) or monetary policy (central bank–caused changes in interest rates) therefore may be needed to try to counter a recession or inflation of any appreciable magnitude.

Evaluating Fiscal Policy

How can we determine whether a government's discretionary fiscal policy is expansionary, neutral, or contractionary? We cannot simply examine the actual budget deficits or surpluses that take place under the current policy because they will necessarily include the automatic changes in tax revenues that accompany every change in GDP. In addition, the expansionary or contractionary strength of any change in discretionary fiscal policy depends not on its absolute size but on how large it is relative to the size of the economy. So, in evaluating the status of fiscal policy, we must adjust deficits and surpluses to eliminate automatic changes in tax revenues and also compare the sizes of the adjusted budget deficits and surpluses to the level of potential GDP.

Cyclically Adjusted Budget

Economists use the **cyclically adjusted budget** (also called the *full-employment budget*) to adjust actual Federal budget deficits and surpluses to account for the changes in tax revenues that happen automatically whenever GDP changes. The cyclically adjusted budget measures what the Federal budget deficit or surplus would have been under existing tax rates and government spending levels if the economy had achieved its full-employment level of GDP (its potential output). The idea essentially is to compare *actual* government expenditures with the tax revenues *that would have occurred* if the economy had achieved full-employment GDP. That procedure removes budget deficits or surpluses that arise simply because of cyclical changes in GDP and thus tell us nothing about whether the government's current discretionary fiscal policy is fundamentally expansionary, contractionary, or neutral.

Consider Figure 13.4a, where line G represents government expenditures and line T represents tax revenues.

In full-employment year 1, government expenditures of $500 billion equal tax revenues of $500 billion, as indicated by the intersection of lines G and T at point a. The cyclically adjusted budget deficit in year 1 is zero—government expenditures equal the tax revenues forthcoming at the full-employment output GDP_1. Obviously, the cyclically adjusted deficit *as a percentage of potential GDP* is also zero. The government's fiscal policy is neutral.

Now suppose that a recession occurs and GDP falls from GDP_1 to GDP_2, as shown in Figure 13.4a. Let's also assume that the government takes no discretionary action, so lines G and T remain as shown in the figure. Tax revenues automatically fall to $450 billion (point c) at GDP_2, while government spending remains unaltered at $500 billion (point b). A $50 billion budget deficit (represented by distance bc) arises. But this **cyclical deficit** is simply a byproduct of the economy's slide into recession, not the result of discretionary fiscal actions by the government. We would be wrong to conclude from this deficit that the government is engaging in an expansionary fiscal policy. The government's fiscal policy has not changed. It is still neutral.

That fact is highlighted when we remove the cyclical part of the deficit and thus consider the cyclically adjusted budget deficit for year 2 in Figure 13.4a. The $500 billion of government expenditures in year 2 is shown by b on line G. And, as shown by a on line T, $500 billion of tax revenues would have occurred if the economy had achieved its full-employment GDP. Because both b and a represent $500 billion, the cyclically adjusted budget deficit in year 2 is zero, as is this deficit as a percentage of potential GDP. Since the cyclically adjusted deficits are zero in both years, we know that government did not change its discretionary fiscal policy, even though a recession occurred and an actual deficit of $50 billion resulted.

Next, consider Figure 13.4b. Suppose that real output declined from full-employment GDP_3 in year 3 to GDP_4 in year 4. Also suppose that government responded to the recession by reducing tax rates in year 4, as represented by the downward shift of the tax line from T_1 to T_2. What has happened to the size of the cyclically adjusted deficit? Government expenditures in year 4 are $500 billion, as shown by e. Compare that amount with the $475 billion of tax revenues that would occur if the economy achieved its full-employment GDP. That is, compare position e on line G with position h on line T_2. The $25 billion of tax revenues by which e exceeds h is the cyclically adjusted budget deficit for year 4. As a percentage of potential GDP, the cyclically adjusted budget deficit has increased from zero in year 3 (before the tax-rate cut) to some positive percent [= ($25 billion/$GDP_3$) $\times$ 100] in year 4. This increase in the relative size of the full-employment deficit

---

[1] Alan J. Auerbach and Daniel Feenberg, "The Significance of Federal Taxes as Automatic Stabilizers," *Journal of Economic Perspectives*, Summer 2000, p. 54.

FIGURE 13.4 Cyclically adjusted deficits. (a) In the left-hand graph, the cyclically adjusted deficit is zero at the full-employment output GDP$_1$. But it is also zero at the recessionary output GDP$_2$ because the $500 billion of government expenditures at GDP$_2$ equals the $500 billion of tax revenues that would be forthcoming at the full-employment GDP$_1$. There has been no change in fiscal policy. (b) In the right-hand graph, discretionary fiscal policy, as reflected in the downward shift of the tax line from T_1 to T_2, has increased the cyclically adjusted budget deficit from zero in year 3 (before the tax cut) to $25 billion in year 4 (after the tax cut). This is found by comparing the $500 billion of government spending in year 4 with the $475 billion of taxes that would accrue at the full-employment GDP$_3$. Such a rise in the cyclically adjusted deficit (as a percentage of potential GDP) identifies an expansionary fiscal policy.

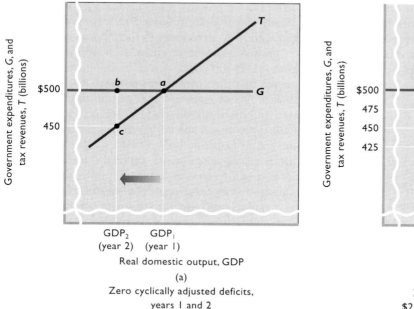

(a)
Zero cyclically adjusted deficits,
years 1 and 2

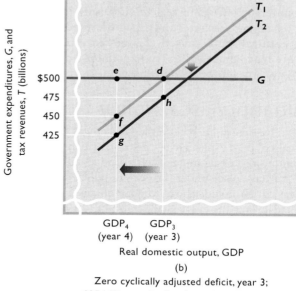

(b)
Zero cyclically adjusted deficit, year 3;
$25 billion cyclically adjusted deficit, year 4

between the two years reveals that the new fiscal policy is *expansionary*.

In contrast, if we observed a cyclically adjusted deficit (as a percentage of potential GDP) of zero in one year, followed by a cyclically adjusted budget surplus in the next, we could conclude that fiscal policy has changed from being neutral to being contractionary. Because the cyclically adjusted budget adjusts for automatic changes in tax revenues, the increase in the cyclically adjusted budget surplus reveals that government either decreased its spending (G) or increased tax rates such that tax revenues (T) increased. These changes in G and T are precisely the discretionary actions that we have identified as elements of a *contractionary* fiscal policy.

Recent U.S. Fiscal Policy

Table 13.1 lists the actual Federal budget deficits and surpluses (column 2) and the cyclically adjusted deficits and surpluses (column 3), as percentages of actual GDP and potential GDP, respectively, between 2000 and 2009. Observe that the cyclically adjusted deficits are generally smaller than the actual deficits. This is because the actual deficits include cyclical deficits, whereas the cyclically

adjusted deficits eliminate them. Only cyclically adjusted surpluses and deficits as percentages of potential GDP (column 3) provide the information needed to assess

TABLE 13.1 Federal Deficits (−) and Surpluses (+) as Percentages of GDP, 2000–2009

(1) Year	(2) Actual Deficit − or Surplus +	(3) Cyclically adjusted Deficit − or Surplus +*
2000	+2.4	+1.1
2001	+1.3	+0.5
2002	−1.5	−1.3
2003	−3.4	−2.7
2004	−3.5	−3.2
2005	−2.6	−2.5
2006	−1.9	−2.0
2007	−1.2	−1.2
2008	−3.2	−2.8
2009	−9.9	−7.3

*As a percentage of potential GDP.

Source: Congressional Budget Office, **www.cbo.gov**.

discretionary fiscal policy and determine whether it is expansionary, contractionary, or neutral.

Fiscal Policy from 2000 to 2007

Take a look at the data for 2000, for example, which shows that fiscal policy was contractionary that year. Note that the actual budget surplus was 2.4 percent of GDP in 2000 and the cyclically adjusted budget surplus was 1.1 percent of potential GDP. Because the economy was fully employed and corporate profits were strong, tax revenues poured into the Federal government and exceeded government expenditures.

But not all was well in 2000. Specifically, the so-called dot-com stock market bubble burst that year, and the U.S. economy noticeably slowed over the latter half of the year. In March 2001 the economy slid into a recession. Congress and the Bush administration responded by cutting taxes by $44 billion in 2001 and scheduling an additional $52 billion of cuts for 2002. These stimulus policies helped boost the economy and offset the recession as well as cushion the economic blow delivered by the September 11, 2001, terrorist attacks. In March 2002 Congress passed further tax cuts totaling $122 billion over two years and extended unemployment benefits.

As Table 13.1 reveals, the cyclically adjusted budget moved from a surplus of 1.1 percent of potential GDP in 2000 to a deficit of −1.3 percent two years later in 2002. Fiscal policy had definitely turned expansionary. Nevertheless, the economy remained sluggish through 2002 and into 2003. In June 2003 Congress again cut taxes, this time by a much larger $350 billion over several years. Specifically, the tax legislation accelerated the reduction of marginal tax rates already scheduled for future years and slashed tax rates on income from dividends and capital gains. It also increased tax breaks for families and small businesses. Note from the table that this tax package increased the cyclically adjusted budget deficit as a percentage of potential GDP to −2.7 percent in 2003. The economy strengthened and both real output and employment grew between 2003 and 2007. By 2007 full employment had been restored, although a −1.2 percent cyclically adjusted budget deficit still remained.

Fiscal Policy during the Great Recession

As pointed out in previous chapters, major economic trouble began in 2007. In the summer of 2007, a crisis in the market for mortgage loans flared up. Later in 2007 that crisis spread rapidly to other financial markets, threatened the survival of several major U.S. financial institutions, and severely disrupted the entire financial system. As credit markets began to freeze, general pessimism spread beyond the financial markets to the overall economy. Businesses and households retrenched on their borrowing and spending, and in December 2007 the economy entered a recession. Over the following two years, it became known as the Great Recession—one of the steepest and longest economic downturns since the 1930s.

In 2008 Congress acted rapidly to pass an economic stimulus package. This law provided a total of $152 billion in stimulus, with some of it coming as tax breaks for businesses, but most of it delivered as checks of up to $600 each to taxpayers, veterans, and Social Security recipients.

As a percentage of GDP, the *actual* Federal budget deficit jumped from −1.2 percent in 2007 to −3.2 percent in 2008. This increase resulted from an automatic drop-off of tax revenues during the recession, along with the tax rebates (fiscal stimulus checks) paid out in 2008. As shown in Table 13.1, the *cyclically adjusted* budget deficit rose from −1.2 percent of potential GDP in 2007 to −2.8 percent in 2008. This increase in the cyclically adjusted budget reveals that fiscal policy in 2008 was expansionary.

The government hoped that those receiving checks would spend the money and thus boost consumption and aggregate demand. But households instead saved substantial parts of the money from the checks or used some of the money to pay down credit card loans. Although this stimulus plan boosted output somewhat in mid-2008, it was neither as expansionary nor long-lasting as policymakers had hoped. The continuing forces of the Great Recession simply overwhelmed the policy.

With the economy continuing its precipitous slide, the Obama administration and Congress enacted the American Recovery and Reinvestment Act of 2009. This gigantic $787 billion program—coming on top of a $700 billion rescue package for financial institutions—consisted of low- and middle-income tax rebates, plus large increases in expenditures on infrastructure, education, and health care. The idea was to flood the economy with additional spending to try to boost aggregate demand and get people back to work.

The tax cuts in the package were aimed at lower- and middle-income individuals and households, who were thought to be more likely than high-income people to spend (rather than save) the extra income from the tax rebates. Rather than sending out lump-sum stimulus checks as in 2008, the new tax rebates showed up as small increases in workers' monthly payroll checks. With smaller amounts per month rather than a single large check, the government hoped that people would spend the bulk of their enhanced income—rather than save it as they had done with the one-time-only, lump-sum checks received in 2008. The second part of the fiscal policy (60 percent of the funding) consisted of increases in government expenditures on a wide assortment of programs, including transportation, education, and aid to state governments. The highly stimulative fiscal policy for 2009 is fully reflected in column 3 of Table 13.1. The cyclically adjusted budget deficit rose dramatically from −2.8 percent of potential GDP in 2008 to a very high −7.3 percent of potential GDP in 2009.

Other nations also experienced recessions and also responded with expansionary fiscal policies. Global Perspective 13.1 shows the magnitudes of the cyclically adjusted surpluses and deficits of a number of countries in 2009.

Budget Deficits and Projections

Figure 13.5 shows the absolute magnitudes of actual (not cyclically adjusted) U.S. budget surpluses and deficits, here from 1994 through 2009. It also shows the projected future deficits through 2014, as estimated by the Congressional Budget Office (CBO). In recession year 2009, the Federal budget deficit reached $1413 billion, mainly but not totally due to reduced tax revenues from lower income and record amounts of stimulus spending. The CBO projects high deficits for several years to come. But projected deficits and surpluses are subject to large and frequent changes, as government alters its fiscal policy and GDP growth accelerates or slows. So we suggest that you update this figure by going to the Congressional Budget Office Web site,

GLOBAL PERSPECTIVE 13.1

Cyclically Adjusted Budget Deficits or Surpluses as a Percentage of Potential GDP, Selected Nations

Because of the global recession, in 2009 all but a few of the world's major nations had cyclically adjusted budget deficits. These deficits varied as percentages of potential GDP, but they each reflected some degree of expansionary fiscal policy.

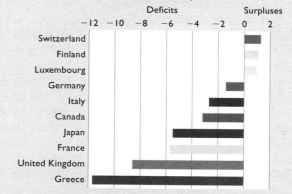

Source: Organization for Economic Cooperation and Development, *OECD Economic Outlook,* **www.oecd.org.**

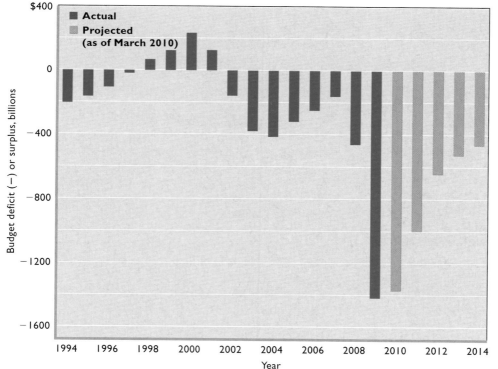

FIGURE 13.5 Federal budget deficits and surpluses, actual and projected, fiscal years 1994–2014 (in billions of nominal dollars). The annual budget deficits of 1992 through 1997 gave way to budget surpluses from 1998 through 2001. Deficits reappeared in 2002 and declined through 2007. They greatly ballooned in recessionary years 2008 and 2009 and are projected to remain high for many years to come.

Source: Congressional Budget Office, **www.cbo.gov**.

www.cbo.gov, and selecting Budget and Economic Outlook and then Executive Summary. The relevant numbers are in Table 1 in the row labeled Total Deficit.

Problems, Criticisms, and Complications

Economists recognize that governments may encounter a number of significant problems in enacting and applying fiscal policy.

Problems of Timing

Several problems of timing may arise in connection with fiscal policy:

- **Recognition lag** The recognition lag is the time between the beginning of recession or inflation and the certain awareness that it is actually happening. This lag arises because the economy does not move smoothly through the business cycle. Even during good times, the economy has slow months interspersed with months of rapid growth and expansion. This makes recognizing a recession difficult since several slow months will have to happen in succession before people can conclude with any confidence that the good times are over and a recession has begun.

  The same is true with inflation. Even periods of moderate inflation have months of high inflation—so that several high-inflation months must come in sequence before people can confidently conclude that inflation has moved to a higher level.

  Attempts to reduce the length of the recognition lag by trying to predict the future course of the economy also have proven to be highly difficult, at best. As a result, the economy is often 4 to 6 months into a recession or inflation before the situation is clearly discernible in the relevant statistics. Due to this recognition lag, the economic downslide or the inflation may become more serious than it would have if the situation had been identified and acted on sooner.

- **Administrative lag** The wheels of democratic government turn slowly. There will typically be a significant lag between the time the need for fiscal action is recognized and the time action is taken. Following the terrorist attacks of September 11, 2001, the U.S. Congress was stalemated for 5 months before passing a compromise economic stimulus law in March 2002. (In contrast, the Federal Reserve began lowering interest rates the week after the attacks.)

- **Operational lag** A lag also occurs between the time fiscal action is taken and the time that action affects output, employment, or the price level. Although changes in tax rates can be put into effect relatively quickly once new laws are passed, government spending on public works—new dams, interstate highways, and so on—requires long planning periods and even longer periods of construction. Such spending is of questionable use in offsetting short (for example, 6- to 12-month) periods of recession. Consequently, discretionary fiscal policy has increasingly relied on tax changes rather than on changes in spending as its main tool.

Political Considerations

Fiscal policy is conducted in a political arena. That reality not only may slow the enactment of fiscal policy but also may create the potential for political considerations swamping economic considerations in its formulation. It is a human trait to rationalize actions and policies that are in one's self-interest. Politicians are very human—they want to get reelected. A strong economy at election time will certainly help them. So they may favor large tax cuts under the guise of expansionary fiscal policy even though that policy is economically inappropriate. Similarly, they may rationalize increased government spending on popular items such as farm subsidies, health care, highways, education, and homeland security.

At the extreme, elected officials and political parties might collectively "hijack" fiscal policy for political purposes, cause inappropriate changes in aggregate demand, and thereby cause (rather than avert) economic fluctuations. For instance, before an election, they may try to stimulate the economy to improve their reelection hopes. And then after the election, they may try to use contractionary fiscal policy to dampen the excessive aggregate demand that they caused with their preelection stimulus. In short, elected officials may cause so-called **political business cycles**—swings in overall economic activity and real GDP resulting from election-motivated fiscal policy, rather than from inherent instability in the private sector. Political business cycles are difficult to document and prove, but there is little doubt that political considerations weigh heavily in the formulation of fiscal policy. The question is how often those political considerations run counter to "sound economics."

Future Policy Reversals

Fiscal policy may fail to achieve its intended objectives if households expect future reversals of policy. Consider a tax cut, for example. If taxpayers believe the tax reduction is temporary, they may save a large portion of their tax cut, reasoning that rates will return to their previous level in the future. They save more now so that they will be able draw on this extra savings to maintain their future consumption levels if taxes do indeed rise again in the future. So a tax reduction thought to be temporary may not increase present consumption spending and aggregate demand by as much as our simple model (Figure 13.1) suggests.

The opposite may be true for a tax increase. If taxpayers think it is temporary, they may reduce their saving to pay the tax while maintaining their present consumption. They may reason they can restore their saving when the tax rate again falls. So the tax increase may not reduce current consumption and aggregate demand by as much as policymakers intended.

To the extent that this so-called *consumption smoothing* occurs over time, fiscal policy will lose some of its strength. The lesson is that tax-rate changes that households view as permanent are more likely to alter consumption and aggregate demand than tax changes they view as temporary.

Offsetting State and Local Finance

The fiscal policies of state and local governments are frequently *pro-cyclical*, meaning that they worsen rather than correct recession or inflation. Unlike the Federal government, most state and local governments face constitutional or other legal requirements to balance their budgets. Like households and private businesses, state and local governments increase their expenditures during prosperity and cut them during recession.

During the Great Depression of the 1930s, most of the increase in Federal spending was offset by decreases in state and local spending. During and immediately following the recession of 2001, many state and local governments had to offset lower tax revenues resulting from the reduced personal income and spending of their citizens. They offset the decline in revenues by raising tax rates, imposing new taxes, and reducing spending.

In view of these past experiences, the $787 billion fiscal package of 2009 made a special effort to reduce this problem by giving substantial aid dollars to state governments. Because of the sizable Federal aid, the states did not have to increase taxes and reduce expenditure by as much as otherwise. So their collective fiscal actions did not fight as much against the increase in aggregate demand that the Federal government wanted to achieve with its tax cuts and expenditure increases.

Crowding-Out Effect

Another potential flaw of fiscal policy is the so-called **crowding-out effect:** An expansionary fiscal policy (deficit spending) may increase the interest rate and reduce investment spending, thereby weakening or canceling the stimulus of the expansionary policy. The rising interest rate might also potentially crowd out interest-sensitive consumption spending (such as purchasing automobiles on credit). But since investment is the most volatile component of GDP, the crowding-out effect focuses its attention on investment and whether the stimulus provided by deficit spending may be partly or even fully neutralized by an offsetting reduction in investment spending.

To see the potential problem, realize that whenever the government borrows money (as it must if it is deficit spending), it increases the overall demand for money. If the monetary authorities are holding the money supply constant, this increase in demand will raise the price paid for borrowing money: the interest rate. Because investment spending varies inversely with the interest rate, some investment will be choked off or "crowded out."

> **ORIGIN OF THE IDEA**
> O 13.2
> Crowding out

Economists vary in their opinions about the strength of the crowding-out effect. An important thing to keep in mind is that crowding out is likely to be less of a problem when the economy is in recession, because investment demand tends to be weak. Why? Because output purchases slow during recessions and therefore most businesses end up with substantial excess capacity. As a result, they do not have much incentive to add new machinery or build new factories. After all, why should they add capacity when some of the capacity they already have is lying idle?

With investment demand weak during a recession, the crowding-out effect is likely to be very small. Simply put, there is not much investment for the government to crowd out. Even if deficit spending does increase the interest rate, the effect on investment may be fully offset by the improved investment prospects that businesses expect from the fiscal stimulus.

By contrast, when the economy is operating at or near full capacity, investment demand is likely to be quite strong so that crowding out will probably be a much more serious problem. When the economy is booming, factories will be running at or near full capacity and firms will have high investment demand for two reasons. First, equipment running at full capacity wears out fast, so firms will be investing substantial amounts just to replace machinery and equipment that wears out and depreciates. Second, the economy is likely to be growing overall so that firms will be heavily investing to *add* to their production capacity to take advantage of the greater anticipated demand for their outputs.

Current Thinking on Fiscal Policy

Where do these complications leave us as to the advisability and effectiveness of discretionary fiscal policy? In view of the complications and uncertain outcomes of fiscal policy, some economists argue that it is better not to engage in it at all. Those holding that view point to the superiority of monetary policy (changes in interest rates engineered by the Federal Reserve) as a stabilizing device or believe that most economic fluctuations tend to be mild and self-correcting.

But most economists believe that fiscal policy remains an important, useful policy lever in the government's macroeconomic toolkit. The current popular view is that fiscal policy can help push the economy in a particular direction but cannot fine-tune it to a precise macroeconomic outcome. Mainstream economists generally agree that monetary policy is the best month-to-month stabilization tool for the U.S. economy. If monetary policy is doing its job, the government should maintain a relatively neutral fiscal policy, with a cyclically adjusted budget deficit or surplus of no more than 2 percent of potential GDP. It should hold major discretionary fiscal policy in reserve to help counter situations where recession threatens to be deep and long lasting, as in 2008 and 2009, or where a substantial reduction in aggregate demand might help the Federal Reserve to quell a major bout of inflation.

Finally, economists agree that proposed fiscal policy should be evaluated for its potential positive and negative impacts on long-run productivity growth. The short-run policy tools used for conducting active fiscal policy often have long-run impacts. Countercyclical fiscal policy should be shaped to strengthen, or at least not impede, the growth of long-run aggregate supply (shown as a rightward shift of the long-run aggregate supply curve in Figure 12.5). For example, a tax cut might be structured to enhance work effort, strengthen investment, and encourage innovation. Alternatively, an increase in government spending might center on preplanned projects for public capital (highways, mass transit, ports, airports), which are complementary to private investment and thus support long-term economic growth.

> ### QUICK REVIEW 13.2
>
> - Automatic changes in net taxes (taxes minus transfers) add a degree of built-in stability to the economy.
> - Cyclical deficits arise from declines in net tax revenues that automatically occur as the economy recedes and incomes and profits fall.
> - The cyclically adjusted budget eliminates cyclical effects on net tax revenues; it compares actual levels of government spending to the projected levels of net taxes that would occur if the economy were achieving its full-employment output.
> - Time lags, political problems, expectations, and state and local finances complicate fiscal policy.
> - The crowding-out effect indicates that an expansionary fiscal policy may increase the interest rate and reduce investment spending.

The U.S. Public Debt

The U.S. national debt, or **public debt,** is essentially the accumulation of all past Federal deficits and surpluses. The deficits have greatly exceeded the surpluses and have emerged mainly from war financing, recessions, and fiscal policy. In 2009 the total public debt was $11.9 trillion—$6.8 trillion held by the public, excluding the Federal Reserve; and $5.1 trillion held by Federal agencies and the Federal Reserve. Between 2007 and 2009, the public debt expanded by a huge $2.9 trillion. During the Great Recession, Federal tax revenues plummeted because incomes and profit fell, and Federal expenditures jumped because of huge spending to rescue failing financial institutions and to stimulate the shrinking economy.

You can find the current size of the public debt at the Web site of the Department of Treasury, Bureau of the Public Debt, at **www.treasurydirect.gov/NP/ BPDLogin?application=np**. At this site, you will see that the U.S. Treasury defines "the public" to include the Federal Reserve. But because the Federal Reserve is the nation's central bank, economists view it as essentially part of the Federal government and not part of the public. Economists typically focus on the part of the debt that is not owned by the Federal government and the Federal Reserve.

Ownership

The total public debt of $11.9 trillion represents the total amount of money owed by the Federal government to the holders of **U.S. securities:** financial instruments issued by the Federal government to borrow money to finance expenditures that exceed tax revenues. These U.S. securities (loan instruments) are of four types: *Treasury bills* (short-

FIGURE 13.6 Ownership of the total public debt, 2009.
The $11.9 trillion public debt can be divided into the proportion held by the public, excluding the Federal Reserve (57 percent), and the proportion held by Federal agencies and the Federal Reserve System (43 percent). Of the total debt, 29 percent is foreign-owned.

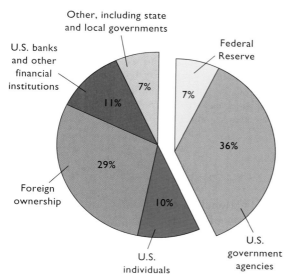

Total debt: $11.9 trillion

Source: Economic Report of the President, 2010, **www.gpoaccess.gov/eop**; authors' derivation from Table B-89, September 2009 data. Federal Reserve percentage is from the U.S. Treasury, **www.fms.treas.gov/bulletin**.

FIGURE 13.7 Federal debt held by the public, excluding the Federal Reserve, as a percentage of GDP, 1970–2009. As a percentage of GDP, the Federal debt held by the public (held outside the Federal Reserve and Federal government agencies) increased sharply over the 1980–1995 period and declined significantly between 1995 and 2001. Since 2001, the percentage has gone up again, and jumped abruptly and sharply in 2008 and 2009.

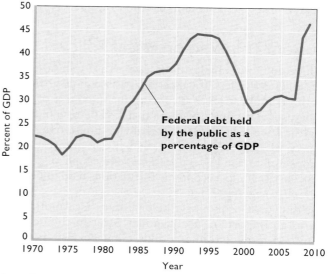

Source: Derived by the authors by subtracting Fed-held debt (**www.fms.treas.gov/bulletin**) from debt held by the public (**www.gpoaccess.gov/eop**).

term securities), *Treasury notes* (medium-term securities), *Treasury bonds* (long-term securities), and *U.S. savings bonds* (long-term, nonmarketable bonds).

Figure 13.6 shows that the public, sans the Federal Reserve, held 57 percent of the Federal debt in 2009 and that Federal government agencies and the Federal Reserve held the remaining 43 percent. The Federal agencies hold U.S. securities as risk-free assets that they can cash in as needed to make latter payments. The Federal Reserve holds these securities to facilitate the "open-market operations" that it uses to control the nation's money supply (Chapter 16). Observe that "the public" in the pie chart consists of individuals here and abroad, state and local governments, and U.S. financial institutions. Foreigners held about 29 percent of the total U.S. public debt in 2009, meaning that most of the U.S. public debt is held internally and not externally. Americans owed 71 percent of the public debt to Americans. Of the $3.7 trillion of debt held by foreigners, China held 24 percent, Japan held 21 percent, and oil-exporting nations held 6 percent.

Debt and GDP

A simple statement of the absolute size of the debt ignores the fact that the wealth and productive ability of the U.S. economy is also vast. A wealthy, highly productive nation can incur and carry a large public debt much more easily than a poor nation can. A more meaningful measure of the public debt relates it to an economy's GDP. Figure 13.7 shows the yearly relative sizes of the U.S. public debt held outside the Federal Reserve and Federal agencies. In 2009 the percentage was 47 percent. Most noticeably, the percentage rose dramatically in 2008 and 2009 because of huge budget deficits together with declining real GDP.

International Comparisons

It is not uncommon for countries to have sizable public debts. As shown in Global Perspective 13.2, the public debt as a percentage of real GDP in the United States is neither particularly high nor low relative to such debt percentages in other advanced industrial nations.

Interest Charges

Many economists conclude that the primary burden of the debt is the annual interest charge accruing on the bonds sold

GLOBAL PERSPECTIVE 13.2

Publicly Held Debt: International Comparisons

Although the United States has the world's largest public debt, a number of other nations have larger debts as percentages of their GDPs.

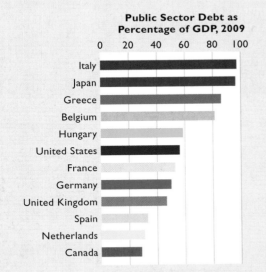

Public Sector Debt as Percentage of GDP, 2009

Source: Organization for Economic Cooperation and Development, *OECD Economic Outlook,* **www.oecd.org**. These debt calculations encompass Federal, state, and local debt, including the debt of government-owned enterprises (not just Federal debt as in Figure 13.7).

to finance the debt. In 2009 interest on the total public debt was $187 billion. Although this amount is sizable in absolute terms, it was only 1.3 percent of GDP for 2009. So, the Federal government had to collect taxes equal to 1.3 percent of GDP to service the total public debt. This percentage was down from 3.2 percent in 1990 and 2.3 percent in 2000, mainly because interest rates in 2009 were extremely low.

False Concerns

You may wonder if the large public debt might bankrupt the United States or at least place a tremendous burden on your children and grandchildren. Fortunately, these are largely false concerns. People were wondering the same things 50 years ago!

Bankruptcy

The large U.S. public debt does not threaten to bankrupt the Federal government, leaving it unable to meet its financial obligations. There are two main reasons: refinancing and taxation.

Refinancing As long as the U.S. public debt is viewed by lenders as manageable and sustainable, the public debt is easily refinanced. As portions of the debt come due on maturing Treasury bills, notes, and bonds each month, the government does not cut expenditures or raise taxes to provide the funds required. Rather, it refinances the debt by selling new bonds and using the proceeds to pay holders of the maturing bonds. The new bonds are in strong demand because lenders can obtain a market-determined interest return with no risk of default by the Federal government.

Of course, refinancing could become an issue with a high enough debt-to-GDP ratio. Some countries such as Greece have run into this problem. High and rising ratios in the United States might raise fears that the U.S. government might be unable to pay back loans as they come due. But, with the present U.S. debt-to-GDP ratio and the prospects of long-term economic growth, this is a false concern for the United States.

Taxation The Federal government has the constitutional authority to levy and collect taxes. A tax increase is a government option for gaining sufficient revenue to pay interest and principal on the public debt. Financially distressed private households and corporations cannot extract themselves from their financial difficulties by taxing the public. If their incomes or sales revenues fall short of their expenses, they can indeed go bankrupt. But the Federal government does have the option to impose new taxes or increase existing tax rates if necessary to finance its debt. Such tax hikes may be politically unpopular and may weaken incentives to work and invest, but they *are* a means of raising funds to finance the debt.

Burdening Future Generations

In 2009 public debt per capita was $37,437. Was each child born in 2009 handed a $37,437 bill from the Federal government? Not really. The public debt does not impose as much of a burden on future generations as commonly thought.

The United States owes a substantial portion of the public debt to itself. U.S. citizens and institutions (banks, businesses, insurance companies, governmental agencies, and trust funds) own about 71 percent of the U.S. government securities. Although that part of the public debt is a liability to Americans (as taxpayers), it is simultaneously an asset to Americans (as holders of Treasury bills, Treasury notes, Treasury bonds, and U.S. savings bonds).

To eliminate the American-owned part of the public debt would require a gigantic transfer payment from Americans to Americans. Taxpayers would pay higher taxes, and holders of the debt would receive an equal amount for their U.S. securities. Purchasing power in the United States would not change. Only the repayment of the 29 percent of the public debt owned by foreigners would negatively impact U.S. purchasing power.

The public debt increased sharply during the Second World War. But the decision to finance military purchases through the sale of government bonds did not shift the economic burden of the war to future generations. The economic cost of the Second World War consisted of the civilian goods society had to forgo in shifting scarce resources to war goods production (recall production possibilities analysis). Regardless of whether society financed this reallocation through higher taxes or through borrowing, the real economic burden of the war would have been the same. That burden was borne almost entirely by those who lived during the war. They were the ones who did without a multitude of consumer goods to enable the United States to arm itself and its allies.

The next generation inherited the debt from the war but also an equal amount of government bonds that would pay them cash in future years. It also inherited the enormous benefits from the victory—namely, preserved political and economic systems at home and the "export" of those systems to Germany, Italy, and Japan. Those outcomes enhanced postwar U.S. economic growth and helped raise the standard of living of future generations of Americans.

Substantive Issues

Although the preceding issues relating to the public debt are false concerns, a number of substantive issues are not. Economists, however, attach varying degrees of importance to them.

Income Distribution

The distribution of ownership of government securities is highly uneven. Some people own much more than the $37,437-per-person portion of government securities; other people own less or none at all. In general, the ownership of the public debt is concentrated among wealthier groups, who own a large percentage of all stocks and bonds. Because the overall Federal tax system is only slightly progressive, payment of interest on the public debt mildly increases income inequality. Income is transferred from people who, on average, have lower incomes to the higher-income bondholders. If greater income equality is one of society's goals, then this redistribution is undesirable.

Incentives

The current public debt necessitates annual interest payments of $187 billion. With no increase in the size of the debt, that interest charge must be paid out of tax revenues. Higher taxes may dampen incentives to bear risk, to innovate, to invest, and to work. So, in this indirect way, a large public debt may impair economic growth and therefore impose a burden of reduced output (and income) on future generations.

Foreign-Owned Public Debt

The 29 percent of the U.S. debt held by citizens and institutions of foreign countries *is* an economic burden to Americans. Because we do not owe that portion of the debt "to ourselves," the payment of interest and principal on this **external public debt** enables foreigners to buy some of our output. In return for the benefits derived from the borrowed funds, the United States transfers goods and services to foreign lenders. Of course, Americans also own debt issued by foreign governments, so payment of principal and interest by those governments transfers some of their goods and services to Americans.

Crowding-Out Effect Revisited

A potentially more serious problem is the financing (and continual refinancing) of the large public debt, which can transfer a real economic burden to future generations by passing on to them a smaller stock of capital goods. This possibility involves the previously discussed crowding-out effect: the idea that public borrowing drives up real interest rates, which reduces private investment spending. If public borrowing only happened during recessions, crowding out would not likely be much of a problem. Because private investment demand tends to be weak during recessions, any increase in interest rates caused by public borrowing will at most cause a small reduction in investment spending.

In contrast, the need to continuously finance a large public debt may be more troublesome. At times, that financing requires borrowing large amounts of money when the economy is near or at its full-employment output. Because this usually is when private demand is strong, any increase in interest rates caused by the borrowing necessary to refinance the debt may result in a substantial decline in investment spending. If the amount of current investment crowded out is extensive, future generations will inherit an economy with a smaller production capacity and, other things equal, a lower standard of living.

FIGURE 13.8 The investment demand curve and the crowding-out effect. If the investment demand curve (ID_1) is fixed, the increase in the interest rate from 6 percent to 10 percent caused by financing a large public debt will move the economy from a to b, crowding out $10 billion of private investment and decreasing the size of the capital stock inherited by future generations. However, if the public goods enabled by the debt improve the investment prospects of businesses, the private investment demand curve will shift rightward, as from ID_1 to ID_2. That shift may offset the crowding-out effect wholly or in part. In this case, it moves the economy from a to c.

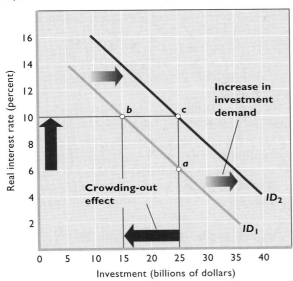

A *Graphical Look at Crowding Out* We know from Chapter 10 that the amount of investment spending is inversely related to the real interest rate. When graphed, that relationship is shown as a downsloping investment demand curve, such as either ID_1 or ID_2 in Figure 13.8. Let's first consider curve ID_1. (Ignore curve ID_2 for now.) Suppose that government borrowing increases the real interest rate from 6 percent to 10 percent. Investment spending will then fall from $25 billion to $15 billion, as shown by the economy's move from a to b. That is, the financing of the debt will compete with the financing of private investment projects and crowd out $10 billion of private investment. So the stock of private capital handed down to future generations will be $10 billion less than it would have been without the need to finance the public debt.

Public Investments and Public-Private Complementarities But even with crowding out, two factors could partly or fully offset the net economic burden shifted to future generations. First, just as private expenditures may involve either consumption or investment, so it is with public goods. Part of the government spending enabled by the

public debt is for public investment outlays (for example, highways, mass transit systems, and electric power facilities) and "human capital" (for example, investments in education, job training, and health). Like private expenditures on machinery and equipment, those **public investments** increase the economy's future production capacity. Because of the financing through debt, the stock of public capital passed on to future generations may be higher than otherwise. That greater stock of public capital may offset the diminished stock of private capital resulting from the crowding-out effect, leaving overall production capacity unimpaired.

So-called public-private complementarities are a second factor that could reduce the crowding out effect. Some public and private investments are complementary. Thus, the public investment financed through debt could spur some private-sector investment by increasing its expected rate of return. For example, a Federal building in a city may encourage private investment in the form of nearby office buildings, shops, and restaurants. Through its complementary effect, the spending on public capital may shift the private investment demand curve to the right, as from ID_1 to ID_2 in Figure 13.8. Even though the government borrowing boosts the interest rate from 6 percent to 10 percent, total private investment need not fall. In the case shown as the move from a to c in Figure 13.8, it remains at $25 billion. Of course, the increase in investment demand might be smaller than that shown. If it were smaller, the crowding-out effect would not be fully offset. But the point is that an increase in investment demand may counter the decline in investment that would otherwise result from the higher interest rate.

QUICK REVIEW 13.3

- The U.S. public debt—$11.9 trillion in 2009—is essentially the total accumulation of all past Federal budget deficits and surpluses; about 29 percent of the U.S. public debt is held by foreigners.
- The U.S. public debt held by the public (excluding the Federal Reserve) was 47 percent of GDP in 2009, up from 30 percent in 2000.
- The Federal government is in no danger of going bankrupt because it needs only to refinance (not retire) the public debt and it can raise revenues, if needed, through higher taxes.
- The borrowing and interest payments associated with the public debt may (a) increase income inequality; (b) require higher taxes, which may dampen incentives; and (c) impede the growth of the nation's stock of capital through crowding out of private investment.

Social Security and Medicare Face Gigantic Future Funding Shortfalls. Metaphorically Speaking, Some Economists See These Programs as Financial and Political Time Bombs.

The American population, on average, is getting decidedly older. The percentage of the population age 62 or older will rise substantially over the next several decades, with the greatest increases for people age 75 and above. In the future, more people will be receiving Social Security benefits (income during retirement) and Medicare (medical care during retirement) for longer periods. Each person's benefits will be paid for by fewer workers. The number of workers per Social Security and Medicare beneficiary was roughly 5:1 in 1960. Today it is 3:1, and by 2040 it will be only 2:1.

The combined cost of the Social Security and Medicare programs was 7.6 percent of GDP in 2008, and that percentage is projected to grow to 12 percent of GDP in 2030 and 17.2 percent of GDP in 2083.*

The Social Security Shortfall Social Security is the major public retirement program in the United States. The program costs $615 billion annually and is financed by a 12.4 percent tax on earnings up to a set level of earnings ($106,800 in 2009). Half the tax (6.2 percent) is paid by the worker; the other half by the employer. Social Security is largely an annual "pay-as-you-go" plan, meaning that most of the current revenues from the Social Security tax are paid to current Social Security retirees.

---

*Social Security and Medicare Board of Trustees, "Status of the Social Security and Medicare Programs: A Summary of the 2009 Annual Reports," **www.ssa.gov**. This publication is also the source of most of the statistical information that follows.

Through the start of 2009, Social Security revenues exceeded Social Security payouts in anticipation of the large benefits promised to the baby boomers when they retire. That excess inflow was used to buy U.S. Treasury securities that were credited to a government account called the Social Security Trust Fund. But the combined accumulation of money in the trust fund through 2009 plus the projected future revenues from the payroll tax in later years was expected to be greatly inadequate for paying the promised retirement benefits to all future retirees.

This underfunding of future retirement promises was brought into sharper focus in the latter half of 2009 when for the first time, Social Security revenues fell below Social Security retirement payouts and the system started shifting money from the trust fund to make up the difference. The trust fund is expected to be exhausted in 2037. For each year thereafter, annual tax revenues will cover only 75 percent of the promised benefits.

The Medicare Shortfall The Medicare program is the U.S. health care program for people age 65 and older in the United States. The program costs $462 billion per year and has been growing at about 9 percent annually. Like Social Security, it also is a pay-as-you-go plan, meaning that current medical benefits for people age 65 or older are being funded by current tax revenues from the 2.9 percent Medicare tax on earnings. Like the Social Security tax, half the Medicare tax is paid by the employer (1.45 percent) and half the by the employee. But the 2.9 percent Medicare tax is applied to all earnings.

The financial status of Medicare is much worse than that of Social Security. To begin with, the Medicare Trust Fund will be depleted in 2017, 20 years before the Social Security Trust Fund is expected to be depleted. Then, in subsequent years, the percentage of scheduled Medicare benefits covered

Summary

1. Fiscal policy consists of deliberate changes in government spending, taxes, or some combination of both to promote full employment, price-level stability, and economic growth. Fiscal policy requires increases in government spending, decreases in taxes, or both—a budget deficit—to increase aggregate demand and push an economy from a recession. Decreases in government spending, increases in taxes, or both—a budget surplus—are appropriate fiscal policy for decreasing aggregate demand to try to slow or halt demand-pull inflation.

by the Medicare tax will decline from 81 percent in 2017 to 50 percent in 2035 and 29 percent in 2080.

The Unpleasant Options To restore long-run balance to Social Security and Medicare, the Federal government must either reduce benefits or increase revenues. It's as simple—and as complicated—as that! The Social Security Administration concludes that bringing projected Social Security revenues and payments into balance over the next 75 years would require a 16 percent permanent reduction in Social Security benefits, a 13 percent permanent increase in tax revenues, or some combination of the two. To bring projected Medicare revenues and expenses into long-run balance would require an increase in the Medicare payroll tax by 122 percent, a 51 percent reduction of Medicare payments from their projected levels, or some combination of each.

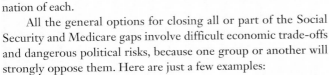

All the general options for closing all or part of the Social Security and Medicare gaps involve difficult economic trade-offs and dangerous political risks, because one group or another will strongly oppose them. Here are just a few examples:

- Increasing the retirement age for collecting Social Security or Medicare benefits will upset preretirement workers who have been paying into the system and will receive their benefits later than they expected.
- Subjecting a larger portion of total earnings to the Social Security tax would constitute a gigantic tax increase on the earnings of the country's highest trained and educated individuals. This might reduce the incentive of younger people to obtain education and advance in their careers.

- Disqualifying wealthy individuals from receiving Social Security and Medicare benefits would tilt the programs toward welfare and redistribution, rather than insurance programs. This would undermine the broad existing political support for the programs.
- Redirecting legal immigration toward high-skilled, high-earning entrants and away from low-skilled, low-earning immigrants to raise Social Security and Medicare revenues would also raise the ire of some native-born high-skilled workers and the proponents of immigration based on family reunification.
- Placing the payroll tax revenues into accounts that individuals, not the government, would own, maintain, and bequeath would transform the Social Security and Medicare programs from guaranteed "defined benefit plans" into much riskier "defined contribution plans." The extreme short-run volatility of the stock market might leave some unlucky people destitute in old age.

The problem is huge and will not go away. One recent attempt to add up the underfunding of all the promised Social Security and Medicare benefits finds that the total underfunding greatly exceeds the combined current wealth (net worth) of everyone in the United States today.[†] Even if this estimate is somewhat extreme, the fact remains: The Federal government and American people eventually will have to face up to the over-promising-underfunding problem and find ways to resolve it.

_____
[†]Bruce Bartlett, "The 81% Tax Increase," Forbes.com, August 8, 2009, **www.forbes.com**.

2. Built-in stability arises from net tax revenues, which vary directly with the level of GDP. During recession, the Federal budget automatically moves toward a stabilizing deficit; during expansion, the budget automatically moves toward an anti-inflationary surplus. Built-in stability lessens, but does not fully correct, undesired changes in real GDP.

3. Actual Federal budget deficits can go up or down because of changes in GDP, changes in fiscal policy, or both. Deficits caused by changes in GDP are called cyclical deficits. The

cyclically adjusted budget removes cyclical deficits from the budget and therefore measures the budget deficit or surplus that would occur if the economy operated at its full-employment output throughout the year. Changes in the cyclical-budget deficit or surplus provide meaningful information as to whether the government's fiscal policy is expansionary, neutral, or contractionary. Changes in the actual budget deficit or surplus do not, since such deficits or surpluses can include cyclical deficits or surpluses.

4. In 2001 the Bush administration and Congress chose to reduce marginal tax rates and phase out the Federal estate tax. A recession occurred in 2001, and Federal spending for the war on terrorism rocketed. The Federal budget swung from a surplus of $128 billion in 2001 to a deficit of $158 billion in 2002. In 2003 the Bush administration and Congress accelerated the tax reductions scheduled under the 2001 tax law and cut tax rates on capital gains and dividends. The purposes were to stimulate a sluggish economy. By 2007 the economy had reached its full employment level of output.

5. The Federal government responded to the deep recession of 2007–2009 by implementing highly expansionary fiscal policy. In 2008 the Federal government passed a tax rebate program that sent $600 dollar checks to qualified individuals. Later that year, it created a $700 billion emergency fund to keep key financial institutions from failing. These and other programs increased the cyclically adjusted budget deficit from −1.2 percent of potential GDP in 2007 to −2.8 percent in 2008. When the economy continued to plunge, the Obama administration and Congress enacted a massive $787 billion stimulus program to be implemented over 2½ years. The cyclically adjusted budget deficit shot up from −2.8 percent of potential GDP in 2008 to −7.3 percent in 2009.

6. Certain problems complicate the enactment and implementation of fiscal policy. They include (a) timing problems associated with recognition, administrative, and operational lags; (b) the potential for misuse of fiscal policy for political rather than economic purposes; (c) the fact that state and local finances tend to be pro-cyclical; (d) potential ineffectiveness if households expect future policy reversals; and (e) the possibility of fiscal policy crowding out private investment.

7. Most economists believe that fiscal policy can help move the economy in a desired direction but cannot reliably be used to fine-tune the economy to a position of price stability and full employment. Nevertheless, fiscal policy is a valuable backup tool for aiding monetary policy in fighting significant recession or inflation.

8. The public debt is the total accumulation of all past Federal government deficits and surpluses and consists of Treasury bills, Treasury notes, Treasury bonds, and U.S. savings bonds. In 2009 the U.S. public debt was $11.9 trillion, or $37,437 per person. The public (which here includes banks and state and local governments) holds 57 percent of that Federal debt; the Federal Reserve and Federal agencies hold the other 43 percent. Foreigners hold 29 percent of the Federal debt. Interest payments as a percentage of GDP were about 1.3 percent in 2009. This is down from 3.2 percent in 1990.

9. The concern that a large public debt may bankrupt the U.S. government is generally a false worry because (a) the debt needs only to be refinanced rather than refunded and (b) the Federal government has the power to increase taxes to make interest payments on the debt.

10. In general, the public debt is not a vehicle for shifting economic burdens to future generations. Americans inherit not only most of the public debt (a liability) but also most of the U.S. securities (an asset) that finance the debt.

11. More substantive problems associated with public debt include the following: (a) Payment of interest on the debt may increase income inequality. (b) Interest payments on the debt require higher taxes, which may impair incentives. (c) Paying interest or principal on the portion of the debt held by foreigners means a transfer of real output abroad. (d) Government borrowing to refinance or pay interest on the debt may increase interest rates and crowd out private investment spending, leaving future generations with a smaller stock of capital than they would have had otherwise.

12. The increase in investment in public capital that may result from debt financing may partly or wholly offset the crowding-out effect of the public debt on private investment. Also, the added public investment may stimulate private investment, where the two are complements.

Terms and Concepts

fiscal policy

Council of Economic Advisers (CEA)

expansionary fiscal policy

budget deficit

contractionary fiscal policy

budget surplus

built-in stabilizer

progressive tax system

proportional tax system

regressive tax system

cyclically adjusted budget

cyclical deficit

political business cycle

crowding-out effect

public debt

U.S. securities

external public debt

public investments

Questions

1. What is the role of the Council of Economic Advisers (CEA) as it relates to fiscal policy? Use an Internet search to find the names and university affiliations of the present members of the CEA. **LO1**

2. What are government's fiscal policy options for ending severe demand-pull inflation? Which of these fiscal options do you think might be favored by a person who wants to preserve the size of government? A person who thinks the public sector is too large? How does the "ratchet effect" affect anti-inflationary fiscal policy? **LO1**

3. (For students who were assigned Chapter 11) Use the aggregate expenditures model to show how government fiscal policy could eliminate either a recessionary expenditure gap or an inflationary expenditure gap (Figure 11.7). Explain how equal-size increases in G and T could eliminate a recessionary gap and how equal-size decreases in G and T could eliminate an inflationary gap. **LO1**

4. Some politicians have suggested that the United States enact a constitutional amendment requiring that the Federal government balance its budget annually. Explain why such an amendment, if strictly enforced, would force the government to enact a contractionary fiscal policy whenever the economy experienced a severe recession. **LO1**

5. Briefly state and evaluate the problem of time lags in enacting and applying fiscal policy. Explain the idea of a political business cycle. How might expectations of a near-term policy reversal weaken fiscal policy based on changes in tax rates? What is the crowding-out effect, and why might it be relevant to fiscal policy? In view of your answers, explain the following statement: "Although fiscal policy clearly is useful in combating the extremes of severe recession and demand-pull inflation, it is impossible to use fiscal policy to fine-tune the economy to the full-employment, noninflationary level of real GDP and keep the economy there indefinitely." **LO1**

6. Explain how built-in (or automatic) stabilizers work. What are the differences between proportional, progressive, and regressive tax systems as they relate to an economy's built-in stability? **LO2**

7. Define the cyclically adjusted budget, explain its significance, and state why it may differ from the actual budget. Suppose the full-employment, noninflationary level of real

output is GDP_3 (not GDP_2) in the economy depicted in Figure 13.3. If the economy is operating at GDP_2, instead of GDP_3, what is the status of its cyclically adjusted budget? The status of its current fiscal policy? What change in fiscal policy would you recommend? How would you accomplish that in terms of the G and T lines in the figure? **LO3**

8. How do economists distinguish between the absolute and relative sizes of the public debt? Why is the distinction important? Distinguish between refinancing the debt and retiring the debt. How does an internally held public debt differ from an externally held public debt? Contrast the effects of retiring an internally held debt and retiring an externally held debt. **LO4**

9. True or false? If false, explain why. **LO4**

   a. The total public debt is more relevant to an economy than the public debt as a percentage of GDP.

   b. An internally held public debt is like a debt of the left hand owed to the right hand.

   c. The Federal Reserve and Federal government agencies hold more than three-fourths of the public debt.

   d. The portion of the U.S. debt held by the public (and not by government entities) was larger as a percentage of GDP in 2009 than it was in 2000.

   e. As a percentage of GDP, the total U.S. public debt is the highest such debt among the world's advanced industrial nations.

10. Why might economists be quite concerned if the annual interest payments on the U.S. public debt sharply increased as a percentage of GDP? **LO4**

11. Trace the cause-and-effect chain through which financing and refinancing of the public debt might affect real interest rates, private investment, the stock of capital, and economic growth. How might investment in public capital and complementarities between public capital and private capital alter the outcome of the cause-effect chain? **LO4**

12. **LAST WORD** What do economists mean when they say Social Security and Medicare are "pay-as-you-go" plans? What are the Social Security and Medicare trust funds, and how long will they have money left in them? What is the key long-run problem of both Social Security and Medicare? Do you favor increasing taxes or do you prefer reducing benefits to fix the problem?

Problems

1. Assume that a hypothetical economy with an MPC of .8 is experiencing severe recession. By how much would government spending have to rise to shift the aggregate demand curve rightward by $25 billion? How large a tax cut would be needed to achieve the same increase in aggregate

demand? Determine one possible combination of government spending increases and tax decreases that would accomplish the same goal. **LO1**

2. Refer back to the table in Figure 12.7 in the previous chapter. Suppose that aggregate demand increases such that the

amount of real output demanded rises by $7 billion at each price level. By what percentage will the price level increase? Will this inflation be demand-pull inflation or will it be cost-push inflation? If potential real GDP (that is, full-employment GDP) is $510 billion, what will be the size of the positive GDP gap after the change in aggregate demand? If government wants to use fiscal policy to counter the resulting inflation without changing tax rates, would it increase government spending or decrease it? **LO1**

3. (For students who were assigned Chapter 11) Assume that, without taxes, the consumption schedule for an economy is as shown below: **LO1**

GDP, Billions	Consumption, Billions
$100	$120
200	200
300	280
400	360
500	440
600	520
700	600

a. Graph this consumption schedule. What is the size of the MPC?

b. Assume that a lump-sum (regressive) tax of $10 billion is imposed at all levels of GDP. Calculate the tax rate at each level of GDP. Graph the resulting consumption schedule and compare the MPC and the multiplier with those of the pretax consumption schedule.

c. Now suppose a proportional tax with a 10 percent tax rate is imposed instead of the regressive tax. Calculate and graph the new consumption schedule and note the MPC and the multiplier.

d. Finally, impose a progressive tax such that the tax rate is 0 percent when GDP is $100, 5 percent at $200, 10 percent at $300, 15 percent at $400, and so forth. Determine and graph the new consumption schedule, noting the effect of this tax system on the MPC and the multiplier.

e. Use a graph similar to Figure 13.3 to show why proportional and progressive taxes contribute to greater economic stability, while a regressive tax does not.

4. Refer to the accompanying table for Waxwania: **LO2, LO3**

Government Expenditures, G	Tax Revenues, T	Real GDP
$160	$100	$500
160	120	600
160	140	700
160	160	800
160	180	900

a. What is the marginal tax rate in Waxwania? The average tax rate? Which of the following describes the tax system: proportional, progressive, regressive?

b. Suppose Waxwania is producing $600 of real GDP, whereas the potential real GDP (or full-employment real GDP) is $700. How large is its budget deficit? Its cyclically adjusted budget deficit? Its cyclically adjusted budget deficit as a percentage of potential real GDP? Is Waxwania's fiscal policy expansionary or is it contractionary?

5. Suppose that a country has no public debt in year 1 but experiences a budget deficit of $40 billion in year 2, a budget deficit of $20 billion in year 3, a budget surplus of $10 billion in year 3, and a budget deficit of $2 billion in year 4. What is the absolute size of its public debt in year 4? If its real GDP in year 4 is $104 billion, what is this country's public debt as a percentage of real GDP in year 4? **LO4**

6. Suppose that the investment demand curve in a certain economy is such that investment declines by $100 billion for every 1 percentage point increase in the real interest rate. Also, suppose that the investment demand curve shifts rightward by $150 billion at each real interest rate for every 1 percentage point increase in the expected rate of return from investment. If stimulus spending (an expansionary fiscal policy) by government increases the real interest rate by 2 percentage points, but also raises the expected rate of return on investment by 1 percentage point, how much investment, if any, will be crowded out? **LO4**

FURTHER TEST YOUR KNOWLEDGE AT
www.mcconnell19e.com

At the text's Online Learning Center (OLC), **www.mcconnell19e.com**, you will find one or more Web-based questions that require information from the Internet to answer. We urge you to check them out; they will familiarize you with Web sites that may be helpful in other courses and perhaps even in your career. The OLC also features multiple-choice questions that give instant feedback and provides other helpful ways to further test your knowledge of the chapter.

MONEY, BANKING, AND MONETARY POLICY

14

AFTER READING THIS CHAPTER, YOU SHOULD BE ABLE TO:

1 Identify and explain the functions of money and the components of the U.S. money supply.

2 Describe what "backs" the money supply, making us willing to accept it as payment.

3 Discuss the makeup of the Federal Reserve and its relationship to banks and thrifts.

4 Identify the functions and responsibilities of the Federal Reserve.

5 Identify and explain the main factors that contributed to the financial crisis of 2007–2008.

6 Discuss the actions of the U.S. Treasury and the Federal Reserve that helped keep the banking and financial crisis of 2007–2008 from worsening.

7 Identify the main subsets of the financial services industry in the United States and provide examples of some firms in each category.

Money, Banking, and Financial Institutions

Money is a fascinating aspect of the economy:

> Money bewitches people. They fret for it, and they sweat for it. They devise most ingenious ways to get it, and most ingenuous ways to get rid of it. Money is the only commodity that is good for nothing but to be gotten rid of. It will not feed you, clothe you, shelter you, or amuse you unless you spend it or invest it. It imparts value only in parting. People will do almost anything for money, and money will do almost anything for people. Money is a captivating, circulating, masquerading puzzle.[1]

In this chapter and the two chapters that follow, we want to unmask the critical role of money and the monetary system in the economy. When the monetary system is working properly, it provides

[1]"Creeping Inflation," *Business Review*, August 1957, p. 3. Federal Reserve Bank of Philadelphia. Used with permission.

the lifeblood of the circular flows of income and expenditure. A well-operating monetary system helps the economy achieve both full employment and the efficient use of resources. A malfunctioning monetary system distorts the allocation of resources and creates severe fluctuations in the economy's levels of output, employment, and prices.

The Functions of Money

Just what is money? There is an old saying that "money *is* what money *does*." In a general sense, anything that performs the functions of money *is* money. Here are those functions:

- *Medium of exchange* First and foremost, money is a **medium of exchange** that is usable for buying and selling goods and services. A bakery worker does not want to be paid 200 bagels per week. Nor does the bakery owner want to receive, say, halibut in exchange for bagels. Money, however, is readily acceptable as payment. As we saw in Chapter 2, money is a social invention with which resource suppliers and producers can be paid and that can be used to buy any of the full range of items available in the marketplace. As a medium of exchange, money allows society to escape the complications of barter. And because it provides a convenient way of exchanging goods, money enables society to gain the advantages of geographic and human specialization.
- *Unit of account* Money is also a **unit of account**. Society uses monetary units—dollars, in the United States—as a yardstick for measuring the relative worth of a wide variety of goods, services, and resources. Just as we measure distance in miles or kilometers, we gauge the value of goods in dollars.

  With money as an acceptable unit of account, the price of each item need be stated only in terms of the monetary unit. We need not state the price of cows in terms of corn, crayons, and cranberries. Money aids rational decision making by enabling buyers and sellers to easily compare the prices of various goods, services, and resources. It also permits us to define debt obligations, determine taxes owed, and calculate the nation's GDP.
- *Store of value* Money also serves as a **store of value** that enables people to transfer purchasing power from the present to the future. People normally do not spend all their incomes on the day they receive them. To buy things later, they store some of their wealth as money. The money you place in a safe or a checking account will still be available to you a few weeks or months from now. When inflation is nonexistent or mild, holding money is a relatively risk-free way to store your wealth for later use.

People can, of course, choose to hold some or all of their wealth in a wide variety of assets besides money. These include real estate, stocks, bonds, precious metals such as gold, and even collectible items like fine art or comic books. But a key advantage that money has over all other assets is that it has the most *liquidity*, or spendability.

An asset's **liquidity** is the ease with which it can be converted quickly into the most widely accepted and easily spent form of money, cash, with little or no loss of purchasing power. The more liquid an asset is, the more quickly it can be converted into cash and used for either purchases of goods and services or purchases of other assets.

Levels of liquidity vary radically. By definition, cash is perfectly liquid. By contrast, a house is highly illiquid for two reasons. First, it may take several months before a willing buyer can be found and a sale negotiated so that its value can be converted into cash. Second, there is a loss of purchasing power when the house is sold because numerous fees have to be paid to real estate agents and other individuals to complete the sale.

As we are about to discuss, our economy uses several different types of money including cash, coins, checking account deposits, savings account deposits, and even more exotic things like deposits in money market mutual funds. As we describe the various forms of money in detail, take the time to compare their relative levels of liquidity—both with each other and as compared to other assets like stocks, bonds, and real estate. Cash is perfectly liquid. Other forms of money are highly liquid, but less liquid than cash.

The Components of the Money Supply

Money is a "stock" of some item or group of items (unlike income, for example, which is a "flow"). Societies have used many items as money, including whales' teeth, circular stones, elephant-tail bristles, gold coins, furs, and pieces of paper. Anything that is widely accepted as a medium of exchange can serve as money. In the United States, currency is not the only form of money. As you will see, certain debts of government and financial institutions also are used as money.

FIGURE 14.1 Components of money supply M1 and money supply M2, in the United States.

(a) *M*1 is a narrow definition of the money supply that includes currency (in circulation) and checkable deposits. (b) *M*2 is a broader definition that includes *M*1 along with several other relatively liquid account balances.

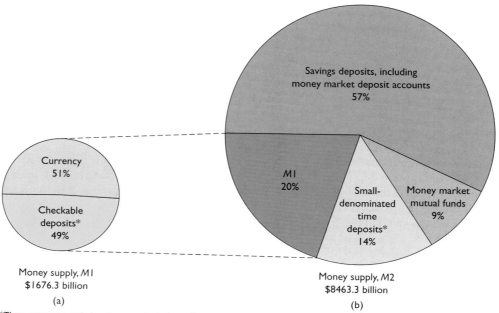

Money supply, M1
$1676.3 billion
(a)

Money supply, M2
$8463.3 billion
(b)

*These categories include other, quantitatively smaller components such as traveler's checks.
Source: Federal Reserve System, **www.federalreserve.gov**. Data are for January 2010.

Money Definition *M1*

The narrowest definition of the U.S. money supply is called **M1.** It consists of two components:

- Currency (coins and paper money) in the hands of the public.
- All checkable deposits (all deposits in commercial banks and "thrift" or savings institutions on which checks of any size can be drawn).[2]

Government and government agencies supply coins and paper money. Commercial banks ("banks") and savings institutions ("thrifts") provide checkable deposits. Figure 14.1a shows that *M*1 is about equally divided between the two components.

Currency: Coins + Paper Money

The currency of the United States consists of metal coins and paper money. The coins are issued by the U.S. Treasury while the paper money consists of **Federal Reserve Notes** issued by the

Federal Reserve System (the U.S. central bank). The coins are minted by the U.S. Mint while the paper money is printed by the Bureau of Engraving and Printing. Both the U.S. Mint and the Bureau of Engraving and Printing are part of the U.S. Department of the Treasury.

As with the currencies of other countries, the currency of the United States is **token money.** This means that the face value of any piece of currency is unrelated to its *intrinsic value*—the value of the physical material (metal or paper and ink) out of which that piece of currency is constructed. Governments make sure that face values exceed intrinsic values to discourage people from destroying coins and bills to resell the material that they are made out of. For instance, if 50-cent pieces each contained 75 cents' worth of metal, then it would be profitable to melt them down and sell the metal. Fifty-cent pieces would disappear from circulation very quickly!

Figure 14.1a shows that currency (coins and paper money) constitutes 51 percent of the *M*1 money supply in the United States.

Checkable Deposits

The safety and convenience of checks has made **checkable deposits** a large component of the *M*1 money supply. You would not think of stuffing $4896 in bills in an envelope and dropping it in a mailbox

---

[2]In the ensuing discussion, we do not discuss several of the quantitatively less significant components of the definitions of money to avoid a maze of details. For example, traveler's checks are included in the *M*1 money supply. The statistical appendix of any recent *Federal Reserve Bulletin* provides more comprehensive definitions.

to pay a debt. But writing and mailing a check for a large sum is commonplace. The person cashing a check must endorse it (sign it on the reverse side); the writer of the check subsequently receives a record of the cashed check as a receipt attesting to the fulfillment of the obligation. Similarly, because the writing of a check requires endorsement, the theft or loss of your checkbook is not nearly as calamitous as losing an identical amount of currency. Finally, it is more convenient to write a check than to transport and count out a large sum of currency. For all these reasons, checkable deposits (checkbook money) are a large component of the stock of money in the United States. About 49 percent of $M1$ is in the form of checkable deposits, on which checks can be drawn.

It might seem strange that checking account balances are regarded as part of the money supply. But the reason is clear: Checks are nothing more than a way to transfer the ownership of deposits in banks and other financial institutions and are generally acceptable as a medium of exchange. Although checks are less generally accepted than currency for small purchases, for major purchases most sellers willingly accept checks as payment. Moreover, people can convert checkable deposits into paper money and coins on demand; checks drawn on those deposits are thus the equivalent of currency.

To summarize:

$$\text{Money, } M1 = \text{currency} + \text{checkable deposits}$$

Institutions That Offer Checkable Deposits

In the United States, a variety of financial institutions allow customers to write checks in any amount on the funds they have deposited. **Commercial banks** are the primary depository institutions. They accept the deposits of households and businesses, keep the money safe until it is demanded via checks, and in the meantime use it to make available a wide variety of loans. Commercial bank loans provide short-term financial capital to businesses, and they finance consumer purchases of automobiles and other durable goods.

Savings and loan associations (S&Ls), mutual savings banks, and credit unions supplement the commercial banks and are known collectively as savings or **thrift institutions,** or simply "thrifts." *Savings and loan associations* and *mutual savings banks* accept the deposits of households and businesses and then use the funds to finance housing mortgages and to provide other loans. *Credit unions* accept deposits from and lend to "members," who usually are a group of people who work for the same company.

The checkable deposits of banks and thrifts are known variously as demand deposits, NOW (negotiable order of withdrawal) accounts, ATS (automatic transfer service) accounts, and share draft accounts. Their commonality is that depositors can write checks on them whenever, and in whatever amount, they choose.

Two Qualifications We must qualify our discussion in two important ways. First, currency held by the U.S. treasury, the Federal Reserve banks, commercial banks, and thrift institutions is *excluded* from $M1$ and other measures of the money supply. A paper dollar or four quarters in the billfold of, say, Emma Buck obviously constitutes just $1 of the money supply. But if we counted currency held by banks as part of the money supply, the same $1 would count for $2 of money supply when Emma deposited the currency into her checkable deposit in her bank. It would count for $1 of checkable deposit owned by Buck and also $1 of currency in the bank's cash drawer or vault. By excluding currency held by banks when determining the total supply of money, we avoid this problem of double counting.

Also *excluded* from the money supply are any checkable deposits of the government (specifically, the U.S. Treasury) or the Federal Reserve that are held by commercial banks or thrift institutions. This exclusion is designed to enable a better assessment of the amount of money available *to the private sector* for potential spending. The amount of money available to households and businesses is of keen interest to the Federal Reserve in conducting its monetary policy (a topic we cover in detail in Chapter 16).

Money Definition *M2*

A second and broader definition of money includes $M1$ plus several near-monies. **Near-monies** are certain highly liquid financial assets that do not function directly or fully as a medium of exchange but can be readily converted into currency or checkable deposits. The *M2* definition of money includes three categories of near-monies.

- *Savings deposits, including money market deposit accounts* A depositor can easily withdraw funds from a **savings account** at a bank or thrift or simply request that the funds be transferred from a savings account to a checkable account. A person can also withdraw funds from a **money market deposit account (MMDA)**, which is an interest-bearing account containing a variety of interest-bearing short-term securities. MMDAs, however, have a minimum-balance requirement and a limit on how often a person can withdraw funds.

- *Small-denominated (less than $100,000) time deposits* Funds from **time deposits** become available at their maturity. For example, a person can convert a 6-month time deposit ("certificate of deposit," or "CD") to currency without penalty 6 months or more after it has been deposited. In return for this withdrawal limitation, the financial institution pays a higher interest rate on such deposits than it does on its MMDAs. Also, a person can "cash in" a CD at any time but must pay a severe penalty.

- ***Money market mutual funds held by individuals*** By making a telephone call, using the Internet, or writing a check for $500 or more, a depositor can redeem shares in a **money market mutual fund (MMMF)** offered by a mutual fund company. Such companies use the combined funds of individual shareholders to buy interest-bearing short-term credit instruments such as certificates of deposit and U.S. government securities. Then they can offer interest on the MMMF accounts of the shareholders (depositors) who jointly own those financial assets. The MMMFs in *M2* include only the MMMF accounts held by individuals; those held by businesses and other institutions are excluded.

All three categories of near-monies imply substantial liquidity. Thus, in equation form,

$$\text{Money, } M2 = \begin{array}{l} M1 + \text{ savings deposits, including} \\ \text{MMDAs} + \text{small-denominated} \\ \text{(less than \$100,000) time deposits} \\ + \text{ MMMFs held by individuals} \end{array}$$

In summary, *M2* includes the immediate medium-of-exchange items (currency and checkable deposits) that constitute *M1* plus certain near-monies that can be easily converted into currency and checkable deposits. In Figure 14.1b we see that the addition of all these items yields an *M2* money supply that is about five times larger than the narrower *M1* money supply.

CONSIDER THIS . . .

Are Credit Cards Money?

You may wonder why we have ignored credit cards such as Visa and MasterCard in our discussion of how the money supply is defined. After all, credit cards are a convenient way to buy things and account for about 25% of the dollar value of all transactions in the United States. The answer is that a credit card is not money. Rather, it is a convenient means of obtaining a short-term loan from the financial institution that issued the card.

What happens when you purchase an item with a credit card? The bank that issued the card will reimburse the seller by making a money payment and charging the establishment a transaction fee, and later you will reimburse the bank for its loan to you by also making a money payment. Rather than reduce your cash or checking account with each purchase, you bunch your payments once a month. You may have to pay an annual fee for the services provided, and if you pay the bank in installments, you will pay a sizable interest charge on the loan. Credit cards are merely a means of deferring or postponing payment for a short period. Your checking account balance that you use to pay your credit card bill *is* money; the credit card is *not* money.*

Although credit cards are not money, they allow individuals and businesses to "economize" in the use of money. Credit cards enable people to hold less currency in their billfolds and, prior to payment due dates, fewer checkable deposits in their bank accounts. Credit cards also help people coordinate the timing of their expenditures with their receipt of income.

---

*A bank debit card, however, is very similar to a check in your checkbook. Unlike a purchase with a credit card, a purchase with a debit card creates a direct "debit" (a subtraction) from your checking account balance. That checking account balance is money—it is part of *M1*.

What "Backs" the Money Supply?

The money supply in the United States essentially is "backed" (guaranteed) by government's ability to keep the value of money relatively stable. Nothing more!

Money as Debt

The major components of the money supply—paper money and checkable deposits—are debts, or promises to pay. In the United States, paper money is the circulating debt of the Federal Reserve Banks. Checkable deposits are the debts of commercial banks and thrift institutions.

Paper currency and checkable deposits have no intrinsic value. A $5 bill is just an inscribed piece of paper. A checkable deposit is merely a bookkeeping entry. And coins, we know, have less intrinsic value than their face value. Nor will government redeem the paper money you hold for anything tangible, such as gold. To many people, the fact that the government does not back the currency with anything tangible seems implausible and insecure. But the decision not to back the currency with anything tangible was made for a very good reason. If the government backed the currency with something tangible like gold, then the supply of money would vary with how much gold was available. By not backing the currency, the government avoids this constraint and indeed receives a key freedom—the ability to provide as much or as little money as needed to maintain the value of money and to best suit the economic needs of the country. In effect, by choosing not to back the currency, the government has chosen to give itself the ability to freely "manage" the nation's money supply. Its monetary authorities attempt to provide the amount of money needed for the particular volume of business activity that will promote full employment, price-level stability, and economic growth.

Nearly all today's economists agree that managing the money supply is more sensible than linking it to gold or to some other commodity whose supply might change arbitrarily and capriciously. For instance, if we used gold to back the money supply so that gold was redeemable for money and vice versa, then a large increase in the nation's gold stock as the result of a new gold discovery might increase the money supply too rapidly and thereby trigger rapid inflation. Or a long-lasting decline in gold production might reduce the money supply to the point where recession and unemployment resulted.

In short, people cannot convert paper money into a fixed amount of gold or any other precious commodity. Money is exchangeable only for paper money. If you ask the government to redeem $5 of your paper money, it will swap one paper $5 bill for another bearing a different serial number. That is all you can get. Similarly, checkable deposits can be redeemed not for gold but only for paper money, which, as we have just seen, the government will not redeem for anything tangible.

Value of Money

So why are currency and checkable deposits money, whereas, say, Monopoly (the game) money is not? What gives a $20 bill or a $100 checking account entry its value? The answer to these questions has three parts.

Acceptability Currency and checkable deposits are money because people accept them as money. By virtue of long-standing business practice, currency and checkable deposits perform the basic function of money: They are acceptable as a medium of exchange. We accept paper money in exchange because we are confident it will be exchangeable for real goods, services, and resources when we spend it.

Legal Tender Our confidence in the acceptability of paper money is strengthened because government has designated currency as **legal tender.** Specifically, each bill contains the statement "This note is legal tender for all debts, public and private." That means paper money is a valid and legal means of payment of any debt that was contracted in dollars. (But private firms and government are not mandated to accept cash. It is not illegal for them to specify payment in noncash forms such as checks, cashier's checks, money orders, or credit cards.)

The general acceptance of paper currency in exchange is more important than the government's decree that money is legal tender, however. The government has never decreed checks to be legal tender, and yet they serve as such in many of the economy's exchanges of goods, services, and resources. But it is true that government agencies—the Federal Deposit Insurance Corporation (FDIC) and the National Credit Union Administration (NCUA)—insure individual deposits of up to $250,000 at commercial banks and thrifts. That fact enhances our willingness to use checkable deposits as a medium of exchange.

Relative Scarcity The value of money, like the economic value of anything else, depends on its supply and demand. Money derives its value from its scarcity relative to its utility (its want-satisfying power). The utility of money lies in its capacity to be exchanged for goods and services, now or in the future. The economy's demand for money thus depends on the total dollar volume of transactions in any period plus the amount of money individuals and businesses want to hold for future transactions. With a reasonably constant demand for money, the supply of money provided by the monetary authorities will determine the domestic value or "purchasing power" of the monetary unit (dollar, yen, peso, or whatever).

Money and Prices

The purchasing power of money is the amount of goods and services a unit of money will buy. When money rapidly loses its purchasing power, it loses its role as money.

The Purchasing Power of the Dollar The amount a dollar will buy varies inversely with the price level; that is, a reciprocal relationship exists between the general price level and the purchasing power of the dollar. When the consumer price index or "cost-of-living" index goes up, the value of the dollar goes down, and vice versa. Higher prices lower the value of the dollar because more dollars are needed to buy a particular amount of goods, services, or resources. For example, if the price level doubles, the value of the dollar declines by one-half, or 50 percent.

Conversely, lower prices increase the purchasing power of the dollar because fewer dollars are needed to obtain a specific quantity of goods and services. If the price level falls by, say, one-half, or 50 percent, the purchasing power of the dollar doubles.

In equation form, the relationship looks like this:

$$\$V = 1/P$$

To find the value of the dollar $\$V$, divide 1 by the price level P expressed as an index number (in hundredths). If the price level is 1, then the value of the dollar is 1. If the price level rises to, say, 1.20, $\$V$ falls to .833; a 20 percent increase in the price level reduces the value of the dollar by 16.67 percent. Check your understanding of this reciprocal relationship by determining the value of $\$V$ and its percentage rise when P falls by 20 percent from $1 to .80.

Inflation and Acceptability In Chapter 9 we noted situations in which a nation's currency became worthless and unacceptable in exchange. These instances of runaway inflation, or *hyperinflation*, happened when the government issued so many pieces of paper currency that the purchasing power of each of those units of money was almost totally undermined. The infamous post–World War I hyperinflation in Germany is an example. In December 1919 there were about 50 billion marks in circulation. Four years later there were 496,585,345,900 billion marks in circulation! The result? The German mark in 1923 was worth an infinitesimal fraction of its 1919 value.[3]

Runaway inflation may significantly depreciate the value of money between the time it is received and the time it is spent. Rapid declines in the value of a currency may cause it to cease being used as a medium of exchange. Businesses and households may refuse to accept paper money in exchange because they do not want to bear the loss in its value that will occur while it is in their possession. (All this despite the fact that the government says that paper currency is legal tender!) Without an acceptable domestic medium of exchange, the economy may simply revert to barter. Alternatively, more stable currencies such as the U.S. dollar or European euro may come into widespread use. At the extreme, a country may adopt a foreign currency as its own official currency as a way to counter hyperinflation.

---

[3]Frank G. Graham, *Exchange, Prices, and Production in Hyperinflation Germany, 1920–1923* (Princeton, N.J.: Princeton University Press, 1930), p. 13.

Similarly, people will use money as a store of value only as long as there is no sizable deterioration in the value of that money because of inflation. And an economy can effectively employ money as a unit of account only when its purchasing power is relatively stable. A monetary yardstick that no longer measures a yard (in terms of purchasing power) does not permit buyers and sellers to establish the terms of trade clearly. When the value of the dollar is declining rapidly, sellers do not know what to charge and buyers do not know what to pay.

Stabilizing Money's Purchasing Power

Rapidly rising price levels (rapid inflation) and the consequent erosion of the purchasing power of money typically result from imprudent economic policies. Since the purchasing power of money and the price level vary inversely, stabilization of the purchasing power of a nation's money requires stabilization of the nation's price level. Such price-level stability (2–3 percent annual inflation) mainly necessitates intelligent management or regulation of the nation's money supply and interest rates (*monetary policy*). It also requires appropriate *fiscal policy* supportive of the efforts of the nation's monetary authorities to hold down inflation. In the United States, a combination of legislation, government policy, and social practice inhibits imprudent expansion of the money supply that might jeopardize money's purchasing power. The critical role of the U.S. monetary authorities (the Federal Reserve) in maintaining the purchasing power of the dollar is the subject of Chapter 16. For now, simply note that they make available a particular quantity of money, such as *M2* in Figure 14.1, and can change that amount through their policy tools.

QUICK REVIEW 14.2

- In the United States, all money consists essentially of the debts of government, commercial banks, and thrift institutions.

- These debts efficiently perform the functions of money as long as their value, or purchasing power, is relatively stable.

- The value of money is rooted not in specified quantities of precious metals but in the amounts of goods, services, and resources that money will purchase.

- The value of the dollar (its domestic purchasing power) is inversely related to the price level.

- Government's responsibility in stabilizing the purchasing power of the monetary unit calls for (a) effective control over the supply of money by the monetary authorities and (b) the application of appropriate fiscal policies by the president and Congress.

The Federal Reserve and the Banking System

In the United States, the "monetary authorities" we have been referring to are the members of the Board of Governors of the **Federal Reserve System** (the "Fed"). As shown in Figure 14.2, the Board directs the activities of the 12 Federal Reserve Banks, which in turn control the lending activity of the nation's banks and thrift institutions. The Fed's major goal is to control the money supply. But since checkable deposits in banks are such a large part of the money supply, an important part of its duties involves assuring the stability of the banking system.

Historical Background

Early in the twentieth century, Congress decided that centralization and public control were essential for an efficient banking system. Decentralized, unregulated banking had fostered the inconvenience and confusion of numerous private bank notes being used as currency. It also had resulted in occasional episodes of monetary mismanagement such that the money supply was inappropriate to the needs of the economy. Sometimes "too much" money precipitated rapid inflation; other times "too little money" stunted the economy's growth by hindering the production and exchange of goods and services. No single entity was charged with creating and implementing nationally consistent banking policies.

Furthermore, acute problems in the banking system occasionally erupted when banks either closed down or insisted on immediate repayment of loans to prevent their own failure. At such times, a banking crisis could emerge, with individuals and businesses who had lost confidence in their banks attempting to simultaneously withdraw all of their money—thereby further crippling the already weakened banks.

An unusually acute banking crisis in 1907 motivated Congress to appoint the National Monetary Commission to study the monetary and banking problems of the economy and to outline a course of action for Congress. The result was the Federal Reserve Act of 1913.

Let's examine the various parts of the Federal Reserve System and their relationship to one another.

Board of Governors

The central authority of the U.S. money and banking system is the **Board of Governors** of the Federal Reserve System. The U.S. president, with the confirmation of the Senate, appoints the seven Board members. Terms are 14 years and staggered so that one member is replaced every 2 years. In addition, new members are appointed when resignations occur. The president selects the chairperson and vice-chairperson of the Board from among the members. Those officers serve 4-year terms and can be reappointed to new 4-year terms by the president. The long-term appointments provide the Board with continuity, experienced membership, and independence from political pressures that could result in inflation.

The 12 Federal Reserve Banks

The 12 **Federal Reserve Banks,** which blend private and public control, collectively serve as the nation's "central bank." These banks also serve as bankers' banks.

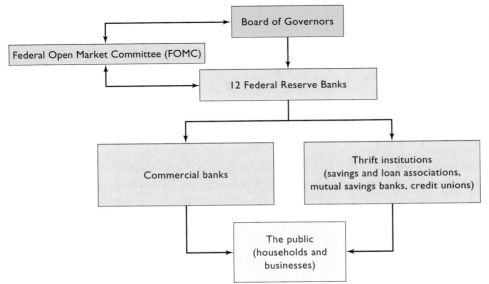

FIGURE 14.2 Framework of the Federal Reserve System and its relationship to the public. The Board of Governors makes the basic policy decisions that provide monetary control of the U.S. money and banking systems. The 12 Federal Reserve Banks implement these decisions. Both the Board of Governors and the 12 Federal Reserve Banks are aided by the Federal Open Market Committee (FOMC).

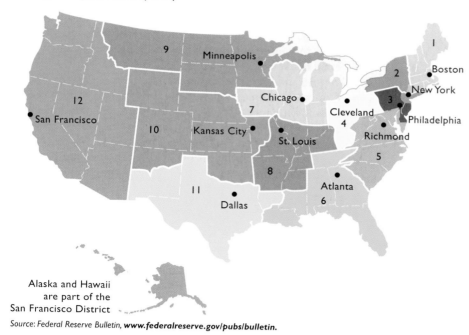

FIGURE 14.3 The 12 Federal Reserve Districts. The Federal Reserve System divides the United States into 12 districts, each having one central bank and in some instances one or more branches of the central bank.

Alaska and Hawaii are part of the San Francisco District

Source: Federal Reserve Bulletin, **www.federalreserve.gov/pubs/bulletin.**

Central Bank Most nations have a single central bank—for example, Britain's Bank of England or Japan's Bank of Japan. The United States' central bank consists of 12 banks whose policies are coordinated by the Fed's Board of Governors. The 12 Federal Reserve Banks accommodate the geographic size and economic diversity of the United States and the nation's large number of commercial banks and thrifts.

Figure 14.3 locates the 12 Federal Reserve Banks and indicates the district that each serves. These banks implement the basic policy of the Board of Governors.

Quasi-Public Banks The 12 Federal Reserve Banks are quasi-public banks, which blend private ownership and public control. Each Federal Reserve Bank is owned by the private commercial banks in its district. (Federally chartered banks are required to purchase shares of stock in the Federal Reserve Bank in their district.) But the Board of Governors, a government body, sets the basic policies that the Federal Reserve Banks pursue.

Despite their private ownership, the Federal Reserve Banks are in practice public institutions. Unlike private firms, they are not motivated by profit. The policies they follow are designed by the Board of Governors to promote the well-being of the economy as a whole. Thus, the activities of the Federal Reserve Banks are frequently at odds with the profit motive.[4] Also, the Federal Reserve Banks do not compete with commercial banks. In general, they do not deal with the public; rather, they interact with the government and commercial banks and thrifts.

Bankers' Banks The Federal Reserve Banks are "bankers' banks." They perform essentially the same functions for banks and thrifts as those institutions perform for the public. Just as banks and thrifts accept the deposits of and make loans to the public, so the central banks accept the deposits of and make loans to banks and thrifts. Normally, these loans average only about $150 million a day. But in emergency circumstances the Federal Reserve Banks become the "lender of last resort" to the banking system and can lend out as much as needed to ensure that banks and thrifts can meet their cash obligations. On the day after terrorists attacked the United States on September 11, 2001, the Fed lent $45 *billion* to U.S. banks and thrifts. The Fed wanted to make sure that the destruction and disruption in New York City and the Washington, D.C., area did not precipitate a nationwide banking crisis.

---

[4]Although it is not their goal, the Federal Reserve Banks have actually operated profitably, largely as a result of the Treasury debts they hold. Part of the profit is used to pay 6 percent annual dividends to the commercial banks that hold stock in the Federal Reserve Banks; the remaining profit is usually turned over to the U.S. Treasury.

The Fed assumed an even greater role as a lender of last resort during the financial crisis of 2007–2008. We discuss that crisis and the Fed's emergency response to the crisis later in this chapter.

But the Federal Reserve Banks have a third function, which banks and thrifts do not perform: They issue currency. Congress has authorized the Federal Reserve Banks to put into circulation Federal Reserve Notes, which constitute the economy's paper money supply.

FOMC

The **Federal Open Market Committee (FOMC)** aids the Board of Governors in conducting monetary policy. The FOMC is made up of 12 individuals:

- The seven members of the Board of Governors.
- The president of the New York Federal Reserve Bank.
- Four of the remaining presidents of Federal Reserve Banks on a 1-year rotating basis.

The FOMC meets regularly to direct the purchase and sale of government securities (bills, notes, bonds) in the open market in which such securities are bought and sold on a daily basis. We will find in Chapter 16 that the purpose of these aptly named *open-market operations* is to control the nation's money supply and influence interest rates. The Federal Reserve Bank in New York City conducts most of the Fed's open-market operations.

Commercial Banks and Thrifts

There are about 6800 commercial banks. Roughly three-fourths are state banks. These are private banks chartered (authorized) by the individual states to operate within those states. One-fourth are private banks chartered by the Federal government to operate nationally; these are national banks. Some of the U.S. national banks are very large, ranking among the world's largest financial institutions (see Global Perspective 14.1).

The 8700 thrift institutions—most of which are credit unions—are regulated by agencies in addition to the Board of Governors and the Federal Reserve Banks. For example, credit unions are regulated and monitored by the National Credit Union Administration (NCUA). But the thrifts *are* subject to monetary control by the Federal Reserve System. In particular, like the banks, thrifts are required to keep a certain percentage of their checkable deposits as "reserves." In Figure 14.2 we use arrows to indicate that the thrift institutions are subject to the control of the Board of Governors and the central banks. Decisions concerning monetary policy affect the thrifts along with the commercial banks.

GLOBAL PERSPECTIVE 14.1

The World's 12 Largest Financial Institutions

The world's 12 largest private sector financial institutions are headquartered in Europe, Japan, and the United States (2009 data).

Assets (trillions of U.S. dollars)

- Royal Bank of Scotland (U.K.)
- Barclays (U.K.)
- Deutsche Bank (Germany)
- BNP Paribas (France)
- HSBC Holdings (U.K.)
- JPMorgan Chase (U.S.)
- Crédit Agricole (France)
- Citigroup (U.S.)
- Mitsubishi UFJ (Japan)
- UBS (Switzerland)
- ING Group (Netherlands)
- Bank of America (U.S.)

Source: Forbes Global 2000, Total Assets, http://www.forbes.com/lists/2009/18/global-09_The-Global-2000_Rank.html. Used with permission of Forbes Media LLC © 2010.

Fed Functions and the Money Supply

The Fed performs several functions, some of which we have already identified but they are worth repeating:

- *Issuing currency* The Federal Reserve Banks issue Federal Reserve Notes, the paper currency used in the U.S. monetary system. (The Federal Reserve Bank that issued a particular bill is identified in black in the upper left of the front of the newly designed bills. "A1," for example, identifies the Boston bank, "B2" the New York bank, and so on.)

- *Setting reserve requirements and holding reserves* The Fed sets reserve requirements, which are the fractions of checking account balances that banks must maintain as currency reserves. The central banks accept as deposits from the banks and thrifts any portion of their mandated reserves not held as vault cash.

- *Lending to financial institutions and serving as an emergency lender of last resort* The Fed makes routine short-term loans to banks and thrifts and charges them an interest rate called the *discount rate*. It also occasionally auctions off loans to banks and thrifts through its *Term Auction Facility*, discussed in Chapter 16. In times of financial emergencies, the Fed serves as a lender of last resort to critical parts of the U.S. financial industry.

- **Providing for check collection** The Fed provides the banking system with a means for collecting on checks. If Sue writes a check on her Miami bank or thrift to Joe, who deposits it in his Dallas bank or thrift, how does the Dallas bank collect the money represented by the check drawn against the Miami bank? Answer: The Fed handles it by adjusting the reserves (deposits) of the two banks.

- **Acting as fiscal agent** The Fed acts as the fiscal agent (provider of financial services) for the Federal government. The government collects huge sums through taxation, spends equally large amounts, and sells and redeems bonds. To carry out these activities, the government uses the Fed's facilities.

- **Supervising banks** The Fed supervises the operations of banks. It makes periodic examinations to assess bank profitability, to ascertain that banks perform in accordance with the many regulations to which they are subject, and to uncover questionable practices or fraud. Following the financial crisis of 2007–2008, Congress expanded the Fed's supervisory powers over banks.[5]

- **Controlling the money supply** Finally, the Fed has ultimate responsibility for regulating the supply of money, and this enables it to influence interest rates. The major task of the Fed under usual economic circumstances is to manage the money supply (and thus interest rates) according to the needs of the economy. This involves making an amount of money available that is consistent with high and rising levels of output and employment *and* a relatively stable price level. While most of the other functions of the Fed are routine activities or have a service nature, managing the nation's money supply requires making basic, but unique, policy decisions. (We discuss those decisions in detail in Chapter 16.)

Federal Reserve Independence

Congress purposely established the Fed as an independent agency of government. The objective was to protect the Fed from political pressures so that it could effectively control the money supply and maintain price stability. Political pressures on Congress and the executive branch may at times result in inflationary fiscal policies, including tax cuts and special-interest spending. If Congress and the executive branch also controlled the nation's monetary policy, citizens and lobbying groups undoubtedly would pressure elected officials to keep interest rates low even though at times high interest rates are necessary to reduce aggregate demand and thus control inflation. An independent monetary authority (the Fed) can take actions to increase interest rates when higher rates are needed to stem inflation. Studies show that countries that have independent central banks like the Fed have lower rates of inflation, on average, than countries that have little or no central bank independence.

The Financial Crisis of 2007 and 2008

As previously noted, a properly functioning monetary system supports the continuous circular flows of income and expenditures in the economy. In contrast, a malfunctioning monetary system causes major problems in credit markets and can cause severe fluctuations in the economy's levels of output, employment, and prices.

"Malfunctioning" is too gentle an adjective to describe the monetary system in late 2007 and 2008. In that period, the U.S. financial system faced its most serious crisis since the Great Depression of the 1930s. The financial crisis soon spread to the entire economy, culminating in the severe recession of 2007–2009. We discussed the recession in detail in previous chapters, and we now want to examine the financial crisis that led up to it. What was the nature of the financial crisis? What caused it? How has it changed the structure of the U.S. financial services industry?

The Mortgage Default Crisis

In 2007 a major wave of defaults on home mortgage loans threatened the health of not only the original mortgage lenders but of any financial institution that had made such loans or invested in such loans either directly or indirectly. A majority of these mortgage defaults were on **subprime mortgage loans**—high-interest-rate loans to home buyers with higher-than-average credit risk. Ironically, the Federal government had encouraged banks to make these types of loans as part of an effort to broaden home ownership to more Americans. But more directly to the point, several of the biggest indirect investors in these subprime loans had been banks. The banks had lent money to investment companies that had purchased many of the mortgages from mortgage lenders. When the mortgages started to go bad, many investment funds "blew up" and

---

[5]The Fed is not alone in this task of supervision. The individual states supervise the banks that they charter. The Office of the Comptroller of the Currency has separate supervisory authority over the banks and the thrifts. Also, the Federal Deposit Insurance Corporation supervises the banks and thrifts whose deposits it insures.

could not repay the loans they had taken out from the banks. The banks thus had to "write off" (declare unrecoverable) the loans they had made to the investment companies, but doing that meant reducing their banks' reserves and limiting their ability to generate new loans. This greatly threatened the economy, because both consumers and businesses rely on loans to finance consumption and investment expenditures.

A strange thing about the crisis was that before it happened, banks and government regulators had mistakenly believed that an innovation known as the "mortgage-backed security" had eliminated most of the bank exposure to mortgage defaults. **Mortgage-backed securities** are bonds backed by mortgage payments. To create them, banks and other mortgage lenders first made mortgage loans. But then instead of holding all of those loans as assets on their balance sheets and collecting the monthly mortgage payments, the banks and other mortgage lenders bundled hundreds or thousands of them together and sold them off as bonds—in essence selling the right to collect all the future mortgage payments. The banks obtained a single, up-front cash payment for the bond and the bond buyer started to collect the mortgage payments as the return on the investment.

From the banks' perspective, this seemed like a smart business decision, because it transferred any future default risk on those mortgages to the buyer of the bond. The banks thought that they were off the hook for these mortgages. Unfortunately for them, however, they lent a substantial portion of the money they received from selling the bonds to investment funds that invested in mortgage-backed bonds. They also purchased large amounts of mortgage-backed securities as financial investments to help meet bank capital requirements set by bank regulators. So while the banks were no longer directly exposed to major portions of the mortgage default risk, they were still indirectly exposed to it. When many homebuyers started to default on their mortgages, the banks lost money on the mortgages they still held. The banks also lost money on the loans they had made to the investors who had purchased mortgage-backed securities, and also on the mortgage-backed securities the banks had purchased from investment firms.

But what had caused the skyrocketing mortgage default rates in the first place? There were many causes, including certain government programs that greatly encouraged and subsidized home ownership for former renters. Also contributing were declining real estate values that arrived at the end of a long housing boom during which house prices had greatly increased. But an equally important factor was the bad incentives provided by the

previously discussed mortgage-backed bonds. Because the banks and other mortgage lenders thought that they were no longer exposed to large portions of their mortgage default risk, they became lax in their lending practices—so much so that people were granted subprime mortgage loans that they were unlikely to be able to repay. Some mortgage companies were so eager to sign up new homebuyers (in order to bundle their loans together to sell bonds) that they stopped running credit checks and even allowed applicants to claim higher incomes than they were actually earning in order to qualify them for big loans. The natural result was that many people took on "too much mortgage" and were soon failing to make their monthly payments.

Securitization

The problems just described relate to **securitization**—the process of slicing up and bundling groups of loans, mortgages, corporate bonds, or other financial debts into distinct new securities. This process was not new and was viewed favorably by government regulators, who thought securitization made the banking system safer by allowing banks to shed risk. As noted in our discussion of mortgages, these securities were sold to financial investors, who purchased them to obtain the interest payments and the eventual return of principal generated by the underlying securities. For example, the mortgage loans provided to the subprime borrowers were bundled together as mortgage-backed securities and sold to private investors, mutual fund firms, and pension funds. These securities were attractive to many private investors and financial institutions alike, because they offered higher-interest returns than securities backed by less-risky mortgages or other safer investments.

Once created, loan-backed securities are bought and sold in financial markets just like other securities such as stocks and bonds. These sorts of securities can therefore end up worldwide in the investment portfolios of banks, thrifts, insurance companies, and pensions, as well as in personal accounts.

To reduce the risk for holders of these securities, a few large insurance companies developed other securities that the holders of loan-backed securities could purchase to insure against losses from defaults. American International Group (AIG), in particular, issued billions of dollars of *collateralized default swaps*—essentially insurance policies—that were designed to compensate the holders of loan-backed securities if the loans underlying these investments went into default and did not pay off. Thus, collateralized default swaps became yet another category of investment security that was highly exposed to mortgage-loan risk.

Securitization is so widespread and so critical to the modern financial system that economists sometimes refer to it as the *shadow banking system*. All sorts of securities backed by loans or other securities are issued, bought, sold, and resold each day in a process that helps to keep credit flowing to the households and firms that rely on it for their personal and business needs. In general, securitization therefore is a positive financial innovation. But mortgage-backed securities, in particular, turned out to contain much more risk than most people thought.

Investors and government regulators failed to ask three related questions about mortgage-backed securities: What would happen if the value of one of the types of loans (say, mortgages) that underlies part of the securitization process unexpectedly plunged? And what then would happen if some of the largest holders of the securities based on these mortgages were major U.S. financial institutions that are vitally important to the day-to-day financing of the credit needed to keep the American economy running smoothly? And what would happen after that if the main insurer of these securities not only was the largest insurance company in the United States but in the world?

All three seemingly improbable "what ifs?" occurred! As previously explained, interest rates on adjustable-rate mortgages increased and house prices fell. Borrowers who had made relatively small down payments on home purchases or had previously cashed out home equity through refinancing discovered that they owed more on their mortgages than their properties were worth. Their loans were said to be "underwater." As interest rates adjusted upward and the economy slowed, borrowers began falling behind on their monthly mortgage payments. Lenders began to foreclose on many houses, while other borrowers literally handed in their house keys and walked away from their houses *and* their mortgages.

Failures and Near-Failures of Financial Firms

When the mortgage loan "card" underpinning mortgage-based securitization fell, the securitization layers above it collapsed like a house of cards. First, the big mortgage lenders faced demise because they still held large amounts of the bad debt. Three huge mortgage lenders collapsed or nearly collapsed. Countrywide, the second largest mortgage lender, was saved from bankruptcy by Bank of America. Regulators also seized Washington Mutual bank, the nation's largest mortgage lender, and arranged a quick takeover by JPMorgan Chase. Wachovia bank's heavy exposure to mortgages through its Golden West

subsidiary resulted in near bankruptcy, and it was rescued through acquisition by Wells Fargo.

The exposure to the growing problem of loan defaults quickly jumped from direct mortgage lenders to other financial institutions. Securities firms and investment banks that held large amounts of loan-backed securities began to suffer huge losses. Merrill Lynch lost more in two years than it made in the prior decade and was acquired at a fire-sale price by Bank of America. Lehman Brothers, a major holder of mortgage-backed securities, declared bankruptcy. Goldman Sachs, Morgan Stanley, and other financial firms that had heavy exposures to mortgage-backed securities and collateralized default swaps rushed to become bank holding companies so they could qualify for the massive emergency loans that the Federal Reserve was making available to banks and bank holding companies. Citibank survived through infusions of Federal government loans. Insurance company AIG suffered enormous losses because it had not set aside sufficient reserves to pay off the unexpectedly large losses that accrued on the insurance policies that it had sold to holders of mortgage-backed securities. The nightmarish thought of a total collapse of the U.S. financial system suddenly became a realistic possibility.

The Treasury Bailout: TARP

In late 2008 Congress passed the **Troubled Asset Relief Program (TARP),** which allocated $700 billion—yes, billion—to the U.S. Treasury to make emergency loans to critical financial and other U.S. firms. Most of this "bailout" money eventually was lent out. In fact, as of March 2009, the Federal government and Federal Reserve had spent $170 billion just keeping insurer AIG afloat. Other major recipients of TARP funds included Citibank, Bank of America, JPMorgan Chase, and Goldman Sachs. Later, nonfinancial firms such as General Motors and Chrysler also received several billion dollars of TARP loans.

TARP indeed saved several financial institutions whose bankruptcy would have caused a tsunami of secondary effects that probably would have brought down other financial firms and frozen credit throughout the economy. But this very fact demonstrates the problem of **moral hazard.** As it relates to financial investment, moral hazard is the tendency for financial investors and financial services firms to take on greater risks because they assume they are at least partially insured against losses. Without TARP, several firms would have gone bankrupt and their stockholders, bondholders, and executives all would have suffered large personal losses. With TARP, those outcomes were at least partially avoided. TARP and similar government bailouts were essentially government-provided insurance payouts to financial firms that never had to pay a single cent in insurance premiums for the massive bailouts that kept them afloat.

The correct assumption by large firms that they were simply too big for government to let them fail may have given them an incentive to make riskier investments than if no government bailouts were likely to be forthcoming.

The Fed's Lender-of-Last-Resort Activities

As noted in our previous list of Fed functions, one of the roles of the Federal Reserve is to serve as the lender of last resort to financial institutions in times of financial emergencies. The Fed performed this vital function well following the 9/11 terrorist attacks. The financial crisis of 2007–2008 presented another, broader-based financial emergency. Under Fed Chair Ben Bernanke, the Fed designed and implemented several highly creative new lender-of-last-resort facilities to pump liquidity into the financial system. These facilities, procedures, and capabilities were in addition to both the TARP efforts by the U.S. Treasury and the Fed's use of standard tools of monetary policy (the subject of Chapter 16) designed to reduce interest rates. All the new Fed facilities had the single purpose and desired outcome of keeping credit flowing.

Total Fed assets rose from $885 billion in February 2008 to $1,903 billion in March 2009. This increase reflected a huge rise in the amount of securities (U.S. securities, mortgage-backed securities, and others) owned by the Fed. In undertaking its lender of last resort functions, the Fed bought these securities from financial institutions. The purpose was to increase liquidity in the financial system by exchanging illiquid bonds (that the firms could not easily sell during the crisis) for cash, the most liquid of all assets.

Many economists believe that TARP and the Fed's actions helped avert a second Great Depression. The following list of new Fed credit facilities underscores the extraordinary extent of the Fed's lender-of-last-resort response to the crisis.

- *Primary Dealer Credit Facility (PDCF)* Provides overnight loans to primary dealers who are willing to post loan-backed securities as collateral. (The Fed keeps the collateral on any loan that is not repaid on time.) Primary dealers are the 16 major financial institutions that the Fed uses to buy and sell U.S. securities.
- *Term Securities Lending Facility (TSLF)* Lends U.S. securities to primary dealers for one-month terms to promote liquidity in the markets for these U.S. securities. The financial institutions obtain the

securities from the Fed through participating in competitive single-bid auctions.
- *Asset-Backed Commercial Paper Money Market Mutual Fund Liquidity Facility* Provides loans to U.S. banks and thrifts to finance their purchases of *commercial paper* from money market mutual funds. Commercial paper consists of asset-backed, short-term IOUs that are mainly issued by corporations. These short-term loans are vital for financing the day-to-day operations of businesses.
- *Commercial Paper Funding Facility (CPFF)* Purchases commercial paper to support the commercial paper market and therefore the short-term credit needs of businesses.
- *Money Market Investor Funding Facility (MMIFF)* Provides funding support to a private-sector initiative designed to ensure the liquidity of U.S. money market mutual funds. Many Americans rely on money market mutual funds as low-risk investments.
- *Term Asset-Backed Securities Loan Facility (TALF)* Helps households and business with their credit needs by providing funding support for asset-backed securities collateralized by student loans, auto loans, credit card loans, and loans guaranteed by the Small Business Administration (SBA).
- *Interest Payments on Reserves* Bolsters the profitability of banks by paying interest on the reserves they hold in their vaults or in the Federal Reserve Banks.

These extraordinary efforts, like those of the Treasury, helped prevent total disarray in the credit markets. But like TARP, the Fed efforts intensified the moral hazard problem by greatly limiting the losses that otherwise would have resulted from bad financial assumptions and decisions.

The Postcrisis U.S. Financial Services Industry

Table 14.1 lists the major categories of firms within the U.S. financial services industry and gives examples of firms in each category. Note that the main categories of the **financial services industry** are commercial banks, thrifts, insurance companies, mutual fund companies, pension funds, security firms, and investment banks. Even before the financial crisis of 2007–2008, the financial services industry was consolidating into fewer, larger firms, each offering a wider spectrum of services. In 1999 Congress ended the Depression-era prohibition against banks selling stocks, bonds, and mutual funds. Thus, the lines between the subsets of the financial industry began to blur.

TABLE 14.1 Major Categories of Financial Institutions within the U.S. Financial Services Industry

Institution	Description	Examples
Commercial banks	State and national banks that provide checking and savings accounts, sell certificates of deposit, and make loans. The Federal Deposit Insurance Corporation (FDIC) insures checking and savings accounts up to $250,000.	JPMorgan Chase, Bank of America, Citibank, Wells Fargo
Thrifts	Savings and loan associations (S&Ls), mutual saving banks, and credit unions that offer checking and savings accounts and make loans. Historically, S&Ls made mortgage loans for houses while mutual savings banks and credit unions made small personal loans, such as automobile loans. Today, major thrifts offer the same range of banking services as commercial banks. The Federal Deposit Insurance Corporation and the National Credit Union Administration insure checking and savings deposits up to $250,000.	Charter One, New York Community Bank, Pentagon Federal Credit Union, Boeing Employees Credit Union (BECU)
Insurance companies	Firms that offer policies (contracts) through which individuals pay premiums to insure against some loss, say, disability or death. In some life insurance policies and annuities, the funds are invested for the client in stocks and bonds and paid back after a specified number of years. Thus, insurance sometimes has a saving or financial-investment element.	Prudential, New York Life, Northwestern Mutual, Hartford, MetLife
Mutual fund companies	Firms that pool deposits by customers to purchase stocks or bonds (or both). Customers thus indirectly own a part of a particular set of stocks or bonds, say stocks in companies expected to grow rapidly (a growth fund) or bonds issued by state governments (a municipal bond fund).	Fidelity, Vanguard, Putnam, Janus, T. Rowe Price
Pension funds	For-profit or nonprofit institutions that collect savings from workers (or from employers on their behalf) throughout their working years and then buy stocks and bonds with the proceeds and make monthly retirement payments.	TIAA-CREF, Teamsters' Union, CalPERs
Securities firms	Firms that offer security advice and buy and sell stocks and bonds for clients. More generally known as *stock brokerage firms*.	Merrill Lynch, Smith Barney, Charles Schwab
Investment banks	Firms that help corporations and governments raise money by selling stocks and bonds. They also typically offer advisory services for corporate mergers and acquisitions as well as brokerage services and advice.	Goldman Sachs, Morgan Stanley, Deutsche Bank, Nomura Securities

Many banks acquired stock brokerage firms and, in a few cases, insurance companies. For example, Citigroup, which was once only into banking, now owns Smith Barney, a large securities firm. Many large banks (for example, Wells Fargo) and pension funds (for example, TIAA-CREF) now provide mutual funds, including money market mutual funds that pay relatively high interest and on which checks of $500 or more can be written.

The upheaval in the financial markets caused by the financial crisis of 2007–2008 further consolidated the industry and further blurred the lines between its segments. Between September 2007 and September 2009, the FDIC shut down more than 200 U.S. banks and transferred their bank deposits to other, usually larger, banks. In 2009 the three largest U.S. banks (JPMorgan Chase, Bank of America, and Wells Fargo) held roughly $3 of every $10 on deposit in the United States.

Also, during the financial crisis of 2007–2008, major investment banks Goldman Sachs and Morgan Stanley opted to become commercial banks to gain access to emergency Federal Reserve loans. The nation's largest thrift—Washington Mutual—was absorbed by commercial bank JPMorgan Chase. But even with all this blending, the categories in Table 14.1 remain helpful. The main lines of a firm's businesses often are in one category or another. For example, even though Goldman Sachs is licensed and regulated as a bank, it is first and foremost an investment company. And the insurance companies and pension funds do most of their business as such.

The financial crisis of 2007–2008 generated much introspection about what went wrong and how to prevent anything like it from happening again. Politicians and financial regulators tightened lending rules to offset the "pass the buck" incentives created by mortgage-backed securities and prevent loans from being issued to people who are unlikely to be able to make the required monthly payments. They also passed legislation to help homeowners who were "underwater" on mortgage loans remain in their homes.

LAST Word Electronic Banking

The Rapid Advance of New Payment Forms and Internet Banking Is Transforming Money, Banking, and Financial Markets.

One of the more significant developments in money and banking during the past few decades is the spread of electronic payments. Households and businesses increasingly use electronic payments rather than currency and checks to buy products, pay bills, pay income taxes, transfer bank funds, and handle recurring mortgage and utility payments. Electronic or digital payment is being widely accepted and embraced by households, businesses, government, and financial institutions.

Several electronic-based means of making payments and transferring funds have pushed currency and checks aside. *Credit cards* enable us to make immediate purchases using credit established in advance with the card provider. In most cases, a swipe of the credit card makes the transaction electronically. Credit card balances can be paid via the Internet, rather than by sending a check to the card provider. *Debit cards* work much like credit

cards but, because no loan is involved, more closely resemble checks. The swipe of the card authorizes an electronic payment directly to the seller from the buyer's bank account.

Other electronic payments include *Fedwire transfers*. This Federal Reserve–maintained system enables banks to transfer funds to other banks. Individuals and businesses can also "wire" funds between financial institutions, domestically or internationally. Households can similarly "send" funds or payments to businesses using *automated clearinghouse transactions (ACHs)*. For example, they can make monthly utility and mortgage payments and transfer funds among financial institutions. The ACH system also allows sellers to scan checks at point of sale, convert them to ACH payments, and move the funds immediately from the buyer's checking account to the seller's checking account. Then the seller immediately hands the check back to the customer.

Some experts believe the next step will be greater use of *electronic money*, which is simply an entry in an electronic file stored in a computer. Electronic money is deposited, or "loaded," into an account through electronic deposits of paychecks, retirement benefits, stock dividends, and other sources of income. The owner of the account withdraws, or "unloads," the money from

his or her account, using the Internet to pay sellers for their goods and services. PayPal—used by 184 million account holders in 190 countries—roughly fits this description and is familiar to eBay users. Buyers and sellers establish accounts based on funds in checking accounts or funds available via credit cards. Customers then can securely make electronic payments or transfer funds to other holders of PayPal accounts.

In the future, the public may be able to use card readers attached to their computers to load electronic money onto so-called smart cards. These plastic cards contain computer chips that store information, including the amount of electronic money the consumer has loaded. When purchases or payments are made, their amounts are automatically deducted from the balance in the card's memory. Consumers will be able to transfer traditional money to their smart cards through computers or cell phones or at automatic teller machines. Thus, it will be possible for nearly all payments to be made through the Internet or a smart card.

A few general-use smart cards with embedded programmable computer chips are available in the United States, including cards issued by Visa, MasterCard, and American Express ("Blue Cards"). More common are *stored-value cards*, which facilitate purchases at the establishments that issued them. Examples are prepaid phone cards, copy-machine cards, mass-transit cards, single-store gift cards, and university meal-service cards. Like the broader smart cards, these cards are "reloadable," meaning the amounts stored on them can be increased. A number of retailers—including FedEx stores, Sears, Starbucks, Walgreens, and Walmart—make stored-value cards available to their customers.

Electronic money also appears poised to make a big impact in developing countries where bank branches are few and far between. Companies like M-PESA in Kenya, Wizzit in South Africa, and G-Cash in the Philippines are now taking advantage of the fact that, while those countries have few banks, they have extensive cellular phone networks. Cell phone subscribers can deposit cash at cell phone stores and then freely send each other electronic payments using their phones. Customers receiving payments can use the electronic money that they receive to make further electronic payments or, if they like, withdraw the money for cash at their local cell phone store. The safety and convenience of these systems is expected to be a substantial aid to local consumers and businesspeople.

In mid-2010 Congress passed and the president signed the **Wall Street Reform and Consumer Protection Act.** This sweeping law includes provisions that:

- Eliminate the Office of Thrift Supervision and give broader authority to the Federal Reserve to regulate all large financial institutions.

- Create a Financial Stability Oversight Council to be on the lookout for risks to the financial system.

- Establish a process for the Federal government to liquidate (sell off) the assets of large failing financial institutions, much like the FDIC does with failing banks.

- Provide Federal regulatory oversight of mortgage-backed securities and other derivatives and require that they be traded on public exchanges.

- Require companies selling asset-backed securities to retain a portion of those securities so the sellers share part of the risk.

- Establish a stronger consumer financial protection role for the Fed through creation of the Bureau of Consumer Financial Protection.

Proponents of the new law say that it will help prevent many of the practices that led up to the financial crisis of 2007–2008. They also contend that the law will send a strong message to stockholders, bondholders, and executives of large financial firms that they will suffer unavoidable and extremely high personal financial losses if they allow their firms to ever again get into serious financial trouble.

Skeptics of the new law say that regulators already had all the tools they needed to prevent the financial crisis. They also point out that the government's own efforts to promote home ownership, via quasi-government institutions that purchased mortgage-backed securities, greatly contributed to the financial crisis. Critics of the new law say that it will simply impose heavy new regulatory costs on the financial industry while doing little to prevent future government bailouts.

Summary

1. Anything that is accepted as (a) a medium of exchange, (b) a unit of monetary account, and (c) a store of value can be used as money.

2. There are two major definitions of the money supply. $M1$ consists of currency and checkable deposits; $M2$ consists of $M1$ plus savings deposits, including money market deposit accounts, small-denominated (less than $100,000) time deposits, and money market mutual fund balances held by individuals.

3. Money represents the debts of government and institutions offering checkable deposits (commercial banks and thrift institutions) and has value because of the goods, services, and resources it will command in the market. Maintaining the purchasing power of money depends largely on the government's effectiveness in managing the money supply.

4. The U.S. banking system consists of (a) the Board of Governors of the Federal Reserve System, (b) the 12 Federal Reserve Banks, and (c) some 6,800 commercial banks and 8,700 thrift institutions (mainly credit unions). The Board of Governors is the basic policymaking body for the entire banking system. The directives of the Board and the Federal Open Market Committee (FOMC) are made effective through the 12 Federal Reserve Banks, which are simultaneously (a) central banks, (b) quasi-public banks, and (c) bankers' banks.

5. The major functions of the Fed are to (a) issue Federal Reserve Notes, (b) set reserve requirements and hold reserves deposited by banks and thrifts, (c) lend money to financial institutions and serve as the lender of last resort in national financial emergencies, (d) provide for the rapid collection of checks, (e) act as the fiscal agent for the Federal government, (f) supervise the operations of the banks, and (g) regulate the supply of money in the best interests of the economy.

6. The Fed is essentially an independent institution, controlled neither by the president of the United States nor by Congress. This independence shields the Fed from political pressure and allows it to raise and lower interest rates (via changes in the money supply) as needed to promote full employment, price stability, and economic growth.

7. The financial crisis of 2007–2008 consisted of an unprecedented rise in mortgage loan defaults, the collapse or near-collapse of several major financial institutions, and the generalized freezing up of credit availability. The crisis resulted from bad mortgage loans together with declining real estate prices. It also resulted from underestimation of risk by holders of mortgage-backed securities and faulty insurance securities designed to protect holders of mortgage-backed securities from the risk of default.

8. In 2008 Congress passed the Troubled Asset Relief Program (TARP), which authorized the U.S. Treasury to spend up to $700 billion to make emergency loans and guarantees to failing financial firms. The Treasury rescue, or bailout, was aided by lender-of-last-resort loans provided by the Federal Reserve to financial institutions through a series of newly established Fed facilities.

9. The TARP loans and the Fed's lender-of-last-resort actions intensify the moral hazard problem. This is the tendency of financial investors and financial firms to take on greater risk when they assume they are at least partially insured against loss.

10. The main categories of the U.S. financial services industry are commercial banks, thrifts, insurance companies, mutual fund companies, pension funds, securities firms, and investment banks. The reassembly of the wreckage from the financial crisis of 2007–2008 has further consolidated the already consolidating financial services industry and has further blurred some of the lines between the subsets of the industry.

11. In response to the financial crisis, Congress passed the Wall Street Reform and Consumer Financial Protection Act of 2010.

Terms and Concepts

medium of exchange

unit of account

store of value

liquidity

M1

Federal Reserve Notes

token money

checkable deposits

commercial banks

thrift institutions

near-monies

M2

savings account

money market deposit account (MMDA)

time deposits

money market mutual fund (MMMF)

legal tender

Federal Reserve System

Board of Governors

Federal Reserve Banks

Federal Open Market Committee (FOMC)

subprime mortgage loans

mortgage-backed securities

securitization

moral hazard

Troubled Asset Relief Program (TARP)

financial services industry

Wall Street Reform and Consumer Protection Act

Questions

1. What are the three basic functions of money? Describe how rapid inflation can undermine money's ability to perform each of the three functions. **LO1**

2. Which two of the following financial institutions offer checkable deposits included within the M1 money supply: mutual fund companies; insurance companies; commercial banks; securities firms; thrift institutions? Which of the following items is not included in either M1 or M2: currency held by the public; checkable deposits; money market mutual fund balances; small-denominated (less than $100,000) time deposits; currency held by banks; savings deposits? **LO1**

3. What are the components of the M1 money supply? What is the largest component? Which of the components of M1 is legal tender? Why is the face value of a coin greater than its intrinsic value? What near-monies are included in the M2 money supply? **LO1, LO2**

4. Explain and evaluate the following statements: **LO2**
   a. The invention of money is one of the great achievements of humankind, for without it the enrichment that comes from broadening trade would have been impossible.
   b. Money is whatever society says it is.
   c. In the United States, the debts of government and commercial banks are used as money.
   d. People often say they would like to have more money, but what they usually mean is that they would like to have more goods and services.
   e. When the price of everything goes up, it is not because everything is worth more but because the currency is worth less.
   f. Any central bank can create money; the trick is to create enough, but not too much, of it.

5. What "backs" the money supply in the United States? What determines the value (domestic purchasing power) of money? How does the purchasing power of money relate to the price level? Who in the United States is responsible for maintaining money's purchasing power? **LO2**

6. How is the chairperson of the Federal Reserve System selected? Describe the relationship between the Board of Governors of the Federal Reserve System and the 12 Federal Reserve Banks. What is the purpose of the Federal Open Market Committee (FOMC)? What is its makeup? **LO3**

7. The following are two hypothetical ways in which the Federal Reserve Board might be appointed. Would you favor either of these two methods over the present method? Why or why not? **LO3**
   a. Upon taking office, the U.S. president appoints seven people to the Federal Reserve Board, including a chair. Each appointee must be confirmed by a majority vote of the Senate, and each serves the same 4-year term as the president.
   b. Congress selects seven members from its ranks (four from the House of Representatives and three from the Senate) to serve at congressional pleasure as the Board of Governors of the Federal Reserve System.

8. What is meant when economists say that the Federal Reserve Banks are central banks, quasi-public banks, and bankers' banks? **LO3**

9. Why do economists nearly uniformly support an independent Fed rather than one beholden directly to either the president or Congress? **LO3**

10. Identify three functions of the Federal Reserve of your choice, other than its main role of controlling the supply of money. **LO4**

11. How do each of the following relate to the financial crisis of 2007–2008: declines in real estate values, subprime mortgage loans, mortgage-backed securities, AIG. **LO5**

12. What is TARP and how was it funded? What is meant by the term "lender of last resort" and how does it relate to the financial crisis of 2007–2008? How do government and Federal Reserve emergency loans relate to the concept of moral hazard? **LO6**

13. What are the major categories of firms that make up the U.S. financial services industry? Are there more or fewer banks today than before the start of the financial crisis of 2007–2008? Why are the lines between the categories of financial firms even more blurred than they were before the crisis? How did the Wall Street Reform and Consumer Protection Act of 2010 try to address some of the problems that helped cause the crisis? **LO7**

14. **LAST WORD** How does a debit card differ from a credit card? How does a stored-value card differ from both? Suppose that a person has a credit card, debit card, and stored-value card. Create a fictional scenario in which the person uses all three cards in the same day. Explain the person's logic for using one card rather than one of the others for each transaction. How do Fedwire and ACH transactions differ from credit card, debit card, and stored-value card transactions?

Problems

1. Assume that the following asset values (in millions of dollars) exist in Ironmania: Federal Reserve Notes in circulation = $700; Money market mutual funds (MMMFs) held by individuals = $400; Corporate bonds = $300; Iron ore deposits = $50; Currency in commercial banks = $100; Savings deposits, including money market deposit accounts (MMDAs) = $140; Checkable deposits = $1500; Small-denominated (less than $100,000) time deposits = $100; Coins in circulation = $40. **LO1**
   a. What is $M1$ in Ironmania?
   b. What is $M2$ in Ironmania?

2. Assume that Jimmy Cash has $2000 in his checking account at Folsom Bank and uses his checking account card to withdraw $200 of cash from the bank's ATM machine. By what dollar amount did the $M1$ money supply change as a result of this single, isolated transaction? **LO1**

3. Suppose the price level and value of the U.S. dollar in year 1 are 1 and $1, respectively. If the price level rises to 1.25 in year 2, what is the new value of the dollar? If, instead, the price level falls to .50, what is the value of the dollar? **LO2**

4. Suppose that Lady Gaga goes to Las Vegas to play poker and at the last minute her record company says it will reimburse her for 50 percent of any gambling losses that she incurs. Will Lady Gaga wager more or less as a result of the reimbursement offer? What economic concept does your answer illustrate? **LO5**

5. Assume that securitization combined with borrowing and irrational exuberance in Hyperville have driven up the value of existing financial securities at a geometric rate, specifically from $2 to $4 to $8 to $16 to $32 to $64 over a six-year time period. Over the same period, the value of the assets underlying the securities rose at an arithmetic rate from $2 to $3 to $4 to $5 to $6 to $7. If these patterns hold for decreases as well as for increases, by how much would the value of the financial securities decline if the value of the underlying asset suddenly and unexpectedly fell by $5? **LO5**

FURTHER TEST YOUR KNOWLEDGE AT
www.mcconnell19e.com

At the text's Online Learning Center (OLC), **www.mcconnell19e.com**, you will find one or more Web-based questions that require information from the Internet to answer. We urge you to check them out; they will familiarize you with Web sites that may be helpful in other courses and perhaps even in your career. The OLC also features multiple-choice questions that give instant feedback and provides other helpful ways to further test your knowledge of the chapter.

AFTER READING THIS CHAPTER, YOU SHOULD BE ABLE TO:

1 Explain the basics of a bank's balance sheet and discuss why the U.S. banking system is called a "fractional reserve" system.

2 Explain the distinction between a bank's actual reserves and its required reserves.

3 Describe how a bank can create money.

4 Describe the multiple expansion of loans and money by the entire banking system.

5 Define the money multiplier, explain how to calculate it, and demonstrate its relevance.

Money Creation

We have seen that the *M1* money supply consists of currency (coins and Federal Reserve Notes) and checkable deposits and that *M1* is a base component of *M2*, a broader measure of the money supply that also includes savings deposits, small-denominated time deposits, and balances in money market mutual funds. The U.S. Mint produces the coins and the U.S. Bureau of Engraving and Printing creates the Federal Reserve Notes. So who creates the checkable deposits? Surprisingly, it is loan officers! Although that may sound like something a congressional committee should investigate, the monetary authorities are well aware that banks and thrifts create checkable deposits. In fact, the Federal Reserve relies on these institutions to create this vital component of the nation's money supply.

The Fractional Reserve System

The United States, like most other countries today, has a **fractional reserve banking system** in which only a portion (fraction) of checkable deposits are backed up by reserves of currency in bank vaults or deposits at the central bank. Our goal is to explain this system and show how commercial banks can create checkable deposits by issuing loans. Our examples will involve commercial banks, but remember that thrift institutions also provide checkable deposits. So the analysis applies to banks and thrifts alike.

Illustrating the Idea: The Goldsmiths

Here is the history behind the idea of the fractional reserve system.

When early traders began to use gold in making transactions, they soon realized that it was both unsafe and inconvenient to carry gold and to have it weighed and assayed (judged for purity) every time they negotiated a transaction. So by the sixteenth century they had begun to deposit their gold with goldsmiths, who would store it in vaults for a fee. On receiving a gold deposit, the goldsmith would issue a receipt to the depositor. Soon people were paying for goods with goldsmiths' receipts, which served as one of the first types of paper money.

At this point the goldsmiths—embryonic bankers—used a 100 percent reserve system; they backed their circulating paper money receipts fully with the gold that they held "in reserve" in their vaults. But because of the public's acceptance of the goldsmiths' receipts as paper money, the goldsmiths soon realized that owners rarely redeemed the gold they had in storage. In fact, the goldsmiths observed that the amount of gold being deposited with them in any week or month was likely to exceed the amount that was being withdrawn.

Then some clever goldsmith hit on the idea that paper "receipts" could be issued in excess of the amount of gold held. Goldsmiths would put these receipts, which were redeemable in gold, into circulation by making interest-earning loans to merchants, producers, and consumers. A borrower might, for instance, borrow $10,000 worth of gold receipts today with the promise to repay $10,500 worth of gold receipts in one year (a 5 percent interest rate). Borrowers were willing to accept loans in the form of gold receipts because the receipts were accepted as a medium of exchange in the marketplace.

This was the beginning of the fractional reserve system of banking, in which reserves in bank vaults are a fraction of the total money supply. If, for example, the goldsmith issued $1 million in receipts for actual gold in storage and another $1 million in receipts as loans, then the total value of paper money in circulation would be $2 million—twice the value of the gold. Gold reserves would be a fraction (one-half) of outstanding paper money.

Significant Characteristics of Fractional Reserve Banking

The goldsmith story highlights two significant characteristics of fractional reserve banking. First, banks can create money through lending. In fact, goldsmiths created money when they made loans by giving borrowers paper money that was not fully backed by gold reserves. The quantity of such money goldsmiths could create depended on the amount of reserves they deemed prudent to have available. The smaller the amount of reserves thought necessary, the larger the amount of paper money the goldsmiths could create. Today, gold is no longer used as bank reserves. Instead, currency itself serves as bank reserves so that the creation of checkable-deposit money by banks (via their lending) is limited by the amount of *currency reserves* that the banks feel obligated, or are required by law, to keep.

A second reality is that banks operating on the basis of fractional reserves are vulnerable to "panics" or "runs." A goldsmith who issued paper money equal to twice the value of his gold reserves would be unable to convert all that paper money into gold in the event that all the holders of that money appeared at his door at the same time demanding their gold. In fact, many European and U.S. banks were once ruined by this unfortunate circumstance. However, a bank panic is highly unlikely if the banker's reserve and lending policies are prudent. Indeed, one reason why banking systems are highly regulated industries is to prevent runs on banks.

This is also why the United States has the system of deposit insurance that we discussed in the last chapter. By guaranteeing deposits, deposit insurance helps to prevent the sort of bank runs that used to happen so often before deposit insurance was available. In these situations, rumors would spread that a bank was about to go bankrupt and that it only had a small amount of reserves left in its vaults. Bank runs are called "bank runs" because depositors would run to the bank trying to be one of the lucky few to withdraw their money while the bank had any reserves left. The rumors were usually totally unfounded. But, unfortunately, the bank would still go bankrupt even if it began the day with its normal amount of reserves. With so many customers withdrawing money simultaneously, it would run out of reserves and be forced to default on its obligations to its remaining depositors.

A Single Commercial Bank

To illustrate the workings of the modern fractional reserve banking system, we need to examine a commercial bank's balance sheet.

The **balance sheet** of a commercial bank (or thrift) is a statement of assets—things owned by the bank or owed to the bank—and claims on those assets. A bank balance sheet summarizes the financial position of the bank at a certain time. Every balance sheet must balance; this means that the value of *assets* must equal the amount of claims against those assets. The claims shown on a balance sheet are divided into two groups: the claims of nonowners of the bank against the firm's assets, called *liabilities*, and the claims of the owners of the firm against the firm's assets, called *net worth*. Liabilities are things owed by the bank to depositors or others. A balance sheet is balanced because

$$Assets = liabilities + net\ worth$$

Every $1 change in assets must be offset by a $1 change in liabilities + net worth. Every $1 change in liabilities + net worth must be offset by a $1 change in assets.

Now let's work through a series of bank transactions involving balance sheets to establish how individual banks can create money.

Transaction 1: Creating a Bank

Suppose some far-sighted citizens of the town of Wahoo, Nebraska (yes, there is such a place), decide their town needs a new commercial bank to provide banking services for that growing community. Once they have secured a state or national charter for their bank, they turn to the task of selling, say, $250,000 worth of stock (equity shares) to buyers, both in and out of the community. Their efforts meet with success and the Bank of Wahoo comes into existence—at least on paper. What does its balance sheet look like at this stage?

The founders of the bank have sold $250,000 worth of shares of stock in the bank—some to themselves, some to other people. As a result, the bank now has $250,000 in cash on hand and $250,000 worth of stock shares outstanding. The cash is an asset to the bank. Cash held by a bank is sometimes called **vault cash** or till money. The shares of stock outstanding constitute an equal amount of claims that the owners have against the bank's assets. Those shares of stock constitute the net worth of the bank. The bank's balance sheet reads:

Creating a Bank Balance Sheet 1: Wahoo Bank		
Assets	Liabilities and net worth	
Cash	$250,000	Stock shares	$250,000

Each item listed in a balance sheet such as this is called an *account*.

Transaction 2: Acquiring Property and Equipment

The board of directors (who represent the bank's owners) must now get the new bank off the drawing board and make it a reality. First, property and equipment must be acquired. Suppose the directors, confident of the success of their venture, purchase a building for $220,000 and pay $20,000 for office equipment. This simple transaction changes the composition of the bank's assets. The bank now has $240,000 less in cash and $240,000 of new property assets. Using blue to denote accounts affected by each transaction, we find that the bank's balance sheet at the end of transaction 2 appears as follows:

Acquiring Property and Equipment Balance Sheet 2: Wahoo Bank		
Assets	Liabilities and net worth	
Cash	$ 10,000	Stock shares	$250,000
Property	240,000		

Note that the balance sheet still balances, as it must.

Transaction 3: Accepting Deposits

Commercial banks have two basic functions: to accept deposits of money and to make loans. Now that the bank is operating, suppose that the citizens and businesses of Wahoo decide to deposit $100,000 in the Wahoo bank. What happens to the bank's balance sheet?

The bank receives cash, which is an asset to the bank. Suppose this money is deposited in the bank as checkable deposits (checking account entries), rather than as savings accounts or time deposits. These newly created *checkable deposits* constitute claims that the depositors have against the assets of the Wahoo bank and thus are a new liability account. The bank's balance sheet now looks like this:

Accepting Deposits Balance Sheet 3: Wahoo Bank		
Assets	Liabilities and net worth	
Cash	$110,000	Checkable deposits	$100,000
Property	240,000	Stock shares	250,000

There has been no change in the economy's total supply of money as a result of transaction 3, but a change has occurred in the composition of the money supply. Bank money, or checkable deposits, has increased by $100,000, and currency held by the public has decreased by $100,000. As explained in the previous chapter, currency held in a bank is not part of the economy's money supply.

A withdrawal of cash will reduce the bank's checkable-deposit liabilities and its holdings of cash by the amount of the withdrawal. This, too, changes the composition, but not the total supply, of money in the economy.

Transaction 4: Depositing Reserves in a Federal Reserve Bank

All commercial banks and thrift institutions that provide checkable deposits must by law keep **required reserves.** Required reserves are an amount of funds equal to a specified percentage of the bank's own deposit liabilities. A bank must keep these reserves on deposit with the Federal Reserve Bank in its district or as cash in the bank's vault. To simplify, we suppose the Bank of Wahoo keeps its required reserves entirely as deposits in the Federal Reserve Bank of its district. But remember that vault cash is counted as reserves and real-world banks keep a significant portion of their own reserves in their vaults.

The "specified percentage" of checkable-deposit liabilities that a commercial bank must keep as reserves is known as the **reserve ratio**—the ratio of the required reserves the commercial bank must keep to the bank's own outstanding checkable-deposit liabilities:

$$\text{Reserve ratio} = \frac{\text{commercial bank's required reserves}}{\text{commercial bank's checkable-deposit liabilities}}$$

If the reserve ratio is $\frac{1}{10}$, or 10 percent, the Wahoo bank, having accepted $100,000 in deposits from the public, would have to keep $10,000 as reserves. If the ratio is $\frac{1}{5}$, or 20 percent, $20,000 of reserves would be required. If $\frac{1}{2}$, or 50 percent, $50,000 would be required.

The Fed has the authority to establish and vary the reserve ratio within limits legislated by Congress. The limits now prevailing are shown in Table 15.1. The first $10.7 million of checkable deposits held by a commercial bank or thrift is exempt from reserve requirements. A 3 percent reserve is required on checkable deposits of between $10.7 million and $55.2 million. A 10 percent reserve is required on checkable deposits over $55.2 million, although the Fed can vary that percentage between 8 and 14 percent. Currently, no reserves are required against

TABLE 15.1 Reserve Requirements (Reserve Ratios) for Banks and Thrifts, 2010

Type of Deposit	Current Requirement	Statutory Limits
Checkable deposits:		
$0–$10.7 million	0%	3%
$10.7–$55.2 million	3	3
Over $55.2 million	10	8–14
Noncheckable nonpersonal savings and time deposits	0	0–9

Source: Federal Reserve, Regulation D, **www.federalreserve.gov**.

noncheckable nonpersonal (business) savings or time deposits, although up to 9 percent can be required. Also, after consultation with appropriate congressional committees, the Fed for 180 days may impose reserve requirements outside the 8–14 percent range specified in Table 15.1. Beginning in late 2008, the Fed began paying banks interest on their required reserves and on their excess reserve balances held at Federal Reserve Banks.

In order to simplify, we will suppose that the reserve ratio for checkable deposits in commercial banks is $\frac{1}{5}$, or 20 percent. Although 20 percent obviously is higher than the requirement really is, the figure is convenient for calculations. Because we are concerned only with checkable (spendable) deposits, we ignore reserves on noncheckable savings and time deposits. The main point is that reserve requirements are fractional, meaning that they are less than 100 percent. This point is critical in our analysis of the lending ability of the banking system.

By depositing $20,000 in the Federal Reserve Bank, the Wahoo bank will just be meeting the required 20 percent ratio between its reserves and its own deposit liabilities. We will use "reserves" to mean the funds commercial banks deposit in the Federal Reserve Banks, to distinguish those funds from the public's deposits in commercial banks.

But suppose the Wahoo bank anticipates that its holdings of checkable deposits will grow in the future. Then, instead of sending just the minimum amount, $20,000, it sends an extra $90,000, for a total of $110,000. In so doing, the bank will avoid the inconvenience of sending additional reserves to the Federal Reserve Bank each time its own checkable-deposit liabilities increase. And, as you will see, it is these extra reserves that enable banks to lend money and earn interest income.

Actually, a real-world bank would not deposit *all* its cash in the Federal Reserve Bank. However, because (1) banks as a rule hold vault cash only in the amount of $1\frac{1}{2}$ or 2 percent of their total assets and (2) vault cash can be counted as reserves, we will assume for simplicity that all of Wahoo's cash is deposited in the Federal Reserve Bank and therefore constitutes the commercial bank's actual reserves. By making this simplifying assumption, we do not need to bother adding two assets—"cash" and "deposits in the Federal Reserve Bank"—to determine "reserves."

After the Wahoo bank deposits $110,000 of reserves at the Fed, its balance sheet becomes:

Depositing Reserves at the Fed
Balance Sheet 4: Wahoo Bank

Assets		Liabilities and net worth	
Cash	$ 0	Checkable deposits	$100,000
Reserves	110,000		
Property	240,000	Stock shares	250,000

There are three things to note about this latest transaction.

Excess Reserves
A bank's **excess reserves** are found by subtracting its *required reserves* from its **actual reserves:**

Excess reserves = actual reserves − required reserves

In this case,

Actual reserves	$110,000
Required reserves	−20,000
Excess reserves	$ 90,000

The only reliable way of computing excess reserves is to multiply the bank's checkable-deposit liabilities by the reserve ratio to obtain required reserves ($100,000 × 20 percent = $20,000) and then to subtract the required reserves from the actual reserves listed on the asset side of the bank's balance sheet.

To test your understanding, compute the bank's excess reserves from balance sheet 4, assuming that the reserve ratio is (1) 10 percent, (2) $33\frac{1}{3}$ percent, and (3) 50 percent.

We will soon demonstrate that the ability of a commercial bank to make loans depends on the existence of excess reserves. Understanding this concept is crucial in seeing how the banking system creates money.

Control
You might think the basic purpose of reserves is to enhance the liquidity of a bank and protect commercial bank depositors from losses. Reserves would constitute a ready source of funds from which commercial banks could meet large, unexpected cash withdrawals by depositors.

But this reasoning breaks down under scrutiny. Although historically reserves have been seen as a source of liquidity and therefore as protection for depositors, a bank's required reserves are not great enough to meet sudden, massive cash withdrawals. If the banker's nightmare should materialize—everyone with checkable deposits appearing at once to demand those deposits in cash—the actual reserves held as vault cash or at the Federal Reserve Bank would be insufficient. The banker simply could not meet this "bank panic." Because reserves are fractional, checkable deposits may be much greater than a bank's required reserves.

So commercial bank deposits must be protected by other means. Periodic bank examinations are one way of promoting prudent commercial banking practices. Furthermore, insurance funds administered by the Federal Deposit Insurance Corporation (FDIC) and the National Credit Union Administration (NCUA) insure individual deposits in banks and thrifts up to $250,000.

If it is not the purpose of reserves to provide for commercial bank liquidity, then what is their function? *Control* is the answer. Required reserves help the Fed control the lending ability of commercial banks. The Fed can take certain actions that either increase or decrease commercial bank reserves and affect the ability of banks to grant credit. The objective is to prevent banks from overextending or underextending bank credit. To the degree that these policies successfully influence the volume of commercial bank credit, the Fed can help the economy avoid business fluctuations. Another function of reserves is to facilitate the collection or "clearing" of checks.

Asset and Liability
Transaction 4 brings up another matter. Specifically, the reserves created in transaction 4 are an asset to the depositing commercial bank because they are a claim this bank has against the assets of another institution—the Federal Reserve Bank. The checkable deposit you get by depositing money in a commercial bank is an asset to you and a liability to the bank (since the bank is liable for repaying you whenever you choose to withdraw your deposit). In the same way, the reserves that a commercial bank establishes by depositing money in a bankers' bank are an asset to the commercial bank and a liability to the Federal Reserve Bank.

Transaction 5: Clearing a Check Drawn against the Bank

Assume that Fred Bradshaw, a Wahoo farmer, deposited a substantial portion of the $100,000 in checkable deposits that the Wahoo bank received in transaction 3. Now suppose that Fred buys $50,000 of farm machinery from the Ajax Farm Implement Company of Surprise, Nebraska. Bradshaw pays for this machinery by writing a $50,000 check against his deposit in the Wahoo bank. He gives the check to the Ajax Company. What are the results?

Ajax deposits the check in its account with the Surprise bank. The Surprise bank increases Ajax's checkable deposits by $50,000 when Ajax deposits the check. Ajax is now paid in full. Bradshaw is pleased with his new machinery.

Now the Surprise bank has Bradshaw's check. This check is simply a claim against the assets of the Wahoo bank. The Surprise bank will collect this claim by sending the check (along with checks drawn on other banks) to the regional Federal Reserve Bank. Here a bank employee will clear, or collect, the check for the Surprise bank by increasing Surprise's reserve in the Federal Reserve Bank by $50,000 and decreasing the Wahoo bank's reserve by that same amount. The check is "collected" merely by making bookkeeping notations to the effect that Wahoo's claim against the Federal Reserve Bank is reduced by $50,000 and Surprise's claim is increased by $50,000.

Finally, the Federal Reserve Bank sends the cleared check back to the Wahoo bank, and for the first time the Wahoo bank discovers that one of its depositors has drawn a check for $50,000 against his checkable deposit. Accordingly, the Wahoo bank reduces Bradshaw's checkable deposit by $50,000 and notes that the collection of this check has caused a $50,000 decline in its reserves at the Federal Reserve Bank. All the balance sheets balance: The Wahoo bank has reduced both its assets (reserves) and its liabilities (checkable deposits) by $50,000. The Surprise bank has $50,000 more in both assets (reserves) and liabilities (checkable deposits). Ownership of reserves at the Federal Reserve Bank has changed—with Wahoo owning $50,000 less and Surprise owning $50,000 more—but total reserves stay the same.

Whenever a check is drawn against one bank and deposited in another bank, collection of that check will reduce both the reserves and the checkable deposits of the bank on which the check is drawn. Conversely, if a bank receives a check drawn on another bank, the bank receiving the check will, in the process of collecting it, have its reserves and deposits increased by the amount of the check. In our example, the Wahoo bank loses $50,000 in both reserves and deposits to the Surprise bank. But there is no loss of reserves or deposits for the banking system as a whole. What one bank loses, another bank gains.

If we bring all the other assets and liabilities back into the picture, the Wahoo bank's balance sheet looks like this at the end of transaction 5:

Clearing a Check
Balance Sheet 5: Wahoo Bank

Assets		Liabilities and net worth	
Reserves	$ 60,000	Checkable deposits	$ 50,000
Property	240,000	Stock shares	250,000

Verify that with a 20 percent reserve requirement, the bank's excess reserves now stand at $50,000.

Money-Creating Transactions of a Commercial Bank

The next two transactions are crucial because they explain (1) how a commercial bank can literally create money by making loans and (2) how banks create money by purchasing government bonds from the public.

Transaction 6: Granting a Loan

In addition to accepting deposits, commercial banks grant loans to borrowers. What effect does lending by a commercial bank have on its balance sheet?

Suppose the Gristly Meat Packing Company of Wahoo decides it is time to expand its facilities. Suppose, too, that the company needs exactly $50,000—which just happens to be equal to the Wahoo bank's excess reserves—to finance this project.

Gristly goes to the Wahoo bank and requests a loan for this amount. The Wahoo bank knows the Gristly Company's fine reputation and financial soundness and is convinced of its ability to repay the loan. So the loan is granted. In return, the president of Gristly hands a promissory note—a fancy IOU—to the Wahoo bank. Gristly wants the convenience and safety of paying its obligations by check. So, instead of receiving a basket full of currency from the bank, Gristly gets a $50,000 increase in its checkable-deposit account in the Wahoo bank.

The Wahoo bank has acquired an interest-earning asset (the promissory note, which it files under "Loans") and has created checkable deposits (a liability) to "pay" for this asset. Gristly has swapped an IOU for the right to draw an additional $50,000 worth of checks against its checkable deposit in the Wahoo bank. Both parties are pleased.

At the moment the loan is completed, the Wahoo bank's position is shown by balance sheet 6a:

When a Loan Is Negotiated
Balance Sheet 6a: Wahoo Bank

Assets		Liabilities and net worth	
Reserves	$ 60,000	Checkable deposits	$100,000
Loans	50,000		
Property	240,000	Stock shares	250,000

All this looks simple enough. But a close examination of the Wahoo bank's balance statement reveals a startling fact: When a bank makes loans, it creates money. The president of Gristly went to the bank with something that is *not* money—her IOU—and walked out with something that *is* money—a checkable deposit.

Contrast transaction 6a with transaction 3, in which checkable deposits were created but only as a result of currency having been taken out of circulation. There was a change in the *composition* of the money supply in that situation but no change in the *total supply* of money. But when banks lend, they create checkable deposits that *are* money. By extending credit, the Wahoo bank has "monetized" an IOU. Gristly and the Wahoo bank have created and then swapped claims. The claim created by Gristly and given to the bank is not money; an individual's IOU is not acceptable as a medium of exchange. But the claim created by the bank and given to Gristly *is* money; checks drawn against a checkable deposit are acceptable as a medium of exchange. Checkable-deposit money like this constitutes about one-half the quantity of $M1$ money in the United States and about 10 percent of $M2$.

Much of the money used in the United States therefore is created through the extension of credit by commercial banks. This checkable-deposit money may be thought of as "debts" of commercial banks and thrift institutions. Checkable deposits are bank debts in the sense that they are claims that banks and thrifts promise to pay "on demand."

But certain factors limit the ability of a commercial bank to create checkable deposits ("bank money") by lending. The Wahoo bank can expect the newly created checkable deposit of $50,000 to be a very active account. Gristly would not borrow $50,000 at, say, 7, 10, or 12 percent interest for the sheer joy of knowing that funds were available if needed.

Assume that Gristly awards a $50,000 building contract to the Quickbuck Construction Company of Omaha. Quickbuck, true to its name, completes the expansion promptly and is paid with a check for $50,000 drawn by Gristly against its checkable deposit in the Wahoo bank. Quickbuck, with headquarters in Omaha, does not deposit this check in the Wahoo bank but instead deposits it in the Fourth National Bank of Omaha. Fourth National now has a $50,000 claim against the Wahoo bank. The check is collected in the manner described in transaction 5. As a result, the Wahoo bank loses both reserves and deposits equal to the amount of the check; Fourth National acquires $50,000 of reserves and deposits.

In summary, assuming a check is drawn by the borrower for the entire amount of the loan ($50,000) and is given to a firm that deposits it in some other bank, the Wahoo bank's balance sheet will read as follows after the check has been cleared against it:

After a Check Is Drawn on the Loan
Balance Sheet 6b: Wahoo Bank

Assets		Liabilities and net worth	
Reserves	$ 10,000	Checkable deposits	$ 50,000
Loans	50,000		
Property	240,000	Stock shares	250,000

After the check has been collected, the Wahoo bank just meets the required reserve ratio of 20 percent (= $10,000/$50,000). The bank has *no* excess reserves. This poses a question: Could the Wahoo bank have lent more than $50,000—an amount greater than its excess reserves—and still have met the 20 percent reserve requirement when a check for the full amount of the loan was cleared against it? The answer is no; the bank is "fully loaned up."

Here is why: Suppose the Wahoo bank had lent $55,000 to the Gristly company and that the Gristly company had spent all of that money by writing a $55,000 check to Quickbuck Construction. Collection of the check against the Wahoo bank would have lowered its reserves to $5,000 (= $60,000 − $55,000), and checkable deposits would once again stand at $50,000 (= $105,000 − $55,000). The ratio of actual reserves to checkable deposits would then be $5,000/$50,000, or only 10 percent. Because the reserve requirement is 20 percent, the Wahoo bank could not have lent $55,000.

WORKED PROBLEMS

W 15.1

Single bank accounting

By experimenting with other amounts over $50,000, you will find that the maximum amount the Wahoo bank could lend at the outset of transaction 6 is $50,000. This amount is identical to the amount of excess reserves the bank had available when the loan was negotiated.

A single commercial bank in a multibank banking system can lend only an amount equal to its initial preloan excess reserves. When it lends, the lending bank faces the possibility that checks for the entire amount of the loan will be drawn and cleared against it. If that happens, it will lose (to other banks) reserves equal to the amount it lends. So, to be safe, it limits its lending to the amount of its excess reserves.

Bank creation of money raises an interesting question: If a bank creates checkable-deposit money when it lends its excess reserves, is money destroyed when borrowers pay off loans? The answer is yes. When loans are paid off, the process works in reverse. The bank's checkable deposits decline by the amount of the loan repayment.

Transaction 7: Buying Government Securities

When a commercial bank buys government bonds from the public, the effect is substantially the same as lending. New money is created.

Assume that the Wahoo bank's balance sheet initially stands as it did at the end of transaction 5. Now suppose that instead of making a $50,000 loan, the bank buys $50,000 of government securities from a securities dealer. The bank receives the interest-bearing bonds, which appear on its balance statement as the asset "Securities," and gives the dealer an increase in its checkable-deposit account. The Wahoo bank's balance sheet appears as follows:

Buying Government Securities Balance Sheet 7: Wahoo Bank		
Assets	Liabilities and net worth	
Reserves $ 60,000	Checkable	
Securities 50,000	deposits	$100,000
Property 240,000	Stock shares	250,000

Checkable deposits, that is, the supply of money, have been increased by $50,000, as in transaction 6. Bond purchases from the public by commercial banks increase the supply of money in the same way as lending to the public does. The bank accepts government bonds (which are not money) and gives the securities dealer an increase in its checkable deposits (which *are* money).

Of course, when the securities dealer draws and clears a check for $50,000 against the Wahoo bank, the bank loses both reserves and deposits in that amount and then just meets the legal reserve requirement. Its balance sheet

now reads precisely as in 6b except that "Securities" is substituted for "Loans" on the asset side.

Finally, the *selling* of government bonds to the public by a commercial bank—like the repayment of a loan—reduces the supply of money. The securities buyer pays by check, and both "Securities" and "Checkable deposits" (the latter being money) decline by the amount of the sale.

Profits, Liquidity, and the Federal Funds Market

The asset items on a commercial bank's balance sheet reflect the banker's pursuit of two conflicting goals:

- *Profit* One goal is profit. Commercial banks, like any other businesses, seek profits, which is why the bank makes loans and buys securities—the two major earning assets of commercial banks.
- *Liquidity* The other goal is safety. For a bank, safety lies in liquidity, specifically such liquid assets as cash and excess reserves. A bank must be on guard for depositors who want to transform their checkable deposits into cash. Similarly, it must guard against more checks clearing against it than are cleared in its favor, causing a net outflow of reserves. Bankers thus seek a balance between prudence and profit. The compromise is between assets that earn higher returns and highly liquid assets that earn no returns.

An interesting way in which banks can partly reconcile the goals of profit and liquidity is to lend temporary excess reserves held at the Federal Reserve Banks to other commercial banks. Normal day-to-day flows of funds to banks rarely leave all banks with their exact levels of required reserves. Also, excess reserves held at the Federal Reserve Banks are highly liquid, but they draw less interest than the banks can make through loans. Banks therefore often lend these excess reserves to other banks on an overnight basis in order to earn additional interest without sacrificing long-term liquidity. Banks that borrow in this Federal funds market—the market for immediately available reserve balances at the Federal Reserve—do so because they are temporarily short of required reserves. The interest rate paid on these overnight loans is called the **Federal funds rate.**

We would show an overnight loan of reserves from the Surprise bank to the Wahoo bank as a decrease in reserves at the Surprise bank and an increase in reserves at the Wahoo bank. Ownership of reserves at the Federal Reserve Bank of Kansas City would change, but total reserves would not be affected. Exercise: Determine what other changes would be required on the Wahoo and Surprise banks' balance sheets as a result of the overnight loan.

- Banks create money when they make loans; money vanishes when bank loans are repaid.
- New money is created when banks buy government bonds from the public; money disappears when banks sell government bonds to the public.
- Banks balance profitability and safety in determining their mix of earning assets and highly liquid assets.
- Although the Fed pays interest on excess reserves, banks may be able to obtain higher interest rates by temporarily lending the reserves to other banks in the Federal funds market; the interest rate on such loans is the Federal funds rate.

The Banking System: Multiple-Deposit Expansion

Thus far we have seen that a single bank in a banking system can lend one dollar for each dollar of its excess reserves. The situation is different for all commercial banks as a group. We will find that the commercial banking system can lend—that is, can create money—by a multiple of its excess reserves. This multiple lending is accomplished even though each bank in the system can lend only "dollar for dollar" with its excess reserves.

How do these seemingly paradoxical results come about? To answer this question succinctly, we will make three simplifying assumptions:

- The reserve ratio for all commercial banks is 20 percent.
- Initially all banks are meeting this 20 percent reserve requirement exactly. No excess reserves exist; or, in the parlance of banking, they are "loaned up" (or "loaned out") fully in terms of the reserve requirement.
- If any bank can increase its loans as a result of acquiring excess reserves, an amount equal to those excess reserves will be lent to one borrower, who will write a check for the entire amount of the loan and give it to someone else, who will deposit the check in another bank. This third assumption means that the worst thing possible happens to every lending bank—a check for the entire amount of the loan is drawn and cleared against it in favor of another bank.

The Banking System's Lending Potential

Suppose a junkyard owner finds a $100 bill while dismantling a car that has been on the lot for years. He deposits the $100 in bank A, which adds the $100 to its reserves.

We will record only changes in the balance sheets of the various commercial banks. The deposit changes bank A's balance sheet as shown by entries (a_1):

		Multiple-Deposit Expansion Process		
		Balance Sheet: Commercial Bank A		
Assets		Liabilities and net worth		
Reserves	$\$+100\ (a_1)$	Checkable		
	$-80\ (a_3)$	deposits	$\$+100\ (a_1)$	
Loans	$+80\ (a_2)$		$+80\ (a_2)$	
			$-80\ (a_3)$	

Recall from transaction 3 that this $100 deposit of currency does not alter the money supply. While $100 of checkable-deposit money comes into being, it is offset by the $100 of currency no longer in the hands of the public (the junkyard owner). But bank A *has* acquired excess reserves of $80. Of the newly acquired $100 in currency, 20 percent, or $20, must be earmarked for the required reserves on the new $100 checkable deposit, and the remaining $80 goes to excess reserves. Remembering that a single commercial bank can lend only an amount equal to its excess reserves, we conclude that bank A can lend a maximum of $80. When a loan for this amount is made, bank A's loans increase by $80 and the borrower gets an $80 checkable deposit. We add these figures—entries (a_2)—to bank A's balance sheet.

But now we make our third assumption: The borrower uses the full amount of the loan ($80) to write a check ($80) to someone else, and that person deposits the amount in bank B, a different bank. As we saw in transaction 6, bank A loses both reserves and deposits equal to the amount of the loan, as indicated in entries (a_3). The net result of these transactions is that bank A's reserves now stand at +$20 (= $100 − $80), loans at +$80, and checkable deposits at +$100 (= $100 + $80 − $80). When the dust has settled, bank A is just meeting the 20 percent reserve ratio.

Recalling our previous discussion, we know that bank B acquires both the reserves and the deposits that bank A has lost. Bank B's balance sheet is changed as in entries (b_1):

		Multiple-Deposit Expansion Process		
		Balance Sheet: Commercial Bank B		
Assets		Liabilities and net worth		
Reserves	$\$+80\ (b_1)$	Checkable		
	$-64\ (b_3)$	deposits	$\$+80\ (b_1)$	
Loans	$+64\ (b_2)$		$+64\ (b_2)$	
			$-64\ (b_3)$	

When the borrower's check is drawn and cleared, bank A loses $80 in reserves and deposits and bank B gains $80 in reserves and deposits. But 20 percent, or $16, of bank B's new reserves must be kept as required reserves against the new $80 in checkable deposits. This means that bank B has $64 (= $80 − $16) in excess reserves. It can therefore lend $64 [entries (b_2)]. When the new borrower writes a check for $64 to buy a product, and the seller deposits the check in bank C, the reserves and deposits of bank B both fall by $64 [entries (b_3)]. As a result of these transactions, bank B's reserves now stand at +$16 (= $80 − $64), loans at +$64, and checkable deposits at +$80 (= $80 + $64 − $64). After all this, bank B is just meeting the 20 percent reserve requirement.

We are off and running again. Bank C acquires the $64 in reserves and deposits lost by bank B. Its balance sheet changes as in entries (c_1):

Multiple-Deposit Expansion Process

Balance Sheet: Commercial Bank C

Assets		Liabilities and net worth	
Reserves	$+64.00 (c_1) −51.20 (c_3)	Checkable deposits	$+64.00 (c_1) +51.20 (c_2)
Loans	+51.20 (c_2)		−51.20 (c_3)

Exactly 20 percent, or $12.80, of these new reserves will be required reserves, the remaining $51.20 being excess reserves. Hence, bank C can safely lend a maximum of $51.20. Suppose it does [entries (c_2)]. And suppose the borrower writes a check for the entire amount ($51.20) to a merchant who deposits it in another bank [entries (c_3)].

We could go ahead with this procedure by bringing banks D, E, F, G, . . . , N, and so on into the picture. In fact, the process will go on almost indefinitely, just as long as banks further down the line receive at least one penny in new reserves that they can use to back another round of lending and money creation. But we suggest that you work through the computations for banks D, E, and F to be sure you understand the procedure.

The entire analysis is summarized in Table 15.2. Data for banks D through N are supplied on their own rows so that you may check your computations. The last row of the table consolidates into one row everything that happens for all banks down the line after bank N. Our conclusion is startling: On the basis of only $80 in excess reserves (acquired by the banking system when someone deposited $100 of currency in bank A), the entire commercial banking system is able to lend $400, the sum of the amounts in column 4. The banking system can lend excess reserves by a multiple of 5 (= $400/$80) when the reserve ratio is 20 percent. Yet each single bank in the banking system is lending only an

TABLE 15.2 Expansion of the Money Supply by the Commercial Banking System

Bank	(1) Acquired Reserves and Deposits	(2) Required Reserves (Reserve Ratio = .2)	(3) Excess Reserves, (1) − (2)	(4) Amount Bank Can Lend; New Money Created = (3)
Bank A	$100.00 (a_1)	$20.00	**$80.00**	$ 80.00 (a_2)
Bank B	80.00 (a_3, b_1)	16.00	64.00	64.00 (b_2)
Bank C	64.00 (b_3, c_1)	12.80	51.20	51.20 (c_2)
Bank D	51.20	10.24	40.96	40.96
Bank E	40.96	8.19	32.77	32.77
Bank F	32.77	6.55	26.21	26.21
Bank G	26.21	5.24	20.97	20.97
Bank H	20.97	4.20	16.78	16.78
Bank I	16.78	3.36	13.42	13.42
Bank J	13.42	2.68	10.74	10.74
Bank K	10.74	2.15	8.59	8.59
Bank L	8.59	1.72	6.87	6.87
Bank M	6.87	1.37	5.50	5.50
Bank N	5.50	1.10	4.40	4.40
Other banks	21.99	4.40	17.59	17.59
Total amount of money created (sum of the amounts in column 4)				**$400.00**

amount equal to its own excess reserves. How do we explain this? How can the banking system as a whole lend by a multiple of its excess reserves, when each individual bank can lend only dollar for dollar with its excess reserves?

The answer is that reserves lost by a single bank are not lost to the banking system as a whole. The reserves lost by bank A are acquired by bank B. Those lost by B are gained by C. C loses to D, D to E, E to F, and so forth. Although reserves can be, and are, lost by individual banks in the banking system, there is no loss of reserves for the banking system as a whole.

An individual bank can safely lend only an amount equal to its excess reserves, *but the commercial banking system can lend by a multiple of its collective excess reserves.* This contrast, incidentally, is an illustration of why it is imperative that we keep the fallacy of composition (Last Word, Chapter 1) firmly in mind. Commercial banks as a group can create money by lending in a manner much different from that of the individual banks in the group.

The Monetary Multiplier

The **monetary multiplier** (or, less commonly, the *checkable deposit multiplier*) defines the relationship between any new excess reserves in the banking system and the magnified creation of new checkable-deposit money by banks as a group. It is a separate idea from the spending-income multiplier of Chapter 10 but shares some mathematical similarities. The spending-income multiplier exists because the expenditures of one household become some other household's income; the multiplier magnifies a change in initial spending into a larger change in GDP. The spending-income multiplier is the reciprocal of the MPS (the leakage into saving that occurs at each round of spending).

Similarly, the monetary multiplier exists because the reserves and deposits lost by one bank become reserves of another bank. It magnifies excess reserves into a larger creation of checkable-deposit money. The monetary multiplier m is the reciprocal of the required reserve ratio R (the leakage into required reserves that occurs at each step in the lending process). In short,

$$\text{Monetary multiplier} = \frac{1}{\text{required reserve ratio}}$$

or, in symbols,

$$m = \frac{1}{R}$$

In this formula, m represents the maximum amount of new checkable-deposit money that can be created by a single dollar of excess reserves, given the value of R. By multiplying the excess reserves E by m, we can find the maximum amount of new checkable-deposit money, D, that can be created by the banking system. That is,

$$\text{Maximum checkable-deposit creation} = \text{excess reserves} \times \text{monetary multiplier}$$

or, more simply,

$$D = E \times m$$

In our example in Table 15.2, R is .20, so m is 5 ($= 1/.20$). This implies that

$$D = \$80 \times 5 = \$400$$

Figure 15.1 depicts the final outcome of our example of a multiple-deposit expansion of the money supply. The initial deposit of $100 of currency into the bank (lower right-hand box) creates new reserves of an equal amount (upper box). With a 20 percent reserve ratio, however, only $20 of reserves are needed to "back up" this $100 checkable deposit. The excess reserves of $80 permit the creation of $400 of new checkable deposits via the making of loans, confirming a monetary multiplier of 5. The $100 of new reserves supports a total supply of money of $500, consisting of the $100 initial checkable deposit plus $400 of checkable deposits created through lending.

WORKED PROBLEMS

W 15.2

Money creation

FIGURE 15.1 The outcome of the money expansion process. A deposit of $100 of currency into a checking account creates an initial checkable deposit of $100. If the reserve ratio is 20 percent, only $20 of reserves is legally required to support the $100 checkable deposit. The $80 of excess reserves allows the banking system to create $400 of checkable deposits through making loans. The $100 of reserves supports a total of $500 of money ($100 + $400).

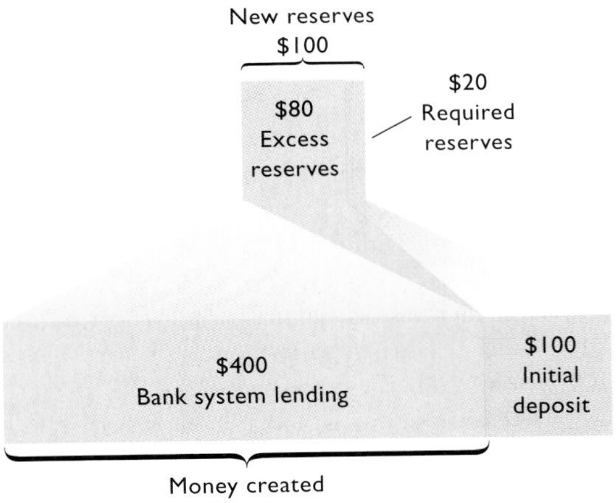

LAST Word The Bank Panics of 1930–1933

A Series of Bank Panics in the Early 1930s Resulted in a Multiple Contraction of the Money Supply.

In the early months of the Great Depression, before there was deposit insurance, several financially weak banks went out of business. As word spread that customers of those banks had lost their deposits, a general concern arose that something similar could happen at other banks. Depositors became frightened that their banks did not, in fact, still have all the money they had deposited. And, of course, in a fractional reserve banking system, that is the reality. Acting on their fears, people went en masse to their banks to withdraw currency—that is, to "cash out" their accounts. They wanted to get their money before it was all gone. Economists liken this sort of collective response to "herd" or "flock" behavior. The sudden "run on the banks" caused many previously financially sound banks to declare bankruptcy. More than 9000 banks failed within three years.

The massive conversion of checkable deposits to currency during 1930–1933 reduced the nation's money supply. This might seem strange, since a check written for "cash" reduces checkable-deposit money and increases currency in the hands of the public by the same amount. So how does the money supply decline? Our discussion of the money-creation process provides the answer, but now the story becomes one of money destruction.

Suppose that people collectively cash out $10 billion from their checking accounts. As an immediate result, checkable-deposit money declines by $10 billion, while currency held by the public increases by $10 billion. But here is the catch: Assuming a reserve ratio of 20 percent, the $10 billion of currency in the banks had been supporting $50 billion of checkable-deposit money, the $10 billion of deposits plus $40 billion created through loans. The $10 billion withdrawal of currency forces banks to reduce loans (and thus checkable-deposit money) by $40 billion to continue to meet their reserve requirement. In short, a $40 billion destruction of checkable-deposit money occurs. This is the scenario that occurred in the early years of the 1930s.

Accompanying this multiple contraction of checkable deposits was the banks' "scramble for liquidity" to try to meet further withdrawals of currency. To obtain more currency, they sold many of their holdings of government securities to the public. You know from this chapter that a bank's sale of government securities to the public, like a reduction in loans, reduces the money supply. People write checks for the securities, reducing their checkable deposits, and the bank uses the currency it obtains to meet the ongoing bank run. In short, the loss of reserves from the banking system, in conjunction with the scramble for security, reduced the amount of checkable-deposit money by far more than the increase in currency in the hands of the public. Thus, the money supply collapsed.

In 1933, President Franklin Roosevelt ended the bank panic by declaring a "national bank holiday," during which all national banks were shut down for one week so that government inspectors could have time to go over each bank's accounting records. Only healthy banks with plenty of reserves were allowed to reopen. This meant that when the holiday was over, people could trust in any bank that had been allowed to reopen. This identification of healthy banks, along with the initiation of the Federal deposit insurance program, reassured depositors and ended the bank panics.

But before these policies could begin to turn things around, the nation's money supply had plummeted by 25 to 33 percent, depending on how narrowly or broadly the money supply is defined. This was the largest drop in the money supply in U.S. history. This decline contributed substantially to the nation's deepest and longest depression. Simply put, less money meant less spending on goods and services as well as fewer loans for businesses. Both effects exacerbated the Great Depression.

Today, a multiple contraction of the money supply of the 1930–1933 magnitude is unthinkable. FDIC insurance has kept individual bank failures from becoming general panics. For example, during the financial crisis of 2007–2008, the FDIC increased deposit insurance from $100,000 per account to $250,000 per account, and the Federal government guaranteed the safety of all balances in money market mutual fund accounts. Also, while the Fed stood idly by during the bank panics of 1930–1933, in 2007–2008 it took immediate and dramatic actions to maintain the banking system's reserves and the nation's money supply. We discussed these lender-of-last-resort actions in the previous chapter. In Chapter 16 we will discuss the interest rate policies that the Fed undertook during the crisis.

Higher reserve ratios mean lower monetary multipliers and therefore less creation of new checkable-deposit money via loans; smaller reserve ratios mean higher monetary multipliers and thus more creation of new checkable-deposit money via loans. With a high reserve ratio, say, 50 percent, the monetary multiplier would be 2 (= 1/.5), and in our example the banking system could create only $100 (= $50 of excess reserves × 2) of new checkable deposits. With a low reserve ratio, say, 5 percent, the monetary multiplier would be 20 (= 1/.05), and the banking system could create $1900 (= $95 of excess reserves × 20) of new checkable deposits.

You might experiment with the following two brainteasers to test your understanding of multiple credit expansion by the banking system:

- Rework the analysis in Table 15.2 (at least three or four steps of it) assuming the reserve ratio is 10 percent. What is the maximum amount of money the banking system can create upon acquiring $100 in new reserves and deposits? (The answer is not $800!)
- Suppose the banking system is loaned up and faces a 20 percent reserve ratio. Explain how it might have to reduce its outstanding loans by $400 when a $100 cash withdrawal from a checkable-deposit account forces one bank to draw down its reserves by $100.

Reversibility: The Multiple Destruction of Money

The process we have described is reversible. Just as checkable-deposit money is created when banks make loans, checkable-deposit money is destroyed when loans are paid off. Loan repayment, in effect, sets off a process of multiple destruction of money the opposite of the multiple creation process. Because loans are both made and paid off in any period, the direction of the loans, checkable deposits, and money supply in a given period will depend on the net effect of the two processes. If the dollar amount of loans made in some period exceeds the dollar amount of loans paid off, checkable deposits will expand and the money supply will increase. But if the dollar amount of loans is less than the dollar amount of loans paid off, checkable deposits will contract and the money supply will decline.

QUICK REVIEW 15.3

- A single bank in a multibank system can safely lend (create money) by an amount equal to its excess reserves; the banking system can lend (create money) by a multiple of its excess reserves.
- The monetary multiplier is the reciprocal of the required reserve ratio; it is the multiple by which the banking system can expand the money supply for each dollar of excess reserves.
- The monetary multiplier works in both directions; it applies to money destruction from the payback of loans as well as the money creation from the making of loans.

Summary

1. Modern banking systems are fractional reserve systems: Only a fraction of checkable deposits is backed by currency.

2. The operation of a commercial bank can be understood through its balance sheet, where assets equal liabilities plus net worth.

3. Commercial banks keep required reserves on deposit in a Federal Reserve Bank or as vault cash. These required reserves are equal to a specified percentage of the commercial bank's checkable-deposit liabilities. Excess reserves are equal to actual reserves minus required reserves.

4. Banks lose both reserves and checkable deposits when checks are drawn against them.

5. Commercial banks create money—checkable deposits, or checkable-deposit money—when they make loans. They convert IOUs, which are *not* money, into checkable-deposits, which *are* money. Money is destroyed when lenders repay bank loans.

6. The ability of a single commercial bank to create money by lending depends on the size of its excess reserves. Generally speaking, a commercial bank can lend only an amount equal to its excess reserves. Money creation is thus limited because, in all likelihood, checks drawn by borrowers will be deposited in other banks, causing a loss of reserves and deposits to the lending bank equal to the amount of money that it has lent.

7. Rather than making loans, banks may decide to use excess reserves to buy bonds from the public. In doing so, banks merely credit the checkable-deposit accounts of the bond sellers, thus creating checkable-deposit money. Money vanishes when banks sell bonds to the public because bond buyers must draw down their checkable-deposit balances to pay for the bonds.

8. Banks earn interest by making loans and by purchasing bonds; they maintain liquidity by holding cash and excess reserves. The Fed pays interest on excess reserves. Nevertheless, banks often can obtain higher interest rates by

lending out excess reserves on an overnight basis to banks that are short of required reserves. These loans are made in the Federal funds market, and the interest paid on the loans is called the Federal funds rate.

9. The commercial banking system as a whole can lend by a multiple of its excess reserves because the system as a whole

cannot lose reserves. Individual banks, however, can lose reserves to other banks in the system.

10. The multiple by which the banking system can lend on the basis of each dollar of excess reserves is the reciprocal of the reserve ratio. This multiple credit expansion process is reversible.

Terms and Concepts

fractional reserve banking system

balance sheet

vault cash

required reserves

reserve ratio

excess reserves

actual reserves

Federal funds rate

monetary multiplier

Questions

1. What is the difference between an asset and a liability on a bank's balance sheet? How does net worth relate to each? Why must a balance sheet always balance? What are the major assets and claims on a commercial bank's balance sheet? **LO1**

2. Explain why merchants accepted gold receipts as a means of payment even though the receipts were issued by goldsmiths, not the government. What risk did goldsmiths introduce into the payments system by issuing loans in the form of gold receipts? **LO1**

3. Why is the banking system in the United States referred to as a fractional reserve bank system? What is the role of deposit insurance in a fractional reserve system? **LO1**

4. Why does the Federal Reserve require commercial banks to have reserves? Explain why reserves are an asset to commercial banks but a liability to the Federal Reserve Banks. What are excess reserves? How do you calculate the amount of excess reserves held by a bank? What is the significance of excess reserves? **LO2**

5. "Whenever currency is deposited in a commercial bank, cash goes out of circulation and, as a result, the supply of money is reduced." Do you agree? Explain why or why not. **LO2**

6. "When a commercial bank makes loans, it creates money; when loans are repaid, money is destroyed." Explain. **LO3**

7. Suppose that Mountain Star Bank discovers that its reserves will temporarily fall slightly below those legally required. How might it temporarily remedy this situation through the Federal funds market? Now assume Mountain Star finds that its reserves will be substantially and permanently deficient. What remedy is available to this bank? (Hint: Recall your answer to question 6.) **LO3**

8. Explain why a single commercial bank can safely lend only an amount equal to its excess reserves but the commercial banking system as a whole can lend by a multiple of its excess reserves. What is the monetary multiplier, and how does it relate to the reserve ratio? **LO4**

9. How would a decrease in the reserve requirement affect the (a) size of the money multiplier, (b) amount of excess reserves in the banking system, and (c) extent to which the system could expand the money supply through the creation of checkable deposits via loans? **LO5**

10. **LAST WORD** Explain how the bank panics of 1930–1933 produced a decline in the nation's money supply. Why are such panics highly unlikely today?

Problems

1. Suppose the assets of the Silver Lode Bank are $100,000 higher than on the previous day and its net worth is up $20,000. By how much and in what direction must its liabilities have changed from the day before? **LO1**

2. Suppose that Serendipity Bank has excess reserves of $8000 and checkable deposits of $150,000. If the reserve ratio is 20 percent, what is the size of the bank's actual reserves? **LO2**

3. Third National Bank has reserves of $20,000 and checkable deposits of $100,000. The reserve ratio is 20 percent. Households deposit $5000 in currency into the bank and

that currency is added to reserves. What level of excess reserves does the bank now have? **LO3**

4. Suppose again that Third National Bank has reserves of $20,000 and checkable deposits of $100,000. The reserve ratio is 20 percent. The bank now sells $5000 in securities to the Federal Reserve Bank in its district, receiving a $5000 increase in reserves in return. What level of excess reserves does the bank now have? By what amount does your answer differ (yes, it does!) from the answer to problem 3? **LO3**

5. The balance sheet at the top of the next page is for Big Bucks Bank. The reserve ratio is 20 percent. **LO3**

Assets		(1)	(2)	Liabilities and net worth		(1')	(2')
Reserves	$22,000	___	___	Checkable deposits	$100,000	___	___
Securities	38,000	___	___				
Loans	40,000	___	___				

a. What is the maximum amount of new loans that Big Bucks Bank can make? Show in columns 1 and 1' how the bank's balance sheet will appear after the bank has lent this additional amount.

b. By how much has the supply of money changed?

c. How will the bank's balance sheet appear after checks drawn for the entire amount of the new loans have been cleared against the bank? Show the new balance sheet in columns 2 and 2'.

d. Answer questions *a*, *b*, and *c* on the assumption that the reserve ratio is 15 percent.

6. Suppose the simplified consolidated balance sheet shown in the right column is for the entire commercial banking system and that all figures are in billions of dollars. The reserve ratio is 25 percent. LO5

a. What is the amount of excess reserves in this commercial banking system? What is the maximum amount the banking system might lend? Show in columns 1 and 1' how the

Assets		(1)	Liabilities and net worth		(1')
Reserves	$ 52	___	Checkable deposits	$200	___
Securities	48	___			
Loans	100	___			

consolidated balance sheet would look after this amount has been lent. What is the size of the monetary multiplier?

b. Answer the questions in part *a* assuming the reserve ratio is 20 percent. What is the resulting difference in the amount that the commercial banking system can lend?

7. If the required reserve ratio is 10 percent, what is the monetary multiplier? If the monetary multiplier is 4, what is the required reserve ratio? LO5

FURTHER TEST YOUR KNOWLEDGE AT
www.mcconnell19e.com

At the text's Online Learning Center (OLC), **www.mcconnell19e.com**, you will find one or more Web-based questions that require information from the Internet to answer. We urge you to check them out; they will familiarize you with Web sites that may be helpful in other courses and perhaps even in your career. The OLC also features multiple-choice questions that give instant feedback and provides other helpful ways to further test your knowledge of the chapter.

16

AFTER READING THIS CHAPTER, YOU SHOULD BE ABLE TO:

1 Discuss how the equilibrium interest rate is determined in the market for money.

2 List and explain the goals and tools of monetary policy.

3 Describe the Federal funds rate and how the Fed directly influences it.

4 Identify the mechanisms by which monetary policy affects GDP and the price level.

5 Explain the effectiveness of monetary policy and its shortcomings.

Interest Rates and Monetary Policy

Some newspaper commentators have stated that the chairperson of the Federal Reserve Board (currently Ben Bernanke) is the second most powerful person in the United States, after the U.S. president. That is undoubtedly an exaggeration because the chair has only a single vote on the 7-person Federal Reserve Board and 12-person Federal Open Market Committee. But there can be no doubt about the chair's influence as well as the overall importance of the Federal Reserve and the **monetary policy** that it conducts. Such policy consists of deliberate changes in the money supply to influence interest rates and thus the total level of spending in the economy. The goal of monetary policy is to achieve and maintain price-level stability, full employment, and economic growth.

Interest Rates

The Fed's primary influence on the economy in normal economic times is through its ability to change the money supply (M1 and M2) and therefore affect interest rates. Interest rates can be thought of in several ways. Most basically, **interest** is the price paid for the use of money. It is also the price that borrowers need to pay lenders for transferring purchasing power to the future. And it can be thought of as the amount of money that must be paid for the use of $1 for 1 year. Although there are many different interest rates that vary by purpose, size, risk, maturity, and taxability, we will simply speak of *the* interest rate unless stated otherwise.

Let's see how the interest rate is determined. Because it is a "price," we again turn to demand and supply analysis for the answer.

The Demand for Money

Why does the public want to hold some of its wealth as *money*? There are two main reasons: to make purchases with it and to hold it as an asset.

Transactions Demand, D_t People hold money because it is convenient for purchasing goods and services. Households usually are paid once a week, every 2 weeks, or monthly, whereas their expenditures are less predictable and typically more frequent. So households must have enough money on hand to buy groceries and pay mortgage and utility bills. Nor are business revenues and expenditures simultaneous. Businesses need to have money available to pay for labor, materials, power, and other inputs. The demand for money as a medium of exchange is called the **transactions demand for money.**

The level of nominal GDP is the main determinant of the amount of money demanded for transactions. The larger the total money value of all goods and services exchanged in the economy, the larger the amount of money needed to negotiate those transactions. The transactions demand for money varies directly with nominal GDP. We specify *nominal* GDP because households and firms will want more money for transactions if prices rise or if real output increases. In both instances a larger dollar volume will be needed to accomplish the desired transactions.

In **Figure 16.1a (Key Graph)** we graph the quantity of money demanded for transactions against the interest rate. For simplicity, let's assume that the amount demanded depends exclusively on the level of nominal GDP and is independent of the interest rate. (In reality, higher interest rates are associated with slightly lower volumes of money demanded for transactions.) Our simplifying assumption allows us to graph the transactions demand, D_t, as a vertical line. This demand curve is positioned at $100 billion, on the assumption that each dollar held for transactions purposes is spent on an average of three times per year and that nominal GDP is $300 billion. Thus the public needs $100 billion (= $300 billion/3) to purchase that GDP.

Asset Demand, D_a The second reason for holding money derives from money's function as a store of value. People may hold their financial assets in many forms, including corporate stocks, corporate or government bonds, or money. To the extent they want to hold money as an asset, there is an **asset demand for money.**

People like to hold some of their financial assets as money (apart from using it to buy goods and services) because money is the most liquid of all financial assets; it is immediately usable for purchasing other assets when opportunities arise. Money is also an attractive asset to hold when the prices of other assets such as bonds are expected to decline. For example, when the price of a bond falls, the bondholder who sells the bond prior to the payback date of the full principal will suffer a loss (called a *capital loss*). That loss will partially or fully offset the interest received on the bond. Holding money presents no such risk of capital loss from changes in interest rates.

The disadvantage of holding money as an asset is that it earns no or very little interest. Checkable deposits pay either no interest or lower interest rates than bonds. Currency itself earns no interest at all.

Knowing these advantages and disadvantages, the public must decide how much of its financial assets to hold as money, rather than other assets such as bonds. The answer depends primarily on the rate of interest. A household or a business incurs an opportunity cost when it holds money; in both cases, interest income is forgone or sacrificed. If a bond pays 6 percent interest, for example, holding $100 as cash or in a noninterest checkable account costs $6 per year of forgone income.

The amount of money demanded as an asset therefore varies inversely with the rate of interest (which is the opportunity cost of holding money as an asset). When the interest rate rises, being liquid and avoiding capital losses becomes more costly. The public reacts by reducing its holdings of money as an asset. When the interest rate falls, the cost of being liquid and avoiding capital losses also declines. The public therefore increases the amount of financial assets that it wants to hold as money. This inverse relationship just described is shown by D_a in Figure 16.1b.

ORIGIN OF THE IDEA

O 16.1

Liquidity preference

FIGURE 16.1 The demand for money, the supply of money, and the equilibrium interest rate. The total demand for money D_m is determined by horizontally adding the asset demand for money D_a to the transactions demand D_t. The transactions demand is vertical because it is assumed to depend on nominal GDP rather than on the interest rate. The asset demand varies inversely with the interest rate because of the opportunity cost involved in holding currency and checkable deposits that pay no interest or very low interest. Combining the money supply (stock) S_m with the total money demand D_m portrays the market for money and determines the equilibrium interest rate i_e.

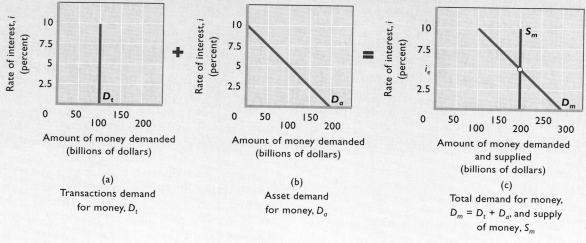

(a)
Transactions demand
for money, D_t

(b)
Asset demand
for money, D_a

(c)
Total demand for money,
$D_m = D_t + D_a$, and supply
of money, S_m

QUICK QUIZ FOR FIGURE 16.1

1. In this graph, at the interest rate i_e (5 percent):
   a. the amount of money demanded as an asset is $50 billion.
   b. the amount of money demanded for transactions is $200 billion.
   c. bond prices will decline.
   d. $100 billion is demanded for transactions, $100 billion is demanded as an asset, and the money supply is $200 billion.

2. In this graph, at an interest rate of 10 percent:
   a. no money will be demanded as an asset.
   b. total money demanded will be $200 billion.
   c. the Federal Reserve will supply $100 billion of money.
   d. there will be a $100 billion shortage of money.

3. Curve D_a slopes downward because:
   a. lower interest rates increase the opportunity cost of holding money.
   b. lower interest rates reduce the opportunity cost of holding money.

   c. the asset demand for money varies directly (positively) with the interest rate.
   d. the transactions-demand-for-money curve is perfectly vertical.

4. Suppose the supply of money declines to $100 billion. The equilibrium interest rate would:
   a. fall, the amount of money demanded for transactions would rise, and the amount of money demanded as an asset would decline.
   b. rise, and the amounts of money demanded both for transactions and as an asset would fall.
   c. fall, and the amounts of money demanded both for transactions and as an asset would increase.
   d. rise, the amount of money demanded for transactions would be unchanged, and the amount of money demanded as an asset would decline.

Answers: 1. d; 2. a; 3. b; 4. d

Total Money Demand, D_m As shown in Figure 16.1, we find the **total demand for money, D_m**, by horizontally adding the asset demand to the transactions demand. The resulting downsloping line in Figure 16.1c represents the total amount of money the public wants to hold, both for transactions and as an asset, at each possible interest rate.

Recall that the transactions demand for money depends on the nominal GDP. A change in the nominal GDP—working through the transactions demand for money—will shift the total money demand curve. Specifi-

WORKED PROBLEMS

W 16.1

Demand for money

cally, an increase in nominal GDP means that the public wants to hold a larger amount of money for transactions, and that extra demand will shift the total money demand curve to the right. In contrast, a decline in the nominal GDP will shift the total money demand curve to the left. As an example, suppose nominal GDP increases from $300 billion to $450 billion and the average dollar held for transactions is still spent three times per year. Then the transactions demand curve will shift from $100 billion (= $300 billion/3) to $150 billion (= $450 billion/3). The total money demand curve will then lie $50 billion farther to the right at each possible interest rate.

The Equilibrium Interest Rate

We can combine the demand for money with the supply of money to determine the equilibrium rate of interest. In Figure 16.1c, the vertical line, S_m, represents the money supply. It is a vertical line because the monetary authorities and financial institutions have provided the economy with some particular stock of money. Here it is $200 billion.

Just as in a product market or a resource market, the intersection of demand and supply determines the equilibrium price in the market for money. In Figure 16.1, this equilibrium price is the equilibrium interest rate, i_e. At this interest rate, the quantity of money demanded (= $200 billion) equals the quantity of money supplied (= $200 billion). The equilibrium interest rate can be thought of as the market-determined price that borrowers must pay for using someone else's money over some period of time.

Changes in the demand for money, the supply of money, or both can change the equilibrium interest rate.

For reasons that will soon become apparent, we are most interested in changes in the supply of money. The important generalization is this: An increase in the supply of money will lower the equilibrium interest rate; a decrease in the supply of money will raise the equilibrium interest rate.

Interest Rates and Bond Prices

Interest rates and bond prices are inversely related. When the interest rate increases, bond prices fall; when the interest rate falls, bond prices rise. Why so? First understand that bonds are bought and sold in financial markets and that the price of bonds is determined by bond demand and bond supply.

Suppose that a bond with no expiration date pays a fixed $50 annual interest payment and is selling for its face value of $1000. The interest yield on this bond is 5 percent:

$$\frac{\$50}{\$1000} = 5\% \text{ interest yield}$$

Now suppose the interest rate in the economy rises to $7\frac{1}{2}$ percent from 5 percent. Newly issued bonds will pay $75 per $1000 lent. Older bonds paying only $50 will not be salable at their $1000 face value. To compete with the $7\frac{1}{2}$ percent bond, the price of this bond will need to fall to $667 to remain competitive. The $50 fixed annual interest payment will then yield $7\frac{1}{2}$ percent to whoever buys the bond:

$$\frac{\$50}{\$667} = 7\frac{1}{2}\%$$

Next suppose that the interest rate falls to $2\frac{1}{2}$ percent from the original 5 percent. Newly issued bonds will pay $25 on $1000 loaned. A bond paying $50 will be highly attractive. Bond buyers will bid up its price to $2000, where the yield will equal $2\frac{1}{2}$ percent:

$$\frac{\$50}{\$2000} = 2\frac{1}{2}\%$$

The point is that bond prices fall when the interest rate rises and rise when the interest rate falls. There is an inverse relationship between the interest rate and bond prices.

- People demand money for transaction and asset purposes.
- The total demand for money is the sum of the transactions and asset demands; it is graphed as an inverse relationship (downsloping line) between the interest rate and the quantity of money demanded.
- The equilibrium interest rate is determined by money demand and supply; it occurs when people are willing to hold the exact amount of money being supplied by the monetary authorities.
- Interest rates and bond prices are inversely related.

The Consolidated Balance Sheet of the Federal Reserve Banks

With this basic understanding of interest rates, we can turn to monetary policy, which relies on changes in interest rates to be effective. The 12 Federal Reserve Banks together constitute the U.S. "central bank," nicknamed the "Fed." (Global Perspective 16.1 also lists some of the other central banks in the world, along with their nicknames.)

The Fed's balance sheet helps us consider how the Fed conducts monetary policy. Table 16.1 consolidates the pertinent assets and liabilities of the 12 Federal Reserve Banks as of March 24, 2010. You will see that some of the Fed's assets and liabilities differ from those found on the balance sheet of a commercial bank.

TABLE 16.1 Consolidated Balance Sheet of the 12 Federal Reserve Banks, March 24, 2010 (in Millions)

Assets		Liabilities and Net Worth	
Securities	$2,017,955	Reserves of commercial banks	$1,147,747
Loans to commercial banks	85,659	Treasury deposits	150,087
All other assets	212,911	Federal Reserve Notes (outstanding)	893,035
		All other liabilities and net worth	125,656
Total	$2,316,525	Total	$2,316,525

Source: Federal Reserve Statistical Release, H.4.1, March 24, 2010, **www.federalreserve.gov**.

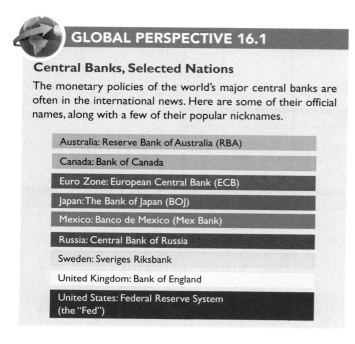

GLOBAL PERSPECTIVE 16.1

Central Banks, Selected Nations

The monetary policies of the world's major central banks are often in the international news. Here are some of their official names, along with a few of their popular nicknames.

Australia: Reserve Bank of Australia (RBA)

Canada: Bank of Canada

Euro Zone: European Central Bank (ECB)

Japan: The Bank of Japan (BOJ)

Mexico: Banco de Mexico (Mex Bank)

Russia: Central Bank of Russia

Sweden: Sveriges Riksbank

United Kingdom: Bank of England

United States: Federal Reserve System (the "Fed")

Assets

The two main assets of the Federal Reserve Banks are securities and loans to commercial banks. (Again, we will simplify by referring only to *commercial banks*, even though the analysis also applies to *thrifts*—savings and loans, mutual savings banks, and credit unions.)

Securities The securities shown in Table 16.1 are government bonds that have been purchased by the Federal Reserve Banks. They consist largely of Treasury bills (short-term securities), Treasury notes (mid-term securities), and Treasury bonds (long-term securities) issued by the U.S. government to finance past budget deficits. These securities are part of the public debt—the money borrowed by the Federal government. The Federal Reserve Banks bought these securities from commercial banks and the public through open-market operations. Although they are an important source of interest income to the

Federal Reserve Banks, they are mainly bought and sold to influence the size of commercial bank reserves and, therefore, the ability of those banks to create money by lending.

Loans to Commercial Banks For reasons that will soon become clear, commercial banks occasionally borrow from Federal Reserve Banks. The IOUs that commercial banks give these "bankers' banks" in return for loans are listed on the Federal Reserve balance sheet as "Loans to commercial banks." They are assets to the Fed because they are claims against the commercial banks. To commercial banks, of course, these loans are liabilities in that they must be repaid. Through borrowing in this way, commercial banks can increase their reserves.

Liabilities

On the "liabilities and net worth" side of the Fed's consolidated balance sheet, three entries are noteworthy: reserves, Treasury deposits, and Federal Reserve Notes.

Reserves of Commercial Banks The Fed requires that the commercial banks hold reserves against their checkable deposits. The Fed pays interest on these required reserves and also on the excess reserves that banks choose to hold at the Fed. Banks held a huge amount of these excess reserves at the Fed during the severe recession of 2007–2009 and on into 2010. Banks simply were highly concerned that loans to some private borrowers might not get paid back. When held in the Federal Reserve Banks, these reserves are listed as a liability on the Fed's balance sheet. They are assets on the books of the commercial banks, which still own them even though they are deposited at the Federal Reserve Banks.

Treasury Deposits The U.S. Treasury keeps deposits in the Federal Reserve Banks and draws checks on them to pay its obligations. To the Treasury these deposits are assets; to the Federal Reserve Banks they are liabilities. The Treasury creates and replenishes these deposits by depositing tax receipts and money borrowed from the public or from the commercial banks through the sale of bonds.

Federal Reserve Notes Outstanding As we have seen, the supply of paper money in the United States consists of Federal Reserve Notes issued by the Federal Reserve Banks. When this money is circulating outside the Federal Reserve Banks, it constitutes claims against the assets of the Federal Reserve Banks. The Fed thus treats these notes as a liability.

Tools of Monetary Policy

With this look at the Federal Reserve Banks' consolidated balance sheet, we can now explore how the Fed can influence the money-creating abilities of the commercial banking system. The Fed has four main tools of monetary control it can use to alter the reserves of commercial banks:

- Open-market operations
- The reserve ratio
- The discount rate
- The term auction facility

Open-Market Operations

Bond markets are "open" to all buyers and sellers of corporate and government bonds (securities). The Federal Reserve is the largest single holder of U.S. government securities. The U.S. government, not the Fed, issued these Treasury bills, Treasury notes, and Treasury bonds to finance past budget deficits. Over the decades, the Fed has purchased these securities from major financial institutions that buy and sell government and corporate securities for themselves or their customers.

The Fed's **open-market operations** consist of buying government bonds (U.S. securities) from or selling government bonds to commercial banks and the general public. The conduit for the Fed's open-market operations is the New York Federal Reserve Bank and a group of 16 or so large financial firms called "primary dealers." These financial institutions, in turn, buy the bonds from and sell the bonds to commercial banks and the general public. Open-market operations are the Fed's most important day-to-day instrument for influencing the money supply.

Buying Securities Suppose that the Fed decides to have the Federal Reserve Banks buy government bonds. They can purchase these bonds either from commercial banks or from the public. In both cases the reserves of the commercial banks will increase.

From Commercial Banks When Federal Reserve Banks buy government bonds *from commercial banks,*

(*a*) The commercial banks give up part of their holdings of securities (the government bonds) to the Federal Reserve Banks.

(*b*) The Federal Reserve Banks, in paying for these securities, place newly created reserves in the accounts of the commercial banks at the Fed. (These reserves are created "out of thin air," so to speak!) The reserves of the commercial banks go up by the amount of the purchase of the securities.

We show these outcomes as (*a*) and (*b*) on the following consolidated balance sheets of the commercial banks and the Federal Reserve Banks:

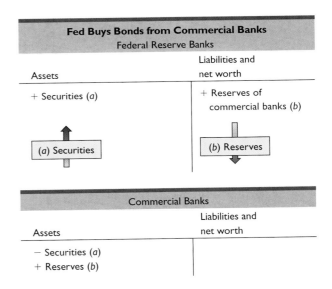

The upward arrow shows that securities have moved from the commercial banks to the Federal Reserve Banks. So we enter "− Securities" (minus securities) in the asset column of the balance sheet of the commercial banks. For the same reason, we enter "+ Securities" in the asset column of the balance sheet of the Federal Reserve Banks.

The downward arrow indicates that the Federal Reserve Banks have provided reserves to the commercial banks. So we enter "+ Reserves" in the asset column of the balance sheet for the commercial banks. In the liability column of the balance sheet of the Federal Reserve Banks, the plus sign indicates that although commercial bank reserves have increased, they are a liability to the Federal Reserve Banks because the reserves are owned by the commercial banks.

What is most important about this transaction is that when Federal Reserve Banks purchase securities from commercial banks, they increase the reserves in the banking

FIGURE 16.2 The Federal Reserve's purchase of bonds and the expansion of the money supply. Assuming all banks are loaded up initially, a Federal Reserve purchase of a $1000 bond from either a commercial bank or the public can increase the money supply by $5000 when the reserve ratio is 20 percent. In the left panel of the diagram, the purchase of a $1000 bond from a commercial bank creates $1000 of excess reserves that support a $5000 expansion of checkable deposits through loans. In the right panel, the purchase of a $1000 bond from the public creates a $1000 checkable deposit but only $800 of excess reserves because $200 of reserves is required to "back up" the $1000 new checkable deposit. The commercial banks can therefore expand the money supply by only $4000 by making loans. This $4000 of checkable-deposit money plus the new checkable deposit of $1000 equals $5000 of new money.

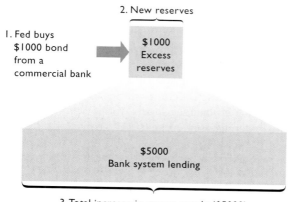
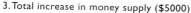
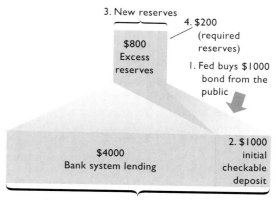

system, which then increases the lending ability of the commercial banks.

From the Public

The effect on commercial bank reserves is much the same when Federal Reserve Banks purchase securities from the general public. Suppose the Gristly Meat Packing Company has government bonds that it sells in the open market to the Federal Reserve Banks. The transaction has several elements:

(*a*) Gristly gives up securities to the Federal Reserve Banks and gets in payment a check drawn by the Federal Reserve Banks on themselves.

(*b*) Gristly promptly deposits the check in its account with the Wahoo bank.

(*c*) The Wahoo bank sends this check against the Federal Reserve Banks to a Federal Reserve Bank for collection. As a result, the Wahoo bank enjoys an increase in its reserves.

To keep things simple, we will dispense with showing the balance sheet changes resulting from the Fed's sale or purchase of bonds from the public. But two aspects of this transaction are particularly important. First, as with Federal Reserve purchases of securities directly from commercial banks, the purchases of securities from the public increase the lending ability of the commercial banking system. Second, the supply of money is directly increased by the Federal Reserve Banks' purchase of government bonds (aside from any expansion of the money supply that may occur from the increase in commercial bank reserves). This direct increase in the money supply has taken the

form of an increased amount of checkable deposits in the economy as a result of Gristly's deposit.

The Federal Reserve Banks' purchases of securities from the commercial banking system differ slightly from their purchases of securities from the public. If we assume that all commercial banks are loaned up initially, Federal Reserve bond purchases *from commercial banks* increase the actual reserves and excess reserves of commercial banks by the entire amount of the bond purchases. As shown in the left panel in Figure 16.2, a $1000 bond purchase from a commercial bank increases both the actual and the excess reserves of the commercial bank by $1000.

In contrast, Federal Reserve Bank purchases of bonds from the public increase actual reserves but also increase checkable deposits when the sellers place the Fed's check into their personal checking accounts. Thus, a $1000 bond purchase from the public would increase checkable deposits by $1000 and hence the actual reserves of the loaned-up banking system by the same amount. But with a 20 percent reserve ratio applied to the $1000 checkable deposit, the excess reserves of the banking system would be only $800 since $200 of the $1000 would have to be held as reserves.

However, in both transactions the end result is the same: When Federal Reserve Banks buy securities in the open market, commercial banks' reserves are increased. When the banks lend out an amount equal to their excess reserves, the nation's money supply will rise. Observe in

WORKED PROBLEMS

W 16.3

Open-market operations

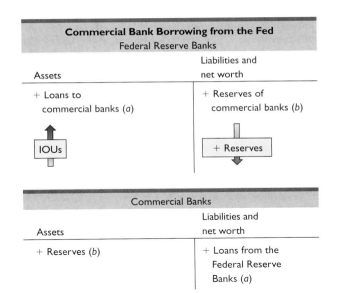

Commercial Bank Borrowing from the Fed

Federal Reserve Banks

Assets	Liabilities and net worth
+ Loans to commercial banks (a)	+ Reserves of commercial banks (b)

IOUs

+ Reserves

Commercial Banks

Assets	Liabilities and net worth
+ Reserves (b)	+ Loans from the Federal Reserve Banks (a)

In providing the loan, the Federal Reserve Bank increases the reserves of the borrowing commercial bank. Since no required reserves need be kept against loans from Federal Reserve Banks, all new reserves acquired by borrowing from Federal Reserve Banks are excess reserves. [These changes are reflected in the two (b) entries on the balance sheets.]

In short, borrowing from the Federal Reserve Banks by commercial banks increases the reserves of the commercial banks and enhances their ability to extend credit.

The Fed has the power to set the discount rate at which commercial banks borrow from Federal Reserve Banks. From the commercial banks' point of view, the discount rate is a cost of acquiring reserves. A lowering of the discount rate encourages commercial banks to obtain additional reserves by borrowing from Federal Reserve Banks. When the commercial banks lend new reserves, the money supply increases.

An increase in the discount rate discourages commercial banks from obtaining additional reserves through borrowing from the Federal Reserve Banks. So the Fed may raise the discount rate when it wants to restrict the money supply.

Term Auction Facility

The fourth Fed tool for altering bank reserves is its **term auction facility.** The Fed holds two auctions each month at which banks bid for the right to borrow reserves for 28-day and 84-day periods. For instance, the Fed might auction off $20 billion in reserves. Banks that want to participate in the auction submit bids that include two pieces of information: how much they wish to borrow and the interest rate that they would be willing to pay. As an example, Wahoo bank

might want to borrow $1 billion and offer to pay an annual interest rate of 4.35 percent.

These bids are submitted secretly. Once they are received, Fed officials arrange them from highest to lowest by interest rate. The limited pool of $20 billion goes to those banks that offer to pay the highest interest rates for the money that they desire to borrow. But the rate that all the auction winners actually pay is the same—it is the rate offered by the lowest bidder whose bid is accepted. For instance, suppose that 56 banks submit bids that total $36 billion. The Fed sorts these from highest to lowest based on interest rates and then goes down the list to see how many banks can get their desired loan amounts before exhausting the $20 billion. Suppose that the top 23 banks together wish to borrow $18 billion and that the 24th bank wishes to borrow the remaining $2 billion. Since its request would exhaust the $20 billion that is being auctioned off, its interest rate is the one that all 24 of the auction-winning banks will have to pay.

Lending through the term auction facility guarantees that the amount of reserves that the Fed wishes to lend will be borrowed. This is true because the auction procedure for determining the interest rate on the loans serves to produce an equilibrium price (interest rate) at which the quantity demanded of loans exactly equals the quantity supplied of loans (the amount of reserves that the Fed is auctioning off). The Fed finds this to be very helpful when it wants to increase reserves by a specific amount because it can be sure that those reserves will, in fact, be borrowed, thereby increasing the overall level of reserves in the banking system. In contrast, lowering the discount rate may or may not produce the exact level of borrowing the Fed desires.

It was this very positive aspect of the term auction facility that caused the Fed to start using it in late 2007 when it wished to increase bank reserves during the mortgage debt crisis. Reserves fell dramatically during that crisis and the Fed wanted to be sure to increase reserves so that banks would have excess reserves and therefore the ability to keep making loans.

In terms of balance sheets, however, loans of reserves borrowed by auction-winning banks under the term auction facility work exactly the same as loans of reserves taken out by banks when they are borrowing at the discount rate. Commercial banks send IOUs to the Fed and the Fed sends reserves to the commercial banks.

The term auction facility allows the Fed to alter the money supply by either increasing or decreasing the amount of reserves it auctions off every two weeks. If it wants to increase the money supply, it auctions off more reserves than those being paid back from previous auctions; if it wants to decrease the money supply, it auctions off fewer such reserves.

Relative Importance

All four of the Fed's instruments of monetary control are useful in particular economic circumstances, but open-market operations are clearly the most important of the four tools over the course of the business cycle. The buying and selling of securities in the open market has the advantage of flexibility—government securities can be purchased or sold daily in large or small amounts—and the impact on bank reserves is prompt. And, compared with reserve-requirement changes, open-market operations work subtly and less directly. Furthermore, the ability of the Federal Reserve Banks to affect commercial bank reserves through the purchase and sale of bonds is virtually unquestionable. The Federal Reserve Banks have very large holdings of government securities ($2018 billion in early 2010, for example). The sale of those securities could theoretically reduce commercial bank reserves to zero.

Changing the reserve requirement is a potentially powerful instrument of monetary control, but the Fed has used this technique only sparingly. Normally, it can accomplish its monetary goals more easily through open-market operations. The last change in the reserve requirement was in 1992, when the Fed reduced the requirement from 12 percent to 10 percent. The main purpose was to shore up the profitability of banks and thrifts in the aftermath of the 1990–1991 recession rather than to reduce interest rates by increasing reserves and expanding the money supply.

Until recently, the discount rate was mainly a passive tool of monetary control, with the Fed raising and lowering the rate simply to keep it in line with other interest rates. However, during the financial crisis of 2007–2008, the Fed aggressively lowered the discount rate independently of other interest rates to provide a cheap and plentiful source of reserves to banks whose reserves were being sharply reduced by unexpectedly high default rates on home mortgage loans. Banks borrowed billions at the lower discount rate. This allowed them to meet reserve ratio requirements and thereby preserved their ability to keep extending loans.

As the financial crisis grew more severe, however, the Fed found that banks became increasingly reluctant to borrow at the discount rate for fear that such borrowing would be interpreted by their own lenders and stockholders as a sign of being in deep financial trouble. This prompted the Fed to create the term auction facility and, perhaps more importantly, to keep the bidding secret. When the Fed holds an auction of reserves using the term auction facility, banks submit their bids in writing and auction winners are given their loans without other bidders or the public knowing who obtained them. This secrecy ensures that banks will participate in the auctions since they do not have to worry about being suspected of being in a financially weak condition.

The success of the term auction facility has led the Fed to adopt the auction of reserves as a fourth permanent tool of monetary policy. That being said, most economists believe that the Fed will mainly use this new tool during times of crisis when it believes that the banking system can be helped by large, quick injections or withdrawals of reserves.

QUICK REVIEW 16.2

- The Fed has four main tools of monetary control, each of which works by changing the amount of reserves in the banking system: (a) conducting open-market operations (the Fed's buying and selling of government bonds to the banks and the public); (b) changing the reserve ratio (the percentage of commercial bank deposit liabilities required as reserves); (c) changing the discount rate (the interest rate the Federal Reserve Banks charge on loans to banks and thrifts); and (d) changing the amount of reserves it auctions to banks through the term auction facility.

- Open-market operations are the Fed's monetary control mechanism of choice for routine increases or decreases in bank reserves over the business cycle; in contrast, changes in reserve requirements, aggressive changes in discount rates, and auctions of reserves are used only in special situations.

Targeting the Federal Funds Rate

The Federal Reserve focuses monetary policy on the interest rate that it can directly influence: the **Federal funds rate.** From the previous chapter, you know that this is the rate of interest that banks charge one another on overnight loans made from temporary excess reserves. Recall that the Federal Reserve requires banks (and thrifts) to deposit in their regional Federal Reserve Bank a certain percentage of their checkable deposits as reserves. At the end of any business day, some banks temporarily have excess reserves (more actual reserves than required) and other banks have reserve deficiencies (fewer reserves than required). Because reserves held at the Federal Reserve Banks earn less interest than commercial banks can obtain from overnight loans to other banks, banks with excess reserves usually desire to make such loans to other banks that temporarily need them to meet their reserve requirements. The funds being lent and borrowed overnight are called "Federal funds" because they are reserves (funds) that are required by the Federal Reserve to meet reserve requirements. An equilibrium interest rate—the Federal funds rate—arises in this market for bank reserves.

The Federal Reserve targets the Federal funds rate by manipulating the supply of reserves that are offered in the Federal funds market. As previously explained, by buying and selling government bonds, the Fed can increase or decrease the reserves in the banking system. These changes in total reserves in turn affect the amount of *excess reserves* that are available for supply to the Federal funds market by whichever banks end up with them on a given day. For instance, suppose that the level of loans and checkable deposits at Wahoo bank are constant on a certain day. If the Fed then engages in open-market operations such that Wahoo's total reserves increase, Wahoo will find that it has excess reserves. It will want to loan out these excess reserves to bank customers as soon as possible. But in the meanwhile it will supply these funds overnight in the Federal funds market.

The Federal Open Market Committee (FOMC) meets regularly to choose a desired Federal funds rate. It then directs the Federal Reserve Bank of New York to undertake whatever open-market operations may be necessary to achieve and maintain the targeted rate. We demonstrate how this works in Figure 16.3, where we initially assume the Fed desires a 4 percent interest rate. The demand curve for Federal funds, D_f, is downsloping because lower interest rates give the banks with reserve deficiencies a greater incentive to borrow Federal funds rather than reduce loans as a way to meet their reserve requirements. The supply curve for Federal funds, S_{f1}, is somewhat unusual. Specifically, it is horizontal at the targeted Federal funds rate, here 4 percent. (Disregard supply curves S_{f2} and S_{f3} for now.) It is horizontal because the Fed uses open-market operations to manipulate the supply of Federal funds so that the quantity supplied of Federal funds will exactly equal the quantity demanded of Federal funds at the targeted interest rate.

In this case, the Fed seeks to achieve an equilibrium Federal funds rate of 4 percent. In Figure 16.3 it is successful. Note that at the 4 percent Federal funds rate, the quantity of Federal funds supplied (Q_{f1}) equals the quantity of funds demanded (also Q_{f1}). This 4 percent Federal funds rate will remain, as long as the supply curve of Federal funds is horizontal at 4 percent. If the demand for Federal funds increases (D_f shifts to the right along S_{f1}), the Fed will use its open-market operations to increase the availability of reserves such that the 4 percent Federal funds rate is retained. If the demand for Federal funds declines (D_f shifts to the left along S_{f1}), the Fed will withdraw reserves to keep the Federal funds rate at 4 percent. In the language of Chapter 4, the Fed ensures that the supply curve is perfectly elastic at its targeted rate.

Expansionary Monetary Policy

Suppose that the economy faces recession and unemployment. How will the Fed respond? It will initiate an **expansionary monetary policy** (or "easy money policy"). This policy will lower the interest rate to bolster borrowing and spending, which will increase aggregate demand and expand real output. The Fed's immediate step will be to announce a lower target for the Federal funds rate, say 3.5 percent instead of 4 percent. To achieve that lower rate, the Fed will use open-market operations to buy bonds from banks and the public. We know from previous discussion that the purchase of bonds increases the reserves in the banking system. Alternatively, the Fed could expand reserves by lowering the reserve requirement, lowering the discount rate, or auctioning off more reserves, but these alternative tools are less frequently used than open-market operations.

The greater reserves in the banking system produce two critical results:

- The supply of Federal funds increases, lowering the Federal funds rate to the new targeted rate. We show this in Figure 16.3 as a downward shift to the horizontal supply curve from S_{f1} to S_{f2}. The equilibrium Federal funds rate falls to 3.5 percent, just as the FOMC wanted. The equilibrium quantity of reserves in the overnight market for reserves rises from Q_{f1} to Q_{f2}.

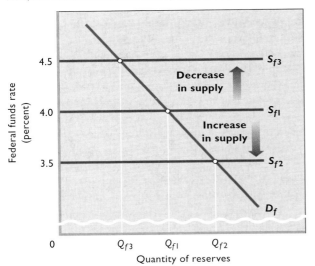

FIGURE 16.3 Targeting the Federal funds rate. In implementing monetary policy, the Federal Reserve determines a desired Federal funds rate and then uses open-market operations (buying and selling of U.S. securities) to add or subtract bank reserves to achieve and maintain that targeted rate. In an expansionary monetary policy, the Fed increases the supply of reserves, for example, from S_{f1} to S_{f2} in this case, to move the Federal funds rate from 4 percent to 3.5 percent. In a restrictive monetary policy, it decreases the supply of reserves, say, from S_{f1} to S_{f3}. Here, the Federal funds rate rises from 4 percent to 4.5 percent.

FIGURE 16.4 **The prime interest rate and the Federal funds rate in the United States, 1998–2010.** The prime interest rate rises and falls with changes in the Federal funds rate.

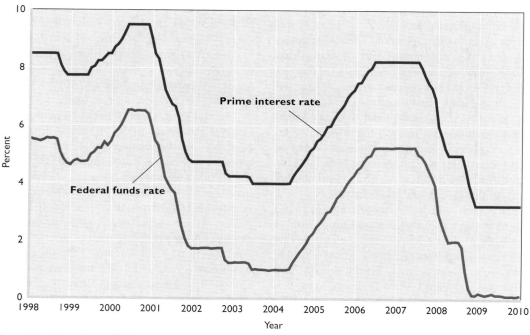

Source: *Federal Reserve Statistical Release*, Historical Data, H.15, **www.federalreserve.gov**.

- A multiple expansion of the nation's money supply occurs (as we demonstrated in Chapter 15). Given the demand for money, the larger money supply places a downward pressure on other interest rates.

One such rate is the **prime interest rate**—the benchmark interest rate used by banks as a reference point for a wide range of interest rates charged on loans to businesses and individuals. The prime interest rate is higher than the Federal funds rate because the prime rate involves longer, more risky loans than overnight loans between banks. But the Federal funds rate and the prime interest rate closely track one another, as evident in Figure 16.4. Also evident are the changes in these rates over the period shown. We will address these changes later in our discussion of recent monetary policy.

Restrictive Monetary Policy

The opposite monetary policy is in order for periods of rising inflation. The Fed will then undertake a **restrictive monetary policy** (or "tight money policy"). This policy will increase the interest rate to reduce borrowing and spending, which will curtail the expansion of aggregate demand and hold down price-level increases. The Fed's immediate step will be to announce a higher target for the Federal funds rate, say 4.5 percent instead of 4 percent. Through open-market operations, the Fed will sell bonds

to the banks and the public and the sale of those bonds will absorb reserves in the banking system. Alternatively, the Fed could absorb reserves by raising the reserve requirement, raising the discount rate, or reducing the amount of reserves that it auctions off. But, open-market operations are usually sufficient to accomplish the goal.

The smaller reserves in the banking system produce two results opposite those discussed for an expansionary monetary policy:

- The supply of Federal funds decreases, raising the Federal funds rate to the new targeted rate. We show this in Figure 16.3 as an upward shift of the horizontal supply curve from S_{f1} to S_{f3}. The equilibrium Federal funds rate rises to 4.5 percent, just as the FOMC wanted, and the equilibrium quantity of funds in this market falls to Q_{f3}.
- A multiple contraction of the nation's money supply occurs (as demonstrated in Chapter 15). Given the demand for money, the smaller money supply places an upward pressure on other interest rates. For example, the prime interest rate rises.

The Taylor Rule

The proper Federal funds rate for a certain period is a matter of policy discretion by the members of the FOMC. At each of their meetings, committee members assess

The Fed as a Sponge

A good way to remember the role of the Fed in setting the Federal funds rate might be to imagine a bowl of water, with the amount of water in the bowl representing the stock of reserves in the banking system. Then think of the FOMC as having a large sponge, labeled open-market operations. When it wants to decrease the Federal funds rate, it uses the sponge—soaked with water (reserves) created by the Fed—to squeeze new reserves into the banking system bowl. It continues this process until the higher supply of reserves reduces the Federal funds rate to the Fed's desired level. If the Fed wants to increase the Federal funds rate, it uses the sponge to absorb reserves from the bowl (banking system). As the supply of reserves falls, the Federal funds rate rises to the Fed's desired level.

whether the current target for the Federal funds rate remains appropriate for achieving the twin goals of low inflation and full employment. If the majority of the FOMC members conclude that a change in the rate is needed, the FOMC sets a new targeted rate. This new target is established without adhering to any particular "inflationary target" or "monetary policy rule." Instead, the committee targets the Federal funds rate at the level most appropriate for the current underlying economic conditions.

A rule of thumb suggested by economist John Taylor, however, roughly matches the actual policy of the Fed over many time periods. This rule of thumb builds on the belief held by many economists that central banks are willing to tolerate a small positive rate of inflation if doing so will help the economy to produce at potential output. The **Taylor rule** assumes that the Fed has a 2 percent "target rate of inflation" that it is willing to tolerate and that the FOMC follows three rules when setting its target for the Federal funds rate:

- When real GDP equals potential GDP and inflation is at its target rate of 2 percent, the Federal funds target rate should be 4 percent, implying a real Federal funds rate of 2 percent (= 4 percent nominal Federal funds rate *minus* 2 percent inflation rate).

- For each 1 percent increase of real GDP above potential GDP, the Fed should raise the *real* Federal funds rate by $\frac{1}{2}$ percentage point.

- For each 1 percent increase in the inflation rate above its 2 percent target rate, the Fed should raise the *real* Federal funds rate by $\frac{1}{2}$ percentage point. (Note, though, that in this case each $\frac{1}{2}$ percentage point increase in the real rate will require a 1.5 percentage point increase in the nominal rate to account for the underlying 1 percent increase in the inflation rate.)

The last two rules are applied independently of each other so that if real GDP is above potential output and at the same time inflation is above the 2 percent target rate, the Fed will apply both rules and raise real interest rates in response to both factors. For instance, if real GDP is 1 percent above potential output and inflation is simultaneously 1 percent above the 2 percent target rate, then the Fed will raise the *real* Federal funds rate by 1 percentage point (= $\frac{1}{2}$ percentage point for the excessive GDP + $\frac{1}{2}$ percentage point for the excessive inflation).

Also notice that the last two rules are reversed for situations in which real GDP falls below potential GDP or inflation falls below 2 percent. Each 1 percent decline in real GDP below potential GDP or fall in inflation below 2 percent calls for a decline of the *real* Federal funds rate by $\frac{1}{2}$ percentage point.

We reemphasize that the Fed has no official allegiance to the Taylor rule. It changes the Federal funds rate to any level that it deems appropriate. During some periods, its policy has diverged significantly from the Taylor rule.

- The Fed conducts its monetary policy by establishing a targeted Federal funds interest rate—the rate that commercial banks charge one another for overnight loans of reserves.

- An expansionary monetary policy (loose money policy) lowers the Federal funds rate, increases the money supply, and lowers other interest rates.

- A restrictive monetary policy (tight money policy) increases the Federal funds rate, reduces the money supply, and increases other interest rates.

- The Fed uses it discretion in setting the Federal funds target rate, but its decisions regarding monetary policy and the target rate appear to be broadly consistent with the Taylor rule.

key graph

FIGURE 16.5 Monetary policy and equilibrium GDP. An expansionary monetary policy that shifts the money supply curve rightward from S_{m1} to S_{m2} in (a) lowers the interest rate from 10 to 8 percent in (b). As a result, investment spending increases from $15 billion to $20 billion, shifting the aggregate demand curve rightward from AD_1 to AD_2 in (c) so that real output rises from the recessionary level of $880 billion to the full employment level $Q_f = $900 billion along the horizontal dashed line. In (d), the economy at point a has an inflationary output gap of $10 billion because it is producing at $910 billion, $10 billion above potential output. A restrictive monetary policy that shifts the money supply curve leftward from $Sm_3 = $175 billion to just $162.5 billion in (a) will increase the interest rate from 6 percent to 7 percent. Investment spending thus falls by $2.5 billion from $25 billion to $22.5 billion in (b). This initial decline is multiplied by 4 by the multiplier process so that the aggregate demand curve shifts leftward in (d) by $10 billion from AD_3 to AD_4, moving the economy along the horizontal dashed line to equilibrium b. This returns the economy to full employment output and eliminates the inflationary output gap.

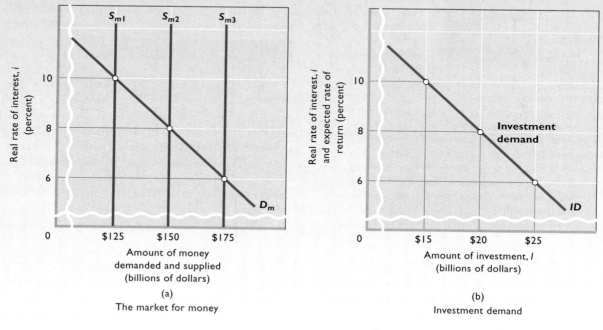

(a) The market for money

(b) Investment demand

QUICK QUIZ FOR FIGURE 16.5

1. The ultimate objective of an expansionary monetary policy is depicted by:
   a. a decrease in the money supply from S_{m3} to S_{m2}.
   b. a reduction of the interest rate from 8 to 6 percent.
   c. an increase in investment from $20 billion to $25 billion.
   d. an increase in real GDP from Q_1 to Q_f.

Monetary Policy, Real GDP, and the Price Level

We have identified and explained the tools of expansionary and contractionary monetary policy. We now want to emphasize how monetary policy affects the economy's levels of investment, aggregate demand, real GDP, and prices.

INTERACTIVE GRAPHS

G 16.2

Monetary policy

Cause-Effect Chain

The four diagrams in **Figure 16.5 (Key Graph)** will help you understand how monetary policy works toward achieving its goals.

Market for Money Figure 16.5a represents the market for money, in which the demand curve for money and the supply curve of money are brought together. Recall that the total demand for money is made up of the transactions and asset demands.

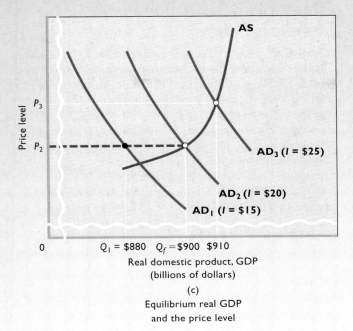

(c)
Equilibrium real GDP
and the price level

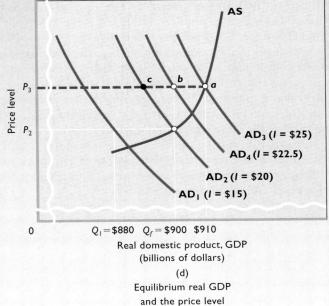

(d)
Equilibrium real GDP
and the price level

2. A successful restrictive monetary policy is evidenced by a shift in the money supply curve from:
   a. S_{m3} to a point half way between S_{m2} and S_{m3}, a decrease in investment from \$25 billion to \$22.5 billion, and a decline in aggregate demand from AD_3 to AD_4.
   b. S_{m1} to S_{m2}, an increase in investment from \$20 billion to \$25 billion, and an increase in real GDP from Q_1 to Q_f.
   c. S_{m3} to S_{m2}, a decrease in investment from \$25 billion to \$20 billion, and a decline in the price level from P_3 to P_2.
   d. S_{m3} to S_{m2}, a decrease in investment from \$25 billion to \$20 billion, and an increase in aggregate demand from AD_2 to AD_3.

3. The Federal Reserve could increase the money supply from S_{m1} to S_{m2} by:
   a. increasing the discount rate.
   b. reducing taxes.
   c. buying government securities in the open market.
   d. increasing the reserve requirement.

4. If the spending-income multiplier is 4 in the economy depicted, an increase in the money supply from \$125 billion to \$150 billion will:
   a. shift the aggregate demand curve rightward by \$20 billion.
   b. increase real GDP by \$25 billion.
   c. increase real GDP by \$100 billion.
   d. shift the aggregate demand curve leftward by \$5 billion.

Answers: 1. d; 2. a; 3. c; 4. a

This figure also shows three potential money supply curves, S_{m1}, S_{m2}, and S_{m3}. In each case, the money supply is shown as a vertical line representing some fixed amount of money determined by the Fed.

The equilibrium interest rate is the rate at which the amount of money demanded and the amount supplied are equal. With money demand D_m in Figure 16.5a, if the supply of money is \$125 billion (S_{m1}), the equilibrium interest rate is 10 percent. With a money supply of \$150 billion (S_{m2}), the equilibrium interest rate is

8 percent; with a money supply of \$175 billion (S_{m3}), it is 6 percent.

You know from Chapter 10 that the real, not the nominal, rate of interest is critical for investment decisions. So here we assume that Figure 16.5a portrays real interest rates.

Investment These 10, 8, and 6 percent real interest rates are carried rightward to the investment demand curve in Figure 16.5b. This curve shows the inverse relationship between the interest rate—the cost of borrowing to invest—and the amount of investment spending. At the 10 percent interest rate, it will be profitable for the nation's businesses to invest $15 billion; at 8 percent, $20 billion; at 6 percent, $25 billion.

Changes in the interest rate mainly affect the investment component of total spending, although they also affect spending on durable consumer goods (such as autos) that are purchased on credit. The impact of changing interest rates on investment spending is great because of the large cost and long-term nature of capital purchases. Capital equipment, factory buildings, and warehouses are tremendously expensive. In absolute terms, interest charges on funds borrowed for these purchases are considerable.

Similarly, the interest cost on a house purchased on a long-term contract is very large: A $\frac{1}{2}$-percentage-point change in the interest rate could amount to thousands of dollars in the total cost of buying a home.

In brief, the impact of changing interest rates is mainly on investment (and, through that, on aggregate demand, output, employment, and the price level). Moreover, as Figure 16.5b shows, investment spending varies inversely with the real interest rate.

Equilibrium GDP Figure 16.5c shows the impact of our three real interest rates and corresponding levels of investment spending on aggregate demand. (Ignore Figure 16.5d for the time being. We will return to it shortly.) As noted, aggregate demand curve AD_1 is associated with the $15 billion level of investment, AD_2 with investment of $20 billion, and AD_3 with investment of $25 billion. That is, investment spending is one of the determinants of aggregate demand. Other things equal, the greater the investment spending, the farther to the right lies the aggregate demand curve.

Suppose the money supply in Figure 16.5a is $150 billion ($S_{m2}$), producing an equilibrium interest rate of 8 percent. In Figure 16.5b we see that this 8 percent interest rate will bring forth $20 billion of investment spending. This $20 billion of investment spending joins with consumption spending, net exports, and government spending to yield aggregate demand curve AD_2 in Figure 16.5c. The equilibrium levels of real output and prices are $Q_f = $900 billion and P_2, as determined by the intersection of AD_2 and the aggregate supply curve AS.

To test your understanding of these relationships, explain why each of the other two levels of money supply in Figure 16.5a results in a different interest rate, level of investment, aggregate demand curve, and equilibrium real output.

Effects of an Expansionary Monetary Policy

Recall that the inflationary ratchet effect discussed in Chapter 12 describes the fact that real-world price levels tend to be downwardly inflexible. Thus, with our economy starting from the initial equilibrium where AD_2 intersects AS, the price level will be downwardly inflexible at P_2 so that aggregate supply will be horizontal to the left of Q_f. This means that if aggregate demand decreases, the economy's equilibrium will move leftward along the dashed horizontal line shown in Figure 16.5c.

Just such a decline would happen if the money supply fell to $125 billion ($S_{m1}$), shifting the aggregate demand curve leftward to AD_1 in Figure 16.5c. This results in a real output of $880 billion, $20 billion less than the economy's full-employment output level of $900 billion. The economy will be experiencing recession, a negative GDP gap, and substantial unemployment. The Fed therefore should institute an expansionary monetary policy.

To increase the money supply, the Fed will take some combination of the following actions: (1) buy government securities from banks and the public in the open market, (2) lower the legal reserve ratio, (3) lower the discount rate, and (4) increase reserve auctions. The intended outcome will be an increase in excess reserves in the commercial banking system and a decline in the Federal funds rate. Because excess reserves are the basis on which commercial banks and thrifts can earn profit by lending and thus creating checkable-deposit money, the nation's money supply will rise. An increase in the money supply will lower the interest rate, increasing investment, aggregate demand, and equilibrium GDP.

For example, an increase in the money supply from $125 billion to $150 billion ($S_{m1}$ to S_{m2}) will reduce the interest rate from 10 to 8 percent, as indicated in Figure 16.5a, and will boost investment from $15 billion to $20 billion, as shown in Figure 16.5b. This $5 billion increase in investment will shift the aggregate demand curve rightward by more than the increase in investment because of the multiplier effect. If the economy's MPC is .75, the multiplier will be 4, meaning that the $5 billion increase in investment will shift the AD curve rightward by $20 billion (= 4 × $5 billion) at each price level. Specifically, aggregate demand will shift from AD_1 to AD_2, as shown in Figure 16.5c. This rightward shift in the aggregate demand curve along the dashed horizontal line will eliminate the negative GDP gap by increasing

TABLE 16.3 Monetary Policies for Recession and Inflation

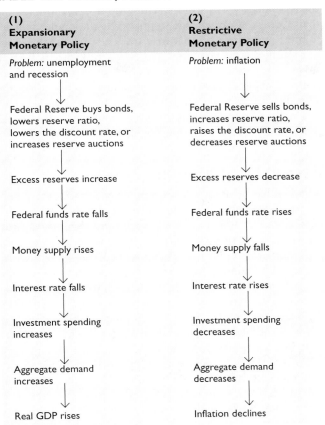

(1) Expansionary Monetary Policy	(2) Restrictive Monetary Policy
Problem: unemployment and recession	Problem: inflation
↓	↓
Federal Reserve buys bonds, lowers reserve ratio, lowers the discount rate, or increases reserve auctions	Federal Reserve sells bonds, increases reserve ratio, raises the discount rate, or decreases reserve auctions
↓	↓
Excess reserves increase	Excess reserves decrease
↓	↓
Federal funds rate falls	Federal funds rate rises
↓	↓
Money supply rises	Money supply falls
↓	↓
Interest rate falls	Interest rate rises
↓	↓
Investment spending increases	Investment spending decreases
↓	↓
Aggregate demand increases	Aggregate demand decreases
↓	↓
Real GDP rises	Inflation declines

GDP from $880 billion to the full-employment GDP of $Q_f =$ $900 billion.[1]

Column 1 in Table 16.3 summarizes the chain of events associated with an expansionary monetary policy.

Effects of a Restrictive Monetary Policy

Next we consider restrictive monetary policy. To prevent overcrowding, we will use graphs *a*, *b*, and *d* (not *c*) in Figure 16.5 to demonstrate the effects of a restrictive monetary policy on the economy. Figure 16.5d represents exactly the same economy as Figure 16.5c but adds some extra curves that relate only to our explanation of restrictive monetary policy.

To see how restrictive monetary policy works, first consider a situation in which the economy moves from a

___

full-employment equilibrium to operating at more than full employment so that inflation is a problem and restrictive monetary policy would be appropriate. Assume that the economy begins at the full-employment equilibrium where AD_2 and AS intersect. At this equilibrium, $Q_f =$ $900 billion and the price level is P_2.

Next, assume that the money supply expands from $150 billion to $175 billion ($S_{m3}$) in Figure 16.5a. This results in an interest rate of 6 percent, investment spending of $25 billion rather than $20 billion, and aggregate demand AD_3. As the AD curve shifts to the right from AD_2 to AD_3 in Figure 16.5d, the economy will move along the upsloping AS curve until it comes to an equilibrium at point *a*, where AD_3 intersects AS. At the new equilibrium, the price level has risen to P_3 and the equilibrium level of real GDP has risen to $910 billion, indicating an inflationary GDP gap of $10 billion (= $910 billion − $900 billion). Aggregate demand AD_3 is excessive relative to the economy's full-employment level of real output $Q_f =$ $900 billion. To rein in spending, the Fed will institute a restrictive monetary policy.

The Federal Reserve Board will direct Federal Reserve Banks to undertake some combination of the following actions: (1) sell government securities to banks and the public in the open market, (2) increase the legal reserve ratio, (3) increase the discount rate, and (4) decrease the amount of reserves auctioned off under the term auction facility. Banks then will discover that their reserves are below those required and that the Federal funds rate has increased. So they will need to reduce their checkable deposits by refraining from issuing new loans as old loans are paid back. This will shrink the money supply and increase the interest rate. The higher interest rate will discourage investment, lowering aggregate demand and restraining demand-pull inflation.

But the Fed must be careful about just how much to decrease the money supply. The problem is that the inflation ratchet will take effect at the new equilibrium point *a*, such that prices will be inflexible at price level P_3. As a result, the dashed horizontal line to the left of point *a* in Figure 16.5d will become relevant. This means that the Fed cannot simply lower the money supply to S_{m2} in Figure 16.5a. If it were to do that, investment demand would fall to $20 billion in Figure 16.5b and the AD curve would shift to the left from AD_3 back to AD_2. But because of inflexible prices, the economy's equilibrium would move to point *c*, where AD_2 intersects the horizontal dashed line to the left of point *a*. This would put the economy into a recession, with equilibrium output below the full-employment output level of $Q_f =$ $900 billion.

What the Fed needs to do to achieve full employment is to move the AD curve back only from AD_3 to AD_4, so that the economy will come to equilibrium at point *b*. This will require a $10 billion decrease in aggregate demand, so that equilibrium output falls from $910 billion at point *a* to Q_f = $900 billion at point *b*. The Fed can achieve this shift by setting the supply of money in Figure 16.5a at $162.5 billion. To see how this works, draw in a vertical money supply curve in Figure 16.5a at $162.5 billion and label it as S_{m4}. It will be exactly halfway between money supply curves S_{m2} and S_{m3}. Notice that the intersection of S_{m4} with the money demand curve D_m will result in an interest rate of 7 percent. In Figure 16.5b, this interest rate of 7 percent will result in investment spending of $22.5 billion (halfway between $20 billion and $25 billion). Thus, by setting the money supply at $162.5 billion, the Fed can reduce investment spending by $2.5 billion, lowering it from the $25 billion associated with AD_3 down to only $22.5 billion. This decline in investment spending will initially shift the AD curve only $2.5 billion to the left of AD_3. But then the multiplier process will work its magic. Since the multiplier is 4 in our model, the AD curve will end up moving by a full $10 billion (= $4 \times$ $2.5 billion) to the left, to AD_4. This shift will move the economy to equilibrium *b*, returning output to the full employment level and eliminating the inflationary GDP gap.[2]

Column 2 in Table 16.3 summarizes the cause-effect chain of a tight money policy.

Monetary Policy: Evaluation and Issues

Monetary policy has become the dominant component of U.S. national stabilization policy. It has two key advantages over fiscal policy:

- Speed and flexibility.
- Isolation from political pressure.

Compared with fiscal policy, monetary policy can be quickly altered. Recall that congressional deliberations may delay the application of fiscal policy for months. In contrast, the Fed can buy or sell securities from day to day and thus affect the money supply and interest rates almost immediately.

Also, because members of the Fed's Board of Governors are appointed and serve 14-year terms, they are relatively isolated from lobbying and need not worry about retaining their popularity with voters. Thus, the Board, more readily than Congress, can engage in politically unpopular policies (higher interest rates) that may be necessary for the long-term health of the economy. Moreover, monetary policy is a subtler and more politically neutral measure than fiscal policy. Changes in government spending directly affect the allocation of resources, and changes in taxes can have extensive political ramifications. Because monetary policy works more subtly, it is more politically palatable.

Recent U.S. Monetary Policy

The Fed has been highly active in its use of monetary policy in recent decades. To demonstrate this fact, let's begin with the year 2000, when the economy abruptly slowed after a long period of full employment and strong economic growth. The Fed responded to the slowdown by cutting the Federal funds interest rate by a full percentage point in two increments in January 2001. Despite those rate cuts, the economy entered a recession in March 2001. Between March 20, 2001, and August 21, 2001, the Fed reduced the Federal funds rate from 5 percent to 3.5 percent in a series of steps. In the 3 months following the terrorist attacks of September 11, 2001, it lowered the Federal funds rate from 3.5 percent to 1.75 percent, and it left the rate there until it lowered it to 1.25 percent in November 2002. Partly because of the Fed's actions, the prime interest rate dropped from 9.5 percent at the end of 2000 to 4.25 percent in December 2002.

Economists generally give the Fed high marks for helping to keep the recession of 2001 relatively mild, particularly in view of the adverse economic impacts of the terrorist attacks of September 11, 2001, and the steep stock-market decline in 2001–2002.

The Fed left the Federal funds rate at historic lows in 2003. But as the economy began to expand robustly in 2004, the Fed engineered a gradual series of rate hikes designed to boost the prime interest rate and other interest rates to make sure that aggregate demand continued to grow at a pace consistent with low inflation. By the summer of 2006, the target for the Federal funds rate had risen to 5.25 percent and the prime rate was 8.25 percent. With the economy enjoying sustainable, noninflationary growth, the Fed left the Federal funds rate at 5.25 percent for over a year.

The mortgage default crisis (discussed in Chapter 14) began during the late summer of 2007 and posed a grave threat to the financial system and the economy. In response, the Fed took several actions. In August it lowered the discount rate by half a percentage point. Then, between September 2007 and April 2008, it lowered the

---

[2]Again, we assume for simplicity that the decrease in nominal GDP does not feed back to reduce the demand for money and thus the interest rate. In reality, this would occur, slightly dampening the increase in the interest rate show in Figure 16.5a.

target for the Federal funds rate from 5.25 percent to 2 percent. The Fed also initiated the term auction facility in December 2007 and, as discussed in Chapter 14, took a series of extraordinary actions to prevent the failure of key financial firms.

In October 2008, the Fed first reduced the Federal funds target rate to 1.5 percent and then later that same month to 1 percent. In December 2008, the Fed lowered it further to a targeted range of 0 percent to 0.25 percent. The Federal funds rate remained in that range through September 2009. Viewed through Figure 16.3, the Fed aggressively pushed the supply of Federal funds curve downward (increased the supply of Federal funds) to lower the actual Federal funds rate to its target level. All these monetary actions and lender-of-last resort functions helped to stabilize the banking sector and keep credit flowing—thereby offsetting at least some of the damage done by the financial crisis.

The decline in the Federal funds rate to near zero during the financial and economic crisis dropped the prime interest rate (review Figure 16.4). In December 2007, the prime interest rate stood at 7.3 percent. By January 2009, it had declined to 3.25 percent, where it remained for the rest of 2009.

The Federal Reserve is lauded by most observers for its quick and innovative actions during the financial crisis and severe recession. Nevertheless, some economists contend that the Fed contributed to the financial crisis by holding the Federal funds interest rate too low for too long during the recovery from the 2001 recession. These critics say that the artificially low interest rates made mortgage and other loans too inexpensive and therefore contributed to the borrowing frenzy by homeowners and other financial investors. Other economists counter that the low mortgage interest rates resulted from huge inflows of savings from abroad to a wide variety of U.S. financial markets.

Problems and Complications

Despite its recent successes in the United States, monetary policy has certain limitations and faces actual-economy complications.

Lags Recall that fiscal policy is hindered by three delays, or lags—a recognition lag, an administrative lag, and an operational lag. Monetary policy also faces a recognition lag and an operational lag, but because the Fed can decide and implement policy changes within days, it avoids the long administrative lag that hinders fiscal policy.

A recognition lag affects monetary policy because normal monthly variations in economic activity and the price level mean that the Fed may not be able to quickly

CONSIDER THIS . . .

Up, Up, and Away

The consolidated balance sheet of the 12 Federal Reserve Banks changed markedly during the severe recession of 2007–2009. Total Fed assets increased from $885 billion in February 2008 to $2317 billion in March 2010. This increase reflected an enormous rise in the number of U.S. securities, mortgage-backed securities, and other financial assets purchased by the Federal Reserve. In undertaking its monetary policy and its lender-of-last-resort functions, the Fed bought these securities from financial institutions—purposely increasing the liquidity of the financial system. The Fed also increased its loans to financial institutions, particularly through the term auction facility. Because term auction loans are "owed to" the Fed, the accounting credits for them are assets on the Fed's balance sheet.

On the liability side, the reserves of commercial banks rose from $43 billion in February 2008 to $1148 billion in March 2010. To make sure they were liquid and the funds were safe, banks placed much of the proceeds from selling securities to the Fed into their respective reserve accounts at the Fed. This flow was strengthened because the Fed began paying interest on the reserves that banks were holding at the Fed.

In March 2010 total bank reserves held at the Fed exceeded total checkable deposits held by the banks. The severe distress in the financial system had voluntarily turned the fractional reserve system into a 100-percent-plus reserve system! The banks had enormous excess reserves from which to increase lending once the banks became more certain of their own financial viability and the likelihood that newly issued loans would be paid back.

The Fed therefore faces a challenging task of using monetary policy to absorb large portions of this overstock of excess reserves as the economy recovers and picks up momentum. It does not want the banks to lend out the full amount of these excess reserves, because that would flood the economy with bank-created money and excessively expand the money supply. During a vigorous economic expansion, the excessive money and resulting very low interest rates could produce such large expansions of aggregate demand that rapid inflation would occur.

recognize when the economy is truly starting to recede or when inflation is really starting to rise. Once the Fed acts, an operation lag of 3 to 6 months affects monetary policy because that much time is typically required for interest-rate changes to have their full impacts on investment,

LAST
Word The "Big Picture"

This Figure Integrates the Various Components of
Macroeconomic Theory and Stabilization Policy.
Determinants That either Constitute Public Policy
or are Strongly Influenced by Public Policy are Shown
in Red.

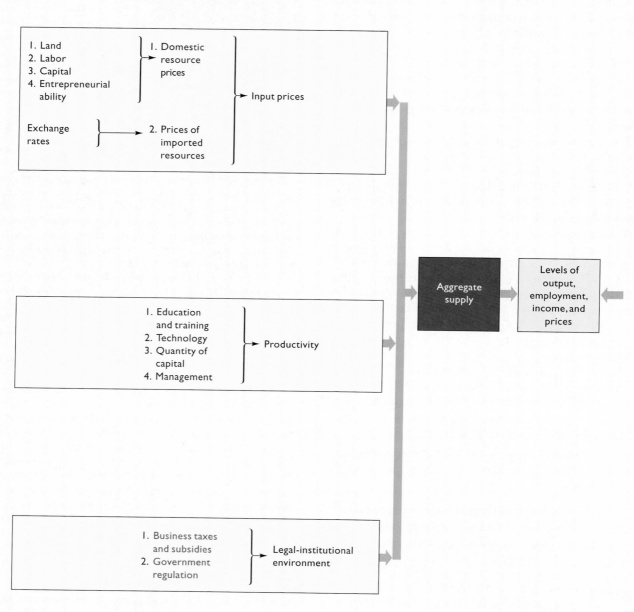

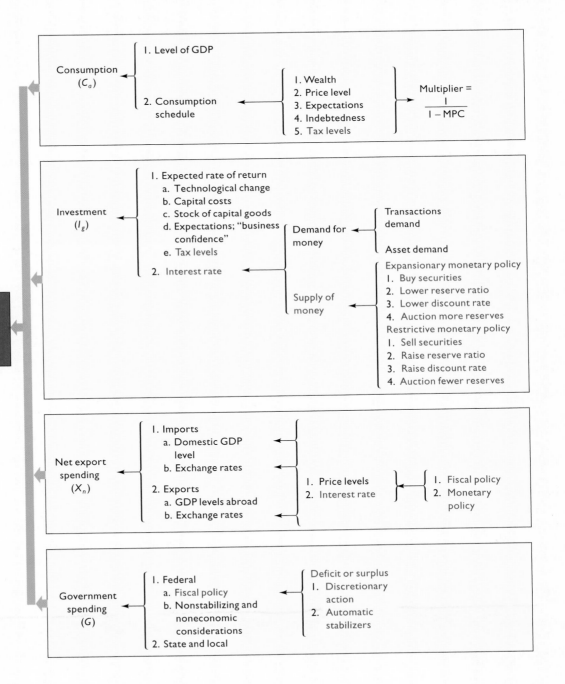

Consumption
(C_a)
1. Level of GDP
2. Consumption schedule
  1. Wealth
  2. Price level
  3. Expectations
  4. Indebtedness
  5. Tax levels

Multiplier = $\dfrac{1}{1 - MPC}$

Investment
(I_g)
1. Expected rate of return
  a. Technological change
  b. Capital costs
  c. Stock of capital goods
  d. Expectations; "business confidence"
  e. Tax levels
2. Interest rate

Demand for money
  Transactions demand
  Asset demand

Supply of money
  Expansionary monetary policy
  1. Buy securities
  2. Lower reserve ratio
  3. Lower discount rate
  4. Auction more reserves
  Restrictive monetary policy
  1. Sell securities
  2. Raise reserve ratio
  3. Raise discount rate
  4. Auction fewer reserves

Net export spending
(X_n)
1. Imports
  a. Domestic GDP level
  b. Exchange rates
2. Exports
  a. GDP levels abroad
  b. Exchange rates

1. Price levels
2. Interest rate

1. Fiscal policy
2. Monetary policy

Government spending
(G)
1. Federal
  a. Fiscal policy
  b. Nonstabilizing and noneconomic considerations
2. State and local

Deficit or surplus
1. Discretionary action
2. Automatic stabilizers

Aggregate demand

aggregate demand, real GDP, and the price level. These two lags complicate the timing of monetary policy.

Cyclical Asymmetry and the Liquidity Trap

Monetary policy may be highly effective in slowing expansions and controlling inflation but may be much less reliable in pushing the economy from a severe recession. Economists say that monetary policy may suffer from **cyclical asymmetry.** The metaphor of "pushing on a string" is often invoked to capture this problem. Imagine the Fed standing on the left-hand side of Figure 16.5d, holding one end of a "monetary-policy string." And imagine that the other end of the monetary-policy string is tied to the AD curve. Because the string would go taut if pulled on, monetary policy may be useful in *pulling* aggregate demand to the left. But because the string would go limp if pushed on, monetary policy will be rather ineffective at *pushing* aggregate demand to the right.

The reason for this asymmetry has to do with the asymmetric way in which people may act in response to changes in bank reserves. If pursued vigorously, a restrictive monetary policy can deplete commercial banking reserves to the point where banks are forced to reduce the volume of loans. That means a contraction of the money supply, higher interest rates, and reduced aggregate demand. The Fed can absorb sufficient reserves and eventually achieve its goal.

But the Fed cannot be certain of achieving its goal when it adds reserves to the banking system because of the so-called **liquidity trap,** in which adding more liquidity to banks has little or no additional positive effect on lending, borrowing, investment, or aggregate demand. For example, during the recent recession, the Fed created billions of dollars of excess reserves that drove down the Federal funds rate to as low as 0.2 percent. The prime interest rate fell from 7.3 percent (December 2007) to 3.25 percent (March 2009). Nevertheless, lending by banks stalled throughout the first 15 months of the recession. The banks were fearful that the loans they would make to households, businesses, and other financial institutions would not be paid back. Consequently, they were content to hold reserves at the Federal Reserve Banks.

To switch analogies, an expansionary monetary policy suffers from a "you can lead a horse to water, but you can't make it drink" problem. The Fed can create excess reserves, but it cannot guarantee that the banks will actually make additional loans and thus promote spending. If commercial banks seek liquidity and are unwilling to lend, the efforts of the Fed will be of little avail. Similarly, households and businesses can frustrate the intentions of the Fed by not borrowing excess reserves being made available as loans. And when the Fed buys securities from the public, people may choose to pay off existing loans with the money received, rather than increasing their spending on goods and services.

Furthermore, a severe recession may so undermine business confidence that the investment demand curve shifts to the left and overwhelms the lower interest rates associated with an expansionary monetary policy. That is what happened in the most recent recession. Although the Fed drove the real interest rate down to zero percent, investment spending remained low and the economy remained mired in recession. The recent U.S. experience reminds us that active monetary policy certainly is not a cure-all for the business cycle. Under some circumstances, monetary policy may be like "pushing on a string."

The liquidity trap that occurred during the severe recession was a primary reason why public policy in the United States turned so significantly and forcefully toward fiscal policy in 2009. Recall our discussion of the American Recovery and Redevelopment Act of 2009, which authorized the infusion of $787 billion of new tax cuts and government spending in 2009 and 2010.

QUICK REVIEW 16.4

- The Fed is engaging in an expansionary monetary policy when it increases the money supply to reduce interest rates and increase investment spending and real GDP; it is engaging in a restrictive monetary policy when it reduces the money supply to increase interest rates and reduce investment spending and inflation.
- The Fed aggressively lowered the Federal funds interest rate following 9/11 and the 2001 recession and also during the severe recession of 2007–2009.
- The main strengths of monetary policy are (a) speed and flexibility and (b) political acceptability; its main weaknesses are (a) time lags and (b) potential ineffectiveness during severe recession.

The "Big Picture"

The Last Word in this chapter brings together the analytical and policy aspects of macroeconomics discussed in this and the eight preceding chapters. This "big picture" shows how the many concepts and principles discussed relate to one another and how they constitute a coherent theory of the price level and real output in a market economy.

Study this diagram and you will see that the levels of output, employment, income, and prices all result from the interaction of aggregate supply and aggregate demand. The items shown in red relate to public policy.

Summary

1. The goal of monetary policy is to help the economy achieve price stability, full employment, and economic growth.

2. The total demand for money consists of the transactions demand for money plus the asset demand for money. The amount of money demanded for transactions varies directly with the nominal GDP; the amount of money demanded as an asset varies inversely with the interest rate. The market for money combines the total demand for money with the money supply to determine equilibrium interest rates.

3. Interest rates and bond prices are inversely related.

4. The four main instruments of monetary policy are (a) open-market operations, (b) the reserve ratio, (c) the discount rate, and (d) the term auction facility.

5. The Federal funds rate is the interest rate that banks charge one another for overnight loans of reserves. The prime interest rate is the benchmark rate that banks use as a reference rate for a wide range of interest rates on short-term loans to businesses and individuals.

6. The Fed adjusts the Federal funds rate to a level appropriate for economic conditions. Under an expansionary monetary policy, it purchases securities from commercial banks and the general public to inject reserves into the banking system. This lowers the Federal funds rate to the targeted level and also reduces other interest rates (such as the prime rate). Under a restrictive monetary policy, the Fed sells securities to commercial banks and the general public via open-market operations. Consequently, reserves are removed from the banking system, and the Federal funds rate and other interest rates rise.

7. Monetary policy affects the economy through a complex cause-effect chain: (a) Policy decisions affect commercial bank reserves; (b) changes in reserves affect the money supply; (c) changes in the money supply alter the interest rate; (d) changes in the interest rate affect investment; (e) changes in investment affect aggregate demand; (f) changes in aggregate demand affect the equilibrium real GDP and the price level. Table 16.3 draws together all the basic ideas relevant to the use of monetary policy.

8. The advantages of monetary policy include its flexibility and political acceptability. In recent years, the Fed has used monetary policy to keep inflation low while helping limit the depth of the recession of 2001, to boost the economy as it recovered from that recession, to help stabilize the banking sector in the wake of the mortgage debt crisis, and to promote recovery from the severe recession of 2007–2009. Today, nearly all economists view monetary policy as a significant stabilization tool.

9. Monetary policy has two major limitations and potential problems: (a) recognition and operation lags complicate the timing of monetary policy; (b) in a severe recession, the reluctance of banks to lend excess reserves and firms to borrow money to spend on capital goods may contribute to a liquidity trap that limits the effectiveness of an expansionary monetary policy.

Terms and Concepts

monetary policy

interest

transactions demand for money

asset demand for money

total demand for money

open-market operations

reserve ratio

discount rate

term auction facility

Federal funds rate

expansionary monetary policy

prime interest rate

restrictive monetary policy

Taylor rule

cyclical asymmetry

liquidity trap

Questions

1. What is the basic determinant of (a) the transactions demand and (b) the asset demand for money? Explain how these two demands can be combined graphically to determine total money demand. How is the equilibrium interest rate in the money market determined? Use a graph to show the effect of an increase in the total demand for money on the equilibrium interest rate (no change in money supply). Use your general knowledge of equilibrium prices to explain why the previous interest rate is no longer sustainable. **LO1**

2. What is the basic objective of monetary policy? What are the major strengths of monetary policy? Why is monetary policy easier to conduct than fiscal policy? **LO2**

3. Use commercial bank and Federal Reserve Bank balance sheets to demonstrate the effect of each of the following transactions on commercial bank reserves: **LO2**
   a. Federal Reserve Banks purchase securities from banks.
   b. Commercial banks borrow from Federal Reserve Banks at the discount rate.

c. The Fed reduces the reserve ratio.

d. Commercial banks borrow from Federal Reserve Banks after winning an auction held as part of the term auction facility.

4. Distinguish between the Federal funds rate and the prime interest rate. Why is one higher than the other? Why do changes in the two rates closely track one another? LO3

5. Why is a decrease in the supply of Federal funds shown as an upshift of the supply curve in Figure 16.3, whereas an increase in Federal funds is shown as a downshift of the supply curve? LO3

6. Suppose that you are a member of the Board of Governors of the Federal Reserve System. The economy is experiencing a sharp rise in the inflation rate. What change in the Federal funds rate would you recommend? How would your recommended change get accomplished? What impact would the actions have on the lending ability of the banking system, the real interest rate, investment spending, aggregate demand, and inflation? LO3, LO4

7. Explain the links between changes in the nation's money supply, the interest rate, investment spending, aggregate demand, real GDP, and the price level. LO4

8. What do economists mean when they say that monetary policy can exhibit cyclical asymmetry? How does the idea of a liquidity trap relate to cyclical asymmetry? Why is this possibility of a liquidity trap significant to policymakers? LO5

9. **LAST WORD** What are the three main aggregate supply factors that determine a nation's potential (or full-employment) level of real output? What are the four main components of aggregate demand? Explain: "Aggregate supply factors determine a nation's potential GDP, whereas aggregate demand factors determine whether or not the nation achieves its full employment GDP." How does fiscal and monetary policy relate to aggregate demand?

Problems

1. Assume that the following data characterize the hypothetical economy of Trance: money supply = $200 billion; quantity of money demanded for transactions = $150 billion; quantity of money demanded as an asset = $10 billion at 12 percent interest, increasing by $10 billion for each 2-percentage-point fall in the interest rate. LO1

   a. What is the equilibrium interest rate in Trance?

   b. At the equilibrium interest rate, what are the quantity of money supplied, the total quantity of money demanded, the amount of money demanded for transactions, and the amount of money demanded as an asset in Trance?

2. Suppose a bond with no expiration date has a face value of $10,000 and annually pays a fixed amount of interest of $800. In the table provided to the right, calculate and enter either the interest rate that the bond would yield to a bond buyer at each of the bond prices listed or the bond price at each of the interest yields shown. What generalization can be drawn from the completed table? LO1

Bond Price	Interest Yield, %
$ 8000	_____
_____	8.9
$10,000	_____
$11,000	_____
_____	6.2

3. In the tables that follow you will find consolidated balance sheets for the commercial banking system and the 12 Federal Reserve Banks. Use columns 1 through 3 to indicate how the balance sheets would read after each of transactions a to c is completed. Do not cumulate your answers; that is, analyze each transaction separately, starting in each case from the numbers provided. All accounts are in billions of dollars. LO2

   a. A decline in the discount rate prompts commercial banks to borrow an additional $1 billion from the Federal

	Consolidated Balance Sheet: All Commercial Banks		
	(1)	(2)	(3)
Assets:			
Reserves $33	_____	_____	_____
Securities 60	_____	_____	_____
Loans 60	_____	_____	_____
Liabilities and net worth:			
Checkable deposits $150	_____	_____	_____
Loans from the Federal			
Reserve Banks 3	_____	_____	_____

	Consolidated Balance Sheet: The 12 Federal Reserve Banks			
		(1)	(2)	(3)
Assets:				
Securities	$60	_____	_____	_____
Loans to commercial banks	3	_____	_____	_____
Liabilities and net worth:				
Reserves of commercial banks	$33	_____	_____	_____
Treasury deposits	3	_____	_____	_____
Federal Reserve Notes	27	_____	_____	_____

Reserve Banks. Show the new balance-sheet numbers in column 1 of each table.

b. The Federal Reserve Banks sell $3 billion in securities to members of the public, who pay for the bonds with checks. Show the new balance-sheet numbers in column 2 of each table.

c. The Federal Reserve Banks buy $2 billion of securities from commercial banks. Show the new balance-sheet numbers in column 3 of each table.

d. Now review each of the above three transactions, asking yourself these three questions: (1) What change, if any, took place in the money supply as a direct and immediate result of each transaction? (2) What increase or decrease in the commercial banks' reserves took place in each transaction? (3) Assuming a reserve ratio of 20 percent, what change in the money-creating potential of the commercial banking system occurred as a result of each transaction?

4. Refer to Table 16.2 and assume that the Fed's reserve ratio is 10 percent and the economy is in a severe recession. Also suppose that the commercial banks are hoarding all excess reserves (not lending them out) because of their fear of loan defaults. Finally, suppose that the Fed is highly concerned that the banks will suddenly lend out these excess reserves and possibly contribute to inflation once the economy begins to recover and confidence is restored. By how many percentage points would the Fed need to increase the reserve ratio to eliminate one-third of the excess reserves?

What would be the size of the monetary multiplier before and after the change in the reserve ratio? By how much would the lending potential of the banks decline as a result of the increase in the reserve ratio? LO2

5. Suppose that the demand for Federal funds curve is such that the quantity of funds demanded changes by $120 billion for each 1 percent change in the Federal funds interest rate. Also, assume that the current Federal funds rate is at the 3 percent rate that is targeted by the Fed. Now suppose that the Fed retargets the rate to 3.5 percent. Assuming no change in demand, will the Fed need to increase or decrease the supply of Federal funds? By how much will the quantity of Federal funds have to change for the equilibrium to occur at the new target rate? LO3

6. Suppose that inflation is 2 percent, the Federal funds rate is 4 percent, and real GDP falls 2 percent below potential GDP. According to the Taylor rule, in what direction and by how much should the Fed change the real Federal funds rate? LO3

7. Refer to the table for Moola at the bottom of this page to answer the following questions. What is the equilibrium interest rate in Moola? What is the level of investment at the equilibrium interest rate? Is there either a recessionary output gap (negative GDP gap) or an inflationary output gap (positive GDP gap) at the equilibrium interest rate and, if either, what is the amount? Given money demand, by how much would the Moola central bank need to change the money supply to close the output gap? What is the expenditure multiplier in Moola? LO4

Money Supply	Money Demand	Interest Rate	Investment at Interest (Rate Shown)	Potential Real GDP	Actual Real GDP at Interest (Rate Shown)
$500	$800	2%	$50	$350	$390
500	700	3	40	350	370
500	600	4	30	350	350
500	500	5	20	350	330
500	400	6	10	350	310

FURTHER TEST YOUR KNOWLEDGE AT
www.mcconnell19e.com

At the text's Online Learning Center (OLC), **www.mcconnell19e.com**, you will find one or more Web-based questions that require information from the Internet to answer. We urge you to check them out; they will familiarize you with Web sites that may be helpful in other courses and perhaps even in your career. The OLC also features multiple-choice questions that give instant feedback and provides other helpful ways to further test your knowledge of the chapter.

EXTENSIONS AND ISSUES

1 Explain the relationship between short-run aggregate supply and long-run aggregate supply.

2 Discuss how to apply the "extended" (short-run/long-run) AD-AS model to inflation, recessions, and economic growth.

3 Explain the short-run trade-off between inflation and unemployment (the Phillips Curve).

4 Discuss why there is no long-run trade-off between inflation and unemployment.

5 Explain the relationship between tax rates, tax revenues, and aggregate supply.

Extending the Analysis of Aggregate Supply

During the early years of the Great Depression, many economists suggested that the economy would correct itself in the *long run* without government intervention. To this line of thinking, economist John Maynard Keynes remarked, "In the long run we are all dead!"

For several decades following the Great Depression, macroeconomists understandably focused on refining fiscal policy and monetary policy to smooth business cycles and address the problems of unemployment and inflation. The main emphasis was on short-run problems and policies associated with the business cycle.

But over people's lifetimes, and from generation to generation, the long run is tremendously important for economic well-being. For that reason, macroeconomists have refocused attention on long-run macroeconomic adjustments, processes, and outcomes. The renewed emphasis on the long run has produced significant insights about aggregate supply, economic growth, and economic development. We will also see in the next chapter that it has renewed historical debates over the causes of macro instability and the effectiveness of stabilization policy.

Our goals in this chapter are to extend the analysis of aggregate supply to the long run, examine the inflation-unemployment relationship, and evaluate the effect of taxes on aggregate supply. The latter is a key concern of so-called *supply-side economics.*

From Short Run to Long Run

In Chapter 12, we noted that in macroeconomics the difference between the **short run** and the **long run** has to do with the flexibility of input prices. Input prices are inflexible or even totally fixed in the short run but fully flexible in the long run. (By contrast, output prices are assumed under these definitions to be fully flexible in both the short run and the long run.)

The assumption that input prices are flexible only in the long run leads to large differences in the shape and position of the short-run aggregate supply curve and the long-run aggregate supply curve. As explained in Chapter 12, the short-run aggregate supply curve is an upsloping line, whereas the long-run aggregate supply curve is a vertical line situated directly above the economy's full-employment output level, Q_f.

We will begin this chapter by discussing how aggregate supply transitions *from* the short run *to* the long run. Once that is done, we will combine the long-run and short-run aggregate supply curves with the aggregate demand curve to form a single model that can provide insights into how the economy adjusts to economic shocks as well as changes in monetary and fiscal policy in both the short run and the long run. That will lead us to discuss how economic growth relates to long-run aggregate supply and how inflation and aggregate supply are related in the long run and the short run. We will conclude with a discussion of a particular set of economic policies that may help increase both short-run aggregate supply and long-run aggregate supply.

Short-Run Aggregate Supply

Our immediate objective is to demonstrate the relationship between short-run aggregate supply and long-run aggregate supply. We begin by briefly reviewing short-run aggregate supply.

Consider the short-run aggregate supply curve AS_1 in Figure 18.1a. This curve is based on three assumptions: (1) The initial price level is P_1, (2) firms and workers have established nominal wages on the expectation that this price level will persist, and (3) the price level is flexible

both upward and downward. Observe from point a_1 that at price level P_1 the economy is operating at its full-employment output Q_f. This output is the real production forthcoming when the economy is operating at its natural rate of unemployment (or potential output).

Now let's review the short-run effects of changes in the price level, say, from P_1 to P_2 in Figure 18.1a. The higher prices associated with price level P_2 increase firms' revenues, and because their nominal wages and other input prices remain unchanged, their profits rise. Those higher profits lead firms to increase their output from Q_f to Q_2, and the economy moves from a_1 to a_2 on aggregate supply AS_1. At output Q_2 the economy is operating beyond its full-employment output. The firms make this possible by extending the work hours of part-time and full-time workers, enticing new workers such as homemakers and retirees into the labor force, and hiring and training the structurally unemployed. Thus, the nation's unemployment rate declines below its natural rate.

How will the firms respond when the price level *falls*, say, from P_1 to P_3 in Figure 18.1a? Because the prices they receive for their products are lower while the nominal wages they pay workers remain unchanged, firms discover that their revenues and profits have diminished or disappeared. So they reduce their production and employment, and, as shown by the movement from a_1 to a_3, real output falls to Q_3. Increased unemployment and a higher unemployment rate accompany the decline in real output. At output Q_3 the unemployment rate is greater than the natural rate of unemployment associated with output Q_f.

Long-Run Aggregate Supply

The outcomes are different in the long run. To see why, we need to extend the analysis of aggregate supply to account for changes in nominal wages that occur in response to changes in the price level. That will enable us to derive the economy's long-run aggregate supply curve.

We illustrate the implications for aggregate supply in Figure 18.1b. Again, suppose that the economy is initially at point a_1 (P_1 and Q_f). As we just demonstrated, an increase in the price level from P_1 to P_2 will move the economy from point a_1 to a_2 along the short-run aggregate

FIGURE 18.1 Short-run and long-run aggregate supply. (a) In the short run, nominal wages and other input prices do not respond to price-level changes and are based on the expectation that price level P_1 will continue. An increase in the price level from P_1 to P_2 increases profits and output, moving the economy from a_1 to a_2; a decrease in the price level from P_1 to P_3 reduces profits and real output, moving the economy from a_1 to a_3. The short-run aggregate supply curve therefore slopes upward. (b) In the long run, a rise in the price level results in higher nominal wages and other input prices and thus shifts the short-run aggregate supply curve to the left. Conversely, a decrease in the price level reduces nominal wages and shifts the short-run aggregate supply curve to the right. After such adjustments, the economy obtains equilibrium of points such as b_1 and c_1. Thus, the long-run aggregate supply curve is vertical at the full-employment output.

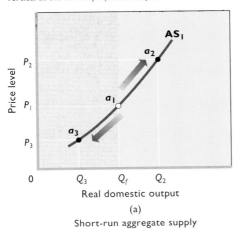

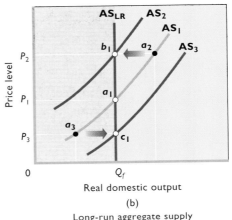

(a)
Short-run aggregate supply

(b)
Long-run aggregate supply

supply curve AS_1. At a_2, the economy is producing at more than its potential output. This implies very high demand for productive inputs, so that input prices will begin to rise. In particular, the high demand for labor will drive up nominal wages, which will increase per unit production costs. As a result, the short-run supply curve shifts leftward from AS_1 to AS_2, which now reflects the higher price level P_2 and the new expectation that P_2, not P_1, will continue. The leftward shift in the short-run aggregate supply curve to AS_2 moves the economy from a_2 to b_1. Real output falls back to its full-employment level Q_f, and the unemployment rate rises to its natural rate.

What is the long-run outcome of a *decrease* in the price level? Assuming eventual downward wage flexibility, a decline in the price level from P_1 to P_3 in Figure 18.1b works in the opposite way from a price-level increase. At first the economy moves from point a_1 to a_3 on AS_1. Profits are squeezed or eliminated because prices have fallen and nominal wages have not. But this movement along AS_1 is the short-run supply response that results only while input prices remain constant. As time passes, input prices will begin to fall because the economy is producing at below its full-employment output level. With so little output being produced, the demand for inputs will be low and their prices will begin to decline. In particular, the low demand for labor will drive down nominal wages and reduce per-unit production costs. Lower nominal wages therefore shift the short-run aggregate supply curve

rightward from AS_1 to AS_3, and real output returns to its full-employment level of Q_f at point c_1.

By tracing a line between the long-run equilibrium points b_1, a_1, and c_1, we obtain a long-run aggregate supply curve. Observe that it is vertical at the full-employment level of real GDP. After long-run adjustments in nominal wages and other nominal input prices, real output is Q_f regardless of the specific price level.

Long-Run Equilibrium in the AD-AS Model

Figure 18.2 helps us understand the long-run equilibrium in the AD-AS model, now extended to include the distinction between short-run and long-run aggregate supply. (Hereafter, we will refer to this model as the extended AD-AS model, with "extended" referring to the inclusion of both the short-run and the long-run aggregate supply curves.)

In the short run, equilibrium occurs wherever the downsloping aggregate demand curve and upsloping short-run aggregate supply curve intersect. This can be at any level of output, not simply the full-employment level. Either a negative GDP gap or a positive GDP gap is possible in the short run.

But in the long run, the short-run aggregate supply curve adjusts as we just described. After those adjustments, long-run equilibrium occurs where the aggregate demand curve, vertical long-run aggregate supply curve, and

FIGURE 18.2 **Equilibrium in the long-run AD-AS model.** The long-run equilibrium price level P_1 and level of real output Q_f occur at the intersection of the aggregate demand curve AD_1, the long-run aggregate supply curve AS_{LR}, and the short-run aggregate supply curve AS_1.

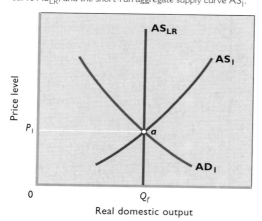

Real domestic output

INTERACTIVE GRAPHS
G 18.1
Extended AD-AS model

short-run aggregate supply curve all intersect. Figure 18.2 shows the long-run outcome. Equilibrium occurs at point *a*, where AD_1 intersects both AS_{LR} and AS_1, and the economy achieves its full-employment (or potential) output, Q_f. At long-run equilibrium price level P_1 and output level Q_f, neither a negative GDP gap nor a positive GDP gap occurs. The economy's *natural rate of unemployment* prevails, meaning that the economy achieves full employment.

In the United States, output Q_f in Figure 18.2 implies a 4-5 percent unemployment rate. The natural rate of unemployment can vary from one time period to another and can differ between countries. But whatever the rate happens to be, it defines the level of potential output and establishes the location of the long-run AS curve.

QUICK REVIEW 18.1

- The short-run aggregate supply curve slopes upward because nominal wages and other input prices are fixed while output prices change.
- The long-run aggregate supply curve is vertical because input prices eventually rise in response to changes in output prices.
- The long-run equilibrium GDP and price level occur at the intersection of the aggregate demand curve, the long-run aggregate supply curve, and the short-run aggregate supply curve.
- In long-run equilibrium, the economy achieves its natural rate of unemployment and its full-potential real output.

Applying the Extended AD-AS Model

The extended AD-AS model helps clarify the long-run aspects of demand-pull inflation, cost-push inflation, and recession.

Demand-Pull Inflation in the Extended AD-AS Model

Recall that demand-pull inflation occurs when an increase in aggregate demand pulls up the price level. Earlier, we depicted this inflation by shifting an aggregate demand curve rightward along a stable aggregate supply curve (see Figure 12.8).

In our more complex version of aggregate supply, however, an increase in the price level eventually leads to an increase in nominal wages and thus a leftward shift of the short-run aggregate supply curve. This is shown in Figure 18.3, where we initially suppose the price level is P_1 at the intersection of aggregate demand curve AD_1, short-run supply curve AS_1, and long-run aggregate supply curve AS_{LR}. Observe that the economy is achieving its full-employment real output Q_f at point *a*.

Now consider the effects of an increase in aggregate demand as represented by the rightward shift from AD_1 to AD_2. This shift might result from any one of a number of factors, including an increase in investment spending or a rise in net exports. Whatever its cause, the increase in aggregate demand boosts the price level from P_1 to P_2 and expands real output from Q_f to Q_2 at point *b*. There, a positive GDP gap of $Q_2 - Q_f$ occurs.

So far, none of this is new to you. But now the distinction between short-run aggregate supply and long-run aggregate supply becomes important. With the economy producing above potential output, inputs will be in high demand. Input prices including nominal wages will rise. As they do, the short-run aggregate supply curve will ultimately shift leftward such that it intersects long-run aggregate supply at point *c*.[1] There, the economy has reestablished long-run equilibrium, with the price level and real output now P_3 and Q_f, respectively. Only at point *c*

---

[1] We say "ultimately" because the initial leftward shift in short-run aggregate supply will intersect the long-run aggregate supply curve AS_{LR} at price level P_2 (review Figure 18.1b). But the intersection of AD_2 and this new short-run aggregate supply curve (that is not shown in Figure 18.3) will produce a price level above P_2. (You may want to pencil this in to make sure that you understand this point.) Again nominal wages will rise, shifting the short-run aggregate supply curve farther leftward. The process will continue until the economy moves to point *c*, where the short-run aggregate supply curve is AS_2, the price level is P_3, and real output is Q_f.

FIGURE 18.3 Demand-pull inflation in the extended AD-AS model. An increase in aggregate demand from AD$_1$ to AD$_2$ drives up the price level and increases real output in the short run. But in the long run, nominal wages rise and the short-run aggregate supply curve shifts leftward, as from AS$_1$ to AS$_2$. Real output then returns to its prior level, and the price level rises even more. In this scenario, the economy moves from a to b and then eventually to c.

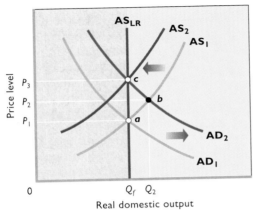

FIGURE 18.4 Cost-push inflation in the extended AD-AS model. Cost-push inflation occurs when the short-run aggregate supply curve shifts leftward, as from AS$_1$ to AS$_2$. If government counters the decline in real output by increasing aggregate demand to the broken line, the price level rises even more. That is, the economy moves in steps from a to b to c. In contrast, if government allows a recession to occur, nominal wages eventually fall and the aggregate supply curve shifts back rightward to its original location. The economy moves from a to b and eventually back to a.

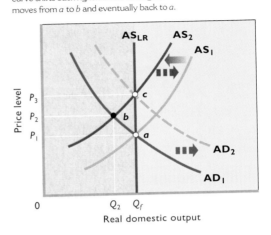

does the new aggregate demand curve AD$_2$ intersect both the short-run aggregate supply curve AS$_2$ and the long-run aggregate supply curve AS$_{LR}$.

In the short run, demand-pull inflation drives up the price level and increases real output; in the long run, only the price level rises. In the long run, the initial increase in aggregate demand moves the economy along its vertical aggregate supply curve AS$_{LR}$. For a while, an economy can operate beyond its full-employment level of output. But the demand-pull inflation eventually causes adjustments of nominal wages that return the economy to its full-employment output Q_f.

Cost-Push Inflation in the Extended AD-AS Model

Cost-push inflation arises from factors that increase the cost of production at each price level, shifting the aggregate supply curve leftward and raising the equilibrium price level. Previously (Figure 12.10), we considered cost-push inflation using only the short-run aggregate supply curve. Now we want to analyze that type of inflation in its long-run context.

Analysis Look at Figure 18.4, in which we again assume that the economy is initially operating at price level P_1 and output level Q_f (point a). Suppose that international oil producers agree to reduce the supply of oil to boost its price by, say, 100 percent. As a result, the per-unit production cost of producing and transporting goods and services

rises substantially in the economy represented by Figure 18.4. This increase in per-unit production costs shifts the short-run aggregate supply curve to the left, as from AS$_1$ to AS$_2$, and the price level rises from P_1 to P_2 (as seen by comparing points a and b). In this case, the leftward shift of the aggregate supply curve is *not a response* to a price-level increase, as it was in our previous discussions of demand-pull inflation; it is the *initiating cause* of the price-level increase.

Policy Dilemma Cost-push inflation creates a dilemma for policymakers. Without some expansionary stabilization policy, aggregate demand in Figure 18.4 remains in place at AD$_1$ and real output declines from Q_f to Q_2. Government can counter this recession, negative GDP gap, and attendant high unemployment by using fiscal policy and monetary policy to increase aggregate demand to AD$_2$. But there is a potential policy trap here: An increase in aggregate demand to AD$_2$ will further raise inflation by increasing the price level from P_2 to P_3 (a move from point b to point c).

Suppose the government recognizes this policy trap and decides not to increase aggregate demand from AD$_1$ to AD$_2$ (you can now disregard the dashed AD$_2$ curve) and instead decides to allow a cost-push-created recession to run its course. How will that happen? Widespread layoffs, plant shutdowns, and business failures eventually occur. At some point the demand for oil, labor, and other inputs will decline so much that oil prices and nominal wages will decline. When that happens, the initial leftward shift of the short-run aggregate supply curve will reverse itself. That is, the declining per-unit production costs caused by the recession will shift the short-run aggregate supply curve rightward from AS_2 to AS_1. The price level will return to P_1, and the full-employment level of output will be restored at Q_f (point a on the long-run aggregate supply curve AS_{LR}).

This analysis yields two generalizations:

- If the government attempts to maintain full employment when there is cost-push inflation, even more inflation will occur.

- If the government takes a hands-off approach to cost-push inflation, the recession will linger. Although falling input prices will eventually undo the initial rise in per-unit production costs, the economy in the meantime will experience high unemployment and a loss of real output.

Recession and the Extended AD-AS Model

By far the most controversial application of the extended AD-AS model is its application to recession (or depression) caused by decreases in aggregate demand. We will look at this controversy in detail in Chapter 19; here we simply identify the key point of contention.

Suppose in Figure 18.5 that aggregate demand initially is AD_1 and that the short-run and long-run aggregate supply curves are AS_1 and AS_{LR}, respectively. Therefore, as

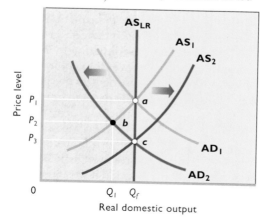

FIGURE 18.5 Recession in the extended AD-AS model. A recession occurs when aggregate demand shifts leftward, as from AD_1 to AD_2. If prices and wages are downwardly flexible, the price level falls from P_1 to P_2 as the economy moves from point a to point b. With the economy in recession at point b, wages eventually fall, shifting the aggregate supply curve from AS_1 to AS_2. The price level declines to P_3, and real output returns to Q_f. The economy moves from a to b to c.

shown by point a, the price level is P_1 and output is Q_f. Now suppose that investment spending declines dramatically, reducing aggregate demand to AD_2. Observe that real output declines from Q_f to Q_1, indicating that a recession has occurred. But if we make the controversial assumption that prices and wages are flexible downward, the price level falls from P_1 to P_2. With the economy producing below potential output at point b, demand for inputs will be low. Eventually, nominal wages themselves fall to restore the previous real wage; when that happens, the short-run aggregate supply curve shifts rightward from AS_1 to AS_2. The negative GDP gap evaporates without the need for expansionary fiscal or monetary policy since real output expands from Q_1 (point b) back to Q_f (point c). The economy is again located on its long-run aggregate supply curve AS_{LR}, but now at lower price level P_3.

There is much disagreement about this hypothetical scenario. The key point of dispute revolves around the degree to which both input and output prices may be downwardly inflexible and how long it would take in the actual economy for the necessary downward price and wage adjustments to occur to regain the full-employment level of output. For now, suffice it to say that most economists believe that if such adjustments are forthcoming, they will occur only after the economy has experienced a relatively long-lasting recession with its accompanying high unemployment and large loss of output. The severity and length of the major recession of 2007–2009 has strengthened this view. Therefore, economists recommend active monetary policy, and perhaps fiscal policy, to counteract recessions.

Economic Growth with Ongoing Inflation

In our analysis so far, we have seen how demand and supply shocks can cause, respectively, demand-push inflation and cost-push inflation. But in these previous cases, the extent of the inflation was *finite* because the size of the initial movement in either the AD curve or the AS curve was *limited*. For instance, in Figure 18.3, the aggregate demand curve shifts right by a limited amount, from AD_1 to AD_2. As the economy's equilibrium moves from a to b to c, the price level rises from P_1 to P_2 to P_3. During this transition, inflation obviously occurs because the price level is rising. But once the economy reaches its new equilibrium at point c, the price level remains constant at P_3 and no further inflation takes place. That is, the limited movement in aggregate demand causes a limited amount of inflation that ends when the economy returns to full employment.

FIGURE 18.6 Production possibilities and long-run aggregate supply. (a) Economic growth driven by supply factors (such as improved technologies or the use of more or better resources) shifts an economy's production possibilities curve outward, as from AB to CD. (b) The same factors shift the economy's long-run aggregate supply curve to the right, as from AS_{LRI} to AS_{LR2}.

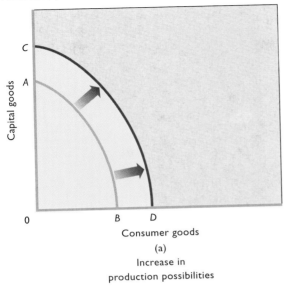

(a)

Increase in
production possibilities

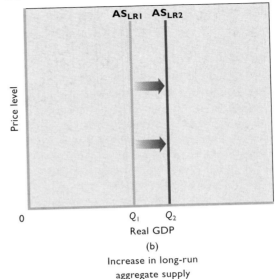

(b)

Increase in long-run
aggregate supply

But the modern economy almost always experiences continuous, but usually mild, positive rates of inflation. That can only happen with ongoing shifts in either the aggregate demand or long-run aggregate supply curves because any single, finite shift will only cause inflation of limited duration. This insight is crucial to understanding why modern economies usually experience ongoing inflation while achieving economic growth. Both aggregate demand and long-run aggregate supply increase over time in the actual economy, and inflation occurs because the increases in aggregate demand generally exceed the increases in long-run aggregate supply. It will be helpful to examine this point graphically.

Increases in Long-Run Aggregate Supply

As discussed in Chapter 8, economic growth is driven by supply factors such as improved technologies and access to more or better resources. Economists illustrate economic growth as either an outward shift of an economy's production possibilities curve or as a rightward shift of its long-run aggregate supply curve. As shown in Figure 18.6, the outward shift of the production possibilities curve from AB to CD in graph a is equivalent to the rightward shift of the economy's long-run aggregate supply curve from AS_{LR1} to AS_{LR2} in graph b.

Let's simply transfer this rightward shift of the economy's long-run aggregate supply curve to Figure 18.7,

which depicts economic growth in the United States in the context of the extended aggregate demand–aggregate supply model. Suppose the economy's long-run aggregate supply curve initially is AS_{LR1}, while its aggregate demand curve and short-run aggregate supply curve are AD_1, and AS_1, as shown. The equilibrium price level is P_1 and the equilibrium level of real output is Q_1.

Now let's assume that economic growth driven by changes in supply factors (quantity and quality of resources and technology) shifts the long-run aggregate supply curve rightward from AS_{LR1} to AS_{LR2} while the economy's aggregate demand curve remains at AD_1. Also, suppose that product and resource prices are flexible downward. The economy's potential output will expand, as reflected by the increase of available real output from Q_1 to Q_2. With aggregate demand constant at AD_1, the rightward shift of the long-run aggregate supply curve will lower the price level from P_1 to P_3. Taken alone, expansions of long-run aggregate supply in the economy are deflationary.

Increases in Aggregate Demand and Inflation

But a decline in the price level, such as the one from P_1 to P_3 in Figure 18.7, is not part of the long-run U.S. growth experience. Why not? The answer is that the nation's central bank—the Federal Reserve—engineers ongoing increases in the nation's money supply to create rightward

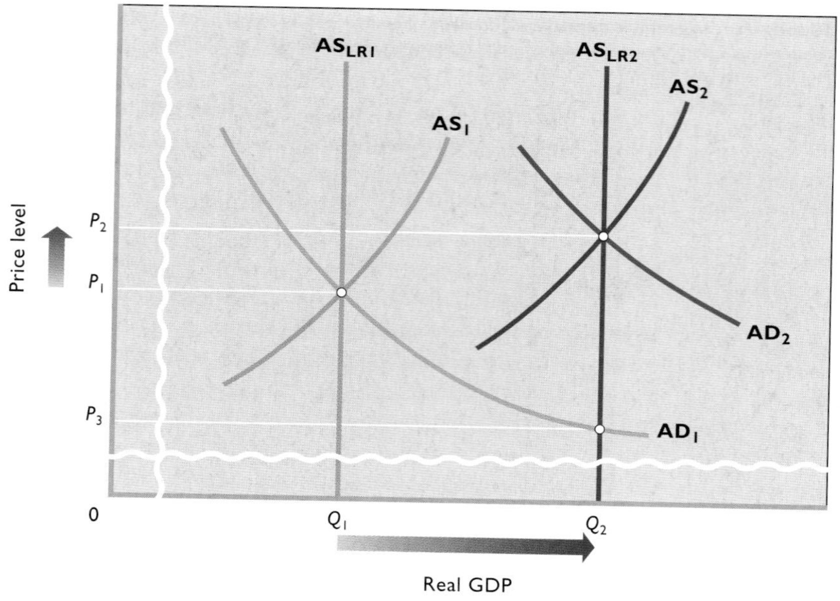

FIGURE 18.7 Depicting U.S. growth via the extended AD-AS model. Long-run aggregate supply and short-run aggregate supply have increased over time, as from AS_{LR1} to AS_{LR2} and AS_1 to AS_2. Simultaneously, aggregate demand has shifted rightward, as from AD_1 to AD_2. The actual outcome of these combined shifts has been economic growth, shown as the increase in real output from Q_1 to Q_2, accompanied by mild inflation, shown as the rise in the price level from P_1 to P_2.

shifts of the aggregate demand curve. These increases in aggregate demand would be highly inflationary absent the increases in long-run aggregate supply. But because the Fed usually makes sure that the inflationary rightward shifts of the aggregate demand curve proceed only slightly faster than the deflationary rightward shifts of the aggregate supply curve, only mild inflation occurs along with economic growth.

We illustrate this outcome in Figure 18.7, where aggregate demand shifts to the right from AD_1 to AD_2 at the same time long-run aggregate supply shifts rightward from AS_{LR1} to AS_{LR2}. Real output expands from Q_1 to Q_2 and the price level increases from P_1 to P_2. At the higher price level P_2, the economy confronts a new short-run aggregate supply curve AS_2. The changes shown in Figure 18.7 describe the actual U.S. experience: economic growth, accompanied by mild inflation. Real output on average increases at about 3.4 percent annually and inflation averages 2–3 percent a year.

Of course, other long-term outcomes besides that depicted are entirely possible. Whether deflation, zero inflation, mild inflation, or rapid inflation accompanies economic growth depends on the extent to which aggregate demand increases relative to long-run aggregate supply. Over long periods, any inflation that accompanies economic growth is exclusively the result of aggregate demand increasing more rapidly than long-run aggregate supply. The expansion of long-run aggregate supply—of potential real GDP—is never the cause of inflation.

QUICK REVIEW 18.2

- In the short run, demand-pull inflation raises both the price level and real output; in the long run, nominal wages rise, the short-run aggregate supply curve shifts to the left, and only the price level increases.
- Cost-push inflation creates a policy dilemma for the government: If it engages in an expansionary policy to increase output, additional inflation will occur; if it does nothing, the recession will linger until input prices have fallen by enough to return the economy to producing at potential output.
- In the short run, a decline in aggregate demand reduces real output (creates a recession); in the long run, prices and nominal wages presumably fall, the short-run aggregate supply curve shifts to the right, and real output returns to its full-employment level.
- The economy has ongoing inflation because the Fed uses monetary policy to shift the AD curve to the right faster than the supply factors of economic growth shift the long-run AS curve to the right.

The Inflation-Unemployment Relationship

We have just seen that the Fed can determine how much inflation occurs in the economy by how much it causes aggregate demand to shift relative to aggregate supply. Given that low inflation and low unemployment rates are the Fed's major economic goals, its ability to control inflation

FIGURE 18.8 The Phillips Curve: concept and empirical data. (a) The Phillips Curve relates annual rates of inflation and annual rates of unemployment for a series of years. Because this is an inverse relationship, there presumably is a trade-off between unemployment and inflation. (b) Data points for the 1960s seemed to confirm the Phillips Curve concept. (Note: The unemployment rates are annual averages and the inflation rates are on a December-to-December basis.)

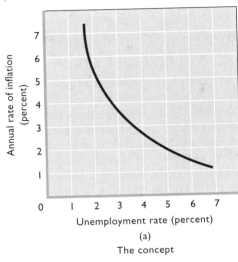

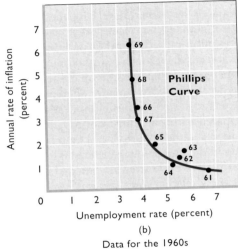

(a)
The concept

(b)
Data for the 1960s

Source: Bureau of Labor Statistics, **www.bls.gov**.

brings up at least two interesting policy questions: Are low unemployment and low inflation compatible goals or conflicting goals? What explains situations in which high unemployment and high inflation coexist?

The extended AD-AS model supports three significant generalizations relating to these questions:

- Under normal circumstances, there is a short-run trade-off between the rate of inflation and the rate of unemployment.
- Aggregate supply shocks can cause both higher rates of inflation and higher rates of unemployment.
- There is no significant trade-off between inflation and unemployment over long periods of time.
  Let's examine each of these generalizations.

The Phillips Curve

We can demonstrate the short-run trade-off between the rate of inflation and the rate of unemployment through the

Phillips Curve, named after A. W. Phillips, who developed the idea in Great Britain. This curve, generalized in Figure 18.8a, suggests an inverse relationship between the rate of inflation and the rate of unemployment. Lower unemployment rates (measured as leftward movements on the horizontal axis) are associated with higher rates of inflation (measured as upward movements on the vertical axis).

FIGURE 18.9 The short-run effect of changes in aggregate demand on real output and the price level. Comparing the effects of various possible increases in aggregate demand leads to the conclusion that the larger the increase in aggregate demand, the higher the rate of inflation and the greater the increase in real output. Because real output and the unemployment rate move in opposite directions, we can generalize that, given short-run aggregate supply, high rates of inflation should be accompanied by low rates of unemployment.

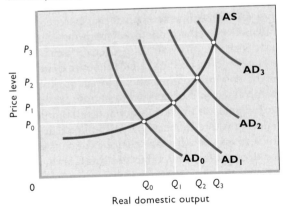

The underlying rationale of the Phillips Curve becomes apparent when we view the short-run aggregate supply curve in Figure 18.9 and perform a simple mental experiment. Suppose that in some short-run period aggregate demand expands from AD_0 to AD_2, either because firms decide to buy more capital goods or the government decides to increase its expenditures. Whatever the cause, in the short run the price level rises from P_0 to P_2 and real output rises from Q_0 to Q_2. As real output rises, the unemployment rate falls.

Now let's compare what would have happened if the increase in aggregate demand had been larger, say, from AD_0 to AD_3. The equilibrium at P_3 and Q_3 indicates that the amount of inflation and the growth of real output would both have been greater (and that the unemployment rate would have been lower). Similarly, suppose aggregate demand during the year had increased only modestly, from AD_0 to AD_1. Compared with our shift from AD_0 to AD_2, the amount of inflation and the growth of real output would have been smaller (and the unemployment rate higher).

The generalization we draw from this mental experiment is this: *Assuming a constant short-run aggregate supply curve*, high rates of inflation are accompanied by low rates of unemployment, and low rates of inflation are accompanied by high rates of unemployment. Other things equal, the expected relationship should look something like Figure 18.8a.

Figure 18.8b reveals that the facts for the 1960s nicely fit the theory. On the basis of that evidence and evidence from other countries, most economists working at the end of the 1960s concluded there was a stable, predictable trade-off between unemployment and inflation. Moreover, U.S. economic policy was built on that supposed trade-off. According to this thinking, it was impossible to achieve "full employment without inflation": Manipulation of aggregate demand through fiscal and monetary measures would simply move the economy along the Phillips Curve. An expansionary fiscal and monetary policy that boosted aggregate demand and lowered the unemployment rate would simultaneously increase inflation. A restrictive fiscal and monetary policy could be used to reduce the rate of inflation but only at the cost of a higher unemployment rate and more forgone production. Society had to choose between the incompatible goals of price stability and full employment; it had to decide where to locate on its Phillips Curve.

For reasons we will soon see, today's economists reject the idea of a stable, predictable Phillips Curve. Nevertheless, they agree there is a short-run trade-off between unemployment and inflation. *Given short-run aggregate supply*, increases in aggregate demand increase real output and reduce the unemployment rate. As the unemployment rate falls and dips below the natural rate, the excessive spending produces demand-pull inflation. Conversely, when recession sets in and the unemployment rate increases, the weak aggregate demand that caused the recession also leads to lower inflation rates.

Periods of exceptionally low unemployment rates and inflation rates do occur, but only under special sets of economic circumstances. One such period was the late 1990s, when faster productivity growth increased aggregate supply and fully blunted the inflationary impact of rapidly rising aggregate demand (review Figure 12.11).

Aggregate Supply Shocks and the Phillips Curve

The unemployment-inflation experience of the 1970s and early 1980s demolished the idea of an always-stable Phillips Curve. In Figure 18.10 we show the Phillips Curve for the 1960s in blue and then add the data points for 1970 through 2009. Observe that in most of the years of the 1970s and early 1980s, the economy experienced both higher inflation rates and higher unemployment rates than it did in the 1960s. In fact, inflation and unemployment rose simultaneously in some of those years. This condition is called **stagflation**—a media term that combines the words "stagnation" and "inflation." If there still was any such thing as a Phillips Curve, it had clearly shifted outward, perhaps as shown.

Adverse Aggregate Supply Shocks The data points for the 1970s and early 1980s support our second generalization: Aggregate supply shocks can cause both higher rates of inflation and higher rates of unemployment. A series of adverse **aggregate supply shocks**—sudden, large increases in resource costs that jolt an economy's short-run aggregate supply curve leftward—hit the economy in the 1970s and early 1980s. The most significant of these shocks was a quadrupling of oil prices by the Organization of Petroleum Exporting Countries (OPEC). Consequently, the cost of producing and distributing virtually every product and service rose rapidly. (Other factors working to increase U.S. costs during this period included major agricultural shortfalls, a greatly depreciated dollar, wage hikes previously held down by wage-price controls, and slower rates of productivity growth.)

These shocks shifted the aggregate supply curve to the left and distorted the usual inflation-unemployment relationship. Remember that we derived the inverse relationship between the rate of inflation and the unemployment rate shown in Figure 18.8a by shifting the aggregate demand curve along a stable short-run aggregate supply curve (Figure 18.9). But the cost-push inflation model shown in Figure 18.4 tells us that a *leftward shift* of the short-run aggregate supply curve increases the price level and reduces real output (and increases the unemployment rate). This, say most economists, is what happened in two periods in the 1970s. The U.S. unemployment rate shot up from 4.9 percent in 1973 to 8.5 percent in 1975,

FIGURE 18.10 Inflation rates and unemployment rates, 1960–2009. A series of aggregate supply shocks in the 1970s resulted in higher rates of inflation *and* higher rates of unemployment. So data points for the 1970s and 1980s tended to be above and to the right of the blue Phillips Curve for the 1960s. In the 1990s the inflation-unemployment data points slowly moved back toward the 1960s Phillips Curve. Points for the late 1990s and 2000s are similar to those from the 1960s. (Note: The unemployment rates are annual averages and the inflation rates are on a December-to-December basis.)

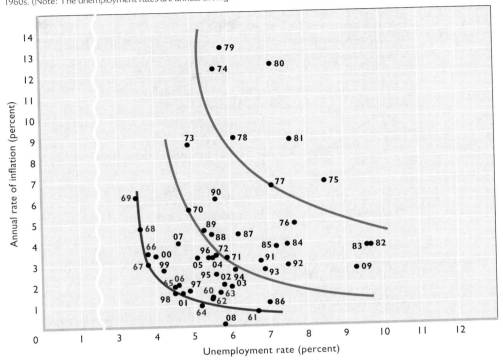

Source: Bureau of Labor Statistics, **www.bls.gov**.

contributing to a significant decline in real GDP. In the same period, the U.S. price level rose by 21 percent. The stagflation scenario recurred in 1978, when OPEC increased oil prices by more than 100 percent. The U.S. price level rose by 26 percent over the 1978–1980 period, while unemployment increased from 6.1 to 7.1 percent.

Stagflation's Demise Another look at Figure 18.10 reveals a generally inward movement of the inflation-unemployment points between 1982 and 1989. By 1989 the lingering effects of the earlier period had subsided. One precursor to this favorable trend was the deep recession of 1981–1982, largely caused by a restrictive monetary policy aimed at reducing double-digit inflation. The recession upped the unemployment rate to 9.5 percent in 1982. With so many workers unemployed, those who were working accepted smaller increases in their nominal wages—or, in some cases, wage reductions—in order to preserve their jobs. Firms, in turn, restrained their price increases to try to retain their relative shares of a greatly diminished market.

Other factors were at work. Foreign competition throughout this period held down wage and price hikes in several basic industries such as automobiles and steel. Deregulation of the airline and trucking industries also resulted in wage reductions or so-called wage givebacks. A significant decline in OPEC's monopoly power and a greatly reduced reliance on oil in the production process produced a stunning fall in the price of oil and its derivative products, such as gasoline.

All these factors combined to reduce per-unit production costs and to shift the short-run aggregate supply curve rightward (as from AS_2 to AS_1 in Figure 18.4). Employment and output expanded, and the unemployment rate fell from 9.6 percent in 1983 to 5.3 percent in 1989. Figure 18.10 reveals that the inflation-unemployment points for recent years are closer to the points associated with the Phillips Curve of the 1960s than to the points in the late 1970s and early 1980s. Even the recession of 2007–2009 did not greatly alter the recent inflation rate–unemployment rate pattern. In 2008, the unemployment rate was 5.8 percent, but the inflation rate was near zero at just 0.1 percent. The

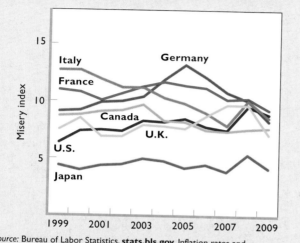

GLOBAL PERSPECTIVE 18.1

The Misery Index, Selected Nations, 1999–2009

The U.S. misery index number (the sum of its unemployment rate and inflation rate) has generally been in the midrange of such numbers relative to other major economies in recent years.

Source: Bureau of Labor Statistics, **stats.bls.gov**. Inflation rates and unemployment rates in this calculation are both on an average-annual basis.

these circumstances causes a huge loss of national output and income (and misery!), even if the higher unemployment rate is partially or fully offset with a decline in the rate of inflation.

The Long-Run Phillips Curve

The overall set of data points in Figure 18.10 supports our third generalization relating to the inflation-unemployment relationship: There is no apparent *long-run* trade-off between inflation and unemployment. Economists point out that when decades as opposed to a few years are considered, any rate of inflation is consistent with the natural rate of unemployment prevailing at that time. We know from Chapter 9 that the natural rate of unemployment is the unemployment rate that occurs when cyclical unemployment is zero; it is the full-employment rate of unemployment, or the rate of unemployment when the economy achieves its potential output.

How can there be a short-run inflation-unemployment trade-off but not a long-run trade-off? Figure 18.11 provides the answer.

inflation-unemployment point for 2009, however, moved up and to the right relative to the point for 2008. In 2009 unemployment was 9.3 percent, while the inflation rate on a December-to-December basis was 2.7 percent.

The media sometimes express the sum of the unemployment rate and the inflation rate as a rough gauge of the economic discomfort that inflation and unemployment jointly impose on an economy in a particular year. The sum of the two rates is used to compute the *misery index*. For example, a nation with a 5 percent unemployment rate and a 5 percent inflation rate has a misery index number of 10, as does a nation with an 8 percent unemployment rate and a 2 percent inflation rate.

Global Perspective 18.1 shows the misery index for several nations between 1999 and 2009. (It uses average annual inflation rates, not the December-to-December inflation rates used to construct Figure 18.10.) The U.S. misery index number has been neither exceptionally low nor exceptionally high relative to the misery index numbers for the other major economies shown. But bear in mind that economists do not put much stock in the misery index because they do not view the national discomfort associated with a 1 percent change in inflation and a 1 percent change in unemployment as necessarily equivalent. In particular, the misery index can greatly disguise the extent of hardship during a recession. The rise in the unemployment rate in

FIGURE 18.11 The long-run vertical Phillips Curve. Increases in aggregate demand beyond those consistent with full-employment output may temporarily boost profits, output, and employment (as from a_1 to b_1). But nominal wages eventually will catch up so as to sustain real wages. When they do, profits will fall, negating the previous short-run stimulus to production and employment (the economy now moves from b_1 to a_2). Consequently, there is no trade-off between the rates of inflation and unemployment in the long run; that is, the long-run Phillips Curve is roughly a vertical line at the economy's natural rate of unemployment.

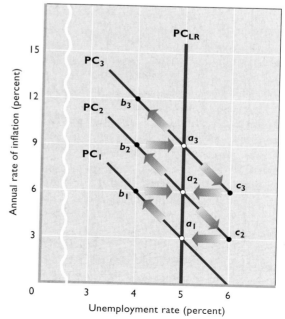

Short-Run Phillips Curve

Consider Phillips Curve PC$_1$ in Figure 18.11. Suppose the economy initially is experiencing a 3 percent rate of inflation and a 5 percent natural rate of unemployment. Such short-term curves as PC$_1$, PC$_2$, and PC$_3$ (drawn as straight lines for simplicity) exist because the actual rate of inflation is not always the same as the expected rate.

Establishing an additional point on Phillips Curve PC$_1$ will clarify this. We begin at a_1, where we assume nominal wages are set on the assumption that the 3 percent rate of inflation will continue. That is, because workers expect output prices to rise by 3 percent per year, they negotiate wage contracts that feature 3 percent per year increases in nominal wages so that these nominal wage increases will exactly offset the expected rise in prices and thereby keep their real wages the same.

But suppose that the rate of inflation rises to 6 percent, perhaps because the Fed has decided to move the AD curve to the right even faster than it had been before. With a nominal wage rate set on the expectation that the 3 percent rate of inflation will continue, the higher product prices raise business profits. Firms respond to the higher profits by hiring more workers and increasing output. In the short run, the economy moves to b_1, which, in contrast to a_1, involves a lower rate of unemployment (4 percent) and a higher rate of inflation (6 percent). The move from a_1 to b_1 is consistent both with an upsloping aggregate supply curve and with the inflation-unemployment trade-off implied by the Phillips Curve analysis. But this short-run Phillips Curve simply is a manifestation of the following principle: *When the actual rate of inflation is higher than expected, profits temporarily rise and the unemployment rate temporarily falls.*

Long-Run Vertical Phillips Curve

But point b_1 is not a stable equilibrium. Workers will recognize that their nominal wages have not increased as fast as inflation and will therefore renegotiate their labor contracts so that they feature faster increases in nominal wages. These faster increases in nominal wages make up for the higher rate of inflation and restore the workers' lost purchasing power. As these new labor contracts kick in, business profits will fall to their prior level. The reduction in profits means that the original motivation to employ more workers and increase output has disappeared.

Unemployment then returns to its natural level at point a_2. Note, however, that the economy now faces a higher actual and expected rate of inflation—6 percent rather than 3 percent. This happens because the new labor contracts feature 6 percent per year increases in wages to make up for the 6 percent per year inflation rate. Because

wages are a production cost, this faster increase in wage rates will imply faster future increases in output prices as firms are forced to raise prices more rapidly to make up for the faster future rate of wage growth. Stated a bit differently, the initial increase in inflation will become *persistent* because it leads to renegotiated labor contracts that will perpetuate the higher rate of inflation. In addition, because the new labor contracts are public, it will also be the case that the higher rates of inflation that they will cause will be *expected* by everyone rather than being a surprise.

In view of the higher 6 percent expected rate of inflation, the short-run Phillips Curve shifts upward from PC$_1$ to PC$_2$ in Figure 18.11. An "along-the-Phillips-Curve" kind of move from a_1 to b_1 on PC$_1$ is merely a short-run or transient occurrence. In the long run, after nominal wage contracts catch up with increases in the inflation rate, unemployment returns to its natural rate at a_2, and there is a new short-run Phillips Curve PC$_2$ at the higher expected rate of inflation.

The scenario repeats if aggregate demand continues to increase. Prices rise momentarily ahead of nominal wages, profits expand, and employment and output increase (as implied by the move from a_2 to b_2). But, in time, nominal wages increase so as to restore real wages. Profits then fall to their original level, pushing employment back to the normal rate at a_3. The economy's "reward" for lowering the unemployment rate below the natural rate is a still higher (9 percent) rate of inflation.

Movements along the short-run Phillips curve (a_1 to b_1 on PC$_1$) cause the curve to shift to a less favorable position (PC$_2$, then PC$_3$, and so on). A stable Phillips Curve with the dependable series of unemployment-rate–inflation-rate trade-offs simply does not exist in the long run. The economy is characterized by a **long-run vertical Phillips Curve.**

The vertical line through a_1, a_2, and a_3 shows the long-run relationship between unemployment and inflation. Any rate of inflation is consistent with the 5 percent natural rate of unemployment. So, in this view, society ought to choose a low rate of inflation rather than a high one.

ORIGIN OF THE IDEA

O 18.2

Long-run vertical
Phillips Curve

Disinflation

The distinction between the short-run Phillips Curve and the long-run Phillips Curve also helps explain **disinflation**—reductions in the inflation rate from year to year. Suppose that in Figure 18.11 the economy is at a_3, where the inflation rate is 9 percent. And suppose that a decline in the rate at which aggregate demand shifts to the right faster than aggregate supply (as happened during the 1981–1982 recession) reduces inflation below the 9 percent expected rate, say, to 6 percent. Business profits fall because prices are rising less rapidly than wages. The nominal wage increases, remember, were set on the assumption that the 9 percent rate of inflation would continue. In response to the decline in profits, firms reduce their employment and consequently the unemployment rate rises. The economy temporarily slides downward from point a_3 to c_3 along the short-run Phillips Curve PC_3. *When the actual rate of inflation is lower than the expected rate, profits temporarily fall and the unemployment rate temporarily rises.*

Firms and workers eventually adjust their expectations to the new 6 percent rate of inflation, and thus newly negotiated wage increases decline. Profits are restored, employment rises, and the unemployment rate falls back to its natural rate of 5 percent at a_2. Because the expected rate of inflation is now 6 percent, the short-run Phillips Curve PC_3 shifts leftward to PC_2.

If the rate at which aggregate demand shifts to the right faster than aggregate supply declines even more, the scenario will continue. Inflation declines from 6 percent to, say, 3 percent, moving the economy from a_2 to c_2 along PC_2. The lower-than-expected rate of inflation (lower prices) squeezes profits and reduces employment. But, in the long run, firms respond to the lower profits by reducing their nominal wage increases. Profits are restored and unemployment returns to its natural rate at a_1 as the short-run Phillips Curve moves from PC_2 to PC_1. Once again, the long-run Phillips Curve is vertical at the 5 percent natural rate of unemployment.

QUICK REVIEW 18.3

- As implied by the upsloping short-run aggregate supply curve, there may be a short-run trade-off between the rate of inflation and the rate of unemployment. This trade-off is reflected in the Phillips Curve, which shows that lower rates of inflation are associated with higher rates of unemployment.

- Aggregate supply shocks that produce severe cost-push inflation can cause stagflation—simultaneous increases in the inflation rate and the unemployment rate. Such stagflation occurred from 1973–1975 and recurred from 1978–1980, producing Phillips Curve data points above and to the right of the Phillips Curve for the 1960s.

- After all nominal wage adjustments to increases and decreases in the rate of inflation have occurred, the economy ends up back at its full-employment level of output and its natural rate of unemployment. The long-run Phillips Curve therefore is vertical at the natural rate of unemployment.

Taxation and Aggregate Supply

A final topic in our discussion of aggregate supply is taxation, a key aspect of **supply-side economics.** "Supply-side economists" or "supply-siders" stress that changes in aggregate supply are an active force in determining the levels of inflation, unemployment, and economic growth. Government policies can either impede or promote rightward shifts of the short-run and long-run aggregate supply curves shown in Figure 18.2. One such policy is taxation.

These economists say that the enlargement of the U.S. tax system has impaired incentives to work, save, and invest. In this view, high tax rates impede productivity growth and hence slow the expansion of long-run aggregate supply. By reducing the after-tax rewards of workers and producers, high tax rates reduce the financial attractiveness of working, saving, and investing.

Supply-siders focus their attention on *marginal tax rates*—the rates on extra dollars of income—because those rates affect the benefits from working, saving, or investing more. In 2010 marginal tax rates varied from 10 to 35 percent in the United States.

Taxes and Incentives to Work

Supply-siders believe that how long and how hard people work depends on the amounts of additional after-tax earnings they derive from their efforts. They say that lower marginal tax rates on earned incomes induce more work, and therefore increase aggregate inputs of labor. Lower marginal tax rates increase the after-tax wage rate and make leisure more expensive and work more attractive. The higher opportunity cost of leisure encourages people to substitute work for leisure. This increase in productive effort is achieved in many ways: by increasing the number of hours worked per day or week, by encouraging workers to postpone retirement, by inducing more people to enter the labor force, by motivating people to work harder, and by avoiding long periods of unemployment.

Incentives to Save and Invest

High marginal tax rates also reduce the rewards for saving and investing. For example, suppose that Tony saves $10,000 at 8 percent interest, bringing him $800 of interest per year. If his marginal tax rate is 40 percent, his after-tax interest earnings will be $480, not $800, and his after-tax interest rate will fall to 4.8 percent. While Tony might be willing to save (forgo current consumption) for an 8 percent return on his saving, he might rather consume when the return is only 4.8 percent.

Saving, remember, is the prerequisite of investment. Thus, supply-side economists recommend lower marginal tax rates on interest earned from saving. They also call for lower taxes on income from capital to ensure that there are ready investment outlets for the economy's enhanced pool of saving. A critical determinant of investment spending is the expected *after-tax* return on that spending.

To summarize: Lower marginal tax rates encourage saving and investing. Workers therefore find themselves equipped with more and technologically superior machinery and equipment. Labor productivity rises, and that expands long-run aggregate supply and economic growth, which in turn keeps unemployment rates and inflation low.

The Laffer Curve

In the supply-side view, reductions in marginal tax rates increase the nation's aggregate supply and can leave the nation's tax revenues unchanged or even enlarge them. Thus, supply-side tax cuts need not produce Federal budget deficits.

This idea is based on the **Laffer Curve,** named after Arthur Laffer, who popularized it. As Figure 18.12 shows, the Laffer Curve depicts the relationship between tax rates and tax revenues. As tax rates increase from 0 to 100 percent, tax revenues increase from zero to some maximum level (at *m*) and then fall to zero. Tax revenues decline beyond some point because higher tax rates discourage economic activity, thereby shrinking the tax base (domestic output and income). This is easiest to see at the extreme, where the tax rate is 100 percent. Tax revenues here are, in theory, reduced to zero because the 100 percent confiscatory tax rate has halted production. A 100 percent tax rate applied to a tax base of zero yields no revenue.

In the early 1980s, Laffer suggested that the United States was at a point such as *n* on the curve in Figure 18.12.

At *n*, tax rates are so high that production is discouraged to the extent that tax revenues are below the maximum at *m*. If the economy is at *n*, then lower tax rates can either increase tax revenues or leave them unchanged. For example, lowering the tax rate from point *n* to point *l* would bolster the economy such that the government would bring in the same total amount of tax revenue as before.

Laffer's reasoning was that lower tax rates stimulate incentives to work, save and invest, innovate, and accept business risks, thus triggering an expansion of real output and income. That enlarged tax base sustains tax revenues even though tax rates are lowered. Indeed, between *n* and *m* lower tax rates result in *increased* tax revenue.

Also, when taxes are lowered, tax avoidance (which is legal) and tax evasion (which is not) decline. High marginal tax rates prompt taxpayers to avoid taxes through various tax shelters, such as buying municipal bonds, on which the interest earned is tax-free. High rates also encourage some taxpayers to conceal income from the Internal Revenue Service. Lower tax rates reduce the inclination to engage in either tax avoidance or tax evasion.

Criticisms of the Laffer Curve

The Laffer Curve and its supply-side implications have been subject to severe criticism.

Taxes, Incentives, and Time A fundamental criticism relates to the degree to which economic incentives are sensitive to changes in tax rates. Skeptics say ample empirical evidence shows that the impact of a tax cut on incentives is small, of uncertain direction, and relatively slow to emerge. For example, with respect to work incentives, studies indicate that decreases in tax rates lead some people to work more but lead others to work less. Those who work more are enticed by the higher after-tax pay; they substitute work for leisure because the opportunity cost of leisure has increased. But other people work less because the higher after-tax pay enables them to "buy more leisure." With the tax cut, they can earn the same level of after-tax income as before with fewer work hours.

Inflation or Higher Real Interest Rates Most economists think that the demand-side effects of a tax cut are more immediate and certain than longer-term supply-side effects. Thus, tax cuts undertaken when the economy is at or near full employment may produce increases in aggregate demand that overwhelm any increase in aggregate supply. The likely result is inflation or restrictive monetary policy to prevent it. If the latter, real interest rates will rise and investment will decline. This will defeat the purpose of the supply-side tax cuts.

FIGURE 18.12 The Laffer Curve. The Laffer Curve suggests that up to point *m* higher tax rates will result in larger tax revenues. But tax rates higher than *m* will adversely affect incentives to work and produce, reducing the size of the tax base (output and income) to the extent that tax revenues will decline. It follows that if tax rates are above *m*, reductions in tax rates will produce increases in tax revenues.

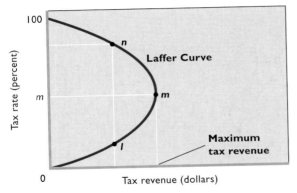

CONSIDER THIS . . .

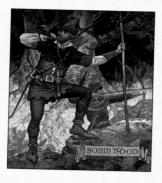

Sherwood Forest

The popularization of the idea that tax-rate reductions may increase tax revenues owes much to Arthur Laffer's ability to present his ideas simply. In explaining his thoughts to a *Wall Street Journal* editor over lunch, Laffer reportedly took out his pen and drew the curve on a napkin. The editor retained the napkin and later reproduced the curve in an editorial in *The Wall Street Journal*. The Laffer Curve was born. The idea it portrayed became the centerpiece of economic policy under the Reagan administration (1981–1989), which cut tax rates on personal income by 25 percent over a 3-year period.

Laffer illustrated his supply-side views with a story relating to Robin Hood, who, you may recall, stole from the rich to give to the poor. Laffer likened people traveling through Sherwood Forest to taxpayers, whereas Robin Hood and his band of merry men were government. As taxpayers passed through the forest, Robin Hood and his men intercepted them and forced them to hand over their money. Laffer asked audiences, "Do you think that travelers continued to go through Sherwood Forest?"

The answer he sought and got, of course, was "no." Taxpayers will avoid Sherwood Forest to the greatest extent possible. They will lower their taxable income by reducing work hours, retiring earlier, saving less, and engaging in tax avoidance and tax evasion activities. Robin Hood and his men may end up with less revenue than if they collected a relatively small "tax" from each traveler for passage through the forest.

Position on the Curve Skeptics say that the Laffer Curve is merely a logical proposition and assert that there must be some level of tax rates between 0 and 100 percent at which tax revenues will be at their maximum. Economists of all persuasions can agree with this. But the issue of where a particular economy is located on its Laffer Curve is an empirical question. If we assume that we are at point *n* in Figure 18.12, then tax cuts will increase tax revenues. But if the economy is at any point below *m* on the curve, tax-rate reductions will reduce tax revenues.

Rebuttal and Evaluation

Supply-side advocates respond to the skeptics by contending that the Reagan tax cuts in the 1980s worked as Laffer predicted. Although the top marginal income tax rates on earned income were cut from 50 to 28 percent in that de-

cade, real GDP and tax revenues were substantially higher at the end of the 1990s than at the beginning.

But the general view among economists is that the Reagan tax cuts, coming at a time of severe recession, helped boost aggregate demand and return real GDP to its full-employment output and normal growth path. As the economy expanded, so did tax revenues despite the lower tax rates. The rise in tax revenues caused by economic growth swamped the declines in revenues from lower tax rates. In essence, the Laffer Curve shown in Figure 18.12 stretched rightward, increasing net tax revenues. But the tax-rate cuts did not produce extraordinary rightward shifts of the long-run aggregate supply curve. Indeed, saving fell as a percentage of personal income during the period and productivity growth was sluggish. Real GDP sprang back vigorously from recessionary levels, but the economic growth rate soon reverted back to its longer-term average.

Because government expenditures rose more rapidly than tax revenues in the 1980s, large budget deficits occurred. In 1993 the Clinton administration increased the top marginal tax rates from 31 to 39.6 percent to address these deficits. The economy boomed in the last half of the 1990s, and by the end of the decade tax revenues were so high relative to government expenditures that budget surpluses emerged. In 2001 the Bush administration reduced marginal tax rates over a series of years, partially "to return excess revenues to taxpayers." In 2003 the top marginal tax rate fell to 35 percent. Also, the income tax rates on capital gains and dividends were reduced to 15 percent. Economists generally agree that the Bush tax cuts, along with a highly expansionary monetary policy, helped revive and expand the economy following the recession of 2001. Strong growth of output and income in 2004 and 2005 produced large increases in tax revenues, although large budget deficits remained because spending also increased rapidly. The 2004 deficit was $413 billion and the 2005 deficit was $318 billion. The deficit fell over the next two years, to $162 billion in 2007. But the previously discussed financial crisis plunged the economy into a severe recession beginning in December 2007 and lasting into 2009. That caused income to fall and tax revenues to plummet. Also, the government implemented highly expansionary fiscal policy. Budget deficits increased to $459 billion in 2008 and $1.4 trillion in 2009.

Today, there is general agreement that the U.S. economy is operating at a point below *m*—rather than above *m*—on the Laffer Curve in Figure 18.12. In this zone, the overall effect is that personal tax-rate increases raise tax revenues while personal tax-rate decreases reduce tax revenues. But at the same time, economists recognize that other things being equal, cuts in tax rates reduce tax revenues in

LAST Word Do Tax Increases Reduce Real GDP?*

Determining the Relationship Between Changes in Taxes and Permanent Changes in Real GDP is Fraught with Complexities and Difficulties. University of California-Berkeley Economists Christina Romer and David Romer have Recently Devised a Novel Way to Approach the Topic. Their Findings Suggest That Tax Increases Reduce Real GDP.[†]

How do changes in the level of taxation affect the level of economic activity? The simple correlation between taxation and economic activity shows that, on average, when economic activity rises more rapidly, tax revenues also are rising more rapidly. But this correlation almost surely does not reflect a positive effect of tax increases on output. Rather, under our tax system, any positive shock to output raises tax revenues by increasing income.

In "The Macroeconomic Effects of Tax Changes: Estimates Based on a New Measure of Fiscal Shocks," authors Christina Romer and David Romer observe that this difficulty is just one of many manifestations of a more general problem. Changes in taxes occur for many reasons. And, because the factors that give rise to tax changes often are correlated with other developments in the economy, disentangling the effects of the tax changes from the other effects of these underlying factors is inherently difficult.

To address this problem, Romer and Romer use the narrative record—presidential speeches, executive branch documents, congressional reports, and so on—to identify the size, timing, and principal motivation for all major tax policy actions in the post-World War II United States. This narrative analysis allows them to separate revenue changes resulting from legislation from changes occurring for other reasons. It also allows them to classify legislated changes according to their primary motivation.

Romer and Romer find that despite the complexity of the legislative process, most significant tax changes have been motivated by one of four factors: counteracting other influences in the economy; paying for increases in government spending (or lowering taxes in conjunction with reductions in spending); addressing an inherited budget deficit; and promoting long-run growth. They observe that legislated tax changes taken to counteract other influences on the economy, or to pay for increases in government spending, are very likely to be correlated with other factors affecting the economy. As a result these observations are likely to lead to unreliable estimates of the effect of tax changes.

Tax changes that are made to promote long-run growth, or to reduce an inherited budget deficit, in contrast, are undertaken for reasons essentially unrelated to other factors influencing output. Thus, examining the behavior of output following these tax changes is likely to provide more reliable estimates of the output effects of tax changes. *The results of this more reliable test indicate that tax changes have very large effects: a tax increase of 1 percent of GDP lowers real GDP by roughly 2 to 3 percent.*

These output effects are highly persistent. The behavior of inflation and unemployment suggests that this persistence reflects long-lasting departures of output from previous levels. Romer and Romer also find that output effects of tax changes are much more closely tied to the actual changes in taxes than news about future changes, and that investment falls sharply in response to tax changes. Indeed, the strong response of investment helps to explain why the output consequences of tax increases are so large.

Romer and Romer find suggestive evidence that tax increases to reduce an inherited budget deficit have much smaller output costs than other tax increases. This is consistent with the idea that deficit-driven tax increases may have important expansionary effects through [improved] expectations and [lower] long-term interest rates, or through [enhanced] confidence.

*Abridged from Les Picker, "Tax Increases Reduce GDP," *The NBER Digest*, February/March 2008. The *Digest* provides synopses of research papers in progress by economists affiliated with the National Bureau of Economic Research (NBER).

[†]Christina Romer and David Romer, "The Macroeconomic Effects of Tax Changes: Estimates Based on a New Measure of Fiscal Shocks," *American Economic Review*, June 2010, pp. 763-801.

percentage terms by less than the tax-rate reductions. Similarly, tax-rate increases do not raise tax revenues by as much in percentage terms as the tax-rate increases. This is true because changes in marginal tax rates alter taxpayer behavior and thus affect taxable income. Although these effects seem to be relatively modest, they need to be considered in designing tax policy—and, in fact, the Federal government's Office of Tax Policy created a special division in 2007 devoted to estimating the magnitude of such effects when it comes to proposed changes in U.S. tax laws. Thus, supply-side economics has contributed to how economists and policymakers design and implement fiscal policy.

Summary

1. In macroeconomics, the short run is a period in which nominal wages do not respond to changes in the price level. In contrast, the long run is a period in which nominal wages fully respond to changes in the price level.

2. The short-run aggregate supply curve is upsloping. Because nominal wages are unresponsive to price-level changes, increases in the price level (prices received by firms) increase profits and real output. Conversely, decreases in the price level reduce profits and real output. However, the long-run aggregate supply curve is vertical. With sufficient time for adjustment, nominal wages rise and fall with the price level, moving the economy along a vertical aggregate supply curve at the economy's full-employment output.

3. In the short run, demand-pull inflation raises the price level and real output. Once nominal wages rise to match the increase in the price level, the temporary increase in real output is reversed.

4. In the short run, cost-push inflation raises the price level and lowers real output. Unless the government expands aggregate demand, nominal wages will eventually decline under conditions of recession and the short-run aggregate supply curve will shift back to its initial location. Prices and real output will eventually return to their original levels.

5. If prices and wages are flexible downward, a decline in aggregate demand will lower output and the price level. The decline in the price level will eventually lower nominal wages and shift the short-run aggregate supply curve rightward. Full-employment output will thus be restored.

6. One-time changes in AD and AS can only cause limited bouts of inflation. Ongoing mild inflation occurs because the Fed purposely increases AD slightly faster than the expansion of long-run AS (driven by the supply factors of economic growth).

7. Assuming a stable, upsloping short-run aggregate supply curve, rightward shifts of the aggregate demand curve of various sizes yield the generalization that high rates of inflation are associated with low rates of unemployment, and vice versa. This inverse relationship is known as the Phillips Curve, and empirical data for the 1960s seemed to be consistent with it.

8. In the 1970s and early 1980s the Phillips Curve apparently shifted rightward, reflecting stagflation—simultaneously rising inflation rates and unemployment rates. The higher unemployment rates and inflation rates resulted mainly from huge oil price increases that caused large leftward shifts in the short-run aggregate supply curve (so-called aggregate supply shocks). The Phillips Curve shifted inward toward its original position in the 1980s. By 1989 stagflation had subsided, and the data points for the late 1990s and first half of the first decade of the 2000s were similar to those of the 1960s. The new pattern continued until 2009, when the unemployment rate jumped to 9.3 percent and the inflation rate rose on a December-to-December basis to 2.7 percent.

9. Although there is a short-run trade-off between inflation and unemployment, there is no long-run trade-off. Workers will adapt their expectations to new inflation realities, and when they do, the unemployment rate will return to the natural rate. So the long-run Phillips Curve is vertical at the natural rate, meaning that higher rates of inflation do not permanently "buy" the economy less unemployment.

10. Supply-side economists focus attention on government policies, such as high taxation, that impede the expansion of aggregate supply. The Laffer Curve relates tax rates to levels of tax revenue and suggests that under some circumstances, cuts in tax rates will expand the tax base (output and income) and increase tax revenues. Most economists, however, believe that the United States is currently operating in the range of the Laffer Curve where tax rates and tax revenues move in the same, not opposite, directions.

11. Today's economists recognize the importance of considering supply-side effects in designing optimal fiscal policy.

Terms and Concepts

short run
long run
Phillips Curve

stagflation
aggregate supply shocks
long-run vertical Phillips Curve

disinflation
supply-side economics
Laffer Curve

Questions

1. Distinguish between the short run and the long run as they relate to macroeconomics. Why is the distinction important? **LO1**

2. Which of the following statements are true? Which are false? Explain why the false statements are untrue. **LO1**
   a. Short-run aggregate supply curves reflect an inverse relationship between the price level and the level of real output.
   b. The long-run aggregate supply curve assumes that nominal wages are fixed.
   c. In the long run, an increase in the price level will result in an increase in nominal wages.

3. Suppose the full-employment level of real output (Q) for a hypothetical economy is $250 and the price level (P) initially is 100. Use the short-run aggregate supply schedules below to answer the questions that follow: **LO1**

AS (P_{100})		AS (P_{125})		AS (P_{75})	
P	**Q**	**P**	**Q**	**P**	**Q**
125	$280	125	$250	125	$310
100	250	100	220	100	280
75	220	75	190	75	250

   a. What will be the level of real output in the short run if the price level unexpectedly rises from 100 to 125 because of an increase in aggregate demand? What if the price level unexpectedly falls from 100 to 75 because of a decrease in aggregate demand? Explain each situation, using numbers from the table.
   b. What will be the level of real output in the long run when the price level rises from 100 to 125? When it falls from 100 to 75? Explain each situation.
   c. Show the circumstances described in parts *a* and *b* on graph paper, and derive the long-run aggregate supply curve.

4. Use graphical analysis to show how each of the following would affect the economy first in the short run and then in the long run. Assume that the United States is initially operating at its full-employment level of output, that

prices and wages are eventually flexible both upward and downward, and that there is no counteracting fiscal or monetary policy. **LO2**
   a. Because of a war abroad, the oil supply to the United States is disrupted, sending oil prices rocketing upward.
   b. Construction spending on new homes rises dramatically, greatly increasing total U.S. investment spending.
   c. Economic recession occurs abroad, significantly reducing foreign purchases of U.S. exports.

5. Between 1990 and 2009, the U.S. price level rose by about 64 percent while real output increased by about 62 percent. Use the aggregate demand–aggregate supply model to illustrate these outcomes graphically. **LO2**

6. Assume there is a particular short-run aggregate supply curve for an economy and the curve is relevant for several years. Use the AD-AS analysis to show graphically why higher rates of inflation over this period would be associated with lower rates of unemployment, and vice versa. What is this inverse relationship called? **LO3**

7. Suppose the government misjudges the natural rate of unemployment to be much lower than it actually is, and thus undertakes expansionary fiscal and monetary policies to try to achieve the lower rate. Use the concept of the short-run Phillips Curve to explain why these policies might at first succeed. Use the concept of the long-run Phillips Curve to explain the long-run outcome of these policies. **LO4**

8. What do the distinctions between short-run aggregate supply and long-run aggregate supply have in common with the distinction between the short-run Phillips Curve and the long-run Phillips Curve? Explain. **LO4**

9. What is the Laffer Curve, and how does it relate to supply-side economics? Why is determining the economy's location on the curve so important in assessing tax policy? **LO5**

10. Why might one person work more, earn more, and pay more income tax when his or her tax rate is cut, while another person will work less, earn less, and pay less income tax under the same circumstance? **LO5**

11. **LAST WORD** On average, does an increase in taxes raise or lower real GDP? If taxes as a percent of GDP go up 1 percent, by how much does real GDP change? Are the decreases in real GDP caused by tax increases temporary or permanent? Does the intention of a tax increase matter?

Problems

1. Use the figure on the next page to answer the following questions. Assume that the economy initially is operating at price level 120 and real output level $870. This output level is the economy's potential (or full-employment) level of output. Next, suppose that the price level rises from 120 to 130. By how much will real output increase in the short run? In the long-run? Instead, now assume that the price level dropped from 120 to 110. Assuming flexible product and resource prices, by how much will real output fall in the short run? In the long run? What is the long-run level of output at each of the three price levels shown? **LO1**

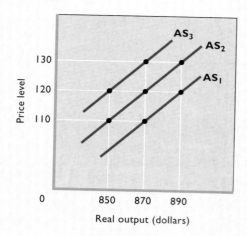

2. ADVANCED ANALYSIS Suppose that the equation for a particular short-run AS curve is $P = 20 + .5Q$, where P is the price level and Q is real output in dollar terms. What is Q if the price level is 120? Suppose that the Q in your answer is the full-employment level of output. By how much will Q increase *in the short run* if the price level unexpectedly rises from 120 to 132? By how much will Q increase *in the long run* due to the price level increase? **LO1**

3. Suppose that over a 30-year period Buskerville's price level increased from 72 to 138, while its real GDP rose from $1.2 trillion to $2.1 trillion. Did economic growth occur in Buskerville? If so, by what average yearly rate in percentage terms (rounded to one decimal place)? Did Buskerville experience inflation? If so, by what average yearly rate in percentage terms (rounded to one decimal place)? Which shifted rightward faster in Buskerville: its long-run aggregate supply curve (AS_{LR}) or its aggregate demand curve (AD)? **LO2**

4. Suppose that for years East Confetti's short-run Phillips Curve was such that each 1 percentage point increase in its unemployment rate was associated with a 2 percentage point decline in its inflation rate. Then, during several recent years, the short-run pattern changed such that its inflation rate rose by 3 percentage points for every 1 percentage point drop in its unemployment rate. Graphically, did East Confetti's Phillips Curve shift upward or did it shift downward? **LO3**

FURTHER TEST YOUR KNOWLEDGE AT
www.mcconnell19e.com

At the text's Online Learning Center (OLC), **www.mcconnell19e.com**, you will find one or more Web-based questions that require information from the Internet to answer. We urge you to check them out; they will familiarize you with Web sites that may be helpful in other courses and perhaps even in your career. The OLC also features multiple-choice questions that give instant feedback and provides other helpful ways to further test your knowledge of the chapter.

Current Issues in Macro Theory and Policy

As any academic discipline evolves, it naturally evokes a number of internal disagreements. Economics is no exception. In this chapter we examine a few alternative perspectives on macro theory and policy. We focus on the disagreements that various economists have about the answers to three interrelated questions: (1) What causes instability in the economy? (2) Is the economy self-correcting? (3) Should government adhere to *rules* or use *discretion* in setting economic policy?

What Causes Macro Instability?

As earlier chapters have indicated, capitalist economies experienced considerable instability during the twentieth century. The United States, for example, experienced the Great Depression, numerous recessions, and periods of inflation. This instability greatly moderated between the early 1980s and 2007, but then the deep recession of 2007–2009 occurred. Economists have different perspectives about why instability like this happens.

Mainstream View

For simplicity, we will use the term "mainstream view" to characterize the prevailing macroeconomic perspective of the majority of economists. According to that view instability in the economy arises from two sources: (1) price stickiness and (2) unexpected shocks to either aggregate demand or aggregate supply.

As we explained in detail in Chapter 18, in the long run, when both input and output prices are fully flexible and have time to adjust to any changes in aggregate demand or short-run aggregate supply, the economy will always return to producing at potential output. In the shorter run, however, stickiness in either input or output prices will mean that any shock to either aggregate demand or aggregate supply will result in changes in output and employment. Although they are not new to you, let's quickly review shocks to aggregate demand and aggregate supply.

Changes in Aggregate Demand
Mainstream macroeconomics focuses on aggregate spending and its components. Recall that the basic equation underlying aggregate expenditures is

$$C_a + I_g + X_n + G = \text{GDP}$$

That is, the aggregate amount of after-tax consumption, gross investment, net exports, and government spending determines the total amount of goods and services produced and sold. In equilibrium, $C_a + I_g + X_n + G$ (aggregate expenditures) is equal to GDP (real output). A decrease in the price level increases equilibrium GDP and thus allows us to trace out a downsloping aggregate demand curve for the economy (see the appendix to Chapter 12). Any change in one of the spending components in the aggregate expenditures equation shifts the aggregate demand curve. This, in turn, changes equilibrium real output, the price level, or both.

Investment spending in particular is subject to wide "booms" and "busts." Significant increases in investment spending are multiplied into even greater increases in aggregate demand and thus can produce demand-pull inflation. In contrast, significant declines in investment spending are multiplied into even greater decreases in aggregate demand and thus can cause recessions.

Adverse Aggregate Supply Shocks
In the mainstream view, the second source of macroeconomic instability arises on the supply side. Occasionally, such external events as wars or an artificial supply restriction of a key resource can boost resource prices and significantly raise per-unit production costs. The result is a sizable decline in a nation's aggregate supply, which destabilizes the economy by simultaneously causing cost-push inflation and recession.

Monetarist View

Monetarism (1) focuses on the money supply, (2) holds that markets are highly competitive, and (3) says that a competitive market system gives the economy a high degree of macroeconomic stability. Monetarists argue that the price and wage flexibility provided by competitive markets should cause fluctuations in aggregate demand to alter product and resource prices rather than output and employment. Thus, the market system would provide substantial macroeconomic stability *were it not for government interference in the economy.*

> **ORIGIN OF THE IDEA**
> O 19.1
> Monetarism

The problem, as monetarists see it, is that government has promoted downward wage inflexibility through the minimum-wage law, pro-union legislation, guaranteed prices for certain farm products, pro-business monopoly legislation, and so forth. The free-market system is capable of providing macroeconomic stability, but, despite good intentions, government interference has undermined that capability. Moreover, monetarists say that government has contributed to the economy's business cycles through its clumsy and mistaken attempts to achieve greater stability through its monetary policies.

Equation of Exchange
The fundamental equation of monetarism is the **equation of exchange:**

$$MV = PQ$$

where M is the supply of money; V is the **velocity** of money, that is, the average number of times per year a dollar is spent on final goods and services; P is the price level or, more specifically, the average price at which each unit of physical output is sold; and Q is the physical volume of all goods and services produced.

> **ORIGIN OF THE IDEA**
> O 19.2
> Equation of exchange

The left side of the equation of exchange, *MV*, represents the total amount spent by purchasers of output, while the right side, *PQ*, represents the total amount received by sellers of that output. The nation's money supply (*M*) multiplied by the number of times it is spent each year (*V*) must equal the nation's nominal GDP (= *P* × *Q*). The dollar value of total spending has to equal the dollar value of total output.

Stable Velocity

Monetarists say that velocity, *V*, in the equation of exchange is relatively stable. To them, "stable" is not synonymous with "constant," however. Monetarists are aware that velocity has generally trended upward over the last several decades. Shorter pay periods, widespread use of credit cards, and faster means of making payments enable people to hold less money and to turn it over more rapidly than was possible in earlier times. These factors have enabled people to reduce their holdings of cash and checkbook money relative to the size of the nation's nominal GDP.

When monetarists say that velocity is stable, they mean that the factors altering velocity change gradually and predictably and that changes in velocity from one year to the next can be readily anticipated. Moreover, they hold that velocity does not change in response to changes in the money supply itself. Instead, people have a stable desire to hold money relative to holding other financial assets, holding real assets, and buying current output. The factors that determine the amount of money the public wants to hold depend mainly on the level of nominal GDP.

Example: Assume that when the level of nominal GDP is $400 billion, the public desires $100 billion of money to purchase that output. That means that *V* is 4 (= $400 billion of nominal GDP/$100 billion of money). If we further assume that the actual supply of money is $100 billion, the economy is in equilibrium with respect to money; the actual amount of money supplied equals the amount the public wants to hold.

If velocity is stable, the equation of exchange suggests that there is a predictable relationship between the money supply and nominal GDP (= *PQ*). An increase in the money supply of, say, $10 billion would upset equilibrium in our example since the public would find itself holding more money or liquidity than it wants. That is, the actual amount of money held ($110 billion) would exceed the amount of holdings desired ($100 billion). In that case, the reaction of the public (households and businesses) is to restore its desired balance of money relative to other items, such as stocks and bonds, factories and equipment, houses and automobiles, and clothing and toys. But the spending of money by individual households and businesses would leave more cash in the checkable deposits or billfolds of other households and firms. And they too would try to "spend down" their excess cash balances. But, overall, the $110 billion supply of money cannot be spent down because a dollar spent is a dollar received.

Instead, the collective attempt to reduce cash balances increases aggregate demand, thereby boosting nominal GDP. Because velocity in our example is 4—that is, the dollar is spent, on average, four times per year—nominal GDP rises from $400 billion to $440 billion. At that higher nominal GDP, the money supply of $110 billion equals the amount of money desired ($440 billion/4 = $110 billion), and equilibrium is reestablished.

The $10 billion increase in the money supply thus eventually increases nominal GDP by $40 billion. Spending on goods, services, and assets expands until nominal GDP has gone up enough to restore the original 4-to-1 equilibrium relationship between nominal GDP and the money supply.

Note that the relationship GDP/*M* defines *V*. A stable relationship between nominal GDP and *M* means a stable *V*. And a change in *M* causes a proportionate change in nominal GDP. Thus, monetarists say that changes in the money supply have a predictable effect on nominal GDP (= *P* × *Q*). An increase in *M* increases *P* or *Q*, or some combination of both; a decrease in *M* reduces *P* or *Q*, or some combination of both.

WORKED PROBLEMS

W 19.1

Equation of exchange

Monetary Causes of Instability

Monetarists say that inappropriate monetary policy is the single most important cause of macroeconomic instability. An increase in the money supply directly increases aggregate demand. Under conditions of full employment, that rise in aggregate demand raises the price level. For a time, higher prices cause firms to increase their real output, and the rate of unemployment falls below its natural rate. But once nominal wages rise to reflect the higher prices and thus to restore real wages, real output moves back to its full-employment level and the unemployment rate returns to its natural rate. The inappropriate increase in the money supply leads to inflation, together with instability of real output and employment.

Conversely, a decrease in the money supply reduces aggregate demand. Real output temporarily falls, and the unemployment rate rises above its natural rate. Eventually, nominal wages fall and real output returns to its full-employment level. The inappropriate decline in the money supply leads to deflation, together with instability of real GDP and employment.

The contrast between mainstream macroeconomics and monetarism on the causes of instability thus comes into sharp focus. Mainstream economists view the instability of investment as the main cause of the economy's instability. They see monetary policy as a stabilizing factor. Changes in the money supply raise or lower interest rates as needed, smooth out swings in investment, and thus reduce macro-economic instability. In contrast, monetarists view changes in the money supply as the main cause of instability in the economy. For example, they say that the Great Depression occurred largely because the Fed allowed the money supply to fall by roughly one-third during that period. According to Milton Friedman, a prominent monetarist,

> And [the money supply] fell not because there were no willing borrowers—not because the horse would not drink. It fell because the Federal Reserve System forced or permitted a sharp reduction in the [money supply], because it failed to exercise the responsibilities assigned to it in the Federal Reserve Act to provide liquidity to the banking system. The Great Contraction is tragic testimony to the power of monetary policy—not, as Keynes and so many of his contemporaries believed, evidence of its impotence.[1]

Real-Business-Cycle View

A third modern view of the cause of macroeconomic instability is that business cycles are caused by real factors that affect aggregate supply rather than by monetary, or spending, factors that cause fluctuations in aggregate demand. In the **real-business-cycle theory,** business fluctuations result from significant changes in technology and resource availability. Those changes affect productivity and thus the long-run growth trend of aggregate supply.

An example focusing on recession will clarify this thinking. Suppose productivity (output per worker) declines sharply because of a large increase in oil prices, which makes it prohibitively expensive to operate certain types of machinery. That decline in productivity implies a reduction in the economy's ability to produce real output. The result would be a decrease in the economy's long-run aggregate supply curve, as represented by the leftward shift from AS_{LR1} to AS_{LR2} in Figure 19.1.

As real output falls from Q_1 to Q_2, the public needs less money to buy the reduced volume of goods and services. So the demand for money falls. Moreover, the slowdown in business activity means that businesses need to borrow less from banks, reducing the part of the money supply created

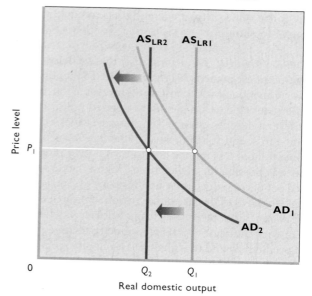

FIGURE 19.1 The real-business-cycle theory. In the real-business-cycle theory, a decline in resource availability shifts the nation's long-run aggregate supply curve to the left from AS_{LR1} to AS_{LR2}. The decline in real output from Q_1 to Q_2, in turn, reduces money demand (less is needed) and money supply (fewer loans are taken out) such that aggregate demand shifts leftward from AD_1 to AD_2. The result is a recession in which the price level remains constant.

by banks through their lending. Thus, the supply of money also falls. In this controversial scenario, changes in the supply of money respond to changes in the demand for money. The decline in the money supply then reduces aggregate demand, as from AD_1 to AD_2 in Figure 19.1. The outcome is a decline in real output from Q_1 to Q_2, with no change in the price level.

Conversely, a large increase in aggregate supply (not shown) caused by, say, major innovations in the production process would shift the long-run aggregate supply curve rightward. Real output would increase, and money demand and money supply would both increase. Aggregate demand would shift rightward by an amount equal to the rightward shift of long-run aggregate supply. Real output would increase, without driving up the price level.

Conclusion: In the real-business-cycle theory, macro instability arises on the aggregate supply side of the economy, not on the aggregate demand side as mainstream economists and monetarists usually claim.

Coordination Failures

A fourth and final modern view of macroeconomic instability relates to so-called **coordination failures.** Such

---

[1] Milton Friedman, *The Optimum Quantity of Money and Other Essays* (Chicago: Aldine, 1969), p. 97.

Too Much Money?

The severe recession of 2007–2009 fits the mainstream view that recessions are caused by AD shocks rather than the real-business-cycle view that they are caused by AS shocks. Recall that the recession began with a financial crisis that caused significant reductions in investment spending and consumption spending and therefore reduced aggregate demand. As inventories increased, businesses further curtailed their investment spending, and aggregate demand, output, and income dropped even more.

Economists with monetarist leanings, however, cite monetary factors as the main cause of the financial crisis that led to the initial declines in aggregate demand. They argue that the Federal Reserve flooded the economy with too much money and held interest rates too low for too long in promoting recovery from the 2001 recession. In this line of reasoning, the excess money and low interest rates contributed to the bubble in the housing market. When that bubble burst, the resulting loan defaults set in motion the forces that produced the declines in AD and therefore the recession.

All economists agree that the bursting of the housing bubble led to the recession. And too-loose monetary policy may have contributed to the bubble. But economists also cite the role of the very large international flows of foreign savings into the United States during this period. These inflows drove down interest rates and helped to fuel the housing bubble. Other factors such as "pass-the-risk" lending practices, government policies promoting home ownership, and poorly designed and enforced financial regulations certainly came into play. The mainstream view is that causes of the financial crisis and recession are numerous and complex.

failures occur when people fail to reach a mutually beneficial equilibrium because they lack a way to coordinate their actions.

Noneconomic Example Consider first a noneconomic example. Suppose you hear that some people might be getting together at the last minute for an informal party at a nearby beach. But because of a chance of rain, there is some doubt about whether people will actually come out. You make a cell phone call or two to try to get a read on what others are thinking, and then base your decision on that limited information. If you expect others to be there, you will decide to go. If you expect that no one will go, you will decide to stay home. There are several possible equilibrium outcomes, depending on the mix of people's expectations. Let's consider just two. If each person assumes that all the others will go to the party, all will go. The party will occur and presumably everyone will have a good time. But if each person assumes that everyone else will stay home, all will stay home and there will be no party. When the party does not take place, even though all would be better off if it did take place, a coordination failure has occurred.

Macroeconomic Example Now let's apply this example to macroeconomic instability, specifically recession. Suppose that individual firms and households expect other firms and consumers to cut back their investment and consumption spending. As a result, each firm and household will anticipate a reduction of aggregate demand. Firms therefore will reduce their own investment spending since they will anticipate that their future production capacity will be excessive. Households will also reduce their own spending (increase their saving) because they anticipate that they will experience reduced work hours, possible layoffs, and falling incomes in the future.

Aggregate demand will indeed decline and the economy will indeed experience a recession in response to what amounts to a self-fulfilling prophecy. Moreover, the economy will stay at a below-full-employment level of output because, once there, producers and households have no individual incentive to increase spending. If all producers and households would agree to increase their investment and consumption spending simultaneously, then aggregate demand would rise, and real output and real income would increase. Each producer and each consumer would be better off. However, this outcome does not occur because there is no mechanism for firms and households to agree on such a joint spending increase.

In this case, the economy is stuck in an *unemployment equilibrium* because of a coordination failure. With a different set of expectations, a coordination failure might leave the economy in an *inflation equilibrium*. In this view, the economy has a number of such potential equilibrium positions, some good and some bad, depending on people's mix of expectations. Macroeconomic instability, then, reflects the movement of the economy from one such equilibrium position to another as expectations change.

Does the Economy "Self-Correct"?

Just as there are disputes over the causes of macroeconomic instability, there are disputes over whether or not the economy will correct itself when instability does occur. And economists also disagree on how long it will take for any such self-correction to take place.

New Classical View of Self-Correction

New classical economists tend to be either monetarists or adherents of **rational expectations theory:** the idea that businesses, consumers, and workers expect changes in policies or circumstances to have certain effects on the economy and, in pursuing their own self-interest, take actions to make sure those changes affect them as little as possible. The **new classical economics** holds that when the economy occasionally diverges from its full-employment output, internal mechanisms within the economy will automatically move it back to that output. Policymakers should stand back and let the automatic correction occur, rather than engage in active fiscal and monetary policy. This perspective is often associated with the vertical long-run Phillips Curve, which we discussed in Chapter 18. But we will analyze it here using the extended AD-AS model that was also developed in Chapter 18.

Graphical Analysis Figure 19.2a relates the new classical analysis to the question of self-correction. Specifically, an increase in aggregate demand, say, from AD_1 to AD_2, moves the economy upward along its short-run aggregate supply curve AS_1 from a to b. The price level rises and real output increases. With the economy producing beyond potential output, high resource demand drives up the prices of labor and other productive inputs. Per-unit production costs increase and the short-run aggregate supply curve shifts leftward, eventually from AS_1 to AS_2. The economy moves from b to c, and real output returns to its full-employment level, Q_1. This level of output is dictated by the economy's vertical long-run aggregate supply curve, AS_{LR}.

FIGURE 19.2 New classical view of self-correction. (a) An unanticipated increase in aggregate demand from AD_1 to AD_2 first moves the economy from a to b. The economy then self-corrects to c. An anticipated increase in aggregate demand moves the economy directly from a to c. (b) An unanticipated decrease in aggregate demand from AD_1 to AD_3 moves the economy from a to d. The economy then self-corrects to e. An anticipated decrease in aggregate demand moves the economy directly from a to e. (Mainstream economists, however, say that if the price level remains at P_1, the economy will move from a to f, and even if the price level falls to P_4, the economy may remain at d because of downward wage inflexibility.)

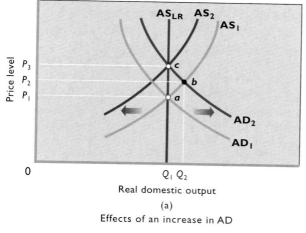

(a)
Effects of an increase in AD

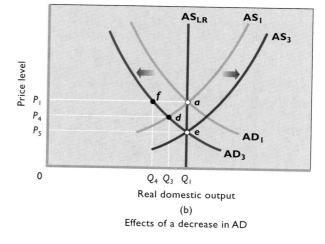

(b)
Effects of a decrease in AD

Conversely, a decrease in aggregate demand from AD_1 to AD_3 in Figure 19.2b first moves the economy downward along its short-run aggregate supply curve AS_1 from point *a* to *d*. The price level declines, as does the level of real output. With the economy producing below potential output, low resource demand drives down the prices of labor and other productive inputs. When that happens, per-unit production costs decline and the short-run aggregate supply curve shifts to the right, eventually from AS_1 to AS_3. The economy moves to *e*, where it again achieves its full-employment level, Q_1. As in Figure 19.2a, the economy in Figure 19.2b has automatically self-corrected to its full-employment output and its natural rate of unemployment.

Speed of Adjustment There is some disagreement among new classical economists on how long it will take for self-correction to occur. Monetarists usually hold the *adaptive expectations* view that people form their expectations on the basis of present realities and only gradually change their expectations as experience unfolds. This means that the shifts in the short-run aggregate supply curves shown in Figure 19.2 may not occur for 2 or 3 years or even longer. Other new classical economists, however, accept the rational expectations assumption that workers anticipate some future outcomes before they occur. When price-level changes are fully anticipated, adjustments of nominal wages are very quick or even instantaneous. Let's see why.

Although several new theories incorporate rational expectations, our interest here is the new classical version of the rational expectations theory (hereafter, RET). RET is based on two assumptions:

- People behave rationally, gathering and intelligently processing information to form expectations about things that are economically important to them. They adjust those expectations quickly as new developments affecting future economic outcomes occur. Where there is adequate information, people's beliefs about future economic outcomes accurately reflect the likelihood that those outcomes will occur. For example, if it is clear that a certain policy will cause inflation, people will recognize that fact and adjust their economic behavior in anticipation of inflation.

- RET economists assume that all product and resource markets are highly competitive and that prices and wages are flexible both upward and downward. But the RET economists go further, assuming that new information is quickly (in some cases, instantaneously) taken into account in the demand and supply curves of such markets. The upshot is that equilibrium prices and quantities adjust rapidly to unforeseen events—say, technological change or

aggregate supply shocks. They adjust instantaneously to events that have known outcomes—for example, changes in fiscal or monetary policy.

Unanticipated Price-Level Changes The implication of RET is not only that the economy is self-correcting but that self-correction occurs quickly. In this thinking, unanticipated changes in the price level—so-called **price-level surprises**—*do* cause temporary changes in real output. Suppose, for example, that an unanticipated increase in foreign demand for U.S. goods increases U.S. aggregate demand from AD_1 to AD_2 in Figure 19.2a. The immediate result is an unexpected increase in the price level from P_1 to P_2.

But now an interesting question arises. If wages and prices are flexible, as assumed in RET, why doesn't the higher price level immediately cause wages and other input prices to rise, such that there is no increase in real output at all? Why does the economy temporarily move from point *a* to *b* along AS_1? In RET, firms increase output from Q_1 to Q_2 because of misperceptions about rising prices of their own products relative to the prices of other products (and to the prices of labor). They mistakenly think the higher prices of their own products have resulted from increased demand for those products relative to the demands for other products. Expecting higher profits, they increase their own production. But in fact *all* prices, including the price of labor (nominal wages), are rising because of the general increase in aggregate demand. Once firms see that *all* prices and wages are rising, they decrease their production to previous levels.

In terms of Figure 19.2a, the increase in nominal wages shifts the short-run aggregate supply curve leftward, ultimately from AS_1 to AS_2, and the economy moves from *b* to *c*. Thus, the increase in real output caused by the price-level surprise corrects itself.

The same analysis in reverse applies to an unanticipated price-level decrease. In the economy represented by Figure 19.2b, firms misperceive that the prices of their own products are falling due to decreases in the demand for those products relative to other products. They incorrectly anticipate declines in profit and cut production. As a result of their collective actions, real output in the economy falls. Once firms see what is really happening—that *all* prices and wages are dropping—they increase their output to prior levels. The short-run aggregate supply curve in Figure 19.2b shifts rightward from AS_1 to AS_3, and the economy "self-corrects" by moving from *d* to *e*.

Fully Anticipated Price-Level Changes In RET, fully *anticipated* price-level changes do not change real output, even for short periods. In Figure 19.2a, again consider the increase in aggregate demand from AD_1 to AD_2. Businesses immediately recognize that the higher prices being paid for their products are part of the inflation they had anticipated. They understand that the same forces that are causing the inflation result in higher nominal wages, leaving their profits unchanged. The economy therefore moves directly from *a* to *c*. The price level rises as expected, and output remains at its full-employment level Q_1.

Similarly, a fully *anticipated* price-level decrease will leave real output unchanged. Firms conclude that nominal wages are declining by the same percentage amount as the declining price level, leaving profits unchanged. The economy represented by Figure 19.2b therefore moves directly from *a* to *e*. Deflation occurs, but the economy continues to produce its full-employment output Q_1. The anticipated decline in aggregate demand causes no change in real output.

Mainstream View of Self-Correction

Almost all economists acknowledge that the new classical economists have made significant contributions to the theory of aggregate supply. In fact, mainstream economists have incorporated some aspects of RET into their own models. However, most economists strongly disagree with RET on the question of downward price and wage flexibility. While the stock market, foreign exchange market, and certain commodity markets experience day-to-day or minute-to-minute price changes, including price declines, that is not true of many product markets and most labor markets. There is ample evidence, say mainstream economists, that many prices and wages are inflexible downward for long periods. As a result, it may take years for the economy to move from recession back to full-employment output, unless it gets help from fiscal and monetary policy.

Graphical Analysis

To understand this mainstream view, again examine Figure 19.2b. Suppose aggregate demand declines from AD_1 to AD_3 because of a significant decline in investment spending. If prices are sticky downward for a while and therefore the price level is temporarily stuck at P_1, the economy will not move from *a* to *d* to *e*, as suggested by RET. Instead, the economy will move from *a* to *f*, as if it were moving along the white horizontal P_1 price line between those two points. Real output will decline from its full-employment level, Q_1, to the recessionary level, Q_4.

But let's assume that large amounts of unsold inventories eventually cause the price level to fall to P_4. Will this lead to the decline in nominal wages needed to shift aggregate supply from AS_1 to AS_3, as suggested by the new classical economists? "Highly unlikely" say mainstream economists. Even more so than prices, nominal wages tend to be inflexible downward. If nominal wages do not decline in response to the decline in the price level, then the short-run aggregate supply curve will not shift rightward. The self-correction mechanism assumed by RET and new classical economists will break down. Instead, the economy will remain at *d*, experiencing less-than-full-employment output and a high rate of unemployment.

INTERACTIVE GRAPHS

G 19.1

Self-correction

Downward Wage Inflexibility

In Chapter 12 we discussed several reasons why firms may not be able to, or may not want to, lower nominal wages. Firms may not be able to cut wages because of wage contracts and the legal minimum wage. And firms may not want to lower wages if they fear potential problems with morale, effort, and efficiency.

While contracts are thought to be the main cause of wage rigidity, so-called efficiency wages and insider-outsider relationships also may play a role. Let's explore both.

Efficiency Wage Theory

Recall from Chapter 12 that an **efficiency wage** is a wage that minimizes the firm's labor cost per unit of output. Normally, we would think that the market wage is the efficiency wage since it is the lowest wage at which a firm can obtain a particular type of labor. But where the cost of supervising workers is high or where worker turnover is great, firms may discover that paying a wage that is higher than the market wage will lower their wage cost per unit of output.

Example: Suppose a firm's workers, on average, produce 8 units of output at a $9 market wage but 10 units of output at a $10 above-market wage. The efficiency wage is $10, not the $9 market wage. At the $10 wage, the labor cost per unit of output is only $1 (= $10 wage/10 units of output), compared with $1.12 (= $9 wage/8 units of output) at the $9 wage.

How can a higher wage result in greater efficiency?

- *Greater work effort* The above-market wage, in effect, raises the cost to workers of losing their jobs as a result of poor performance. Because workers have a strong incentive to retain their relatively high-paying jobs, they are more likely to provide greater work effort. Looked at differently, workers are more reluctant to shirk (neglect or avoid work) because the higher wage makes job loss more costly to them. Consequently, the above-market wage can be the efficient wage; it can enhance worker productivity so much that the higher wage more than pays for itself.

- *Lower supervision costs* With less incentive among workers to shirk, the firm needs fewer supervisory personnel to monitor work performance. This, too, can lower the firm's overall wage cost per unit of output.
- *Reduced job turnover* The above-market pay discourages workers from voluntarily leaving their jobs. The lower turnover rate reduces the firm's cost of hiring and training workers. It also gives the firm a more experienced, more productive workforce.

The key implication for macroeconomic instability is that efficiency wages add to the downward inflexibility of wages. Firms that pay efficiency wages will be reluctant to cut wages

ORIGIN OF THE IDEA

O 19.4

Efficiency wages

when aggregate demand declines, since such cuts may encourage shirking, require more supervisory personnel, and increase turnover. In other words, wage cuts that reduce productivity and raise per-unit labor costs are self-defeating.

Insider-Outsider Relationships Other economists theorize that downward wage inflexibility may relate to relationships between "insiders" and "outsiders." Insiders are workers who retain employment even during recession. Outsiders are workers who have been laid off from a firm and unemployed workers who would like to work at that firm.

When recession produces layoffs and widespread unemployment, we might expect outsiders to offer to work for less than the current wage rate, in effect, bidding down wage rates. We also might expect firms to hire such workers to reduce their costs. But, according to the **insider-outsider theory**, outsiders may not be able to underbid existing wages because employers may view the nonwage cost of hiring them to be prohibitive. Employers might fear that insiders would view acceptance of such underbidding as undermining years of effort to increase wages or, worse, as "stealing" jobs. So insiders may refuse to cooperate with new workers who have undercut their pay. Where teamwork is critical for production, such lack of cooperation will reduce overall productivity and thereby lower the firms' profits.

Even if firms are willing to employ outsiders at less than the current wage, those workers might refuse to work for less than the existing wage. To do so might invite harassment from the insiders whose pay they have undercut. Thus, outsiders may remain unemployed, relying on past saving, unemployment compensation, and other social programs to make ends meet.

As in the efficiency wage theory, the insider-outsider theory implies that wages will be inflexible downward

when aggregate demand declines. Self-correction may eventually occur but not nearly as rapidly as the new classical economists contend.

QUICK REVIEW 19.2

- New classical economists believe that the economy "self-corrects" when unanticipated events divert it from its full-employment level of real output.
- In RET, unanticipated price-level changes cause changes in real output in the short run but not in the long run.
- According to RET, market participants immediately change their actions in response to anticipated price-level changes such that no change in real output occurs.
- Mainstream economists say that the economy can get mired in recession for several months or more because of downward price and wage inflexibility.
- Sources of downward wage inflexibility include contracts, efficiency wages, and insider-outsider relationships.

Rules or Discretion?

These different views on the causes of instability and on the speed of self-correction have led to vigorous debate on macro policy. Should the government adhere to policy rules that prohibit it from causing instability in an economy that is otherwise stable? Or should it use discretionary fiscal and monetary policy, when needed, to stabilize a sometimes-unstable economy?

In Support of Policy Rules

Monetarists and other new classical economists believe policy rules would reduce instability in the economy. They believe that such rules would prevent government from trying to "manage" aggregate demand. That would be a desirable trend because, in their view, such management is misguided and thus is likely to *cause* more instability than it cures.

Monetary Rule Since inappropriate monetary policy is the major source of macroeconomic instability, say monetarists, the enactment of a **monetary rule** would make sense. One such rule would be a requirement that the Fed expand the money supply each year at the same annual rate as the typical growth of the economy's production capacity. That fixed-rate expansion of the money supply would occur whatever the state of the economy. The Fed's sole monetary role would be to use its tools (open-market operations, the discount rate, the term auction facility, and reserve requirements) to ensure that the nation's money

CONSIDER THIS . . .

On the Road Again

Economist Abba Lerner (1903–1982) likened the economy to an automobile traveling down a road that had traffic barriers on each side. The problem was that the car had no steering wheel. It would hit one barrier, causing the car to veer to the opposite side of the road. There it would hit the other barrier, which in turn would send it careening to the opposite side. To avoid such careening in the form of business cycles, said Lerner, society must equip the economy with a steering wheel. Discretionary fiscal and monetary policy would enable government to steer the economy safely between the problems of recession and demand-pull inflation.

Economist Milton Friedman (1912–2006) modified Lerner's analogy, giving it a different meaning. He said that the economic vehicle does not need a skillful driver who is continuously turning the wheel to adjust to the unexpected irregularities of the route. Instead, the economy needs a way to prohibit the monetary passenger in the back seat from occasionally leaning over and giving the steering wheel a jerk that sends the car off the road. According to Friedman, the car will travel down the road just fine unless the Federal Reserve destabilizes it.

Lerner's analogy implied an internally unstable economy that needs steering through discretionary government stabilization policy. Friedman's modification of the analogy implied a generally stable economy that is destabilized by inappropriate monetary policy by the Federal Reserve. For Lerner, stability required active use of fiscal and monetary policy. For Friedman, macroeconomic stability required a monetary rule forcing the Federal Reserve to increase the money supply at a set, steady annual rate.*

_____
*In his later years, Friedman softened his call for a monetary rule, acknowledging that the Fed had become much more skillful at keeping the rate of inflation in check through prudent monetary policy.

supply grew steadily by, say, 3 to 5 percent a year. According to Milton Friedman,

> Such a rule . . . would eliminate . . . the major cause of instability in the economy—the capricious and unpredictable impact of countercyclical monetary policy. As long as the money supply grows at a constant rate each year, be it 3, 4, or 5 percent, any decline into recession will be temporary. The liquidity

FIGURE 19.3 Rationale for a monetary rule. A monetary rule that required the Fed to increase the money supply at an annual rate linked to the long-run increase in potential GDP would shift aggregate demand rightward, as from AD$_1$ to AD$_2$, at the same pace as the shift in long-run aggregate supply, here, AS$_{LR1}$ to AS$_{LR2}$. Thus the economy would experience growth without inflation or deflation.

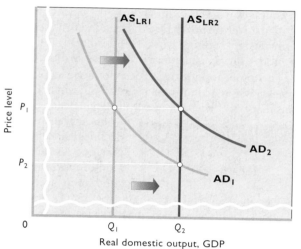

provided by a constantly growing money supply will cause aggregate demand to expand. Similarly, if the supply of money does not rise at a more than average rate, any inflationary increase in spending will burn itself out for lack of fuel.[2]

Figure 19.3 illustrates the rationale for a monetary rule. Suppose the economy represented there is operating at its full-employment real output, Q_1. Also suppose the nation's long-run aggregate supply curve shifts rightward, as from AS$_{LR1}$ to AS$_{LR2}$, each year, signifying the average annual increase in potential real output. As you saw in earlier chapters, such annual increases in "potential GDP" result from added resources, improved resources, and improved technology.

Monetarists argue that a monetary rule would tie increases in the money supply to the typical rightward shift of long-run aggregate supply. In view of the direct link between changes in the money supply and aggregate demand, this would ensure that the AD curve would shift rightward, as from AD$_1$ to AD$_2$, each year. As a result, while GDP increases from Q_1 to Q_2, the price level would remain constant at P_1. A monetary rule, then, would promote steady growth of real output along with price stability.

Generally, rational expectations economists also support a monetary rule. They conclude that an expansionary or re-

_____
[2]As quoted in Lawrence S. Ritter and William L. Silber, *Money*, 5th ed. (New York: Basic Books, 1984), pp. 141–142.

strictive monetary policy would alter the rate of inflation but not real output. Suppose, for example, the Fed implements an easy money policy to reduce interest rates, expand investment spending, and boost real GDP. On the basis of past experience and economic knowledge, the public would anticipate that this policy is inflationary and would take protective actions. Workers would press for higher nominal wages; firms would raise their product prices; and lenders would lift their nominal interest rates on loans.

All these responses are designed to prevent inflation from having adverse effects on the real income of workers, businesses, and lenders. But collectively they would immediately raise wage and price levels. So the increase in aggregate demand brought about by the expansionary monetary policy would be completely dissipated in higher prices and wages. Real output and employment would not be increased by the easy money policy.

In this view, the combination of rational expectations and instantaneous market adjustments dooms discretionary monetary policy to ineffectiveness. If discretionary monetary policy produces only inflation (or deflation), say the RET economists, then it makes sense to limit the Fed's discretion and to require that Congress enact a monetary rule consistent with price stability at all times.

In recent decades, the call for a Friedman-type monetary rule has faded. Some economists who tend to favor monetary rules have advocated **inflation targeting,** under which the Fed would be required to announce a targeted band of inflation rates, say, 1 to 2 percent, for some future period such as the following 2 years. It would then be expected to use its monetary policy tools to keep inflation rates within that range. If it did not hit the inflation target, it would have to explain why it failed.

Strictly interpreted, inflation targeting would focus the Fed's attention nearly exclusively on controlling inflation and deflation, rather than on counteracting business fluctuations. Proponents of inflation targeting generally believe the economy will have fewer, shorter, and less severe business cycles if the Fed adheres to the rule "Set a known inflation goal and achieve it."

We discussed another modern monetary rule—the Taylor rule—in Chapter 16 on monetary policy. This rule specifies how the Fed should alter the Federal funds rate under differing economic circumstances. We discuss this rule in more depth in this chapter's Last Word.

Balanced Budget Monetarists and new classical economists question the effectiveness of fiscal policy. At the extreme, a few of them favor a constitutional amendment requiring that the Federal government balance its budget annually. Others simply suggest that government be "pas-

sive" in its fiscal policy, not intentionally creating budget deficits or surpluses. They believe that deficits and surpluses caused by recession or inflationary expansion will eventually correct themselves as the economy self-corrects to its full-employment output.

Monetarists are particularly strong in their opposition to expansionary fiscal policy. They believe that the deficit spending accompanying such a policy has a strong tendency to "crowd out" private investment. Suppose government runs a budget deficit by printing and selling U.S. securities—that is, by borrowing from the public. By engaging in such borrowing, the government is competing with private businesses for funds. The borrowing increases the demand for money, which then raises the interest rate and crowds out a substantial amount of private investment that would otherwise have been profitable. The net effect of a budget deficit on aggregate demand therefore is unpredictable and, at best, modest.

RET economists reject discretionary fiscal policy for the same reason they reject active monetary policy: They don't think it works. Business and labor will immediately adjust their behavior in anticipation of the price-level effects of a change in fiscal policy. The economy will move directly to the anticipated new price level. Like monetary policy, say the RET theorists, fiscal policy can move the economy along its vertical long-run aggregate supply curve. But because its effects on inflation are fully anticipated, fiscal policy cannot alter real GDP even in the short run. The best course of action for government is to balance its budget.

In Defense of Discretionary Stabilization Policy

Mainstream economists oppose both a strict monetary rule and a balanced-budget requirement. They believe that monetary policy and fiscal policy are important tools for achieving and maintaining full employment, price stability, and economic growth.

Discretionary Monetary Policy In supporting discretionary monetary policy, mainstream economists argue that the rationale for the Friedman monetary rule is flawed. While there is indeed a close relationship between the money supply and nominal GDP over long periods, in shorter periods this relationship breaks down. The reason is that the velocity of money has proved to be more variable and unpredictable than monetarists contend. Arguing that velocity is variable both cyclically and over time, mainstream economists contend that a constant annual rate of increase in the money supply might not eliminate fluctuations in aggregate demand. In terms of the equation of exchange, a steady rise of M does not guarantee a steady expansion of aggregate demand because V—the rate at which money is spent—can change.

Look again at Figure 19.3, in which we demonstrated the monetary rule: Expand the money supply annually by a fixed percentage, regardless of the state of the economy. During the period in question, optimistic business expectations might create a boom in investment spending and thus shift the aggregate demand curve to some location to the right of AD_2. (You may want to pencil in a new AD curve, labeling it AD_3.) The price level would then rise above P_1; that is, demand-pull inflation would occur. In this case, the monetary rule will not accomplish its goal of maintaining price stability. Mainstream economists say that the Fed can use a restrictive monetary policy to reduce the excessive investment spending and thereby hold the rightward shift of aggregate demand to AD_2, thus avoiding inflation.

Similarly, suppose instead that investment declines because of pessimistic business expectations. Aggregate demand will then increase by some amount less than the increase from AD_1 to AD_2 in Figure 19.3. Again, the monetary rule fails the stability test: The price level sinks below P_1 (deflation occurs). Or if the price level is inflexible downward at P_1, the economy will not achieve its full-employment output (unemployment rises). An expansionary monetary policy can help avoid each outcome.

Mainstream economists quip that the trouble with the monetary rule is that it tells the policymaker, "Don't do something, just stand there."

Discretionary Fiscal Policy Mainstream economists support the use of fiscal policy to keep recessions from deepening or to keep mild inflation from becoming severe inflation. They recognize the possibility of crowding out but do not think it is a serious problem when business borrowing is depressed, as is usually the case in recession. Because politicians can abuse fiscal policy, most economists feel that it should be held in reserve for situations where monetary policy appears to be ineffective or working too slowly.

As indicated earlier, mainstream economists oppose requirements to balance the budget annually. Tax revenues fall sharply during recessions and rise briskly during periods of demand-pull inflation. Therefore, a law or a constitutional amendment mandating an annually balanced budget would require that the government increase tax rates and reduce government spending during recession and reduce tax rates and increase government spending during economic booms. The first set of actions would worsen recession, and the second set would fuel inflation.

Policy Successes

Finally, mainstream economists point out several specific policy successes in the past three decades:

- A tight money policy dropped inflation from 13.5 percent in 1980 to 3.2 percent in 1983.
- An expansionary fiscal policy reduced the unemployment rate from 9.7 percent in 1982 to 5.5 percent in 1988.
- An easy money policy helped the economy recover from the 1990–1991 recession.
- Judicious tightening of monetary policy in the mid-1990s, and then again in the late 1990s, helped the economy remain on a noninflationary, full-employment growth path.
- In late 2001 and 2002, expansionary fiscal and monetary policy helped the economy recover from a series of economic blows, including the collapse of numerous Internet start-up firms, a severe decline in investment spending, the impacts of the terrorist attacks of September 11, 2001, and a precipitous decline in stock values.
- In 2004 and 2005 the Fed tempered continued expansionary fiscal policy by increasing the Federal funds rate in $\frac{1}{4}$ percentage-point increments from 1 percent to 4.25 percent. The economy expanded briskly in those years, while inflation stayed in check. The mild inflation was particularly impressive because the average price of a barrel of crude oil rose from $24 in 2002 to $55 in 2005. The Fed's further increases in interest rates to 5.25 percent in 2006 also kept inflation mild that year and the next despite continued strong growth and oil reaching $99 per barrel in late 2007.
- In 2007 the Fed vigorously responded to a crisis in the mortgage market by ensuring monetary liquidity in the banking system. Besides aggressively lowering the Federal funds rate from 5.25 percent in the summer of 2007 to just 2 percent in April 2008, the Fed greatly increased the reserves of the banking system by creating and using its term auction facility. It also undertook other lender-of-last resort actions to unfreeze credit and prevent a possible collapse of the entire financial system. During the severe recession of 2007–2009, the Fed lowered the Federal funds rate further, holding it in the 0 to 0.25 percent range to break the downward slide of the economy and help promote economic recovery.

LAST

Word The Taylor Rule: Could a Robot Replace Ben Bernanke?

Macroeconomist John Taylor of Stanford University Calls for a New Monetary Rule That Would Institutionalize Appropriate Fed Policy Responses to Changes in Real Output and Inflation.

In our discussion of rules versus discretion, "rules" were associated with a *passive* monetary policy—one in which the monetary rule required that the Fed expand the money supply at a fixed annual rate regardless of the state of the economy. "Discretion," on the other hand, was associated with an *active* monetary policy in which the Fed changed interest rates in response to actual or anticipated changes in the economy.

Economist John Taylor has put a new twist on the rules-versus-discretion debate by suggesting a hybrid policy rule that dictates the precise active monetary actions the Fed should take when changes in the economy occur. You first encountered this Taylor rule in our discussion of monetary policy in Chapter 16. The **Taylor rule** combines traditional monetarism, with its emphasis on a monetary rule, and the more mainstream view that active monetary policy is a useful tool for taming inflation and limiting recession. Unlike the Friedman monetary rule, the Taylor rule holds, for example, that monetary policy should respond to changes in both real GDP and inflation, not simply inflation. The key adjustment instrument is the interest rate, not the money supply.

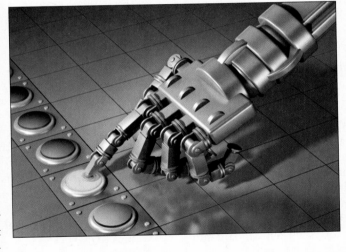

The Taylor rule builds on the belief held by many economists that central banks are willing to tolerate a small positive rate of inflation if doing so will help the economy to produce at potential output. The Taylor rule assumes that the Fed has a 2 percent "target rate of inflation" that it is willing to tolerate and that the Fed follows three rules when setting its target for the Federal funds rate (the rate of interest that commercial banks with excess reserves charge on overnight loans to banks that wish to borrow reserves in order to meet their reserve requirements). The three rules are

- When real GDP equals potential GDP and inflation is at its target rate of 2 percent, the Federal funds target rate should be 4 percent, implying a *real* Federal funds rate of 2 percent (= 4 percent nominal Federal funds rate *minus* 2 percent inflation rate).
- For each 1 percent increase of real GDP above potential GDP, the Fed should raise the *real* Federal funds rate by $\frac{1}{2}$ percentage point.
- For each 1 percent increase in the inflation rate above its 2 percent target rate, the Fed should raise the *real* Federal funds rate by $\frac{1}{2}$ percentage point.[*]

Taylor has neither suggested nor implied that a robot, programmed with the Taylor rule, should replace Ben Bernanke, chairman of the Federal Reserve System. The Fed's discretion to override the rule (or "contingency plan for policy") would be retained, but the Fed would have to explain why its policies diverged from the rule. So the rule would remove the "mystery" associated with monetary policy and increase the Fed's accountability. Also, says Taylor, if used consistently, the rule would enable market participants to predict Fed behavior, and this would increase Fed credibility and reduce uncertainty.

Critics of the Taylor rule acknowledge that it is closer in tune with actual Fed countercyclical policy than is the Friedman monetary rule. They also acknowledge that adherence to the Taylor rule would have raised interest rates more rapidly during the two years prior to the mortgage debt crisis of 2007. Those higher interest rates might have reduced the excessive mortgage borrowing that eventually led to the crisis. But critics of the Taylor rule say that it is unwise to limit the Fed's future discretion in adjusting interest rates as it deems necessary. They note that the Fed has successfully kept inflation in check over the past two decades and has used monetary policy creatively and decisively when necessary during financial and economic emergencies. In view of the overall success, critics conclude that a mechanical monetary rule is certainly unnecessary and might even be detrimental.

---

[*]John Taylor, *Inflation, Unemployment, and Monetary Policy* (Cambridge, Mass.: MIT Press, 1998), pp. 44–47.

TABLE 19.1 Summary of Alternative Macroeconomic Views

Issue	Mainstream Macroeconomics	New Classical Economics	
		Monetarism	Rational Expectations
View of the private economy	Potentially unstable	Stable in long run at natural rate of unemployment	Stable in long run at natural rate of unemployment
Cause of the observed instability of the private economy	Investment plans unequal to saving plans (changes in AD); AS shocks	Inappropriate monetary policy	Unanticipated AD and AS shocks in the short run
Assumptions about short-run price and wage stickiness	Both prices and wages stuck in the immediate short run; in the short run, wages sticky while prices inflexible downward but flexible upward	Prices flexible upward and downward in the short run; wages sticky in the short run	Prices and wages flexible both upward and downward in the short run
Appropriate macro policies	Active fiscal and monetary policy	Monetary rule	Monetary rule
How changes in the money supply affect the economy	By changing the interest rate, which changes investment and real GDP	By directly changing AD, which changes GDP	No effect on output because price-level changes are anticipated
View of the velocity of money	Unstable	Stable	No consensus
How fiscal policy affects the economy	Changes AD and GDP via the multiplier process	No effect unless money supply changes	No effect because price-level changes are anticipated
View of cost-push inflation	Possible (AS shock)	Impossible in the long run in the absence of excessive money supply growth	Impossible in the long run in the absence of excessive money supply growth

Summary of Alternative Views

In Table 19.1 we summarize the fundamental ideas and policy implications of three macroeconomic theories: mainstream macroeconomics, monetarism, and rational expectations theory. Note that we have broadly defined new classical economics to include both monetarism and the rational expectations theory since both adhere to the view that the economy tends automatically to achieve equilibrium at its full-employment output.

These different perspectives have obliged mainstream economists to rethink some of their fundamental principles and to revise many of their positions. Although considerable disagreement remains, mainstream macroeconomists agree with monetarists that "money matters" and that excessive growth of the money supply is the major cause of long-lasting, rapid inflation. They also agree with RET proponents and theorists of coordination failures that expectations matter. If government can create expectations of price stability, full employment, and economic growth, households and firms will tend to act in ways to make them happen. In short, thanks to ongoing challenges to conventional wisdom, macroeconomics continues to evolve.

Summary

1. The mainstream view is that macro instability is caused by a combination of price stickiness and shocks to aggregate demand or aggregate supply. With prices inflexible in the shorter run, changes in aggregate demand or short-run aggregate supply result in changes in output and employment. In the long run when both input and output prices are fully flexible, the economy will produce at potential output.

2. Monetarism focuses on the equation of exchange: $MV = PQ$. Because velocity is thought to be stable, changes in M create changes in nominal GDP ($= PQ$). Monetarists believe that the most significant cause of macroeconomic instability has been inappropriate monetary policy. Rapid increases in M cause inflation; insufficient growth of M causes recession. In this view, a major cause of the Great Depression was inappropriate monetary policy, which allowed the money supply to decline by roughly one-third.

3. Real-business-cycle theory views changes in resource availability and technology (real factors), which alter productivity,

as the main causes of macroeconomic instability. In this theory, shifts of the economy's long-run aggregate supply curve change real output. In turn, money demand and money supply change, shifting the aggregate demand curve in the same direction as the initial change in long-run aggregate supply. Real output thus can change without a change in the price level.

4. A coordination failure is said to occur when people lack a way to coordinate their actions in order to achieve a mutually beneficial equilibrium. Depending on people's expectations, the economy can come to rest at either a good equilibrium (noninflationary full-employment output) or a bad equilibrium (less-than-full-employment output or demand-pull inflation). A bad equilibrium is a result of a coordination failure.

5. The rational expectations theory rests on two assumptions: (1) With sufficient information, people's beliefs about future economic outcomes accurately reflect the likelihood that those outcomes will occur; and (2) markets are highly competitive, and prices and wages are flexible both upward and downward.

6. New classical economists (monetarists and rational expectations theorists) see the economy as automatically correcting itself when disturbed from its full-employment level of real output. In RET, unanticipated changes in aggregate demand change the price level, and in the short run this leads firms to change output. But once the firms realize that all prices are changing (including nominal wages) as part of general inflation or deflation, they restore their output to the previous

level. Anticipated changes in aggregate demand produce only changes in the price level, not changes in real output.

7. Mainstream economists reject the new classical view that all prices and wages are flexible downward. They contend that nominal wages, in particular, are inflexible downward because of several factors, including labor contracts, efficiency wages, and insider-outsider relationships. This means that declines in aggregate demand lower real output, not only wages and prices.

8. Monetarist and rational expectations economists say the Fed should adhere to some form of policy rule, rather than rely exclusively on discretion. The Friedman rule would direct the Fed to increase the money supply at a fixed annual rate equal to the long-run growth of potential GDP. An alternative approach—inflation targeting—would direct the Fed to establish a targeted range of inflation rates, say, 1 to 2 percent, and focus monetary policy on meeting that goal. They also support maintaining a "neutral" fiscal policy, as opposed to using discretionary fiscal policy to create budget deficits or budget surpluses. A few monetarists and rational expectations economists favor a constitutional amendment requiring that the Federal government balance its budget annually.

9. Mainstream economists oppose strict monetary rules and a balanced-budget requirement, and defend discretionary monetary and fiscal policies. They say that both theory and evidence suggest that such policies are helpful in achieving full employment, price stability, and economic growth.

Terms and Concepts

monetarism	rational expectations theory	monetary rule
equation of exchange	new classical economics	inflation targeting
velocity	price-level surprises	Taylor rule
real-business-cycle theory	efficiency wage	
coordination failures	insider-outsider theory	

Questions

1. First, imagine that both input and output prices are fixed in the economy. What does the aggregate supply curve look like? If AD decreases in this situation, what will happen to equilibrium output and the price level? Next, imagine that input prices are fixed, but output prices are flexible. What does the aggregate supply curve look like? In this case, if AD decreases, what will happen to equilibrium output and the price level? Finally, if both input and output prices are fully flexible, what does the aggregate supply curve look like? In this case, if AD decreases, what will happen to equilibrium output and the price level? (To check your answers, review Figures 12.3, 12.4, and 12.5 in Chapter 12). **LO1**

2. According to mainstream economists, what is the usual cause of macroeconomic instability? What role does the spending-income multiplier play in creating instability? How might adverse aggregate supply factors cause instability, according to mainstream economists? **LO1**

3. What is an efficiency wage? How might payment of an above-market wage reduce shirking by employees and reduce worker turnover? How might efficiency wages contribute to downward wage inflexibility, at least for a time, when aggregate demand declines? **LO1**

4. How might relationships between so-called insiders and outsiders contribute to downward wage inflexibility? **LO1**

396 | PART SIX
Extensions and Issues

5. Briefly describe the difference between a so-called real business cycle and a more traditional "spending" business cycle. LO1

6. Craig and Kris were walking directly toward each other in a congested store aisle. Craig moved to his left to avoid Kris, and at the same time Kris moved to his right to avoid Craig. They bumped into each other. What concept does this example illustrate? How does this idea relate to macroeconomic instability? LO1

7. State and explain the basic equation of monetarism. What is the major cause of macroeconomic instability, as viewed by monetarists? LO2

8. Use the equation of exchange to explain the rationale for a monetary rule. Why will such a rule run into trouble if V unexpectedly falls because of, say, a drop in investment spending by businesses? LO2

9. Use an AD-AS graph to demonstrate and explain the price-level and real-output outcome of an anticipated decline in aggregate demand, as viewed by RET economists. (Assume that the economy initially is operating at its full-employment level of output.) Then demonstrate and explain on the same graph the outcome as viewed by mainstream economists. LO3

10. Explain the difference between "active" discretionary fiscal policy advocated by mainstream economists and "passive" fiscal policy advocated by new classical economists. Explain: "The problem with a balanced-budget amendment is that it would, in a sense, require active fiscal policy—but in the wrong direction—as the economy slides into recession." LO4

11. Place "MON," "RET," or "MAIN" beside the statements that most closely reflect monetarist, rational expectations, or mainstream views, respectively: LO4
    a. Anticipated changes in aggregate demand affect only the price level; they have no effect on real output.
    b. Downward wage inflexibility means that declines in aggregate demand can cause long-lasting recession.
    c. Changes in the money supply M increase PQ; at first only Q rises, because nominal wages are fixed, but once workers adapt their expectations to new realities, P rises and Q returns to its former level.
    d. Fiscal and monetary policies smooth out the business cycle.
    e. The Fed should increase the money supply at a fixed annual rate.

12. You have just been elected president of the United States, and the present chairperson of the Federal Reserve Board has resigned. You need to appoint a new person to this position, as well as a person to chair your Council of Economic Advisers. Using Table 19.1 and your knowledge of macroeconomics, identify the views on macro theory and policy you would want your appointees to hold. Remember, the economic health of the entire nation—and your chances for reelection—may depend on your selections. LO4

13. **LAST WORD** Compare and contrast the Taylor rule for monetary policy with the older, simpler monetary rule advocated by Milton Friedman.

Problems

1. Suppose that the money supply and the nominal GDP for a hypothetical economy are $96 billion and $336 billion, respectively. What is the velocity of money? How will households and businesses react if the central bank reduces the money supply by $20 billion? By how much will nominal GDP have to fall to restore equilibrium, according to the monetarist perspective? LO2

2. Assume the following information for a hypothetical economy in year 1: money supply = $400 billion; long-term annual growth of potential GDP = 3 percent; velocity = 4. Assume that the banking system initially has no excess reserves and that the reserve requirement is 10 percent. Also suppose that velocity is constant and that the economy initially is operating at its full-employment real output. LO2
    a. What is the level of nominal GDP in year 1?
    b. Suppose the Fed adheres to a monetary rule through open-market operations. What amount of U.S. securities will it have to sell to, or buy from, banks or the public between years 1 and 2 to meet its monetary rule?

FURTHER TEST YOUR KNOWLEDGE AT
www.mcconnell19e.com

At the text's Online Learning Center (OLC), **www.mcconnell19e.com**, you will find one or more Web-based questions that require information from the Internet to answer. We urge you to check them out; they will familiarize you with Web sites that may be helpful in other courses and perhaps even in your career. The OLC also features multiple-choice questions that give instant feedback and provides other helpful ways to further test your knowledge of the chapter.

INTERNATIONAL ECONOMICS

20

AFTER READING THIS CHAPTER, YOU SHOULD BE ABLE TO:

1 List and discuss several key facts about international trade.

2 Define comparative advantage, and demonstrate how specialization and trade add to a nation's output.

3 Describe how differences between world prices and domestic prices prompt exports and imports.

4 Analyze the economic effects of tariffs and quotas.

5 Analyze the validity of the most frequently presented arguments for protectionism.

6 Identify and explain the objectives of GATT, WTO, EU, Euro Zone, and NAFTA, and discuss offshoring and trade adjustment assistance.

International Trade*

Backpackers in the wilderness like to think they are "leaving the world behind," but, like Atlas, they carry the world on their shoulders. Much of their equipment is imported—knives from Switzerland, rain gear from South Korea, cameras from Japan, aluminum pots from England, sleeping bags from China, and compasses from Finland. Moreover, they may have driven to the trailheads in Japanese-made Toyotas or German-made BMWs, sipping coffee from Brazil or snacking on bananas from Honduras.

International trade and the global economy affect all of us daily, whether we are hiking in the wilderness, driving our cars, buying groceries, or working at our jobs. We cannot "leave the world behind." We are enmeshed in a global web of economic relationships, such as trading of goods and

---

*Note to Instructors: This chapter is a consolidation of Chapters 5 and 37 of *Economics* 18e. If you prefer to cover international trade early in your course, you can assign this chapter at the end of either Part 1 or Part 2. This chapter builds on the introductory ideas of opportunity costs, supply and demand analysis, and economic efficiency but does not require an understanding of either elasticity or market failures.

services, multinational corporations, cooperative ventures among the world's firms, and ties among the world's financial markets.

The focus of this chapter is the trading of goods and services. Then in Chapter 21, we examine the U.S. balance of payments, exchange rates, and U.S. trade deficits. In Chapter 22W on our Web site, we look at the economics of developing nations.

Some Key Trade Facts

The following are several important facts relating to international trade.

- U.S. exports and imports have more than doubled as percentages of GDP since 1980.
- A *trade deficit* occurs when imports exceed exports. The United States has a trade deficit in goods. In 2009 U.S. imports of goods exceeded U.S. exports of goods by $517 billion.
- A *trade surplus* occurs when exports exceed imports. The United States has a trade surplus in services (such as air transportation services and financial services). In 2009 U.S. exports of services exceeded U.S. imports of services by $138 billion.
- Principal U.S. exports include chemicals, agricultural products, consumer durables, semiconductors, and aircraft; principal imports include petroleum, automobiles, metals, household appliances, and computers.
- As with other advanced industrial nations, the United States imports many goods that are in some of the same categories as the goods that it exports. Examples: automobiles, computers, chemicals, semiconductors, and telecommunications equipment.
- Canada is the United States' most important trading partner quantitatively. In 2009 about 20 percent of U.S. exported goods were sold to Canadians, who in turn provided 15 percent of imported U.S. goods.
- The United States has a sizable trade deficit with China. In 2009 it was $220 billion.
- The U.S. dependence on foreign oil is reflected in its trade with members of OPEC. In 2009 the United States imported $112 billion of goods (mainly oil) from OPEC members, while exporting $48 billion of goods to those countries.
- The United States leads the world in the combined volume of exports and imports, as measured in dollars. China, Germany, the United States, Japan, and the Netherlands were the top five exporters by dollar in 2009.
- Currently, the United States provides about 8.5 percent of the world's exports. (See Global Perspective 20.1.)
- Exports of goods and services (on a national income account basis) make up about 13 percent of total U.S.

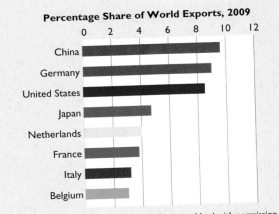

GLOBAL PERSPECTIVE 20.1

Shares of World Exports, Selected Nations

China has the largest share of world exports, followed by Germany and the United States. The eight largest export nations account for about 46 percent of world exports.

Percentage Share of World Exports, 2009

China
Germany
United States
Japan
Netherlands
France
Italy
Belgium

Source: International Trade Statistics, WTO Publications. Used with permission of the World Trade Organization, www.wto.org.

output. That percentage is much lower than the percentage in many other nations, including Canada, France, Germany, the Netherlands, and South Korea. (See Global Perspective 20.2.)

- China has become a major international trader, with an estimated $1.2 trillion of exports in 2009. Other Asian economies—including South Korea, Taiwan, and Singapore—are also active in international trade. Their combined exports exceed those of France, Britain, or Italy.
- International trade links world economies. Through trade, changes in economic conditions in one place on the globe can quickly affect other places.
- International trade is often at the center of debates over economic policy, both within the United States and internationally.

With this information in mind, let's turn to the economics of international trade.

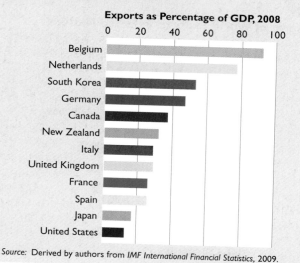

Source: Derived by authors from *IMF International Financial Statistics,* 2009.

The Economic Basis for Trade

Sovereign nations, like individuals and the regions of a nation, can gain by specializing in the products they can produce with the greatest relative efficiency and by trading for the goods they cannot produce as efficiently. The simple answer to the question "Why do nations trade?" is "They trade because it is beneficial." The benefits that emerge relate to three underlying facts:

- The distribution of natural, human, and capital resources among nations is uneven; nations differ in their endowments of economic resources.

- Efficient production of various goods requires different technologies, and not all nations have the same level of technological expertise.

- Products are differentiated as to quality and other attributes, and some people may prefer certain goods imported from abroad rather than similar goods produced domestically.

To recognize the character and interaction of these three facts, think of China, which has abundant and inexpensive labor. As a result, China can produce efficiently (at low cost of other goods forgone) a variety of **labor-intensive goods,** such as textiles, electronics, apparel, toys, and sporting goods.

In contrast, Australia has vast amounts of land and can inexpensively produce such **land-intensive goods** as beef, wool, and meat. Mexico has the soil, tropical climate, rainfall, and ready supply of unskilled labor that allow for the efficient, low-cost production of vegetables. Industrially advanced economies such as the United States and Germany that have relatively large amounts of capital can inexpensively produce goods whose production requires much capital, including such **capital-intensive goods** as airplanes, automobiles, agricultural equipment, machinery, and chemicals.

Also, regardless of their resource intensities, nations can develop individual products that are in demand worldwide because of their special qualities. Examples: fashions from Italy, chocolates from Belgium, software from the United States, and watches from Switzerland.

The distribution of resources, technology, and product distinctiveness among nations is relatively stable in short time periods but certainly can change over time. When that distribution changes, the relative efficiency and success that nations have in producing and selling goods also changes. For example, in the past several decades, South Korea has greatly expanded its stock of capital. Although South Korea was primarily an exporter of agricultural products and raw materials a half-century ago, it now exports large quantities of manufactured goods. Similarly, the new technologies that gave us synthetic fibers and synthetic rubber drastically altered the resource mix needed to produce fibers and rubber and changed the relative efficiency of nations in manufacturing them.

As national economies evolve, the size and quality of their labor forces may change, the volume and composition of their capital stocks may shift, new technologies may develop, and even the quality of land and the quantity of natural resources may be altered. As such changes take place, the relative efficiency with which a nation can produce specific goods will also change. As economists would say, comparative advantage can and does sometimes change.

Comparative Advantage

In an open economy (one with an international sector), a country produces more of certain goods (exports) and fewer of other goods (imports) than it would otherwise. Thus, the country shifts the use of labor and other productive resources toward export industries and away from import industries. For example, in the presence of international trade, the United States uses more resources to make commercial aircraft and to grow wheat and fewer resources to make television sets and sew clothes. So we ask: Do such shifts of resources make economic sense? Do they enhance U.S. total output and thus the U.S. standard of living?

The answers are affirmative. Specialization and international trade increase the productivity of U.S. resources and allow the United States to obtain greater total output than otherwise would be possible. These benefits are the result of exploiting both *absolute advantages* and *comparative advantages*. A country is said to have an *absolute advantage* over other producers of a product if it is the most efficient producer of that product (by which we mean that it can produce more output of that product from any given amount of resource inputs than can any other producer). A country is said to have a *comparative advantage* over other producers of a product if it can produce the product at a lower opportunity cost (by which we mean that it must forgo less output of alternative products when allocating productive resources to producing the product in question).

In 1776 Adam Smith used the concept of absolute advantage to argue for international specialization and trade. His point was that nations would be better off if they each specialized in the production of those products in which they had an absolute advantage and were therefore the most efficient producers:

> It is the maxim of every prudent master of a family, never to attempt to make at home what it will cost him more to make than to buy. The taylor does not attempt to make his own shoes, but buys them of the shoemaker. The shoemaker does not attempt to make his own clothes, but employs a taylor. The farmer attempts to make neither the one nor the other, but employs those different artificers. . . .
>
>   What is prudence in the conduct of every private family, can scarce be folly in that of a great kingdom. If a foreign country can supply us with a commodity cheaper than we can make it, better buy it of them with some part of the produce of our own industry, employed in a way in which we have some advantage.[1]

In the early 1800s, David Ricardo extended Smith's idea by demonstrating that it is advantageous for a country to specialize and trade with another country even if it is more productive in all economic activities than that other country. Stated more formally, a nation does not need Smith's absolute advantage—total superiority in the efficiency with which it produces products—to benefit from specialization and trade. It needs only a comparative advantage.

The nearby Consider This box provides a simple, two-person illustration of Ricardo's principle of comparative

---

[1]Adam Smith, *The Wealth of Nations* (originally published, 1776; New York: Modern Library, 1937), p. 424.

CONSIDER THIS . . .

A CPA and a House Painter

Suppose that Madison, a certified public accountant (CPA), is a swifter painter than Mason, the professional painter she is thinking of hiring. Also assume that Madison can earn $50 per hour as an accountant but would have to pay Mason $15 per hour. And suppose that Madison would need 30 hours to paint her house but Mason would need 40 hours.

Should Madison take time from her accounting to paint her own house, or should she hire the painter? Madison's opportunity cost of painting her house is $1500 (= 30 hours of sacrificed CPA time × $50 per CPA hour). The cost of hiring Mason is only $600 (= 40 hours of painting × $15 per hour of painting). Although Madison is better at both accounting and painting, she will get her house painted at lower cost by specializing in accounting and using some of her earnings from accounting to hire a house painter.

Similarly, Mason can reduce his cost of obtaining accounting services by specializing in painting and using some of his income to hire Madison to prepare his income tax forms. Suppose Mason would need 10 hours to prepare his tax return, while Madison could handle the task in 2 hours. Mason would sacrifice $150 of income (= 10 hours of painting time × $15 per hour) to do something he could hire Madison to do for $100 (= 2 hours of CPA time × $50 per CPA hour). By specializing in painting and hiring Madison to prepare his tax return, Mason lowers the cost of getting his tax return prepared.

We will see that what is true for our CPA and house painter is also true for nations. Specializing on the basis of comparative advantage enables nations to reduce the cost of obtaining the goods and services they desire.

advantage. Be sure to read it now, because it will greatly help you understand the graphical analysis that follows.

Two Isolated Nations

Our goal is to place the idea of comparative advantage into the context of trading nations. Our method is to build a simple model that relies on the familiar concepts of production possibilities curves. Suppose the world consists of just two nations, the United States and Mexico. Also for simplicity, suppose that the labor forces in the United States and Mexico are of equal size. Each nation can

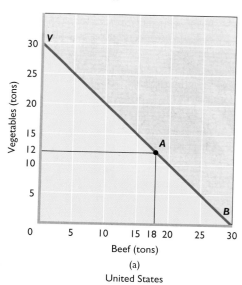

(a)
United States

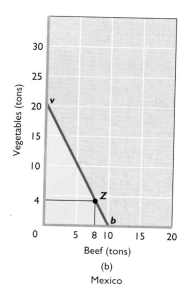

(b)
Mexico

FIGURE 20.1 Production possibilities for the United States and Mexico. The two production possibilities curves show the combinations of vegetables and beef that (a) the United States and (b) Mexico can produce domestically. The curves for both countries are straight lines because we are assuming constant opportunity costs. The different cost ratios, 1 vegetables ≡ 1 beef for the United States, and 2 vegetables ≡ 1 beef for Mexico, are reflected in the different slopes of the two lines.

produce both beef and raw (unprocessed) vegetables but at different levels of economic efficiency. Suppose the U.S. and Mexican domestic production possibilities curves for beef and vegetables are those shown in Figure 20.1a and Figure 20.1b. Note three realities relating to the production possibilities curves in the two graphs:

- **Constant costs** The curves derive from the tables and are drawn as straight lines, in contrast to the bowed-outward production possibilities frontiers we examined in Chapter 1. This means that we have replaced the law of increasing opportunity costs with the assumption of constant costs. This substitution simplifies our discussion but does not impair the validity of our analysis and conclusions. Later we will consider the effects of increasing opportunity costs.

- **Different costs** The production possibilities curves of the United States and Mexico reflect different resource mixes and differing levels of technology. Specifically, the differing slopes of the two curves reflect the numbers in the figures and reveal that the opportunity costs of producing beef and vegetables differ between the two nations.

- **U.S. absolute advantage in both** A producer (an individual, firm, or country) has an *absolute advantage* over another producer if it can produce more of a product than the other producer using the same amount of resources. Because of our convenient assumption that the U.S. and Mexican labor forces are the same size, the two production possibilities curves show that the United States has an absolute advantage in producing both products. If the United States and Mexico use

their entire (equal-size) labor forces to produce either vegetables or beef, the United States can produce more of either than Mexico. The United States, using the same number of workers as Mexico, has greater production possibilities. So output per worker—labor productivity—in the United States exceeds that in Mexico in producing both products.

Opportunity-Cost Ratio in the United States In Figure 20.1a, with full employment, the United States will operate at some point on its production possibilities curve. On that curve, it can increase its output of beef from 0 tons to 30 tons by forgoing 30 tons of vegetables output. So the slope of the production possibilities curve is 1 (= 30 vegetables/30 beef), meaning that 1 ton of vegetables must be sacrificed for each extra ton of beef. In the United States the **opportunity-cost ratio** (domestic exchange ratio) for the two products is 1 ton of vegetables (V) for 1 ton of beef (B), or

United States: $1V \equiv 1B$ (The "≡" sign simply means "equivalent to.")

Within its borders, the United States can "exchange" a ton of vegetables from itself for a ton of beef from itself. Our constant-cost assumption means that this exchange or opportunity-cost relationship prevails for all possible moves from one point to another along the U.S. production possibilities curve.

Opportunity-Cost Ratio in Mexico Mexico's production possibilities curve in Figure 20.1b represents a

TABLE 20.1 International Specialization According to Comparative Advantage and the Gains from Trade

Country	(1) Outputs before Specialization	(2) Outputs after Specialization	(3) Amounts Exported (−) and Imported (+)	(4) Outputs Available after Trade	(5) Gains from Specialization and Trade (4) − (1)
United States	18 beef 12 vegetables	30 beef 0 vegetables	−10 beef +15 vegetables	20 beef 15 vegetables	2 beef 3 vegetables
Mexico	8 beef 4 vegetables	0 beef 20 vegetables	+10 beef −15 vegetables	10 beef 5 vegetables	2 beef 1 vegetables

different full-employment opportunity-cost ratio. In Mexico, 20 tons of vegetables must be given up to obtain 10 tons of beef. The slope of the production possibilities curve is 2 (= 20 vegetables/10 beef). This means that in Mexico the opportunity-cost ratio for the two goods is 2 tons of vegetables for 1 ton of beef, or

$$\text{Mexico: } 2V \equiv 1B$$

Self-Sufficiency Output Mix

If the United States and Mexico are isolated and self-sufficient, then each country must choose some output mix on its production possibilities curve. It will select the mix that provides the greatest total utility or satisfaction. Let's assume that combination point *A* in Figure 20.1a is the optimal mix in the United States. That is, society deems the combination of 18 tons of beef and 12 tons of vegetables preferable to any other combination of the goods available along the production possibilities curve. Suppose Mexico's optimal product mix is 8 tons of beef and 4 tons of vegetables, indicated by point *Z* in Figure 20.1b. These choices by the two countries are reflected in column 1 of Table 20.1.

Specializing Based on Comparative Advantage

A producer (an individual, firm, or nation) has a **comparative advantage** in producing a particular product if it can produce that product at a lower opportunity cost than other producers. Comparative advantage is the key determinant in whether or not nations can gain from specialization and trade. In fact, absolute advantage turns out to be irrelevant.

In our example, for instance, the United States has an absolute advantage over Mexico in producing both vegetables and beef. But it is still the case that the United States can gain from specialization and trade with Mexico. That is because what actually matters is whether the opportunity costs of producing the two products (beef and vegetables) differ in the two countries. If they do, then each nation will enjoy a comparative advantage in one of the products,

meaning that it can produce that product at a lower opportunity cost than the other country. As a result, total output can increase if each country specializes in the production of the good in which it has the lower opportunity cost.

This idea is summarized in the **principle of comparative advantage,** which says that total output will be greatest when each good is produced by the nation that has the lowest domestic opportunity cost for producing that good. In our two-nation illustration, the United States has the lower domestic opportunity cost for beef; the United States must forgo only 1 ton of vegetables to produce 1 ton of beef, whereas Mexico must forgo 2 tons of vegetables for 1 ton of beef. The United States has a comparative (cost) advantage in beef and should specialize in beef production. The "world" (that is, the United States and Mexico) in our example would clearly not be economizing in the use of its resources if a high-cost producer (Mexico) produced a specific product (beef) when a low-cost producer (the United States) could have produced it. Having Mexico produce beef would mean that the world economy would have to give up more vegetables than is necessary to obtain a ton of beef.

Mexico has the lower domestic opportunity cost for vegetables. It must sacrifice only $\frac{1}{2}$ ton of beef to produce 1 ton of vegetables, while the United States must forgo 1 ton of beef to produce 1 ton of vegetables. Mexico has a comparative advantage in vegetables and should specialize in vegetable production. Again, the world would not be employing its resources economically if vegetables were produced by a high-cost producer (the United States) rather than by a low-cost producer (Mexico). If the United States produced vegetables, the world would be giving up more beef than necessary to obtain each ton of vegetables. Economizing requires that any particular good be produced by the nation having the lowest domestic opportunity cost or the nation having the comparative advantage for that good. The United States should produce beef, and Mexico should produce vegetables. The situation is summarized in Table 20.2.

TABLE 20.2 Comparative-Advantage Example: A Summary

Beef	Vegetables
Mexico: Must give up 2 tons of vegetables to get 1 ton of beef.	**Mexico:** Must give up $\frac{1}{2}$ ton of beef to get 1 ton of vegetables.
United States: Must give up 1 ton of vegetables to get 1 ton of beef.	**United States:** Must give up 1 ton of beef to get 1 ton of vegetables.
Comparative advantage: United States	**Comparative advantage:** Mexico

A comparison of columns 1 and 2 in Table 20.1 verifies that specialized production enables the world to obtain more output from its fixed amount of resources. By

ORIGIN OF THE IDEA

O 20.1

Absolute and comparative advantage

specializing completely in beef, the United States can produce 30 tons of beef and no vegetables. Mexico, by specializing completely in vegetables, can produce 20 tons of vegetables and no beef. These figures exceed the yields generated without specialization: 26 tons of beef (= 18 in the United States + 8 in Mexico) and 16 tons of vegetables (= 12 in the United States + 4 in Mexico). As a result, the world ends up with 4 more tons of beef (= 30 tons − 26 tons) and 4 more tons of vegetables (= 20 tons − 16 tons) than it would if there were self-sufficiency and unspecialized production.

Terms of Trade

We have just seen that specialization in production will allow for the largest possible amounts of both beef and vegetables to be produced. But with each country specializing in the production of only one item, how will the vegetables that are all produced by Mexico and the beef that is all produced by the United States be divided between consumers in the two countries? The key turns out to be the **terms of trade,** the exchange ratio at which the United States and Mexico trade beef and vegetables.

Crucially, the terms of trade also establish whether each country will find it in its own better interest to bother specializing at all. This is because the terms of trade determine whether each country can "get a better deal" by specializing and trading than it could if it opted instead for self sufficiency. To see how this works, note that because $1B \equiv 1V$ (= $1V \equiv 1B$) in the United States, it must get more than 1 ton of vegetables for each 1 ton of beef exported; otherwise, it will not benefit from exporting beef in exchange for Mexican vegetables. The United States must get a better

"price" (more vegetables) for its beef through international trade than it can get domestically; otherwise, no gain from trade exists and such trade will not occur.

Similarly, because $1B \equiv 2V$ (= $2V \equiv 1B$) in Mexico, Mexico must obtain 1 ton of beef by exporting less than 2 tons of vegetables to get it. Mexico must be able to pay a lower "price" for beef in the world market than it must pay domestically, or else it will not want to trade. The international exchange ratio or terms of trade must therefore lie somewhere between

$$1B \equiv 1V \text{ (United States' cost conditions)}$$

and

$$1B \equiv 2V \text{ (Mexico's cost conditions)}$$

Where between these limits will the world exchange ratio fall? The United States will prefer a rate close to $1B \equiv 2V$, say, $1B \equiv 1\frac{3}{4} V$. The United States wants to obtain as many vegetables as possible for each 1 ton of beef it exports. By contrast, Mexico wants a rate near $1B \equiv 1V$, say, $1B \equiv 1\frac{1}{4} V$. This is true because Mexico wants to export as few vegetables as possible for each 1 ton of beef it receives in exchange.

The actual exchange ratio depends on world supply and demand for the two products. If overall world demand for vegetables is weak relative to its supply and if the demand for beef is strong relative to its supply, the price of vegetables will be lower and the price of beef will be higher. The exchange ratio will settle nearer the $1B \equiv 2V$ figure the United States prefers. If overall world demand for vegetables is great relative to its supply and if the demand for beef is weak relative to its supply, the ratio will settle nearer the $1B \equiv 1V$ level favorable to Mexico. In this manner, the actual exchange ratio that is set by world supply and demand determines how the gains from international specialization and trade are divided between the two nations and, consequently, how the beef that is all produced in the United States and the vegetables that are all produced in Mexico get divided among consumers in the two countries. (We discuss equilibrium world prices later in this chapter.)

Gains from Trade

Suppose the international terms of trade are $1B \equiv 1\frac{1}{2} V$. The possibility of trading on these terms permits each nation to supplant its domestic production possibilities curve with a trading possibilities line (or curve), as shown in **Figure 20.2 (Key Graph).** Just as a production possibilities curve shows the amounts of these products that a full-employment economy can obtain by shifting resources from one to the other, a **trading possibilities line** shows

key graph

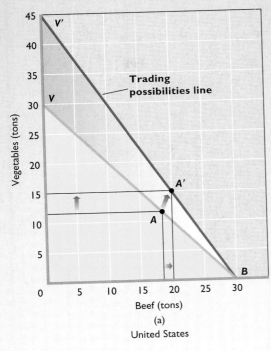

(a)
United States

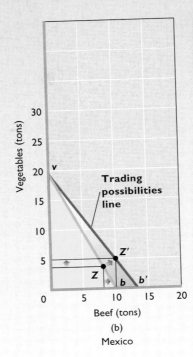

(b)
Mexico

FIGURE 20.2 Trading possibilities lines and the gains from trade. As a result of specialization and trade, both the United States and Mexico can have higher levels of output than the levels attainable on their domestic production possibilities curves. (a) The United States can move from point A on its domestic production possibilities curve to, say, A' on its trading possibilities line. (b) Mexico can move from Z to Z'.

QUICK QUIZ FOR FIGURE 20.2

1. The production possibilities curves in graphs (a) and (b) imply:
   a. increasing domestic opportunity costs.
   b. decreasing domestic opportunity costs.
   c. constant domestic opportunity costs.
   d. first decreasing, then increasing, domestic opportunity costs.

2. Before specialization, the domestic opportunity cost of producing 1 unit of beef is:
   a. 1 unit of vegetables in both the United States and Mexico.
   b. 1 unit of vegetables in the United States and 2 units of vegetables in Mexico.
   c. 2 units of vegetables in the United States and 1 unit of vegetables in Mexico.
   d. 1 unit of vegetables in the United States and $\frac{1}{2}$ unit of vegetables in Mexico.

3. After specialization and international trade, the world output of beef and vegetables is:
   a. 20 tons of beef and 20 tons of vegetables.
   b. 45 tons of beef and 15 tons of vegetables.
   c. 30 tons of beef and 20 tons of vegetables.
   d. 10 tons of beef and 30 tons of vegetables.

4. After specialization and international trade:
   a. the United States can obtain units of vegetables at less cost than it could before trade.
   b. Mexico can obtain more than 20 tons of vegetables, if it so chooses.
   c. the United States no longer has a comparative advantage in producing beef.
   d. Mexico can benefit by prohibiting vegetables imports from the United States.

Answers: 1. c; 2. b; 3. c; 4. a

the amounts of the two products that a nation can obtain by specializing in one product and trading for the other. The trading possibilities lines in Figure 20.2 reflect the assumption that both nations specialize on the basis of comparative advantage: The United States specializes completely in beef (at point *B* in Figure 20.2a), and Mexico specializes completely in vegetables (at point *v* in Figure 20.2b).

Improved Alternatives With specialization and trade, the United States is no longer constrained by its domestic production possibilities line, which requires it to give up 1 ton of beef for every 1 ton of vegetables it wants as it moves up its domestic production possibilities line from, say, point *B*. Instead, the United States, through trade with Mexico, can get 1$\frac{1}{2}$ tons of vegetables for every ton of beef that it exports to Mexico, as long as Mexico has vegetables

405

to export. Trading possibilities line BV' thus represents the $1B \equiv 1\frac{1}{2} V$ trading ratio.

Similarly, Mexico, starting at, say, point v, no longer has to move down its domestic production possibilities curve, giving up 2 tons of vegetables for each ton of beef it wants. It can now export just $1\frac{1}{2}$ tons of vegetables for each 1 ton of beef that it wants by moving down its trading possibilities line vb'.

Specialization and trade create a new exchange ratio between beef and vegetables, and that ratio is reflected in each nation's trading possibilities line. For both nations, this exchange ratio is superior to the unspecialized exchange ratio embodied in their respective production possibilities curves. By specializing in beef and trading for Mexico's vegetables, the United States can obtain more than 1 ton of vegetables for 1 ton of beef. By specializing in vegetables and trading for U.S. beef, Mexico can obtain 1 ton of beef for less than 2 tons of vegetables. In both cases, self-sufficiency is inefficient and therefore undesirable.

Greater Output
By specializing on the basis of comparative advantage and by trading for goods that are produced in the nation with greater domestic efficiency, the United States and Mexico can achieve combinations of beef and vegetables beyond their own individual production possibilities curves. Specialization according to comparative advantage results in a more efficient allocation of world resources, and larger outputs of both products are therefore available to both nations.

Suppose that at the $1B \equiv 1\frac{1}{2} V$ terms of trade, the United States exports 10 tons of beef to Mexico and in return Mexico exports 15 tons of vegetables to the United States. How do the new quantities of beef and vegetables available to the two nations compare with the optimal product mixes that existed before specialization and trade? Point A in Figure 20.2a reminds us that the United States chose 18 tons of beef and 12 tons of vegetables originally. But by producing 30 tons of beef and no vegetables and by trading 10 tons of beef for 15 tons of vegetables, the United States can obtain 20 tons of beef and 15 tons of vegetables. This new, superior combination of beef and vegetables is indicated by point A' in Figure 20.2a. Compared with the no-trade amounts of 18 tons of beef and 12 tons of vegetables, the United States' **gains from trade** are 2 tons of beef and 3 tons of vegetables.

Similarly, recall that Mexico's optimal product mix was 4 tons of vegetables and 8 tons of beef (point Z) before specialization and trade. Now, after specializing in vegetables and trading for beef, Mexico can have 5 tons of vegetables and 10 tons of beef. It accomplishes that by producing 20 tons of vegetables and no beef and exporting 15 tons of its vegetables in exchange for 10 tons of American beef. This new position is indicated by point Z' in Figure 20.2b. Mexico's gains from trade are 1 ton of vegetables and 2 tons of beef.

Points A' and Z' in Figure 20.2 are superior economic positions to points A and Z. This fact is enormously important! We know that a nation can expand its production possibilities boundary by (1) expanding the quantity and improving the quality of its resources or (2) realizing technological progress. We have now established that international trade can enable a nation to circumvent the output constraint illustrated by its production possibilities curve. An economy can grow by expanding international trade. The outcome of international specialization and trade is equivalent to having more and better resources or discovering and implementing improved production techniques.

Table 20.1 summarizes the transactions and outcomes in our analysis. Please give it one final careful review.

INTERACTIVE GRAPHS

G 20.1

Comparative advantage

WORKED PROBLEMS

W 20.1

Gains from trade

CONSIDER THIS . . .

Misunderstanding the Gains from Trade

It is a common myth that the greatest benefit to be derived from international trade is greater domestic employment in the export sector. This suggests that exports are "good" because they increase domestic employment, whereas imports are "bad" because they deprive people of jobs at home. As we have demonstrated, the true benefit created by international trade is the overall increase in output available through specialization and exchange.

A nation does not need international trade to operate *on* its production possibilities curve. It can fully employ its resources, including labor, with or without international trade. International trade, however, enables a country to reach a point of consumption beyond its domestic production possibilities curve. The gain from trade to a nation is the extra output obtained from abroad—the imports obtained for less sacrifice of other goods than if they were produced at home.

Trade with Increasing Costs

To explain the basic principles underlying international trade, we simplified our analysis in several ways. For example, we limited discussion to two products and two nations. But multiproduct and multinational analysis yield the same conclusions. We also assumed constant opportunity costs (linear production possibilities curves), which is a more substantive simplification. Let's consider the effect of allowing increasing opportunity costs (concave-to-the-origin production possibilities curves) to enter the picture.

Suppose that the United States and Mexico initially are at positions on their concave production possibilities curves where their domestic cost ratios are $1B \equiv 1V$ and $1B \equiv 2V$, as they were in our constant-cost analysis. As before, comparative advantage indicates that the United States should specialize in beef and Mexico in vegetables. But now, as the United States begins to expand beef production, its cost of beef will rise; it will have to sacrifice more than 1 ton of vegetables to get 1 additional ton of beef. Resources are no longer perfectly substitutable between alternative uses, as the constant-cost assumption implied. Resources less and less suitable to beef production must be allocated to the U.S. beef industry in expanding beef output, and that means increasing costs—the sacrifice of larger and larger amounts of vegetables for each additional ton of beef.

Similarly, suppose that Mexico expands vegetable production starting from its $1B \equiv 2V$ cost ratio position. As production increases, it will find that its $1B \equiv 2V$ cost ratio begins to rise. Sacrificing 1 ton of beef will free resources that are capable of producing only something less than 2 tons of vegetables, because those transferred resources are less suitable to vegetable production.

As the U.S. cost ratio falls from $1B \equiv 1V$ and the Mexican ratio rises from $1B \equiv 2V$, a point will be reached where the cost ratios are equal in the two nations, perhaps at $1B \equiv 1\frac{3}{4}V$. At this point the underlying basis for further specialization and trade—differing cost ratios—has disappeared, and further specialization is therefore uneconomical. And, most important, this point of equal cost ratios may be reached while the United States is still producing some vegetables along with its beef and Mexico is producing some beef along with its vegetables. The primary effect of increasing opportunity costs is less-than-complete specialization. For this reason, we often find domestically produced products competing directly against identical or similar imported products within a particular economy.

The Case for Free Trade

The case for free trade reduces to one compelling argument: Through free trade based on the principle of comparative advantage, the world economy can achieve a more efficient allocation of resources and a higher level of material well-being than it can without free trade.

Since the resource mixes and technological knowledge of the world's nations are all somewhat different, each nation can produce particular commodities at different real costs. Each nation should produce goods for which its domestic opportunity costs are lower than the domestic opportunity costs of other nations and exchange those goods for products for which its domestic opportunity costs are high relative to those of other nations. If each nation does this, the world will realize the advantages of geographic and human specialization. The world and each free-trading nation can obtain a larger real income from the fixed supplies of resources available to it.

Government trade barriers lessen or eliminate gains from specialization. If nations cannot trade freely, they must shift resources from efficient (low-cost) to inefficient (high-cost) uses to satisfy their diverse wants. A recent study suggests that the elimination of trade barriers since the Second World War has increased the income of the average U.S. household by at least $7000 and perhaps by as much as $13,000. These income gains are recurring; they happen year after year.[2]

One side benefit of free trade is that it promotes competition and deters monopoly. The increased competition from foreign firms forces domestic firms to find and use the lowest-cost production techniques. It also compels them to be innovative with respect to both product quality and production methods, thereby contributing to economic growth. And free trade gives consumers a wider range of product choices. The reasons to favor free trade are the same as the reasons to endorse competition.

A second side benefit of free trade is that it links national interests and breaks down national animosities. Confronted with political disagreements, trading partners tend to negotiate rather than make war.

QUICK REVIEW 20.1

- International trade enables nations to specialize, increase productivity, and increase output available for consumption.
- Comparative advantage means total world output will be greatest when each good is produced by the nation that has the lowest domestic opportunity cost.
- Specialization is less than complete among nations because opportunity costs normally rise as any specific nation produces more of a particular good.

---

[2]Scott C. Bradford, Paul L. E. Grieco, and Gary C. Hufbauer, "The Payoff to America from Globalization," *The World Economy*, July 2006, pp. 893–916.

Supply and Demand Analysis of Exports and Imports

Supply and demand analysis reveals how equilibrium prices and quantities of exports and imports are determined. The amount of a good or a service a nation will export or import depends on differences between the equilibrium world price and the equilibrium domestic price. The interaction of *world* supply and demand determines the equilibrium **world price**—the price that equates the quantities supplied and demanded globally. *Domestic* supply and demand determine the equilibrium **domestic price**—the price that would prevail in a closed economy that does not engage in international trade. The domestic price equates quantity supplied and quantity demanded domestically.

In the absence of trade, the domestic prices in a closed economy may or may not equal the world equilibrium prices. When economies are opened for international trade, differences between world and domestic prices encourage exports or imports. To see how, consider the international effects of such price differences in a simple two-nation world, consisting of the United States and Canada, that are both producing aluminum. We assume there are no trade barriers, such as tariffs and quotas, and no international transportation costs.

Supply and Demand in the United States

Figure 20.3a shows the domestic supply curve S_d and the domestic demand curve D_d for aluminum in the United States, which for now is a closed economy. The intersection of S_d and D_d determines the equilibrium domestic price of $1 per pound and the equilibrium domestic quantity of 100 million pounds. Domestic suppliers produce 100 million pounds and sell them all at $1 a pound. So there are no domestic surpluses or shortages of aluminum.

But what if the U.S. economy were opened to trade and the world price of aluminum were above or below this $1 domestic price?

U.S. Export Supply If the aluminum price in the rest of the world (that is, Canada) exceeds $1, U.S. firms will produce more than 100 million pounds and will export the excess domestic output. First, consider a world price of

FIGURE 20.3 U.S. export supply and import demand. (a) Domestic supply S_d and demand D_d set the domestic equilibrium price of aluminum at $1 per pound. At world prices above $1 there are domestic surpluses of aluminum. At prices below $1 there are domestic shortages. (b) Surpluses are exported (top curve), and shortages are met by importing aluminum (lower curve). The export supply curve shows the direct relationship between world prices and U.S. exports; the import demand curve portrays the inverse relationship between world prices and U.S. imports.

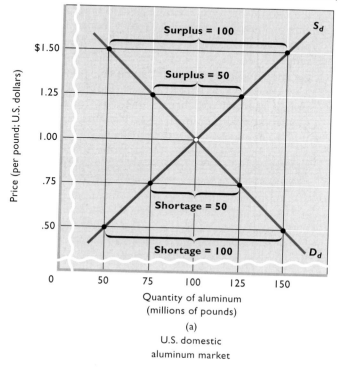

(a)
U.S. domestic
aluminum market

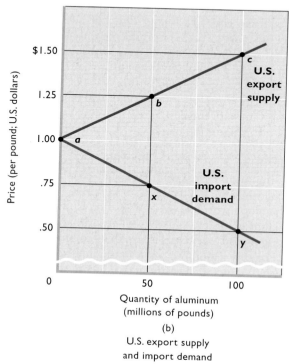

(b)
U.S. export supply
and import demand

$1.25. We see from the supply curve S_d that U.S. aluminum firms will produce 125 million pounds of aluminum at that price. The demand curve D_d tells us that the United States will purchase only 75 million pounds at $1.25. The outcome is a domestic surplus of 50 million pounds of aluminum. U.S. producers will export those 50 million pounds at the $1.25 world price.

What if the world price were $1.50? The supply curve shows that U.S. firms will produce 150 million pounds of aluminum, while the demand curve tells us that U.S. consumers will buy only 50 million pounds. So U.S. producers will export the domestic surplus of 100 million pounds.

Toward the top of Figure 20.3b we plot the domestic surpluses—the U.S. exports—that occur at world prices above the $1 domestic equilibrium price. When the world and domestic prices are equal (= $1), the quantity of exports supplied is zero (point *a*). There is no surplus of domestic output to export. But when the world price is $1.25, U.S. firms export 50 million pounds of surplus aluminum (point *b*). At a $1.50 world price, the domestic surplus of 100 million pounds is exported (point *c*).

The U.S. **export supply curve,** found by connecting points *a*, *b*, and *c*, shows the amount of aluminum U.S. producers will export at each world price above $1. This curve *slopes upward*, indicating a direct or positive relationship between the world price and the amount of U.S. exports. As world prices increase relative to domestic prices, U.S. exports rise.

U.S. Import Demand If the world price is below the domestic $1 price, the United States will import aluminum. Consider a $.75 world price. The supply curve in Figure 20.3a reveals that at that price U.S. firms produce only 75 million pounds of aluminum. But the demand curve shows that the United States wants to buy 125 million pounds at that price. The result is a domestic shortage of 50 million pounds. To satisfy that shortage, the United States will import 50 million pounds of aluminum.

At an even lower world price, $.50, U.S. producers will supply only 50 million pounds. Because U.S. consumers want to buy 150 million pounds at that price, there is a domestic shortage of 100 million pounds. Imports will flow to the United States to make up the difference. That is, at a $.50 world price U.S. firms will supply 50 million pounds and 100 million pounds will be imported.

In Figure 20.3b we plot the U.S. **import demand curve** from these data. This *downsloping curve* shows the amounts of aluminum that will be imported at world prices below the $1 U.S. domestic price. The relationship between world prices and imported amounts is inverse or negative. At a world price of $1, domestic output will sat-

isfy U.S. demand; imports will be zero (point *a*). But at $.75 the United States will import 50 million pounds of aluminum (point *x*); at $.50, the United States will import 100 million pounds (point *y*). Connecting points *a*, *x*, and *y* yields the *downsloping* U.S. import demand curve. It reveals that as world prices fall relative to U.S. domestic prices, U.S. imports increase.

Supply and Demand in Canada

We repeat our analysis in Figure 20.4, this time from the viewpoint of Canada. (We have converted Canadian dollar prices to U.S. dollar prices via the exchange rate.) Note that the domestic supply curve S_d and the domestic demand curve D_d for aluminum in Canada yield a domestic price of $.75, which is $.25 lower than the $1 U.S. domestic price.

The analysis proceeds exactly as above except that the domestic price is now the Canadian price. If the world price is $.75, Canadians will neither export nor import aluminum (giving us point *q* in Figure 20.4b). At world prices above $.75, Canadian firms will produce more aluminum than Canadian consumers will buy. Canadian firms will export the surplus. At a $1 world price, Figure 20.4b tells us that Canada will have and export a domestic surplus of 50 million pounds (yielding point *r*). At $1.25, it will have and will export a domestic surplus of 100 million pounds (point *s*). Connecting these points yields the upsloping Canadian export supply curve, which reflects the domestic surpluses (and hence the exports) that occur when the world price exceeds the $.75 Canadian domestic price.

At world prices below $.75, domestic shortages occur in Canada. At a $.50 world price, Figure 20.4a shows that Canadian consumers want to buy 125 million pounds of aluminum but Canadian firms will produce only 75 million pounds. The shortage will bring 50 million pounds of imports to Canada (point *t* in Figure 20.4b). The Canadian import demand curve in that figure shows the Canadian imports that will occur at all world aluminum prices below the $.75 Canadian domestic price.

Equilibrium World Price, Exports, and Imports

We now have the tools for determining the **equilibrium world price** of aluminum and the equilibrium world levels of exports and imports when the world is opened to trade. Figure 20.5 combines the U.S. export supply curve and import demand curve in Figure 20.3b and the Canadian export supply curve and import demand curve in Figure 20.4b. The two U.S. curves proceed rightward from the $1 U.S. domestic price; the two Canadian curves proceed rightward from the $.75 Canadian domestic price.

FIGURE 20.4 **Canadian export supply and import demand.** (a) At world prices above the $.75 domestic price, production in Canada exceeds domestic consumption. At world prices below $.75, domestic shortages occur. (b) Surpluses result in exports, and shortages result in imports. The Canadian export supply curve and import demand curve depict the relationships between world prices and exports or imports.

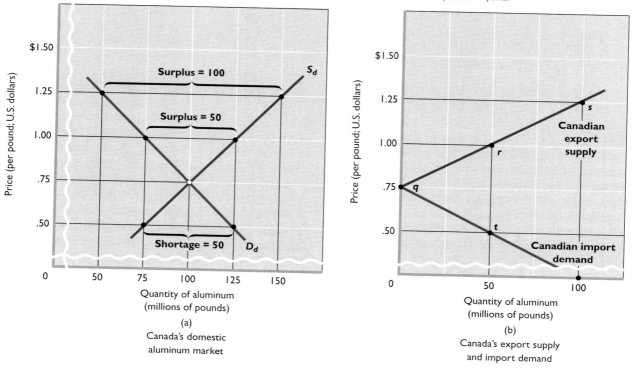

(a)
Canada's domestic
aluminum market

(b)
Canada's export supply
and import demand

FIGURE 20.5 **Equilibrium world price and quantity of exports and imports.** In a two-nation world, the equilibrium world price (= $.88) is determined by the intersection of one nation's export supply curve and the other nation's import demand curve. This intersection also decides the equilibrium volume of exports and imports. Here, Canada exports 25 million pounds of aluminum to the United States.

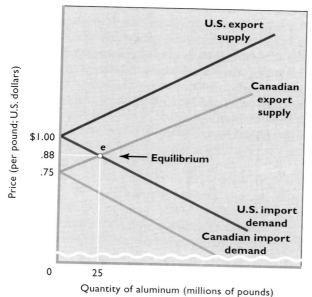

Quantity of aluminum (millions of pounds)

WORKED PROBLEMS

W 20.2

Equilibrium world price, exports, and imports

International equilibrium occurs in this two-nation model where one nation's import demand curve intersects another nation's export supply curve. In this case the U.S. import demand curve intersects Canada's export supply curve at *e*. There, the world price of aluminum is $.88. The Canadian export supply curve indicates that Canada will export 25 million pounds of aluminum at this price. Also at this price the United States will import 25 million pounds from Canada, indicated by the U.S. import demand curve. The $.88 world price equates the quantity of imports demanded and the quantity of exports supplied (25 million pounds). Thus, there will be world trade of 25 million pounds of aluminum at $.88 per pound.

Note that after trade, the single $.88 world price will prevail in both Canada and the United States. Only one price for a standardized commodity can persist in a highly competitive world market. With trade, all consumers can buy a pound of aluminum for $.88, and all producers can sell it for that price. This world price means that Canadians will pay more for aluminum with trade ($.88) than without it ($.75). The increased Canadian output caused by trade raises Canadian per-unit production costs and therefore raises the price of aluminum in Canada. The United States, however, pays less for aluminum with trade ($.88) than without it ($1). The U.S. gain comes from Canada's comparative cost advantage in producing aluminum.

Why would Canada willingly send 25 million pounds of its aluminum output to the United States for U.S. consumption? After all, producing this output uses up scarce Canadian resources and drives up the price of aluminum for Canadians. Canadians are willing to export aluminum to the United States because Canadians gain the means—the U.S. dollars—to import other goods, say, computer software, from the United States. Canadian exports enable Canadians to acquire imports that have greater value to Canadians than the exported aluminum. Canadian exports to the United States finance Canadian imports from the United States.

CONSIDER THIS . . .

Buy American?

Will "buying American" make Americans better off? No, says Dallas Federal Reserve economist W. Michael Cox:

A common myth is that it is better for Americans to spend their money at home than abroad. The best way to expose the fallacy of this argument is to take it to its logical extreme. If it is better for me to spend my money here than abroad, then it is even better yet to buy in Texas than in New York, better yet to buy in Dallas than in Houston . . . in my own neighborhood . . . within my own family . . . to consume only what I can produce. Alone and poor.*

———
* "The Fruits of Free Trade," 2002 Annual Report, by W. Michael Cox and Richard Alm, p. 16, Federal Reserve Bank of Dallas. Used with permission.

QUICK REVIEW 20.2

- A nation will export a particular product if the world price exceeds the domestic price; it will import the product if the world price is less than the domestic price.
- In a two-country world model, equilibrium world prices and equilibrium quantities of exports and imports occur where one nation's export supply curve intersects the other nation's import demand curve.

Trade Barriers and Export Subsidies

While a nation as a whole gains from trade, trade may harm particular domestic industries and their workers. Those industries might seek to preserve their economic positions by persuading their respective governments to protect them from imports—perhaps through tariffs, import quotas, or other trade barriers.

Indeed, the public may be won over by the apparent plausibility ("Cut imports and prevent domestic unemployment") and the patriotic ring ("Buy American!") of the arguments. The alleged benefits of tariffs are immediate and clear-cut to the public, but the adverse effects cited by economists are obscure and dispersed over the entire economy. When political deal-making is added in—"You back tariffs for the apparel industry in my state, and I'll back tariffs for the auto industry in your state"—the outcome can be a politically robust network of trade barriers. These impediments to free international trade can take several forms.

Tariffs are excise taxes or "duties" on the dollar values or physical quantities of imported goods. They may be imposed to obtain revenue or to protect domestic firms. A **revenue tariff** is usually applied to a product that is not being produced domestically, for example, tin, coffee, or bananas in the case of the United States. Rates on revenue tariffs tend to be modest and are designed to provide the Federal government with revenue. A **protective tariff** is implemented to shield domestic producers from foreign competition. These tariffs impede free trade by increasing the prices of imported goods and therefore shifting sales toward domestic producers. Although protective tariffs are usually not high enough to stop the importation of foreign goods, they put foreign producers at a competitive disadvantage. A tariff on imported auto tires, for example, would make domestically produced tires more attractive to consumers.

An **import quota** is a limit on the quantities or total values of specific items that are imported in some period. Once a quota is filled, further imports of that product are choked off. Import quotas are more effective than tariffs in impeding international trade. With a tariff, a product can go on being imported in large quantities. But with an import quota, all imports are prohibited once the quota is filled.

A **nontariff barrier (NTB)** includes onerous licensing requirements, unreasonable standards pertaining to product quality, or simply bureaucratic hurdles and delays in customs procedures. Some nations require that importers of foreign goods obtain licenses and then restrict the number of licenses issued. Although many nations carefully inspect imported agricultural products to prevent the introduction of potentially harmful insects, some countries use lengthy inspections to impede imports. Japan and the European countries frequently require that their domestic importers of foreign goods obtain licenses. By restricting the issuance of licenses, governments can limit imports.

A **voluntary export restriction (VER)** is a trade barrier by which foreign firms "voluntarily" limit the amount of their exports to a particular country. VERs have the same effect as import quotas and are agreed to by exporters to avoid more stringent tariffs or quotas. In the late 1990s, for example, Canadian producers of softwood lumber (fir, spruce, cedar, pine) agreed to a VER on exports to the United States under the threat of a permanently higher U.S. tariff.

ORIGIN OF THE IDEA

O 20.2

Trade protectionism

An **export subsidy** consists of a government payment to a domestic producer of export goods and is designed to aid that producer. By reducing production costs, the subsidies enable the domestic firm to charge a lower price and thus to sell more exports in world markets. Two examples: Some European governments have heavily subsidized Airbus Industries, a European firm that produces commercial aircraft. The subsidies help Airbus compete against the American firm Boeing. The United States and other nations have subsidized domestic farmers to boost the domestic food supply. Such subsidies have artificially lowered export prices on agricultural produce.

Later in this chapter we will discuss some of the specific arguments and appeals that are made to justify protection.

Economic Impact of Tariffs

We will confine our in-depth analysis of the effects of trade barriers to the two most common forms: tariffs and quotas. Once again, we turn to supply and demand analysis for help. Curves D_d and S_d in Figure 20.6 show domestic demand and supply for a product in which a nation, say, the United States, does *not* have a comparative advantage—for example, DVD players. (Disregard curve $S_d + Q$ for now.) Without world trade, the domestic price and output would be P_d and q, respectively.

Assume now that the domestic economy is opened to world trade and that Japan, which *does* have a comparative advantage in DVD players, begins to sell its players in the United States. We assume that with free trade the domestic price cannot differ from the world price, which here is P_w. At P_w domestic consumption is d and domestic production is a.

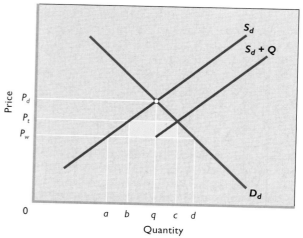

FIGURE 20.6 The economic effects of a protective tariff or an import quota. A tariff that increases the price of a good from P_w to P_t will reduce domestic consumption from d to c. Domestic producers will be able to sell more output (b rather than a) at a higher price (P_t rather than P_w). Foreign exporters are injured because they sell less output (bc rather than ad). The yellow area indicates the amount of tariff paid by domestic consumers. An import quota of bc units has the same effect as the tariff, with one exception: The amount represented by the yellow area will go to foreign producers rather than to the domestic government.

The horizontal distance between the domestic supply and demand curves at P_w represents imports of ad. Thus far, our analysis is similar to the analysis of world prices in Figure 20.3.

Direct Effects Suppose now that the United States imposes a tariff on each imported DVD player. The tariff, which raises the price of imported players from P_w to P_t, has four effects:

- *Decline in consumption* Consumption of DVD players in the United States declines from d to c as the higher price moves buyers up and to the left along their demand curve. The tariff prompts consumers to buy fewer players, and reallocate a portion of their expenditures to less desired substitute products. U.S. consumers are clearly injured by the tariff, since they pay $P_t - P_w$ more for each of the c units they buy at price P_t.

- *Increased domestic production* U.S. producers—who are not subject to the tariff—receive the higher price P_t per unit. Because this new price is higher than the pretariff world price P_w, the domestic DVD-player industry moves up and to the right along its supply curve S_d, increasing domestic output from a to b. Domestic producers thus enjoy both a higher price and expanded sales; this explains why domestic producers lobby for protective tariffs. But from a social point of view, the increase in domestic production from *a* to *b* means that the tariff permits domestic producers of players to bid resources away from other, more efficient, U.S. industries.

- **Decline in imports** Japanese producers are hurt. Although the sales price of each player is higher by $P_t - P_w$, that amount accrues to the U.S. government, not to Japanese producers. The after-tariff world price, or the per-unit revenue to Japanese producers, remains at P_w, but the volume of U.S. imports (Japanese exports) falls from *ad* to *bc*.

- **Tariff revenue** The yellow rectangle represents the amount of revenue the tariff yields. Total revenue from the tariff is determined by multiplying the tariff, $P_t - P_w$ per unit, by the number of players imported, *bc*. This tariff revenue is a transfer of income from consumers to government and does not represent any net change in the nation's economic well-being. The result is that government gains this portion of what consumers lose by paying more for DVD players.

Indirect Effect Tariffs have a subtle effect beyond what our supply and demand diagram can show. Because Japan sells fewer DVD players in the United States, it earns fewer dollars and so must buy fewer U.S. exports. U.S. export industries must then cut production and release resources. These are highly efficient industries, as we know from their comparative advantage and their ability to sell goods in world markets.

Tariffs directly promote the expansion of inefficient industries that do not have a comparative advantage; they also indirectly cause the contraction of relatively efficient industries that do have a comparative advantage. Put bluntly, tariffs cause resources to be shifted in the wrong direction—and that is not surprising. We know that specialization and world trade lead to more efficient use of world resources and greater world output. But protective tariffs reduce world trade. Therefore, tariffs also reduce efficiency and the world's real output.

Economic Impact of Quotas

We noted earlier that an import quota is a legal limit placed on the amount of some product that can be imported in a given year. Quotas have the same economic impact as a tariff, with one big difference: While tariffs generate revenue for the domestic government, a quota transfers that revenue to foreign producers.

Suppose in Figure 20.6 that, instead of imposing a tariff, the United States prohibits any imports of Japanese DVD players in excess of *bc* units. In other words, an import quota

of *bc* players is imposed on Japan. We deliberately chose the size of this quota to be the same amount as imports would be under a $P_t - P_w$ tariff so that we can compare "equivalent" situations. As a consequence of the quota, the supply of players is $S_d + Q$ in the United States. This supply consists of the domestic supply plus the fixed amount *bc* (= Q) that importers will provide at each domestic price. The supply curve $S_w + Q$ does not extend below price P_w because Japanese producers would not export players to the United States at any price below P_w; instead, they would sell them to other countries at the world market price of P_w.

Most of the economic results are the same as those with a tariff. Prices of DVD players are higher (P_t instead of P_w) because imports have been reduced from *ad* to *bc*. Domestic consumption of DVD players is down from *d* to *c*. U.S. producers enjoy both a higher price (P_t rather than P_w) and increased sales (*b* rather than *a*).

The difference is that the price increase of $P_t - P_w$ paid by U.S. consumers on imports of *bc*—the yellow area—no longer goes to the U.S. Treasury as tariff (tax) revenue but flows to the Japanese firms that have acquired the quota rights to sell DVD players in the United States. For consumers in the United States, a tariff produces a better economic outcome than a quota, other things being the same. A tariff generates government revenue that can be used to cut other taxes or to finance public goods and services that benefit the United States. In contrast, the higher price created by quotas results in additional revenue for foreign producers.

Net Costs of Tariffs and Quotas

Figure 20.6 shows that tariffs and quotas impose costs on domestic consumers but provide gains to domestic producers and, in the case of tariffs, revenue to the Federal government. The consumer costs of trade restrictions are calculated by determining the effect the restrictions have on consumer prices. Protection raises the price of a product in three ways: (1) The price of the imported product goes up; (2) the higher price of imports causes some consumers to shift their purchases to higher-priced domestically produced goods; and (3) the prices of domestically produced goods rise because import competition has declined.

Study after study finds that the costs to consumers substantially exceed the gains to producers and government. A sizable net cost or efficiency loss to society arises from trade protection. Furthermore, industries employ large amounts of economic resources to influence Congress to pass and retain protectionist laws. Because these rent-seeking efforts divert resources away from more socially desirable purposes, trade restrictions impose these additional costs on society as well.

Conclusion: The gains that U.S. trade barriers create for protected industries and their workers come at the expense of much greater losses for the entire economy. The result is economic inefficiency, reduced consumption, and lower standards of living.

The Case for Protection: A Critical Review

Despite the logic of specialization and trade, there are still protectionists in some union halls, corporate boardrooms, and congressional conference rooms. What arguments do protectionists make to justify trade barriers? How valid are those arguments?

Military Self-Sufficiency Argument

The argument here is not economic but political-military: Protective tariffs are needed to preserve or strengthen industries that produce the materials essential for national defense. In an uncertain world, the political-military objectives (self-sufficiency) sometimes must take precedence over economic goals (efficiency in the use of world resources).

Unfortunately, it is difficult to measure and compare the benefit of increased national security against the cost of economic inefficiency when protective tariffs are imposed. The economist can only point out that when a nation levies tariffs to increase military self-sufficiency it incurs economic costs.

All people in the United States would agree that relying on hostile nations for necessary military equipment is not a good idea, yet the self-sufficiency argument is open to serious abuse. Nearly every industry can claim that it makes direct or indirect contributions to national security and hence deserves protection from imports.

Diversification-for-Stability Argument

Highly specialized economies such as Saudi Arabia (based on oil) and Cuba (based on sugar) are dependent on international markets for their income. In these economies, wars, international political developments, recessions abroad, and random fluctuations in world supply and demand for one or two particular goods can cause deep declines in export revenues and therefore in domestic income. Tariff and quota protection are allegedly needed in such nations to enable greater industrial diversification. That way, these economies will not be so dependent on exporting one or two products to obtain the other goods they need. Such goods will be available domestically, thereby providing greater domestic stability.

There is some truth in this diversification-for-stability argument. But the argument has little or no relevance to the United States and other advanced economies. Also, the economic costs of diversification may be great; for example, one-crop economies may be highly inefficient at manufacturing.

Infant Industry Argument

The infant industry argument contends that protective tariffs are needed to allow new domestic industries to establish themselves. Temporarily shielding young domestic firms from the severe competition of more mature and more efficient foreign firms will give infant industries a chance to develop and become efficient producers.

This argument for protection rests on an alleged exception to the case for free trade. The exception is that young industries have not had, and if they face mature foreign competition will never have, the chance to make the long-run adjustments needed for larger scale and greater efficiency in production. In this view, tariff protection for such infant industries will correct a misallocation of world resources perpetuated by historically different levels of economic development between domestic and foreign industries.

There are some logical problems with the infant industry argument. In the developing nations it is difficult to determine which industries are the infants that are capable of achieving economic maturity and therefore deserving protection. Also, protective tariffs may persist even after industrial maturity has been realized.

Most economists feel that if infant industries are to be subsidized, there are better means than tariffs for doing so. Direct subsidies, for example, have the advantage of making explicit which industries are being aided and to what degree.

Protection-against-Dumping Argument

The protection-against-dumping argument contends that tariffs are needed to protect domestic firms from "dumping" by foreign producers. **Dumping** is the sale of a product in a foreign country at prices either below cost or below the prices commonly charged at home.

Economists cite two plausible reasons for this behavior. First, with regard to below-cost dumping, firms in country A may dump goods at below cost into country B in an attempt to drive their competitors in country B out of business. If the firms in country A succeed in driving their competitors in country B out of business, they will enjoy monopoly power and monopoly prices and profits on the goods they subsequently sell in country B. Their hope is that the longer-term monopoly profits will more than offset the losses from below-cost sales that must take place while they are attempting to drive their competitors in country B out of business.

Second, dumping that involves selling abroad at a price that is below the price commonly charged in the home country (but that is still at or above production costs) may be a form of price discrimination, which is charging different prices to different customers. As an example, a foreign seller that has a monopoly in its home market may find that it can maximize its overall profit by charging a high price in its monopolized domestic market while charging a lower price in the United States, where it must compete with U.S. producers. Curiously, it may pursue this strategy even if it makes no profit at all from its sales in the United States, where it must charge the competitive price. So why bother selling in the United States? Because the increase in overall production that comes about by exporting to the United States may allow the firm to obtain the per-unit cost savings often associated with large-scale production. These cost savings imply even higher profits in the monopolized domestic market.

Because dumping is an "unfair trade practice," most nations prohibit it. For example, where dumping is shown to injure U.S. firms, the Federal government imposes tariffs called *antidumping duties* on the goods in question. But relatively few documented cases of dumping occur each year, and specific instances of unfair trade do not justify widespread, permanent tariffs. Moreover, antidumping duties can be abused. Often, what appears to be dumping is simply comparative advantage at work.

Increased Domestic Employment Argument

Arguing for a tariff to "save U.S. jobs" becomes fashionable when the economy encounters a recession (such as the severe recession of 2007–2009 in the United States). In an economy that engages in international trade, exports involve spending on domestic output and imports reflect spending to obtain part of another nation's output. So, in this argument, reducing imports will divert spending on another nation's output to spending on domestic output. Thus, domestic output and employment will rise. But this argument has several shortcomings.

While imports may eliminate some U.S. jobs, they create others. Imports may have eliminated the jobs of some U.S. steel and textile workers in recent years, but other workers have gained jobs unloading ships, flying imported aircraft, and selling imported electronic equipment. Import restrictions alter the composition of employment, but they may have little or no effect on the volume of employment.

The *fallacy of composition*—the false idea that what is true for the part is necessarily true for the whole—is also present in this rationale for tariffs. All nations cannot simultaneously succeed in restricting imports while maintaining their exports; what is true for one nation is not true for all nations. The exports of one nation must be the imports of another nation. To the extent that one country is able to expand its economy through an excess of exports over imports, the resulting excess of imports over exports worsens another economy's unemployment problem. It is no wonder that tariffs and import quotas meant to achieve domestic full employment are called "beggar my neighbor" policies: They achieve short-run domestic goals by making trading partners poorer.

Moreover, nations adversely affected by tariffs and quotas are likely to retaliate, causing a "trade war" (more precisely, a *trade barrier war*) that will choke off trade and make all nations worse off. The **Smoot-Hawley Tariff Act** of 1930 is a classic example. Although that act was meant to reduce imports and stimulate U.S. production, the high tariffs it authorized prompted adversely affected nations to retaliate with tariffs equally high. International trade fell, lowering the output and income of all nations. Economic historians generally agree that the Smoot-Hawley Tariff Act was a contributing cause of the Great Depression.

Finally, forcing an excess of exports over imports cannot succeed in raising domestic employment over the long run. It is through U.S. imports that foreign nations earn dollars for buying U.S. exports. In the long run, a nation must import in order to export. The long-run impact of tariffs is not an increase in domestic employment but, at best, a reallocation of workers away from export industries and to protected domestic industries. This shift implies a less efficient allocation of resources.

Cheap Foreign Labor Argument

The cheap foreign labor argument says that domestic firms and workers must be shielded from the ruinous competition of countries where wages are low. If protection is not provided, cheap imports will flood U.S. markets and the prices of U.S. goods—along with the wages of U.S. workers—will be pulled down. That is, domestic living standards in the United States will be reduced.

This argument can be rebutted at several levels. The logic of the argument suggests that it is not mutually beneficial for rich and poor persons to trade with one another. However, that is not the case. A low-income farmworker may pick lettuce or tomatoes for a rich landowner, and both may benefit from the transaction. And both U.S. consumers and Chinese workers gain when they "trade" a pair of athletic shoes priced at $30 as opposed to U.S. consumers being restricted to buying a similar shoe made in the United States for $60.

Also, recall that gains from trade are based on comparative advantage, not on absolute advantage. Look back at Figure 20.1, where we supposed that the United States and Mexico had labor forces of exactly the same size. Noting the positions of the production possibilities curves, observe that U.S. labor can produce more of either good. Thus, it is more productive. Because of this greater productivity, we can expect wages and living standards to be higher for U.S. labor. Mexico's less productive labor will receive lower wages.

The cheap foreign labor argument suggests that, to maintain its standard of living, the United States should not trade with low-wage Mexico. What if it does not trade with Mexico? Will wages and living standards rise in the United States as a result? No. To obtain vegetables, the United States will have to reallocate a portion of its labor from its relatively more-efficient beef industry to its relatively less-efficient vegetables industry. As a result, the average productivity of U.S. labor will fall, as will real wages and living standards. The labor forces of both countries will have diminished standards of living because without specialization and trade they will have less output available to them. Compare column 4 with column 1 in Table 20.1 or points A' and Z' with A and Z in Figure 20.2 to confirm this point.

Another problem with the cheap foreign labor argument is that its proponents incorrectly focus on labor costs per hour when what really matters is labor costs per unit of output. As an example, suppose that a U.S. factory pays its workers $20 per hour while a factory in a developing country pays its workers $4 per hour. The proponents of the cheap foreign labor argument look at these numbers and conclude—incorrectly—that it is impossible for the U.S. factory to compete with the factory in the developing country. But this conclusion fails to take into account two crucial facts:

- What actually matters is labor costs per *unit of output*, not labor costs per *hour of work*.
- Differences in productivity typically mean that labor costs per unit of output are often nearly identical despite huge differences in hourly labor costs.

To see why these points matter so much, let's take into account how productive the two factories are. Because the U.S. factory uses much more sophisticated technology, better trained workers, and a lot more capital per worker, one worker in one hour can produce 20 units of output. Since the U.S. workers get paid $20 per hour, this means the U.S. factory's labor cost *per unit of output* is $1. The factory in the developing country is much less productive

since it uses less efficient technology and its relatively untrained workers have a lot less machinery and equipment to work with. A worker there produces only 4 units per hour. Given the foreign wage of $4 per hour, this means that the labor cost per unit of output at the factory in the developing country is also $1.

As you can see, the lower wage rate per hour at the factory in the developing country does not translate into lower labor costs per unit—meaning that it won't be able to undersell its U.S. competitor just because its workers get paid lower wages per hour.

Proponents of the cheap foreign labor argument tend to focus exclusively on the large international differences that exist in labor costs per hour. They typically fail to mention that these differences in labor costs per hour are mostly the result of tremendously large differences in productivity and that these large differences in productivity serve to equalize labor costs per unit of output. As a result, firms in developing countries only *sometimes* have an advantage in terms of labor costs per unit of output. Whether they do in any specific situation will vary by industry and firm and will depend on differences in productivity as well as differences in labor costs per hour. For many goods, labor productivity in high-wage countries like the United States is so much higher than labor productivity in low-wage countries that it is actually cheaper *per unit of output* to manufacture those goods in high-wage countries. That is why, for instance, Intel still makes microchips in the United States and why most automobiles are still produced in the United States, Japan, and Europe rather than in low-wage countries.

QUICK REVIEW 20.3

- A tariff on a product increases its price, reduces its consumption, increases its domestic production, reduces its imports, and generates tariff revenue for government; an import quota does the same, except a quota generates revenue for foreign producers rather than for the government imposing the quota.
- Most rationales for trade protections are special-interest requests that, if followed, would create gains for protected industries and their workers at the expense of greater losses for the economy.

Multilateral Trade Agreements and Free-Trade Zones

Aware of the detrimental effects of trade wars and the general weaknesses of arguments for trade protections, nations have worked to lower tariffs worldwide. Their pursuit of freer trade has been aided by recently emerged special-interest groups that have offset the more-established special-interest groups that have traditionally supported tariffs and quotas. Specifically, lower tariffs are now supported by exporters of goods and services, importers of foreign components used in "domestic" products, and domestic sellers of imported products.

General Agreement on Tariffs and Trade

In 1947, 23 nations, including the United States, signed the **General Agreement on Tariffs and Trade (GATT)**. GATT was based on three principles: (1) equal, nondiscriminatory trade treatment for all member nations; (2) the reduction of tariffs by multilateral negotiation; and (3) the elimination of import quotas. Basically, GATT provided a forum for the multilateral negotiation of reduced trade barriers.

Since the Second World War, member nations have completed eight "rounds" of GATT negotiations to reduce trade barriers. The eighth round of negotiations began in Uruguay in 1986. After seven years of complex discussions, in 1993 a new agreement was reached by the 128 nations that were by that time members of GATT. The Uruguay Round agreement took effect on January 1, 1995, and its provisions were phased in through 2005.

Under this agreement, tariffs on thousands of products were eliminated or reduced, with overall tariffs dropping by 33 percent. The agreement also liberalized government rules that in the past impeded the global market for such services as advertising, legal services, tourist services, and financial services. Quotas on imported textiles and apparel were phased out and replaced with tariffs. Other provisions reduced agricultural subsidies paid to farmers and protected intellectual property (patents, trademarks, and copyrights) against piracy.

World Trade Organization

The Uruguay Round agreement established the **World Trade Organization (WTO)** as GATT's successor. Some 153 nations belonged to the WTO in 2010. The WTO oversees trade agreements reached by the member nations, and rules on trade disputes among them. It also provides forums for further rounds of trade negotiations. The ninth and latest round of negotiations—the **Doha Development Agenda**—was launched in Doha, Qatar, in late 2001. (The trade rounds occur over several years in several venues but are named after the city or country of origination.) The negotiations are aimed at further reducing tariffs and quotas, as well as agricultural subsidies that distort trade. You can get an update on the status of the complex negotiations at **www.wto.org**.

GATT and the WTO have been positive forces in the trend toward liberalized world trade. The trade rules agreed upon by the member nations provide a strong and necessary bulwark against the protectionism called for by the special-interest groups in the various nations.

For that reason and others, the WTO is quite controversial. Critics are concerned that rules crafted to expand international trade and investment enable firms to circumvent national laws that protect workers and the environment. Critics ask: What good are minimum-wage laws, worker-safety laws, collective-bargaining rights, and environmental laws if firms can easily shift their production to nations that have weaker laws or if consumers can buy goods produced in those countries?

Proponents of the WTO respond that labor and environmental protections should be pursued directly in nations that have low standards and via international organizations other than the WTO. These issues should not be linked to the process of trade liberalization, which confers widespread economic benefits across nations. Moreover, say proponents of the WTO, many environmental and labor concerns are greatly overblown. Most world trade is among advanced industrial countries, not between them and countries that have lower environmental and labor standards. Moreover, the free flow of goods and resources raises output and income in the developing nations. Historically, such increases in living standards have eventually resulted in stronger, not weaker, protections for the environment and for workers.

The European Union

Countries have also sought to reduce tariffs by creating regional free-trade zones. The most dramatic example is the **European Union (EU)**. Initiated in 1958 as the Common Market, in 2003 the EU comprised 15 European nations—Austria, Belgium, Denmark, Finland, France, Germany, Greece, Ireland, Italy, Luxembourg, the Netherlands, Portugal, Spain, Sweden, and the United Kingdom. In 2004, the EU expanded by 10 additional European countries—Cyprus, the Czech Republic, Estonia, Hungary, Latvia, Lithuania, Malta, Poland, Slovakia, and Slovenia. In 2007, the addition of Bulgaria and Romania expanded the EU to its present size of 27 nations.

The EU has abolished tariffs and import quotas on nearly all products traded among the participating nations and established a common system of tariffs applicable to all goods received from nations outside the EU. It has also liberalized the movement of capital and labor within the EU and has created common policies in other economic matters of joint concern, such as agriculture, transportation, and business practices.

EU integration has achieved for Europe what the U.S. constitutional prohibition on tariffs by individual states has achieved for the United States: increased regional specialization, greater productivity, greater output, and faster economic growth. The free flow of goods and services has created large markets for EU industries. The resulting economies of large-scale production have enabled these industries to achieve much lower costs than they could have achieved in their small, single-nation markets.

One of the most significant accomplishments of the EU was the establishment of the so-called **Euro Zone** in the early 2000s. As of 2010, 16 members of the EU (Austria, Belgium, Cyprus, Germany, Greece, Ireland, Finland, France, Italy, Luxembourg, Malta, the Netherlands, Portugal, Slovenia, Slovakia, and Spain) use the euro as a common currency. Notably, the United Kingdom, Denmark, and Sweden have opted not to use the common currency, at least for now. But gone are French francs, German marks, Italian liras, and other national currencies that were once used by Euro Zone countries.

Economists expect the adoption of the euro to raise the standard of living in the Euro Zone nations over time. By ending the inconvenience and expense of exchanging currencies, the euro has enhanced the free flow of goods, services, and resources among the Euro Zone members. Companies that previously sold products in only one or two European nations have found it easier to price and sell their products in all 16 Euro Zone countries. The euro has also allowed consumers and businesses to comparison shop for outputs and inputs, and this capability has increased competition, reduced prices, and lowered costs.

North American Free Trade Agreement

In 1993 Canada, Mexico, and the United States created a major free-trade zone. The **North American Free Trade Agreement (NAFTA)** established a free-trade area that has about the same combined output as the EU but encompasses a much larger geographic area. NAFTA has eliminated tariffs and other trade barriers between Canada, Mexico, and the United States for most goods and services.

Critics of NAFTA feared that it would cause a massive loss of U.S. jobs as firms moved to Mexico to take advantage of lower wages and weaker regulations on pollution and workplace safety. Also, they were concerned that Japan and South Korea would build plants in Mexico and transport goods tariff-free to the United States, further hurting U.S. firms and workers.

In retrospect, critics were much too pessimistic. Since the passage of NAFTA in 1993, employment in the United States has increased by more than 20 million workers.

NAFTA has increased trade among Canada, Mexico, and the United States and has enhanced the standard of living in all three countries.

Trade Adjustment Assistance

Shifts in patterns of comparative advantage and removal of long-standing trade protection can hurt specific groups of workers. For example, the erosion of the United States' once strong comparative advantage in steel has caused production plant shutdowns and layoffs in the U.S. steel industry. The textile and apparel industries in the United States face similar difficulties. Clearly, not everyone wins from free trade (or freer trade). Some workers lose.

The **Trade Adjustment Assistance Act** of 2002 introduced some innovative policies to help those hurt by shifts in international trade patterns. The law provides cash assistance (beyond unemployment insurance) for up to 78 weeks for workers displaced by imports or plant relocations abroad. To obtain the assistance, workers must participate in job searches, training programs, or remedial education. Also provided are relocation allowances to help displaced workers move geographically to new jobs within the United States. Refundable tax credits for health insurance serve as payments to help workers maintain their insurance coverage during the retraining and job-search period. Workers who are 50 years of age or older are eligible for "wage insurance," which replaces some of the difference in pay (if any) between their old and new jobs. Many economists support trade adjustment assistance because it not only helps workers hurt by international trade but also helps create the political support necessary to reduce trade barriers and export subsidies.

But not all economists favor trade adjustment assistance. Loss of jobs from imports, sending some work abroad, and plant relocations to other countries are only a small fraction (about 4 percent in recent years) of total job losses in the economy each year. Many workers also lose their jobs because of changing patterns of demand, changing technology, bad management, and other dynamic aspects of a market economy. Some critics ask, "What makes losing one's job to international trade worthy of such special treatment, compared to losing one's job to, say, technological change or domestic competition?" Economists can find no totally satisfying answer.

Offshoring of Jobs

Not only are some U.S. jobs lost because of international trade, but some are lost because of globalization of resource markets. In recent years U.S. firms have found the

LAST Word   Petition of the Candlemakers, 1845

French Economist Frédéric Bastiat (1801–1850) Devastated the Proponents of Protectionism by Satirically Extending Their Reasoning to Its Logical and Absurd Conclusions.

Petition of the Manufacturers of Candles, Waxlights, Lamps, Candlesticks, Street Lamps, Snuffers, Extinguishers, and of the Producers of Oil Tallow, Rosin, Alcohol, and, Generally, of Everything Connected with Lighting.

TO MESSIEURS THE MEMBERS OF THE CHAMBER OF DEPUTIES.

Gentlemen—You are on the right road. You reject abstract theories, and have little consideration for cheapness and plenty. Your chief care is the interest of the producer. You desire to emancipate him from external competition, and reserve the national market for national industry.

We are about to offer you an admirable opportunity of applying your—what shall we call it? your theory? No; nothing is more deceptive than theory; your doctrine? your system? your principle? but you dislike doctrines, you abhor systems, and as for principles, you deny that there are any in social economy: we shall say, then, your practice, your practice without theory and without principle.

We are suffering from the intolerable competition of a foreign rival, placed, it would seem, in a condition so far superior to ours for the production of light, that he absolutely inundates our national market with it at a price fabulously reduced. The moment he shows himself, our trade leaves us—all consumers apply to him; and a branch of native industry, having countless ramifi-cations, is all at once rendered completely stagnant. This rival . . . is no other than the Sun.

What we pray for is, that it may please you to pass a law ordering the shutting up of all windows, skylights, dormer windows, outside and inside shutters, curtains, blinds, bull's-eyes; in a word, of all openings, holes, chinks, clefts, and fissures, by or through which the light of the sun has been in use to enter houses, to the prejudice of the meritorious manufacturers with which we flatter ourselves we have accommodated our country,—a country which, in gratitude, ought not to abandon us now to a strife so unequal.

If you shut up as much as possible all access to natural light, and create a demand for artificial light, which of our French manufacturers will not be encouraged by it? If more tallow is consumed, then there must be more oxen and sheep; and, consequently, we shall behold the multiplication of artificial meadows, meat, wool, hides, and, above all, manure, which is the basis and foundation of all agricultural wealth.

The same remark applies to navigation. Thousands of vessels will proceed to the whale fishery; and, in a short time, we shall possess a navy capable of maintaining the honor of France, and gratifying the patriotic aspirations of your petitioners, the undersigned candlemakers and others.

Only have the goodness to reflect, Gentlemen, and you will be convinced that there is, perhaps, no Frenchman, from the wealthy coalmaster to the humblest vender of lucifer matches, whose lot will not be ameliorated by the success of this our petition.

Source: Frédéric Bastiat, *Economic Sophisms* (Irvington-on-Hudson, NY: The Foundation for Economic Education, Inc., 1996), abridged. Used with permission of Foundation for Economic Education, **www.FEE.org**.

outsourcing of work abroad to be increasingly profitable. Economists call this business activity **offshoring**—shifting work previously done by American workers to workers located in other nations. Offshoring is not a new practice but traditionally has involved components for U.S. manufacturing goods. For example, Boeing has long offshored the production of major airplane parts for its "American" aircraft.

Recent advances in computer and communications technology have enabled U.S. firms to offshore service jobs such as data entry, book composition, software coding, call-center operations, medical transcription, and claims processing to countries such as India. Where off-shoring occurs, some of the value added in the production process accrues to foreign countries rather than the United States. So part of the income generated from the production of U.S. goods is paid to foreigners, not to American workers.

Offshoring is a wrenching experience for many Americans who lose their jobs, but it is not necessarily bad for the overall economy. Offshoring simply reflects growing specialization and international trade in services, or, more descriptively, "tasks." That growth has been made possible by recent trade agreements and new information and communication technologies. As with trade in goods, trade in services reflects comparative advantage and is beneficial to both trading parties. Moreover, the United States has a sizable trade surplus with other nations in services. The United States gains by specializing in high-valued services such as transportation services, accounting services, legal services, and advertising services, where it still has a comparative advantage. It then "trades" to obtain lower-valued services such as call-center and data-entry work, for which comparative advantage has gone abroad.

Offshoring also increases the demand for complementary jobs in the United States. Jobs that are close substitutes for existing U.S. jobs are lost, but complementary jobs in the United States are expanded. For example, the lower price of writing software code in India may mean a lower cost of software sold in the United States and abroad. That, in turn, may create more jobs for U.S.-based workers such as software designers, marketers, and distributors. Moreover, offshoring may encourage domestic investment and the expansion of firms in the United States by reducing their production costs and keeping them competitive worldwide. In some instances, "offshoring jobs" may equate to "importing competitiveness." Entire firms that might otherwise disappear abroad may remain profitable in the United States only because they can offshore some of their work.

QUICK REVIEW 20.4

- The General Agreement on Tariffs and Trade (GATT) of 1947 reduced tariffs and quotas and established a process for numerous subsequent rounds of multinational trade negotiations that have liberalized international trade.
- The World Trade Organization (WTO)—GATT's successor—rules on trade disputes and provides forums for negotiations on further rounds of trade liberalization. The current round of negotiations is called the Doha Development Agenda.
- The European Union (EU) and the North American Free Trade Agreement (NAFTA) have reduced internal trade barriers among their member nations by establishing multination free-trade zones.
- Increased international trade and offshoring of jobs have harmed some specific U.S. workers and have led to policies such as trade adjustment assistance to try to help them with their transitions to new lines of work.

Summary

1. The United States leads the world in the combined volume of exports and imports. Other major trading nations are Germany, Japan, the western European nations, and the Asian economies of China, South Korea, Taiwan, and Singapore. The United States' principal exports include chemicals, agricultural products, consumer durables, semiconductors, and aircraft; principal imports include petroleum, automobiles, metals, household appliances, and computers.

2. World trade is based on three considerations: the uneven distribution of economic resources among nations, the fact that efficient production of various goods requires particular techniques or combinations of resources, and the differentiated products produced among nations.

3. Mutually advantageous specialization and trade are possible between any two nations if they have different domestic opportunity-cost ratios for any two products. By specializing on the basis of comparative advantage, nations can obtain larger real incomes with fixed amounts of resources. The terms of trade determine how this increase in world output is shared by the trading nations. Increasing (rather than constant) opportunity costs limit specialization and trade.

4. A nation's export supply curve shows the quantities of a product the nation will export at world prices that exceed the domestic price (the price in a closed, no-international-trade economy). A nation's import demand curve reveals the quantities of a product it will import at world prices below the domestic price.

5. In a two-nation model, the equilibrium world price and the equilibrium quantities of exports and imports occur where one nation's export supply curve intersects the other nation's import demand curve. A nation will export a particular product if the world price exceeds the domestic price; it will import the product if the world price is less than the domestic price. The country with the lower costs of production will be the exporter and the country with the higher costs of production will be the importer.

6. Trade barriers take the form of protective tariffs, quotas, nontariff barriers, and "voluntary" export restrictions. Export subsidies also distort international trade. Supply and demand analysis demonstrates that protective tariffs and quotas increase the prices and reduce the quantities demanded of the affected goods. Sales by foreign exporters diminish; domestic producers, however, gain higher prices and enlarged sales. Consumer losses from trade restrictions greatly exceed producer and government gains, creating an efficiency loss to society.

7. The strongest arguments for protection are the infant industry and military self-sufficiency arguments. Most other arguments for protection are interest-group appeals or reasoning fallacies that emphasize producer interests over consumer interests or stress the immediate effects of trade barriers while ignoring long-run consequences.

8. The cheap foreign labor argument for protection fails because it focuses on labor costs per hour rather than on what really matters, labor costs per unit of output. Due to higher productivity, firms in high-wage countries like the United States can have lower wage costs per unit of output than competitors in low-wage countries. Whether they do will depend on how their particular wage and productivity levels compare with those of their competitors in low-wage countries.

9. In 1947 the General Agreement on Tariffs and Trade (GATT) was formed to encourage nondiscriminatory treatment for all member nations, to reduce tariffs, and to eliminate import quotas. The Uruguay Round of GATT negotiations (1993) reduced tariffs and quotas, liberalized trade in services, reduced agricultural subsidies, reduced pirating of intellectual property, and phased out quotas on textiles.

10. GATT's successor, the World Trade Organization (WTO), had 153 member nations in 2010. It implements WTO agreements, rules on trade disputes between members, and provides forums for continued discussions on trade liberalization. The latest round of trade negotiations—the Doha Development Agenda—began in late 2001 and as of 2010 was still in progress.

11. Free-trade zones liberalize trade within regions. Two examples of free-trade arrangements are the 27-member European Union (EU) and the North American Free Trade Agreement (NAFTA), comprising Canada, Mexico, and the United States. Sixteen EU nations have abandoned their national currencies for a common currency called the euro.

12. The Trade Adjustment Assistance Act of 2002 recognizes that trade liberalization and increased international trade can create job loss for many workers. The Act therefore provides cash assistance, education and training benefits, health care subsidies, and wage subsidies (for persons aged 50 or older) to qualified workers displaced by imports or relocations of plants from the United States to abroad.

13. Offshoring is the practice of shifting work previously done by Americans in the United States to workers located in other nations. Although offshoring reduces some U.S. jobs, it lowers production costs, expands sales, and therefore may create other U.S. jobs. Less than 4 percent of all job losses in the United States each year are caused by imports, offshoring, and plant relocation abroad.

Terms and Concepts

labor-intensive goods

land-intensive goods

capital-intensive goods

opportunity-cost ratio

comparative advantage

principle of comparative advantage

terms of trade

trading possibilities line

gains from trade

world price

domestic price

export supply curve

import demand curve

equilibrium world price

tariffs

revenue tariff

protective tariff

import quota

nontariff barrier (NTB)

voluntary export restriction (VER)

export subsidy

dumping

Smoot-Hawley Tariff Act

General Agreement on Tariffs and Trade (GATT)

World Trade Organization (WTO)

Doha Development Agenda

European Union (EU)

Euro Zone

North American Free Trade Agreement (NAFTA)

Trade Adjustment Assistance Act

offshoring

Questions

1. Quantitatively, how important is international trade to the United States relative to the importance of trade to other nations? What country is the United States' most important trading partner, quantitatively? With what country does the United States have the largest trade deficit? **LO1**

2. Distinguish among land-, labor-, and capital-intensive goods, citing an example of each without resorting to book examples. How do these distinctions relate to international trade? How do distinctive products, unrelated to resource intensity, relate to international trade? **LO1, LO2**

3. Explain: "The United States can make certain toys with greater productive efficiency than can China. Yet we import those toys from China." Relate your answer to the ideas of Adam Smith and David Ricardo. LO2

4. Suppose Big Country can produce 80 units of X by using all its resources to produce X or 60 units of Y by devoting all its resources to Y. Comparable figures for Small Nation are 60 units of X and 60 units of Y. Assuming constant costs, in which product should each nation specialize? Explain why. What are the limits of the terms of trade between these two countries? How would rising costs (rather than constant costs) affect the extent of specialization and trade between these two countries? LO2

5. What is an export demand curve? What is an import supply curve? How do such curves relate to the determination of the equilibrium world price of a tradable good? LO3

6. Why is a quota more detrimental to an economy than a tariff that results in the same level of imports as the quota? What is the net outcome of either tariffs or quotas for the world economy? LO4

7. Draw a domestic supply-and-demand diagram for a product in which the United States does not have a comparative advantage. What impact do foreign imports have on domestic price and quantity? On your diagram show a protective tariff that eliminates approximately one-half of the assumed imports. What are the price-quantity effects of this tariff on (a) domestic consumers, (b) domestic producers, and (c) foreign exporters? How would the effects of a quota that creates the same amount of imports differ? LO4

8. "The potentially valid arguments for tariff protection—military self-sufficiency, infant industry protection, and diversification for stability—are also the most easily abused." Why are these arguments susceptible to abuse? LO4

9. Evaluate the effectiveness of artificial trade barriers, such as tariffs and import quotas, as a way to achieve and maintain full employment throughout the U.S. economy. How might such policies reduce unemployment in one U.S. industry but increase it in another U.S. industry? LO4

10. In 2007, manufacturing workers in the United States earned average compensation of $30.56 per hour. That same year, manufacturing workers in Mexico earned average compensation of $3.91 per hour. How can U.S. manufacturers possibly compete? Why isn't all manufacturing done in Mexico and other low-wage countries? LO4

11. How might protective tariffs reduce both the imports and the exports of the nation that levies tariffs? In what way do foreign firms that "dump" their products onto the U.S. market in effect provide bargains to American consumers? How might the import competition lead to quality improvements and cost reductions by American firms? LO4

12. Identify and state the significance of each of the following trade-related entities: (a) the WTO; (b) the EU; (c) the Euro Zone; and (d) NAFTA. LO5

13. What form does trade adjustment assistance take in the United States? How does such assistance promote political support for free-trade agreements? Do you think workers who lose their jobs because of changes in trade laws deserve special treatment relative to workers who lose their jobs because of other changes in the economy, say, changes in patterns of government spending? LO6

14. What is offshoring of white-collar service jobs and how does that practice relate to international trade? Why has offshoring increased over the past few decades? Give an example (other than that in the textbook) of how offshoring can eliminate some American jobs while creating other American jobs. LO6

15. **LAST WORD** What was the central point that Bastiat was trying to make in his imaginary petition of the candlemakers?

Problems

1. Assume that the comparative-cost ratios of two products—baby formula and tuna fish—are as follows in the nations of Canswicki and Tunata:

   Canswicki: 1 can baby formula ≡ 2 cans tuna fish
   Tunata: 1 can baby formula ≡ 4 cans tuna fish

   In what product should each nation specialize? Which of the following terms of trade would be acceptable to both nations: (a) 1 can baby formula ≡ $2\frac{1}{2}$ cans tuna fish; (b) 1 can baby formula ≡ 1 can tuna fish; (c) 1 can baby formula ≡ 5 cans tuna fish? LO2

2. The accompanying hypothetical production possibilities tables are for New Zealand and Spain. Each country can produce apples and plums. Plot the production possibilities data for each of the two countries separately. Referring to your graphs, answer the following: LO2

New Zealand's Production Possibilities Table (Millions of Bushels)

Product	A	B	C	D
	Production Alternatives			
Apples	0	20	40	60
Plums	15	10	5	0

Spain's Production Possibilities Table (Millions of Bushels)

Product	R	S	T	U
	Production Alternatives			
Apples	0	20	40	60
Plums	60	40	20	0

a. What is each country's cost ratio of producing plums and apples?

b. Which nation should specialize in which product?

c. Show the trading possibilities lines for each nation if the actual terms of trade are 1 plum for 2 apples. (Plot these lines on your graph.)

d. Suppose the optimum product mixes before specialization and trade were alternative B in New Zealand and alternative S in Spain. What would be the gains from specialization and trade?

3. The following hypothetical production possibilities tables are for China and the United States. Assume that before specialization and trade the optimal product mix for China is alternative B and for the United States is alternative U. LO2

a. Are comparative-cost conditions such that the two areas should specialize? If so, what product should each produce?

b. What is the total gain in apparel and chemical output that would result from such specialization?

c. What are the limits of the terms of trade? Suppose that the actual terms of trade are 1 unit of apparel for 1½ units of chemicals and that 4 units of apparel are exchanged for 6 units of chemicals. What are the gains from specialization and trade for each nation?

Product	China Production Possibilities					
	A	B	C	D	E	F
Apparel (in thousands)	30	24	18	12	6	0
Chemicals (in tons)	0	6	12	18	24	30

Product	U.S. Production Possibilities					
	R	S	T	U	V	W
Apparel (in thousands)	10	8	6	4	2	0
Chemicals (in tons)	0	4	8	12	16	20

4. Refer to Figure 3.6, page 57. Assume that the graph depicts the U.S. domestic market for corn. How many bushels of corn, if any, will the United States export or import at a world price of $1, $2, $3, $4, and $5? Use this information to construct the U.S. export supply curve and import demand curve for corn. Suppose that the only other corn-producing nation is France, where the domestic price is $4. Which country will export corn; which county will import it? LO3

FURTHER TEST YOUR KNOWLEDGE AT
www.mcconnell19e.com

At the text's Online Learning Center (OLC), **www.mcconnell19e.com**, you will find one or more Web-based questions that require information from the Internet to answer. We urge you to check them out; they will familiarize you with Web sites that may be helpful in other courses and perhaps even in your career. The OLC also features multiple-choice questions that give instant feedback and provides other helpful ways to further test your knowledge of the chapter.

21

AFTER READING THIS CHAPTER, YOU SHOULD BE ABLE TO:

1 Explain how currencies of different nations are exchanged when international transactions take place.

2 Analyze the balance sheet the United States uses to account for the international payments it makes and receives.

3 Discuss how exchange rates are determined in currency markets.

4 Describe the difference between flexible exchange rates and fixed exchange rates.

5 Identify the causes and consequences of recent U.S. trade deficits.

The Balance of Payments, Exchange Rates, and Trade Deficits

If you take a U.S. dollar to the bank and ask to exchange it for U.S. currency, you will get a puzzled look. If you persist, you may get a dollar's worth of change: One U.S. dollar can buy exactly one U.S. dollar. But on April 4, 2010, for example, 1 U.S. dollar could buy 1922 Colombian pesos, 1.09 Australian dollars, .66 British pound, 1.01 Canadian dollars, .74 European euro, 94.61 Japanese yen, or 12.30 Mexican pesos. What explains this seemingly haphazard array of exchange rates?

In Chapter 20 we examined comparative advantage as the underlying economic basis of world trade and discussed the effects of barriers to free trade. Now we introduce the highly important monetary and financial aspects of international trade.

International Financial Transactions

This chapter focuses on international financial transactions, the vast majority of which fall into two broad categories: international trade and international asset transactions. International trade involves either purchasing or selling currently produced goods or services across an international border. Examples include an Egyptian firm exporting cotton to the United States and an American company hiring an Indian call center to answer its phones. International asset transactions involve the transfer of the property rights to either real or financial assets between the citizens of one country and the citizens of another country. It includes activities like buying foreign stocks or selling your house to a foreigner.

These two categories of international financial transactions reflect the fact that whether they are from different countries or the same country, individuals and firms can only exchange two things with each other: currently produced goods and services or preexisting assets. With regard to assets, however, money is by far the most commonly exchanged asset. Only rarely would you ever find a barter situation in which people directly exchanged other assets—such as trading a car for 500 shares of Microsoft stock or a cow for 30 chickens and a tank of diesel fuel.

As a result, there are two basic types of transactions:

- People trading either goods or services for money.
- People trading assets for money.

In either case, money flows from the buyers of the goods, services, or assets to the sellers of the goods, services, or assets.

When the people engaged in any such transactions are both from places that use the same currency, what type of money to use is not an issue. Americans from California and Wisconsin will use their common currency, the dollar. People from France and Germany will use their common currency, the euro. However, when the people involved in an exchange are from places that use different currencies, intermediate asset transactions have to take place: the buyers must convert their own currencies into the currencies that the sellers use and accept.

As an example, consider the case of an English software design company that wants to buy a supercomputer made by an American company. The American company sells these high-powered machines for $300,000. To pay for the machine, the English company has to convert some of the money it has (British pounds sterling) into the money that the American company will accept (U.S. dollars). This process is not difficult. As we will soon explain in

detail, there are many easy-to-use foreign exchange markets in which those who wish to sell pounds and buy dollars can interact with others who wish to sell dollars and buy pounds. The demand and supply created by these two groups determine the equilibrium exchange rate, which, in turn, determines how many pounds our English company will have to convert to pay for the supercomputer. If, for instance, the exchange rate is $2 = £1, then the English company will have to convert £150,000 to obtain the $300,000 necessary to purchase the computer.

The Balance of Payments

A nation's **balance of payments** is the sum of all the financial transactions that take place between its residents and the residents of foreign nations. Most of these transactions fall into the two main categories that we have just discussed: international trade and international asset transactions. As a result, nearly all the items included in the balance of payments are things such as exports and imports of goods, exports and imports of services, and international purchases and sales of financial and real assets. But the balance of payments also includes international transactions that fall outside of these main categories—things such as tourist expenditures, interest and dividends received or paid abroad, debt forgiveness, and remittances made by immigrants to their relatives back home.

The U.S. Commerce Department's Bureau of Economic Analysis compiles a balance-of-payments statement each year. This statement summarizes all of the millions of payments that individuals and firms in the United States receive from foreigners as well as all of the millions of payments that individuals and firms in the United States make to foreigners. It shows "flows" of inpayments of money *to* the United States and outpayments of money *from* the United States. For convenience, all of these money payments are given in terms of dollars. This is true despite the fact that some of them actually may have been made using foreign currencies—as when, for instance, an American company converts dollars into euros to buy something from an Italian company. When including this outpayment of money from the United States, the accountants who compile the balance-of-payments statement use the number of dollars the American company converted—rather than the number of euros that were actually used to make the purchase.

Table 21.1 is a simplified balance-of-payments statement for the United States in 2009. Because most international financial transactions fall into only two categories—international trade and international asset exchanges—the balance-of-payments statement is organized into two broad

TABLE 21.1 The U.S. Balance of Payments, 2009 (in Billions)

CURRENT ACCOUNT		
(1) U.S. goods exports	$+1046	
(2) U.S. goods imports	−1563	
(3) *Balance on goods*		$−517
(4) U.S. exports of services	+509	
(5) U.S. imports of services	−371	
(6) *Balance on services*		+138
(7) *Balance on goods and services*		−379
(8) Net investment income	+89*	
(9) Net transfers	−130	
(10) **Balance on current account**		**−420**
CAPITAL AND FINANCIAL ACCOUNT		
Capital account		
(11) *Balance on capital account*		−3
Financial account		
(12) Foreign purchases of assets in the United States	+548†	
(13) U.S. purchases of assets abroad	−125†	
(14) *Balance on financial account*		+423
(15) **Balance on capital and financial account**		**+420**
		$ 0

*Includes other, less significant, categories of income.
†Includes one-half of a $225 billion statistical discrepancy that is listed in the capital account.
Source: U.S. Department of Commerce, Bureau of Economic Analysis, **www.bea.gov**. Preliminary 2009 data. The export and import data are on a "balance-of-payment basis," and usually vary from the data on exports and imports reported in the National Income and Product Accounts.

categories. *The current account* located at the top of the table primarily treats international trade. *The capital and financial account* at the bottom of the table primarily treats international asset exchanges.

Current Account

The top portion of Table 21.1 that mainly summarizes U.S. trade in currently produced goods and services is called the **current account.** Items 1 and 2 show U.S. exports and imports of goods (merchandise) in 2009. U.S. exports have a *plus* (+) sign because they are a *credit*; they generate flows of money toward the United States. U.S. imports have a *minus* (−) sign because they are a *debit*; they cause flows of money out of the United States.

Balance on Goods Items 1 and 2 in Table 21.1 reveal that in 2009 U.S. goods exports of $1046 billion were less than U.S. goods imports of $1563 billion. A country's *balance of trade on goods* is the difference between its exports and its imports of goods. If exports exceed imports, the result is a surplus on the balance of goods. If imports exceed exports, there is a trade deficit on the balance of goods.

We note in item 3 that in 2009 the United States incurred a trade deficit on goods of $517 billion.

Balance on Services The United States exports not only goods, such as airplanes and computer software, but also services, such as insurance, consulting, travel, and investment advice, to residents of foreign nations. Item 4 in Table 21.1 shows that these service "exports" totaled $509 billion in 2009. Since they generate flows of money toward the United States, they are a credit (thus the + sign). Item 5 indicates that the United States "imports" similar services from foreigners. Those service imports were $371 billion in 2009, and since they generate flows of money out of the United States, they are a debit (thus the − sign). Summed together, items 4 and 5 indicate that the balance on services (item 6) in 2009 was $138 billion. The **balance on goods and services** shown as item 7 is the difference between U.S. exports of goods and services (items 1 and 4) and U.S. imports of goods and services (items 2 and 5). In 2009, U.S. imports of goods and services exceeded U.S. exports of goods and services by $379 billion. So a **trade deficit** of that amount occurred. In contrast, a **trade surplus** occurs

U.S. Trade Balances in Goods and Services, Selected Nations, 2009

The United States has large trade deficits in goods and services with several nations, in particular, China, Mexico, and Germany.

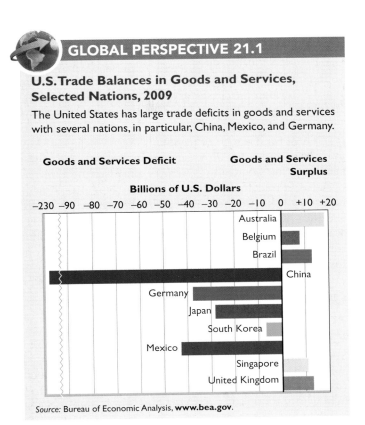

Source: Bureau of Economic Analysis, **www.bea.gov**.

when exports of goods and services exceed imports of goods and services. (Global Perspective 21.1 shows U.S. trade deficits and surpluses with selected nations.)

Balance on Current Account Items 8 and 9 are not items relating directly to international trade in goods and services. But they are listed as part of the current account (which is mostly about international trade in goods and services) because they are international financial flows that in some sense compensate for things that can be conceptualized as being *like* international trade in either goods or services. For instance, item 8, *net investment income*, represents the difference between (1) the interest and dividend payments foreigners paid U.S. citizens and companies for the services provided by U.S. capital invested abroad ("exported" capital) and (2) the interest and dividends the U.S. citizens and companies paid for the services provided by foreign capital invested here ("imported" capital). Observe that in 2009 U.S. net investment income was a positive $89 billion.

Item 9 shows net transfers, both public and private, between the United States and the rest of the world. Included here is foreign aid, pensions paid to U.S. citizens

living abroad, and remittances by immigrants to relatives abroad. These $130 billion of transfers are net U.S. outpayments (and therefore listed as a negative number in Table 21.1). They are listed as part of the current account because they can be thought of as the financial flows that accompany the exporting of goodwill and the importing of "thank you notes."

By adding all transactions in the current account, we obtain the **balance on current account** shown in item 10. In 2009 the United States had a current account deficit of $420 billion. This means that the U.S. current account transactions created outpayments from the United States greater than inpayments to the United States.

Capital and Financial Account

The bottom portion of the current account statement summarizes U.S. international asset transactions. It is called the **capital and financial account** and consists of two separate accounts: the *capital account* and the *financial account*.

Capital Account The capital account mainly measures debt forgiveness—which is an asset transaction because the person forgiving a debt essentially hands the IOU back to the borrower. It is a "net" account (one that can be either + or −). The $3 billion listed in line 11 tells us that in 2009 Americans forgave $3 billion more of debt owed to them by foreigners than foreigners forgave debt owed to them by Americans. The − sign indicates a debit; it is an "on-paper" outpayment (asset transfer) by the net amount of debt forgiven.

Financial Account The financial account summarizes international asset transactions having to do with international purchases and sales of real or financial assets. Line 12 lists the amount of foreign purchases of assets in the United States. It has a + sign because any purchase of an American-owned asset by a foreigner generates a flow of money toward the American who sells the asset. Line 13 lists U.S. purchases of assets abroad. These have a − sign because such purchases generate a flow of money from the Americans who buy foreign assets toward the foreigners who sell them those assets.

Items 11 and 12 combined yielded a $423 billion balance on the financial account for 2009 (line 14). In 2009 the United States "exported" $548 billion of ownership of its real and financial assets and "imported" $125 billion. Thought of differently, this surplus in the financial account brought in income of $423 billion to the United States. The **balance on the capital and financial account** (line 15) is $420 billion. It is the sum of the $3 billion deficit on the capital account and the $423 billion surplus on the financial account. Observe that this $420 billion surplus in the capital and financial account equals the $420 billion deficit in the current account. This is not an accident. The two numbers always equal—or "balance." That's why the statement is called the *balance* of payments. It has to balance. Let's see why.

Why the Balance?

The balance on the current account and the balance on the capital and financial account must always sum to zero because any deficit or surplus in the current account automatically creates an offsetting entry in the capital and financial account. People can only trade one of two things with each other: currently produced goods and services or preexisting assets. Therefore, if trading partners have an imbalance in their trade of currently produced goods and services, the only way to make up for that imbalance is with a net transfer of assets from one party to the other.

To see why this is true, suppose that John (an American) makes shoes and Henri (a Swiss citizen) makes watches and that the pair only trade with each other. Assume that their financial assets consist entirely of money, with each beginning the year with $1000 in his bank account. Suppose that this year John exports $300 of shoes to Henri and imports $500 of watches from Henri. John therefore ends the year with a $200 goods deficit with Henri.

John and Henri's goods transactions, however, also result in asset exchanges that cause a net transfer of assets from John to Henri equal in size to John's $200 goods deficit with Henri. This is true because Henri pays John $300 for his shoes while John pays Henri $500 for his watches. The *net* result of these opposite-direction asset movements is that $200 of John's initial assets of $1000 are transferred to Henri. This is unavoidable, because the $300 John receives from his exports pays for only the first $300 of his $500 of imports. The only way for John to pay for the remaining $200 of imports is for him to transfer $200 of his initial asset holdings to Henri. Consequently, John's assets decline by $200 from $1000 to $800, and Henri's assets rise from $1000 to $1200.

Consider how the transaction between John and Henri affects the U.S. balance-of-payments statement (Table 21.1), other things equal. John's $200 goods deficit with Henri shows up in the U.S. current account as a −$200 entry in the balance on goods account (line 3) and carries down to a −$200 entry in the balance on current account (line 10).

In the capital and financial account, this $200 is recorded as +$200 in the account labeled foreign purchases of assets in the United States (line 12). This +$200 then

carries down to the balance on capital and financial account (line 15). Think of it this way: Henri has in essence used $200 worth of watches to purchase $200 of John's initial $1000 holding of assets. The +$200 entry in line 12 (foreign purchases of assets in the United States) simply recognizes this fact. This +$200 exactly offsets the −$200 in the current account.

Thus, the balance of payments always balances. Any current account deficit or surplus in the top half of the statement automatically generates an offsetting international asset transfer that shows up in the capital and financial account in the bottom half of the statement. More specifically, current account deficits simultaneously generate transfers of assets to foreigners, while current account surpluses automatically generate transfers of assets from foreigners.

Official Reserves, Payments Deficits, and Payments Surpluses

Some of the foreign purchases of assets in the United States (line 12, Table 21.1) and the U.S. assets purchased abroad (line 13) are of so-called official reserves. **Official reserves** consist of foreign currencies, certain reserves held with the International Monetary Fund, and stocks of gold. These reserves are owned by governments or their central banks. For simplicity, we will assume for now that the entire stock of U.S. official reserves consists of foreign currency so we can speak of official reserves and foreign currency reserves interchangeably.

Although the balance of payments must always sum to zero, as in Table 21.1, in some years a net sale of official reserves by a nation's treasury or central bank occurs in the process of bringing the capital and financial account into balance with the current account. In such years, a **balance-of-payments deficit** is said to occur. This deficit is in a subset of the overall balance statement and *is not a deficit in the overall account*. Remember, the overall balance of payments is always in balance. But in this case the balancing of the overall account includes sales of official reserves to create an inflow of dollars to the United States. In selling foreign currency in the foreign exchange market, the treasury or central bank must draw down its stock of reserves. This drawdown is an indicator of a balance-of-payments deficit.

These net sales of official reserves in the foreign exchange market show up as a *plus* (+) item on the U.S. balance-of-payments statement, specifically as are foreign purchases of U.S. assets (line 12). They are a credit or an inflow of dollars to the United States, just as are John's proceeds from the sale of $200 of his assets to Henri in our previous example.

In other years, the capital and financial account balances the current account because of government purchases of official reserves from foreigners. The treasury or central bank engineers this balance by selling dollars to obtain foreign currency, and then adding the newly acquired foreign currency to its stock of official reserves. In these years, a **balance-of-payments surplus** is said to exist. This payments surplus therefore can be thought of as either net purchases of official reserves in the balance of payments or, alternatively, as the resulting increase in the stock of official reserves held by the government.

Net purchases of official reserves by the treasury or central bank appear on the U.S. balance sheet as U.S. purchases of foreign assets (line 13)—a *negative* (−) item. These purchases are a debit because they represent an outflow of dollars.

A balance-of-payments deficit is not necessarily bad, just as a balance-of-payments surplus is not necessarily good. Both simply happen. However, any nation's official reserves are limited. Persistent payments deficits must be financed by drawing down those reserves, which would ultimately deplete the reserves. That nation would have to adopt policies to correct its balance of payments. Such policies might require painful macroeconomic adjustments, trade barriers and similar restrictions, or a major depreciation of its currency. For this reason, nations strive for payments balance, at least over several-year periods.

> **WORKED PROBLEMS**
>
> **W 21.1**
>
> Balance of payments

> **QUICK REVIEW 21.1**
>
> - A nation's balance-of-payments statement summarizes all of the international financial transactions that take place between its residents and the residents of all foreign nations. It includes the current account balance and the capital and financial account balance.
> - The current account balance is a nation's exports of goods and services less its imports of goods and services plus its net investment income and net transfers.
> - The capital and financial account balance includes the net amount of the nation's debt forgiveness as well as the nation's sale of real and financial assets to people living abroad less its purchases of real and financial assets from foreigners.
> - The current account balance and the capital and financial account balance always sum to zero because any current account imbalance automatically generates an offsetting international asset transfer.
> - A balance-of-payments deficit exists when net sales of official reserves (mainly foreign currency) occur in the balance-of-payments statement; in contrast, a balance-of-payments surplus exists when net purchases of official reserves occur.

Flexible Exchange Rates

Both the size and the persistence of a nation's balance-of-payments deficits and surpluses and the adjustments it must make to correct those imbalances depend on the system of exchange rates being used. There are two pure types of exchange-rate systems:

- A **flexible- or floating-exchange-rate system** through which demand and supply determine exchange rates and in which no government intervention occurs.
- A **fixed-exchange-rate system** through which governments determine exchange rates and make necessary adjustments in their economies to maintain those rates.

We begin by looking at flexible exchange rates. Let's examine the rate, or price, at which U.S. dollars might be exchanged for British pounds. In

> **INTERACTIVE GRAPHS**
>
> **G 21.1**
>
> Flexible exchange rates

Figure 21.1 (Key Graph) we show demand D_1 and supply S_1 of pounds in the currency market.

The *demand-for-pounds curve* is downsloping because all British goods and services will be cheaper to the United States if pounds become less expensive to the United States. That is, at lower dollar prices for pounds, the United States can obtain more pounds and therefore more British goods and services per dollar. To buy those cheaper British goods, U.S. consumers will increase the quantity of pounds they demand.

The *supply-of-pounds curve* is upsloping because the British will purchase more U.S. goods when the dollar price of pounds rises (that is, as the pound price of dollars falls). When the British buy more U.S. goods, they supply a greater quantity of pounds to the foreign exchange market. In other words, they must exchange pounds for dollars to purchase U.S. goods. So, when the dollar price of pounds rises, the quantity of pounds supplied goes up.

The intersection of the supply curve and the demand curve will determine the dollar price of pounds. Here, that price (exchange rate) is $2 for £1. At this exchange rate, the quantities of pounds supplied and demanded are equal; neither a shortage nor a surplus of pounds occurs.

Depreciation and Appreciation

An exchange rate determined by market forces can, and often does, change daily like stock and bond prices. When the dollar price of pounds *rises*, for example, from $2 = £1 to $3 = £1, the dollar has *depreciated* relative to the pound (and the pound has appreciated relative to the dollar). When a currency depreciates, more units of it (dollars)

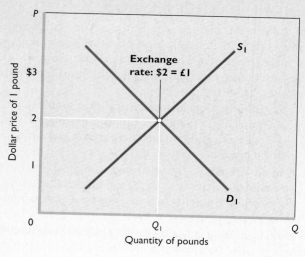

FIGURE 21.1 The market for foreign currency (pounds). The intersection of the demand-for-pounds curve D_1 and the supply-of-pounds curve S_1 determines the equilibrium dollar price of pounds, here, $2. That means that the exchange rate is $2 = £1. Not shown, an increase in demand for pounds or a decrease in supply of pounds will increase the dollar price of pounds and thus cause the pound to appreciate. Also not shown, a decrease in demand for pounds or an increase in the supply of pounds will reduce the dollar price of pounds, meaning that the pound has depreciated.

QUICK QUIZ FOR FIGURE 21.1

1. Which of the following statements is true?
   a. The quantity of pounds demanded falls when the dollar appreciates.
   b. The quantity of pounds supplied declines as the dollar price of the pound rises.
   c. At the equilibrium exchange rate, the pound price of $1 is $£\frac{1}{2}$.
   d. The dollar appreciates if the demand for pounds increases.

2. At the price of $2 for £1 in this figure:
   a. the dollar-pound exchange rate is unstable.
   b. the quantity of pounds supplied equals the quantity demanded.
   c. the dollar price of £1 equals the pound price of $1.
   d. U.S. goods exports to Britain must equal U.S. goods imports from Britain.

3. Other things equal, a leftward shift of the demand curve in this figure:
   a. would depreciate the dollar.

   b. would create a shortage of pounds at the previous price of $2 for £1.
   c. might be caused by a major recession in the United States.
   d. might be caused by a significant rise of real interest rates in Britain.

4. Other things equal, a rightward shift of the supply curve in this figure would:
   a. depreciate the dollar and might be caused by a significant rise of real interest rates in Britain.
   b. depreciate the dollar and might be caused by a significant fall of real interest rates in Britain.
   c. appreciate the dollar and might be caused by a significant rise of real interest rates in the United States.
   d. appreciate the dollar and might be caused by a significant fall of interest rates in the United States.

Answers: 1. c; 2. b; 3. c; 4. c

---

are needed to buy a single unit of some other currency (a pound).

When the dollar price of pounds *falls*, for example, from $2 = £1 to $1 = £1, the dollar has *appreciated* relative to the pound. When a currency appreciates, fewer units of it (dollars) are needed to buy a single unit of some other currency (pounds).

In our U.S.-Britain illustrations, depreciation of the dollar means an appreciation of the pound, and vice versa. When the dollar price of a pound jumps from $2 = £1 to $3 = £1, the pound has appreciated relative to the dollar because it takes fewer pounds to buy $1. At $2 = £1, it took $£\frac{1}{2}$ to buy $1; at $3 = £1, it takes only $£\frac{1}{3}$ to buy $1.

Conversely, when the dollar appreciated relative to the pound, the pound depreciated relative to the dollar. More pounds were needed to buy a dollar.

In general, the relevant terminology and relationships between the U.S. dollar and another currency are as follows.

- Dollar price of foreign currency increases ≡ dollar depreciates relative to the foreign currency ≡ foreign currency price of dollar decreases ≡ foreign currency appreciates relative to the dollar.
- Dollar price of foreign currency decreases ≡ dollar appreciates relative to the foreign currency ≡ foreign currency price of dollar increases ≡ foreign currency depreciates relative to the dollar.

Determinants of Exchange Rates

What factors would cause a nation's currency to appreciate or depreciate in the market for foreign exchange? Here are three generalizations:

- If the demand for a nation's currency increases (other things equal), that currency will appreciate; if the demand declines, that currency will depreciate.
- If the supply of a nation's currency increases, that currency will depreciate; if the supply decreases, that currency will appreciate.
- If a nation's currency appreciates, some foreign currency depreciates relative to it.

With these generalizations in mind, let's examine the determinants of exchange rates—the factors that shift the demand or supply curve for a certain currency. As we do so, keep in mind that the other-things-equal assumption is always in force. Also note that we are discussing factors *that change the exchange rate*, not things that change *as a result of* a change in the exchange rate.

Changes in Tastes
Any change in consumer tastes or preferences for the products of a foreign country may alter the demand for that nation's currency and change its exchange rate. If technological advances in U.S. wireless phones make them more attractive to British consumers and businesses, then the British will supply more pounds in the exchange market to purchase more U.S. wireless phones. The supply-of-pounds curve will shift to the right, causing the pound to depreciate and the dollar to appreciate.

In contrast, the U.S. demand-for-pounds curve will shift to the right if British woolen apparel becomes more fashionable in the United States. So the pound will appreciate and the dollar will depreciate.

Relative Income Changes
A nation's currency is likely to depreciate if its growth of national income is more rapid than that of other countries. Here's why: A country's imports vary directly with its income level. As total income rises in the United States, people there buy both more domestic goods and more foreign goods. If the U.S. economy is expanding rapidly and the British economy is stagnant, U.S. imports of British goods, and therefore U.S. demands for pounds, will increase. The dollar price of pounds will rise, so the dollar will depreciate.

Relative Inflation Rate Changes
Other things equal, changes in the relative rates of inflation of two nations change their relative price levels and alter the exchange rate between their currencies. The currency of the nation with the higher inflation rate—the more rapidly rising price level—tends to depreciate. Suppose,

for example, that inflation is zero percent in Great Britain and 5 percent in the United States so that prices, on average, are rising by 5 percent per year in the United States while, on average, remaining unchanged in Great Britain. U.S. consumers will seek out more of the now relatively lower-priced British goods, increasing the demand for pounds. British consumers will purchase less of the now relatively higher-priced U.S. goods, reducing the supply of pounds. This combination of increased demand for pounds and reduced supply of pounds will cause the pound to appreciate and the dollar to depreciate.

According to the **purchasing-power-parity theory**, exchange rates should eventually adjust such that they equate the purchasing power of various currencies. If a certain market basket of identical products costs \$10,000 in the United States and £5000 in Great Britain, the exchange rate should move to \$2 = £1. That way, a dollar spent in the United States will buy exactly as much output as it would if it were first converted to pounds (at the \$2 = £1 exchange rate) and used to buy output in Great Britain.

In terms of our example, 5 percent inflation in the United States will increase the price of the market basket from \$10,000 to \$10,500, while the zero percent inflation in Great Britain will leave the market basket priced at £5000. For purchasing power parity to hold, the exchange rate would have to move from \$2 = £1 to \$2.10 = £1. That means the dollar therefore would depreciate and the pound would appreciate. In practice, however, not all exchange rates move precisely to equate the purchasing power of various currencies and thereby achieve "purchasing power parity," even over long periods.

Relative Interest Rates
Changes in relative interest rates between two countries may alter their exchange rate. Suppose that real interest rates rise in the United States but stay constant in Great Britain. British citizens will then find the United States a more attractive place in which to loan money directly or loan money indirectly by buying bonds. To make these loans, they will have to supply pounds in the foreign exchange market to obtain dollars. The increase in the supply of pounds results in depreciation of the pound and appreciation of the dollar.

Changes in Relative Expected Returns on Stocks, Real Estate, and Production Facilities
International investing extends beyond buying foreign bonds. It includes international investments in stocks and real estate as well as foreign purchases of factories and production facilities. Other things equal, the extent of this foreign investment depends on relative expected returns. To make the investments, investors in one country must sell their

currencies to purchase the foreign currencies needed for the foreign investments.

For instance, suppose that investing in England suddenly becomes more popular due to a more positive outlook regarding expected returns on stocks, real estate, and production facilities there. U.S. investors therefore will sell U.S. assets to buy more assets in England. The U.S. assets will be sold for dollars, which will then be brought to the foreign exchange market and exchanged for pounds, which will in turn be used to purchase British assets. The increased demand for pounds in the foreign exchange market will cause the pound to appreciate and therefore the dollar to depreciate relative to the pound.

Speculation Currency speculators are people who buy and sell currencies with an eye toward reselling or repurchasing them at a profit. Suppose speculators expect the U.S. economy to (1) grow more rapidly than the British economy and (2) experience more rapid inflation than Britain. These expectations translate into an anticipation that the pound will appreciate and the dollar will depreciate. Speculators who are holding dollars will therefore try to convert them into pounds. This effort will increase the demand for pounds and cause the dollar price of pounds to rise (that is, cause the dollar to depreciate). A self-fulfilling prophecy occurs: The pound appreciates and the dollar depreciates because speculators act on the belief that these changes will in fact take place. In this way, speculation can cause changes in exchange rates. (We discuss currency speculation in more detail in this chapter's Last Word.)

Table 21.2 has more illustrations of the determinants of exchange rates; the table is worth careful study.

Flexible Rates and the Balance of Payments

Flexible exchange rates have an important feature: They automatically adjust and eventually eliminate balance-of-payments deficits or surpluses. We can explain this idea through Figure 21.2, in which S_1 and D_1 are the supply and demand curves for pounds from Figure 21.1. The equilibrium exchange rate of $2 = £1 means that there is no balance-of-payments deficit or surplus between the United States and Britain. At that exchange rate, the quantity of pounds demanded by U.S. consumers to import British goods, buy British transportation and insurance services, and pay interest and dividends on British investments in the United States equals the amount of pounds supplied by the British in buying U.S. exports, purchasing services from the United States, and making interest and dividend payments on U.S. investments in Britain. The United States would have no need to either draw down or build up its official reserves to balance its payments.

Suppose tastes change and U.S. consumers buy more British automobiles; the U.S. inflation rate increases relative to Britain's; or interest rates fall in the United States compared to those in Britain. Any or all of these changes will increase the U.S. demand for British pounds, for example, from D_1 to D_2 in Figure 21.2.

If the exchange rate remains at the initial $2 = £1, a U.S. balance-of-payments deficit will occur in the amount of *ab*. At the $2 = £1 rate, U.S. consumers will demand the quantity of pounds shown by point *b*, but Britain will supply only the amount shown by *a*. There will be a shortage of pounds. But this shortage will not last because this is a

TABLE 21.2 Determinants of Exchange Rates: Factors That Change the Demand for or the Supply of a Particular Currency and Thus Alter the Exchange Rate

Determinant	Examples
Change in tastes	Japanese electronic equipment declines in popularity in the United States (Japanese yen depreciates; U.S. dollar appreciates).
	European tourists reduce visits to the United States (U.S. dollar depreciates; European euro appreciates).
Change in relative incomes	England encounters a recession, reducing its imports, while U.S. real output and real income surge, increasing U.S. imports (British pound appreciates; U.S. dollar depreciates).
Change in relative inflation rates	Switzerland experiences a 3% inflation rate compared to Canada's 10% rate (Swiss franc appreciates; Canadian dollar depreciates).
Change in relative real interest rates	The Federal Reserve drives up interest rates in the United States, while the Bank of England takes no such action (U.S. dollar appreciates; British pound depreciates).
Changes in relative expected returns on stocks, real estate, or production facilities	Corporate tax cuts in the United States raise expected after-tax investment returns in the United States relative to those in Europe (U.S. dollar appreciates; the euro depreciates).
Speculation	Currency traders believe South Korea will have much greater inflation than Taiwan (South Korean won depreciates; Taiwanese dollar appreciates).
	Currency traders think Norway's interest rates will plummet relative to Denmark's rates (Norway's krone depreciates; Denmark's krone appreciates).

FIGURE 21.2 Adjustments under flexible exchange rates and fixed exchange rates. Under flexible exchange rates, a shift in the demand for pounds from D_1 to D_2, other things equal, would cause a U.S. balance-of-payments deficit ab. That deficit would be corrected by a change in the exchange rate from $2 = £1 to $3 = £1. Under fixed exchange rates, the United States would cover the shortage of pounds ab by selling official reserves (here pounds), restricting trade, implementing exchange controls, or enacting a contractionary stabilization policy.

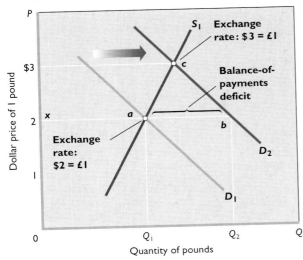

From Britain's standpoint, the exchange rate (the pound price of dollars) has fallen (from $£\frac{1}{2}$ to $£\frac{1}{3}$ for $1). The international value of the pound has appreciated. The British previously got only $2 for £1; now they get $3 for £1. U.S. goods are therefore cheaper to the British, and U.S. exports to Britain will rise.

The two adjustments—a decrease in U.S. imports from Britain and an increase in U.S. exports to Britain—are just what are needed in terms of Figure 21.2 to decrease the quantity of pounds demanded from b to c, increase the quantity of pounds supplied from a to c, and thus correct the U.S. balance-of-payments deficit. These changes end when, at point c, the quantities of British pounds demanded and supplied are equal.

Disadvantages of Flexible Exchange Rates

Even though flexible exchange rates automatically work to eliminate payment imbalances, they may cause several significant problems. These are all related to the fact that flexible exchange rates are often volatile and can change by a large amount in just a few weeks or months. In addition, they often take substantial swings that can last several years or more. This can be seen in Figure 21.3, which plots the dollar-pound exchange rate from 1970 through 2009. (You can track other exchange rates, for example, the dollar-euro or dollar-yen rate, by going to the Federal Reserve Web site, **www.federalreserve.gov**, selecting Economic Research & Data, Statistical Releases and Historical Data, and finally, Exchange Rates and International Data.)

Uncertainty and Diminished Trade The risks and uncertainties associated with flexible exchange rates may discourage the flow of trade. Suppose a U.S. automobile dealer contracts to purchase 10 British cars for £150,000. At the current exchange rate of, say, $2 for £1, the U.S. importer expects to pay $300,000 for these automobiles. But if during the 3-month delivery period the rate of exchange shifts to $3 for £1, the £150,000 payment contracted by the U.S. importer will be $450,000.

That increase in the dollar price of pounds may thus turn the U.S. importer's anticipated profit into a substantial loss. Aware of the possibility of an adverse change in the exchange rate, the U.S. importer may not be willing to assume the risks involved. The U.S. firm may confine its operations to domestic automobiles, so international trade in this product will not occur.

The same thing can happen with investments. Assume that when the exchange rate is $3 to £1, a U.S. firm invests $30,000 (or £10,000) in a British enterprise. It

competitive foreign exchange market. Instead, the dollar price of pounds will rise (the dollar will depreciate) until the balance-of-payments deficit is eliminated. That occurs at the new equilibrium exchange rate of $3 = £1, where the quantities of pounds demanded and supplied are again equal.

To explain why the increase in the dollar price of pounds—the dollar depreciation—eliminates the balance-of-payments deficit ab in Figure 21.2, we need to reemphasize that the exchange rate links all domestic (U.S.) prices with all foreign (British) prices. The dollar price of a foreign good is found by multiplying the foreign price by the exchange rate (in dollars per unit of the foreign currency). At an exchange rate of $2 = £1, a British automobile priced at £15,000 will cost a U.S. consumer $30,000 (= 15,000 × $2).

A change in the exchange rate alters the prices of all British goods to U.S. consumers and all U.S. goods to British buyers. The shift in the exchange rate (here from $2 = £1 to $3 = £1) changes the relative attractiveness of U.S. imports and exports and restores equilibrium in the U.S. (and British) balance of payments. From the U.S. view, as the dollar price of pounds changes from $2 to $3, the British auto priced at £15,000, which formerly cost a U.S. consumer $30,000, now costs $45,000 (= 15,000 × $3). Other British goods will also cost U.S. consumers more, so that U.S. imports of British goods will decline.

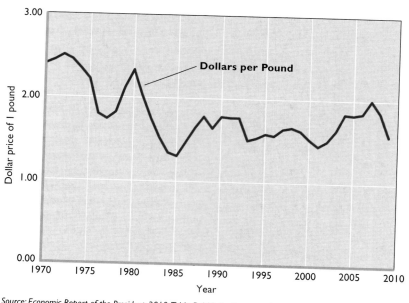

FIGURE 21.3 The dollar-pound exchange rate, 1970–2009. Before January 1971, the dollar-pound exchange rate was fixed at $2.40 = £1. Since that time, its value has been determined almost entirely by market forces, with only occasional government interventions. Under these mostly flexible conditions, the dollar-pound exchange rate has varied considerably. For instance, in 1981 it took $2.02 to buy a pound but by 1985 only $1.50 was needed to buy a pound. In contrast, between 2001 and 2007 the dollar price of a pound rose from $1.44 to $2.00, indicating that the dollar had depreciated relative to the pound. The dollar then sank back to $1.57 per British pound in 2009.

Source: *Economic Report of the President, 2010*, Table B-110. Earlier years from prior *Economic Reports*.

estimates a return of 10 percent; that is, it anticipates annual earnings of $3000 or £1000. Suppose these expectations prove correct in that the British firm earns £1000 in the first year on the £10,000 investment. But suppose that during the year, the value of the dollar appreciates to $2 = £1. The absolute return is now only $2000 (rather than $3000), and the rate of return falls from the anticipated 10 percent to only $6\frac{2}{3}$ percent (= $2000/$30,000). Investment is risky in any case. The added risk of changing exchange rates may persuade the U.S. investor not to venture overseas.[1]

Terms-of-Trade Changes A decline in the international value of its currency will worsen a nation's terms of trade. For example, an increase in the dollar price of a pound will mean that the United States must export more goods and services to finance a specific level of imports from Britain.

Instability Flexible exchange rates may destabilize the domestic economy because wide fluctuations stimulate and then depress industries producing exported goods. If the U.S. economy is operating at full employment and its currency depreciates, as in our illustration, the results will

be inflationary, for two reasons. (1) Foreign demand for U.S. goods may rise, increasing total spending and pulling up U.S. prices. Also, the prices of all U.S. imports will increase. (2) Conversely, appreciation of the dollar will lower U.S. exports and increase imports, possibly causing unemployment.

Flexible or floating exchange rates also may complicate the use of domestic stabilization policies in seeking full employment and price stability. This is especially true for nations whose exports and imports are large relative to their total domestic output.

Fixed Exchange Rates

To circumvent the disadvantages of flexible exchange rates, at times nations have fixed or "pegged" their exchange rates. For our analysis of fixed exchange rates, we assume that the United States and Britain agree to maintain a $2 = £1 exchange rate.

The problem is that such a government agreement cannot keep from changing the demand for and the supply of pounds. With the rate fixed, a shift in demand or supply will threaten the fixed-exchange-rate system, and government must intervene to ensure that the exchange rate is maintained.

In Figure 21.2, suppose the U.S. demand for pounds increases from D_1 to D_2 and a U.S. payment deficit *ab* arises. Now, the new equilibrium exchange rate ($3 = £1) is above the fixed exchange rate ($2 = £1). How can the

---

[1]You will see in this chapter's Last Word, however, that a trader can circumvent part of the risk of unfavorable exchange-rate fluctuations by "hedging" in the "futures market" or "forward market" for foreign exchange.

United States prevent the shortage of pounds from driving the exchange rate up to the new equilibrium level? How can it maintain the fixed exchange rate? The answer is by altering market demand or market supply or both so that they will intersect at the $2 = £1$ rate. There are several ways to do this.

Use of Official Reserves

One way to maintain a fixed exchange rate is to engage in **currency interventions.** These are situations in which governments or their central banks manipulate an exchange rate through the use of official reserves. For instance, by selling some of its reserves of pounds, the U.S. government could increase the supply of pounds, shifting supply curve S_1 to the right so that it intersects D_2 at b in Figure 21.2, thereby maintaining the exchange rate at $2 = £1$.

Notice that when the U.S. government sells some of its reserves of pounds, it is transferring assets to foreigners (since they gain ownership of the pounds). In terms of the balance-of-payments statement shown in Table 21.1, this transfer of assets enters positively on line (12), "Foreign purchases of assets in the United States." This positive entry is what offsets the balance-of-payments deficit caused by the fixed exchange rate and ensures that the U.S. balance of payments does in fact balance.

How do official reserves originate? Perhaps a balance-of-payments surplus occurred in the past. The U.S. government would have purchased that surplus. That is, at some earlier time, the U.S. government may have spent tax dollars to buy the surplus pounds that were threatening to reduce the exchange rate to below the $2 = £1$ fixed rate. Those purchases would have bolstered the stock of U.S. official reserves of pounds.

Nations also have used gold as "international money" to obtain official reserves. In our example, the U.S. government could sell some of its gold to Britain to obtain pounds. It could then sell pounds for dollars. That would shift the supply-of-pounds curve to the right, and the $2 = £1$ exchange rate could be maintained.

It is critical that the amount of reserves and gold be enough to accomplish the required increase in the supply of pounds. There is no problem if deficits and surpluses occur more or less randomly and are of similar size. Then, last year's balance-of-payments surplus with Britain will increase the U.S. reserve of pounds, and that reserve can be used to "finance" this year's deficit. But if the United States encounters persistent and sizable deficits for an extended period, it may exhaust its reserves, and thus be forced to abandon fixed exchange rates. Or, at the least, a nation whose reserves are inadequate must use less–appealing options to maintain exchange rates. Let's consider some of those options.

Trade Policies

To maintain fixed exchange rates, a nation can try to control the flow of trade and finance directly. The United States could try to maintain the $2 = £1$ exchange rate in the face of a shortage of pounds by discouraging imports (thereby reducing the demand for pounds) and encouraging exports (thus increasing the supply of pounds). Imports could be reduced by means of new tariffs or import quotas; special taxes could be levied on the interest and dividends U.S. financial investors receive from foreign investments. Also, the U.S. government could subsidize certain U.S. exports to increase the supply of pounds.

The fundamental problem is that these policies reduce the volume of world trade and change its makeup from what is economically desirable. When nations impose tariffs, quotas, and the like, they lose some of the economic benefits of a free flow of world trade. That loss should not be underestimated: Trade barriers by one nation lead to retaliatory responses from other nations, multiplying the loss.

Exchange Controls and Rationing

Another option is to adopt exchange controls and rationing. Under **exchange controls** the U.S. government could handle the problem of a pound shortage by requiring that all pounds obtained by U.S. exporters be sold to the Federal government. Then the government would allocate or ration this short supply of pounds (represented by xa in Figure 21.2) among various U.S. importers, who demand the quantity xb. This policy would restrict the value of U.S. imports to the amount of foreign exchange earned by U.S. exports. Assuming balance in the capital and financial account, there would then be no balance-of-payments deficit. U.S. demand for British imports with the value ab would simply not be fulfilled.

There are major objections to exchange controls:

- *Distorted trade* Like *trade controls* (tariffs, quotas, and export subsidies), exchange controls would distort the pattern of international trade away from the pattern suggested by comparative advantage.
- *Favoritism* The process of rationing scarce foreign exchange might lead to government favoritism toward selected importers (big contributors to reelection campaigns, for example).

- *Restricted choice* Controls would limit freedom of consumer choice. The U.S. consumers who prefer Volkswagens might have to buy Chevrolets. The business opportunities for some U.S. importers might be impaired if the government were to limit imports.

- *Black markets* Enforcement problems are likely under exchange controls. U.S. importers might want foreign exchange badly enough to pay more than the $2 = £1 official rate, setting the stage for black-market dealings between importers and illegal sellers of foreign exchange.

Domestic Macroeconomic Adjustments

A final way to maintain a fixed exchange rate would be to use domestic stabilization policies (monetary policy and fiscal policy) to eliminate the shortage of foreign currency. Tax hikes, reductions in government spending, and a high-interest-rate policy would reduce total spending in the U.S. economy and, consequently, domestic income. Because the volume of imports varies directly with domestic income, demand for British goods, and therefore for pounds, would be restrained.

If these "contractionary" policies served to reduce the domestic price level relative to Britain's, U.S. buyers of consumer and capital goods would divert their demands from British goods to U.S. goods, reducing the demand for pounds. Moreover, the high-interest-rate policy would lift U.S. interest rates relative to those in Britain.

Lower prices on U.S. goods and higher U.S. interest rates would increase British imports of U.S. goods and would increase British financial investment in the United States. Both developments would increase the supply of pounds. The combination of a decrease in the demand for and an increase in the supply of pounds would reduce or eliminate the original U.S. balance-of-payments deficit. In Figure 21.2 the new supply and demand curves would intersect at some new equilibrium point on line *ab*, where the exchange rate remains at $2 = £1.

Maintaining fixed exchange rates by such means is hardly appealing. The "price" of exchange-rate stability for the United States would be a decline in output, employment, and price levels—in other words, a recession. Eliminating a balance-of-payments deficit and achieving domestic stability are both important national economic goals, but to sacrifice macroeconomic stability simply to balance international payments would be to let the tail wag the dog.

QUICK REVIEW 21.2

- In a system in which exchange rates are flexible (meaning that they are free to float), the rates are determined by the demand for and supply of individual national currencies in the foreign exchange market.

- Determinants of flexible exchange rates (factors that shift currency supply and demand curves) include changes in (a) tastes; (b) relative national incomes; (c) relative inflation rates; (d) real interest rates; (e) relative expected returns on stocks, real estate, and production facilities; and (f) speculation.

- Under a system of fixed exchange rates, nations set their exchange rates and then maintain them by buying or selling official reserves of currencies, establishing trade barriers, employing exchange controls, or incurring inflation or recession.

The Current Exchange Rate System: The Managed Float

Over the past 130 years, the world's nations have used three different exchange-rate systems. From 1879 to 1934, most nations used a gold standard, which implicitly created fixed exchange rates. From 1944 to 1971, most countries participated in the Bretton Woods system, which was a fixed-exchange-rate system indirectly tied to gold. And since 1971, most have used managed floating exchange rates, which mix mostly flexible exchange rates with occasional currency interventions. Naturally, our focus here is on the current exchange rate system. However, the history of the previous systems and why they broke down is highly fascinating. For that reason, we have included a discussion of these systems at the book's Web site (see Content Option for Instructors 2 [COI 2]).

The current international exchange-rate system (1971–present) is an "almost" flexible system called **managed floating exchange rates.** Exchange rates among major currencies are free to float to their equilibrium market levels, but nations occasionally use currency interventions in the foreign exchange market to stabilize or alter market exchange rates.

Normally, the major trading nations allow their exchange rates to float up or down to equilibrium levels based on supply and demand in the foreign exchange market. They recognize that changing economic conditions among nations require continuing changes in equilibrium exchange rates to avoid persistent payments deficits or surpluses. They rely on freely operating foreign exchange markets to accomplish the necessary adjustments. The result has been considerably more volatile exchange rates than those during the Bretton Woods era.

But nations also recognize that certain trends in the movement of equilibrium exchange rates may be at odds with national or international objectives. On occasion, nations therefore intervene in the foreign exchange market by buying or selling large amounts of specific currencies. This way, they can "manage" or stabilize exchange rates by influencing currency demand and supply.

The leaders of the *G8 nations* (Canada, France, Germany, Italy, Japan, Russia, United Kingdom, and United States) meet regularly to discuss economic issues and try to coordinate economic policies. At times they have collectively intervened to try to stabilize currencies. For example, in 2000 they sold dollars and bought euros in an effort to stabilize the falling value of the euro relative to the dollar. In the previous year the euro (€) had depreciated from €1 = \$1.17 to €1 = \$.87.

The current exchange-rate system is thus an "almost" flexible exchange-rate system. The "almost" refers mainly to the occasional currency interventions by governments; it also refers to the fact that the actual system is more complicated than described. While the major currencies such as dollars, euros, pounds, and yen fluctuate in response to changing supply and demand, some developing nations peg their currencies to the dollar and allow their currencies to fluctuate with it against other currencies. Also, some nations peg the value of their currencies to a "basket" or group of other currencies.

How well has the managed float worked? It has both proponents and critics.

In Support of the Managed Float

Proponents of the managed-float system argue that it has functioned far better than many experts anticipated. Skeptics had predicted that fluctuating exchange rates would reduce world trade and finance. But in real terms world trade under the managed float has grown tremendously over the past several decades. Moreover, as supporters are quick to point out, currency crises such as those in Mexico and southeast Asia in the last half of the 1990s were not the result of the floating-exchange-rate system itself. Rather, the abrupt currency devaluations and depreciations resulted from internal problems in those nations, in conjunction with the nations' tendency to peg their currencies to the dollar or to a basket of currencies. In some cases, flexible exchange rates would have made these adjustments far more gradual.

Proponents also point out that the managed float has weathered severe economic turbulence that might have caused a fixed-rate system to break down. Such events as extraordinary oil price increases in 1973–1974 and again in 1981–1983, inflationary recessions in several nations in the mid-1970s, major national recessions in the early 1980s, and large U.S. budget deficits in the 1980s and the first half of the 1990s all caused substantial imbalances in international trade and finance, as did the large U.S. budget deficits and soaring world oil prices that occurred in the middle of the first decade of the 2000s. The U.S. financial crisis and the severe recession of 2007–2009 greatly disrupted world trade. Flexible rates enabled the system to adjust to all these events, whereas the same events would have put unbearable pressures on a fixed-rate system.

Concerns with the Managed Float

There is still much sentiment in favor of greater exchange-rate stability. Those favoring more stable exchange rates see problems with the current system. They argue that the excessive volatility of exchange rates under the managed float threatens the prosperity of economies that rely heavily on exports. Several financial crises in individual nations (for example, Mexico, South Korea, Indonesia, Thailand, Russia, and Brazil) have resulted from abrupt changes in exchange rates. These crises have led to massive "bailouts" of those economies via loans from the International Monetary Fund (IMF). The IMF bailouts, in turn, may encourage nations to undertake risky and inappropriate economic policies since they know that, if need be, the IMF will come to the rescue. Moreover, some exchange-rate volatility has occurred even when underlying economic and financial conditions were relatively stable, suggesting that speculation plays too large a role in determining exchange rates.

Skeptics say the managed float is basically a "nonsystem" because the guidelines as to what each nation may or may not do with its exchange rates are not specific enough to keep the system working in the long run. Nations inevitably will be tempted to intervene in the foreign exchange market, not merely to smooth out short-term fluctuations in exchange rates but to prop up their currency if it is chronically weak or to manipulate the exchange rate to achieve domestic stabilization goals.

So what are we to conclude? Flexible exchange rates have not worked perfectly, but they have not failed miserably. Thus far they have survived, and no doubt have eased, several major shocks to the international trading system. Meanwhile, the "managed" part of the float has given nations some sense of control over their collective economic destinies. On balance, most economists favor continuation of the present system of "almost" flexible exchange rates.

Recent U.S. Trade Deficits

As shown in Figure 21.4a, the United States has experienced large and persistent trade deficits in recent years. These deficits rose rapidly between 2001 and 2006 before declining when consumers and businesses greatly curtailed their purchase of imports during the recession of 2007–2009. Even in 2009, however, the trade deficit on goods was still at $517 billion and the trade deficit on goods and services was $379 billion. The current account deficit (Figure 21.4b) reached a record high of $806 billion in 2006, and that amount was 6.0 percent of GDP. The current account deficit declined to $420 billion—2.9 percent of GDP—in the recession year 2009. Economists expect the trade deficits to expand, absolutely and relatively, toward prerecession levels when the economy recovers and U.S. income and imports again rise.

Causes of the Trade Deficits

The large U.S. trade deficits have several causes. First, the U.S. economy expanded more rapidly between 2001 and 2007 than the economies of several U.S. trading partners. The strong U.S. income growth that accompanied that economic growth enabled Americans to greatly increase their purchases of imported products. In contrast, Japan and some European nations suffered recession or experienced relatively slow income growth over that same period. So consumers in those countries increased their purchases of U.S. exports much less rapidly than Americans increased their purchases of foreign imports.

Another factor explaining the large trade deficits is the enormous U.S. trade imbalance with China. In 2007 the United States imported $257 billion more of goods and services than it exported to China. Even in the recession year 2009, the trade deficit with China was $220 billion.

FIGURE 21.4 U.S. trade deficits, 2001–2009. (a) The United States experienced large deficits in *goods* and in *goods and services* between 2001 and 2009. (b) The U.S. current account, generally reflecting the goods and services deficit, was also in substantial deficit. Although reduced significantly by the recession of 2007–2009, large trade deficits are expected to continue for many years to come.

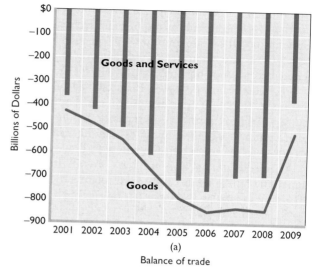

(a)
Balance of trade

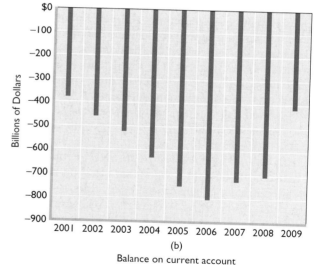

(b)
Balance on current account

Source: Bureau of Economic Analysis, **www.bea.gov**.

That deficit was double the combined deficits with Mexico ($43 billion), Germany ($37 billion), and Japan ($28 billion). The United States is China's largest export market, and although China has greatly increased its imports from the United States, its standard of living has not yet risen sufficiently for its households to afford large quantities of U.S. products. Adding to the problem, China's government has fixed the exchange rate of it currency, the yuan, to a basket of currencies that includes the U.S. dollar.

Therefore, China's large trade surpluses with the United States have not caused the yuan to appreciate much against the U.S. dollar. Greater appreciation of the yuan would have made Chinese goods more expensive in the United States and reduced U.S. imports from China. In China a stronger yuan would have reduced the dollar price of U.S. goods and increased Chinese purchases of U.S. exports. That combination—reduced U.S. imports from China and increased U.S. exports to China—would have reduced the large U.S. trade imbalance.

Another factor underlying the large U.S. trade deficits is a continuing trade deficit with oil-exporting nations. For example, in 2009 the United States had a $54 billion trade deficit with the OPEC countries.

A declining U.S. saving rate (= saving/total income) also contributed to the large U.S. trade deficits. Up until the recession of 2007–2009, the U.S. saving rate declined substantially, while its investment rate (= investment/total income) increased. The gap between U.S. investment and U.S. saving was filled by foreign purchases of U.S. real and financial assets, which created a large surplus on the U.S. capital and financial account. Because foreign savers were willing to finance a large part of U.S. investment, Americans were able to save less and consume more. Part of that added consumption spending was on imported goods.

Finally, many foreigners simply view U.S. assets favorably because of the relatively high risk-adjusted rates of return they provide. The purchase of those assets provides foreign currency to Americans that enables them to finance their strong appetite for imported goods. The capital account surpluses therefore may partially cause the high U.S. trade deficits, not just result from those high deficits. The point is that the causes of the high U.S. trade deficits are numerous and not so easy to disentangle.

Implications of U.S. Trade Deficits

The prerecession U.S. trade deficits were the largest ever run by a major industrial nation. Whether the large trade deficits should be of significant concern to the United States and the rest of the world is debatable. Most economists see both benefits and costs to trade deficits.

Increased Current Consumption   At the time a trade deficit or a current account deficit is occurring, American consumers benefit. A trade deficit means that the United States is receiving more goods and services as imports from abroad than it is sending out as exports. Taken alone, a trade deficit allows the United States to consume outside its production possibilities curve. It augments the domestic standard of living. But here is a catch: The gain in present consumption may come at the expense of reduced future consumption. When and if the current account deficit declines, Americans may have to consume less than before and perhaps even less than they produce.

Increased U.S. Indebtedness   A trade deficit is considered unfavorable because it must be financed by borrowing from the rest of the world, selling off assets, or dipping into official reserves. Recall that current account deficits are financed by surpluses in the capital and financial accounts. Such surpluses require net inpayments of dollars to buy U.S. assets, including debt issued by Americans. Therefore, when U.S. exports are insufficient to finance U.S. imports, the United States increases both its debt to people abroad and the value of foreign claims against assets in the United States. Financing of the U.S. trade deficit has resulted in a larger foreign accumulation of claims against U.S. financial and real assets than the U.S. claim against foreign assets. In 2008, foreigners owned about $3.5 trillion more of U.S. assets (corporations, land, stocks, bonds, loan notes) than U.S. citizens and institutions owned in foreign assets.

If the United States wants to regain ownership of these domestic assets, at some future time it will have to export more than it imports. At that time, domestic consumption will be lower because the United States will need to send more of its output abroad than it receives as imports. Therefore, the current consumption gains delivered by U.S. current account deficits may mean permanent debt, permanent foreign ownership, or large sacrifices of future consumption.

We say "may mean" above because the foreign lending to U.S. firms and foreign investment in the United States increases the U.S. capital stock. U.S. production capacity therefore might increase more rapidly than otherwise because of a large surplus on the capital and financial account. Faster increases in production capacity and real GDP enhance the economy's ability to service foreign debt and buy back real capital, if that is desired.

Trade deficits therefore are a mixed blessing. The long-term impacts of the record-high U.S. trade deficits are largely unknown. That "unknown" worries some economists, who are concerned that foreigners will lose financial confidence in the United States. If that happens, they would restrict their lending to American households and businesses and also reduce their purchases of U.S. assets. Both actions would decrease the demand for U.S. dollars in the foreign exchange market and cause the U.S. dollar to depreciate. A sudden, large depreciation of the U.S. dollar might disrupt world trade and negatively affect economic growth worldwide. Other economists, however, downplay this scenario. Because any decline in the U.S. capital and financial account surplus is automatically met with a decline in the current account deficit, U.S. net exports would rise and the overall impact on the American economy would be slight.

Word Speculation in Currency Markets

Are Speculators a Negative or a Positive Influence in Currency Markets and International Trade?

Most people buy foreign currency to facilitate the purchase of goods, services, or assets from another country. A U.S. importer buys Japanese yen to purchase Japanese autos. A Hong Kong financial investor purchases Australian dollars to invest in the Australian stock market. But there is another group of participants in the currency market—speculators—that buys and sells foreign currencies in the hope of reselling or rebuying them later at a profit.

Contributing to Exchange-Rate Fluctuations Speculators were much in the news in late 1997 and 1998 when they were widely accused of driving down the values of the South Korean won, Thai baht, Malaysian ringgit, and Indonesian rupiah. The value of these currencies fell by as much as 50 percent within one month, and speculators undoubtedly contributed to the swiftness of those declines. The expectation of currency depreciation (or appreciation) can be self-fulfilling. If speculators, for example, expect the Indonesian rupiah to be devalued or to depreciate, they quickly sell rupiah and buy currencies that they think will increase in relative value. The sharp increase in the supply of rupiah indeed reduces its value; this reduction then may trigger further selling of rupiah in expectation of further declines in its value.

But changed economic realities, not speculation, are normally the underlying causes of changes in currency values. That was largely the case with the southeast Asian countries in which actual and threatened bankruptcies in the financial and manufacturing sectors undermined confidence in the strength of the currencies. Anticipating the eventual declines in currency values, speculators simply hastened those declines. That is, the declines in value probably would have occurred with or without speculators.

Moreover, on a daily basis, speculation clearly has positive effects in foreign exchange markets.

Smoothing Out Short-Term Fluctuations in Currency Prices When temporarily weak demand or strong supply reduces a currency's value, speculators quickly buy the currency, adding to its demand and strengthening its value. When temporarily strong demand or weak supply increases a currency's value, speculators sell the currency. That selling increases the supply of the currency and reduces its value. In this way speculators smooth out supply and demand, and thus exchange rates, over short time periods. This day-to-day exchange-rate stabilization aids international trade.

Absorbing Risk Speculators also absorb risk that others do not want to bear. Because of potential adverse changes in exchange rates, international transactions are riskier than

Summary

1. International financial transactions involve trade either in currently produced goods and services or in preexisting assets. Exports of goods, services, and assets create inflows of money, while imports cause outflows of money. If buyers and sellers use different currencies, then foreign exchange transactions take place so that the exporter can be paid in his or her own currency.

2. The balance of payments records all international trade and financial transactions taking place between a given nation and the rest of the world. The balance on goods and services (the trade balance) compares exports and imports of both goods and services. The current account balance includes not only goods and services transactions but also net investment income and net transfers.

3. The capital and financial account includes (a) the net amount of the nation's debt forgiveness and (b) the nation's sale of real and financial assets to people living abroad less its purchases of real and financial assets from foreigners.

4. The current account and the capital and financial account always sum to zero. A deficit in the current account is always offset by a surplus in the capital and financial account. Conversely, a surplus in the current account is always offset by a deficit in the capital and financial account.

5. Official reserves are owned by national governments and their central banks and consist of stocks of foreign currencies, certain reserves held with the International Monetary Fund, and stocks of gold.

domestic transactions. Suppose AnyTime, a hypothetical retailer, signs a contract with a Swiss manufacturer to buy 10,000 Swatch watches to be delivered in three months. The stipulated price is 75 Swiss francs per watch, which in dollars is $50 per watch at the present exchange rate of, say, $1 = 1.5 francs. AnyTime's total bill for the 10,000 watches will be $500,000 (= 750,000 francs).

But if the Swiss franc were to appreciate, say, to $1 = 1 franc, the dollar price per watch would rise from $50 to $75 and Any-

Time would owe $750,000 for the watches (= 750,000 francs). AnyTime may reduce the risk of such an unfavorable exchange-rate fluctuation by hedging in the futures market. Hedging is an action by a buyer or a seller to protect against a change in future prices. The futures market is a market in which currencies are bought and sold at prices fixed now, for delivery at a specified date in the future.

AnyTime can purchase the needed 750,000 francs at the current $1 = 1.5 francs exchange rate, but with delivery in three months when the Swiss watches are delivered. And here is where speculators come in. For a price determined in the futures market, they agree to deliver the 750,000 francs to AnyTime in three months at the $1 = 1.5 francs exchange rate, regardless of the exchange rate then. The speculators need not own francs when the agreement is made. If the Swiss franc depreciates to, say, $1 = 2 francs in this period, the speculators profit. They can buy the 750,000 francs stipulated in the contract for $375,000, pocketing the difference between that amount and the $500,000 AnyTime has agreed to pay for the 750,000 francs. If the Swiss franc appreciates, the speculators, but not AnyTime, suffer a loss.

The amount AnyTime must pay for this "exchange-rate insurance" will depend on how the market views the likelihood of the franc depreciating, appreciating, or staying constant over the three-month period. As in all competitive markets, supply and demand determine the price of the futures contract.

The futures market thus eliminates much of the exchange-rate risk associated with buying foreign goods for future delivery. Without it, AnyTime might have decided against importing Swiss watches. But the futures market and currency speculators greatly increase the likelihood that the transaction will occur. Operating through the futures market, speculation promotes international trade.

In short, although speculators in currency markets occasionally contribute to swings in exchange rates, on a day-to-day basis they play a positive role in currency markets.

6. A balance-of-payments deficit is said to occur when a nation draws down its stock of official reserves to purchase dollars from abroad to balance the capital and financial account with the current account. A balance-of-payments surplus occurs when a nation adds to its stock of official reserves by selling dollars to foreigners to obtain foreign currencies to balance the two accounts. The desirability of a balance-of-payments deficit or surplus depends on its size and its persistence.

7. Flexible or floating exchange rates between international currencies are determined by the demand for and supply of those currencies. Under flexible rates, a currency will depreciate or appreciate as a result of changes in tastes, relative income changes, relative changes in inflation rates, relative changes in real interest rates, and speculation.

8. The maintenance of fixed exchange rates requires adequate official reserves to accommodate periodic payments deficits. If reserves are inadequate, nations must invoke protectionist trade policies, engage in exchange controls, or endure undesirable domestic macroeconomic adjustments.

9. Since 1971 the world's major nations have used a system of managed floating exchange rates. Market forces generally set rates, although governments intervene with varying frequency to alter their exchange rates.

10. Between 1997 and 2007, the United States had large and rising trade deficits, which are projected to last well into the future. Causes of the trade deficits include (a) more rapid income growth in the United States than in Japan and some European nations, resulting in expanding U.S. imports

relative to exports, (b) the emergence of a large trade deficit with China, (c) continuing large trade deficits with oil-exporting nations, and (d) a large surplus in the capital and financial account, which enabled Americans to reduce their saving and buy more imports. The severe recession of 2007–2009 in the United States substantially lowered the U.S. trade deficit by reducing American spending on imports.

11. U.S. trade deficits have produced current increases in the living standards of U.S. consumers. The accompanying surpluses on the capital and financial account have increased U.S. debt to the rest of the world and increased foreign ownership of assets in the United States. This greater foreign investment in the United States, however, has undoubtedly increased U.S. production possibilities.

Terms and Concepts

balance of payments

current account

balance on goods and services

trade deficit

trade surplus

balance on current account

capital and financial account

balance on capital and financial account

official reserves

balance-of-payments deficits and surpluses

flexible- or floating-exchange-rate system

fixed-exchange-rate system

purchasing-power-parity theory

currency interventions

exchange controls

managed floating exchange rates

Questions

1. Do all international financial transactions necessarily involve exchanging one nation's distinct currency for another? Explain. Could a nation that neither imports goods and services nor exports goods and services still engage in international financial transactions? LO1

2. Explain: "U.S. exports earn supplies of foreign currencies that Americans can use to finance imports." Indicate whether each of the following creates a demand for or a supply of European euros in foreign exchange markets: LO1

   a. A U.S. airline firm purchases several Airbus planes assembled in France.

   b. A German automobile firm decides to build an assembly plant in South Carolina.

   c. A U.S. college student decides to spend a year studying at the Sorbonne in Paris.

   d. An Italian manufacturer ships machinery from one Italian port to another on a Liberian freighter.

   e. The U.S. economy grows faster than the French economy.

   f. A U.S. government bond held by a Spanish citizen matures, and the loan amount is paid back to that person.

   g. It is widely expected that the euro will depreciate in the near future.

3. What do the plus signs and negative signs signify in the U.S. balance-of-payments statement? Which of the following items appear in the current account and which appear in the capital and financial account? U.S. purchases of assets abroad; U.S. services imports; foreign purchases of assets in the United States; U.S. good exports, U.S. net investment income. Why must the current account and the capital and financial account sum to zero? LO2

4. What are official reserves? How do net sales of official reserves to foreigners and net purchases of official reserves from foreigners relate to U.S. balance-of-payment deficits and surpluses? Explain why these deficits and surpluses are not actual deficits and surpluses in the *overall* balance-of-payments statement. LO2

5. Generally speaking, how is the dollar price of euros determined? Cite a factor that might increase the dollar price of euros. Cite a different factor that might decrease the dollar price of euros. Explain: "A rise in the dollar price of euros necessarily means a fall in the euro price of dollars." Illustrate and elaborate: "The dollar-euro exchange rate provides a direct link between the prices of goods and services produced in the Euro Zone and in the United States." Explain the purchasing-power-parity theory of exchange rates, using the euro-dollar exchange rate as an illustration. LO3

6. Suppose that a Swiss watchmaker imports watch components from Sweden and exports watches to the United States. Also suppose the dollar depreciates, and the Swedish krona appreciates, relative to the Swiss franc. Speculate as to how each would hurt the Swiss watchmaker. LO3

7. Explain why the U.S. demand for Mexican pesos is downsloping and the supply of pesos to Americans is upsloping. Assuming a system of flexible exchange rates between Mexico and the United States, indicate whether each of the following would cause the Mexican peso to appreciate or depreciate, other things equal: LO3

   a. The United States unilaterally reduces tariffs on Mexican products.

   b. Mexico encounters severe inflation.

c. Deteriorating political relations reduce American tourism in Mexico.

d. The U.S. economy moves into a severe recession.

e. The United States engages in a high-interest-rate monetary policy.

f. Mexican products become more fashionable to U.S. consumers.

g. The Mexican government encourages U.S. firms to invest in Mexican oil fields.

h. The rate of productivity growth in the United States diminishes sharply.

8. Explain why you agree or disagree with the following statements. Assume other things equal. **LO3**

a. A country that grows faster than its major trading partners can expect the international value of its currency to depreciate.

b. A nation whose interest rate is rising more rapidly than interest rates in other nations can expect the international value of its currency to appreciate.

c. A country's currency will appreciate if its inflation rate is less than that of the rest of the world.

9. "Exports pay for imports. Yet in 2009 the nations of the world exported about $379 billion more of goods and services to the United States than they imported from the United States." Resolve the apparent inconsistency of these two statements. **LO2**

10. Diagram a market in which the equilibrium dollar price of 1 unit of fictitious currency zee (Z) is $5 (the exchange rate is $5 = Z1). Then show on your diagram a decline in the demand for zee. **LO4**

a. Referring to your diagram, discuss the adjustment options the United States would have in maintaining the exchange rate at $5 = Z1 under a fixed-exchange-rate system.

b. How would the U.S. balance-of-payments surplus that is caused by the decline in demand be resolved under a system of flexible exchange rates?

11. Suppose that a country follows a managed-float policy but that its exchange rate is currently floating freely. In addition, suppose that it has a massive current account deficit. Does it also necessarily have a balance-of-payments deficit? If it decides to engage in a currency intervention to reduce the size of its current account deficit, will it buy or sell its own currency? As it does so, will its official reserves of foreign currencies get larger or smaller? Would that outcome indicate a balance-of-payments deficit or a balance-of-payments surplus? **LO4**

12. What have been the major causes of the large U.S. trade deficits in recent years? What are the major benefits and costs associated with trade deficits? Explain: "A trade deficit means that a nation is receiving more goods and services from abroad than it is sending abroad." How can that be considered to be "unfavorable"? **LO5**

13. **LAST WORD** Suppose Super D'Hiver—a hypothetical French snowboard retailer—wants to order 5000 snowboards made in the United States. The price per board is $200, the present exchange rate is 1 euro = $1, and payment is due in dollars when the boards are delivered in 3 months. Use a numerical example to explain why exchange-rate risk might make the French retailer hesitant to place the order. How might speculators absorb some of Super D'Hiver's risk?

Problems

1. Alpha's balance-of-payments data for 2010 are shown below. All figures are in billions of dollars. What are the (*a*) balance on goods, (*b*) balance on goods and services, (*c*) balance on current account, and (*d*) balance on capital and financial account? Suppose Alpha sold $10 billion of official reserves abroad to balance the capital and financial account with the current account. Does Alpha have a balance-of-payments deficit or does it have a surplus? **LO2**

Goods exports	$+40
Goods imports	−30
Service exports	+15
Service imports	−10
Net investment income	−5
Net transfers	+10
Balance on capital account	0
Foreign purchases of Alpha assets	+20
Alpha purchases of assets abroad	−40

2. China had a $372 billion overall current account surplus in 2007. Assuming that China's net debt forgiveness was zero in 2007 (its capital account balance was zero), by how much did Chinese purchases of financial and real assets abroad exceed foreign purchases of Chinese financial and real assets? **LO2**

3. Refer to the following table, in which Q_d is the quantity of yen demanded, P is the dollar price of yen, Q_s is the quantity of yen supplied in year 1, and Q_s' is the quantity of yen supplied in year 2. All quantities are in billions and the dollar-yen exchange rate is fully flexible. **LO3**

Q_d	P	Q_s	Q_s'
10	125	30	20
15	120	25	15
20	115	20	10
25	110	15	5

a. What is the equilibrium dollar price of yen in year 1?
b. What is the equilibrium dollar price of yen in year 2?
c. Did the yen appreciate or did it depreciate relative to the dollar between years 1 and 2?
d. Did the dollar appreciate or did it depreciate relative to the yen between years 1 and 2?
e. Which one of the following could have caused the change in relative values of the dollar and yen between years 1 and 2: (1) More rapid inflation in the United States than in Japan, (2) an increase in the real interest rate in the United States but not in Japan, or (3) faster income growth in the United States than in Japan.

4. Suppose that the current Canadian dollar (CAD) to U.S. dollar exchange rate is $.85 CAD = $1 US and that the U.S. dollar price of an Apple iPhone is $300. What is the Canadian dollar price of an iPhone? Next, suppose that the CAD to U.S. dollar exchange rate moves to $.96 CAD = $1 US. What is the new Canadian dollar price of an iPhone? Other things equal, would you expect Canada to import more or fewer iPhones at the new exchange rate? **LO3**

5. Return to problem 3 and assume the exchange rate is fixed against the dollar at the equilibrium exchange rate that occurs in year 1. Also suppose that Japan and the United States are the only two countries in the world. In year 2, what quantity of yen would the Japanese government have to buy or sell to balance its capital and financial account with its current account? In what specific account would this purchase or sale show up in Japan's balance-of-payments statement: Foreign purchases of assets in Japan or Japanese purchase of assets abroad? Would this transaction increase Japan's stock of official reserves or decrease its stock? **LO5**

FURTHER TEST YOUR KNOWLEDGE AT
www.mcconnell19e.com

At the text's Online Learning Center (OLC), **www.mcconnell19e.com**, you will find one or more Web-based questions that require information from the Internet to answer. We urge you to check them out; they will familiarize you with Web sites that may be helpful in other courses and perhaps even in your career. The OLC also features multiple-choice questions that give instant feedback and provides other helpful ways to further test your knowledge of the chapter.

AFTER READING THIS CHAPTER, YOU SHOULD BE ABLE TO:

1 **Describe how the World Bank distinguishes between industrially advanced countries (high-income nations) and developing countries (middle-income and low-income nations).**

2 **List some of the obstacles to economic development.**

3 **Explain the vicious circle of poverty that afflicts low-income nations.**

4 **Discuss the role of government in promoting economic development within low-income nations.**

5 **Describe how industrial nations attempt to aid low-income countries.**

The Economics of Developing Countries

It is difficult for those of us in the United States, where per capita GDP in 2009 was about $48,000, to grasp the fact that about 2.5 billion people, or nearly half the world's population, live on $2 or less a day. And about 1.4 billion live on less than $1.25 a day. Hunger, squalor, and disease are the norm in many nations of the world.

In this bonus Web chapter (at our Web site, **www.mcconnell19e.com**), we identify the developing countries, discuss their characteristics, and explore the obstacles that have impeded their growth. We also examine the appropriate roles of the private sector and government in economic development. Finally, we look at policies that might help developing countries increase their growth rates.

Note: Terms set in *italic* type are defined separately in this glossary.

absolute advantage A situation in which a person or country can produce more of a particular product from a specific quantity of resources than some other person or country.

actively managed funds *Mutual funds* that have portfolio managers who constantly buy and sell *assets* in an attempt to generate higher returns that some benchmark rate of return for similar *portfolios*.

actual investment The amount that *firms* invest; equal to *planned investment* plus *unplanned investment*.

actual reserves The funds that a bank has on deposit at the *Federal Reserve Bank* of its district (plus its *vault cash*).

aggregate A collection of specific economic units treated as if they were one. For example, all prices of individual goods and services are combined into a *price level*, or all units of output are aggregated into *gross domestic product*.

aggregate demand A schedule or curve that shows the total quantity of goods and services demanded (purchased) at different *price levels*.

aggregate demand–aggregate supply (AD-AS) model The macroeconomic model that uses *aggregate demand* and *aggregate supply* to determine and explain the *price level* and the real *domestic output*.

aggregate expenditures The total amount spent for final goods and services in an economy.

aggregate expenditures–domestic output approach Determination of the equilibrium *gross domestic product* by finding the real GDP at which *aggregate expenditures* equal *domestic output*.

aggregate expenditures schedule A schedule or curve showing the total amount spent for final goods and services at different levels of *real GDP*.

aggregate supply A schedule or curve showing the total quantity of goods and services supplied (produced) at different *price levels*.

aggregate supply shocks Sudden, large changes in resource costs that shift an economy's aggregate supply curve.

allocative efficiency The apportionment of resources among firms and industries to obtain the production of the products most wanted by society (consumers); the output of each product at which its *marginal cost* and *price* or *marginal benefit* are equal.

anticipated inflation Increases in the price level (*inflation*) that occur at the expected rate.

appreciation (of the dollar) An increase in the value of the dollar relative to the currency of another nation, so a dollar buys a larger amount of the foreign currency and thus of foreign goods.

arbitrage The activity that generates riskless profits by selling one *asset* and buying an identical or nearly identical asset to benefit from temporary differences in prices or rates of return; the practice that equalizes prices or returns on similar financial instruments and thus eliminates further opportunities for riskless financial gains.

asset Anything of monetary value owned by a firm or individual.

asset demand for money The amount of *money* people want to hold as a *store of value*; this amount varies inversely with the *interest rate*.

average expected rate of return The *probability-weighted average* of an investment's possible future returns.

average propensity to consume (APC) Fraction (or percentage) of *disposable income* that households plan to spend for consumer goods and services; consumption divided by *disposable income*.

average propensity to save (APS) Fraction (or percentage) of *disposable income* that households save; *saving* divided by *disposable income*.

average tax rate Total tax paid divided by total *taxable income* or some other base (such as total income) against which to compare the amount of tax paid. Expressed as a percentage.

balance of payments (See *international balance of payments*.)

balance-of-payments deficit The net amount of *official reserves* (mainly foreign currencies) that a nation's treasury or central bank must sell to achieve balance between that nation's *capital and financial account* and its *current account* (in its *balance of payments*).

balance-of-payments surplus The net amount of *official reserves* (mainly foreign currencies) that a nation's treasury or central bank must buy to achieve balance between that nation's *capital and financial account* and its *current account* (in its *balance of payments*).

balance on capital and financial account The sum of the *capital account balance* and the *financial account balance*.

balance on current account The exports of goods and services of a nation less its imports of goods and services plus its *net investment income* and *net transfers* in a year.

balance on goods and services The exports of goods and services of a nation less its imports of goods and services in a year.

balance sheet A statement of the *assets*, *liabilities*, and *net worth* of a firm or individual at some given time.

bank deposits The deposits that individuals or firms have at banks (or thrifts) or that banks have at the *Federal Reserve Banks*.

bankers' bank A bank that accepts the deposits of and makes loans to *depository institutions*; in the United States, a *Federal Reserve Bank*.

bank reserves The deposits of commercial banks and thrifts at *Federal Reserve Banks* plus bank and thrift *vault cash*.

bankrupt A legal situation in which an individual or *firm* finds that it cannot make timely interest payments on money it has borrowed. In such cases, a bankruptcy judge can order the individual or firm to liquidate (turn into cash) its assets in order to pay lenders at least some portion of the amount they are owed.

barter The exchange of one good or service for another good or service.

base year The year with which other years are compared when an index is constructed; for example, the base year for a *price index*.

beta A relative measure of *nondiversifiable risk* that measures how the nondiversifiable risk of a given *asset* or *portfolio* compares with that of the *market portfolio* (the portfolio that contains every asset available in the financial markets).

Board of Governors The seven-member group that supervises and controls the money and banking system of the United States; the Board of Governors of the *Federal Reserve System;* the Federal Reserve Board.

bond A financial device through which a borrower (a firm or government) is obligated to pay the principal and interest on a loan at a specific date in the future.

break-even income The level of *disposable income* at which *households* plan to consume (spend) all their income and to save none of it.

budget deficit The amount by which the expenditures of the Federal government exceed its revenues in any year.

budget line A line that shows the different combinations of two products a consumer can purchase with a specific money income, given the products' prices.

budget surplus The amount by which the revenues of the Federal government exceed its expenditures in any year.

built-in stabilizer A mechanism that increases government's budget deficit (or reduces its surplus) during a recession and increases government's budget surplus (or reduces its deficit) during an expansion without any action by policymakers. The tax system is one such mechanism.

Bureau of Economic Analysis (BEA) An agency of the U.S. Department of Commerce that compiles the national income and product accounts.

business cycle Recurring increases and decreases in the level of economic activity over periods of years; consists of peak, recession, trough, and expansion phases.

businesses Economic entities (*firms*) that purchase resources and provide goods and services to the economy.

business firm (See *firm.*)

capital Human-made resources (buildings, machinery, and equipment) used to produce goods and services; goods that do not directly satisfy human wants; also called capital goods.

capital and financial account The section of a nation's *international balance of payments* that records (1) debt forgiveness by and to foreigners and (2) foreign purchases of assets in the United States and U.S. purchases of assets abroad.

capital and financial account deficit A negative balance on its *capital and financial account* in a country's *international balance of payments*.

capital and financial account surplus A positive balance on its *capital and financial account* in a country's *international balance of payments*.

capital flight (Web chapter) The transfer of savings from *developing countries* to *industrially advanced countries* to avoid government expropriation, taxation, higher rates of inflation, or simply to realize greater returns on *financial investments*.

capital gain The gain realized when securities or properties are sold for a price greater than the price paid for them.

capital goods (See *capital.*)

capital-intensive goods Products that require relatively large amounts of *capital* to produce.

capitalism An economic system in which property resources are privately owned and markets and prices are used to direct and coordinate economic activities.

capital-saving technology (Web chapter) An improvement in *technology* that permits a greater quantity of a product to be produced with a specific amount of *capital* (or permits the same amount of the product to be produced with a smaller amount of capital).

capital stock The total available *capital* in a nation.

capital-using technology (Web chapter) An improvement in *technology* that requires the use of a greater amount of *capital* to produce a specific quantity of a product.

capricious-universe view (Web chapter) The view held by some people that fate and outside events, rather than hard work and enterprise, will determine their economic destinies.

cartel A formal agreement among firms (or countries) in an industry to set the price of a product and establish the outputs of the individual firms (or countries) or to divide the market for the product geographically.

causation A relationship in which the occurrence of one or more events brings about another event.

CEA (See *Council of Economic Advisers.*)

ceiling price (See *price ceiling.*)

central bank A bank whose chief function is the control of the nation's *money supply;* in the United States, the *Federal Reserve System.*

central economic planning Government determination of the objectives of the economy and how resources will be directed to attain those goals.

ceteris paribus assumption (See *other-things-equal assumption.*)

change in demand A movement of an entire *demand curve* or schedule such that the *quantity demanded* changes at every particular price; caused by a change in one or more of the *determinants of demand*.

change in quantity demanded A change in the *quantity demanded* along a fixed *demand curve* (or within a fixed demand schedule) as a result of a change in the product's price.

change in quantity supplied A change in the *quantity supplied* along a fixed *supply curve* (or within a fixed supply schedule) as a result of a change in the product's price.

change in supply A movement of an entire *supply curve* or schedule such that the *quantity supplied* changes at every particular price; caused by a change in one or more of the *determinants of supply*.

checkable deposit Any deposit in a *commercial bank* or *thrift institution* against which a check may be written.

checkable-deposit multiplier (See *monetary multiplier*.)

check clearing The process by which funds are transferred from the checking accounts of the writers of checks to the checking accounts of the recipients of the checks.

checking account A *checkable deposit* in a *commercial bank* or *thrift institution*.

circular flow diagram An illustration showing the flow of resources from *households* to *firms* and of products from firms to households. These flows are accompanied by reverse flows of money from firms to households and from households to firms.

closed economy An economy that neither exports nor imports goods and services.

Coase theorem The idea, first stated by economist Ronald Coase, that some *externalities* can be resolved through private negotiations of the affected parties.

coincidence of wants A situation in which the good or service that one trader desires to obtain is the same as that which another trader desires to give up and an item that the second trader wishes to acquire is the same as that which the first trader desires to surrender.

COLA (See *cost-of-living adjustment*.)

command system A method of organizing an economy in which property resources are publicly owned and government uses *central economic planning* to direct and coordinate economic activities; command economy; communism.

commercial bank A firm that engages in the business of banking (accepts deposits, offers checking accounts, and makes loans).

commercial banking system All *commercial banks* and *thrift institutions* as a group.

communism (See *command system*.)

comparative advantage A situation in which a person or country can produce a specific product at a lower opportunity cost than some other person or country; the basis for specialization and trade.

compensation to employees *Wages* and salaries plus wage and salary supplements paid by employers to workers.

competition The presence in a market of independent buyers and sellers competing with one another along with the freedom of buyers and sellers to enter and leave the market.

complementary goods Products and services that are used together. When the price of one falls, the demand for the other increases (and conversely).

compound interest The accumulation of money that builds over time in an investment or interest-bearing account as new interest is earned on previous interest that is not withdrawn.

conglomerates Firms that produce goods and services in two or more separate industries.

constant opportunity cost An *opportunity cost* that remains the same for each additional unit as a consumer (or society) shifts purchases (production) from one product to another along a straight-line *budget line* (*production possibilities curve*).

consumer goods Products and services that satisfy human wants directly.

Consumer Price Index (CPI) An index that measures the prices of a fixed "market basket" of some 300 goods and services bought by a "typical" consumer.

consumer sovereignty Determination by consumers of the types and quantities of goods and services that will be produced with the scarce resources of the economy; consumers' direction of production through their *dollar votes*.

consumption of fixed capital An estimate of the amount of *capital* worn out or used up (consumed) in producing the *gross domestic product*; also called depreciation.

consumption schedule A schedule showing the amounts *households* plan to spend for *consumer goods* at different levels of *disposable income*.

contractionary fiscal policy A decrease in *government purchases* of goods and services, an increase in *net taxes*, or some combination of the two, for the purpose of decreasing *aggregate demand* and thus controlling inflation.

coordination failure A situation in which people do not reach a mutually beneficial outcome because they lack some way to jointly coordinate their actions; a possible cause of macroeconomic instability.

core inflation The underlying increases in the *price level* after volatile food and energy prices are removed.

corporate income tax A tax levied on the net income (accounting profit) of corporations.

corporation A legal entity ("person") chartered by a state or the Federal government that is distinct and separate from the individuals who own it.

correlation A systematic and dependable association between two sets of data (two kinds of events); does not necessarily indicate causation.

corruption The misuse of government power, with which one has been entrusted or assigned, to obtain private gain; includes payments from individuals or companies to secure advantages in obtaining government contracts, avoiding government regulations, or obtaining inside knowledge about forthcoming policy changes.

cost-benefit analysis A comparison of the *marginal costs* of a government project or program with the *marginal benefits* to decide whether or not to employ resources in that project or program and to what extent.

cost-of-living adjustment (COLA) An automatic increase in the incomes (wages) of workers when inflation occurs; guaranteed by a collective bargaining contract between firms and workers.

cost-push inflation Increases in the price level (inflation) resulting from an increase in resource costs (for example, raw-material prices) and hence in *per-unit production costs;* inflation caused by reductions in *aggregate supply.*

Council of Economic Advisers (CEA) A group of three persons that advises and assists the president of the United States on economic matters (including the preparation of the annual *Economic Report of the President*).

creative destruction The hypothesis that the creation of new products and production methods simultaneously destroys the market power of existing monopolies.

credit An accounting item that increases the value of an asset (such as the foreign money owned by the residents of a nation).

credit union An association of persons who have a common tie (such as being employees of the same firm or members of the same labor union) that sells shares to (accepts deposits from) its members and makes loans to them.

cross elasticity of demand The ratio of the percentage change in *quantity demanded* of one good to the percentage change in the price of some other good. A positive coefficient indicates the two products are *substitute goods;* a negative coefficient indicates they are *complementary goods.*

crowding-out effect A rise in interest rates and a resulting decrease in *planned investment* caused by the Federal government's increased borrowing to finance budget deficits and refinance debt.

currency Coins and paper money.

currency appreciation (See *exchange-rate appreciation.*)

currency depreciation (See *exchange-rate depreciation.*)

currency intervention A government's buying and selling of its own currency or foreign currencies to alter international exchange rates.

current account The section in a nation's *international balance of payments* that records its exports and imports of goods and services, its net *investment income,* and its *net transfers.*

cyclical asymmetry The idea that *monetary policy* may be more successful in slowing expansions and controlling *inflation* than in extracting the economy from severe recession.

cyclical deficit A Federal *budget deficit* that is caused by a recession and the consequent decline in tax revenues.

cyclically adjusted budget A comparison of the government expenditures and tax collections that would occur if the economy operated at *full employment* throughout the year; the full-employment budget.

cyclical unemployment A type of *unemployment* caused by insufficient total spending (or by insufficient *aggregate demand*).

debit An accounting item that decreases the value of an asset (such as the foreign money owned by the residents of a nation).

defaults Situations in which borrowers stop making loan payments or do not pay back loans that they took out and are now due.

deflating Finding the *real gross domestic product* by decreasing the dollar value of the GDP for a year in which prices were higher than in the *base year.*

deflation A decline in the economy's *price level.*

demand A schedule showing the amounts of a good or service that buyers (or a buyer) wish to purchase at various prices during some time period.

demand curve A curve illustrating *demand.*

demand factor (in growth) The increase in the level of *aggregate demand* that brings about the *economic growth* made possible by an increase in the production potential of the economy.

demand management The use of *fiscal policy* and *monetary policy* to increase or decrease *aggregate demand.*

demand-pull inflation Increases in the price level (inflation) resulting from an excess of demand over output at the existing price level, caused by an increase in *aggregate demand.*

demand schedule (See *demand.*)

demand shocks Sudden, unexpected changes in demand.

demand-side market failures Underallocations of resources that occur when private demand curves understate consumers' full willingness to pay for a good or service.

demographers Scientists who study the characteristics of human populations.

demographic transition (Web chapter) The idea that population growth slows once a developing country achieves higher standards of living because the perceived marginal cost of additional children begins to exceed the perceived marginal benefit.

dependent variable A variable that changes as a consequence of a change in some other (independent) variable; the "effect" or outcome.

depository institutions Firms that accept deposits of *money* from the public (businesses and persons); *commercial banks, savings and loan associations, mutual savings banks,* and *credit unions.*

depreciation (See *consumption of fixed capital.*)

depreciation (of the dollar) A decrease in the value of the dollar relative to another currency, so a dollar buys a smaller amount of the foreign currency and therefore of foreign goods.

derived demand The demand for a resource that depends on the demand for the products it helps to produce.

determinants of aggregate demand Factors such as consumption spending, *investment,* government spending, and *net exports* that, if they change, shift the aggregate demand curve.

determinants of aggregate supply Factors such as input prices, *productivity,* and the legal-institutional environment that, if they change, shift the aggregate supply curve.

determinants of demand Factors other than price that determine the quantities demanded of a good or service.

determinants of supply Factors other than price that determine the quantities supplied of a good or service.

developing countries Many countries of Africa, Asia, and Latin America that are characterized by lack of capital goods, use of nonadvanced technologies, low literacy rates, high unemployment, rapid population growth, and labor forces heavily committed to agriculture.

direct foreign investment (See *foreign direct investment*.)

direct relationship The relationship between two variables that change in the same direction, for example, product price and quantity supplied; positive relationship.

discount rate The interest rate that the *Federal Reserve Banks* charge on the loans they make to *commercial banks* and *thrift institutions*.

discouraged workers Employees who have left the *labor force* because they have not been able to find employment.

discretionary fiscal policy Deliberate changes in taxes (tax rates) and government spending by Congress to promote full employment, price stability, and economic growth.

discrimination The practice of according individuals or groups inferior treatment in hiring, occupational access, education and training, promotion, wage rates, or working conditions even though they have the same abilities, education, skills, and work experience as other workers.

disinflation A reduction in the rate of *inflation*.

disposable income (DI) *Personal income* less personal taxes; income available for *personal consumption expenditures* and *personal saving*.

dissaving Spending for consumer goods and services in excess of *disposable income*; the amount by which *personal consumption expenditures* exceed disposable income.

diversifiable risk Investment *risk* that investors can reduce via *diversification*; also called idiosyncratic risk.

diversification The strategy of investing in a large number of investments in order to reduce the overall risk to an entire investment *portfolio*.

dividends Payments by a corporation of all or part of its profit to its stockholders (the corporate owners).

division of labor The separation of the work required to produce a product into a number of different tasks that are performed by different workers; *specialization* of workers.

Doha Development Agenda The latest, uncompleted (as of mid-2010) sequence of trade negotiations by members of the *World Trade Organization*; named after Doha, Qatar, where the set of negotiations began. Also called the Doha Round.

dollar votes The "votes" that consumers and entrepreneurs cast for the production of consumer and capital goods, respectively, when they purchase those goods in product and resource markets.

domestic capital formation The process of adding to a nation's stock of *capital* by saving and investing part of its own domestic output.

domestic output *Gross* (or net) *domestic product*; the total output of final goods and services produced in the economy.

domestic price The price of a good or service within a country, determined by domestic demand and supply.

dumping The sale of a product in a foreign country at prices either below cost or below the prices commonly charged at home.

durable good A consumer good with an expected life (use) of three or more years.

earnings The money income received by a worker; equal to the *wage* (rate) multiplied by the amount of time worked.

economic cost A payment that must be made to obtain and retain the services of a *resource*; the income a firm must provide to a resource supplier to attract the resource away from an alternative use; equal to the quantity of other products that cannot be produced when resources are instead used to make a particular product.

economic efficiency The use of the minimum necessary resources to obtain the socially optimal amounts of goods and services; entails both *productive efficiency* and *allocative efficiency*.

economic growth (1) An outward shift in the *production possibilities curve* that results from an increase in resource supplies or quality or an improvement in *technology*; (2) an increase of real output (*gross domestic product*) or real output per capita.

economic investment (See *investment*.)

economic law An *economic principle* that has been tested and retested and has stood the test of time.

economic model A simplified picture of economic reality; an abstract generalization.

economic perspective A viewpoint that envisions individuals and institutions making rational decisions by comparing the marginal benefits and marginal costs associated with their actions.

economic policy A course of action intended to correct or avoid a problem.

economic principle A widely accepted generalization about the economic behavior of individuals or institutions.

economic profit The *total revenue* of a firm less its *economic costs* (which include both *explicit costs* and *implicit costs*); also called "pure profit" and "above-normal profit."

economic resources The *land, labor, capital,* and *entrepreneurial ability* that are used in the production of goods and services; productive agents; factors of production.

economics The social science concerned with how individuals, institutions, and society make optimal (best) choices under conditions of scarcity.

economic system A particular set of institutional arrangements and a coordinating mechanism for solving the economizing problem; a method of organizing an economy, of which the *market system* and the *command system* are the two general types.

economic theory A statement of a cause-effect relationship; when accepted by all or nearly all economists, an *economic principle*.

economies of scale Reductions in the *average total cost* of producing a product as the firm expands the size of plant (its output) in the *long run*; the economies of mass production.

economizing problem The choices necessitated because society's economic wants for goods and services are unlimited but the resources available to satisfy these wants are limited (scarce).

efficiency factors (in growth) The capacity of an economy to combine resources effectively to achieve growth of real output that the *supply factors* (of growth) make possible.

efficiency loss Reduction in combined consumer and producer surplus caused by an underallocation or overallocation of resources to the production of a good or service. Also called *deadweight loss.*

efficiency wage A wage that minimizes wage costs per unit of output by encouraging greater effort or reducing turnover.

efficient allocation of resources That allocation of an economy's resources among the production of different products that leads to the maximum satisfaction of consumers' wants, thus producing the socially optimal mix of output with society's scarce resources.

elastic demand Product or resource demand whose *price elasticity* is greater than 1. This means the resulting change in *quantity demanded* is greater than the percentage change in *price.*

elasticity coefficient The number obtained when the percentage change in *quantity demanded* (or supplied) is divided by the percentage change in the *price* of the commodity.

elasticity formula (See *price elasticity of demand.*)

elastic supply Product or resource supply whose price elasticity is greater than 1. This means the resulting change in quantity supplied is greater than the percentage change in price.

electronic payments Purchases made by transferring funds electronically. Examples: Fedwire transfers, automated clearinghouse transactions (ACHs), payments via the PayPal system, and payments made through stored-value cards.

employment rate The percentage of the *labor force* employed at any time.

entrepreneurial ability The human resource that combines the other resources to produce a product, makes nonroutine decisions, innovates, and bears risks.

equation of exchange $MV = PQ$, in which M is the supply of money, V is the *velocity* of money, P is the *price level*, and Q is the physical volume of *final goods and services* produced.

equilibrium GDP (See *equilibrium real domestic output.*)

equilibrium price The *price* in a competitive market at which the *quantity demanded* and the *quantity supplied* are equal, there is neither a shortage nor a surplus, and there is no tendency for price to rise or fall.

equilibrium price level The price level at which the aggregate demand curve intersects the aggregate supply curve.

equilibrium quantity (1) The quantity at which the intentions of buyers and sellers in a particular market match at a particular price such that the *quantity demanded* and the *quantity supplied* are equal; (2) the profit-maximizing output of a firm.

equilibrium real domestic output The *gross domestic product* at which the total quantity of final goods and services purchased *(aggregate expenditures)* is equal to the total quantity of final goods and services produced (the real domestic output); the real domestic output at which the aggregate demand curve intersects the aggregate supply curve.

equilibrium real output (See *equilibrium real domestic output.*)

equilibrium world price The price of an internationally traded product that equates the quantity of the product demanded by importers with the quantity of the product supplied by exporters; the price determined at the intersection of the export supply curve and the import demand curve.

euro The common currency unit used by 16 European nations (as of 2010) in the *Euro Zone*, which consists of Austria, Belgium, Cyprus, Finland, France, Germany, Greece, Ireland, Italy, Luxembourg, Malta, the Netherlands, Portugal, Slovakia, Slovenia, and Spain.

European Union (EU) An association of 27 European nations (as of 2010) that has eliminated tariffs and quotas among them, established common tariffs for imported goods from outside the member nations, eliminated barriers to the free movement of capital, and created other common economic policies.

Euro Zone The 16 nations (as of 2010) of the 25-member (as of 2010) *European Union* that use the *euro* as their common currency. The Euro Zone countries are Austria, Belgium, Cyprus, Finland, France, Germany, Greece, Ireland, Italy, Luxembourg, Malta, the Netherlands, Portugal, Slovakia, Slovenia, and Spain.

excess reserves The amount by which a bank's or thrift's *actual reserves* exceed its *required reserves*; actual reserves minus required reserves.

exchange controls (See *foreign exchange controls.*)

exchange rate The *rate of exchange* of one nation's currency for another nation's currency.

exchange-rate appreciation An increase in the value of a nation's currency in foreign exchange markets; an increase in the *rate of exchange* with foreign currencies.

exchange-rate depreciation A decrease in the value of a nation's currency in foreign exchange markets; a decrease in the *rate of exchange* with foreign currencies.

exchange-rate determinant Any factor other than the *rate of exchange* that determines a currency's demand and supply in the *foreign exchange market.*

excise tax A tax levied on the production of a specific product or on the quantity of the product purchased.

excludability The characteristic of a *private good*, for which the seller can keep nonbuyers from obtaining the good.

exhaustive expenditure An expenditure by government resulting directly in the employment of *economic resources* and in the absorption by government of the goods and services those resources produce; a *government purchase.*

expansion A phase of the *business cycle* in which *real GDP*, *income*, and employment rise.

expansionary fiscal policy An increase in *government purchases* of goods and services, a decrease in *net taxes*, or some combination of the two for the purpose of increasing *aggregate demand* and expanding real output.

expansionary monetary policy *Federal Reserve System* actions to increase the *money supply*, lower *interest rates*, and expand *real GDP*; an easy money policy.

expectations The anticipations of consumers, firms, and others about future economic conditions.

expected rate of return The increase in profit a firm anticipates it will obtain by purchasing capital (or engaging in research and development); expressed as a percentage of the total cost of the investment (or R&D) activity.

expenditures approach The method that adds all expenditures made for *final goods and services* to measure the *gross domestic product*.

expenditures-output approach (See *aggregate expenditures–domestic output approach*.)

exports Goods and services produced in a nation and sold to buyers in other nations.

export subsidy A government payment to a domestic producer to enable the firm to reduce the price of a good or service to foreign buyers.

export supply curve An upward-sloping curve that shows the amount of a product that domestic firms will export at each *world price* that is above the *domestic price*.

export transaction A sale of a good or service that increases the amount of foreign currency flowing to a nation's citizens, firms, and government.

external benefit (See *positive externality*.)

external cost (See *negative externality*.)

external debt Private or public debt owed to foreign citizens, firms, and institutions.

externality A cost or benefit from production or consumption, accruing without compensation to someone other than the buyers and sellers of the product (see *negative externality* and *positive externality*).

external public debt The portion of the public debt owed to foreign citizens, firms, and institutions.

face value The dollar or cents value placed on a U.S. coin or piece of paper money.

factors of production *Economic resources: land, capital, labor,* and *entrepreneurial ability.*

fallacy of composition The false notion that what is true for the individual (or part) is necessarily true for the group (or whole).

FDIC (See *Federal Deposit Insurance Corporation*.)

Federal Deposit Insurance Corporation (FDIC) The federally chartered corporation that insures deposit liabilities (up to $250,000 per account) of *commercial banks* and *thrift institutions*

(excluding *credit unions*, whose deposits are insured by the *National Credit Union Administration*).

Federal funds rate The interest rate banks and other depository institutions charge one another on overnight loans made out of their *excess reserves*.

Federal government The government of the United States, as distinct from the state and local governments.

Federal Open Market Committee (FOMC) The 12-member group that determines the purchase and sale policies of the *Federal Reserve Banks* in the market for U.S. government securities.

Federal Reserve Banks The 12 banks chartered by the U.S. government to control the *money supply* and perform other functions. (See *central bank, quasi-public bank,* and *bankers' bank*.)

Federal Reserve Note Paper money issued by the *Federal Reserve Banks*.

Federal Reserve System The U.S. central bank, consisting of the *Board of Governors* of the Federal Reserve and the 12 *Federal Reserve Banks*, which controls the lending activity of the nation's banks and thrifts and thus the *money supply*; commonly referred to as the "Fed."

fiat money Anything that is *money* because government has decreed it to be money.

final goods Goods that have been purchased for final use and not for resale or further processing or manufacturing.

financial capital (See *money capital*.)

financial investment The purchase of a financial asset (such as a *stock, bond,* or *mutual fund*) or real asset (such as a house, land, or factories) or the building of such assets in the expectation of financial gain.

financial services industry The broad category of firms that provide financial products and services to help households and businesses earn *interest*, receive *dividends*, obtain *capital gains*, insure against losses, and plan for retirement. Includes *commercial banks*, thrifts, insurance companies, mutual fund companies, pension funds, investment banks, and securities firms.

firm An organization that employs resources to produce a good or service for profit and owns and operates one or more *plants*.

fiscal policy Changes in government spending and tax collections designed to achieve a full-employment and noninflationary domestic output; also called *discretionary fiscal policy*.

fixed exchange rate A *rate of exchange* that is set in some way and therefore prevented from rising or falling with changes in currency supply and demand.

fixed resource Any resource whose quantity cannot be changed by a firm in the *short run*.

flexible exchange rate A *rate of exchange* determined by the international demand for and supply of a nation's money; a rate free to rise or fall (to float).

flexible prices Product prices that freely move upward or downward when product demand or supply changes.

floating exchange rate (See *flexible exchange rate*.)

follower countries As it relates to *economic growth*, countries that adopt advanced technologies that previously were developed and used by *leader countries*.

foreign competition (See *import competition*.)

foreign direct investment (Web chapter) Investments made to obtain a lasting interest in firms operating outside of the economy of the investor; may involve purchasing existing assets or building new production facilities.

foreign exchange controls Controls a government may exercise over the quantity of foreign currency demanded by its citizens and firms and over the *rates of exchange* as a way to limit the nation's quantity of *outpayments* relative to its quantity of *inpayments* (to eliminate a *payments deficit*).

foreign exchange market A market in which the money (currency) of one nation can be used to purchase (can be exchanged for) the money of another nation; currency market.

foreign exchange rate (See *rate of exchange*.)

foreign purchase effect The inverse relationship between the *net exports* of an economy and its price level relative to foreign price levels.

45° (degree) line A line along which the value of *GDP* (measured horizontally) is equal to the value of *aggregate expenditures* (measured vertically).

fractional reserve banking system A system in which *commercial banks* and *thrift institutions* hold less than 100 percent of their checkable-deposit liabilities as *required reserves*.

freedom of choice The freedom of owners of property resources to employ or dispose of them as they see fit, of workers to enter any line of work for which they are qualified, and of consumers to spend their incomes in a manner that they think is appropriate.

freedom of enterprise The freedom of *firms* to obtain economic resources, to use those resources to produce products of the firm's own choosing, and to sell their products in markets of their choice.

free-rider problem The inability of potential providers of an economically desirable good or service to obtain payment from those who benefit, because of *nonexcludability*.

free trade The absence of artificial (government-imposed) barriers to trade among individuals and firms in different nations.

frictional unemployment A type of unemployment caused by workers voluntarily changing jobs and by temporary layoffs; unemployed workers between jobs.

full employment (1) The use of all available resources to produce want-satisfying goods and services; (2) the situation in which the *unemployment rate* is equal to the *full-employment rate of unemployment* and where *frictional* and *structural* unemployment occur but not *cyclical unemployment* (and the *real GDP* of the economy equals *potential output*).

full-employment rate of unemployment The *unemployment rate* at which there is no *cyclical unemployment* of the *labor force*; equal to between 4 and 5 percent in the United States because some *frictional* and *structural unemployment* is unavoidable.

functional distribution of income The manner in which *national income* is divided among the functions performed to earn it (or the kinds of resources provided to earn it); the division of national income into wages and salaries, proprietors' income, corporate profits, interest, and rent.

future value The amount to which some current amount of money will grow if the interest earned on the amount is left to compound over time. *See compound interest*.

gains from trade The extra output that trading partners obtain through specialization of production and exchange of goods and services.

GDP (See *gross domestic product*.)

GDP gap Actual *gross domestic product* minus potential output; may be either a positive amount (a *positive GDP gap*) or a negative amount (a *negative GDP gap*).

GDP price index A *price index* for all the goods and services that make up the *gross domestic product*; the price index used to adjust *nominal gross domestic product* to *real gross domestic product*.

G8 nations A group of eight major nations (Canada, France, Germany, Italy, Japan, Russia, United Kingdom, and United States) whose leaders meet regularly to discuss common economic problems and try to coordinate economic policies.

General Agreement on Tariffs and Trade (GATT) The international agreement reached in 1947 in which 23 nations agreed to give equal and nondiscriminatory treatment to one another, to reduce tariff rates by multinational negotiations, and to eliminate *import quotas*. It now includes most nations and has become the *World Trade Organization*.

generalization Statement of the nature of the relationship between two or more sets of facts.

gold standard A historical system of fixed exchange rates in which nations defined their currencies in terms of gold, maintained a fixed relationship between their stocks of gold and their money supplies, and allowed gold to be freely exported and imported.

government purchases (G) Expenditures by government for goods and services that government consumes in providing public goods and for public (or social) capital that has a long lifetime; the expenditures of all governments in the economy for those *final goods and services*.

government transfer payment The disbursement of money (or goods and services) by government for which government receives no currently produced good or service in return.

gross domestic product (GDP) The total market value of all *final goods and services* produced annually within the boundaries of the United States, whether by U.S.- or foreign-supplied resources.

gross private domestic investment (I_g) Expenditures for newly produced *capital goods* (such as machinery, equipment, tools, and buildings) and for additions to inventories.

growth accounting   The bookkeeping of the supply-side elements such as productivity and labor inputs that contribute to changes in *real GDP* over some specific time period.

guiding function of prices   The ability of price changes to bring about changes in the quantities of products and resources demanded and supplied.

horizontal axis   The "left-right" or "west-east" measurement line on graph or grid.

households   Economic entities (of one or more persons occupying a housing unit) that provide *resources* to the economy and use the *income* received to purchase goods and services that satisfy economic wants.

human capital   The knowledge and skills that make a person productive.

human capital investment   Any expenditure undertaken to improve the education, skills, health, or mobility of workers, with an expectation of greater productivity and thus a positive return on the investment.

hyperinflation   A very rapid rise in the price level; an extremely high rate of inflation.

hypothesis   A tentative explanation of cause and effect that requires testing.

IMF   (See *International Monetary Fund*.)

immediate short-run aggregate supply curve   An aggregate supply curve for which real output, but not the price level, changes when the aggregate demand curves shifts; a horizontal aggregate supply curve that implies an inflexible price level.

import competition   The competition that domestic firms encounter from the products and services of foreign producers.

import demand curve   A downsloping curve showing the amount of a product that an economy will import at each *world price* below the *domestic price*.

import quota   A limit imposed by a nation on the quantity (or total value) of a good that may be imported during some period of time.

imports   Spending by individuals, *firms*, and governments for goods and services produced in foreign nations.

import transaction   The purchase of a good or service that decreases the amount of foreign money held by citizens, firms, and governments of a nation.

income   A flow of dollars (or purchasing power) per unit of time derived from the use of human or property resources.

income approach   The method that adds all the income generated by the production of *final goods and services* to measure the *gross domestic product*.

income effect   A change in the quantity demanded of a product that results from the change in *real income (purchasing power)* caused by a change in the product's price.

income elasticity of demand   The ratio of the percentage change in the *quantity demanded* of a good to a percentage change in consumer income; measures the responsiveness of consumer purchases to income changes.

income inequality   The unequal distribution of an economy's total income among households or families.

increase in demand   An increase in the *quantity demanded* of a good or service at every price; a shift of the *demand curve* to the right.

increase in supply   An increase in the *quantity supplied* of a good or service at every price; a shift of the *supply curve* to the right.

increasing returns   An increase in a firm's output by a larger percentage than the percentage increase in its inputs.

independent goods   Products or services for which there is little or no relationship between the price of one and the demand for the other. When the price of one rises or falls, the demand for the other tends to remain constant.

independent variable   The variable causing a change in some other (dependent) variable.

index funds   *Mutual funds* that select stock or bond *portfolios* to exactly match a stock or bond index (a collection of stocks or bonds meant to capture the overall behavior of a particular category of investments) such as the Standard & Poor's 500 Index or the Russell 3000 Index.

individual demand   The demand schedule or *demand curve* of a single buyer.

individual supply   The supply schedule or *supply curve* of a single seller.

industrially advanced countries   High-income countries such as the United States, Canada, Japan, and the nations of western Europe that have highly developed *market economies* based on large stocks of technologically advanced capital goods and skilled labor forces.

industry   A group of (one or more) *firms* that produce identical or similar products.

inelastic demand   Product or resource demand for which the *elasticity coefficient* for price is less than 1. This means the resulting percentage change in *quantity demanded* is less than the percentage change in *price*.

inelastic supply   Product or resource supply for which the price elasticity coefficient is less than 1. The percentage change in *quantity supplied* is less than the percentage change in *price*.

inferior good   A good or service whose consumption declines as income rises, prices held constant.

inflating   Determining *real gross domestic product* by increasing the dollar value of the *nominal gross domestic product* produced in a year in which prices are lower than those in a *base year*.

inflation   A rise in the general level of prices in an economy.

inflationary expectations   The belief of workers, firms, and consumers about future rates of inflation.

inflationary expenditure gap   The amount by which the *aggregate expenditures schedule* must shift downward to decrease the *nominal GDP* to its full-employment noninflationary level.

inflation premium The component of the *nominal interest rate* that reflects anticipated inflation.

inflation targeting The annual statement by a *central bank* of a goal for a specific range of inflation in a future year, coupled with monetary policy designed to achieve the goal.

inflexible prices Product prices that remain in place (at least for a while) even though supply or demand has changed; stuck prices or sticky prices.

information technology New and more efficient methods of delivering and receiving information through the use of computers, fax machines, wireless phones, and the Internet.

infrastructure The capital goods usually provided by the *public sector* for use by its citizens and firms (for example, highways, bridges, transit systems, wastewater treatment facilities, municipal water systems, and airports).

injection An addition of spending to the income-expenditure stream: *investment, government purchases,* and *net exports.*

innovation The first commercially successful introduction of a new product, the use of a new method of production, or the creation of a new form of business organization.

inpayments The receipts of domestic or foreign money that individuals, firms, and governments of one nation obtain from the sale of goods and services abroad, as investment income and remittances, and from foreign purchases of domestic assets.

insider-outsider theory The hypothesis that nominal wages are inflexible downward because firms are aware that workers ("insiders") who retain employment during recession may refuse to work cooperatively with previously unemployed workers ("outsiders") who offer to work for less than the current wage.

insurable risk An event that would result in a loss but whose frequency of occurrence can be estimated with considerable accuracy. Insurance companies are willing to sell insurance against such losses.

interest The payment made for the use of money (of borrowed funds).

interest income Payments of income to those who supply the economy with *capital.*

interest rate The annual rate at which *interest* is paid; a percentage of the borrowed amount.

interest-rate effect The tendency for increases in the *price level* to increase the demand for money, raise interest rates, and, as a result, reduce total spending and real output in the economy (and the reverse for price-level decreases).

intermediate goods Products that are purchased for resale or further processing or manufacturing.

internally held public debt *Public debt* owed to citizens, firms, and institutions of the same nation that issued the debt.

international balance of payments A summary of all the transactions that took place between the individuals, firms, and government units of one nation and those of all other nations during a year.

international balance-of-payments deficit (See *balance-of-payments deficit.*)

international balance-of-payments surplus (See *balance-of-payments surplus.*)

international gold standard (See *gold standard.*)

International Monetary Fund (IMF) The international association of nations that was formed after the Second World War to make loans of foreign monies to nations with temporary *payments deficits* and, until the early 1970s, to administer the *adjustable pegs.* It now mainly makes loans to nations facing possible defaults on private and government loans.

international monetary reserves The foreign currencies and other assets such as gold that a nation can use to settle a *balance-of-payments deficit.*

international value of the dollar The price that must be paid in foreign currency (money) to obtain one U.S. dollar.

intertemporal choice Choices between benefits obtainable in one time period and benefits achievable in a later time period; comparisons that individuals and society must make between the reductions in current consumption that are necessary to fund current investments and the higher levels of future consumption that those current investments can produce.

intrinsic value The market value of the metal within a coin.

inventories Goods that have been produced but remain unsold.

inverse relationship The relationship between two variables that change in opposite directions, for example, product price and quantity demanded; a negative relationship.

investment In economics, spending for the production and accumulation of *capital* and additions to inventories. (For contrast, see *financial investment.*)

investment banks Firms that help corporations and government raise money by selling stocks and bonds; they also offer advisory services for corporate mergers and acquisitions in addition to providing brokerage services and advice.

investment demand curve A curve that shows the amounts of *investment* demanded by an economy at a series of *real interest rates.*

investment goods Same as *capital* or capital goods.

investment in human capital (See *human capital investment.*)

investment schedule A curve or schedule that shows the amounts firms plan to invest at various possible values of *real gross domestic product.*

"invisible hand" The tendency of firms and resource suppliers that seek to further their own self-interests in competitive markets to also promote the interests of society.

Joint Economic Committee (JEC) Committee of senators and representatives that investigates economic problems of national interest.

labor People's physical and mental talents and efforts that are used to help produce goods and services.

labor force Persons 16 years of age and older who are not in institutions and who are employed or are unemployed and seeking work.

labor-force participation rate The percentage of the working-age population that is actually in the *labor force*.

labor-intensive goods Products requiring relatively large amounts of *labor* to produce.

labor productivity Total output divided by the quantity of labor employed to produce it; the *average product* of labor or output per hour of work.

labor union A group of workers organized to advance the interests of the group (to increase wages, shorten the hours worked, improve working conditions, and so on).

Laffer Curve A curve relating government tax rates and tax revenues and on which a particular tax rate (between zero and 100 percent) maximizes tax revenues.

laissez-faire capitalism (See *capitalism*.)

land Natural resources ("free gifts of nature") used to produce goods and services.

land-intensive goods Products requiring relatively large amounts of *land* to produce.

land reform (Web chapter) A set of policies designed to create more efficient distribution of land ownership in developing countries; policies vary country to country and can involve everything from government purchasing large land estates and dividing the land into smaller farms to consolidating tiny plots of land into larger, more efficient private farms.

law of demand The principle that, other things equal, an increase in a product's price will reduce the quantity of it demanded, and conversely for a decrease in price.

law of increasing opportunity costs The principle that as the production of a good increases, the *opportunity cost* of producing an additional unit rises.

law of supply The principle that, other things equal, an increase in the price of a product will increase the quantity of it supplied, and conversely for a price decrease.

leader countries As it relates to *economic growth*, countries that develop and use advanced technologies, which then become available to *follower countries*.

leakage (1) A withdrawal of potential spending from the income-expenditures stream via *saving*, tax payments, or *imports*; (2) a withdrawal that reduces the lending potential of the banking system.

learning by doing Achieving greater *productivity* and lower *average total cost* through gains in knowledge and skill that accompany repetition of a task; a source of *economies of scale*.

legal tender A nation's official currency (bills and coins). Payment of debts must be accepted in this monetary unit, but creditors can specify the form of payment, for example, "cash only" or "check or credit card only."

lending potential of an individual commercial bank The amount by which a single bank can increase the *money supply* by making new loans to (or buying securities from) the public; equal to the bank's excess reserves.

lending potential of the banking system The amount by which the banking system can increase the *money supply* by making new loans to (or buying securities from) the public; equal to the *excess reserves* of the banking system multiplied by the *monetary multiplier*.

liability A debt with a monetary value; an amount owed by a firm or an individual.

limited liability rule Rule limiting the risks involved in investing in corporations and encouraging investors to invest in stocks by capping their potential losses at the amount that they paid for their shares.

liquidity The ease with which an asset can be converted quickly into cash with little or no loss of purchasing power. Money is said to be perfectly liquid, whereas other assets have a lesser degree of liquidity.

liquidity trap A situation in a severe *recession* in which the Fed's injection of additional reserves into the banking system has little or no additional positive impact on lending, borrowing, *investment*, or *aggregate demand*.

long run (1) In *microeconomics*, a period of time long enough to enable producers of a product to change the quantities of all the resources they employ; period in which all resources and costs are variable and no resources or costs are fixed. (2) In *macroeconomics*, a period sufficiently long for *nominal wages* and other input prices to change in response to a change in a nation's *price level*.

long-run aggregate supply curve The aggregate supply curve associated with a time period in which input prices (especially *nominal wages*) are fully responsive to changes in the *price level*.

long-run competitive equilibrium The price at which firms in *pure competition* neither obtain *economic profit* nor suffer economic losses in the *long run* and in which the total quantity demanded and supplied are equal; a price equal to the *marginal cost* and the minimum long-run *average total cost* of producing the product.

long-run supply curve As it applies to macroeconomics, a supply curve for which price, but not real output, changes when the demand curves shifts; a vertical supply curve that implies fully flexible prices.

long-run vertical Phillips Curve The *Phillips Curve* after all nominal wages have adjusted to changes in the rate of inflation; a line emanating straight upward at the economy's *natural rate of unemployment*.

lump-sum tax A tax that collects a constant amount (the tax revenue of government is the same) at all levels of GDP.

M1 The most narrowly defined *money supply*, equal to *currency* in the hands of the public and the *checkable deposits* of commercial banks and thrift institutions.

M2 A more broadly defined *money supply*, equal to *M1* plus *noncheckable savings accounts* (including *money market deposit accounts*), small *time deposits* (deposits of less than $100,000), and individual *money market mutual fund* balances.

macroeconomics The part of economics concerned with the economy as a whole; with such major aggregates as the household, business, and government sectors; and with measures of the total economy.

managed floating exchange rate An *exchange rate* that is allowed to change (float) as a result of changes in currency supply and demand but at times is altered (managed) by governments via their buying and selling of particular currencies.

marginal analysis The comparison of marginal ("extra" or "additional") benefits and marginal costs, usually for decision making.

marginal benefit The extra (additional) benefit of consuming 1 more unit of some good or service; the change in total benefit when 1 more unit is consumed.

marginal cost (MC) The extra (additional) cost of producing 1 more unit of output; equal to the change in *total cost* divided by the change in output (and, in the short run, to the change in total *variable cost* divided by the change in output).

marginal propensity to consume (MPC) The fraction of any change in *disposable income* spent for *consumer goods*; equal to the change in consumption divided by the change in disposable income.

marginal propensity to save (MPS) The fraction of any change in *disposable income* that households save; equal to the change in *saving* divided by the change in disposable income.

marginal tax rate The tax rate paid on an additional dollar of income.

marginal utility The extra *utility* a consumer obtains from the consumption of 1 additional unit of a good or service; equal to the change in total utility divided by the change in the quantity consumed.

market Any institution or mechanism that brings together buyers (demanders) and sellers (suppliers) of a particular good or service.

market demand (See *total demand*.)

market economy An economy in which the private decisions of consumers, resource suppliers, and firms determine how resources are allocated; the *market system*.

market failure The inability of a market to bring about the allocation of resources that best satisfies the wants of society; in particular, the overallocation or underallocation of resources to the production of a particular good or service because of *externalities* or informational problems or because markets do not provide desired *public goods*.

market period A period in which producers of a product are unable to change the quantity produced in response to a change in its price and in which there is a *perfectly inelastic supply*.

market portfolio The portfolio consisting of every financial asset (including every *stock* and *bond*) traded in the financial markets. The market portfolio is used to calculate *beta* (a measure of the degree of riskiness) for specific stocks, bonds, and mutual funds.

market system All the product and resource markets of a *market economy* and the relationships among them; a method that allows the prices determined in those markets to allocate the economy's scarce resources and to communicate and coordinate the decisions made by consumers, firms, and resource suppliers.

Medicaid A Federal program that helps finance the medical expenses of individuals covered by the *Supplemental Security Income (SSI)* and *Temporary Assistance for Needy Families (TANF)* programs.

Medicare A Federal program that is financed by *payroll taxes* and provides for (1) compulsory hospital insurance for senior citizens, (2) low-cost voluntary insurance to help older Americans pay physicians' fees, and (3) subsidized insurance to buy prescription drugs.

medium of exchange Any item sellers generally accept and buyers generally use to pay for a good or service; *money*; a convenient means of exchanging goods and services without engaging in *barter*.

menu costs The reluctance of firms to cut prices during recessions (that they think will be short-lived) because of the costs of altering and communicating their price reductions; named after the cost associated with printing new menus at restaurants.

microeconomics The part of economics concerned with decision making by individual units such as a *household*, a *firm*, or an *industry* and with individual markets, specific goods and services, and product and resource prices.

microfinance (Web chapter) A credit system through which groups of people pool their money and make small loans to budding *entrepreneurs* and owners of small businesses in *developing countries*.

midpoint formula A method for calculating *price elasticity of demand* or *price elasticity of supply* that averages the two prices and two quantities as the reference points for computing percentages.

minimum wage The lowest *wage* that employers may legally pay for an hour of work.

modern economic growth The historically recent phenomenon in which nations for the first time have experienced sustained increases in *real GDP per capita*.

monetarism The macroeconomic view that the main cause of changes in aggregate output and *price level* is fluctuations in the *money supply*; espoused by advocates of a *monetary rule*.

monetary multiplier The multiple of its *excess reserves* by which the banking system can expand *checkable deposits* and thus the *money supply* by making new loans (or buying securities); equal to 1 divided by the *reserve requirement*.

monetary policy A central bank's changing of the *money supply* to influence interest rates and assist the economy in achieving price stability, full employment, and economic growth.

monetary rule The rule suggested by *monetarism*. As traditionally formulated, the rule says that the *money supply* should be expanded each year at the same annual rate as the potential rate of growth of the *real gross domestic product*; the supply of money should be increased steadily between 3 and 5 percent per year. (Also see *Taylor rule*.)

money Any item that is generally acceptable to sellers in exchange for goods and services.

money capital Money available to purchase *capital*; simply *money*, as defined by economists.

money income (See *nominal income.*)

money market The market in which the demand for and the supply of money determine the *interest rate* (or the level of interest rates) in the economy.

money market deposit accounts (MMDAs) Bank- and thrift-provided interest-bearing accounts that contain a variety of short-term securities; such accounts have minimum balance requirements and limits on the frequency of withdrawals.

money market mutual funds (MMMFs) Interest-bearing accounts offered by investment companies, which pool depositors' funds for the purchase of short-term securities. Depositors can write checks in minimum amounts or more against their accounts.

money supply Narrowly defined, *M1*; more broadly defined, *M2*. (See *M1* and *M2*)

monopoly A market structure in which there is only a single seller of a good, service, or resource. In antitrust law, a dominant firm that accounts for a very high percentage of total sales within a particular market.

monopsony A market structure in which there is only a single buyer of a good, service, or resource.

mortgage-backed securities *Bonds* that represent claims to all or part of the monthly mortgage payments from the pools of mortgage loans made by lenders to borrowers to help them purchase residential property.

mortgage debt crisis The period beginning in late 2007 when thousands of homeowners defaulted on mortgage loans when they experienced a combination of higher mortgage interest rates and falling home prices.

multinational corporations Firms that own production facilities in two or more countries and produce and sell their products globally.

multiple counting Wrongly including the value of *intermediate goods* in the *gross domestic product;* counting the same good or service more than once.

multiplier The ratio of a change in equilibrium GDP to the change in *investment* or in any other component of *aggregate expenditures* or *aggregate demand;* the number by which a change in any such component must be multiplied to find the resulting change in the equilibrium GDP.

multiplier effect The effect on equilibrium GDP of a change in *aggregate expenditures* or *aggregate demand* (caused by a change in the *consumption schedule, investment,* government expenditures, or *net exports*).

mutual funds *Portfolios* of *stocks* and *bonds* selected and purchased by mutual fund companies, which finance the purchases by pooling money from thousands of individual fund investors; includes both *index funds* as well as *actively managed funds.* Fund returns (profits or losses) pass through to the individual fund investors who invest in the funds.

national bank A *commercial bank* authorized to operate by the U.S. government.

National Credit Union Administration (NCUA) The federally chartered agency that insures deposit liabilities (up to $250,000 per account) in *credit unions.*

national income Total income earned by resource suppliers for their contributions to *gross domestic product* plus *taxes on production and imports;* the sum of wages and salaries, rent, interest, profit, proprietors' income, and such taxes.

national income accounting The techniques used to measure the overall production of the economy and other related variables for the nation as a whole.

natural monopoly An industry in which *economies of scale* are so great that a single firm can produce the product at a lower average total cost than would be possible if more than one firm produced the product.

natural rate of unemployment (NRU) The *full-employment rate of unemployment;* the unemployment rate occurring when there is no cyclical unemployment and the economy is achieving its potential output; the unemployment rate at which actual inflation equals expected inflation.

near-money Financial assets, the most important of which are *noncheckable savings accounts, time deposits,* and U.S. short-term securities and savings bonds, which are not a medium of exchange but can be readily converted into money.

negative externality A cost imposed without compensation on third parties by the production or consumption of sellers or buyers. Example: A manufacturer dumps toxic chemicals into a river, killing fish prized by sports fishers; an external cost or a spillover cost.

negative GDP gap A situation in which actual *gross domestic product* is less than *potential output.* Also known as a recessionary output gap.

negative relationship (See *inverse relationship.*)

net benefits The total benefits of some activity or policy less the total costs of that activity or policy.

net domestic product (NDP) *Gross domestic product* less the part of the year's output that is needed to replace the *capital goods* worn out in producing the output; the nation's total output available for consumption or additions to the *capital stock.*

net exports (X_n) *Exports* minus *imports.*

net foreign factor income Receipts of resource income from the rest of the world minus payments of resource income to the rest of the world.

net investment income The interest and dividend income received by the residents of a nation from residents of other nations less the interest and dividend payments made by the residents of that nation to the residents of other nations.

net private domestic investment *Gross private domestic investment* less *consumption of fixed capital;* the addition to the nation's stock of *capital* during a year.

net taxes The taxes collected by government less *government transfer payments.*

net transfers The personal and government transfer payments made by one nation to residents of foreign nations less the personal and government transfer payments received from residents of foreign nations.

network effects Increases in the value of a product to each user, including existing users, as the total number of users rises.

net worth The total *assets* less the total *liabilities* of a firm or an individual; for a firm, the claims of the owners against the firm's total assets; for an individual, his or her wealth.

new classical economics The theory that, although unanticipated price-level changes may create macroeconomic instability in the short run, the economy is stable at the full-employment level of domestic output in the long run because prices and wages adjust automatically to correct movements away from the full-employment, noninflationary output.

nominal gross domestic product (GDP) *GDP* measured in terms of the price level at the time of measurement; *GDP* not adjusted for *inflation*.

nominal income number of dollars received by an individual or group for its resources during some period of time.

nominal interest rate The interest rate expressed in terms of annual amounts currently charged for interest and not adjusted for inflation.

nominal wage The amount of money received by a worker per unit of time (hour, day, etc.); money wage.

nondiscretionary fiscal policy (See *built-in stabilizer*.)

nondiversifiable risk Investment *risk* that investors are unable to reduce via *diversification*; also called systemic risk.

nondurable good A *consumer good* with an expected life (use) of less than three years.

nonexcludability The inability to keep nonpayers (free riders) from obtaining benefits from a certain good; a characteristic of a *public good*.

nonexhaustive expenditure An expenditure by government that does not result directly in the use of economic resources or the production of goods and services; see *government transfer payment*.

nonincome determinants of consumption and saving All influences on consumption and saving other than the level of *GDP*.

noninterest determinants of investment All influences on the level of investment spending other than the *interest rate*.

noninvestment transaction An expenditure for stocks, bonds, or secondhand *capital goods*.

nonmarket transactions The value of the goods and services that are not included in the *gross domestic product* because they are not bought and sold.

nonproduction transaction The purchase and sale of any item that is not a currently produced good or service.

nonrivalry The idea that one person's benefit from a certain good does not reduce the benefit available to others; a characteristic of a *public good*.

nontariff barriers (NTBs) All barriers other than *protective tariffs* that nations erect to impede international trade, including *import quotas*, licensing requirements, unreasonable product-quality standards, unnecessary bureaucratic detail in customs procedures, and so on.

normal good A good or service whose consumption increases when income increases and falls when income decreases, price remaining constant.

normal profit The payment made by a firm to obtain and retain *entrepreneurial ability*; the minimum income entrepreneurial ability must receive to induce it to perform entrepreneurial functions for a firm.

normative economics The part of economics involving value judgments about what the economy should be like; focused on which economic goals and policies should be implemented; policy economics.

North American Free Trade Agreement (NAFTA) A 1993 agreement establishing, over a 15-year period, a free-trade zone composed of Canada, Mexico, and the United States.

official reserves Foreign currencies owned by the central bank of a nation.

offshoring The practice of shifting work previously done by American workers to workers located abroad.

Okun's law The generalization that any 1-percentage-point rise in the *unemployment rate* above the *full-employment rate of unemployment* is associated with a rise in the negative *GDP gap* by 2 percent of *potential output* (potential GDP).

OPEC (See *Organization of Petroleum Exporting Countries*.)

open economy An economy that exports and imports goods and services.

open-market operations The buying and selling of U.S. government securities by the *Federal Reserve Banks* for purposes of carrying out *monetary policy*.

opportunity cost The amount of other products that must be forgone or sacrificed to produce a unit of a product.

opportunity-cost ratio An equivalency showing the number of units of two products that can be produced with the same resources; the cost 1 corn ≡ 3 olives shows that the resources required to produce 3 units of olives must be shifted to corn production to produce 1 unit of corn.

optimal reduction of an externality The reduction of a *negative externality* such as pollution to the level at which the *marginal benefit* and *marginal cost* of reduction are equal.

Organization of Petroleum Exporting Countries (OPEC) A cartel of 12 oil-producing countries (Algeria, Angola, Ecuador, Iran, Iraq, Kuwait, Libya, Nigeria, Qatar, Saudi Arabia, Venezuela, and the United Arab Emirates) that attempts to control the quantity and price of crude oil exported by its members and that accounts for a large percentage of the world's export of oil.

other-things-equal assumption The assumption that factors other than those being considered are held constant; *ceteris paribus* assumption.

outpayments The expenditures of domestic or foreign currency that the individuals, firms, and governments of one nation make to purchase goods and services, for remittances, to pay investment income, and for purchases of foreign assets.

output effect The situation in which an increase in the price of one input will increase a firm's production costs and reduce its level of output, thus reducing the demand for other inputs; conversely for a decrease in the price of the input.

paper money Pieces of paper used as a *medium of exchange*; in the United States, *Federal Reserve Notes*.

paradox of thrift The seemingly self-contradictory but nevertheless true statement that increased *saving* can be both good and bad for the economy. It is good in the long run when matched with increased *investment* spending, but bad during a *recession* because it reduces spending, which further reduces output and employment. In fact, attempts by *households* to save more during a recession may simply worsen the recession and result in less saving.

partnership An unincorporated firm owned and operated by two or more persons.

passively managed funds *Mutual funds* whose *portfolios* are not regularly updated by a fund manager attempting to generate high returns. Rather, once an initial portfolio is selected, it is left unchanged so that investors receive whatever return that unchanging portfolio subsequently generates. *Index funds* are a type of passively managed fund.

patent An exclusive right given to inventors to produce and sell a new product or machine for 20 years from the time of patent application.

payments deficit (See *balance-of-payments deficit*.)

payments surplus (See *balance-of-payments surplus*.)

payroll tax A tax levied on employers of labor equal to a percentage of all or part of the wages and salaries paid by them and on employees equal to a percentage of all or part of the wages and salaries received by them.

peak The point in a business cycle at which business activity has reached a temporary maximum; the economy is near or at full employment and the level of real output is at or very close to the economy's capacity.

per capita GDP *Gross domestic product* (GDP) per person; the average GDP of a population.

per capita income A nation's total income per person; the average income of a population.

percentage rate of return The percentage gain or loss, relative to the buying price, of an *economic investment* or *financial investment* over some period of time.

perfectly inelastic demand Product or resource demand in which *price* can be of any amount at a particular quantity of the product or resource demanded; *quantity demanded* does not respond to a change in price; graphs as a vertical *demand curve*.

perfectly inelastic supply Product or resource supply in which *price* can be of any amount at a particular quantity of the product or resource demanded; *quantity supplied* does not respond to a change in price; graphs as a vertical *supply curve*.

personal consumption expenditures (C) The expenditures of *households* for *durable* and *nondurable consumer goods* and *services*.

personal distribution of income The manner in which the economy's *personal* or *disposable income* is divided among different income classes or different households or families.

personal income (PI) The earned and unearned income available to resource suppliers and others before the payment of personal taxes.

personal income tax A tax levied on the taxable income of individuals, households, and unincorporated firms.

personal saving The *personal income* of households less personal taxes and *personal consumption expenditures; disposable income* not spent for *consumer goods*.

per-unit production cost The average production cost of a particular level of output; total input cost divided by units of output.

Phillips Curve A curve showing the relationship between the *unemployment rate* (on the horizontal axis) and the annual rate of increase in the *price level* (on the vertical axis).

planned investment The amount that *firms* plan or intend to invest.

plant A physical establishment that performs one or more functions in the production, fabrication, and distribution of goods and services.

policy economics The formulation of courses of action to bring about desired economic outcomes or to prevent undesired occurrences.

political business cycle Fluctuations in the economy caused by the alleged tendency of Congress to destabilize the economy by reducing taxes and increasing government expenditures before elections and to raise taxes and lower expenditures after elections.

Ponzi scheme A financial fraud in which the returns paid to earlier investors come from contributions made by later investors (rather than from the financial investment that the perpetrator of the fraud claims to be making). Named after notorious fraudster Charles Ponzi.

portfolio A specific collection of *stocks, bonds,* or other *financial investments* held by an individual or a *mutual fund*.

positive economics The analysis of facts or data to establish scientific generalizations about economic behavior.

positive externality A benefit obtained without compensation by third parties from the production or consumption of sellers or buyers. Example: A beekeeper benefits when a neighboring farmer plants clover. An *external benefit* or a spillover benefit.

positive GDP gap A situation in which actual *gross domestic product* exceeds *potential output*. Also known as an inflationary output gap.

positive relationship (See *direct relationship*.)

post hoc, ergo propter hoc fallacy The false belief that when one event precedes another, the first event must have caused the second event.

potential output The real output (*GDP*) an economy can produce when it fully employs its available resources.

poverty A situation in which the basic needs of an individual or family exceed the means to satisfy them.

poverty rate The percentage of the population with incomes below the official poverty income levels that are established by the Federal government.

present value Today's value of some amount of money that is to be received sometime in the future.

price The amount of money needed to buy a particular good, service, or resource.

price ceiling A legally established maximum price for a good or service.

price elasticity of demand The ratio of the percentage change in *quantity demanded* of a product or resource to the percentage change in its *price*; a measure of the responsiveness of buyers to a change in the price of a product or resource.

price elasticity of supply The ratio of the percentage change in *quantity supplied* of a product or resource to the percentage change in its *price*; a measure of the responsiveness of producers to a change in the price of a product or resource.

price floor A legally determined minimum price above the *equilibrium price*.

price index An index number that shows how the weighted-average price of a "market basket" of goods changes over time.

price level The weighted average of the prices of all the final goods and services produced in an economy.

price-level stability A steadiness of the price level from one period to the next; zero or low annual inflation; also called "price stability."

price-level surprises Unanticipated changes in the price level.

price war Successive and continued decreases in the prices charged by firms in an oligopolistic industry. Each firm lowers its price below rivals' prices, hoping to increase its sales and revenues at its rivals' expense.

prime interest rate The benchmark *interest rate* that banks use as a reference point for a wide range of loans to businesses and individuals.

principle of comparative advantage The proposition that an individual, region, or nation will benefit if it specializes in producing goods for which its own *opportunity costs* are lower than the opportunity costs of a trading partner, and then exchanging some of the products in which it specializes for other desired products produced by others.

private good A good or service that is individually consumed and that can be profitably provided by privately owned firms because they can exclude nonpayers from receiving the benefits.

private property The right of private persons and firms to obtain, own, control, employ, dispose of, and bequeath *land*, *capital*, and other property.

private sector The *households* and business *firms* of the economy.

probability-weighted average Each of the possible future rates of return from an investment multiplied by its respective probability (expressed as a decimal) of happening.

producer surplus The difference between the actual price a producer receives (or producers receive) and the minimum acceptable price; the triangular area above the supply curve and below the market price.

production possibilities curve A curve showing the different combinations of two goods or services that can be produced in a *full-employment, full-production* economy where the available supplies of resources and technology are fixed.

productive efficiency The production of a good in the least costly way; occurs when production takes place at the output at which *average total cost* is a minimum and *marginal product* per dollar's worth of input is the same for all inputs.

productivity A measure of average output or real output per unit of input. For example, the productivity of labor is determined by dividing real output by hours of work.

productivity growth The increase in *productivity* from one period to another.

product market A market in which products are sold by *firms* and bought by *households*.

profit The return to the resource *entrepreneurial ability* (see *normal profit*); *total revenue* minus *total cost* (see *economic profit*).

progressive tax A tax whose *average tax rate* increases as the taxpayer's income increases and decreases as the taxpayer's income decreases.

property tax A tax on the value of property (*capital, land, stocks* and *bonds*, and other *assets*) owned by *firms* and *households*.

proportional tax A tax whose *average tax rate* remains constant as the taxpayer's income increases or decreases.

proprietor's income The net income of the owners of unincorporated firms (proprietorships and partnerships).

protective tariff A *tariff* designed to shield domestic producers of a good or service from the competition of foreign producers.

public debt The total amount owed by the Federal government to the owners of government securities; equal to the sum of past government *budget deficits* less government *budget surpluses*.

public good A good or service that is characterized by *nonrivalry* and *nonexcludability*; a good or service with these characteristics provided by government.

public investments Government expenditures on public capital (such as roads, highways, bridges, mass-transit systems, and electric power facilities) and on *human capital* (such as education, training, and health).

public sector The part of the economy that contains all government entities; government.

purchasing power The amount of goods and services that a monetary unit of income can buy.

purchasing power parity The idea that exchange rates between nations equate the purchasing power of various currencies. Exchange rates between any two nations adjust to reflect the price-level differences between the countries.

pure rate of interest An essentially risk-free, long-term interest rate that is free of the influence of market imperfections.

quantity demanded The amount of a good or service that buyers (or a buyer) are willing and able to purchase at a specific price during a specified period of time.

quantity supplied The amount of a good or service that producers (or a producer) are willing and able to make available for sale at a specific price during a specified period of time.

quasi-public bank A bank that is privately owned but governmentally (publicly) controlled; each of the U.S. *Federal Reserve Banks*.

quasi-public good A good or service to which excludability could apply but that has such a large *positive externality* that government sponsors its production to prevent an underallocation of resources.

R&D Research and development activities undertaken to bring about *technological advance*.

rate of exchange The price paid in one's own money to acquire 1 unit of a foreign currency; the rate at which the money of one nation is exchanged for the money of another nation.

rate of return The gain in net revenue divided by the cost of an investment or an *R&D* expenditure; expressed as a percentage.

rational behavior Human behavior based on comparison of marginal costs and marginal benefits; behavior designed to maximize total utility.

rational expectations theory The hypothesis that firms and households expect monetary and fiscal policies to have certain effects on the economy and (in pursuit of their own self-interests) take actions that make these policies ineffective.

rationing function of prices The ability of market forces in competitive markets to equalize *quantity demanded* and *quantity supplied* and to eliminate shortages and surpluses via changes in prices.

real-balances effect The tendency for increases in the *price level* to lower the real value (or purchasing power) of financial assets with fixed money value and, as a result, to reduce total spending and real output, and conversely for decreases in the price level.

real-business-cycle theory A theory that *business cycles* result from changes in technology and resource availability, which affect *productivity* and thus increase or decrease long-run aggregate supply.

real capital (See *capital*.)

real GDP (See *real gross domestic product*.)

real GDP per capita *Inflation*-adjusted output per person; *real GDP*/population.

real gross domestic product (GDP) *Gross domestic product* adjusted for inflation; gross domestic product in a year divided by the GDP *price index* for that year, the index expressed as a decimal.

real income The amount of goods and services that can be purchased with *nominal income* during some period of time; nominal income adjusted for inflation.

real interest rate The interest rate expressed in dollars of constant value (adjusted for *inflation*) and equal to the *nominal interest rate* less the expected rate of inflation.

real wage The amount of goods and services a worker can purchase with his or her *nominal wage;* the purchasing power of the nominal wage.

recession A period of declining real GDP, accompanied by lower real income and higher unemployment.

recessionary expenditure gap The amount by which the *aggregate expenditures schedule* must shift upward to increase the real GDP to its full-employment, noninflationary level.

refinancing the public debt Selling new government securities to owners of expiring securities or paying them money gained from the sale of new securities to others.

regressive tax A tax whose *average tax rate* decreases as the taxpayer's income increases and increases as the taxpayer's income decreases.

rental income The payments (income) received by those who supply *land* to the economy.

required reserves The funds that banks and thrifts must deposit with the *Federal Reserve Bank* (or hold as *vault cash*) to meet the legal *reserve requirement;* a fixed percentage of the bank's or thrift's checkable deposits.

reserve ratio The fraction of *checkable deposits* that a bank must hold as reserves in a *Federal Reserve Bank* or in its own bank vault; also called the *reserve requirement.*

reserve requirement The specified minimum percentage of its checkable deposits that a bank or thrift must keep on deposit at the Federal Reserve Bank in its district or hold as *vault cash*.

resource A natural, human, or manufactured item that helps produce goods and services; a productive agent or factor of production.

resource market A market in which *households* sell and *firms* buy resources or the services of resources.

restrictive monetary policy *Federal Reserve System* actions to reduce the *money supply*, increase *interest rates*, and reduce *inflation;* a tight money policy.

revenue tariff A *tariff* designed to produce income for the Federal government.

risk The uncertainty as to the actual future returns of a particular *financial investment* or *economic investment.*

risk-free interest rate The *interest rate* earned on short-term U.S. government bonds.

risk premium The *interest rate* above the *risk-free* interest rate that must be paid and received to compensate a lender or investor for *risk*.

rivalry (1) The characteristic of a *private good*, the consumption of which by one party excludes other parties from obtaining the benefit; (2) the attempt by one firm to gain strategic advantage over another firm to enhance market share or profit.

rule of 70 A method for determining the number of years it will take for some measure to double, given its annual percentage increase. Example: To determine the number of years it will take for the *price level* to double, divide 70 by the annual rate of *inflation*.

sales tax A tax levied on the cost (at retail) of a broad group of products.

saving Disposable income not spent for consumer goods; equal to *disposable income* minus *personal consumption expenditures;* saving is a flow.

savings The accumulation of funds that results when people in an economy spend less (consume less) than their incomes during a given time period; savings are a stock.

savings account A deposit in a *commercial bank* or *thrift institution* on which interest payments are received; generally used for saving rather than daily transactions; a component of the *M2* money supply.

savings and loan association (S&L) A firm that accepts deposits primarily from small individual savers and lends primarily to individuals to finance purchases such as autos and homes; now nearly indistinguishable from a *commercial bank*.

saving schedule A schedule that shows the amounts *households* plan to save (plan not to spend for *consumer goods*), at different levels of *disposable income*.

savings deposit A deposit that is interest-bearing and that the depositor can normally withdraw at any time.

savings institution (See *thrift institution*.)

Say's law The largely discredited macroeconomic generalization that the production of goods and services (supply) creates an equal *demand* for those goods and services.

scarce resources The limited quantities of *land, capital, labor,* and *entrepreneurial ability* that are never sufficient to satisfy people's virtually unlimited economic wants.

scientific method The procedure for the systematic pursuit of knowledge involving the observation of facts and the formulation and testing of hypotheses to obtain theories, principles, and laws.

secular trend A long-term tendency; a change in some variable over a very long period of years.

securitization The process of aggregating many individual financial debts, such as mortgages or student loans, into a pool and then issuing new securities (financial instruments) backed by the pool. The holders of the new securities are entitled to receive the debt payments made on the individual financial debts in the pool.

Security Market Line (SML) A line that shows the average expected rate of return of all financial investments at each level of *nondiversifiable risk*, the latter measured by *beta*.

self-interest That which each firm, property owner, worker, and consumer believes is best for itself and seeks to obtain.

seniority The length of time a worker has been employed absolutely or relative to other workers; may be used to determine which workers will be laid off when there is insufficient work for them all and who will be rehired when more work becomes available.

separation of ownership and control The fact that different groups of people own a *corporation* (the stockholders) and manage it (the directors and officers).

service An (intangible) act or use for which a consumer, firm, or government is willing to pay.

shirking Workers' neglecting or evading work to increase their *utility* or well-being.

shocks Sudden, unexpected changes in *demand* (or *aggregate demand*) or supply (or *aggregate supply*).

shortage The amount by which the *quantity demanded* of a product exceeds the *quantity supplied* at a particular (below-equilibrium) price.

short run (1) In microeconomics, a period of time in which producers are able to change the quantities of some but not all of the resources they employ; a period in which some resources (usually plant) are fixed and some are variable. (2) In macroeconomics, a period in which nominal wages and other input prices do not change in response to a change in the price level.

short-run aggregate supply curve An *aggregate supply* curve relevant to a time period in which input prices (particularly *nominal wages*) do not change in response to changes in the *price level*.

simple multiplier The *multiplier* in any economy in which government collects no *net taxes*, there are no *imports*, and *investment* is independent of the level of income; equal to 1 divided by the *marginal propensity to save*.

simultaneous consumption The same-time derivation of *utility* from some product by a large number of consumers.

slope of a line The ratio of the vertical change (the rise or fall) to the horizontal change (the run) between any two points on a line. The slope of an upward-sloping line is positive, reflecting a direct relationship between two variables; the slope of a downward-sloping line is negative, reflecting an inverse relationship between two variables.

Smoot-Hawley Tariff Act Legislation passed in 1930 that established very high tariffs. Its objective was to reduce imports and stimulate the domestic economy, but it resulted only in retaliatory tariffs by other nations.

Social Security The social insurance program in the United States financed by Federal payroll taxes on employers and employees and designed to replace a portion of the earnings lost when workers become disabled, retire, or die.

Social Security trust fund A Federal fund that saves excessive Social Security tax revenues received in one year to meet Social

Security benefit obligations that exceed Social Security tax revenues in some subsequent year.

sole proprietorship   An unincorporated *firm* owned and operated by one person.

specialization   The use of the resources of an individual, a firm, a region, or a nation to concentrate production on one or a small number of goods and services.

speculation   The activity of buying or selling with the motive of later reselling or rebuying for profit.

stagflation   Inflation accompanied by stagnation in the rate of growth of output and an increase in unemployment in the economy; simultaneous increases in the *inflation rate* and the *unemployment rate*.

start-up firm   A new firm focused on creating and introducing a particular new product or employing a specific new production or distribution method.

state bank   A *commercial bank* authorized by a state government to engage in the business of banking.

sticky prices   (See *inflexible prices*.)

stock (corporate)   An ownership share in a corporation.

store of value   An *asset* set aside for future use; one of the three functions of *money*.

structural unemployment   Unemployment of workers whose skills are not demanded by employers, who lack sufficient skill to obtain employment, or who cannot easily move to locations where jobs are available.

subprime mortgage loans   High-interest rate loans to home buyers with above-average credit risk.

subsidy   A payment of funds (or goods and services) by a government, firm, or household for which it receives no good or service in return. When made by a government, it is a *government transfer payment*.

substitute goods   Products or services that can be used in place of each other. When the price of one falls, the demand for the other product falls; conversely, when the price of one product rises, the demand for the other product rises.

substitution effect   (1) A change in the quantity demanded of a *consumer good* that results from a change in its relative expensiveness caused by a change in the product's price; (2) the effect of a change in the price of a *resource* on the quantity of the resource employed by a firm, assuming no change in its output.

supply   A schedule showing the amounts of a good or service that sellers (or a seller) will offer at various prices during some period.

supply curve   A curve illustrating *supply*.

supply factor (in growth)   An increase in the availability of a resource, an improvement in its quality, or an expansion of technological knowledge that makes it possible for an economy to produce a greater output of goods and services.

supply schedule   (See *supply*.)

supply shocks   Sudden, unexpected changes in *aggregate supply*.

supply-side economics   A view of macroeconomics that emphasizes the role of costs and *aggregate supply* in explaining *inflation*, *unemployment*, and *economic growth*.

supply-side market failures   Overallocations of resources that occur when private supply curves understate the full cost of producing a good or service.

surplus   The amount by which the *quantity supplied* of a product exceeds the *quantity demanded* at a specific (above-equilibrium) price.

tariff   A tax imposed by a nation on an imported good.

tax   An involuntary payment of money (or goods and services) to a government by a *household* or *firm* for which the household or firm receives no good or service directly in return.

taxes on production and imports   A *national income accounting* category that includes such taxes as *sales*, *excise*, business property taxes, and *tariffs* which firms treat as costs of producing a product and pass on (in whole or in part) to buyers by charging a higher price.

tax incidence   The degree to which a *tax* falls on a particular person or group.

tax subsidy   A grant in the form of reduced taxes through favorable tax treatment. For example, employer-paid health insurance is exempt from Federal income and payroll taxes.

tax-transfer disincentives   Decreases in the incentives to work, save, invest, innovate, and take risks that result from high *marginal tax rates* and *transfer payments*.

Taylor rule   A modern monetary rule proposed by economist John Taylor that would stipulate exactly how much the Federal Reserve should change real interest rates in response to divergences of real GDP from potential GDP and divergences of actual rates of inflation from a target rate of inflation.

technological advance   New and better goods and services and new and better ways of producing or distributing them.

technology   The body of knowledge and techniques that can be used to combine *economic resources* to produce goods and services.

Temporary Assistance for Needy Families (TANF)   A state-administered and partly federally funded program in the United States that provides financial aid to poor families; the basic welfare program for low-income families in the United States; contains time limits and work requirements.

term auction facility   The *monetary policy* procedure used by the Federal Reserve, in which commercial banks anonymously bid to obtain loans being made available by the Fed as a way to expand reserves in the banking system.

terms of trade   The rate at which units of one product can be exchanged for units of another product; the price of a good or service; the amount of one good or service that must be given up to obtain 1 unit of another good or service.

theoretical economics   The process of deriving and applying economic theories and principles.

thrift institution A *savings and loan association, mutual savings bank,* or *credit union.*

till money (See *vault cash.*)

time deposit An interest-earning deposit in a *commercial bank* or *thrift institution* that the depositor can withdraw without penalty after the end of a specified period.

time preference The human tendency for people, because of impatience, to prefer to spend and consume in the present rather than save and wait to spend and consume in the future; this inclination varies in strength among individuals.

time-value of money The idea that a specific amount of money is more valuable to a person the sooner it is received because the money can be placed in a financial account or investment and earn *compound interest* over time; the *opportunity cost* of receiving a sum of money later rather than earlier.

token money Bills or coins for which the amount printed on the *currency* bears no relationship to the value of the paper or metal embodied within it; for currency still circulating, money for which the face value exceeds the commodity value.

total demand The demand schedule or the *demand curve* of all buyers of a good or service; also called market demand.

total demand for money The sum of the *transactions demand for money* and the *asset demand for money.*

total revenue (TR) The total number of dollars received by a firm (or firms) from the sale of a product; equal to the total expenditures for the product produced by the firm (or firms); equal to the quantity sold (demanded) multiplied by the price at which it is sold.

total-revenue test A test to determine elasticity of *demand* between any two prices: Demand is elastic if *total revenue* moves in the opposite direction from price; it is inelastic when it moves in the same direction as price; and it is of unitary elasticity when it does not change when price changes.

total spending The total amount that buyers of goods and services spend or plan to spend; also called *aggregate expenditures.*

total supply The supply schedule or the *supply curve* of all sellers of a good or service; also called market supply.

Trade Adjustment Assistance Act A U.S. law passed in 2002 that provides cash assistance, education and training benefits, health care subsidies, and wage subsidies (for persons age 50 or older) to workers displaced by imports or relocations of U.S. plants to other countries.

trade balance The export of goods (or goods and services) of a nation less its imports of goods (or goods and services).

trade controls *Tariffs, export subsidies, import quotas,* and other means a nation may employ to reduce *imports* and expand *exports.*

trade deficit The amount by which a nation's *imports* of goods (or goods and services) exceed its *exports* of goods (or goods and services).

trademark A legal protection that gives the originators of a product an exclusive right to use the brand name.

trade-off The sacrifice of some or all of one economic goal, good, or service to achieve some other goal, good, or service.

trade surplus The amount by which a nation's *exports* of goods (or goods and services) exceed its *imports* of goods (or goods and services).

trading possibilities line A line that shows the different combinations of two products that an economy is able to obtain (consume) when it specializes in the production of one product and trades (exports) it to obtain the other product.

transactions demand for money The amount of money people want to hold for use as a *medium of exchange* (to make payments); varies directly with *nominal GDP.*

transfer payment A payment of *money* (or goods and services) by a government to a *household* or *firm* for which the payer receives no good or service directly in return.

Troubled Asset Relief Program (TARP) A 2008 Federal government program that authorized the U.S. Treasury to loan up to $700 billion to critical financial institutions and other U.S. firms that were in extreme financial trouble and therefore at high risk of failure.

trough The point in a *business cycle* at which business activity has reached a temporary minimum; the point at which a *recession* has ended and an expansion (recovery) begins.

unanticipated inflation Increases in the price level (*inflation*) at a rate greater than expected.

underemployment (Web chapter) A situation in which workers are employed in positions requiring less education and skill than they have.

undistributed corporate profits After-tax corporate profits not distributed as dividends to stockholders; corporate or business saving; also called retained earnings.

unemployment The failure to use all available *economic resources* to produce desired goods and services; the failure of the economy to fully employ its *labor force.*

unemployment compensation (See *unemployment insurance*).

unemployment insurance The social insurance program that in the United States is financed by state *payroll taxes* on employers and makes income available to workers who become unemployed and are unable to find jobs.

unemployment rate The percentage of the *labor force* unemployed at any time.

unfulfilled expectations Situations in which households and businesses were expecting one thing to happen but instead find that something else has happened; unrealized anticipations or plans relating to future economic conditions and outcomes.

uninsurable risk An event that would result in a loss and whose occurrence is uncontrollable and unpredictable. Insurance companies are not willing to sell insurance against such a loss.

unit elasticity   Demand or supply for which the *elasticity coefficient* is equal to 1; means that the percentage change in the quantity demanded or supplied is equal to the percentage change in price.

unit labor cost   Labor cost per unit of output; total labor cost divided by total output; also equal to the *nominal wage* rate divided by the *average product* of labor.

unit of account   A standard unit in which prices can be stated and the value of goods and services can be compared; one of the three functions of *money*.

unlimited wants   The insatiable desire of consumers for goods and services that will give them satisfaction or *utility*.

unplanned changes in inventories   Changes in inventories that firms did not anticipate; changes in inventories that occur because of unexpected increases or decreases of aggregate spending (or of *aggregate expenditures*).

unplanned investment   Actual investment less *planned investment*; increases or decreases in the *inventories* of firms resulting from production greater than sales.

Uruguay Round   A 1995 trade agreement (fully implemented in 2005) that established the *World Trade Organization (WTO)*, liberalized trade in goods and services, provided added protection to intellectual property (for example, *patents* and *copyrights*), and reduced farm subsidies.

U.S. securities   U.S. Treasury bills, notes, and bonds used to finance *budget deficits*; the components of the *public debt*.

utility   The want-satisfying power of a good or service; the satisfaction or pleasure a consumer obtains from the consumption of a good or service (or from the consumption of a collection of goods and services).

value added   The value of the product sold by a *firm* less the value of the products (materials) purchased and used by the firm to produce the product.

value judgment   Opinion of what is desirable or undesirable; belief regarding what ought or ought not to be in terms of what is right (or just) and wrong (or unjust).

value of money   The quantity of goods and services for which a unit of money (a dollar) can be exchanged; the purchasing power of a unit of money; the reciprocal of the *price index*.

vault cash   The *currency* a bank has in its vault and cash drawers.

velocity   The number of times per year that the average dollar in the *money supply* is spent for *final goods and services*; nominal GDP divided by the money supply.

venture capital   (Web chapter) That part of household saving used to finance high-risk business enterprises in exchange for shares of the profit if the enterprise succeeds.

vertical axis   The "up-down" or "north-south" measurement line on a graph or grid.

vertical intercept   The point at which a line meets the vertical axis of a graph.

vicious circle of poverty   (Web chapter) A problem common in some *developing countries* in which their low *per capita incomes* are an obstacle to realizing the levels of saving and investment needed to achieve rates of growth of output that exceed their rates of population growth.

voluntary export restrictions (VER)   Voluntary limitations by countries or firms of their exports to a particular foreign nation to avoid enactment of formal trade barriers by that nation.

wage   The price paid for the use or services of *labor* per unit of time (per hour, per day, and so on).

wage rate   (See *wage*.)

wages   The income of those who supply the economy with *labor*.

Wall Street Reform and Consumer Protection Act of 2010   A law that gave authority to the *Federal Reserve System* to regulate all large financial institutions, created an oversight council to look for growing risk to the financial system, established a process for the Federal government to sell off the assets of large failing financial institutions, provided Federal regulatory oversight of asset-backed securities, and created a financial consumer protection bureau within the Fed.

wealth   Anything that has value because it produces income or could produce income. Wealth is a stock; *income* is a flow. Assets less liabilities; net worth.

wealth effect   The tendency for people to increase their consumption spending when the value of their financial and real assets rises and to decrease their consumption spending when the value of those assets falls.

will to develop   (Web chapter) The state of wanting *economic growth* strongly enough to change from old to new ways of doing things.

World Bank   (Web chapter) A bank that lends (and guarantees loans) to developing nations to assist them in increasing their *capital stock* and thus in achieving *economic growth*.

world price   The international market price of a good or service, determined by world demand and supply.

World Trade Organization (WTO)   An organization of 153 nations (as of mid-2010) that oversees the provisions of the current world trade agreement, resolves trade disputes stemming from it, and holds forums for further rounds of trade negotiations.

WTO   (See *World Trade Organization*.)